Perspectives on American Politics

Perspectives on American Politics

FOURTH EDITION

William Lasser

Clemson University

Houghton Mifflin Company

Boston   New York

Publisher: Charles Hartford
Editor-in-Chief: Jean Woy
Sponsoring Editor: Katherine Meisenheimer
Associate Editor: Julie Hassel
Editorial Assistant: Sabrina Abhyankar
Senior Project Editor: Rosemary R. Jaffe
Senior Production/Design Coordinator: Jennifer Meyer Dare
Senior Manufacturing Coordinator: Priscilla Bailey
Marketing Manager: Nicola Poser

Cover Image: U.S.A., Washington, D.C., columns of Jefferson Memorial
© Paul Edmondson/Getty.

Printed in the U.S.A.

Library of Congress Control Number: 2002109503

ISBN: 0-618-31200-5

56789-QWF-09 08 07 06 05

To Susan J. S. Lasser, with love

Contents

us into remoteness and invisibility. . . . We stepped under the white canopy that extends from the side doorway . . . and into a building that was humming back to life after the longest session of inactivity perhaps in its existence."

Readings by Perspective

Foundations

American Politics Today

 ## The International Context

View from the Inside

Federalist Papers

Supreme Court Decisions

Preface

A great deal has happened in American politics since the publication of the last edition of this anthology three years ago. The election of 2000 brought us the excitement of a photo finish that took five weeks—and two Supreme Court decisions—to resolve. The stock market bubble of the late 1990s popped, bringing with it economic distress, major corporate scandals, and rising federal budget deficits. But above all came September 11, 2001, when terrorists attacked the World Trade Center in New York and the Pentagon in Washington, killing thousands and leaving us in a seemingly permanent state of war and fear.

The fourth edition of *Perspectives on American Politics* reflects both the new realities of life in America and long-standing matters of concern to students and professors of American government. Like its predecessors, the fourth edition is organized in a manner that provides a variety of perspectives on these issues, from classic works in American politics to contemporary accounts and analyses by both academics and nonacademics. But new issues are clearly allowed to take center stage. The war on terrorism is featured in several selections—from a discussion of its implications for civil liberties to an account of what September 11 was like inside the White House. And the election of 2000 is featured prominently in selections that reveal what election night was like behind the CNN anchor desk and what happened inside the Supreme Court on the days leading up to *Bush* v. *Gore*.

As in all previous editions, a central feature of this reader is the emphasis on examining American politics from several key viewpoints. Every chapter is organized around four essential perspectives—Foundations, American Politics Today, The International Context, and View from the Inside. Every selection has been chosen for its ability to inform, educate, and engage undergraduate students.

The Purpose of This Reader

My goal in *Perspectives on American Politics* has been to develop a collection of readings that is clearly organized, that can be easily integrated into an American government course and actually help in teaching the course, and that will hold the students' (and professor's) attention by presenting a wide variety of viewpoints, writing styles, and approaches. Above all, I have endeavored to create a reader that shows students just why I—and all other professors of American government—find this subject so meaningful and important.

The challenge in compiling an American government reader is to maintain structure and coherence without sacrificing the extraordinary eclecticism that marks the enormous body of writings about American government. The solution incorporated here is to begin each chapter with certain key questions in mind and then to present a set of readings designed to provide various perspectives on those questions. This approach allows students to focus on a manageable number of crit-ical issues, while at the same time giving them a variety of perspectives on those issues. All of the readings, however diverse they might be, revolve around the central chapter questions and thus maintain a clear and cohesive relationship with each other and with the readings in earlier and later chapters.

Another key goal has been to produce a reader that professors and students alike will find easy to use. The thirteen chapters of this book correspond to the most frequently assigned chapters of most American government textbooks, so they should fit neatly into any standard syllabus. Furthermore, many of the chap-ter and reading questions can serve as essay assignments, and the selections can be used as a starting point for class discussions of controversial or important issues.

The Fourth Edition

In preparing the fourth edition, I carefully scrutinized each selection for readability, usefulness, and timeliness. The following features are particularly worth noting:

- *Four essential perspectives in each chapter.* To make this reader easy to use and to provide a consistent chapter structure, each chapter contains one or more se-lections under each of the following headings: Foundations, American Politics Today, The International Context, and View from the Inside. These perspec-tives make it easy for professors to include or exclude specific material and make it easy for students to find their way around the book. At the same time, however, these perspectives are diverse enough to give students a wide range of vantage points on American politics. These four perspectives appear in the same order in every chapter.
- *Selections reflecting dramatic recent developments in American politics.* In addition to the war on terrorism and the elections of 2000 and 2002, these new develop-ments include continuing debates over affirmative action; new developments in the federal system; an end (at least for the moment) of divided government, with Republican control of the House, the Senate, and the presidency; and a renewed debate (intensified by the 2003 Iraq War) over whether the United States should act unilaterally or multilaterally in foreign policy.
- *Expanded international emphasis.* The selections included under the heading The International Context have been expanded and broadened. This heading now includes not only readings that contain a comparative perspective, but also readings that provide insights on foreign policy or international relations. These include a selection on the controversial Arab news network, Al Jazeera, which came to prominence after September 11 and again during the Iraq War.

The Perspectives

All of the readings are grouped into four perspectives that are presented in every chapter in the order listed here:

- **Foundations.** The first perspective presents a classic work in American poli-tics, an important theoretical reading, or a seminal work in American political science. Examples include selections from the *Federalist Papers;* important

Supreme Court decisions, such as *Brown* v. *Board of Education* or *Marbury* v. *Madison;* and excerpts from works such as John Stuart Mill's *On Liberty* and E.E. Schattschneider's *The Scope and Bias of the Pressure System.*

- **American Politics Today.**   The second perspective provides a snapshot of the current state of American politics. This section often comprises works by political scientists and others who do not merely describe the current state of affairs, but seek to analyze and understand it. These selections may also include contemporary Supreme Court cases or other works that present new developments in American politics. Examples include a thought-provoking article on protecting civil liberties in the age of terror and an analysis of George W. Bush's leadership style both before and after September 11.

- **The International Context.**   Each chapter includes a reading or readings chosen to provide a global or comparative perspective on American politics. Choosing the selections for this category was not easy, particularly since I could not presume that students would have preexisting knowledge of international affairs or other political systems. In every case my aim was to choose a reading that casts light on issues of concern to students of American politics. Examples include a comparison of American and European federalism, an analysis of how lobbying the European Union differs from lobbying the U.S. government, a comparison of presidential and parliamentary systems, and an analysis of the advantages and disadvantages of American unilateralism in foreign policy.

- **View from the Inside.**   This popular perspective from earlier editions appears in every chapter. These readings provide an inside view of American politics and government. In addition to insider accounts of September 11 and the 2000 election, I have included a minute-by-minute report of the hunt for the snipers who terrorized Washington, D.C., in October and November 2002 and a brief excerpt from the U.S. government's legal challenge to the exclusion of women from the Virginia Military Institute's cadet program.

Pedagogy

Like earlier editions, the fourth edition of *Perspectives on American Politics* includes pedagogical devices designed to make life easier for students and professors alike. These include chapter, category, and reading introductions and questions that orient students to the key themes, promote critical thinking, and make essential background information available. The questions can also be used by students for review purposes and by instructors for generating class discussion. Outlines for difficult readings, such as the *Federalist Papers,* provide some help to students approaching these works for the first time. Finally, I have provided a separate Instructor's Resource Manual, which features teaching hints for each chapter and each selection, ideas for assignments and class discussions, additional readings, and Internet links.

Some Technical Notes

I have used several standard conventions throughout the text. The omission of large amounts of material is indicated by centered bullets (• • •); smaller omissions are indicated by ellipses (. . .). In general, I have not corrected antique spellings, nor have I modified older styles of punctuation or capitalization. I have eliminated virtually all footnotes; readers who are interested in source notes and other references should go directly to the originals. Where necessary, I have inserted explanatory or additional matter within brackets. For the sake of clarity, I have frequently shortened selection titles, and in some cases I have modified them substantially.

An Apology, More or Less

No anthology can contain everything. Undoubtedly, there will be some who are dismayed or scandalized at the omission or inclusion of a particular article, case, or essay. To some extent, the fourth edition reflects the criticisms, compliments, or suggestions offered by particular readers. All such communications are welcome and appreciated; my email address is william.lasser@hubcap.clemson.edu.

Acknowledgments

I am grateful for the advice and assistance of editors, colleagues, and friends both in the preparation of the original manuscript and in the revisions for the fourth edition. Above all, I would like to thank my editors at Houghton Mifflin— Katherine Meisenheimer, Julie Hassel, Rosemary Jaffe, and Sabrina Abhyankar. It is a great comfort to be able to rely on their knowledge and expertise, and I very much appreciate their contributions to this book.

My colleagues at Clemson and elsewhere have provided advice and counsel in the preparation of this and previous editions. I would particularly like to thank Chuck Dunn, R. Shep Melnick, Laura Olson, Marty Slann, Robert Vipond, and Dave Woodard. A number of others read and critiqued various parts of this manuscript and gave many helpful suggestions, including Jasmine L. Farrier, University of Louisville; Irwin Morris, University of Maryland; Rickey Hill, DePauw University; and Robert Weissberg, University of Illinois-Urbana. Many other users have provided useful comments over the years, and this fourth edition reflects many of their suggestions.

Finally, I thank my children, Max Hoffman and Adina Rose. Their very existence is a constant reminder of what really matters. Above all, I thank my wife, Susan J.S. Lasser, who after twenty-four years, two children, and four editions remains a source of inspiration. As with the earlier editions, this remains, with love and gratitude, her book.

W.L.

Perspectives on American Politics

 Chapter 1

The Constitution

The United States Constitution forms the basis of the American political system. Despite extraordinary changes in the American economy and in the nation's role and responsibilities in the world, the Constitution remains essentially the same document as written in Philadelphia in the summer of 1787. Over the years, several amendments have made it more inclusive and extended the "blessings of liberty" to previously excluded groups, including blacks and women. At the same time, countless decisions of the United States Supreme Court have altered the nuances and interpretations of the original text. Still, the original document and the political philosophy that lies behind it are well worth studying.

The political philosophy of the Constitution is largely that of the Federalists, its primary supporters. The Federalists were less than a political party; they were a loosely organized group of individuals who shared a commitment to the proposed Constitution and the ideas it represented. Because they won and because they counted among their number such leading figures as Alexander Hamilton and James Madison, the Federalists are far better known than their opponents, who went by the unfortunately negative-sounding name "Antifederalists." To understand the Federalists and their political philosophy, however, it is essential to understand the views and opinions of the opposition.

Chapter 1 begins by presenting the major ideas of the Federalists and Antifederalists (selections 1.1 through 1.5). It then provides a modern example—drawn from the debates over the meaning of the Second Amendment—that suggests that the ideas of the Founding Generation still have relevance today (selection 1.6). It concludes with articles on the influence of the United States Constitution abroad, particularly with respect to developments in Eastern Europe in the early 1990s (selection 1.7), and with an inside view of the political realities of the Constitutional Convention of 1787 (selection 1.8).

Chapter Questions

1. In what senses are the Federalists properly described as "aristocrats" and the Antifederalists as "democrats"? Consider both the social standing of the two groups and their ideas about politics.
2. Did the Federalists believe in democracy? What evidence is there that they did? That they did not? How can these two views be reconciled?
3. Were the Antifederalists correct in at least some of their charges against the Constitution? Which of their complaints look more reasonable after two hundred years? Which look less so?

 # Foundations

There is no better way to understand the political philosophy of the Federalists than to read the *Federalist Papers.* Originally a selection of newspaper columns written during the debate over the ratification of the Constitution in New York State, the *Federalist Papers* are a compendium of eighty-five essays explaining, defending, and elaborating on the proposed Constitution. The *Federalist,* as it is known, is widely regarded as the definitive statement of the Federalists' views on the Constitution and thus is a frequent reference point for those (federal judges, for example) who seek to know the intent of those who wrote the Constitution. The essays that make up the *Federalist* were written by three prominent proponents of the Constitution: John Jay, Alexander Hamilton, and James Madison. Following the style of the day, the articles were signed by the pseudonym Publius, a name that perhaps sought to imply that the authors spoke for the public interest.

Federalist No. 10, written by James Madison, is concerned with the problem of factions. Frequently, it appears in a textbook chapter on interest groups, and it might profitably be reread along with the selections in Chapter 6. Its real importance, however, lies in Publius's discussion of human nature and representative government. Publius believes that in a free society, there will soon arise factions, or groups of individuals motivated by a common interest or passion adverse to the interests of other citizens or to the public interest. These factions arise because individuals are free to think for themselves about "religion . . . government, and many other points" and because they have different abilities for acquiring property. Once factions arise, it is in the nature of human beings that they will attempt to use the government to advance their own interests, even at the expense of others. In a pure democracy, the majority faction will pursue its own interest at the expense of the minority, with the result that rational government is impossible. The solution is to construct a representative government covering a large area, so that each representative will represent many diverse interests, and no one faction will be able to dominate.

Notice the consequences of Publius's theory: representative government is not merely a means of approximating a direct democracy but an improvement on it, and representatives are expected not merely to echo the interests of their constituents but to refine and filter those interests and balance them against the interests of others and against the public interest.

In *Federalist* Nos. 47–51, James Madison lays out his theory of the separation of powers. Contrary to the assumption of most other Americans, Madison did not believe that legislative, executive, and judicial power should be rigidly constrained, each to its own branch of government. In fact, *Federalist* No. 47 was written explicitly to challenge the assumption that the separation of powers means that the three departments of government "ought to have no *partial agency* in, or no *control* over, the acts of each other." Quite the opposite is true, in Madison's opinion: each branch should be given a share of the others' powers. It is only if "the *whole* power of one department is exercised by the same hands which possess the whole power of another department" that liberty is threatened.

Having demonstrated that the separation of powers does not demand a strict separation of functions, Madison then lays out the psychological basis for the separation of powers. Put simply, human beings are not angels; they are and will always be ambitious and power hungry. The only security against such individuals (and politicians are especially likely to possess such qualities) is to make sure that ambition checks ambition. By dividing power among ambitious people and then making them compete for power among themselves, liberty is protected.

All of this may be a sad commentary on human nature, as Madison suggests, but "what is government itself but the greatest of all reflections on human nature?" Madison's political theory here tracks the Scottish economist Adam Smith's theory of capitalism: we rely on the baker for bread not on the assumption that the baker will want to feed his fellow human beings but on his personal desire for money. Similarly, Madison relies for the protection of liberty not on politicians' love of the people but on their desire to protect their own power.

Also included here is a selection from the Antifederalists, who opposed the Constitution. That they lost their battle does not mean that their arguments were without merit. The Antifederalists were in general educated and intelligent men whose ideas on politics presented a viable alternative to that presented by the Federalists. In fact, the Antifederalists' views typically represented the conventional eighteenth-century wisdom as compared to the much more innovative—and therefore controversial—ideas of the Federalists.

The Antifederalists produced no such book as the *Federalist Papers*. Their writings were diverse, uncoordinated, and of uneven quality. One example—the report of the minority of the Pennsylvania ratifying convention of 1787—is given below. This report presents one of the most systematic statements of the Antifederalists' arguments. Notice in particular the minority's fearful and suspicious tone—justifiable, considering the way they were treated by the majority—along with their objections to a large republic; the mixing of legislative, executive, and judicial power; the lack of limits to federal authority over the states; and the absence of a bill of rights.

Other selections from the *Federalist Papers* are contained in Chapters 2, 9, 10, and 12.

Questions

1. What is a faction? Why are majority factions more dangerous than minority factions, according to Madison?
2. According to Madison, what advantages does a large republic have over a smaller one? How might the Antifederalists respond to Madison's position?
3. How does Madison respond to the Antifederalists' charge that the Constitution impermissibly blends executive, legislative, and judicial power? Why, in Madison's view, is it necessary to blend the three types of power?
4. Compare and contrast the Federalists' and Antifederalists' views on human nature. Pay particular attention to Madison's argument in *Federalist* No. 51.

1.1 *Federalist* No. 10 (1787)

James Madison

Outline

I. Republican governments are prone to the disease of *factions;* protecting against factions is critical to the success of any design for republican government.

II. Definition of faction.

III. The problem of factions can be cured by removing the causes of factions or by controlling their effects.

    A. It is impractical and unwise to try to remove the causes of factions; they are "sown in the nature of man."

    B. Therefore factions must be controlled.

        1. Minority factions can be controlled by the principle of majority rule.

        2. Minority factions can be controlled by creating a large republic and by creating a system of representation to "refine and enlarge" the views of the public.

Among the numerous advantages promised by a well-constructed Union, none deserves to be more accurately developed than its tendency to break and control the violence of faction. The friend of popular governments never finds himself so much alarmed for their character and fate as when he contemplates their propensity to this dangerous vice. He will not fail, therefore, to set a due value on any plan which, without violating the principles to which he is attached, provides a proper cure for it. The instability, injustice, and confusion introduced into the public councils have, in truth, been the mortal diseases under which popular governments have everywhere perished, as they continue to be the favorite and fruitful topics from which the adversaries to liberty derive their most specious declamations. The valuable improvements made by the American constitutions on the popular models, both ancient and modern, cannot certainly be too much admired; but it would be an unwarrantable partiality to contend that they have as effectually obviated the danger on this side, as was wished and expected. Complaints are everywhere heard from our most considerate and virtuous citizens, equally the friends of public and private faith and of public and personal liberty, that our governments are too unstable, that the public good is disregarded in the conflicts of rival parties, and that measures are too often decided, not according to the rules of justice and the rights of the minor party, but by the superior force of an interested and overbearing majority. However anxiously we may wish that these complaints had no foundation, the evidence of known facts will not permit us to deny that they are in some degree true. It will be found, indeed, on a candid review of our situation, that some of the distresses under which we labor have been erroneously charged on the operation of our governments; but it will be found, at the same time, that other causes will not alone account for many of our heaviest misfortunes; and, particularly, for that prevailing and increasing distrust of public engagements and alarm for private rights which are echoed from one end of the continent to the other. These must be chiefly, if not wholly, effects of the unsteadiness and injustice with which a factious spirit has tainted our public administration.

By a faction I understand a number of citizens, whether amounting to a majority or minority of the whole, who are united and actuated by some common impulse of passion, or of interest, adverse to the rights of other citizens, or to the permanent and aggregate interests of the community.

There are two methods of curing the mischiefs of faction: the one, by removing its causes; the other, by controlling its effects.

There are again two methods of removing the causes of faction: the one, by destroying the liberty which is essential to its existence; the other, by giving to every citizen the same opinions, the same passions, and the same interests.

It could never be more truly said than of the first remedy that it was worse than the disease. Liberty is to faction what air is to fire, an aliment without which it instantly expires. But it could not be a less folly to abolish liberty, which is essential to political life, because it nourishes faction than it would be to wish the annihilation of air, which is essential to animal life, because it imparts to fire its destructive agency.

The second expedient is as impracticable as the first would be unwise. As long as the reason of man continues fallible, and he is at liberty to exercise it, different opinions will be formed. As long as the connection subsists between his reason and his self-love, his opinions and his passions will have a reciprocal influence on each other; and the former will be objects to which the latter will attach themselves. The diversity in the faculties of men, from which the rights of property originate, is not less an insuperable obstacle to a uniformity of interests. The protection of these faculties is the first object of government. From the protection of different and unequal faculties of acquiring property, the possession of different degrees and kinds of property immediately results; and from the influence of these on the sentiments and views of the respective proprietors ensues a division of the society into different interests and parties.

The latent causes of faction are thus sown in the nature of man; and we see them everywhere brought into different degrees of activity, according to the different circumstances of civil society. A zeal for different opinions concerning religion, concerning government, and many other points, as well of speculation as of practice; an attachment to different leaders ambitiously contending for preeminence and power; or to persons of other descriptions whose fortunes have been interesting to the human passions, have, in turn, divided mankind into parties, inflamed them with mutual animosity, and rendered them much more disposed to vex and oppress each other than to cooperate for their common good. So strong is this propensity of mankind to fall into mutual animosities that where no substantial occasion presents itself the most frivolous and fanciful distinctions have been sufficient to kindle their unfriendly passions and excite their most violent conflicts. But the most common and durable source of factions has been the various and unequal distribution of property. Those who hold and those who are without property have ever formed distinct interests in society. Those who are creditors, and those who are debtors, fall under a like discrimination. A landed interest, a manufacturing interest, a mercantile interest, a moneyed interest, with many lesser interests, grow up of necessity in civilized nations, and divide them into different classes, actuated by different sentiments and views. The regulation of these various and interfering interests forms the principal task of modern legislation and involves the spirit of party and faction in the necessary and ordinary operations of government.

No man is allowed to be a judge in his own cause, because his interest would certainly bias his judgment, and, not improbably, corrupt his integrity. With equal, nay with greater reason, a body of men are unfit to be both judges and parties at the same time; yet what are many of the most important acts of legislation but so many judicial determinations, not indeed concerning the rights of single persons, but concerning the rights of large bodies of citizens? And what are the different classes of legislators but advocates and parties to the causes which they determine? Is a law proposed concerning private debts? It is a question to which the creditors are parties on one side and the debtors on the other. Justice ought to hold the balance between them. Yet the parties are, and must be, themselves the judges; and the most numerous party, or in other words, the most powerful faction must be expected to prevail. Shall domestic manufacturers be encouraged, and in what degree, by restrictions on foreign manufacturers? are questions which would be differently decided by the landed and the manufacturing classes, and probably by neither with a sole regard to justice and the public good. The apportionment of taxes on the various descriptions of property is an act which seems to require the most exact impartiality; yet there is, perhaps, no legislative act in which greater opportunity and temptation are given to a predominant party to trample on the rules of justice. Every shilling with which they overburden the inferior number is a shilling saved to their own pockets.

It is in vain to say that enlightened statesmen will be able to adjust these clashing interests and render them all subservient to the public good. Enlightened statesmen will not always be at the helm. Nor, in many cases, can such an adjustment be made at all without taking into view indirect and remote considerations, which will rarely prevail over the immediate interest which one party may find in disregarding the rights of another or the good of the whole.

The inference to which we are brought is that the *causes* of faction cannot be removed and that relief is only to be sought in the means of controlling its *effects*.

If a faction consists of less than a majority, relief is supplied by the republican principle, which enables the majority to defeat its sinister views by regular vote. It may clog the administration, it may convulse the society; but it will be unable to execute and mask its violence under the forms of the Constitution. When a majority is included in a faction, the form of popular government, on the other hand, enables it to sacrifice to its ruling passion or interest both the public good and the rights of other citizens. To secure the public good and private rights against the danger of such a faction, and at the same time to preserve the spirit and the form of popular government, is then the great object to which our inquiries are directed. Let me add that it is the great desideratum by which alone this form of government can be rescued from the opprobrium under which it has so long labored and be recommended to the esteem and adoption of mankind.

By what means is this object attainable? Evidently by one of two only. Either the existence of the same passion or interest in a majority at the same time must be prevented, or the majority, having such coexistent passion or interest, must be rendered, by their number and local situation, unable to concert and carry into effect schemes of oppression. If the impulse and the opportunity be suffered to coincide, we well know that neither moral nor religious motives can be relied on as an adequate control. They are not found to be such on the injustice and violence of individuals, and lose their efficacy in proportion to the number combined together, that is, in proportion as their efficacy becomes needful.

From this view of the subject it may be concluded that a pure democracy, by which I mean a society consisting of a small number of citizens, who assemble and administer the government in person, can admit of no cure for the mischiefs of faction. A common passion or interest will, in almost every case, be felt by a majority of the whole; a communication and concert results from the form of government itself; and there is nothing to check the inducements to sacrifice the weaker party or an obnoxious individual. Hence it is that such democracies have ever been spectacles of turbulence and contention; have ever been found incompatible with personal security or the rights of property; and have in general been as short in their lives as they have been violent in their deaths. Theoretic politicians, who have patronized this species of government, have erroneously supposed that by reducing mankind to a perfect equality in their political rights, they would at the same time be perfectly equalized and assimilated in their possessions, their opinions, and their passions.

A republic, by which I mean a government in which the scheme of representation takes place, opens a different prospect and promises the cure for which we are seeking. Let us examine the points in which it varies from pure democracy, and we shall comprehend both the nature of the cure and the efficacy which it must derive from the Union.

The two great points of difference between a democracy and a republic are: first, the delegation of the government, in the latter, to a small number of citizens elected by the rest; secondly, the greater number of citizens and greater sphere of country over which the latter may be extended.

The effect of the first difference is, on the one hand, to refine and enlarge the public views by passing them through the medium of a chosen body of citizens, whose wisdom may best discern the true interest of their country and whose patriotism and love of justice will be least likely to sacrifice it to temporary or partial considerations. Under such a regulation it may well happen that the public voice, pronounced by the representatives of the people, will be more consonant to the public good than if pronounced by the people themselves, convened for the purpose. On the other hand, the effect may be inverted. Men of factious tempers, of local prejudices, or of sinister designs, may, by intrigue, by corruption, or by other means, first obtain the suffrages, and then betray the interests of the people. The question resulting is, whether small or extensive republics are most favorable to the election of proper guardians of the public weal; and it is clearly decided in favor of the latter by two obvious considerations.

In the first place it is to be remarked that however small the republic may be the representatives must be raised to a certain number in order to guard against the cabals of a few; and that however large it may be they must be limited to a certain number in order to guard against the confusion of a multitude. Hence, the number of representatives in the two cases not being in proportion to that of the constituents, and being proportionally greatest in the small republic, it follows that if the proportion of fit characters be not less in the large than in the small republic, the former will present a greater option, and consequently a greater probability of a fit choice.

In the next place, as each representative will be chosen by a greater number of citizens in the large than in the small republic, it will be more difficult for unworthy candidates to practise with success the vicious arts by which elections are too often carried; and the suffrages of the people being more free, will be more likely to center on men who possess the most attractive merit and the most diffusive and established characters.

It must be confessed that in this, as in most other cases, there is a mean, on both sides of which inconveniences will be found to lie. By enlarging too much the number of electors, you render the representative too little acquainted with all their local circumstances and lesser interests; as by reducing it too much, you render him unduly attached to these, and too little fit to comprehend and pursue great and national objects. The federal Constitution forms a happy combination in this respect; the great and aggregate interests being referred to the national, the local and particular to the State legislatures.

The other point of difference is the greater number of citizens and extent of territory which may be brought within the compass of republican than of democratic government; and it is this circumstance principally which renders factious combinations less to be dreaded in the former than in the latter. The smaller the society, the fewer probably will be the distinct parties and interests composing it; the fewer the distinct parties and interests, the more frequently will a majority be found of the same party; and the smaller the number of individuals composing a majority, and the smaller the compass within which they are placed, the more easily will they concert and execute their plans of oppression. Extend the sphere and you take in a greater variety of parties and interests; you make it less probable that a majority of the whole will have a common motive to invade the rights of other citizens; or if such a common motive exists, it will be more difficult for all who feel it to discover their own strength and to act in unison with each other. Besides other impediments, it may be remarked that, where there is a consciousness of unjust or dishonorable purposes, communication is always checked by distrust in proportion to the number whose concurrence is necessary.

Hence, it clearly appears that the same advantage which a republic has over a democracy in controlling the effects of faction is enjoyed by a large over a small republic—is enjoyed by the Union over the States composing it. Does this advantage consist in the substitution of representatives whose enlightened views and virtuous sentiments render them superior to local prejudices and to schemes of injustice? It will not be denied that the representation of the Union will be most likely to possess these requisite endowments. Does it consist in the greater security afforded by a greater variety of parties, against the event of any one party being able to outnumber and oppress the rest? In an equal degree does the increased variety of parties comprised within the Union increase this security. Does it, in fine, consist in the greater obstacles opposed to the concert and accomplishment of the secret wishes of an unjust and interested majority? Here again the extent of the Union gives it the most palpable advantage.

The influence of factious leaders may kindle a flame within their particular States but will be unable to spread a general conflagration through the other States. A religious sect may degenerate into a political faction in a part of the Confederacy; but the variety of sects dispersed over the entire face of it must secure the national councils against any danger from that source. A rage for paper money, for an abolition of debts, for an equal division of property, or for any other improper or wicked project, will be less apt to pervade the whole body of the Union than a particular member of it, in the same proportion as such a malady is more likely to taint a particular county or district than an entire State.

In the extent and proper structure of the Union, therefore, we behold a republican remedy for the diseases most incident to republican government. And according to the degree of pleasure and pride we feel in being republicans ought to be our zeal in cherishing the spirit and supporting the character of federalists. ■

1.2 *Federalist* No. 47 (1787)

James Madison

Outline

I. The charge that the Constitution violates the separation of powers principle is based on a misinterpretation of the separation of powers.

  A. The Constitution is consistent with Montesquieu's view of the separation of powers.

    1. Montesquieu's view based on the British Constitution.

    2. Discussion of Montesquieu's theory.

  B. The Constitution is consistent with the implementation of the separation of powers in the constitutions of the several states.

. . . One of the principal objections inculcated by the more respectable adversaries to the Constitution is its supposed violation of the political maxim that the legislative, executive, and judiciary departments ought to be separate and distinct. In the structure of the federal government no regard, it is said, seems to have been paid to this essential precaution in favor of liberty. The several departments of power are distributed and blended in such a manner as at once to destroy all symmetry and beauty of form, and to expose some of the essential parts of the edifice to the danger of being crushed by the disproportionate weight of other parts.

No political truth is certainly of greater intrinsic value, or is stamped with the authority of more enlightened patrons of liberty than that on which the objection is founded. The accumulation of all powers, legislative, executive, and judiciary, in the same hands, whether of one, a few, or many, and whether hereditary, self-appointed, or elective, may justly be pronounced the very definition of tyranny.

Were the federal Constitution, therefore, really chargeable with this accumulation of power, or with a mixture of powers, having a dangerous tendency to such an accumulation, no further arguments would be necessary to inspire a universal reprobation of the system. I persuade myself, however, that it will be made apparent to everyone that the charge cannot be supported, and that the maxim on which it relies has been totally misconceived and misapplied. In order to form correct ideas on this important subject it will be proper to investigate the sense in which the preservation of liberty requires that the three great departments of power should be separate and distinct.

The oracle who is always consulted and cited on this subject is the celebrated Montesquieu. If he be not the author of this invaluable precept in the science of politics, he has the merit at least of displaying and recommending it most effectually to the attention of mankind. Let us endeavor, in the first place, to ascertain his meaning on this point.

The British Constitution was to Montesquieu what Homer has been to the didactic writers on epic poetry. As the latter have considered the work of the immortal bard as the perfect model from which the principles and rules of the epic art were to be drawn, and by which all similar works were to be judged, so this great political critic appears to have viewed the Constitution of England as the standard, or to use his own expression, as the mirror of political liberty; and to have delivered, in the form of elementary truths, the several characteristic principles of that particular system. That we may be sure, then, not to mistake his meaning in this case, let us recur to the source from which the maxim was drawn.

On the slightest view of the British Constitution, we must perceive that the legislative, executive, and judiciary departments are by no means totally separate and distinct from each other. The executive magistrate forms an integral part of the legislative authority. He alone has the prerogative of making treaties with foreign sovereigns which, when made, have, under certain limitations, the force of legislative acts. All the members of the judiciary department are appointed by him, can be removed by him on the address of the two Houses of Parliament, and form, when he pleases to consult them, one of his constitutional councils. One branch of the legislative department forms also a great constitutional council to the executive chief, as, on another hand, it is the sole depositary of judicial power in cases of impeachment, and is invested with the supreme appellate jurisdiction in all other cases. The judges, again, are so far connected with the legislative department as often to attend and participate in its deliberations, though not admitted to a legislative vote.

From these facts, by which Montesquieu was guided, it may clearly be inferred that in saying "There can be no liberty where the legislative and executive powers are united in the same person, or body of magistrates," or, "if the power of judging be not separated from the legislative and executive powers," he did not mean that these departments ought to have no *partial agency* in, or no *control* over, the acts of each other. His meaning, as his own words import, and still more conclusively as illustrated by the example in his eye, can amount to no more than this, that where the *whole* power of one department is exercised by the same hands which possess the *whole* power of another department, the fundamental principles of a free constitution are subverted. This would have been the case in the constitution examined by him, if the king, who is the sole executive magistrate, had possessed also the complete legislative power, or the supreme administration of justice; or if the entire legislative body had possessed the supreme judiciary, or the supreme executive authority. This, however, is not among the vices of that constitution. The magistrate in whom the whole executive power resides cannot of himself make a law, though he can put a negative on every law; nor administer justice in person, though he has the appointment of those who do administer it. The judges can exercise no executive prerogative, though they are shoots from the executive stock; nor any legislative function, though they may be advised by the legislative councils. The entire legislature can perform no judiciary act, though by the joint act of two of its branches the judges may be removed from their offices, and though one of its branches is possessed of the judicial power in the last resort. The entire legislature, again, can exercise no executive prerogative, though one of its branches constitutes the supreme executive magistracy, and another, on the impeachment of a third, can try and condemn all the subordinate officers in the executive department.

The reasons on which Montesquieu grounds his maxim are a further demonstration of his meaning. "When the legislative and executive powers are united in the same person or body," says he, "there can be no liberty, because apprehensions may arise lest *the same* monarch or senate should *enact* tyrannical laws to *execute* them in a tyrannical manner." Again: "Were the power of judging joined with the legislative, the life and liberty of the subject would be exposed to arbitrary control, for *the judge* would then be *the legislator*. Were it joined to the executive power, *the judge* might behave with all the violence of *an oppressor*." Some of these reasons are more fully explained in other passages; but briefly stated as they are here they sufficiently establish the meaning which we have put on this celebrated maxim of this celebrated author.

If we look into the constitutions of the several States we find that, notwithstanding the emphatical and, in some instances, the unqualified terms in which this axiom has been laid down, there is not a single instance in which the several departments of power have been kept absolutely separate and distinct. New Hampshire, whose constitution was the last formed, seems to have been fully aware of the impossibility and inexpediency of avoiding any mixture whatever of these departments, and has qualified the doctrine by declaring "that the legislative, executive, and judiciary powers ought to be kept as separate from, and independent of, each other *as the nature of a free government will admit; or as is consistent with that chain of connection that binds the whole fabric of the constitution in one indissoluble bond of unity and amity.*" Her constitution accordingly mixes these departments in several respects. The Senate, which is a branch of the legislative department, is also a judicial tribunal for the trial of impeachments; The President, who is the head of the executive department, is the presiding member also of the Senate; and, besides an equal vote in all cases, has a casting vote in case of a tie. The executive head is himself eventually elective every year by the legislative department, and his council is every year chosen by and from the members of the same department. Several of the officers of state are also appointed by the legislature. And the members of the judiciary department are appointed by the executive department.

The constitution of Massachusetts has observed a sufficient though less pointed caution in expressing this fundamental article of liberty. It declares "that the legislative department shall never exercise the executive and judicial powers, or either of them; the executive shall never exercise the legislative and judicial powers, or either of them; the judicial shall never exercise the legislative and executive powers, or either of them." This declaration corresponds precisely with the doctrine of Montesquieu, as it has been explained, and is not in a single point violated by the plan of the convention. It goes no farther than to prohibit any one of the entire departments from exercising the powers of another department. In the very Constitution to which it is prefixed, a partial mixture of powers has been admitted. The executive magistrate has a qualified negative on the legislative body, and the Senate, which is a part of the legislature, is a court of impeachment for members both of the executive and judiciary departments. The members of the judiciary department, again, are appointable by the executive department, and removable by the same authority on the address of the two legislative branches. Lastly, a number of the officers of government are annually appointed by the legislative department. As the appointment to offices, particularly executive offices, is in its nature an executive function, the compilers of the Constitution have, in this last point at least, violated the rule established by themselves. . . . [Publius next reviews other state constitutions.]

In citing these cases, in which the legislative, executive, and judiciary departments have not been kept totally separate and distinct, I wish not to be regarded as an advocate for the particular organizations of the several State governments. I am fully aware that among the many excellent principles which they exemplify they carry strong marks of the haste, and still stronger of the inexperience, under which they were framed. It is but too obvious that in some instances the fundamental principle under consideration has been violated by too great a mixture, and even an actual consolidation of the different powers; and that in no instance has a competent provision been made for maintaining in practice the separation delineated on paper. What I have wished to evince is that the charge brought against the proposed Constitution of violating the sacred maxim of free government is warranted neither by the real meaning annexed to that maxim by its author, nor by the sense in which it has hitherto been understood in America. This interesting subject will be resumed in the ensuing paper. ∎

1.3 *Federalist* No. 48 (1787)

James Madison

Outline

I. The separation of powers requires that the three departments be connected and blended, giving each control over the others.

   A. Encroaching nature of political power.

   B. Inadequacy of "parchment (or paper) barriers."

II. Preeminent danger of legislative power makes it necessary to give the other two branches some control.

It was shown in the last paper that the political apothegm there examined does not require that the legislative, executive, and judiciary departments should be wholly unconnected with each other. I shall undertake, in the next place, to show that unless these departments be so far connected and blended as to give to each a constitutional control over the others, the degree of separation which the maxim requires, as essential to a free government, can never in practice be duly maintained.

It is agreed on all sides that the powers properly belonging to one of the departments ought not to be directly and completely administered by either of the other departments. It is equally evident that none of them ought to possess, directly or indirectly, an overruling influence over the others in the administration of their respective powers. It will not be denied that power is of an encroaching nature and that it ought to be effectually restrained from passing the limits assigned to it. After discriminating, therefore, in theory, the several classes of power, as they may in their nature be legislative, executive, or judiciary, the next and most difficult task is to provide some practical security for each, against the invasion of the others. What this security ought to be is the great problem to be solved.

Will it be sufficient to mark, with precision, the boundaries of these departments in the constitution of the government, and to trust to these parchment barriers against the encroaching spirit of power? This is the security which appears to have been principally relied on by the compilers of most of the American constitutions. But experience assures us that the efficacy of the provision has been greatly overrated; and that some more adequate defense is indispensably necessary for the more feeble against the more powerful members of the government. The legislative department is everywhere extending the sphere of its activity and drawing all power into its impetuous vortex.

The founders of our republics have so much merit for the wisdom which they have displayed that no task can be less pleasing than that of pointing out the errors into which they have fallen. A respect for truth, however, obliges us to remark that they seem never for a moment to have turned their eyes from the danger, to liberty, from the overgrown and all-grasping prerogative of an hereditary magistrate, supported and fortified by an hereditary branch of the legislative authority. They seem never to have recollected the danger from legislative usurpations, which, by assembling all power in the same hands, must lead to the same tyranny as is threatened by executive usurpations.

In a government where numerous and extensive prerogatives are placed in the hands of an hereditary monarch, the executive department is very justly regarded as the source of danger, and watched with all the jealousy which a zeal for liberty ought to inspire. In a democracy, where a multitude of people exercise in person the legislative functions and are continually exposed, by their incapacity for regular deliberation and concerted measures, to the ambitious intrigues of their executive magistrates, tyranny may well be apprehended, on some favorable emergency, to start up in the same quarter. But in a representative republic where the executive magistracy is carefully limited, both in the extent and the duration of its power; and where the legislative power is exercised by an assembly, which is inspired by a supposed influence over the people with an intrepid confidence in its own strength; which is sufficiently numerous to feel all the passions which actuate a multitude, yet not so numerous as to be incapable of pursuing the objects of its passions by means which reason prescribes; it is against the enterprising ambition of this department that the people ought to indulge all their jealousy and exhaust all their precautions.

The legislative department derives a superiority in our governments from other circumstances. Its constitutional powers being at once more extensive, and less susceptible of precise limits, it can, with the greater facility, mask, under complicated and indirect measures, the encroachments which it makes on the co-ordinate departments. It is not unfrequently a question of real nicety in legislative bodies whether the operation of a particular measure will, or will not, extend beyond the legislative sphere. On the other side, the executive power being restrained within a narrower compass and being more simple in its nature, and the judiciary being described by landmarks still less uncertain, projects of usurpation by either of these departments would immediately betray and defeat themselves. Nor is this all; as the legislative department alone has access to the pockets of the people, and has in some constitutions full discretion, and in all a prevailing influence, over the pecuniary rewards of those who fill the other departments, a dependence is thus created in the latter, which gives still greater facility to encroachments of the former. . . .

The conclusion which I am warranted in drawing from these observations is that a mere demarcation on parchment of the constitutional limits of the several departments is not a sufficient guard against those encroachments which lead to a tyrannical concentration of all the powers of government in the same hands. ■

1.4 *Federalist* No. 51 (1787)

James Madison

Outline

I. Maintaining the separation of powers in practice requires giving each branch the means of checking the others.

   A. Members of one branch should not appoint members of the other branches, but an exception is made in the case of the judiciary.

   B. Members of one branch should not be dependent on the other branches for pay and perks.

   C. Above all, each branch must have the *means* and the *motive* to check and balance the others.

   D. Overwhelming power of the legislature requires dividing it into two parts and strengthening the executive branch.

II. Protection of liberty further enhanced by dividing power between the national and state governments and by diluting the influence of majority factions.

T o what expedient, then, shall we finally resort, for maintaining in practice the necessary partition of power among the several departments as laid down in the Constitution? The only answer that can be given is that as all these exterior provisions are found to be inadequate the defect must be supplied by so contriving the interior structure of the government as that its several constituent parts may, by their mutual relations, be the means of keeping each other in their proper places. Without presuming to undertake a full development of this important idea I will hazard a few general observations which may perhaps place it in a clearer light, and enable us to form a more correct judgment of the principles and structure of the government planned by the convention.

In order to lay a due foundation for that separate and distinct exercise of the different powers of government, which to a certain extent is admitted on all hands to be essential to the preservation of liberty, it is evident that each department should have a will of its own; and consequently should be so constituted that the members of each should have as little agency as possible in the appointment of the members of the others. Were this principle rigorously adhered to, it would require that all the appointments for the supreme executive, legislative, and judiciary magistracies should be drawn from the same fountain of authority, the people, through channels having no communication whatever with one another. Perhaps such a plan of constructing the several departments would be less difficult in practice than it may in contemplation appear. Some difficulties, however, and some additional expense would attend the execution of it. Some deviations, therefore, from the principle must be admitted. In the constitution of the judiciary department in particular, it might be inexpedient to insist rigorously on the principle: first, because peculiar qualifications being essential in the members, the primary consideration ought to be to select that mode of choice which best secures these qualifications; second, because the permanent tenure by which the appointments are held in that department must soon destroy all sense of dependence on the authority conferring them.

It is equally evident that the members of each department should be as little dependent as possible on those of the others for the emoluments annexed to their offices. Were the executive magistrate, or the judges, not independent of the legislature in this particular, their independence in every other would be merely nominal.

But the great security against a gradual concentration of the several powers in the same department consists in giving to those who administer each department the necessary constitutional means and personal motives to resist encroachments of the others. The provision for defense must in this, as in all other cases, be made commensurate to the danger of attack. Ambition must be made to counteract ambition. The interest of the man must be connected with the constitutional rights of the place. It may be a reflection on human nature that such devices should be necessary to control the abuses of government. But what is government itself but the greatest of all reflections on human nature? If men were angels, no government would be necessary. If angels were to govern men, neither external nor internal controls on government would be necessary. In framing a government which is to be administered by men over men, the great difficulty lies in this: you must first enable the government to control the governed; and in the next place oblige it to control itself. A dependence on the people is, no doubt, the primary control on the government; but experience has taught mankind the necessity of auxiliary precautions.

This policy of supplying, by opposite and rival interests, the defect of better motives, might be traced through the whole system of human affairs, private as well as public. We see it particularly displayed in all the subordinate distributions of power, where the constant aim is to divide and arrange the several offices in such a manner as that each may be a check on the other—that the private interest of every individual may be a sentinel over the public rights. These inventions of prudence cannot be less requisite in the distribution of the supreme powers of the State.

But it is not possible to give to each department an equal power of self-defense. In republican government, the legislative authority necessarily predominates. The remedy for this inconveniency is to divide the legislature into different branches; and to render them, by different modes of election and different principles of action, as little connected with each other as the nature of their common functions and their common dependence on the society will admit. It may even be necessary to guard against dangerous encroachments by still further precautions. As the weight of the legislative authority requires that it should be thus divided, the weakness of the executive may require, on the other hand, that it should be fortified. An absolute negative on the legislature appears, at first view, to be the natural defense with which the executive magistrate should be armed. But perhaps it would be neither altogether safe nor alone sufficient. On ordinary occasions it might not be exerted with the requisite firmness, and on extraordinary occasions it might be perfidiously abused. May not this defect of an absolute negative be supplied by some qualified connection between this weaker department and the weaker branch of the stronger department, by which the latter may be led to support the constitutional rights of the former, without being too much detached from the rights of its own department?

If the principles on which these observations are founded be just, as I persuade myself they are, and they be applied as a criterion to the several State constitutions, and to the federal Constitution, it will be found that if the latter does not perfectly correspond with them, the former are infinitely less able to bear such a test.

There are, moreover, two considerations particularly applicable to the federal system of America, which place that system in a very interesting point of view.

First. In a single republic, all the power surrendered by the people is submitted to the administration of a single government; and the usurpations are guarded against by a division of the government into distinct and separate departments. In the compound republic of America, the power surrendered by the people is first divided between two distinct governments, and then the portion allotted to each subdivided among distinct and separate departments. Hence a double security arises to the rights of the people. The different governments will control each other, at the same time that each will be controlled by itself.

Second. It is of great importance in a republic not only to guard the society against the oppression of its rulers, but to guard one part of the society against the injustice of the other part. Different interests necessarily exist in different classes of citizens. If a majority be united by a common interest, the rights of the minority will be insecure. There are but two methods of providing against this evil: the one by creating a will in the community independent of the majority— that is, of the society itself; the other, by comprehending in the society so many separate descriptions of citizens as will render an unjust combination of a majority of the whole very improbable, if not impracticable. The first method prevails in all governments possessing an hereditary or self-appointed authority. This, at best, is but a precarious security; because a power independent of the society may as well espouse the unjust views of the major as the rightful interests of the minor party, and may possibly be turned against both parties. The second method will be exemplified in the federal republic of the United States. Whilst all authority in it will be derived from and dependent on the society, the society itself will be broken into so many parts, interests and classes of citizens, that the rights of individuals, or of the minority, will be in little danger from interested combinations of the majority. In a free government the security for civil rights must be the same as that for religious rights. It consists in the one case in the multiplicity of interests, and in the other in the multiplicity of sects. The degree of security in both cases will depend on the number of interests and sects; and this may be presumed to depend on the extent of country and number of people comprehended under the same government. This view of the subject must particularly recommend a proper federal system to all the sincere and considerate friends of republican government, since it shows that in exact proportion as the territory of the Union may be formed into more circumscribed Confederacies, or States, oppressive combinations of a majority will be facilitated; the best security, under the republican forms, for the rights of every class of citizen, will be diminished; and consequently the stability and independence of some member of the government, the only other security, must be proportionally increased. Justice is the end of government. It is the end of civil society. It ever has been and ever will be pursued until it be obtained, or until liberty be lost in the pursuit. In a society under the forms of which the stronger faction can readily unite and oppress the weaker, anarchy may as truly be said to reign as in a state of nature, where the weaker individual is not secured against the violence of the stronger; and as, in the latter state, even the stronger individuals are prompted, by the uncertainty of their condition, to submit to a government which may protect the weak as well as themselves; so, in the former state, will the more powerful factions or parties be gradually induced, by a like motive, to wish for a government which will protect all parties, the weaker as well as the more powerful. It can be little doubted that if the State of Rhode Island was separated from the Confederacy and left to itself, the insecurity of rights under the popular form of government within such narrow limits would be displayed by such reiterated oppressions of factious majorities that some power altogether independent of the people would soon be called for by the voice of the very factions whose misrule had proved the necessity of it. In the extended republic of the United States, and among the great variety of interests, parties, and sects which it embraces, a coalition of a majority of the whole society could seldom take place on any other principles than those of justice and the general good; whilst there being thus less danger to a minor from the will of a major party, there must be less pretext, also, to provide for the security of the former, by introducing into the government a will not dependent on the latter, or, in other words, a will independent of the society itself. It is no less certain than it is important, notwithstanding the contrary opinions which have been entertained, that the larger the society, provided it lie within a practicable sphere, the more duly capable it will be of self-government. And happily for the *republican cause*, the practicable sphere may be carried to a very great extent by a judicious modification and mixture of the *federal principle*. ■

1.5 The Address and Reasons of Dissent of the Minority of the Convention of Pennsylvania to Their Constituents (1788)

I t was not until after the termination of the late glorious contest, which made the people of the United States, an independent nation, that any defect was discovered in the present confederation. It was formed by some of the ablest patriots in America. It carried us successfully through the war; and the virtue and patriotism of the people, with their disposition to promote the common cause, supplied the want of power in Congress. . . .

It was at the end of the war . . . that the want of an efficient federal government was first complained of, and that the powers vested in Congress were found to be inadequate to the procuring of the benefits that should result from the union. . . . [Many states refused to grant Congress the funds it needed to carry out its responsibilities.] . . . It was found that our national character was sinking in the opinion of foreign nations. The Congress could make treaties of commerce, but could not enforce the observance of them. We were suffering from the restrictions of foreign nations, who had shackled our commerce, while we were unable to retaliate: and all now agreed that it would be advantageous to the union to enlarge the powers of Congress; that they should be enabled in the amplest manner to regulate commerce, and to lay and collect duties on the imports throughout the United States. With this view a convention was first proposed by Virginia, and finally recommended by Congress for the different states to appoint deputies to meet in convention, "for the purposes of revising and amending the present articles of confederation, so as to make them adequate to the exigencies of the union." This recommendation the legislatures of twelve states complied with so hastily as not to consult their constituents on the subject; and though the different legislatures had no authority from their constituents for the purpose, they probably apprehended the necessity would justify the measure; and none of them extended their ideas at that time further than "revising and amending the present articles of confederation." Pennsylvania by the act appointing deputies expressly confined their powers to this object; and though it is probable that some of the members of the assembly of this state had at that time in contemplation to annihilate the present confederation, as well as the constitution of

Pennsylvania, yet the plan was not sufficiently matured to communicate it to the public.

The majority of the legislature of this commonwealth, were at that time under the influence of the members from the city of Philadelphia. They agreed that the deputies sent by them to convention should have no compensation for their services, which determination was calculated to prevent the election of any member who resided at a distance from the city. It was in vain for the minority to attempt electing delegates to the convention, who understood the circumstances, and the feelings of the people, and had a common interest with them. They found a disposition in the leaders of the majority of the house to chuse themselves and some of their dependants. The minority attempted to prevent this by agreeing to vote for some of the leading members, who they knew had influence enough to be appointed at any rate, in hopes of carrying with them some respectable citizens of Philadelphia, in whose principles and integrity they could have more confidence; but even in this they were disappointed, except in one member: the eighth member was added at a subsequent session of the assembly.

The Continental convention met in the city of Philadelphia at the time appointed. It was composed of some men of excellent characters; of others who were more remarkable for their ambition and cunning, than their patriotism; and of some who had been opponents to the independence of the United States. The delegates from Pennsylvania were, six of them, uniform and decided opponents to the constitution of this commonwealth. The convention sat upwards of four months. The doors were kept shut, and the members brought under the most solemn engagements of secrecy. Some of those who opposed their going so far beyond their powers, retired, hopeless, from the convention, others had the firmness to refuse signing the plan altogether; and many who did sign it, did it not as a system they wholly approved, but as the best that could be then obtained, and notwithstanding the time spent on this subject, it is agreed on all hands to be a work of haste and accommodation.

Whilst the gilded chains were forging in the secret conclave, the meaner instruments of despotism without, were busily employed in alarming the fears of the people with dangers which did not exist, and exciting their hopes of greater advantages from the expected plan than even the best government on earth could produce.

The proposed plan had not many hours issued forth from the womb of suspicious secrecy, until such as were prepared for the purpose, were carrying about petitions for people to sign, signifying their approbation of the system, and requesting the legislature to call a convention. While every measure was taken to intimidate the people against opposing it, the public papers teemed with the most violent threats against those who should dare to think for themselves, and *tar and feathers* were liberally promised to all those who would not immediately join in supporting the proposed government be it what it would. Under such circumstances petitions in favour of calling a convention were signed by great numbers in and about the city, before they had leisure to read and examine the system, many of whom, now they are better acquainted with it, and have had time to investigate its principles, are heartily opposed to it. The petitions were speedily handed into the legislature. . . .

In this situation of affairs were the subscribers elected members of the convention of Pennsylvania. A convention called by a legislature in direct violation of their duty, and composed in part of members, who were compelled to attend for that purpose, to consider of a constitution proposed by a convention of the United States, who were not appointed for the purpose of framing a new form of government, but whose powers were expressly confined to altering and amending the present articles of confederation.—Therefore the members of the continental convention in proposing the plan acted as individuals, and not as deputies from Pennsylvania. The assembly who called the state convention acted as individuals, and not as the legislature of Pennsylvania; nor could they or the convention chosen on their recommendation have authority to do any act or thing, that can alter or annihilate the constitution of Pennsylvania (both of which will be done by the new constitution) nor are their proceedings in our opinion, at all binding on the people.

The election for members of the convention was held at so early a period and the want of information was so great, that some of us did not know of it until after it was over, and we have reason to believe that great numbers of the people of Pennsylvania have not yet had an opportunity of sufficiently examining the proposed constitution.—We apprehend that no change can take place that will affect the internal government or constitution of this commonwealth, unless a majority of the people should evidence a wish for such a change; but on examining the number of votes given for members of the present state convention, we find that of upwards of *seventy thousand* freemen who are intitled to vote in Pennsylvania, the whole convention has been elected by about *thirteen thousand* voters, and though *two thirds* of the members of the convention have thought proper to ratify the proposed constitution, yet those *two thirds* were elected by the votes of only *six thousand and eight hundred* freemen.

In the city of Philadelphia and some of the eastern counties, the junto that took the lead in the business agreed to vote for none but such as would solemnly promise to adopt the system *in toto*, without exercising their judgment. In many of the counties the people did not attend the elections as they had not an opportunity of judging of the plan. Others did not consider themselves bound by the call of a set of men who assembled at the statehouse in Philadelphia, and assumed the name of the legislature of Pennsylvania; and some were prevented from voting by the violence of the party who were determined at all events to force down the measure. To such lengths did the tools of despotism carry their outrage, that in the night of the election for members of convention, in the city of Philadelphia, several of the subscribers (being then in the city to transact your business) were grossly abused, ill-treated and insulted while they were quiet in their lodgings, though they did not interfere, nor had any thing to do with the said election, but as they apprehend, because they were supposed to be adverse to the proposed constitution, and would not tamely surrender those sacred rights, which you had committed to their charge.

The convention met, and the same disposition was soon manifested in considering the proposed constitution, that had been exhibited in every other stage of the business. We were prohibited by an express vote of the convention, from taking any question on the separate articles of the plan, and reduced to the necessity of adopting or rejecting *in toto.*—'Tis true the majority permitted us to debate on each article, but restrained us from proposing amendments.—They also determined not to permit us to enter on the minutes our reasons of dissent against any of the articles, nor even on the final question our reasons of dissent against the whole. Thus situated we entered on the examination of the proposed system of government, and found it to be such as we could not adopt, without, as we conceived, surrendering up your dearest rights. We offered our objections to the convention, and opposed those parts of the plan, which, in our opinion, would be injurious to you, in the best manner we were able; and closed our arguments by offering the following propositions to the convention.

1. The right of conscience shall be held inviolable; and neither the legislative, executive nor judicial powers of the United States shall have authority to alter, abrogate, or infringe any part of the constitution of the several states, which provide for the preservation of liberty in matters of religion.

2. That in controversies respecting property, and in suits between man and man, trial by jury shall remain as heretofore, as well in the federal courts, as in those of the several states.

3. That in all capital and criminal prosecutions, a man has a right to demand the cause and nature of his accusation, as well in the federal courts, as in those of the several states; to be heard by himself and his counsel; to be confronted with the accusers and witnesses; to call for evidence in his favor, and a speedy trial by an impartial jury of his vicinage, without whose unanimous consent, he cannot be found guilty, nor can he be compelled to give evidence against himself; and that no man be deprived of his liberty, except by the law of the land or the judgment of his peers.

4. That excessive bail ought not to be required, nor excessive fines imposed, nor cruel nor unusual punishments inflicted.

5. That warrants unsupported by evidence, whereby any officer or messenger may be commanded or required to search suspected places, or to seize any person or persons, his or their property, not particularly described, are grievous and oppressive, and shall not be granted either by the magistrates of the federal government or others.

6. That the people have a right to the freedom of speech, of writing and publishing their sentiments, therefore, the freedom of the press shall not be restrained by any law of the United States.

7. That the people have a right to bear arms for the defence of themselves and their own state, or the United States, or for the purpose of killing game; and no law shall be passed for disarming the people or any of them, unless for crimes committed, or real danger of public injury from individuals; and as standing armies in the time of peace are dangerous to liberty, they ought not to be kept up; and that the military shall be kept under strict subordination to and be governed by the civil powers.

8. The inhabitants of the several states shall have liberty to fowl and hunt in seasonable times, on the lands they hold, and on all other lands in the United States not inclosed, and in like manner to fish in all navigable waters, and others

not private property, without being restrained therein by any laws to be passed by the legislature of the United States.

9. That no law shall be passed to restrain the legislatures of the several states from enacting laws for imposing taxes, except imposts and duties on goods imported or exported, and that no taxes, except imposts and duties upon goods imported and exported, and postage on letters shall be levied by the authority of Congress.

10. That the house of representatives be properly increased in number; that elections shall remain free; that the several states shall have power to regulate the elections for senators and representatives, without being controuled either directly or indirectly by any interference on the part of the Congress; and that elections of representatives be annual.

11. That the power of organizing, arming and disciplining the militia (the manner of disciplining the militia to be prescribed by Congress) remain with the individual states, and that Congress shall not have authority to call or march any of the militia out of their own state, without the consent of such state, and for such length of time only as such state shall agree.

That the sovereignty, freedom and independency of the several states shall be retained, and every power, jurisdiction and right which is not by this constitution expressly delegated to the United States in Congress assembled.

12. That the legislative, executive, and judicial powers be kept separate; and to this end that a constitutional council be appointed, to advise and assist the president, who shall be responsible for the advice they give, hereby the senators would be relieved from almost constant attendance; and also that the judges be made completely independent.

13. That no treaty which shall be directly opposed to the existing laws of the United States in Congress assembled, shall be valid until such laws shall be repealed, or made conformable to such treaty; neither shall any treaties be valid which are in contradiction to the constitution of the United States, or the constitutions of the several states.

14. That the judiciary power of the United States shall be confined to cases affecting ambassadors, other public ministers and consuls; to cases of admiralty and maritime jurisdiction; to controversies to which the United States shall be a party; to controversies between two or more states—between a state and citizens of different states—between citizens claiming lands under grants of different states; and between a state or the citizen thereof and foreign states, and in criminal cases, to such only as are expressly enumerated in the constitution, and that the United States in Congress assembled, shall not have power to enact laws, which shall alter the laws of descents and distribution of the effects of deceased persons, the titles of lands or goods, or the regulation of contracts in the individual states.

After reading these propositions, we declared our willingness to agree to the plan, provided it was so amended as to meet these propositions, or something similar to them; and finally moved the convention to adjourn, to give the people of Pennsylvania time to consider the subject, and determine for themselves; but these were all rejected, and the final vote was taken, when our duty to you induced us to vote against the proposed plan, and to decline signing the ratification of the same.

During the discussion we met with many insults, and some personal abuse; we were not even treated with decency, during the sitting of the convention, by the persons in the gallery of the house; however, we flatter ourselves that in contending for the preservation of those invaluable rights you have thought proper to commit to our charge, we acted with a spirit becoming freemen, and being desirous that you might know the principles which actuated our conduct, and being prohibited from inserting our reasons of dissent on the minutes of the convention, we have subjoined them for your consideration, as to you alone we are accountable. It remains with you whether you will think those inestimable privileges, which you have so ably contended for, should be sacrificed at the shrine of despotism, or whether you mean to contend for them with the same spirit that has so often baffled the attempts of an aristocratic faction, to rivet the shackles of slavery on you and your unborn posterity.

Our objections are comprised under three general heads of dissent, viz.

We dissent, first, because it is the opinion of the most celebrated writers on government, and confirmed by uniform experience, that a very extensive territory cannot be governed on the principles of freedom, otherwise than by a confederation of republics, possessing all the powers of internal government; but united in the management of their general, and foreign concerns.

● ● ●

We dissent, secondly, because the powers vested in Congress by this constitution, must necessarily annihilate and absorb the legislative, executive, and judicial powers of the several states, and produce from their ruins one consolidated government, which from the nature of things will be *an iron handed despotism*, as nothing short of the supremacy of despotic sway could connect and govern these United States under one government.

● ● ●

. . . We dissent, Thirdly, Because if it were practicable to govern so extensive a territory as these United States includes, on the plan of a consolidated government, consistent with the principles of liberty and the happiness of the people, yet the construction of this constitution is not calculated to attain the object, for independent of the nature of the case, it would of itself, necessarily, produce a despotism, and that not by the usual gradations, but with the celerity that has hitherto only attended revolutions effected by the sword.

To establish the truth of this position, a cursory investigation of the principles and form of this constitution will suffice.

The first consideration that this review suggests, is the omission of a BILL of RIGHTS, ascertaining and fundamentally establishing those unalienable and personal rights of men, without the full, free, and secure enjoyment of which there can be no liberty, and over which it is not necessary for a good government to have the controul. The principal of which are the rights of conscience, personal liberty by the clear and unequivocal establishment of the writ of *habeas corpus*, jury trial in criminal and civil cases, by an impartial jury of the vicinage or county, with the common-law proceedings, for the safety of the accused in criminal prosecutions; and the liberty of the press, that scourge of tyrants, and the grand bulwark of every other liberty and privilege; the stipulations heretofore made in favor of them in the state constitutions, are entirely superceded by this constitution.

• • •

We will now bring the legislature under this constitution to the test of the foregoing principles, which will demonstrate, that it is deficient in every essential quality of a just and safe representation.

The house of representatives is to consist of 65 members; that is one for about every 50,000 inhabitants, to be chosen every two years. Thirty-three members will form a quorum for doing business; and 17 of these, being the majority, determine the sense of the house.

The senate, the other constituent branch of the legislature, consists of 26 members being *two* from each state, appointed by their legislatures every six years—fourteen senators make a quorum; the majority of whom, eight, determines the sense of that body; except in judging on impeachments, or in making treaties, or in expelling a member, when two thirds of the senators present, must concur.

The president is to have the controul over the enacting of laws, so far as to make the concurrence of *two* thirds of the representatives and senators present necessary, if he should object to the laws.

Thus it appears that the liberties, happiness, interests, and great concerns of the whole United States, may be dependent upon the integrity, virtue, wisdom, and knowledge of 25 or 26 men—How unadequate and unsafe a representation! Inadequate, because the sense and views of 3 or 4 millions of people diffused over so extensive a territory comprising such various climates, products, habits, interests, and opinions, cannot be collected in so small a body; and besides, it is not a fair and equal representation of the people even in proportion to its number, for the smallest state has as much weight in the senate as the largest, and from the smallness of the number to be chosen for both branches of the legislature; and from the mode of election and appointment, which is under the controul of Congress; and from the nature of the thing, men of the most elevated rank in life, will alone be chosen. The other orders in the society, such as farmers, traders, and mechanics, who all ought to have a competent number of their best informed men in the legislature, will be totally unrepresented.

The representation is unsafe, because in the exercise of such great powers and trusts, it is so exposed to corruption and undue influence, by the gift of the numerous places of honor and emoluments at the disposal of the executive; by the arts and address of the great and designing; and by direct bribery.

The representation is moreover inadequate and unsafe, because of the long terms for which it is appointed, and the mode of its appointment, by which Congress may not only controul the choice of the people, but may so manage as to divest the people of this fundamental right, and become self-elected.

The number of members in the house of representatives *may* be increased to one for every 30,000 inhabitants. But when we consider, that this cannot be done without the consent of the senate, who from their share in the legislative, in the executive, and judicial departments, and permanency of appointment, will be the great efficient body in this government, and whose weight and predominancy would be abridged by an increase of the representatives, we are persuaded that this is a circumstance that cannot be expected. On the contrary, the number of representatives will probably be continued at 65, although the population of the country may swell to treble what it now is; unless a revolution should effect a change.

• • •

The next consideration that the constitution presents, is the undue and dangerous mixture of the powers of government; the same body possessing legislative, executive, and judicial powers. The senate is a constituent branch of the legislature, it has judicial power in judging on impeachments, and in this case unites in some measure the characters of judge and party, as all the principal officers are appointed by the president-general, with the concurrence of the senate and therefore they derive their offices in part from the senate. This may bias the judgments of the senators and tend to screen great delinquents from punishment. And the senate has, moreover, various and great executive powers, viz. in concurrence with the president-general, they form treaties with foreign nations, that may controul and abrogate the constitutions and laws of the several states. Indeed, there is no power, privilege or liberty of the state governments, or of the people, but what may be affected by virtue of this power. For all treaties, made by them, are to be the "supreme law of the land, any thing in the constitution or laws of any state, to the contrary notwithstanding."

And this great power may be exercised by the president and 10 senators (being two-thirds of 14, which is a quorum of that body). What an inducement would this offer to the ministers of foreign powers to compass by bribery *such concessions* as could not otherwise be obtained. It is the unvaried usage of all free states, whenever treaties interfere with the positive laws of the land, to make the intervention of the legislature necessary to give them operation. This became necessary, and was afforded by the parliament of Great-Britain. In consequence of the late commercial treaty between that kingdom and France—As the senate judges on impeachments, who is to try the members of the senate for the abuse of this power! And none of the great appointments to office can be made without the consent of the senate.

Such various, extensive, and important powers combined in one body of men, are inconsistent with all freedom; the celebrated Montesquieu tells us, that "when the legislative and executive powers are united in the same person, or in the same body or magistrates, there can be no liberty, because apprehensions may arise, lest the same monarch or *senate* should enact tyrannical laws, to execute them in a tyrannical manner."

"Again, there is no liberty, if the power of judging be not separated from the legislative and executive powers. Were it joined with the legislative, the life and liberty of the subject would be exposed to arbitrary controul; for the judge would then be legislator. Were it joined to the executive power, the judge might behave with all the violence of an oppressor. There would be an end of every thing, were the same man, or the same body of the nobles, or of the people, to exercise those three powers; that of enacting laws; that of executing the public resolutions; and that of judging the crimes or differences of individuals."

The president-general is dangerously connected with the senate; his coincidence with the views of the ruling junto in that body, is made essential to his weight and importance in the government, which will destroy all independency and purity in the executive department, and having the power of pardoning without the concurrence of a council, he may skreen from punishment the most treasonable attempts that may be made on the liberties of the people, when instigated by his coadjutors in the senate. Instead of this dangerous and improper mixture of the executive with the legislative and judicial, the supreme executive powers ought to have been placed in the president, with a small independent council, made personally responsible for every appointment to office or other act, by having their opinions recorded; and that without the concurrence of the majority of the quorum of this council, the president should not be capable of taking any step.

• • •

From the foregoing investigation, it appears that the Congress under this constitution will not possess the confidence of the people, which is an essential requisite in a good government; for unless the laws command the confidence and respect of the great body of the people, so as to induce them to support them, when called on by the civil magistrate, they must be executed by the aid of a numerous standing army, which would be inconsistent with every idea of liberty; for the same force that may be employed to compel obedience to good laws, might and probably would be used to wrest from the people their constitutional liberties. The framers of this constitution appear to have been aware of this great deficiency; to have been sensible that no dependence could be placed on the people for their support; but on the contrary, that the government must be executed by force. They have therefore made a provision for this purpose in a permanent STANDING ARMY, and a MILITIA that may be subjected to as strict discipline and government.

• • •

As this government will not enjoy the confidence of the people, but be executed by force, it will be a very expensive and burthensome government. The standing army must be numerous, and as a further support, it will be the policy of this government to multiply officers in every department: judges, collectors, tax gatherers, excisemen and the whole host of revenue officers will swarm over the land, devouring the hard earnings of the industrious. Like the locusts of old, impoverishing and desolating all before them.

We have not noticed the smaller, nor many of the considerable blemishes, but have confined our objections to the great and essential defects; the main pillars of the constitution; which we have shewn to be inconsistent with the liberty and happiness of the people, as its establishment will annihilate the state governments, and produce one consolidated government that will eventually and speedily issue in the supremacy of despotism. ∎

American Politics Today

Because the Supreme Court plays such a key role in interpreting the United States Constitution (see Chapter 12), constitutional debates in the United States can quickly become mired in legal details and technicalities. The debate over the Second Amendment—which protects the right of the people to "keep and bear arms"—is in this regard the exception that proves the rule. Because the Court has been largely silent on the meaning and application of the Second Amendment, both supporters and opponents of gun control make arguments that more closely reflect the debates of the Founding Generation than the thinking of modern justices. As Wendy Kaminer points out, the Second Amendment debate brings out "the fundamental tension between republicanism and individualism" in the American constitutional system.

Questions

1. What are the meanings of "republicanism" and "individualism," particularly in the context of the Second Amendment debate?
2. What are the strongest points in favor of those who argue that the Second Amendment should be interpreted to guarantee the right *of the individual* to keep and bear arms? What are the strongest points in favor of those who argue that the amendment protects the right of the people to bear arms collectively?

1.6 Second Thoughts on the Second Amendment (1996)

Wendy Kaminer

Debates about gun ownership and gun control are driven more by values and ideology than by pragmatism—and hardly at all by the existing empirical research, which is complex and inconclusive. . . . As for legal debates about the existence of constitutional rights, empirical data is irrelevant, or at best peripheral. But the paucity of proof that gun controls lessen crime is particularly galling to people who believe that they have a fundamental right to bear arms. In theory, at least, we restrict constitutional rights only when the costs of exercising them seem unbearably high. In fact we argue continually about what those costs are: Does violence in the media cause violence in real life? Did the release of the Pentagon Papers

Excerpted from Wendy Kaminer, "Second Thoughts on the Second Amendment," *The Atlantic Monthly* (March 1996), Volume 277, pp. 32–45—abridged. A longer version of this article first appeared in *The Atlantic Monthly,* March 1995. Copyright Wendy Kaminer. Reprinted with permission.

endanger the national security? Does hate speech constitute discrimination? In the debate about firearms, however, we can't even agree on the principles that should govern restrictions on guns, because we can't agree about the right to own them.

How could we, given the importance of the competing values at stake—public safety and the right of self-defense—and the opacity of the constitutional text? The awkwardly drafted Second Amendment doesn't quite make itself clear: "A well regulated Militia, being necessary to the security of a free State, the right of the people to keep and bear Arms, shall not be infringed." Is the reference to a militia a limitation on the right to bear arms or merely an explanation of an armed citizenry's role in a government by consent? There is little dispute that one purpose of the Second Amendment was to ensure that the people would be able to resist a central government should it ever devolve into despotism. But there is little agreement about what that capacity for resistance was meant to entail— armed citizens acting under the auspices of state militias or armed citizens able to organize and act on their own. And there is virtually no consensus about the constitutional right to own a gun in the interests of individual self-defense against crime, rather than communal defense against tyranny. Is defense of the state, and of the common good, the *raison d'être* of the Second Amendment or merely one use of it?

The Supreme Court has never answered these fundamental questions about the constitutional uses of guns. It has paid scant attention to the Second Amendment, providing little guidance in the gun-control debate. Two frequently cited late-nineteenth-century cases relating to the Second Amendment were more about federalism than about the right to bear arms. *Presser* v. *Illinois*, decided in 1886, involved a challenge to a state law prohibiting private citizens from organizing their own military units and parades. The Court held that the Second Amendment was a limitation on federal, not state, power, reflecting the prevailing view (now discredited) that the Bill of Rights in general applied only to the federal government, not to the states. (A hundred years ago the Court did not apply the First Amendment to the states either.) *Presser* followed *U.S.* v. *Cruikshank*, which held that the federal government could not protect people from private infringement of their rights to assemble and bear arms. *Cruikshank*, decided in 1876, invalidated the federal convictions of participants in the lynching of two black men. This ruling, essentially concerned with limiting federal police power, is virtually irrelevant to Second Amendment debates today, although it has been cited to support the proposition that an oppressed minority has a compelling need (or a natural right) to bear arms in self-defense.

The most significant Supreme Court decision on the Second Amendment was *U.S.* v. *Miller* (1939), a less-than-definitive holding now cited approvingly by both sides in the gun-control debate. *Miller* involved a prosecution under the 1934 National Firearms Act. Jack Miller and his accomplice had been convicted of transporting an unregistered shotgun of less than regulation length across state lines. In striking down their Second Amendment claim and upholding their conviction, the Court noted that no evidence had been presented that a shotgun was in fact a militia weapon, providing no factual basis for a Second Amendment claim. This ruling implies that the Second Amendment could protect the right to bear arms suitable for a militia.

Advocates of gun control or prohibition like the *Miller* case because it makes the right to bear arms dependent on at least the possibility of service in a militia. They cite the Court's declaration that the Second Amendment was obviously intended to "assure the continuation and render possible the effectiveness" of state militias; they place less emphasis on the Court's apparent willingness to permit private citizens to possess military weapons. Citing *Miller*, a dealer at a gun show told me that the Second Amendment protects the ownership of only such devices as machine guns, Stingers, and grenade throwers. But advocates of gun ownership don't generally emphasize this awkward implication of *U.S. v. Miller* any more than their opponents do: it could lead to prohibitions on handguns. They like the *Miller* decision because it delves into the history of the Second Amendment and stresses that for the framers, the militia "comprised all males physically capable of acting in concert for the common defense."

This view of the militia as an inchoate citizens' army, not a standing body of professionals, is central to the claim that the Second Amendment protects the rights of individual civilians, not simply the right of states to organize and arm militias. And, in fact, fear and loathing of standing armies did underlie the Second Amendment, which was at least partly intended to ensure that states would be able to call up citizens in defense against a tyrannical central government. (Like the Bill of Rights in general, the Second Amendment was partly a response to concerns about federal abuses of power.) James Madison, the author of the Second Amendment, invoked in *The Federalist Papers* the potential force of a citizen militia as a guarantee against a federal military coup.

> Let a regular army, fully equal to the resources of the country, be formed; and let it be entirely at the devotion of the federal government: still it would not be going too far to say that the State governments with the people on their side would be able to repel the danger. . . . To [the regular army] would be opposed a militia amounting to near half a million of citizens with arms in their hands, officered by men chosen from among themselves, fighting for their common liberties and united and conducted by governments possessing their affection and confidence. It may well be doubted whether a militia thus circumstanced could ever be conquered by such a proportion of regular troops. Those who are best acquainted with the late successful resistance of this country against the British arms will be most inclined to deny the possibility of it. Besides the advantage of being armed, which the Americans possess over the people of almost every other nation, the existence of subordinate governments, to which the people are attached and by which the militia officers are appointed, forms a barrier against the enterprises of ambition, more insurmountable than any which a simple government of any form can admit of.

This passage is enthusiastically cited by advocates of the right to bear arms, because it supports their notion of the militia as the body of people, privately armed; but it's also cited by their opponents, because it suggests that the militia is activated and "conducted" by the states, and it stresses that citizens are "attached" to their local governments. The militia envisioned by Madison is not simply a "collection of unorganized, privately armed citizens," Dennis Henigan, a handgun-control advocate, has argued.

That Madison's reflections on the militia and the Supreme Court's holding in *U.S. v. Miller* can be cited with some accuracy by both sides in the debate testifies to the hybrid nature of Second Amendment rights. The Second Amendment presumes (as did the framers) that private citizens will possess private arms; Madison referred offhandedly to "the advantage of being armed, which the Americans possess." But Madison also implied that the right to bear arms is based in the obligation of citizens to band together as a militia to defend the common good, as opposed to the prerogative of citizens to take up arms individually in pursuit of self-interest and happiness.

The tension at the heart of the Second Amendment, which makes it so difficult to construe, is the tension between republicanism and liberal individualism. (To put it very simply, republicanism calls for the subordination of individual interests to the public good; liberalism focuses on protecting individuals against popular conceptions of the good.) A growing body of scholarly literature on the Second Amendment locates the right to bear arms in republican theories of governance. In a 1989 article in the *Yale Law Journal* that helped animate the Second Amendment debate, the University of Texas law professor Sanford Levinson argued that the Second Amendment confers an individual right to bear arms so that, in the republican tradition, armed citizens might rise up against an oppressive state. Wendy Brown, a professor of women's studies at the University of California at Santa Cruz, and David C. Williams, a law professor at Cornell University, have questioned the validity of a republican right to bear arms in a society that lacks the republican virtue of being willing to put communal interests first. Pro-gun activists don't generally acknowledge the challenge posed by republicanism to the individualist culture that many gun owners inhabit. They embrace republican justifications for gun ownership, stressing the use of arms in defending the community, at the same time that they stress the importance of guns in protecting individual autonomy.

Advocates of the right to bear arms often insist that the Second Amendment is rooted in both collective and individual rights of self-defense—against political oppression and crime—without recognizing how those rights conflict. The republican right to resist oppression is the right of the majority, or the people, not the right of a small religious cult in Waco, Texas, or of a few survivalist tax protesters in Idaho. The members of these groups have individual rights against the government, state and federal. (Both the American Civil Liberties Union and the NRA protested the government's actions in Waco and its attack on the survivalist Randy Weaver and his family.) But refuseniks and refugees from society are not republicans. They do not constitute the citizen militia envisioned by the framers, any more than they stand for the American community; indeed, they stand against it—withdrawing from the body politic, asserting their rights to alienation and anomie or membership in exclusionary alternative communities of their own. Republicanism can't logically be invoked in the service of libertarianism. It elevates civic virtue over individualism, consensus over dissent.

Nor can social-contract theory be readily invoked in support of a right to arm yourself in a war against street crime, despite the claims of some gun-ownership advocates. The right or power to engage in punishment or retribution is precisely what is given up when you enter an ordered civil society. The loss of self-help remedies is the price of the social contract. "God hath certainly appointed Government to restrain the partiality and violence of Men," John Locke wrote. A person may always defend his or her life when threatened, but only when there is no chance to appeal to the law. If a man points his sword at me and demands my purse, Locke explained, I may kill him. But if he steals my purse by stealth and then raises a sword to defend it, I may not use force to get it back. "My Life not being in danger, I may have the *benefit of appealing* to the Law, and have Reparation for my 100£ that way."

Locke was drawing a line between self-defense and vigilantism which many gun owners would no doubt respect. Others would point to the inability of the criminal-justice system to avenge crimes and provide reparation to victims, and thus they would assert a right to engage in self-help. Social-contract theory, however, might suggest that if the government is no longer able to provide order, or justice, the remedy is not vigilantism but revolution; the utter failure of law enforcement is a fundamental breach of trust. And, in fact, there are large pockets of disaffected citizens who do not trust the government to protect them or to provide impartial justice, and who might be persuaded to rise up against it, as evidenced by the disorder that followed the 1992 acquittal of police officers who assaulted Rodney King. Was Los Angeles the scene of a riot or of an uprising?

Injustice, and the sense of oppression it spawns, are often matters of perspective—particularly today, when claims of political victimization abound and there is little consensus on the demands of public welfare. We use the term "oppression" promiscuously, to describe any instance of discrimination. In this climate of grievance and hyperbole, many acts of violence are politicized. How do we decide whether an insurrection is just? Don Kates observes that the Second Amendment doesn't exactly confer the right to resist. He says, "It gives you a right to win."

The prospect of armed resistance, however, is probably irrelevant to much public support for gun ownership, which reflects a fear of crime more than a fear or loathing of government. People don't buy guns in order to overthrow or even to thwart the government; in the belief that the police can't protect them, people buy guns to protect themselves and their families. Recognizing this, the NRA appeals to fear of crime, particularly crime against women. ("Choose to refuse to be a victim," NRA ads proclaim, showing a woman and her daughter alone in a desolate parking lot at night.) And it has countered demands for tougher gun controls not with radical individualist appeals for insurrection but with statist appeals for tougher anti-crime laws, notably stringent mandatory-minimum sentences and parole reform. There is considerable precedent for the NRA's appeal to state authority: founded after the Civil War, with the mission of teaching soldiers to shoot straight, in its early years the NRA was closely tied to the military and dependent on government largesse; until recently it drew considerable moral support from the police. Today, however, statist anti-crime campaigns are mainly matters of politics for the NRA and for gun advocates in general; laws mandating tough sentences for the criminal use of firearms defuse demands for firearm controls. Personal liberty—meaning the liberty to own guns and use them against the government if necessary—is these people's passion.

Gun advocates are apt to be extravagantly libertarian when the right to own guns is at stake. At heart many are insurrectionists—at least, they need to feel prepared. Nothing arouses their anger more, I've found, than challenges to the belief that private gun ownership is an essential check on political oppression. . . .

. . . "Using a national epidemic of crime and violence as their justification, media pundits and collectivist politicians are aggressively campaigning to disarm private citizens and strengthen federal law enforcement powers," proclaims a special edition of *The New American*, a magazine on sale at gun shows. After gun control, the editors suggest, the greatest threat to individual liberty is the Clinton plan for providing local police departments with federal assistance. "Is it possible that some of those who are advocating a disarmed populace and a centralized police system have totalitarian designs in mind? It is worth noting that this is exactly what happened in many countries during this century."

This can be dismissed as ravings on the fringe, but it captures in crazed form the hostility toward a powerful central government which inspired the adoption of the Second Amendment right to bear arms 200 years ago and fuels support for it today. Advocates of First Amendment rights, who believe firmly that free speech is both a moral imperative and an instrument of democratic governance, should understand the passion of Second Amendment claims.

They should be sympathetic as well to the more dispassionate constitutional arguments of gun owners. Civil libertarians who believe that the Bill of Rights in general protects individuals have a hard time explaining why the Second Amendment protects only groups. They have a hard time reconciling their opposition to prohibitions of problematic behavior, such as drug abuse, with their support for the prohibition of guns. (Liberals tend to demonize guns and gun owners the way conservatives tend to demonize drugs and pornography and the people who use them.) In asserting that the Second Amendment provides no individual right to bear arms or that the right provided is anachronistic and not worth its cost, civil libertarians place themselves in the awkward position of denying the existence of a constitutional right because they don't value its exercise.

The civil-libertarian principles at issue in the gun debate are made clear by the arguments of First Amendment and Second Amendment advocates, which are strikingly similar—as are the arguments their opponents use. Pornography rapes, some feminists say. Words oppress, according to advocates of censoring hate speech. "Words Kill," declared a Planned Parenthood ad following the abortion-clinic shootings in Brookline, Massachusetts, last year. And all you can say in response is "Words don't kill people; people kill people." To an anti-libertarian, the literature sold at gun shows may seem as dangerous as the guns; at a recent gun show I bought *Incendiaries*, an army manual on unconventional warfare; *Exotic Weapons: An Access Book; Gunrunning for Fun and Profit;* and *Vigilante Handbook,* which tells me how to harass, torture, and assassinate people. Should any of this material be censored? If it were, it would be sold on the black market; and the remedy for bad speech is good speech, First Amendment devotees point out. According to Second Amendment supporters, gun-control laws affect only law-abiding gun owners, and the best defense against armed criminals is armed victims; the remedy for the bad use of guns in violent crime is the good use of guns in self-defense.

Of course, guns do seem a bit more dangerous than books, and apart from a few anti-pornography feminists, most of us would rather be accosted by a man with a video than a man with a gun. But none of our constitutional rights are absolute. Recognizing that the Second Amendment confers an individual right to bear arms would not immunize guns from regulation; it would require that the government establish a necessity, not just a desire, to regulate. The majority of gun owners, Don Kates suggests, would be amenable to gun controls, such as waiting periods and even licensing and training requirements, if they didn't perceive them as preludes to prohibition. The irony of the Second Amendment debate is that acknowledging an individual right to bear arms might facilitate gun control more than denying it ever could.

But it will not facilitate civic engagement or the community that Americans are exhorted to seek. The civil-libertarian defense of Second Amendment rights is not a republican one. It does not derive the individual right to bear arms from republican notions of the militia; instead it relies on traditional liberal views of personal autonomy. It is a communitarian nightmare. If the war against crime has replaced the Cold War in popular culture, a private storehouse of guns has replaced the fallout shelter in the psyche of Americans who feel besieged. Increasingly barricaded, mistrustful of their neighbors, they've sacrificed virtue to fear. ■

 # The International Context

Since the days of the French Revolution, other nations have looked to the United States for advice and inspiration on constitutions and constitutionalism. The impact of the United States Constitution was especially pronounced after World War II; the constitutions of Germany and Japan were strongly influenced by American ideas.

The collapse of communism in the late 1980s and early 1990s provided a similar opportunity. Like their counterparts in earlier eras, the men and women who drafted constitutions for the new regimes of Eastern Europe also sought guidance from the United States. As the law professor A. E. Dick Howard explains, constitution writers in Europe and elsewhere faced the challenging task of grafting American ideas about rights, consent of the governed, limited government, and the rule of law onto their own cultures and experiences. Americans, he suggests, learned from the new European constitutions just as Europeans can learn from us.

Questions

1. What ideas from the U.S. Constitution are reflected in the Eastern European constitutions of the 1990s and what ideas are not?
2. What can Americans learn about constitutions and constitutionalism from the experiences of these other nations?

1.7 How Ideas Travel: Rights at Home and Abroad (1993)

A.E. Dick Howard

Neither time nor place can cabin ideas. In 1987 United States citizens celebrated the two hundredth anniversary of their Constitution, and in 1991 they marked the bicentennial of their Bill of Rights. At just the same time—as if history were a creative choreographer—the peoples of Central and Eastern Europe were proving the resilience of old ideas about freedom, human dignity, and democracy. After living for so many years under oppressive one-party regimes, people in Central and Eastern Europe and the Soviet sphere . . . [found] themselves questing for choices long denied them.

New times require new constitutions. Nearly every country, even the most repressive, has a "constitution." We are all too familiar with constitutions, such as the Soviet Union's 1936 Constitution, whose glowing promises of justice and human dignity have little relation to reality. Such documents must be discarded, and authentic constitutionalism planted in their place.

Thus, as the United States reflected on the two-hundred-year odyssey of its Bill of Rights, Russians, Poles, Bulgarians, and others began to write new constitutions. At the core of each of these new documents lies a bill of rights. Indeed, in January 1991 the national assembly of the Czech and Slovak Federal Republic gave priority to the adoption of a new bill of rights; meanwhile debate continued on other constitutional provisions—in particular, those effecting a division of powers between the federal government and the two republics.

Those who draft a bill of rights must understand the history and traditions of the country for which the document is being created. One who sought to write a bill of rights for Hungary, for example, would need to know about the great Golden Bull of 1222 (which is to Hungarian history what Magna Carta is to that of England), the impact of Enlightenment thought on eighteenth-century Hungary, and the reformist thrust of the 1848 revolution. Likewise, a Polish drafter would wish to recall the legacy of Polish Constitutionalism, including the notable Constitution of 3 May 1791—the world's second national constitution (after the Philadelphia Constitution of 1787).

Stating a people's rights is not, however, a parochial exercise. Drafters of bills of rights look not only to their own country's experience but also to that of other countries. Professors and scholars who work with constitutional commissions in Central and Eastern Europe are well read; they know the *Federalist Papers* and the writings of Western theorists such as John Locke and Montesquieu. Drafting commissions invite experts from other countries to pore over drafts and offer comments and advice.

A.E. Dick Howard, "How Ideas Travel: Rights at Home and Abroad," in A.E. Dick Howard, ed., *Constitution Making in Eastern Europe* (Washington, D.C.: Woodrow Wilson Center Press, 1993), pp. 9–10, 14–20. Reprinted with the permission of the author.

Traffic is heavy between the United States and the emerging democracies, as well as between those countries and the capitals of Western Europe. Americans who travel to consult on new constitutions are sometimes dubbed "constitutional Johnny Appleseeds." West European experts are equally in demand. . . .

In the years immediately following World War II, it was possible to speak of the "American century." With much of Europe in ashes, and Asia yet to become a major economic force, the United States enjoyed immense influence. In Japan, the staff of General Douglas MacArthur's headquarters drafted a new constitution in seven days for that defeated country. Similarly, the mark of American ideas on West Germany's postwar constitution is evident.

Even in the period after World War II, however, the influence of American constitutionalism was variable. In Africa, for example, British barristers and scholars were enlisted to work on constitutions for British colonies, such as Ghana, that were becoming independent nations.

The upheavals in Central and Eastern Europe since the winter of 1989 have brought a burst of attention to constitutions and bills of rights. An American who reads the draft of a bill of rights or constitution for one of the region's fledgling democracies will find much that is familiar but also much that is not.

Two hundred years after their drafting, the United States Constitution and the Bill of Rights are widely recognized as furnishing paradigms of the fundamental principles that define constitutional democracy. These principles include:

1. *Consent of the governed.* The first three words of the United States Constitution—"We the People"—embody the principle of consent of the governed. But American constitutionalism has also worked out the modes by which genuinely representative government can exist, including freedom to form political parties, fair apportionment of legislative seats, a liberal franchise, and free and fair elections.

2. *Limited government.* Constitutionalism pays special attention—through devices such as separation of powers and checks and balances—to preventing power from being concentrated in such a way that it becomes a threat to individual liberty.

3. *The open society.* Central to American precepts of individual liberty are the rights to believe what one will, to embrace what religious beliefs one chooses, to engage in free and robust debate, to oppose the orthodoxy of the moment. No part of the Constitution is a more powerful beacon than the First Amendment.

4. *Human dignity and the sanctity of the individual.* It is no accident that the Bill of Rights accords such detailed attention to criminal procedure. A good measure of the respect accorded human rights is how the state treats those charged with or suspected of criminal activity. The sanctity of the individual also connotes aspects of personal privacy and autonomy, those zones of private life into which the state may not intrude at all or only for demonstrable and pressing public needs.

5. *The rule of law.* The principle of due process of law, an idea as old as Magna Carta, requires fairness and impartiality in both criminal and civil proceedings. A corollary of fairness is equality. Constitutionalism's moral fabric is put to special test by discrimination involving race, religion, or similar factors. Liberty and equality may, at times, seem to be in tension with each other, but by and large they go hand in hand.

Bills of rights...drafted in Central and Eastern Europe parallel, in some respects, the principles flowing from the Bill of Rights of the United States Constitution and from American constitutionalism. Every draft bill of rights contains, in one form or another, assurances of free speech, freedom of conscience, and the right to form political parties. No draft fails to include some version of the antidiscrimination principle, which bans discrimination on the basis of nationality, ethnicity, religion, or other enumerated grounds. Procedural protections for those accused of crime are invariably included.

Other provisions of bills of rights being proposed or adopted in Central and Eastern Europe, however, will strike the American observer as less familiar, and in some cases disturbing. There are respects in which the bills of rights in the region go beyond the requirements of American constitutional law. There are other ways in which they fall short.

The Bill of Rights of the United States Constitution declares what government may *not* do; it is what Justice Hugo L. Black once called a list of "thou shalt nots." The document reflects the view that the function of a bill of rights is to limit government's powers. Central and East European drafters have enlarged this meaning of "rights." A legacy of the twentieth-century notion of positive government, an age of entitlements, is bills of rights that declare affirmative rights. Such bills include, of course, the traditional, negative rights, but they also spell out claims upon government, such as the right to an education, the right to a job, or the benefits of care in one's old age.

It may well be that, notwithstanding the language of the United States Bill of Rights, judicial gloss on the Constitution has brought American jurisprudence closer to the idea of affirmative rights than theory might suggest. The United States Supreme Court has rejected the argument that education is a "fundamental" right under the Fourteenth Amendment. Yet one who reads the many cases (especially those in lower courts) regarding school desegregation, education for the children of illegal aliens, and other school cases may well conclude that, in many respects, education is indeed a protected constitutional right. Be that as it may, bills of rights in the newer nations make explicit rights (such as education) that are, at most, only implicit in American constitutional law.

Thus the Charter of Fundamental Rights and Freedoms of the Czech and Slovak Federal Republic, adopted in January 1991, declares that workers "are entitled to fair remuneration for work and to satisfactory working conditions." Other sections decree free medical care, material security in one's old age, maternity benefits, and assistance to assure the needy of "basic living conditions." At the same time, some new bills of rights promise less than they seem to. Free speech will enjoy only qualified protection. Although stating that one may speak freely, the typical draft bill of rights proceeds to list significant exceptions. Drafts commonly state that advocacy of "fascism" or "communism" is excepted from the constitution's protection, or that speech may be forbidden if it conflicts with "public morality" or with the "constitutional order." Such exceptions overshadow the rule, especially when a draft (as always seems the case) does not require some finding of "clear and present danger" or a similar standard to justify a restriction on speech.

For example, Romania's Constitution, adopted in 1991, declares the "freedom to express ideas, opinions, and beliefs" to be "inviolable." But the document then adds that the law "prohibits defamation of the country and the nation; provocation to war or aggression, and to ethnic, racial, class, or religious hatred; incitement to discrimination, territorial separatism, or public violence; and obscene acts, contrary to good morals." What ethnic Hungarian, inclined to complain about conditions in Transylvania, would care to rely on his or her right to speak freely as being "inviolable" in the face of such sweeping and malleable exceptions?

Draft bills of rights, in addition to banning various forms of discrimination, often declare affirmative rights of culture, language, and education. The Czech and Slovak charter, for example, guarantees national and ethnic minorities the right to education in their language, the right to use that language in official settings, and the right to participation (form unspecified) in the settlement of matters concerning those minorities. But left unaddressed in most drafts is the explosive question whether rights of national minorities are simply rights of the individuals who make up those minorities or take on the character of group rights—an issue of utmost gravity wherever, as in so much of Central and Eastern Europe, disparate racial and ethnic groups are involved.

A constitution must, of course, be planted in a country's own soil to take root. One should not expect that a Bulgarian or Pole drafting a constitution or bill of rights will copy the American model, or any other model. Moreover, one should not be surprised that Central and East Europeans will draft documents that, at least in their specific provisions, bear more resemblance to fundamental laws in Western Europe than to American documents.

Several forces pull Central and East European drafters and lawmakers into the European orbit. After decades of an Iron Curtain, the people of the region yearn to rejoin the "family of Europe." Ties of tradition include the strong appeal of French ideas in some intellectual circles and the long-standing custom of legal scholars in many countries to view German scholarship as offering the highest and most rigorous standards.

New bills of rights also reflect the hope of the emerging democracies to be fully accepted as members of the civilized community of nations. Drafters thus study such documents as the Universal Declaration of Human Rights and the European Convention on Human Rights. Lofty aspirations are also coupled with more practical considerations: countries aspiring to membership in such regional arrangements as the European Community want to be seen as having fundamental laws in line with principles accepted in Western Europe.

Increasingly in this century, bills of rights have come to resemble political party platforms that appeal to this or that constituency, though in the poorest countries such rhetoric inevitably confronts the hard realities of poverty and privation. The revolutionaries who drafted Mexico's 1917 Constitution paid special attention to labor and social welfare, decreeing the rights to an eight-hour workday, a minimum wage, and workers' compensation—subjects on which constitutions are commonly silent. That document's Article 123 is considered so important that a street in Mexico City is named for it.

India's 1950 Constitution reflects the ethos of a Ghandian state. Its Directive Principles of State Policy point India toward the goal of a welfare state, the creation of a "casteless and classless society," and the promotion of world peace.

Perhaps the most baroque use of a bill of rights to legislate public policy is found in Brazil's 1988 Constitution. Rather than convene a constituent assembly, Brazil's leaders asked their Congress to draft a new constitution. All 559 members of Congress participated, dividing themselves into eight committees, each with three subcommittees. These twenty-four subcommittees worked without any master plan. The resulting document is unrivaled among constitutions for conferring favors on special-interest groups. There are, for example, thirty-seven sections dealing with just the rights of workers. Some rights, such as one day off in seven, derived from Brazil's 1946 Constitution; others, such as a forty-four–hour work week, had not been legally mandated before the adoption of the 1988 Constitution.

In South Africa, delegates to the drafting table consider[ed] proposals to use the bill of rights to compensate for past inequalities. An African National Congress draft provide[d] for diverting resources from richer to poorer areas "in order to achieve a common floor of rights for the whole country." The judiciary would be "transformed in such a way as to consist of men and women drawn from all sections of South African society." The nation's land, waters, and sky are declared to be the "common heritage" of the people of South Africa, and the state's agencies and organs are admonished to take measures against air and water pollution and other kinds of environmental harm.

The use of a bill of rights as an affirmative tool presents special problems. The traditional rights, such as expression or assembly, tell government what it *cannot* do and may be enforced through injunctions and other familiar judicial remedies. Affirmative rights tell government what it *must* do. Here enforcement is more problematic. Affirmative rights commonly entail legislative implementation or decisions about allocation of resources, tasks for which courts are often ill-suited. Anyone familiar with cases in which American judges have become administrators of school systems, prisons, or other public institutions will understand the skewing effect that decreeing affirmative rights has on public budgets.

The fortunes of Americans and peoples in the new democracies intertwine in many ways. Bills of rights—verbal declarations of fundamental aspirations—are a visible reflection of a shared legacy and common concerns. To flourish, however, constitutionalism requires skillful political leadership, viable political parties, a healthy press and media, an independent bench and bar, a sound economy, and a system of education in which young minds will prosper. A good constitution and bill of rights can foster these things but cannot assure them.

Ultimately, for rights to be respected there must be a mature civic spirit—an attitude in the minds of ordinary citizens. A nation of people who do not understand the basic precepts of free government are unlikely to keep it alive and vibrant. Describing his Bill for the More General Diffusion of Knowledge, Thomas Jefferson called for "rendering the people the safe, as they are the ultimate, guardians of their own liberty."

This lesson is as cogent in Washington or Albany as it is in Moscow or Warsaw. Americans have good cause to celebrate two hundred years of the Bill of Rights. They likewise have every reason to hope for the principles of that document to take root in the lands now free of tyrannical rule.

Neither East nor West can take liberty for granted. Witnessing the making of constitutions in the emerging democracies is an occasion for probing the lessons implicit therein: the nature and meaning of rights, the means by which they are enforced, and the habits of mind that keep them alive. ∎

View from the Inside

It is all too easy to view the participants in the constitutional debate as detached philosophers crafting a new system of government in a political vacuum. The political scientist John P. Roche, by contrast, sees the men who met in Philadelphia in 1787 as practical politicians operating within very real political constraints. In Roche's view, much of the elegant political philosophy that emerged from the debate, especially in the *Federalist Papers,* originated as simple matters of political compromise. Roche's treatment of the Framers as politicians is probably overstated, but it offers a welcome perspective on the constitutional debate.

Questions

1. Madison, Roche suggests, was originally in favor of a "unitary central government" but compromised over the course of the convention. What factors created the necessity for such a compromise? What were the essential outlines of the compromise?
2. What features of the Constitution reflect the Framers' practical—in contrast to their philosophical—concerns?

1.8 The Founding Fathers: A Reform Caucus in Action (1961)

John P. Roche

S tandard treatments of the Convention divide the delegates into "nationalists" and "states'-righters" with various improvised shadings ("moderate nationalists," etc.), but these are *a posteriori* categories which obfuscate more than they clarify. What is striking to one who analyzes the Convention as a case-study in democratic politics is the lack of clear-cut ideological divisions in the Convention. Indeed, I submit that the evidence—Madison's *Notes,* the correspondence of the delegates, and debates on ratification—indicates that this was a remarkably homogeneous body on the ideological level. Yates and Lansing, Clinton's two chaperones for Hamilton, left in disgust on July 10. (Is there anything more tedious than sitting through endless disputes on matters one deems fundamentally misconceived. It takes an iron will to spend a hot summer as an ideological *agent provocateur.*) Luther Martin, Maryland's bibulous narcissist, left on September 4 in a huff when he discovered that others did not share his

---

John P. Roche, "The Founding Fathers: A Reform Caucus in Action," *American Political Science Review* 55 (1961), pp. 799–816. Reprinted by permission.

self-esteem; others went home for personal reasons. But the hard core of delegates accepted a grinding regimen throughout the attrition of a Philadelphia summer precisely because they shared the Constitutionalist goal.

Basic differences of opinion emerged, of course, but these were not ideological; they were *structural*. If the so-called "states'-rights" group had not accepted the fundamental purposes of the Convention, they could simply have pulled out and by doing so have aborted the whole enterprise. Instead of bolting, they returned day after day to argue and to compromise. An interesting symbol of this basic homogeneity was the initial agreement on secrecy: these professional politicians did not want to become prisoners of publicity; they wanted to retain that freedom of maneuver which is only possible when men are not forced to take public stands in the preliminary stages of negotiation. There was no legal means of binding the tongues of the delegates: at any stage in the game a delegate with basic principled objections to the emerging project could have taken the stump (as Luther Martin did after his exit) and denounced the convention to the skies. Yet Madison did not even inform Thomas Jefferson in Paris of the course of the deliberations and available correspondence indicates that the delegates generally observed the injunction. Secrecy is certainly uncharacteristic of any assembly marked by strong ideological polarization. This was noted at the time: the *New York Daily Advertiser*, August 14, 1787, commented that the " . . . profound secrecy hitherto observed by the Convention [we consider] a happy omen, as it demonstrates that the spirit of party on any great and essential point cannot have arisen to any height."

Commentators on the Constitution who have read *The Federalist* in lieu of reading the actual debates have credited the Fathers with the invention of a sublime concept called "Federalism." Unfortunately *The Federalist* is probative evidence for only one proposition: that Hamilton and Madison were inspired propagandists with a genius for retrospective symmetry. Federalism, as the theory is generally defined, was an improvisation which was later prompted into a political theory. Experts on "Federalism" should take to heart the advice of David Hume, who warned in his *Of the Rise and Progress of the Arts and Sciences* that ". . . there is no subject in which we must proceed with more caution than in [history], lest we assign causes which never existed and reduce what is merely contingent to stable and universal principles." In any event, the final balance in the Constitution between the states and the nation must have come as a great disappointment to Madison, while Hamilton's unitary views are too well known to need elucidation.

It is indeed astonishing how those who have glibly designated James Madison the "father" of Federalism have overlooked the solid body of fact which indicates that he shared Hamilton's quest for a unitary central government. To be specific, they have avoided examining the clear import of the Madison-Virginia Plan, and have disregarded Madison's dogged inch-by-inch retreat from the bastions of centralization. The Virginia Plan envisioned a unitary national government effectively freed from and dominant over the states. The lower house of the national legislature was to be elected directly by the people of the states with membership proportional to population. The upper house was to be selected by the lower and the two chambers would elect the executive and choose the judges. The national government would be thus cut completely loose from the states.

The structure of the general government was freed from state control in a truly radical fashion, but the scope of the authority of the national sovereign as Madison initially formulated it was breathtaking. . . . The national legislature was to be empowered to disallow the acts of state legislatures and the central government was vested in addition to the powers of the nation under the Articles of Confederation, with plenary authority wherever ". . . the separate States are incompetent or in which the harmony of the United States may be interrupted by the exercise of individual legislation." Finally, just to lock the door against state intrusion, the national Congress was to be given the power to use military force on recalcitrant states. This was Madison's "model" of an ideal national government, though it later received little publicity in *The Federalist*.

The interesting thing was the reaction of the Convention to this militant program for a strong autonomous central government. Some delegates were startled, some obviously leery of so comprehensive a project of reform, but nobody set off any fireworks and nobody walked out. Moreover, in the two weeks that followed, the Virginia Plan received substantial endorsement *en principe*; the initial temper of the gathering can be deduced from the approval "without debate or dissent," on May 31, of the Sixth Resolution which granted Congress the authority to disallow state legislation ". . . contravening *in its opinion* the Articles of Union." Indeed, an amendment was included to bar states from contravening national treaties.

The Virginia Plan may therefore be considered, in ideological terms, as the delegates' Utopia, but as the discussions continued and became more specific, many of those present began to have second thoughts. After all, they were not residents of Utopia or guardians in Plato's Republic who could simply impose a philosophical ideal on subordinate strata of the population. They were practical politicians in a democratic society, and no matter what their private dreams might be, they had to take home an acceptable package and defend it—and their own political futures—against predictable attack. On June 14 the breaking point between dream and reality took place. Apparently realizing that under the Virginia Plan, Massachusetts, Virginia and Pennsylvania could virtually dominate the national government—and probably appreciating that to sell this program to "the folks back home" would be impossible—the delegates from the small states dug in their heels and demanded time for a consideration of alternatives. One gets a graphic sense of the inner politics from John Dickinson's reproach to Madison: "You see the consequences of pushing things too far. Some of the members from the small States wish for two branches in the General Legislature and are friends to a good National Government; but we would sooner submit to a foreign power than . . . be deprived of an equality of suffrage in both branches of the Legislature, and thereby be thrown under the domination of the large States."

The bare outline of the *Journal* entry for Tuesday, June 14, is suggestive to anyone with extensive experience in deliberative bodies. "It was moved by Mr. Patterson [*sic*, Paterson's name was one of those consistently misspelled by Madison and everybody else] seconded by Mr. Randolph that the further consideration of the report from the Committee of the whole House [endorsing the Virginia Plan] be postponed til tomorrow, and before the question for postponement was taken. It was moved by Mr. Randolph seconded by Mr. Patterson that the House adjourn." The House adjourned by obvious prearrangement of the two principals:

since the preceding Saturday when Brearley and Paterson of New Jersey had announced their fundamental discontent with the representational features of the
Virginia Plan, the informal pressure had certainly been building up to slow down
the streamroller. Doubtless there were extended arguments at the Indian Queen
between Madison and Paterson, the latter insisting that events were moving
rapidly towards a probably disastrous conclusion, towards a political suicide pact.
Now the process of accommodation was put into action smoothly—and wisely,
given the character and strength of the doubters. Madison had the votes, but this
was one of those situations where the enforcement of mechanical majoritarianism
could easily have destroyed the objectives of the majority: the Constitutionalists
were in quest of a qualitatitve as well as a quantitative consensus. This was hardly
from deference to local Quaker custom; it was a political imperative if they were
to attain ratification.

[I]

According to the standard script, at this point the "states'-rights" group inter-
vened in force behind the New Jersey Plan, which has been characteristically por-
trayed as a reversion to the *status quo* under the Articles of Confederation with
but minor modifications. A careful examination of the evidence indicates that
only in a marginal sense is this an accurate description. It is true that the New Jersey Plan put the states back into the institutional picture, but one could argue that
to do so was a recognition of political reality rather than an affirmation of states'-
rights. A serious case can be made that the advocates of the New Jersey Plan, far
from being ideological addicts of states'-rights, intended to substitute for the Virginia Plan a system which would both retain strong national power and have a
chance of adoption in the states. The leading spokesman for the project asserted
quite clearly that his views were based more on counsels of expediency than on
principle; said Paterson on June 16: "I came here not to speak my own sentiments,
but the sentiments of those who sent me. Our object is not such a Governmt. as
may be best in itself, but such a one as our Constituents have authorized us to prepare, and as they will approve." This is Madison's version; in Yates' transcription,
there is a crucial sentence following the remarks above: "I believe that a little
practical virtue is to be preferred to the finest theoretical principles, which cannot
be carried into effect." In his preliminary speech on June 9, Paterson had stated
". . . to the public mind we must accommodate ourselves," and in his notes for this
and his later effort as well, the emphasis is the same. The *structure* of government
under the Articles should be retained:

  2. Because it accords with the Sentiments of the People

     [Proof:] 1. Coms. [Commissions from state legislatures defining the jurisdiction of the
              delegates]
           2. News-papers—Political Barometer. Jersey never would have sent Dele-
              gates under the first [Virginia] Plan—

  Not here to sport Opinions of my own. Wt. [What] can be done. A little practicable
  Virtue preferrable to Theory.

This was a defense of political acumen, not of states'-rights. In fact, Paterson's notes of his speech can easily be construed as an argument for attaining the substantive objectives of the Virginia Plan by a sound political route, *i.e.*, pouring the new wine in the old bottles. With a shrewd eye, Paterson queried:

> Will the Operation and Force of the [central] Govt. depend upon the mode of Representn.—No—it will depend upon the Quantum of Power lodged in the leg. ex. and judy. Departments—Give [the existing] Congress the same Powers that you intend to give the two Branches, [under the Virginia Plan] and I apprehend they will act with as much Propriety and more Energy . . .

In other words, the advocates of the New Jersey Plan concentrated their fire on what they held to be the *political liabilities* of the Virginia Plan—which were matters of institutional structure—rather than on the proposed scope of national authority. Indeed, the Supremacy Clause of the Constitution first saw the light of day in Paterson's Sixth Resolution; the New Jersey Plan contemplated the use of military force to secure compliance with national law; and finally Paterson made clear his view that under either the Virginia or the New Jersey systems, the general government would ". . . act on individuals and not on states." From the states'-rights viewpoint, this was heresy; the fundament of that doctrine was the proposition that any central government had as its constituents the states, not the people, and could only reach the people through the agency of the state government.

Paterson then reopened the agenda of the Convention, but he did so within a distinctly nationalist framework. Paterson's position was one of favoring a strong central government in principle, but opposing one which in fact *put the big states in the saddle*. (The Virginia Plan, for all its abstract merits, did very well by Virginia.) As evidence for this speculation, there is a curious and intriguing proposal among Paterson's preliminary drafts of the New Jersey Plan:

> Whereas it is necessary in Order to form the People of the U.S. of America in to a Nation, that the States should be consolidated, by which means all the Citizens thereof will become equally intitled to and will equally participate in the same Privileges and Rights . . . it is therefore resolved that all the Lands contained within the Limits of each state individually, and of the U.S. generally be considered as constituting one Body or Mass, and be divided into thirteen or more integral parts.
> Resolved, That such Divisions or integral Parts shall be styled Districts.

This makes it sound as though Paterson was prepared to accept a strong unified central government along the lines of the Virginia Plan if the existing states were eliminated. He may have gotten the idea from his New Jersey colleague Judge David Brearley, who on June 9 had commented that the only remedy to the dilemma over representation was ". . . that a map of the U.S. be spread out, that all the existing boundaries be erased, and that a new partition of the whole be made into 13 equal parts." According to Yates, Brearley added at this point, ". . . then a government on the present [Virginia Plan] system will be just."

This proposition was never pushed—it was patently unrealistic—but one can appreciate its purpose: it would have separated the men from the boys in the large-state delegations. How attached would the Virginians have been to their reform principles if Virginia were to disappear as a component geographical unit (the largest) for representational purposes? Up to this point, the Virginians had been in the happy position of supporting high ideals with that inner confidence born of knowledge that the "public interest" they endorsed would nourish their private interest. Worse, they had shown little willingness to compromise. Now the delegates from the small states announced that they were unprepared to be offered up as sacrificial victims to a "national interest" which reflected Virginia's parochial ambition. Caustic Charles Pinckney was not far off when he remarked sardonically that "... the whole [conflict] comes to this": "Give N. Jersey an equal vote, and she will dismiss her scruples, and concur in the Natil. system." What he rather unfairly did not add was that the Jersey delegates were not free agents who could adhere to their private convictions; they had to take back, sponsor and risk their reputations on the reforms approved by the Convention—and in New Jersey, not in Virginia.

Paterson spoke on Saturday, and one can surmise that over the weekend there was a good deal of consultation, argument, and caucusing among the delegates. One member at least prepared a full length address: on Monday Alexander Hamilton, previously mute, rose and delivered a six-hour oration. It was a remarkably apolitical speech; the gist of his position was that *both* the Virginia and New Jersey Plans were inadequately centralist, and he detailed a reform program which was reminiscent of the Protectorate under the Cromwellian *Instrument of Government* of 1653. It has been suggested that Hamilton did this in the best political tradition to emphasize the moderate character of the Virginia Plan, to give the cautious delegates something *really* to worry about; but this interpretation seems somehow too clever. Particularly since the sentiments Hamilton expressed happened to be completely consistent with those he privately—and sometimes publicly—expressed throughout his life. He wanted, to take a striking phrase from a letter to George Washington, a "strong well mounted government"; in essence, the Hamilton Plan contemplated an elected life monarch, virtually free of public control, on the Hobbesian ground that only in this fashion could strength and stability be achieved. The other alternatives, he argued, would put policymaking at the mercy of the passions of the mob; only if the sovereign was beyond the reach of selfish influence would it be possible to have government in the interests of the whole community.

From all accounts, this was a masterful and compelling speech, but (aside from furnishing John Lansing and Luther Martin with ammunition for later use against the Constitution) it made little impact. Hamilton was simply transmitting on a different wave-length from the rest of the delegates; the latter adjourned after his great effort, admired his rhetoric, and then returned to business. It was rather as if they had taken a day off to attend the opera. Hamilton, never a particularly patient man or much of a negotiator, stayed for another ten days and then left, in considerable disgust, for New York. Although he came back to Philadelphia sporadically and attended the last two weeks of the Convention, Hamilton played no part in the laborious task of hammering out the Constitution. His day came later when he led the New York Constitutionalists into the savage imbroglio over ratification—an arena in which his unmatched talent for dirty political infighting may well have won the day. For instance, in the New York Ratifying Convention,

Lansing threw back into Hamilton's teeth the sentiments the latter had expressed in his June 18 oration in the Convention. However, having since retreated to the fine defensive positions immortalized in *The Federalist*, the Colonel flatly denied that he had ever been an enemy of the states, or had believed that conflict between states and nation was inexorable! As Madison's authoritative *Notes* did not appear until 1840, and there had been no press coverage, there was no way to verify his assertions, so in the words of the reporter, ". . . a warm personal altercation between [Lansing and Hamilton] engrossed the remainder of the day [June 28, 1788]."

[II]

On Tuesday morning, June 19, the vacation was over. James Madison led off with a long, carefully reasoned speech analyzing the New Jersey Plan which, while intellectually vigorous in its criticisms, was quite conciliatory in mood. "The great difficulty," he observed, "lies in the affair of Representation; and if this could be adjusted, all others would be surmountable." (As events were to demonstrate, this diagnosis was correct.) When he finished, a vote was taken on whether to continue with the Virginia Plan as the nucleus for a new constitution: seven states voted "Yes"; New York, New Jersey, and Delaware voted "No"; and Maryland, whose position often depended on which delegates happened to be on the floor, divided. Paterson, it seems, lost decisively; yet in a fundamental sense he and his allies had achieved their purpose: from that day onward, it could never be forgotten that the state governments loomed ominously in the background and that no verbal incantations could exorcise their power. Moreover, nobody bolted the convention: Paterson and his colleagues took their defeat in stride and set to work to modify the Virginia Plan, particularly with respect to its provisions on representation in the national legislature. Indeed, they won an immediate rhetorical bonus; when Oliver Ellsworth of Connecticut rose to move that the word "national" be expunged from the Third Virginia Resolution ("Resolved that a *national* Government ought to be established consisting of a *supreme* Legislative, Executive and Judiciary"), Randolph agreed and the motion passed unanimously. The process of compromise had begun.

For the next two weeks, the delegates circled around the problem of legislative representation. The Connecticut delegation appears to have evolved a possible compromise quite early in the debates, but the Virginians and particularly Madison (unaware that he would later be acclaimed as the prophet of "federalism") fought obdurately against providing for equal representation of states in the second chamber. There was a good deal of acrimony and at one point Benjamin Franklin—of all people—proposed the institution of a daily prayer; practical politicians in the gathering, however, were mediating more on the merits of a good committee than on the utility of Divine intervention. On July 2, the ice began to break when through a number of fortuitous events—and one that seems deliberate—the majority against equality of representation was converted into a dead tie. The Convention had reached the stage where it was "ripe" for a solution (presumably all the therapeutic speeches had been made), and the South Carolinians proposed a committee. Madison and James Wilson wanted none of it, but with only Pennsylvania dissenting, the body voted to establish a working party on the problem of representation.

The members of this committee, one from each state, were elected by the delegates—and a very interesting committee it was. Despite the fact that the Virginia Plan had held majority support up to that date, neither Madison nor Randolph was selected (Mason was the Virginian) and Baldwin of Georgia, whose shift in position had resulted in the tie, was chosen. From the composition, it was clear that this was not to be a "fighting" committee: the emphasis in membership was on what might be described as "second-level political entrepreneurs." On the basis of the discussions up to that time, only Luther Martin of Maryland could be described as a "bitter-ender." Admittedly, some divination enters into this sort of analysis, but one does get a sense of the mood of the delegates from these choices—including the interesting selection of Benjamin Franklin, despite his age and intellectual wobbliness, over the brilliant and incisive Wilson or the sharp, polemical Gouverneur Morris, to represent Pennsylvania. His passion for conciliation was more valuable at this juncture than Wilson's logical genius, or Morris' acerbic wit.

There is a common rumor that the Framers divided their time between philosophical discussions of government and reading the classics in political theory. Perhaps this is as good a time as any to note that their concerns were highly practical, that they spent little time canvassing abstractions. A number of them had some acquaintance with the history of political theory (probably gained from reading John Adams' monumental compilation *A Defense of the Constitutions of Government,* the first volume of which appeared in 1786), and it was a poor rhetorician indeed who could not cite Locke, Montesquieu, or Harrington *in support* of a desired goal. Yet up to this point in the deliberations, no one had expounded a defense of states'-rights or the "separation of powers" on anything resembling a theoretical basis. It should be reiterated that the Madison model had no room either for the states or for the "separation of powers": effectively *all* governmental power was vested in the national legislature. The merits of Montesquieu did not turn up until *The Federalist;* and although a perverse argument could be made that Madison's ideal was truly in the tradition of John Locke's *Second Treatise of Government,* the Locke whom the American rebels treated as an honorary president was a pluralistic defender of vested rights, not of parliamentary supremacy.

It would be tedious to continue a blow-by-blow analysis of the work of the delegates; the critical fight was over representation of the states and once the Connecticut Compromise was adopted on July 17, the Convention was over the hump. Madison, James Wilson, and Gouverneur Morris of New York (who was there representing Pennsylvania!) fought the compromise all the way in a last-ditch effort to get a unitary state with parliamentary supremacy. But their allies deserted them and they demonstrated after their defeat the essentially opportunist character of their objections—using "opportunist" here in a non-pejorative sense, to indicate a willingness to swallow their objections and get on with the business. Moreover, once the compromise had carried (by five states to four, with one state divided), its advocates threw themselves vigorously into the job of strengthening the general government's substantive powers—as might have been predicted, indeed, from Paterson's early statements. It nourishes an increased respect for Madison's devotion to the art of politics, to realize that this dogged fighter could sit down six months later and prepare essays for *The Federalist* in contradiction to his basic convictions about the true course the Convention should have taken. . . .

[III]

Drawing on their vast collective political experience, utilizing every weapon in the politician's arsenal, looking constantly over their shoulders at their constituents, the delegates put together a Constitution. It was a makeshift affair; some sticky issues (for example, the qualification of voters) they ducked entirely; others they mastered with that ancient instrument of political sagacity, studied ambiguity (for example, citizenship), and some they just overlooked. In this last category, I suspect, fell the matter of the power of the federal courts to determine the constitutionality of acts of Congress. When the judicial article was formulated (Article III of the Constitution), deliberations were still in the stage where the legislature was endowed with broad power under the Randolph formulation, authority which by its own terms was scarcely amenable to judicial review. In essence, courts could hardly determine when ". . . the separate States are incompetent or . . . the harmony of the United States may be interrupted"; the National Legislature, as critics pointed out, was free to define its own jurisdiction. Later the definition of legislative authority was changed into the form we know, a series of stipulated powers, *but the delegates never seriously reexamined the jurisdiction of the judiciary under this new limited formulation.* All arguments on the intention of the Framers in this matter are thus deductive and *a posteriori*, though some obviously make more sense than others.

The Framers were busy and distinguished men, anxious to get back to their families, their positions, and their constituents, not members of the French Academy devoting a lifetime to a dictionary. They were trying to do an important job, and do it in such a fashion that their handiwork would be acceptable to very diverse constituencies. No one was rhapsodic about the final document, but it was a beginning, a move in the right direction, and one they had reason to believe the people would endorse. In addition, since they had modified the impossible amendment provisions of the Articles (the requirement of unanimity which could always be frustrated by "Rogues Island") to one demanding approval by only three-quarters of the states, they seemed confident that gaps in the fabric which experience would reveal could be rewoven without undue difficulty. . . . ■

Chapter 2

Federalism

The idea of dividing political power between a central government and its component parts while preserving both elements was one of the great innovations of American political thought. In the eighteenth century, the accepted wisdom was that sovereignty—that is, the ultimate political power in a community—could not be divided. In a confederation, either the states would have to retain sovereignty, authorizing the national government to take on only certain specific tasks with the approval of all the states, or the states would lose their power and identity and be swallowed up into one great whole. There was, according to this line of thought, no middle ground.

Throughout the constitutional debate of the 1780s, the Antifederalists clung to this traditional point of view. The Articles of Confederation, after all, were just that: a confederation of fully sovereign states that came together in a league, much like a modern alliance, for certain limited purposes. The Articles began, in fact, "We the . . . Delegates of the States." The Antifederalists conceded that the Articles needed modification, but they resisted attempts to strengthen the national government too much, fearing that it would become a threat to the sovereignty of the states.

The Federalists' great innovation was the creation of a new conception of federalism. Under this theory, ultimate sovereignty rested in the people; they delegated some of their sovereignty to the national government and some to the states, and retained some for themselves. Within their respective spheres of authority, both the states and the national government were supreme.

The Antifederalists' charge that such a system could not work was dismissed out of hand by the Federalists. Nevertheless, in the more than two hundred years since the ratification of the Constitution, power has definitely shifted from the states to the national government. This shift of power began in the early days of the Republic, when Congress claimed broad powers to regulate commerce and encourage economic expansion. It accelerated in the late 1800s and early 1900s as the national government expanded its regulation of railroads and other national industries, established a national banking system, and began to enforce the provisions of the Bill of Rights against the states. But the most dramatic expansion of national power came during and after the New Deal of the 1930s, when Washington took on a wide range of new responsibilities in regulating the national economy. After a brief effort to block these programs on constitutional grounds, the Supreme Court reversed itself, upholding New Deal programs across the board. By the 1960s, the Court's decisions led many scholars to conclude that there were no real constitutional limitations on the powers of the national government.

The 1960s and 1970s also saw a dramatic increase in the amount and scope of federal grants to the states. Along with federal money came increased federal influence on the states. Federal highway money, for example, was conditioned on the states' compliance with a national speed limit and a legal drinking age of twenty-one. In general, the Supreme Court upheld these indirect applications of national power.

By the 1970s and 1980s, however, critics of national power began to score points with their efforts to restrain the role of the national government and return power to the states. Supporters of this "new federalism" urged the national government to give the states money with few or no strings attached; to refrain from "unfunded mandates," which impose costly requirements on the states without reimbursement; and, in general, to scale back the breadth and scope of its regulatory activities. These efforts to shift the long-term balance of power away from Washington took on new momentum after the Republican party gained control of Congress in the 1990s. Moreover, in recent years the Supreme Court has shown a new willingness to police the boundaries of national and state power, and to impose new restraints on the national government.

Throughout the centuries, a major player in the struggle between the national government and the states has been the United States Supreme Court. Early on, the Court made a series of critical decisions—the most important of which was *McCulloch* v. *Maryland* (1819)—establishing itself as the key arbiter between the national government and the states and laying the foundation for a broad expansion of national power. Since at least the 1950s, the Court has been a key actor in applying to the states national standards on civil rights and civil liberties. Given that the Court is and always has been a component part of the national government, is it any surprise that the national government seems to have emerged triumphant from its power struggles with the states?

The readings in this chapter begin with a series of selections presenting early views on federalism (selections 2.1–2.3). Next comes an assessment of current trends in federalism, with an eye on possible future developments (selection 2.4); a look at federalism issues in the European Union (selection 2.5); and two views of the national-state relationship in the wake of September 11, 2001.

Chapter Questions

1. What is the meaning of "dual federalism"? How does the theory of dual federalism differ from traditional understandings of the nature of sovereignty?
2. How does federalism in practice differ from federalism in theory? Is there a difference between the national government's theoretical power over the states and the relationship, in practice, between the national government and the states?
3. What are the advantages and disadvantages of a federal system of government?

 # Foundations

One of the key differences of opinion between the Federalists and the Antifederalists, as their names imply, was over the question of federalism. The Antifederalists, as the political scientist Herbert Storing explains in selection 2.1, objected to the Constitution above all because they feared that it would concentrate power in the national government at the expense of the states. Rather than throw away the Articles of Confederation and start over with the Constitution, the Antifederalists advocated merely modifying and updating the Articles, leaving sovereignty in the states. The Federalists, by contrast, viewed the weakness of the national government as the principal problem with the Articles of Confederation, and urged that its powers and responsibilities be significantly expanded.

In *The Federalist* Nos. 39 and 45, James Madison (author of the *Federalist Papers* with John Jay and Alexander Hamilton), makes general arguments in favor of the new system of government. In No. 39, he defends the Constitution against charges that it would be anti-Republican and that it would allow the states to be swallowed up by the national government. In No. 45, he again makes the argument that the national government will never threaten the sovereignty or authority of the states. Just beneath the surface, however, Madison's tilt toward a strong national government becomes clear. All prior confederacies have perished because the central government was too weak, he writes in No. 45; moreover, "as far as the sovereignty of the States cannot be reconciled to the happiness of the people," he declares, "let the former be sacrificed to the latter."

Madison's argument that the "powers delegated by the proposed Constitution to the federal government are few and defined," while "those which are to remain in the State governments are numerous and indefinite" is still formally true. All actions of the national government must be justified with reference to a specific provision of the Constitution granting that power (see the Constitution, Article I, section 8). By contrast, the states possess broadly defined "police" powers—that is, powers to regulate the public health, safety, welfare, and morals.

The powers of the national government may be limited in theory, but in practice the Supreme Court has interpreted the Constitution's grants of power in broad terms. The key case was *McCulloch* v. *Maryland* (1819), which held that the Constitution gave Congress sweeping powers and broad discretion to choose how to carry out those powers. Although on occasion the Court has deviated from this principle, in general it has followed the logic of *McCulloch* and refused to interfere with congressional attempts to assert national authority.

Thus Madison's argument in *Federalist* No. 45 that "the State governments will have the advantage of the federal government . . . [in] the disposition and faculty of resisting and frustrating the measures of the other" has been disproved by history. Throughout American history, there have been no successful threats to federal supremacy. In any event, Madison's emphasis in No. 45 on the importance of a strong national government makes one wonder whether the argument was made seriously in the first place.

Although the Antifederalists lost the debate over the Constitution, it would be unfair to dismiss their views as narrow-minded, unsophisticated, or incorrect. As you read the selections in this section, remember that the Antifederalists were not merely "against" the Constitution; like the Federalists, they had strong beliefs and political principles and a coherent way of looking at politics.

Questions

1. How did the Antifederalists define federalism?
2. What did they view as the major threat posed by the new "federalism" of the United States Constitution?
3. What are the reasons Madison gives for his argument that the states will be able to resist the encroachments of the national government—just as the members of earlier confederations were able to do so? How does the Court's decision in *McCulloch* affect this argument?
4. Why do you think that threats to the supremacy of the federal government have been unsuccessful?

2.1 What the Antifederalists Were For (1981)

Herbert Storing

Far from straying from the principles of the American Revolution, as some of the Federalists accused them of doing, the Anti-Federalists saw themselves as the true defenders of those principles. "I am fearful," said Patrick Henry, "I have lived long enough to become an old fashioned fellow: Perhaps an invincible attachment to the dearest rights of man, may, in these refined enlightened days, be deemed *old fashioned*: If so, I am contented to be so: I say, the time has been, when every pore of my heart beat for American liberty, and which, I believe, had a counterpart in the breast of every true American." The Anti-Federalists argued, as some historians have argued since, that the Articles of Confederation were the constitutional embodiment of the principles on which the Revolution was based:

> Sir, I venerate the spirit with which every thing was done at the trying time in which the Confederation was formed. America had then a sufficiency of this virtue to resolve to resist perhaps the first nation in the universe, even unto bloodshed. What was her aim? Equal liberty and safety. What ideas had she of this equal liberty? Read them in her Articles of Confederation.

The innovators were impatient to change this "most excellent constitution," which was "sent like a blessing from heaven," for a constitution "essentially differing from the principles of the revolution, and from freedom," and thus destructive of the whole basis of the American community. "Instead of repairing the old and venerable fabrick, which sheltered the United States, from the dreadful and cruel

---

Herbert Storing, *What the Antifederalists Were For* (Chicago: University of Chicago Press, 1981), pp. 9–14. Reprinted by permission of the publisher, The University of Chicago Press.

storms of a tyrannical British ministry, they built a stately palace after their own fancies. . . ."

The principal characteristic of that "venerable fabrick" was its federalism: the Articles of Confederation established a league of sovereign and independent states whose representatives met in congress to deal with a limited range of common concerns in a system that relied heavily on voluntary cooperation. Federalism means that the states are primary, that they are equal, and that they possess the main weight of political power. The defense of the federal character of the American union was the most prominent article of Anti-Federalist conservative doctrine. While some of the other concerns were intrinsically more fundamental, the question of federalism was central and thus merits fuller discussion here, as it did in that debate.

To begin with an apparently small terminological problem, if the Constitution was opposed because it was anti-federal how did the opponents come to be called Anti-Federalists? They usually denied, in fact, that the name was either apt or just, and seldom used it themselves. They were, they often claimed, the true federalists. Some of them seemed to think that their proper name had been filched, while their backs were turned, as it were, by the pro-Constitution party, which refused to give it back; and versions of this explanation have been repeated by historians. Unquestionably the Federalists saw the advantage of a label that would suggest that those who opposed the Constitution also opposed such a manifestly good thing as federalism. But what has not been sufficiently understood is that the term "federal" had acquired a specific ambiguity that enabled the Federalists not merely to take but to keep the name.

One of the perennial issues under the Articles of Confederation involved the degree to which the general government—or the instrumentality of the federation per se—was to be supported or its capacity to act strengthened. In this context one was "federal" or "anti-federal" according to his willingness or unwillingness to strengthen or support the institutions of the federation. This was James Wilson's meaning when he spoke of the "fœderal disposition and character" of Pennsylvania. It was Patrick Henry's meaning when he said that, in rejecting the Constitution, New Hampshire and Rhode Island "have refused to become federal." It was the meaning of the New York Assembly when in responding coolly to the recommendations of the Annapolis Convention it nevertheless insisted on its "truly federal" disposition. This usage had thoroughly penetrated political discussion in the United States. In the straightforward explanation of Anti-Federalist George Bryan, "The name of Federalists, or Federal men, grew up at New York and in the eastern states, some time before the calling of the Convention, to denominate such as were attached to the general support of the United States, in opposition to those who preferred local and particular advantages. . . ." Later, according to Bryan, "this name was taken possession of by those who were in favor of the new federal government, as they called it, and opposers were called Anti-Federalists." Recognizing the pre-1787 usage, Jackson Turner Main tries, like Bryan, to preserve the spirit of Federalist larceny by suggesting that during the several years before 1787 "the men who wanted a strong national government, who might more properly be called 'nationalists,' began to appropriate the term 'federal' for themselves" and to apply the term "antifederal" to those hostile to the measures of Congress and thus presumably unpatriotic. But there was nothing exceptional or improper in the use of the term "federal" in this way; the shift in meaning was less an "appropriation" than a natural extension of the language, which the Federalists fully exploited.

The point of substance is that the Federalists had a legitimate *claim* to their name and therefore to their name for their opponents. Whether they had a better claim than their opponents cannot be answered on the basis of mere linguistic usage but only by considering the arguments. When, during the years of the Confederation, one was called a "federal man," his attachment to the principles of federalism was not at issue; that was taken for granted, and the point was that he was a man who (given this federal system) favored strengthening the "federal" or general authority. The ambiguity arose because strengthening the federal *authority* could be carried so far as to undermine the federal *principle*; and that was precisely what the Anti-Federalists claimed their opponents were doing. Thus *The Impartial Examiner* argued that, despite the "sound of names" on which the advocates of the Constitution "build their fame," it is the opponents who act "on the broader scale of true *fœderal principles*." They desire "a continuance of each distinct sovereignty—and are anxious for such a degree of energy in the general government, as will cement the union in the strongest manner." It was possible (or so the Anti-Federalists believed) to be a federalist in the sense of favoring a strong agency of the federation and, at the same time, to be a federalist in the sense of adhering to the principle of league of independent states. In the name of federalism in the former sense, it was claimed, the proponents of the Constitution had abandoned federalism in the latter (and fundamental) sense.

The Anti-Federalists stood, then, for federalism in opposition to what they called the consolidating tendency and intention of the Constitution—the tendency to establish one complete national government, which would destroy or undermine the states. They feared the implications of language like Washington's reference, in transmitting the Constitution to Congress, to the need for "the consolidation of our Union." They saw ominous intentions in Publius' opinion that "a NATION, without a NATIONAL GOVERNMENT, is, in my view, an awful spectacle." They resented and denied suggestions that "we must forget our local habits and attachments" and "be reduced to one faith and one government." They saw in the new Constitution a government with authority extending "to every case that is of the least importance" and capable of acting (preeminently in the crucial case of taxation) at discretion and independently of any agency but its own. Instead of thus destroying the federal character of the Union, "the leading feature of every amendment" of the Articles of Confederation ought to be, as Yates and Lansing expressed it, "the preservation of the individual states, in their uncontrouled constitutional rights, and . . . in reserving these, a mode might have been devised of granting to the confederacy, the monies arising from a general system of revenue; the power of regulating commerce, and enforcing the observance of foreign treaties, and other necessary matters of less moment."

A few of the Anti-Federalists were not sure, it is true, that consolidation would be so bad, if it were really feasible. James Monroe went so far as to say that "to collect the citizens of America, who have fought and bled together, by whose joint and common efforts they have been raised to the comparatively happy and exalted theatre on which they now stand; to lay aside all those jarring interests and discordant principles, which state legislatures if they do not create, certainly foment and increase, arrange them under one government and make them one people, is an idea not only elevated and sublime, but equally benevolent and humane." And, on the other hand, most of the Federalists agreed or professed to agree that consolidation was undesirable. Fisher Ames, defending the Constitution in Massachusetts, spoke the language of many Federalists when he insisted that "too much provision cannot be made against a consolidation. The state governments represent the wishes, and feelings, and local interests of the people. They are the safeguard and ornament of the Constitution; they will protract the period of our liberties; they will afford a shelter against the abuse of power, and will be the natural avengers of our violated rights." Indeed, expressions of rather strict federal principles were not uncommon on the Federalist side, although they were often perfunctory or shallow.

Perhaps the most conciliatory Federalist defense of federalism, and not accidentally one of the least satisfactory in principle, was contained in a line of argument put forward by James Wilson and some others to the effect that, just as individuals have to give up some of their natural rights to civil government to secure peaceful enjoyment of civil rights, so states must give up some of theirs to federal government in order to secure peaceful enjoyment of federal liberties. But the analogy of civil liberty and federal liberty concedes the basic Anti-Federal contentions, and Wilson did not consistently adhere to it. As each individual has one vote in civil society, for example, so each state ought, on this analogy, to have one vote in federal society. As the preservation of the rights of individuals is the object of civil society, so the preservation of the rights of states (not individuals) ought to be the object of federal society. But these are Anti-Federal conclusions. Thus, when Agrippa assessed the proposed Constitution from the point of view of the interests of Massachusetts, he did so on *principled* ground, the same ground that properly leads any man to consider the civil society of which he is or may become a member, not exclusively but first and last, from the point of view of his interest in his life, liberty, and property. Wilson, on the other hand, argued for the priority of the general interest of the Union over the particular interests of the states. And this position is not defensible—as Wilson's own argument sufficiently demonstrates— on the basis of the federal liberty–civil liberty analogy.

The more characteristic Federalist position was to deny that the choice lay between confederation and consolidation and to contend that in fact the Constitution provided a new form, partly national and partly federal. This was Publius' argument in *The Federalist,* no. 39. It was Madison's argument in the Virginia ratifying convention. And it was the usual argument of James Wilson himself, who emphasized the strictly limited powers of the general government and the essential part to be played in it by the states. The Anti-Federalists objected that all such arguments foundered on the impossibility of dual sovereignty. "It is a solecism in politics for two coordinate sovereignties to exist together. . . ." A mixture may exist for a time, but it will inevitably tend in one direction or the other, subjecting the country in the meantime to "all the horrors of a divided sovereignty." Luther Martin agreed with Madison that the new Constitution presented a novel mixture of federal and national elements; but he found it "just so much federal in appearance as to give its advocates in some measure, an opportunity of passing it as such upon the unsuspecting multitude, before they had time and opportunity to examine it, and yet so predominantly national as to put it in the power of its movers, whenever the machine shall be set agoing, to strike out every part that has the appearance of being federal, and to render it wholly and entirely a national government."

The first words of the preamble sufficiently declare the anti-federal (in the strict sense) character of the Constitution, Patrick Henry thought; and his objection thundered over the Virginia convention sitting in Richmond:

> [W]hat right had they to say, *We the People?* My political curiosity, exclusive of my anxious solicitude for the public welfare, leads me to ask, who authorised them to speak the language of, *We, the People,* instead of *We, the States?* States are the characteristics, and the soul of a confederation. If the States be not the agents of this compact, it must be one great consolidated National Government of the people of all the States.

The clearest minds among the Federalists agreed that states are the soul of a confederacy. That is what is wrong with confederacies: "The fundamental principle of the old Confederation is defective; we must totally eradicate and discard this principle before we can expect an efficient government."

Here lies the main significance of the mode of ratification in the proposed Constitution. The new procedure—ratification by special state conventions rather than by Congress and the state legislatures and provision that the Constitution shall be established on ratification of nine states (as between them), rather than all thirteen states as required under the Articles of Confederation—was not merely illegal; it struck at the heart of the old Confederation. It denied, as Federalists like Hamilton openly admitted, the very basis of legality under the Articles of Confederation. The requirement in the Articles of Confederation for unanimous consent of the states to constitutional changes rested on the assumption that the states are the basic political entities, permanently associated indeed, but associated entirely at the will and in the interest of each of the several states. Even if it were granted that government under the Articles had collapsed (which most Anti-Federalists did not grant), there was no justification for abandoning the principles of state equality and unanimous consent to fundamental constitutional change. As William Paterson had put it in the Philadelphia Convention,

> If we argue the matter on the supposition that no Confederacy at present exists, it cannot be denied that all the States stand on the footing of equal sovereignty. All therefore must concur before any can be bound. . . . If we argue on the fact that a federal compact actually exists, and consult the articles of it we still find an equal Sovereignty to be the basis of it.

Whether in the Articles of Confederation or outside, the essential principle of American union was the equality of the states. As Luther Martin had argued in Philadelphia, "the separation from G. B. placed the 13 States in a state of nature towards each other; [and] they would have remained in that state till this time, but for the confederation. . . ."

The provision for ratifying the Constitution rested, in the main, on the contrary assumption that the American states are not several political wholes, associated together according to their several wills and for the sake of their several interests, but are, and always were from the moment of their separation from the King of England, parts of one whole. Thus constitutional change is the business of the people, not of the state legislatures, though the people act in (or through) their states. As one nation divided into several states, moreover, constitutional change is to be decided, not by unanimous consent of separate and equal entities, but by the major part of a single whole—an extraordinary majority because of the importance of the question. The Federalists contended that the colonies declared their independence not individually but unitedly, and that they had never been independent of one another. And the implication of this view is that the foundation of government in the United States is the interest of the nation and not the interests of the states. "The Union is essential to our being as a nation. The pillars that prop it are crumbling to powder," said Fisher Ames, staggering through a metaphorical forest. "The Union is the vital sap that nourishes the tree." The Articles of Confederation, in this view, were a defective instrument of a preexisting union. The congressional resolution calling for the Philadelphia Convention had described a means—"for the sole and express purpose of revising the Articles of Confederation"—and an end—to "render the federal constitution adequate to the exigencies of Government & the preservation of the Union." If there was any conflict, the means ought to be sacrificed to the end. The duty of the Philadelphia Convention and the members of the ratifying conventions was to take their bearings, not from the defective means, but from the great end, the preservation and well-being of the Union. ■

2.2 *Federalist* No. 39 (1788)

James Madison

Outline

I. The nature of republican government and whether the Constitution is truly republican in form and substance.

II. Whether the government of the United States is *federal* or *national* in character, or a combination of the two.

   A. The establishment of the Union.

   B. The establishment of the institutions of the U.S. government.

   C. The operation of the government.

   D. The scope of the government's powers.

   E. The process of amending the Constitution.

III. Conclusion: the mixed nature of the U.S. government as partly federal, partly national.

• • •

The first question that offers itself is whether the general form and aspect of the government be strictly republican. It is evident that no other form would be reconcilable with the genius of the people of America; with the fundamental principles of the Revolution; or with that honorable determination which animates every votary of freedom to rest all our political experiments on the capacity of mankind for self-government. If the plan of the convention, therefore, be found to depart from the republican character, its advocates must abandon it as no longer defensible.

What, then, are the distinctive characters of the republican form? Were an answer to this question to be sought, not by recurring to principles but in the application of the term by political writers to the constitutions of different States, no satisfactory one would ever be found. Holland, in which no particle of the supreme authority is derived from the people, has passed almost universally under the denomination of a republic. The same title has been bestowed on Venice, where absolute power over the great body of the people is exercised in the most absolute manner by a small body of hereditary nobles. Poland, which is a mixture of aristocracy and of monarchy in their worst forms, has been dignified with the same appellation. The government of England, which has one republican branch only, combined with an hereditary aristocracy and monarchy, has with equal impropriety been frequently placed on the list of republics. These examples, which are nearly as dissimilar to each other as to a genuine republic, show the extreme inaccuracy with which the term has been used in political disquisitions.

If we resort for a criterion to the different principles on which different forms of government are established, we may define a republic to be, or at least may bestow that name on, a government which derives all its powers directly or indirectly from the great body of the people, and is administered by persons holding their offices during pleasure for a limited period, or during good behavior. It is *essential* to such a government that it be derived from the great body of the society, not from an inconsiderable proportion or a favored class of it; otherwise a handful of tyrannical nobles, exercising their oppressions by a delegation of their powers, might aspire to the rank of republicans and claim for their government the honorable title of republic. It is *sufficient* for such a government that the persons administering it be appointed, either directly or indirectly, by the people; and that they hold their appointments by either of the tenures just specified; otherwise every government in the United States, as well as every other popular government that has been or can be well organized or well executed, would be degraded from the republican character. According to the constitution of every State in the Union, some or other of the officers of government are appointed indirectly only by the people. According to most of them, the chief magistrate himself is so appointed. And according to one, this mode of appointment is extended to one of the co-ordinate branches of the legislature. According to all the constitutions, also, the tenure of the highest offices is extended to a definite period, and in many instances, both within the legislative and executive departments, to a period of years. According to the provisions of most of the constitutions, again, as well as according to the most respectable and received opinions on the subject, the members of the judiciary department are to retain their offices by the firm tenure of good behavior.

On comparing the Constitution planned by the convention with the standard here fixed, we perceived at once that it is, in the most rigid sense, conformable to it. The House of Representatives, like that of one branch at least of all the State legislatures, is elected immediately by the great body of the people. The Senate, like the present Congress and the Senate of Maryland, derives its appointment indirectly from the people. The President is indirectly derived from the choice of the people, according to the example in most of the States. Even the judges, with all other officers of the Union, will, as in the several States, be the choice, though a remote choice, of the people themselves. The duration of the appointments is equally conformable to the republican standard and to the model of State constitutions. The House of Representatives is periodically elective, as in all the States; and for the period of two years, as in the State of South Carolina. The Senate is elective for the period of six years, which is but one year more than the period of the Senate of Maryland, and but two more than that of the Senates of New York and Virginia. The President is to continue in office for the period of four years; as in New York and Delaware the chief magistrate is elected for three years, and in South Carolina for two years. In the other States the election is annual. In several of the States, however, no explicit provision is made for the impeachment of the chief magistrate. And in Delaware and Virginia he is not impeachable till out of office. The President of the United States is impeachable at any time during his continuance in office. The tenure by which the judges are to hold their places is, as it unquestionably ought to be, that of good behavior. The tenure of the ministerial offices generally will be a subject of legal regulation, conformably to the reason of the case and the example of the State constitutions.

Could any further proof be required of the republican complexion of this system, the most decisive one might be found in its absolute prohibition of titles of nobility, both under the federal and the State governments; and in its express guaranty of the republican form to each of the latter.

"But it was not sufficient," say the adversaries of the proposed Constitution, "for the convention to adhere to the republican form. They ought with equal care to have preserved the *federal* form, which regards the Union as a *Confederacy* of sovereign states; instead of which they have flamed a *national* government, which regards the Union as a *consolidation* of the States." And it is asked by what authority this bold and radical innovation was undertaken? The handle which has been made of this objection requires that it should be examined with some precision.

Without inquiring into the accuracy of the distinction on which the objection is founded, it will be necessary to a just estimate of its force, first, to ascertain the real character of the government in question; secondly, to inquire how far the convention were authorized to propose such a government; and thirdly, how far the duty they owed to their country could supply any defect of regular authority.

First.—In order to ascertain the real character of the government, it may be considered in relation to the foundation on which it is to be established; to the sources from which its ordinary powers are to be drawn; to the operation of those powers; to the extent of them; and to the authority by which future changes in the government are to be introduced.

On examining the first relation, it appears, on one hand, that the Constitution is to be founded on the assent and ratification of the people of America, given by deputies elected for the special purpose; but, on the other, that this assent and ratification is to be given by the people, not as individuals composing one entire nation, but as composing the distinct and independent States to which they respectively belong. It is to be the assent and ratification of the several States, derived from the supreme authority in each State—the authority of the people themselves. The act, therefore, establishing the Constitution will not be a *national* but a *federal* act.

That it will be a federal and not a national act, as these terms are understood by the objectors—the act of the people, as forming so many independent States, not as forming one aggregate nation—is obvious from this single consideration: that it is to result neither from the decision of a *majority* of the people of the Union, nor from that of a *majority* of the States. It must result from the *unanimous* assent of the several States that are parties to it differing no otherwise from their ordinary assent than in its being expressed, not by the legislative authority, but by that of the people themselves. Were the people regarded in this transaction as forming one nation, the will of the majority of the whole people of the United States would bind the minority, in the same manner as the majority in each State must bind the minority; and the will of the majority must be determined either by a comparison of the individual votes, or by considering the will of the majority of the States as evidence of the will of a majority of the people of the United States. Neither of these rules has been adopted. Each State, in ratifying the Constitution, is considered as a sovereign body independent of all others, and only to be bound by its own voluntary act. In this relation, then, the new Constitution will, if established, be a *federal* and not a *national* constitution.

The next relation is to the sources from which the ordinary powers of government are to be derived. The House of Representatives will derive its powers from the people of America; and the people will be represented in the same proportion and on the same principle as they are in the legislature of a particular State. So far the government is *national*, not *federal*. The Senate, on the other hand, will derive its powers from the States as political and coequal societies; and these will be represented on the principle of equality in the Senate, as they now are in the existing Congress. So far the government is *federal*, not *national*. The executive power will be derived from a very compound source. The immediate election of the President is to be made by the States in their political characters. The votes allotted to them are in a compound ratio, which considers them partly as distinct and coequal societies, partly as unequal members of the same society. The eventual election, again, is to be made by that branch of the legislature which consists of the national representatives; but in this particular act they are to be thrown into the form of individual delegations from so many distinct and coequal bodies politic. From this aspect of the government it appears to be of a mixed character, presenting at least as many *federal* as *national* features.

The difference between a federal and national government, as it relates to the *operation of the government*, is by the adversaries of the plan of the convention supposed to consist in this, that in the former the powers operate on the political bodies composing the Confederacy in their political capacities; in the latter, on the individual citizens composing the nation in their individual capacities. On trying the Constitution by this criterion, it fails under the *national* not the *federal* character; though perhaps not so completely as has been understood. In several cases, and particularly in the trial of controversies to which States may be parties, they must be viewed and proceeded against in their collective and political capacities only.

But the operation of the government on the people in their individual capacities, in its ordinary and most essential proceedings, will, in the sense of its opponents, on the whole, designate it, in this relation, a *national* government.

But if the government be national with regard to the *operation* of its powers, it changes its aspect again when we contemplate it in relation to the extent of its powers. The idea of a national government involves in it not only an authority over the individual citizens, but an indefinite supremacy over all persons and things, so far as they are objects of lawful government. Among a people consolidated into one nation, this supremacy is completely vested in the national legislature. Among communities united for particular purposes, it is vested partly in the general and partly in the municipal legislatures. In the former case, all local authorities are subordinate to the supreme; and may be controlled, directed, or abolished by it at pleasure. In the latter, the local or municipal authorities form distinct and independent portions of the supremacy, no more subject, within their respective spheres, to the general authority than the general authority is subject to them, within its own sphere. In this relation, then, the proposed government cannot be deemed a *national* one; since its jurisdiction extends to certain enumerated objects only, and leaves to the several States a residuary and inviolable sovereignty over all other objects. It is true that in controversies relating to the boundary between the two jurisdictions, the tribunal which is ultimately to decide is to be established under the general government. But this does not change the principle of the case. The decision is to be impartially made, according to the rules of the Constitution; and all the usual and most effectual precautions are taken to secure this impartiality. Some such tribunal is clearly essential to prevent an appeal to the sword and a dissolution of the compact; and that it ought to be established under the general rather than under the local governments, or, to speak more properly, that it could be safely established under the first alone, is a position not likely to be combated.

If we try the Constitution by its last relation to the authority by which amendments are to be made, we find it neither wholly *national* nor wholly *federal*. Were it wholly national, the supreme and ultimate authority would reside in the *majority* of the people of the Union; and this authority would be competent at all times, like that of a majority of every national society to alter or abolish its established government. Were it wholly federal, on the other hand, the concurrence of each State in the Union would be essential to every alteration that would be binding on all. The mode provided by the plan of the convention is not founded on either of these principles. In requiring more than a majority, and particularly in computing the proportion by *States*, not by *citizens*, it departs from the national and advances towards the *federal* character; in rendering the concurrence of less than the whole number of States sufficient, it loses again the federal and partakes of the *national* character.

The proposed Constitution, therefore, even when tested by the rules laid down by its antagonists, is, in strictness, neither a national nor a federal Constitution, but a composition of both. In its foundation it is federal, not national; in the sources from which the ordinary powers of the government are drawn, it is partly federal and partly national; in the operation of these powers, it is national, not federal; in the extent of them, again, it is federal, not national; and, finally in the authoritative mode of introducing amendments, it is neither wholly federal nor wholly national. ■

2.3 *Federalist* No. 45 (1788)

James Madison

Outline

 I. Importance of increasing the powers of the national government at the expense of the states.
 II. Historical weakness of central governments in confederacies.
   A. Ancient times.
   B. Feudal times.
 III. Advantages of the states in their relations with the national government.
   A. States as constituent and essential parts of the national government.
   B. Relatively small size of the national government.
   C. Few and defined powers of the national government.
   D. Advantages of the states in times of peace.
 IV. Conclusion: Constitution as invigorating the powers of the national government more than adding to them.

• • •

The adversaries to the plan of the convention, instead of considering in the first place what degree of power was absolutely necessary for the purposes of the federal government, have exhausted themselves in a secondary inquiry into the possible consequences of the proposed degree of power to the governments of the particular States. But if the Union, as has been shown, be essential to the security of the people of America against foreign danger; if it be essential to their security against contentions and wars among the different States; if it be essential to guard them against those violent and oppressive factions which embitter the blessings of liberty and against those military establishments which must gradually poison its very fountain; if, in a word, the Union be essential to the happiness of the people of America, is it not preposterous to urge as an objection to a government, without which the objects of the Union cannot be attained, that such a government may derogate from the importance of the governments of the individual States? Was, then, the American Revolution effected, was the American Confederacy formed, was the precious blood of thousands spilt, and the hard-earned substance of millions lavished, not that the people of America should enjoy peace, liberty, and safety, but that the governments of the individual States, that particular municipal establishments, might enjoy a certain extent of power and be arrayed with certain dignities and attributes of sovereignty? We have heard of the impious doctrine in the old world, that the people were made for kings, not kings for the people. Is the same doctrine to be revived in the new, in another shape—that the solid happiness of the people is to be sacrificed to the views of political institutions of a different form? It is too early for politicians to presume on our forgetting that the public good, the real welfare of the great body of the people, is the supreme object to be pursued; and that no form of government whatever has any other value than as it may be fitted for the attainment of this object. Were the plan of the convention adverse to the public happiness, my voice would be, Reject the plan. Were the Union itself inconsistent with the public happiness, it would be, Abolish the Union. In like manner, as far as the sovereignty of the States cannot be reconciled to the happiness of the people, the voice of every good citizen must be, Let the former be sacrificed to the latter. How far the sacrifice is necessary has been shown. How far the unsacrificed residue will be endangered is the question before us.

Several important considerations have been touched in the course of these papers, which discountenance the supposition that the operation of the federal government will by degrees prove fatal to the State governments. The more I revolve the subject, the more fully I am persuaded that the balance is much more likely to be disturbed by the preponderancy of the last than of the first scale.

We have seen, in all the examples of ancient and modern confederacies, the strongest tendency continually betraying itself in the members to despoil the general government of its authorities, with a very ineffectual capacity in the latter to defend itself against the encroachments. Although, in most of these examples, the system has been so dissimilar from that under consideration as greatly to weaken any inference concerning the latter from the fate of the former, yet, as the States will retain under the proposed Constitution a very extensive portion of active sovereignty, the inference ought not to be wholly disregarded. In the [ancient] Achæan league it is probable that the federal head had a degree and species of power which gave it a considerable likeness to the government framed by the convention. The Lycian Confederacy, as far as its principles and form are transmitted, must have borne a still greater analogy to it. Yet history does not inform us that either of them ever degenerated, or tended to degenerate, into one consolidated government. On the contrary, we know that the ruin of one of them proceeded from the incapacity of the federal authority to prevent the dissensions, and finally the disunion, of the subordinate authorities. These cases are the more worthy of our attention as the external causes by which the component parts were pressed together were much more numerous and powerful than in our case; and consequently less powerful ligaments within would be sufficient to bind the members to the head and to each other.

In the feudal system, we have seen a similar propensity exemplified. Notwithstanding the want of proper sympathy in every instance between the local sovereigns and the people, and the sympathy in some instances between the general sovereign and the latter, it usually happened that the local sovereigns prevailed in the rivalship for encroachments. Had no external dangers enforced internal harmony and subordination, and particularly, had the local sovereigns possessed the affections of the people, the great kingdoms in Europe would at this time consist of as many independent princes as there were formerly feudatory barons.

The State governments will have the advantage of the federal government, whether we compare them in respect to the immediate dependence of the one on the other; to the weight of personal influence which each side will possess; to the powers respectively vested in them; to the predilection and probable support of the people; to the disposition and faculty of resisting and frustrating the measures of each other.

The State governments may be regarded as constituent and essential parts of the federal government; whilst the latter is nowise essential to the operation or organization of the former. Without the intervention of the State legislatures, the President of the United States cannot be elected at all. They must in all cases have a great share in his appointment, and will, perhaps, in most cases, of themselves determine it. The Senate will be elected absolutely and exclusively by the State legislatures. Even the House of Representatives, though drawn immediately from the people, will be chosen very much under the influence of that class of men whose influence over the people obtains for themselves an election into the State legislatures. Thus, each of the principal branches of the federal government will owe its existence more or less to the favor of the State governments, and must consequently feel a dependence, which is much more likely to beget a disposition too obsequious than too overbearing towards them. On the other side, the component parts of the State governments will in no instance be indebted for their appointment to the direct agency of the federal government, and very little, if at all, to the local influence of its members.

The number of individuals employed under the Constitution of the United States will be much smaller than the number employed under the particular States. There will consequently be less of personal influence on the side of the former than of the latter. The members of the legislative, executive, and judiciary departments of thirteen and more States, the justices of peace, officers of militia, ministerial officers of justice, with all the county, corporation, and town officers, for three millions and more of people, intermixed and having particular acquaintance with every class and circle of people must exceed, beyond all proportion, both in number and influence, those of every description who will be employed in the administration of the federal system. Compare the members of the three great departments of the thirteen States, excluding from the judiciary department the justices of peace, with the members of the corresponding departments of the single government of the Union; compare the militia officers of three millions of people with the military and marine officers of any establishment which is within the compass of probability, or, I may add, of possibility, and in this view alone, we may pronounce the advantage of the States to be decisive. If the federal government is to have collectors of revenue, the State governments will have theirs also. And as those of the former will be principally on the seacoast, and not very numerous, whilst those of the latter will be spread over the face of the country, and will be very numerous, the advantage in this view also lies on the same side. It is true that the Confederacy is to possess, and may exercise, the power of collecting internal as well as external taxes throughout the States; but it is probable that this power will not be resorted to, except for supplemental purposes of revenue; that an option will then be given to the States to supply their quotas by previous collections of their own; and that the eventual collection, under the immediate authority of the Union, will generally be made by the officers, and according to the rules, appointed by the several States. Indeed it is extremely probable that in other instances, particularly in the organization of the judicial power, the officers of the States will be clothed with the correspondent authority of the Union. Should it happen, however, that separate collectors of internal revenue should be appointed under the federal government, the influence of the whole number would not bear a comparison with that of the multitude of State officers in the opposite scale. Within every district to which a federal collector would be allotted, there would not be less than thirty or forty, or even more, officers of different descriptions, and many of them persons of character and weight whose influence would lie on the side of the State.

The powers delegated by the proposed Constitution to the federal government are few and defined. Those which are to remain in the State governments are numerous and indefinite. The former will be exercised principally on external objects, as war, peace, negotiation, and foreign commerce; with which last the power of taxation will, for the most part, be connected. The powers reserved to the several States will extend to all the objects which, in the ordinary course of affairs, concern the lives, liberties, and properties of the people, and the internal order, improvement, and prosperity of the State.

The operations of the federal government will be most extensive and important in times of war and danger; those of the State governments in times of peace and security. As the former periods will probably bear a small proportion of the latter, the State governments will here enjoy another advantage over the federal government. The more adequate, indeed, the federal powers may be rendered to the national defense, the less frequent will be those scenes of danger which might favor their ascendancy over the governments of the particular States.

If the new Constitution be examined with accuracy and candor, it will be found that the change which it proposes consists much less in the addition of NEW POWERS to the Union than in the invigoration of its ORIGINAL POWERS. The regulation of commerce, it is true, is a new power; but that seems to be an addition which few oppose and from which no apprehensions are entertained. The powers relating to war and peace, armies and fleets, treaties and finance, with the other more considerable powers, are all vested in the existing Congress by the Articles of Confederation. The proposed change does not enlarge these powers; it only substitutes a more effectual mode of administering them. The change relating to taxation may be regarded as the most important; and yet the present Congress have as complete authority to REQUIRE of the States indefinite supplies of money for the common defense and general welfare as the future Congress will have to require them of individual citizens; and the latter will be no more bound than the States themselves have been to pay the quotas respectively taxed on them. Had the States complied punctually with the Articles of Confederation, or could their compliance have been enforced by as peaceable means as may be used with success towards single persons, our past experience is very far from countenancing an opinion that the State governments would have lost their constitutional powers, and have gradually undergone an entire consolidation. To maintain that such an event would have ensued would be to say at once that the existence of the State governments is incompatible with any system whatever that accomplishes the essential purposes of the Union. ■

 # American Politics Today

This past decade has seen a significant shift of power from Washington to the state capitals. Support for this "new federalism" has come from the Republican-controlled Congress, a sympathetic Supreme Court, and presidents who have either actively supported "states' rights" or at least been willing to compromise. In this selection, the political scientist Ann O'M. Bowman surveys the possibilities for American federalism in the twenty-first century.

Questions

1. How has the distribution of power between Washington and the states changed in recent years? What implications do these changes have for the shape of American public policy?
2. How would the Federalists and Antifederalists (see selections 2.1 through 2.3) evaluate the trends in American federalism described in this selection?

2.4 American Federalism on the Horizon (2002)

Ann O'M. Bowman

This article takes a prospective look at American federalism by reflecting on current trends and likely futures. The central question is: What will the first decade of the twenty-first century mean for American federalism? In other words, how will American federalism shape the next ten years or so and how will the federal system itself evolve during that period? This is a two-part question because federalism is both a cause and an effect. As a structure and system, it determines outcomes such as governmental policies and behaviors. But federalism also is an effect; it is influenced and molded by societal conditions, economic

Excerpted from Ann O'M. Bowman, "American Federalism on the Horizon," *Publius: The Journal of Federalism* 32 (Spring 2002): 3–22. Reprinted by permission.

trends, and political events. The near future for federalism holds a range of possibilities. . . .

Prospective American Federalism

During the twentieth century, the American federal system became extremely intergovernmental. By 2001, few functions belonged exclusively to one level of government. The growing intergovernmentalism led to calls for a sorting out of functions between the federal and state governments, a realignment of sorts. Those calls have had little effect, however, as the number of governmental connections has increased, leading one observer to advocate the replacement of common federalism metaphors of marble cakes and picket fences with another: spider webs.

Five Possible Paths   Peering into the future is an exercise best undertaken cautiously. There are five possible paths that American federalism can take in the early twenty-first century. These include (1) continuation of current trends at a similar pace in a similar style, (2) great acceleration of current trends, an exponential increase, (3) the stabilization of current trends, slow movement with little increase or decrease, (4) actual reversal of current trends, albeit modest, and (5) substantial reversal of current trends, extensive and system-changing.

A linearity assumption underlies the first scenario: yesterday is the best predictor of tomorrow. Substantial disruption is not anticipated; incrementalism rules. With the second scenario, the factors that have produced the current situation increase dramatically, thus producing an exponential acceleration of the contemporary trends. Yesterday may still predict tomorrow but only if yesterday's trends are squared. The third scenario, stabilization of conditions and patterns of federalism at today's level, represents a diversion from the growth-over-time expectations. Stabilization assumes that an optimal point has been reached and that it ought to be maintained, not expanded or contracted. In the fourth scenario, factors are disrupted sufficiently to generate a reversal in the trend. This new trend takes the federal system in a different direction. The fifth scenario is the transformational reversal that is likely to follow major shocks. It is the mirror image of the exponential increase, but the change is in the inverse direction. Figure 1 displays the five possible federalism paths.

The federalism scenarios make no assumptions about the length of time represented by the dotted lines. It is quite possible, even likely, that the next decade or two will see several of these trends unfold at different periods. Increases may be followed by decreases, periods of no change could be interspersed among upward or downward trends. However, if in 2010 or 2020, one were to look back in an attempt to measure the direction of federalism since 2001, one of these five paths will be proven accurate. . . .

Federalism as a Political Tool

In the contemporary political dialogue in the United States, the concept of federalism has regained some luster. Politicians, pundits, and scholars alike, reacting to

Figure 1 ■ Future Federalism Paths

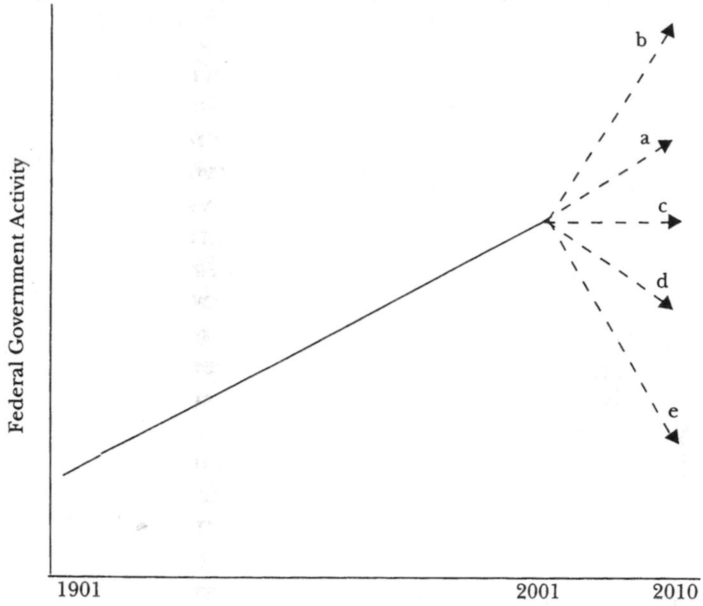

(a) continuation of twentieth century trend
(b) great acceleration of twentieth century trend
(c) stabilization at end of twentieth century level
(d) modest reversal of twentieth century trend
(e) substantial reversal of twentieth century trend

the centralization of the past century, have embraced federalism as a solution. Seeking to avoid the "states' rights" rhetoric of the past, this newer federalism envisions a shift in the relative power positions of the federal government and the states.

In 1981, newly elected Republican President Ronald Reagan promised to "restore the balance between levels of government." Although his commitment to that goal eventually wavered, Reagan was successful in bringing federalism into the political debate. Issuance of Executive Order 12372 in 1982, for example, gave state and local governments more flexibility in reviewing and managing federal grant programs; Executive Order 12612 (1987) established "fundamental federalism principles" to guide the policies of federal departments and agencies. Subsequent presidents have followed Reagan's lead with their own versions of federalism principles. Even for Democrats, federalism has become something to support. Thus, it was little surprise to hear Democratic President Bill Clinton declare in his 1996 State of the Union message that "the era of big government is over." The point is not the accuracy of the statement but its utility as a symbol. In the 2000 presidential election, both George W. Bush and Al Gore subscribed to a "less national government–more state government" perspective. The differences between the candidates were matters of degree. The Bush approach tended to be more market-driven, Gore's approach retained a larger role for government. Still, both of the candidates sought to portray themselves as federalism-friendly.

Among the states, efforts to advance the cause of federalism have been sustained. It was governors who issued one of the earliest calls for a sorting out of functions between the federal government and the states. Particularly galling to state and local officials were federal mandates that lacked sufficient funding, thus forcing states to assume additional financial burdens. State and local leaders were successful in capturing public attention with their "National Unfunded Mandates Day" events in the fall of 1993. By 1995, with Republicans controlling the U.S. House of Representatives, the climate was right for the passage of the Unfunded Mandates Reform Act of 1995, a bill supported by state and local government interest groups. Governors such as Republicans Michael Leavitt of Utah and Tommy Thompson of Wisconsin emerged as leaders in the sorting-out-functions movement, issuing occasional anti-national government, pro-state pronouncements. Federalism became good politics. . . .

The use of federalism as a political tool is likely to endure, at least in the short term. If federalism's value is primarily as a symbol, then it is not surprising that the chief institutional engine for advancing the cause of federalism, the bipartisan U.S. Advisory Commission on Intergovernmental Relations, met its demise at the hands of a budget-cutting Congress in 1996. But if the pro-federalism sentiment is more than symbolic, that is, if it has sufficient depth to produce the restoration of the federal-state balance, then the path labeled (d) in Figure 1 may be heavily traveled over the next decade. This and related questions are taken up in the next section.

The Distribution of Power

During the past century, centripetal forces pulled power toward the federal government. Centralization has been rapid in some decades; in other periods, it has been countered by varied efforts at decentralization. The most recent decentralization attempts have been the most successful, albeit only modest success. At the start of the twenty-first century, the balance of power between the federal and state governments remains the fundamental federalism issue.

Devolution   Toward the end of the twentieth century, some analysts contended that the country was poised on the brink of a massive restructuring, a "devolution revolution." The concept of devolution, or a shifting of power to state governments, captured the hearts and minds of many Americans. Devolution is associated with several positive outcomes. Its proponents contend that it will provide (1) more efficient provision and production of public services, (2) better alignment of the costs and benefits of government for a diverse citizenry, (3) better fits between public goods and their spatial characteristics, (4) increased competition, experimentation, and innovation in the public sector, (5) greater responsiveness to citizen preferences, and (6) more transparent accountability in policy-making.

Public support for devolution has been strong since the Reagan era. In a survey of Michigan residents, for example, fully 70 percent responded positively to a general question about shifting functions from the federal government to the states. National polls found that two-thirds of Americans supported a plan in which Congress would lessen its involvement in a series of domestic programs, and instead give program funds to the states. However, the Michigan study suggests that public sentiment about devolution is more complex than typically assumed. With regard to eleven specific governmental services (e.g., providing airports and highways, providing police protection and prisons, stimulating economic development, and preventing pollution), a majority of respondents wanted some federal government involvement in all but two of them. (The two were elementary and secondary education and police protection.)

During the 1990s, federal institutions appeared to be converging in a pro-devolution direction. Republicans, the party advocating smaller, closer-to-the-people government, controlled both houses of Congress. The president, although a Democrat, was a former governor who spoke the language of the states. The U.S. Supreme Court issued several state-empowering rulings (e.g., its decision that the Gun Free School Zone Act was unconstitutional).

From the state side, the time for broadening the states' role seemed propitious. As noted earlier, state and local leaders found a unifying issue in mandate reform. Enthusiasm for devolution among governors was high, especially in the Republican ranks. Most states were enjoying nearly record-level budget surpluses, thus giving them the financial basis to assume a greater role in the federal system. Several states, with Wisconsin at the forefront, began to tinker with their welfare systems, using waiver provisions provided under section 1115 of the Social Security Act.

Federalism advocates cheered when the Republican-controlled Congress enacted the Personal Responsibility and Work Opportunity Reconciliation Act of 1996, a welfare-reform bill containing many devolutionary features. States were to use their Temporary Assistance for Needy Families (TANF) block grant funds in any way reasonably calculated to accomplish the purposes of the legislation. The discretion of states extended to the determination of eligibility, the design of methods of assistance, and the establishment of benefit levels. States could decide whether to operate new food stamp and employment and training programs, or whether to shift some welfare functions to local governments. Subsequent research on the law's impact suggests that one area in which welfare reform has produced the intended consequences is in program diversity, that is, in letting states and localities design their programs to fit their circumstances. It is no wonder that welfare reform was hailed by many as a major first step in shifting power and responsibility to the states.

Yet, as the new century opens, the devolutionary trend in federalism—akin to trend line (d) in Figure 1—appears to be somewhat equivocal. In other words, the devolution era thus far has delivered a lot less than promised. Welfare reform, for all its celebration, contained other decidedly nondevolutionary elements that limit flexibility (e.g., states must spend at least 4 percent of their TANF funds for child care), impose mandates (states must record Social Security numbers on official documents such as drivers' licenses), and reduce funding (states can lose a portion of their TANF allocation if they fail to meet work-participation requirements).

Analysts seeking evidence of the impact of devolution have not been able to uncover much. Paul Posner's research on federal mandates found that, even in the aftermath of passage of the Unfunded Mandates Reform Act, new federal mandates were imposed and more preemptions were enacted. A 1998 survey of city officials conducted by Richard Cole and his colleagues showed that "very little by way of real devolution" had taken place. Robert Dilger's analysis of spending patterns from 1990 to 1999 revealed that federal intergovernmental grant-in-aid expenditures were on the rise in almost all functional categories, hardly the pattern of devolution. Republican control of Congress, despite a Contract with America that extolled the virtues of devolution, did not produce as much new federalism as anticipated, thus reaffirming the logic that elected federal policymakers like to make policy in Washington, D.C. Furthermore, the decisions rendered by the U.S. Supreme Court were less state empowering than they were federal discouraging. That is, rather than shifting power to the states, the rulings tended to hold the line on the extension of federal power. The devolution that has occurred has tended to be of an administrative variety (e.g., the federal government's granting of a waiver to a state implementing a federal statute); meaningful substantive devolution is notably absent, as John Kincaid has concluded. Thus, it appears that devolution may be more hyperbole than empirical fact. But even if interest in devolution *per se* fades away, the issue of the federal-state balance is at the heart of federalism and will undoubtedly remain central to public debate.

• • •

Emerging Issues of Consequence

The Composition of the U.S. Supreme Court   The cumulative effect of the Rehnquist Court's federalism decisions has enhanced state power vis-a-vis the federal government. As Susan Gluck Mezey notes,

> the federalism decisions of the 1990s have shielded states from the authority of the federal government in a variety of ways. Through its interpretations of the interstate commerce clause and of the Tenth and Eleventh Amendments, primarily the latter, the Court has reminded Congress that its authority to govern has limits. [But] . . . the Court has largely refrained from effecting wholesale changes in its Tenth Amendment and commerce clause doctrines.

The slight "pro-state" balance on the Court is fragile, with most federalism cases decided with 5–4 margins. With more federalism cases coming before the Court, a change in the Court's composition could have a greater impact than usual on its federalism jurisprudence. This issue loomed large in the 2000 presidential election and, if no vacancies occur in the interim, will undoubtedly re-emerge in 2004. . . .

An Assortment of Issues   [Other issues in addition to the Supreme Court] affect (and are effected by) federalism. Demographic changes—an aging population and increased ethnic diversity—will reverberate across governmental levels. Population mobility, especially the re-centering of the populace in a southern and western direction, continues. The economic boom of the late 1990s has slowed; now many state governments are falling victim to overly optimistic revenue projections. Health-care costs are escalating rapidly, and some of the most innovative state managed-care plans are threatened. Federal grants to state and local governments are on the rise, constituting 17.9 percent of the fiscal year 2002 budget. However, payments to individuals constitute an ever-increasing proportion of those federal outlays: 11.4 percent in 2002, compared to 8.0 percent in 1992.

The issues run the gamut. The federalization of crime continues with the Bush administration's proposals for additional federal gun-crimes. With the reauthorization of the 1965 Elementary and Secondary Education Act, more federal government involvement in public schools is a certainty. President Bush has stated repeatedly that education is his number-one priority, and the reauthorization bills passed by the House and Senate emphasize testing and accountability—accountability not only for schools and school districts, but for states as well. At the same time, the growing threat of catastrophic terrorism on U.S. soil is encouraging a new form of intergovernmental cooperation: terrorism prevention. Interstate cooperation is on the rise. The number of interstate compacts has reached an all-time high; the use of joint legal action by states has never been greater. In states with direct democracy, the increased use of ballot initiatives is posing real challenges to representative democracy. In the international environmental arena, the United States is likely to face demands that it lower its emission of greenhouse gases, an action that would have broad domestic consequences. The list of federalism-relevant conditions goes on and on. The only certain outcome is the continued evolution of the federal system. As Martha Derthick has said, "American federalism is a highly protean form, long on change and confusion, short on fixed, generally accepted principles."

Conclusion

What makes it difficult to predict federalism over the course of the next decade is the existence of the five different paths set out in Figure 1. None of the paths has a zero probability, although the two most extreme (trend lines [b] and [e]) are certainly least likely. But are we going to see the "authentic rebirth of federalism" that David Walker has called for?

If federalism travels along a path toward decentralization (trend line [d]), it would likely mean greater policy diversity and greater inequality across constituent units. Is inequality an acceptable trade-off for policy diversity? But then again, states may embrace harmonization more than customization. State leaders, as political realists, may conclude that working in concert with other states to achieve a common outcome is preferable to federal preemptions and mandates. Thus, a decentralized future could actually mean state-generated commonalities across the states.

John Kincaid is probably not too far off the mark with his assessment that what is occurring "appears to be a process involving restoration, deaccession, and rebalancing, that is, restorations of powers to the states and their local governments as well as deaccessions of unwanted functions, which, together, could produce a rebalancing of power between the federal government and the states." That would be somewhere between trend line (c) and trend line (d). ∎

The International Context

The American model of federalism holds great attraction to many Europeans, who see the American constitutional system as a blueprint for the evolving European Union (EU). But the history of American federalism offers little hope that the road to a federal Europe will be perfectly smooth and direct. The fierce battles over federal and state power in the nineteenth century, and the continued debate over fundamental principles in the twentieth and twenty-first centuries, testify to the difficulty of the task of making "one out of many." In this cautionary article, the editors of the British magazine *The Economist* warn Europe's people and its politicians not to copy the New World's example without first studying its history. As Europe has moved steadily toward economic and political integration over the past decade, and as the EU has added new members from Central and Eastern Europe, the issues raised in this selection have become increasingly relevant and important.

Questions

1. What aspects of the American experience might provide advocates of a "United States of Europe" with a sense of optimism about the future of Europe? What aspects might produce pessimism?
2. What advice does *The Economist* give to advocates of a more united Europe? Why?

2.5 If You Sincerely Want to Be a United States . . . (1991)

The Economist

I magine a hot summer in Paris. By grace of a kindly time-warp, a group of European eminences have assembled for a conference. Charles de Gaulle is their chairman. Among those attending are John Maynard Keynes (who has a continent-wide reputation, though he is still only 29) and Albert Einstein.

Bertrand Russell is not there—he is holidaying on Cape Cod—but he barrages the proceedings by fax. Russell is kept abreast of things by young King Juan Carlos of Spain, who, with Keynes, provides the driving force of the conference.

Impossible, except in one of those rosy early-morning dreams. Now remember the men who gathered at Philadelphia in the summer of 1787. George Washington was the chairman. Alexander Hamilton, whose short life never knew a dull moment, was there, as was James Madison, a pragmatic man of principle who would later become president. Together, they directed the conference. Benjamin Franklin was there too, though somewhat in his dotage. Thomas Jefferson (compared with whom Bertrand Russell was a startlingly narrow fellow) was not there, but kept an eye on things from Paris.

It is no offence to Jacques Delors and his friends to say that the people now charged with trying to create a political union in Europe do not inspire such awe. Yet the job of the two intergovernmental conferences the European Community has assembled this year is not different in kind from that which faced America's constitutional convention 204 years ago. Constitution-writing is also in vogue in the Soviet Union, as that country's central government and its 15 surly republics struggle to redefine their relations with each other; though that is a matter of trying to stop a bad union falling apart, not creating a good new one. Might the most mature and successful constitutional settlement in the world have some lessons for these European parvenus?

They Were One, and They Knew It

Start with two great differences between America then and Europe now. The America that declared its independence from Britain in 1776 was, except for its black slaves, an extraordinarily homogeneous society.

Think of those huge distances, and those primitive communications, and wonder at the early Americans' sense of cohesion. Although North and South already showed the difference that had to be bridged by war in 1861–65, Americans shared some essential attributes. A few German and Dutch dissenters apart, their stock was solidly British. Their intellectual heroes (a nod to Montesquieu notwithstanding) were from the British tradition: Hobbes and Locke, Smith and Hume. Their language was English; their law was English law; their God an English God.

Wherever on the coast they settled, they had originally had to win the land by backbreaking struggle (even in the Carolinas, whose plantations were far bigger than New England farms). Three thousand perilous miles from England, they had all learnt the same self-sufficiency. Most of them, or their fathers, had fought Indians.

And those who did not leave for Canada after the break with Britain had a second thing in common: they had all won their independence from an external power, by force of arms. Their successful war of liberation made them feel more clearly "American" than ever before.

Yet that war had been prosecuted by 13 states, not one; and it did not forge anything that, to modern eyes, looks like a nation-state. Indeed, this absence of unity was made explicit by the articles of confederation, which the 13 states signed in 1781. Article 2 said that the states retained their "sovereignty, freedom and independence." They merely (article 3) entered into a "firm league of friendship with each other."

After only six years, the articles of 1781 were deemed unsatisfactory enough to warrant revision. The result—today's constitution—provided a system of government that was federal in form, but with a much stronger central government than had existed before. So, if Europe wants to learn from America, it had better start with a look at the supposed defects of those articles.

In broad terms, critics of the confederation argued that it was unstable, an awkward half-way house between a collection of independent states and a truly single country. Their criticisms concentrated on two things: economics, in particular the internal market of the 13 states; and foreign policy, the ability of the states to fend off foreign dangers.

Take economics first. The monetary and fiscal policy of the America that had just chucked out the British was chaotic. Congress (the body of delegates that had, so far as possible, directed the war against Britain, and whose position was formalised by the articles) could not pay off its creditors. It had no taxing power, and could only issue "requisitions" (in effect, requests for money) to the states. Some paid; some did not. Some states took over the responsibility for the part of the national debt that was owed to their own citizens, and then paid this in securities they issued themselves. There was a shortage of sound money (coin). Some states issued paper money themselves; much of it soon lost its face value. The currency of one state was not normally legal tender in another.

Tariff policy was a particular bugbear. States with small towns and few ports, such as New Jersey and Connecticut, were at the mercy of big states like Pennsylvania and New York, through whose ports America's imports flowed. Tariffs levied by New York would be paid by consumers in (say) Connecticut; but Connecticut's treasury derived no benefit from these tariffs. In short, the internal barriers to trade were big.

Abroad, the 13 states faced a ring of dangers. Britain still held Canada and a string of forts to the west of the United States. If it wished, it could have encircled the 13 states; its troops burnt Washington in 1812. Spain controlled Florida and—worse—it presided over navigation on the Mississippi.

Americans with a sense of where history was taking them (meaning most Americans of the time) well knew that, in Europe, loose confederations were vulnerable to their enemies. Some members of Congress compared that body to the Polish parliament, whose every member had a veto. The comparison hurt: at that time, Poland was being divided three ways by its enemies. The German confederation, or Holy Roman Empire, was notoriously feeble. It was characterised, said Madison, by "the licentiousness of the strong and the oppression of the weak"—a "nerveless" body "agitated with unceasing fermentation in its bowels."

The Americans decided they wanted calmer bowels and a better circulation. In the *Federalist Papers*—the collection of essays written by Hamilton, Madison and John Jay after the convention of 1787—Hamilton was to weave together the economic and political arguments. Trade wars between the states, he suggested, would sooner or later turn into shooting wars. Given the lack of unity of the

American states, European powers (with their "pernicious labyrinths of politics and wars") would divide and rule. The destiny to which God had pointed America would vanish in the ensuing strife.

That was putting it a bit high. Many historians today argue that, far from being on the edge of economic collapse, the America of the 1780s was happy and rich. Peter Aranson of Emory University in Georgia says that, although there was little immigration, the new country's population grew as fast in that decade as at almost any time in American history. No sign of hardship there. Trade wars were ending as the states found ways to reduce or remove the tariffs on goods passing through their territory to another state. Had each state's currency been legal tender elsewhere, good money might sooner or later have driven out bad.

The Three Big Things of 1787

For all that, Hamilton and the others who wanted a stronger central government won the day in Philadelphia. The convention's report was adopted by the states, though not without a few close shaves. And America got the constitution it still has. How has it lasted so long? For three main reasons that should interest today's Europeans.

The first was that the constitution created an executive—the president—where none had existed before. The president embodied a response to those external threats. He was to be the commander-in-chief of the armed forces. Although Congress had the power to declare war (and jealously preserves it), the president, with the advice and consent of the Senate, could conclude treaties and appoint ambassadors. He was to be the instrument of a unified foreign policy. This was made explicit by the constitution's first article, which prohibited any of the states from entering into any treaty, alliance or confederation, and from keeping troops, and from engaging in war unless it was invaded or was in imminent danger.

Second, the constitution was a document of limited powers. It gave to the central government (or so went the theory) only those powers specifically allocated to it. The tenth amendment made plain what Hamilton and Madison thought implicit: "The powers not delegated to the United States by the Constitution," it says, "nor prohibited to it by the states, are reserved to the states respectively, or to the people."

Third, the constitution recognised a "judicial power," and established a Supreme Court. The court, among other things, was to have jurisdiction over all cases arising "under the constitution" (and the constitution itself was declared to be "the supreme law of the land"). It also had jurisdiction over disputes between any one of the states and the United States, and between two or more states themselves. Members of the Supreme Court had no date of retirement. In other words, the Supreme Court was to be charged with deciding whether the practice of government conformed with the theory as laid down in the constitution.

How might modern Europeans use the American experience? Those who believe that the European Community is destined to be more than a collection of nation-states—an argument heard since the days of Monnet and Schuman—concentrate on the supposed instability of the original American confederation. Look at the Soviet Union, on the other hand, and you may conclude that that argument cuts the other way. It is the tight union of Stalin and Brezhnev that is unstable; it will survive, if it survives at all, only if it is converted into a much looser confederation.

Western Europe's federalists have a reply. In two respects, they argue, the Community has already learnt the lesson of the American constitution's success. Since the late 1950s the European Court of Justice has arrogated to itself the power to declare acts of member states or of Community institutions to have no effect if they contravene the Treaty of Rome, the EC's founding charter. And the notion of subsidiarity—that decisions in the Community should be taken at the lowest governmental level possible—is a rough-and-ready approximation to the American constitution's commitment to limited powers. Subsidiarity is not, or not yet, a matter of general Community law, but the idea is treated with growing respect.

Moreover, late 20th-century Europeans share the 18th-century American desire to create a single market and remove barriers to internal trade. Here the Americans found it necessary to make the states cede some sovereignty, and to grant the union some powers it had not previously possessed. The states were forbidden to levy their own external tariffs. In the so-called "commerce clause" of the constitution, the federal government was given the exclusive power to "regulate commerce with foreign nations, and among the several states."

In much the same way, Project 1992 is designed to realise the Community's dream of a single market, free of all internal impediments. European federalists would argue that the goal of monetary union is all of a piece with this. If a single trading block has 12 national currencies, the transactions costs of trade will always be higher than if there was but one. Americans at the 1787 convention would have recognised the force of this; the constitution they wrote forbids states to coin their own money. (Still, it was not until 1913 that America established a stable system for guiding national monetary policy.)

But that is not the whole of the American lesson. Those Europeans who doubt whether the American experience of federalism can be applied to Europe will find Americans ready to argue their case for them. One argument of America's own anti-federalists (still around, two centuries later) strikes a particular chord.

America's anti-federalists say the combination of a broad commerce clause and a powerful Supreme Court has been disastrous. It is a simple matter to show that almost anything is a matter of "inter-state commerce." Even if a company does almost all its business within one state, for instance, it may still use the federal postal service. Once interstate commerce has been proved, the central government can easily decide that such commerce is within its regulatory competence. As Mr Aranson has pointed out, as early as 1870 the Supreme Court held that Congress could insist on the inspection of steamships travelling entirely within the waters of one state, if other vessels on those waters carried goods bound for other states.

According to the anti-federalists, the breadth of the commerce clause means that an activist Supreme Court, given an inch, takes a mile. The power of states to regulate their own affairs has been diminished, and the power of the central government has been allowed to increase excessively.

Non-Americans living in America, wrapped in the red tape of federalism (try working out where to get your car exhaust tested each year if you bought the car in Virginia, live in Maryland and work in the District of Columbia), may think the argument over-done; they usually pray for less power for the individual states, not more. But many Americans still worry about excessive centralisation. So do people on the other side of the Atlantic.

Europeans fearful of being turned into "identikit Europeans," in Margaret Thatcher's phrase, therefore have American allies. Such Europeans will note Mr Aranson's warning that America's commerce clause "sustains national cartels that cross state boundaries and empower states, often with federal assistance, to cartelise markets." These Europeans suspect that a Community "social charter" will mean all European states sooner or later being required to have the same laws on health and welfare.

The Right to Opt Out

Europe's anti-federalists can draw further succour from America. The part of a future Europe that most Europeans find it hardest to picture clearly is the idea of Europe acting towards the outside world with a united mind, a single will.

Different Europeans, faced with a challenge abroad, can behave in radically different ways. This is partly because Europe is still far from being the homogeneous society that America was from the start. Europe is still a place of separate nationalisms, to an extent that America never was; those nationalisms have grown milder in the past half-century, but they have not vanished. Although almost all of Europe suffered the same frightful war 50 years ago, the various Europeans have very different memories of it. And this past year they have displayed very different feelings about such things as standing up to Saddam Hussein, and rebuking Mikhail Gorbachev for re-embracing his country's old guard.

This has a direct constitutional implication. Recall how important foreign policy, the threat abroad, was to Madison and Hamilton. They would have considered a union without a single foreign and defence policy to be a nonsense on stilts. So they created a powerful executive, independent of the states, to take control of that policy. Even those Europeans who want a single foreign policy shy away from a European equivalent of the American presidency. Yet without a president, embodying within his person a common will towards the world outside, it is hard to see how Europeans can create what Americans would regard as a federal Europe.

The non-homogeneity, and the hesitation about a European president as powerful as America's, will not necessarily remain as influential as they are today. But one awkward lesson from America is permanent. This is the fact that America did not take its final political shape in 1787; three-quarters of a century later, the founding fathers' structure blew up.

Most non-Americans do not realise how large the civil war of 1861-65 looms in America's collective memory. It killed more than 600,000 people, foreshadowing the efficient slaughter that Europe did not experience until Verdun and the Somme 50 years later. In its last year, when the North's armies under Grant and Sherman marched into the South's heartland, it became unbearably brutal. If you are going to have a constitution linking several states that cherish their sovereignty, it is worth making sure in advance that it does not lead to the kind of war America's constitution led to.

Unfair! yell Northern historians, for whom it is an article of faith that the civil war was fought not over a constitutional principle (the right of states to secede from the union) but over a social injustice (slavery). The Northerners have a case, even though—as Southerners never tire of pointing out—the abolition of slavery was not formally an original aim of the war: the fact is that, without slavery, the Southerners would not have wanted to secede. Since Europe's federalists would argue that nothing divides European countries from each other as passionately as slavery divided North and South, they may feel justified in ignoring the terrible warning of the civil war.

They would be wrong. Nobody knows what explosive arguments the future of Europe will bring. Some countries may see relations with Russia as the right centerpiece for Europe's foreign policy; others may put relations with America in that place; still others will focus on the Arab world to Europe's south. Some Europeans may want far more restrictive immigration policies than others, which could lead to some sharp intra-European border tensions. Country X will favour fewer controls on arms sales abroad than Country Y. Europe's capacity to speak and act as one is still almost entirely theoretical. If Europeans are genuinely interested in learning from the American experience, this lesson should be taken to heart: make it clear in advance that, whatever union is to be forged, states can leave it, unhindered, at will. ■

 # View from the Inside

Coping with the terrorist attacks of September 11, 2001, required the full attention not only of the federal government but also of state and local governments. There were some well-publicized problems—emergency workers from the various federal, state, and local governments had trouble communicating, for example, because their radios operated on different frequencies. But these difficulties were overshadowed, at least on the ground, by a general spirit of teamwork and cooperation.

The two selections in this section highlight the nature of the federal-state relationship in the aftermath of September 11. The first profiles Richard Sheirer, New York City's director of the Office of Emergency Management (OEM), who took charge of coordinating the many agencies involved in responding to the attacks. The second shines a spotlight on the negotiations in Washington over how much federal money to allocate for New York's recovery effort.

Questions

1. What factors brought Sheirer to the fore of the cleanup effort? Consider not only his style and personality, but also the nature of his local (rather than national) office.
2. Who led the fight for a large appropriation of federal funds for New York City? Who opposed the effort? What factors motivated those on either side of this policy struggle?

2.6 The Man Behind the Mayor (2001)

Amanda Griscom

On the morning of September 12, Richard Sheirer, director of the mayor's Office of Emergency Management, was scheduled to conduct a biological-terrorism drill in a cavernous commercial warehouse on the Hudson. Known as TRIPOD—short for "trial point of distribution"—the exercise was to test how quickly Sheirer's staff could administer treatments at the kind of ad hoc medical centers that would be set up all over the city in the event of an actual attack. For an audience, Sheirer had lined up Mayor Rudy Giuliani, the police and fire commissioners, and representatives of the FBI and the Federal Emergency Management Agency (FEMA). He had hired over 1,000 Police Academy cadets and Fire Department trainees to play terrified civilians afflicted with various medical conditions, allergies, and panic attacks. He had even arranged for a shipment of 70,000 M&Ms to be delivered and divided by color into medical packets representing different prophylactics and vaccines. But the M&Ms never arrived.

On the morning of September 11, Sheirer got to City Hall at 8 A.M. for a meeting about the Jackie Robinson–Pee Wee Reese memorial planned for Coney Island. "I was in heaven, sitting between Ralph Branca and Joe Black," he remembers. "We were about to select the statue, and then we heard the pop." At first he thought a transformer had exploded in an underground substation. Then he got a flash report from Watch Command in OEM headquarters.

As his driver barreled down Broadway, Sheirer recalls, "my first move was to clear the streets so we could get emergency vehicles in and people out." He radioed the police department and told them to shut down traffic below Canal Street and close every bridge and tunnel in the city.

Down at the scene, he joined Fire Commissioner Tom Von Essen and his chiefs Pete Ganci and Bill Feehan—old friends from Sheirer's 26 years with the New York Fire Department. They were establishing a command post at the base of the burning tower. Then the second airplane hit. "At that point there was no more doubt," he says ruefully. "We were under attack." He picked up one of the three cell phones strapped to his belt and started giving orders: to the Coast Guard to seal the harbor, and to the State Emergency Management Office to send back-up search and rescue teams and get the Pentagon to freeze the city's airspace. Then he lost his signal.

As Sheirer helped move the Fire Department command post, he saw a cloud of smoke and debris engulf his own command center, on the twenty-third floor of 7 World Trade Center. His staff was inside sending alerts to representatives of nearly 100 organizations—everyone from Con Edison to the Department of Health. One of his deputies radioed him to report that the OEM would have to evacuate.

Then his radio buzzed again: Giuliani was with Police Commissioner Bernard Kerik at an NYPD [New York Police Department] command post two blocks

From "The Man Behind the Mayor," by Amanda Griscom. *New York Magazine,* October 15, 2001, pp. 78–82. Reprinted by permission of the author.

north, at 75 Barclay Street. Sheirer and Von Essen were needed at the mayor's side, so they bolted north, leaving chiefs Ganci and Feehan in charge.

Minutes after they arrived at Barclay, the second tower collapsed. "It was a tremendous *whoosh,* roaring like a train in a tunnel," Sheirer remembers. The doors were jammed with piles of debris, but a janitor led the mayor and his commissioners out through the basement. Their cars were crushed, so they trudged uptown to a firehouse at Houston and Sixth Avenue.

As soon as he had access to land lines, Sheirer ordered fuel reserves for the fire boats that pump water from the Hudson, called the Department of Buildings to send down a team of structural engineers, and made arrangements to establish a temporary command center in the Police Academy at Third Avenue and 20th. Then a retired fireman named Dennis Conway, whom Sheirer had known for decades, limped in. "He sat down next to me and said, 'Feehan and Ganci ordered me to go north, but they went south to get the other troops,'" Sheirer remembers. "'Ritchie,' he said, 'they're gone. The tower swallowed them up.' It was so far beyond my wildest dreams. When I left the post at the scene, there was no thought in my mind that I wasn't going to see my friends again."

As Sheirer struggled to catch his breath, one of his deputies put a phone up to his ear. "He said, 'It's the missus—tell her you're alive.' I could hear my wife crying. She knows when there's an accident, I'm down on the scene. I told her, 'I'm still here, baby. It wasn't my time.'". . .

Since September 11, Sheirer has taken charge of the biggest cleanup effort in American history, coordinating 100 federal, state, and local agencies, including FEMA. He's become, in effect, the CEO of a company with thousands of workers and a budget that could run up to $40 billion—or, if you prefer, the mayor of the hot zone. He calls in the city's Department of Transportation to patch up the streets and has the Department of Design and Construction hang netting so broken glass won't fall on workers below. He orders Con Ed and Verizon to rehabilitate buildings without power or phone service, then gets the Department of Environmental Protection and the Department of Design and Construction to make sure they're safe. If they pass the test, he signs the documents that open them up to the public. "OEM is in charge," says Mike Byrne, deputy federal coordinating officer of FEMA for this incident. "Sheirer gives the marching orders. So far, we're blown away by OEM's performance."

Late on a Sunday night, two weeks after the attack, Sheirer is riding shotgun in his silver GMC Yukon. He's heading down to the on-scene OEM command bus to coordinate supplies for debris removal—wrecking balls, jackhammers, Tyvec suits, even tetanus shots. "Whatever the guys need down there to fight the devil," he says, "I make sure they have it."

As he flashes his badge out the window at one of the checkpoints, the Dixie Chicks are playing on the stereo. "Turn it up, Johnny," he says to his driver. "I need a calming influence. My favorite is Billy Joel, but I also go for the Dixies and Barenaked Ladies." Sheirer attributes his taste in music to the five sons he has with Barbara, his wife of 27 years.

Sheirer cuts off the music as he rolls through ground zero, glaring at the contorted remains like it's the first time he's seen them. "I do this trip three, four times a day, and still it turns my stomach," he says. "Some of the men buried in that pile I've worked with for 30 years. I know men out here who are digging for their sons, sons who are digging for their fathers." He sighs, then rolls down the window: "Hiya, Jimmy, Carlos, Lou. You boys are doing a yeoman's job!"

Parked near the remains of 7 World Trade Center, the OEM command bus is glossy blue, 50 feet long, and divided into two sections. Up front, the control room has dozens of wall-mounted monitors and a built-in Motorola radio center; in back, the conference room has track lighting, leather bunks, and a table piled with two six-foot subs, a platter of sausage dogs, and red binders labeled FEMA: CLASSIFIED.

Sheirer takes a seat, scarfs down a dog, and calls out a name: "Ray Lynch!" Responsible for coordinating the Urban Search and Rescue (USAR) teams, Lynch appears in full gear—body suit, hard hat, face mask, rubber boots—and offers an update: He's got teams in from Pennsylvania, Ohio, Indiana, Arizona, California, Utah, and Florida, with more help on the way. Right now he's working with experts in structural collapse and confined-space rescue. "I don't want anybody in there for more than twelve hours," Sheirer tells him. "Make sure those guys get sleep."

"You got it, boss," Lynch replies. "There's still hope. We're only fourteen days into it. USAR teams have found survivors up to sixteen days after an incident without food and water."

Sheirer radios the on-site rep of the Department of Design and Construction to offer an update on the hundred-ton crane he had FEMA fly in from Germany. Then he reports that he was able to get permission to dredge the Hudson so the Department of Sanitation can send garbage barges closer to the scene instead of taking debris away by truck.

Then it's back to the conference room to meet with his senior staff. Schools near the scene need to be reopened, so he asks his deputy of planning to find alternative buildings to store supplies; volunteer ironworkers and machine operators need to be taken care of, so he reviews their food and housing situation. "These construction guys are like family," says Sheirer. "They consider this sacred ground just like we do."

Around midnight, Sheirer stumbles out of the bus, leans up against a chain-link fence, and flips open his cell phone. "Hiya, hon," he says. "I know it's Sunday, I know. I'm comin' home." Just next to where he's standing, there's a printed flyer pinned to a fence: "Tempest-tossed soul, keep your hand firmly upon the helm of thought. In the bark of your soul reclines the Commanding Master. Self-control is strength, Right thought is mastery, Calmness is power."

"Nobody understands his stamina," Sheirer's driver says, as he waits in the Yukon. "Last night, I took him home to Staten Island at 2 A.M. When I picked him up at six this morning, his wife met me at the door and said he'd been on the phone until four. Then he jumps in the car with a stack of reports to get ready for his morning meeting with the mayor. He's unbelievable. This has been going on for two weeks straight."

The night of Tuesday the 11th, Sheirer and his staff never left the Police Academy. "It was dreadful," says Henry Jackson, Sheirer's deputy director for administration, who was responsible for setting up the temporary command post. "The phones kept going down. The little computer network we jerry-rigged kept going down, so everything had to be done with pen and paper."

Sheirer knew he needed another building, one big enough to house a command center the size of a football field, but also secure enough to house the mayor. The location was obvious: He commandeered the facility on the Hudson where he had been scheduled to do his TRIPOD drill the following day. It was a space Sheirer knew well—when he was a rookie in the Fire Department, he had organized quilting and antique fairs there as a side job.

When Action Jackson, as the deputy administrator is known at OEM, got the order to build a new command center, it was 8 A.M. Wednesday morning; he had slept for two hours on a cot in the Police Academy gym and was still covered in a film of debris. "I loaded up on coffee and smokes," says Jackson with a Han Solo grimace, "and brought a team of ten guys from logistics, telecom, and security to check the place out." By midnight Wednesday, "there were 150 people crawling all over the place," he says. "We gathered the whole crowd of laborers and gave 'em a little Knute Rockne, a little Vince Lombardi speech—some inspiration. Boom! We got the place up and running and functional in 32 hours." He pauses. "The mayor keeps saying it was 48, but it was 32."

Cement floors were carpeted, tablecloths stapled to tables, areas sectioned off with drywall. The ground level hummed with forklifts moving in mountains of computers, giant spools of cable, and bulk shipments of food and toiletries. The Navy sailed in the U.S.S. *Comfort,* a medical ship with 900 beds and a full kitchen, and docked it next to the warehouse to serve as a relief hotel.

"I could have asked for anything in the world and gotten it," says Jackson. "Everybody knew we were in charge." Compaq shipped hundreds of computers, Cisco sent servers, Nextel brought in a cell site to boost its signal. By the end of the day, vendors were vying to donate their products. "Now Microsoft is calling me and wants to know why we aren't using Microsoft," sighs Jackson.

Finally, there was the issue of décor: "I'm like, we don't have an American flag here," says Jackson. "I'm like, we *need* American flags here. I said *get* American flags! So I had some of the laborers run up and down the place hanging flags." By Friday night, 500 representatives from various city agencies had added their own personal touches, and aerial photographs of the site shared wall space with posters reading STRENGTH AND HONOR and hundreds of handmade cards from kids around the country.

The new command center is organized just the way the original was: FEMA and OEM officials sit on a raised platform known as Command and Control. Surrounding them are ten sections: Health and Medical, Logistics, Transportation, Infrastructure, Law Enforcement, Debris Removal, Aerial Imaging and Mapping, Machinery, Utilities, and Joint Information Center.

By the time Friday night rolled around, Jackson hadn't slept or showered in four days. "I literally hadn't been able to dust myself off," he says. "I hadn't even been able to think. Then somebody gave me a box of Girl Scout cookies that had a little note on it, from some Girl Scout somewhere. And that's when I lost it. I just started bawling."

Sheirer says the next [New York mayoral] administration will have to increase building security, step up drills to prepare for biological and chemical terrorism as well as natural disasters and day-to-day emergencies, boost the back-up electricity reserves and more frequently test the water supply. "It's not cheap to be prepared," says Sheirer. "But if there's one good thing to come out of this, it's political support to commit the necessary resources."

From a federal point of view, New York is already ahead of the rest of the nation. "It should be used as a model to build other OEMs across the country," says Byrne of FEMA. There are not many leaders in the U.S. like Sheirer. There will be a boom in demand for these kind of experts. ■

2.7 The Out-of-Towners (2001)

Michael Tomasky

. . . The narrative begins the day after the attack, Wednesday, when Senators Chuck Schumer and Hillary Clinton met with Governor Pataki and Mayor Giuliani, urging them to assess the scope of the damage and agree to a dollar amount they could then take to Capitol Hill. The $20 billion figure was agreed upon, and Schumer and Clinton made their way back to Washington.

The next part of the story has been widely retailed. Thursday afternoon, Schumer and Clinton met with President Bush in the Oval Office. They described the scale of the carnage, and Schumer pressed the case that New York needed a cash infusion of perhaps staggering proportions. "How much?" Schumer says the president asked. "Twenty billion," came the reply. "You've got it," Bush said.

What unfolded during the evening hours that Thursday, according to four sources who followed the events closely, provides for an eye-popping lesson both in the ways of Capitol Hill and in the reality behind all the lovely rhetoric about unity.

The $20 billion was to be delivered to New York through an emergency supplemental-appropriations measure. The Office of Management and Budget [OMB] drafted the language, calling for a total appropriation of $40 billion, half for military preparedness, national security, and transportation security, and half for "disaster-recovery activities and assistance" in New York. (Technically, this half was earmarked for New York, Virginia, and Pennsylvania, the latter two having also been attacked, though the bulk of the money was meant for . . . New York.)

That's how things stood at eight o'clock. Around this time, an aide to Hillary Clinton left the office and went to the Senate floor, where Clinton was checking on the status of the bill. So, the aide said, I guess everything looks pretty good. "Well, no," Clinton said. "It's falling apart. We've got to go talk to Daschle right now."

What had happened, as Clinton and Schumer both were now learning, was that a second version of the bill had mysteriously emerged from OMB. This language called for only $20 billion, not $40 billion. It also noted that, after the first $20 billion was spent, an additional $20 billion could be allocated "in a subsequent Act of Congress attendant to a specific emergency request proposed by the President." In other words, weeks or months later, when New York's grief had left the front pages. In other words, maybe some money, but nothing close to $20 billion.

Where did this mystery language come from? My sources didn't know for sure, but as we shall see, a meeting that took place in House Speaker Dennis Hastert's office later that night provides a likely suspect list of two. "It's clear to me," says Congressman Jerry Nadler, "that Gramm and Nickles tried to take out the earmark."

Schumer and Clinton charged up to Majority Leader Tom Daschle's office, where they met with Daschle, Majority Whip Harry Reid of Nevada, and Robert Byrd of West Virginia. They were trying to figure out how to respond when, one source says, "somebody came in and said, 'Gramm and Nickles are down in the speaker's office right now.' Byrd said, 'Let's go.'"

Schumer and Clinton decided their presence in the speaker's office might be counterproductive. They went instead to the Senate Democratic cloakroom, where they furiously made calls. Schumer called Andrew Card, the president's chief of staff—a call, as described by my sources, that Card will not soon forget. Clinton called around to members of the New York House delegation, Democrat and Republican, to enroll them in the fight. Nadler and Nita Lowey were particularly involved, as were upstate Republicans James Walsh and John Sweeney, who has especially close ties to the White House.

The New Yorkers converged outside Hastert's office. Inside were the Speaker, Byrd, Daschle, Dick Gephardt, and House Appropriations Committee leaders Bill Young and David Obey. And Phil Gramm and Don Nickles, who have nothing to do with appropriations but who had barged their way in just to argue against the bill. [Senator John] McCain had raised objections earlier, on the confusing—not to say offensive—grounds that the money somehow constituted pork, but "he made his peace with it and left," one source says. Of the other two, says the source, "Gramm just doesn't want to spend any money. And Nickles . . . he's just anti–New York. He was saying that Oklahoma City didn't get anything like this amount after the bombing there."

As the night pressed on, the good guys circled the wagons. Gramm and Nickles surrendered, and even voted for the package in the end. But the story, besides telling us that our senators earned their paychecks, leaves at least two distinct foul odors hanging in the air. There is, first, the rank indecency of the two men's objections. Granted, $20 billion is a lot of money, and New York must spend it wisely. But to try to block this money under these circumstances, forcing the city to rattle the cup for some much smaller amount at some undetermined point in the future, leaves one speechless. Gramm is retiring, but when Nickles runs again, I hope the police officers and firefighters of his state ask him why he deemed the widows and children of more than 350 heroic cops and firefighters unworthy of federal support.

And second, the senators' shenanigans reveal the hypocrisy of those who are given to thinking of New York as anti-American—a sentiment not, alas, limited to right-wing senators. Andrew Sullivan, in an obscene epistolary excretion that appeared in the *Times* of London, wrote adoringly of the humble red states that are behind the president, as opposed to the "decadent" blue states that will, in the coming months, constitute a veritable "fifth column" against America. Sullivan provides here the intellectual (so to speak) groundwork upon which the likes of Gramm and Nickles can justify themselves: An attack on the blue zone is somehow not *really* an attack on America. This may not make them fifth columnists, but it sure doesn't make them good Americans. ∎

 Chapter 3

Civil Liberties

The American commitment to individual rights and liberties is one of the distinguishing characteristics of our political system. Even more striking is the fact that we have a written Bill of Rights and that we rely to a great extent on the judicial system to define and defend the rights enumerated there.

Originally, the Bill of Rights applied only to the federal government. The First Amendment, for example, states explicitly that "*Congress* shall make no law ... abridging the freedom of speech." An 1833 case, *Barron* v. *Baltimore,* made it clear that the restrictions of the first eight amendments were not intended to interfere with laws passed by the states. Over the course of the twentieth century, however, the Supreme Court applied the various provisions of the Bill of Rights, one by one, to the states.

The emphasis in American politics on individual rights raises two sorts of problems. The first involves balancing competing rights. The publication of the name of a rape victim, for example, might violate the victim's right to privacy; but punishing such publication might interfere with a newspaper's right to free speech. Such problems can be extremely troubling, but even more serious are problems that pit the interests of an individual against those of society. How far can society go in limiting the civil liberties of individuals in order to protect itself? Might the police be justified, for example, in torturing suspects in order to prevent a catastrophic terrorist attack.

The selections in this chapter examine these questions from a variety of different viewpoints. Selection 3.1, from John Stuart Mill's *On Liberty,* presents the classic liberal argument for individuality. In selection 3.2, the law professor Michael J. Glennon argues that society must find the appropriate balance between protecting civil liberties and waging an effective war on terrorism. Selection 3.3 discusses the impact of American ideas on the Universal Declaration of Human Rights, and selection 3.4 presents an inside account of a team of lawyers who defended a very unpopular client in order to protect the right to free speech.

Chapter Questions

1. What are "civil liberties"? Why are they important in a society that values freedom? Why is freedom of thought and expression particularly important?
2. How are individual rights defined and balanced against the rights of other citizens and against the interests of society at large? What factors work to tip such a balancing process in favor of society? In favor of individual rights?

Foundations

One of the greatest advocates of civil liberties was the English philosopher John Stuart Mill. Published in 1859, Mill's *On Liberty* is perhaps the most important statement of the "importance of freedom for the discovery of truth and for the full development of individuality."* Although written in England, Mill's argument found a more receptive audience in the United States; his ideas greatly influenced the United States Supreme Court in later years, especially the opinions of Justices Oliver Wendell Holmes, who served on the Court from 1902 to 1932, and Louis Brandeis, who served from 1916 to 1939.

Mill was a utilitarian; he believed that all arguments had to be grounded in practical reason and justified with reference to the social good that would be brought about or the social evils that would be prevented. Therefore, his argument for allowing the individual the maximum freedom to decide how to live stresses the reasons that such freedom ultimately is good for society, even if the opinions expressed are clearly wrong. Note that his argument—unlike American constitutional arguments—is not based on claims of individual rights. Still, Mill's reasoning lies behind American liberal arguments as to the importance of protecting liberty under the Bill of Rights.

Questions

1. How does Mill justify the protection of individuality even when an individual's actions are clearly detrimental to that person's own well-being?
2. What does Mill mean by the "despotism of custom"? How does it operate? What effect does it have? Is Mill's characterization of his society applicable as well to our own? Why or why not?

3.1 On Liberty (1859)

John Stuart Mill

We have now recognised the necessity to the mental well-being of mankind (on which all their other well-being depends) of freedom of opinion, and freedom of the expression of opinion, on four distinct grounds; which we will now briefly recapitulate.

First, if any opinion is compelled to silence, that opinion may, for aught we can certainly know, be true. To deny this is to assume our own infallibility.

Secondly, though the silenced opinion be an error, it may, and very commonly does, contain a portion of truth; and since the general or prevailing opinion on

---

John Stuart Mill, *On Liberty* (London: J. W. Parker and Son, 1859).

*David Spitz, Preface to John Stuart Mill, *On Liberty* (New York: W. W. Norton and Co., 1975), p. vii.

any subject is rarely or never the whole truth, it is only by the collision of adverse opinions that the remainder of the truth has any chance of being supplied.

Thirdly, even if the received opinion be not only true, but the whole truth; unless it is suffered to be, and actually is, vigorously and earnestly contested, it will, by most of those who receive it, be held in the manner of a prejudice, with little comprehension or feeling of its rational grounds. And not only this, but, fourthly, the meaning of the doctrine itself will be in danger of being lost, or enfeebled, and deprived of its vital effect on the character and conduct; the dogma becoming a mere formal profession, inefficacious for good, but cumbering the ground, and preventing the growth of any real and heartfelt conviction from reason or personal experience.

• • •

Such being the reasons which make it imperative that human beings should be free to form opinions, and to express their opinions without reserve; and such the baneful consequences to the intellectual, and through that to the moral nature of man, unless this liberty is either conceded, or asserted in spite of prohibition; let us next examine whether the same reasons do not require that men should be free to act upon their opinions— to carry these out in their lives, without hindrance, either physical or moral, from their fellow-men, so long as it is at their own risk and peril. This last proviso is of course indispensable. No one pretends that actions should be as free as opinions. On the contrary, even opinions lose their immunity when the circumstances in which they are expressed are such as to constitute their expression a positive instigation to some mischievous act. An opinion that corn-dealers are starvers of the poor, or that private property is robbery, ought to be unmolested when simply circulated through the press, but may justly incur punishment when delivered orally to an excited mob assembled before the house of a corn-dealer, or when handed about among the same mob in the form of a placard. Acts, of whatever kind, which, without justifiable cause, do harm to others, may be, and in the more important cases absolutely require to be, controlled by the unfavourable sentiments, and, when needful, by the active interference of mankind. The liberty of the individual must be thus far limited; he must not make himself a nuisance to other people. But if he refrains from molesting others in what concerns them, and merely acts according to his own inclination and judgment in things which concern himself, the same reasons which show that opinion should be free, prove also that he should be allowed, without molestation, to carry his opinions into practice at his own cost. That mankind are not infallible; that their truths, for the most part, are only half-truths; that unity of opinion, unless resulting from the fullest and freest comparison of opposite opinions, is not desirable, and diversity not an evil, but a good, until mankind are much more capable than at present of recognising all sides of the truth, are principles applicable to men's modes of action, not less than to their opinions. As it is useful that while mankind are imperfect there should be different opinions, so it is that there should be different experiments of living; that free scope should be given to varieties of character, short of injury to others; and that the worth of different modes of life should be proved practically, when any one thinks fit to try them. It is desirable, in short, that in things which do not primarily concern others, individuality should assert itself. Where, not the person's own character, but the traditions or customs of other people are the rule of conduct, there is wanting one of the principal ingredients of human happiness, and quite the chief ingredient of individual and social progress.

In maintaining this principle, the greatest difficulty to be encountered does not lie in the appreciation of means towards an acknowledged end, but in the indifference of persons in general to the end itself. If it were felt that the free development of individuality is one of the leading essentials of well-being; that it is not only a coordinate element with all that is designated by the terms civilisation, instruction, education, culture, but is itself a necessary part and condition of all those things; there would be no danger that liberty should be undervalued, and the adjustment of the boundaries between it and social control would present no extraordinary difficulty. But the evil is, that individual spontaneity is hardly recognised by the common modes of thinking as having any intrinsic worth, or deserving any regard on its own account. The majority, being satisfied with the ways of mankind as they now are (for it is they who make them what they are), cannot comprehend why those ways should not be good enough for everybody; and what is more, spontaneity forms no part of the ideal of the majority of moral and social reformers, but is rather looked on with jealousy, as a troublesome and perhaps rebellious obstruction to the general acceptance of what these reformers, in their own judgment, think would be best for mankind. Few persons, out of Germany, even comprehend the meaning of the doctrine which Wilhelm von Humboldt, so eminent both as a *savant* and as a politician, made the text of a treatise— that "the end of man, or that which is prescribed by the eternal or immutable dictates of reason, and not suggested by vague and transient desires, is the highest and most harmonious development of his powers to a complete and consistent whole"; that, therefore, the object "towards which every human being must ceaselessly direct his efforts, and on which especially those who design to influence their fellow-men must ever keep their eyes, is the individuality of power and development"; that for this there are two requisites, "freedom, and variety of situations"; and that from the union of these arise "individual vigour and manifold diversity," which combine themselves in "originality."

Little, however, as people are accustomed to a doctrine like that of von Humboldt, and surprising as it may be to them to find so high a value attached to individuality, the question, one must nevertheless think, can only be one of degree. No one's idea of excellence in conduct is that people should do absolutely nothing but copy one another. No one would assert that people ought not to put into their mode of life, and into the conduct of their concerns, any impress whatever of their own judgment, or of their own individual character. On the other hand, it would be absurd to pretend that people ought to live as if nothing whatever had been known in the world before they came into it; as if experience had as yet done nothing towards showing that one mode of existence, or of conduct, is preferable to another. Nobody denies that people should be so taught and trained in youth as to know and benefit by the ascertained results of human experience. But it is the privilege and proper condition of a human being, arrived at the maturity of his faculties, to use and interpret experience in his own way. It is for him to find out what part of recorded experience is properly applicable to his own circumstances and character. The traditions and customs of other people are, to a certain extent, evidence of what their experience has taught *them*; presumptive evidence, and as such, have a claim to his deference: but, in the first place, their experience may be too narrow; or they may not have interpreted it rightly. Secondly, their interpretation of experience may be correct, but unsuitable to him. Customs are made for customary circumstances and customary characters; and his circumstances or his character may be uncustomary. Thirdly, though the customs be both good as customs, and suitable to him, yet to conform to custom, merely *as* custom, does not educate or develop in him any of the qualities which are the distinctive endowment of a human being. The human faculties of perception, judgment, discriminative feeling, mental activity, and even moral preference, are exercised only in making a choice. He who does anything because it is the custom makes no choice. He gains no practice either in discerning or in desiring what is best. The mental and moral, like the muscular powers, are improved only by being used. The faculties are called into no exercise by doing a thing merely because others do it, no more than by believing a thing only because others believe it. If the grounds of an opinion are not conclusive to the person's own reason, his reason cannot be strengthened, but is likely to be weakened, by his adopting it: and if the inducements to an act are not such as are consentaneous to his own feelings and character (where affection, or the rights of others, are not concerned) it is so much done towards rendering his feelings and character inert and torpid, instead of active and energetic.

He who lets the world, or his own portion of it, choose his plan of life for him, has no need of any other faculty than the ape-like one of imitation. He who chooses his plan for himself, employs all his faculties. He must use observation to see, reasoning and judgment to foresee, activity to gather materials for decision, discrimination to decide, and when he has decided, firmness and self-control to hold to his deliberate decision. And these qualities he requires and exercises exactly in proportion as the part of his conduct which he determines according to his own judgment and feelings is a large one. It is possible that he might be guided in some good path, and kept out of harm's way, without any of these things. But what will be his comparative worth as a human being? It really is of importance, not only what men do, but also what manner of men they are that do it. Among the works of man, which human life is rightly employed in perfecting and beautifying, the first in importance surely is man himself. Supposing it were possible to get houses built, corn grown, battles fought, causes tried, and even churches erected and prayers said, by machinery—by automatons in human form—it would be a considerable loss to exchange for these automatons even the men and women who at present inhabit the more civilised parts of the world, and who assuredly are but starved specimens of what nature can and will produce. Human nature is not a machine to be built after a model, and set to do exactly the work prescribed for it, but a tree, which requires to grow and develop itself on all sides, according to the tendency of the inward forces which make it a living thing.

It will probably be conceded that it is desirable people should exercise their understandings, and that an intelligent following of custom, or even occasionally an intelligent deviation from custom, is better than a blind and simply mechanical adhesion to it. To a certain extent it is admitted that our understanding should be our own: but there is not the same willingness to admit that our desires and impulses should be our own likewise; or that to possess impulses of our own, and of any strength, is anything but a peril and a snare. Yet desires and impulses are as much a part of a perfect human being as beliefs and restraints: and strong impulses are only perilous when not properly balanced; when one set of aims and inclinations is developed into strength, while others, which ought to co-exist with them, remain weak and inactive. It is not because men's desires are strong that they act ill; it is because their consciences are weak. There is no natural connection between strong impulses and a weak conscience. The natural connection is the other way. To say that one person's desires and feelings are stronger and more various than those of another, is merely to say that he has more of the raw material of human nature, and is therefore capable, perhaps of more evil, but certainly of more good. Strong impulses are but another name for energy. Energy may be turned to bad uses; but more good may always be made of an energetic nature, than of an indolent and impassive one. Those who have most natural feeling, are always those whose cultivated feelings may be made the strongest. The same strong susceptibilities which make the personal impulses vivid and powerful, are also the source from whence are generated the most passionate love of virtue, and the sternest self-control. It is through the cultivation of these that society both does its duty and protects its interests: not by rejecting the stuff of which heroes are made, because it knows not how to make them. A person whose desires and impulses are his own—are the expression of his own nature, as it has been developed and modified by his own culture—is said to have a character. One whose desires and impulses are not his own, has no character, no more than a steam-engine has a character. If, in addition to being his own, his impulses are strong, and are under the government of a strong will, he has an energetic character. Whoever thinks that individuality of desires and impulses should not be encouraged to unfold itself, must maintain that society has no need of strong natures—is not the better for containing many persons who have much character—and that a high general average of energy is not desirable.

In some early states of society, these forces might be, and were, too much ahead of the power which society then possessed of disciplining and controlling them. There has been a time when the element of spontaneity and individuality was in excess, and the social principle had a hard struggle with it. The difficulty then was to induce men of strong bodies or minds to pay obedience to any rules which required them to control their impulses. To overcome this difficulty, law and discipline, like the Popes struggling against the Emperors, asserted a power over the whole man, claiming to control all his life in order to control his character—which society had not found any other sufficient means of binding. But society has now fairly got the better of individuality; and the danger which threatens human nature is not the excess, but the deficiency, of personal impulses and preferences. Things are vastly changed since the passions of those who were strong by station or by personal endowment were in a state of habitual rebellion against laws and ordinances, and required to be rigorously chained up to enable the persons within their reach to enjoy any particle of security. In our times, from the highest class of society down to the lowest, every one lives as under the eye of a hostile and dreaded censorship. Not only in what concerns others, but in what concerns only themselves, the individual or the family do not ask themselves—what do I prefer? or, what would suit my character and disposition? or, what would allow the best and highest in me to have fair play, and enable it to grow and thrive? They ask themselves, what is suitable to my position? what is usually done by persons of my station and pecuniary circumstances? or (worse still) what is usually done by persons of a station and circumstances superior to mine? I do not mean that they choose what is customary in preference to what suits their own inclination. It does not occur to them to have any inclination, except for what is customary. Thus the mind itself is bowed to the yoke: even in what people do for pleasure, conformity is the first thing thought of; they like in crowds; they exercise choice only among things commonly done: peculiarity of taste, eccentricity of conduct, are shunned equally with crimes: until by dint of not following their own nature they have no nature to follow: their human capacities are withered and starved: they become incapable of any strong wishes or native pleasures, and are generally without either opinions or feelings of home growth, or properly their own.

• • •

It is not by wearing down into uniformity all that is individual in themselves, but by cultivating it, and calling it forth, within the limits imposed by the rights and interests of others, that human beings become a noble and beautiful object of contemplation; and as the works partake the character of those who do them, by the same process human life also becomes rich, diversified, and animating, furnishing more abundant aliment to high thoughts and elevating feelings, and strengthening the tie which binds every individual to the race, by making the race infinitely better worth belonging to. In proportion to the development of his individuality, each person becomes more valuable to himself, and is therefore capable of being more valuable to others. There is a greater fulness of life about his own existence, and when there is more life in the units there is more in the mass which is composed of them. As much compression as is necessary to prevent the stronger specimens of human nature from encroaching on the rights of others, cannot be dispensed with; but for this there is ample compensation even in the point of view of human development. The means of development which the individual loses by being prevented from gratifying his inclinations to the injury of others, are chiefly obtained at the expense of the development of other people. And even to himself there is a full equivalent in the better development of the social part of his nature, rendered possible by the restraint put upon the selfish part. To be held to rigid rules of justice for the sake of others, develops the feelings and capacities which have the good of others for their object. But to be restrained in things not affecting their good, by their mere displeasure, develops nothing valuable, except such force of character as may unfold itself in resisting the restraint. If acquiesced in, it dulls and blunts the whole nature. To give any fair play to the nature of each, it is essential that different persons should be allowed to lead different lives. In proportion as this latitude has been exercised in any age, has that age been noteworthy to posterity. Even despotism does not produce its worst effects, so long as individuality exists under it; and whatever crushes individuality is despotism, by whatever name it may be called, and whether it professes to be enforcing the will of God or the injunctions of men.

Having said that the individuality is the same thing with development, and that it is only the cultivation of individuality which produces, or can produce, well-developed human beings, I might here close the argument: for what more or better can be said of any condition of human affairs than that it brings human beings themselves nearer to the best things they can be? or what worse can be said of any obstruction to good than that it prevents this? Doubtless, however, these considerations will not suffice to convince those who most need convincing; and it is necessary further to show, that these developed human beings are of some use to the undeveloped—to point out to those who do not desire liberty, and would not avail themselves of it, that they may be in some intelligible manner rewarded for allowing other people to make use of it without hindrance.

In the first place, then, I would suggest that they might possibly learn something from them. It will not be denied by anybody, that originality is a valuable element in human affairs. There is always need of persons not only to discover new truths, and point out when what were once truths are true no longer, but also to commence new practices, and set the example of more enlightened conduct, and better taste and sense in human life. This cannot well be gainsaid by anybody who does not believe that the world has already attained perfection in all its ways and practices. It is true that this benefit is not capable of being rendered by everybody alike: there are but few persons, in comparison with the whole of mankind, whose experiments, if adopted by others, would be likely to be any improvement on established practice. But these few are the salt of the earth; without them, human life would become a stagnant pool. Not only is it they who introduce good things which did not before exist; it is they who keep the life in those which already exist. If there were nothing new to be done, would human intellect cease to be necessary? Would it be a reason why those who do the old things should forget why they are done, and do them like cattle, not like human beings? There is only too great a tendency in the best beliefs and practices to degenerate into the mechanical; and unless there were a succession of persons whose ever-recurring originality prevents the grounds of those beliefs and practices from becoming merely traditional, such dead matter would not resist the smaller shock from anything really alive, and there would be no reason why civilisation should not die out, as in the Byzantine Empire. Persons of genius, it is true, are, and are always likely to be, a small minority; but in order to have them, it is necessary to preserve the soil in which they grow. Genius can only breathe freely in an *atmosphere* of freedom. Persons of genius are, *ex vi termini*, more individual than any other people—less capable, consequently, of fitting themselves, without hurtful compression, into any of the small number of moulds which society provides in order to save its members the trouble of forming their own character. If from timidity they consent to be forced into one of these moulds, and to let all that part of themselves which cannot expand under the pressure remain unexpanded, society will be little the better for their genius. If they are of a strong character, and break their fetters, they become a mark for the society which has not succeeded in reducing them to commonplace, to point out with solemn warning as "wild," "erratic," and the like; much as if one should complain of the Niagara river for not flowing smoothly between its banks like a Dutch canal.

I insist thus emphatically on the importance of genius, and the necessity of allowing it to unfold itself freely both in thought and in practice, being well aware that no one will deny the position in theory, but knowing also that almost every one, in reality, is totally indifferent to it. People think genius a fine thing if it enables a man to write an exciting poem, or paint a picture. But in its true sense, that of originality in thought and action, though no one says that it is not a thing to be admired, nearly all, at heart, think that they can do very well without it. Unhappily this is too natural to be wondered at. Originality is the one thing which unoriginal minds cannot feel the use of. They cannot see what it is to do for them: how should they? If they could see what it would do for them, it would not be originality. The first service which originality has to render them, is that of opening their eyes: which being once fully done, they would have a chance of being themselves original. Meanwhile, recollecting that nothing was ever yet done which some one was not the first to do, and that all good things which exist are the fruits of originality, let them be modest enough to believe that there is something still left for it to accomplish, and assure themselves that they are more in need of originality, the less they are conscious of the want. . . .

The despotism of custom is everywhere the standing hindrance to human advancement, being in unceasing antagonism to that disposition to aim at something better than customary, which is called, according to circumstances, the spirit of liberty, or that of progress or improvement. . . .

[I]t is not easy to see how [individuality] can stand its ground [against the despotism of custom and other influences that stand against it]. It will do so with increasing difficulty, unless the intelligent part of the public can be made to feel its value—to see that it is good there should be differences, even though not for the better, even though, as it may appear to them, some should be for the worse. If the claims of individuality are ever to be asserted, the time is now, while much is still wanting to complete the enforced assimilation. It is only in the earlier stages that any stand can be successfully made against the encroachment. The demand that all other people shall resemble ourselves grows by what it feeds on. If resistance waits till life is reduced *nearly* to one uniform type, all deviations from that type will come to be considered impious, immoral, even monstrous and contrary to nature. Mankind speedily become unable to conceive diversity, when they have been for some time unaccustomed to see it. ∎

 # American Politics Today

Times of war are never kind to civil liberties, and the war against terrorism has been no exception. With the safety of the nation and its citizens at stake, the U.S. government has moved vigorously to investigate and disrupt suspected and potential terrorists, often at the expense of civil liberties. The government has detained an unspecified number of individuals as "material witnesses"; held suspects—including at least one American citizen—in military custody without access to a lawyer; and expanded its legal authority to place wiretaps on terrorism suspects and to investigate alleged terrorist groups.

Both critics and defenders of the government's policies have been quick to weigh in with their opinions. On the one side are those who argue that such tactics undermine the very Constitution that the government is trying to protect, damaging democracy and thus handing a kind of victory to the terrorists. On the other are those who assert that the government's first duty is the protection of the people, and that security is worth some cost in diminished liberty.

In this selection, the law professor Michael J. Glennon aims to find a balance between these two positions.

Questions

1. What competing values are at stake in the argument between those who would tilt the balance between civil liberties and the war against terrorism in one direction or the other? How would each side answer the "ticking time bomb" hypothetical described in this selection?
2. What are the implications of Glennon's argument for American policy in the war against terrorism?

3.2 Terrorism and the Limits of Law (2002)

Michael J. Glennon

Cries of outrage erupted around the world this past January when the Pentagon released pictures of Taliban and Al Qaeda prisoners shackled, blindfolded by strange-looking goggles, and forced to kneel during their captivity at the U.S. military base at Guantánamo Bay in Cuba. Secretary of Defense Donald H. Rumsfeld's explanation that such methods were not inhumane and were used only when the men—dangerous terrorist suspects, after all—were moved from place to place did little to still the protests. But millions of Americans, and doubtless many abroad, thought to themselves: So what? It is likely, in fact, that many thought the prisoners deserved far worse. A CNN/USA Today/Gallup poll in early October revealed that 45 percent of those surveyed would approve the torture of captured terrorists who knew details of future attacks in the United States. One prominent American law professor has even suggested that judges be empowered to issue "torture warrants."

There is no evidence that the roughly 300 men held at Guantánamo have been tortured, but there is no question that America since September 11 has experienced a sharp clash of values, pitting freedom against security, and law against politics. Yet the months since terrorists brought down the World Trade towers also show how the United States has come to balance competing constitutional values, and—perhaps paradoxically—the way it has come to recognize the limits of the law as a tool for striking that balance.

From "Terrorism and the Limits of Law," by Michael J. Glennon, *Wilson Quarterly* 22, Spring 2002, pp. 12–19. Reprinted by permission of the author.

Why not torture the terrorists? The answer is not as obvious as it may seem—and some of the most obvious answers don't hold up under scrutiny. In 20 years of teaching constitutional law, I have found that considering hypothetical cases can be a useful way to get at bigger truths. Many of these "hypos," as they are called in law schools, are simply outlandish, but one has turned out, alas, to be a lot less improbable than it seemed before September 11. That is the famous, or infamous, "ticking time bomb" hypo:

> Assume that the police capture a terrorist whom they know has planted a nuclear bomb somewhere in New York City. The police know that the bomb will explode very soon; the city cannot possibly be evacuated. The terrorist refuses to talk. Question: Should the police torture him?

Some students always answer with a flat no: Torture, they argue, can never be conducted under any circumstances. They usually give two kinds of reasons, one practical, the other theoretical. On the practical side, students cite the familiar "slippery slope" argument: Once we accept the permissibility of torture under any circumstances, we will end up torturing under many circumstances. The theoretical reason can best be described as a natural rights argument—it is an almost instinctive American response. It holds that human beings have certain rights that no government can take away, and that one of those rights is the right not to be tortured. Some natural rights proponents would add that it is impermissible to do evil even if good may come of it, or that the end can never justify the means.

Each of these arguments has flaws. The answer to the "slippery slope" view is simply that we have not yet reached the bottom of the slope, indeed, that we are far from it, and that long before we do reach the bottom we will stop. We can torture terrorists without opening the way to the torture of, say, car thieves. It is irrational not to act where we must act just because, some day, we may act where we ought not act.

The answer to the theoretical, natural rights argument is complex, as is the natural rights argument itself. At bottom, though, the response is that the natural rights argument is not really an argument at all, but rather an assertion—an assertion that is as unproved as it is unprovable. It hinges on a set of presuppositions. The most prominent of these is the assumption of eternal right and wrong, of an overarching morality contingent upon neither circumstance nor culture, a "truth" that all rational people everywhere—all persons of "right reason"—must accept. . . .

On the other side of the debate over our hypothetical are students—most students, these days—who respond that of course we should torture the terrorist. Many of these students believe that this is simply a practical argument. They justify torturing, or even killing, the terrorist by relying on simple arithmetic: The lives of eight million are worth more than the life of one. No great philosophical inquiry is needed. Unlike natural rights, utilitarianism is modern and seemingly scientific—"empirical." So it's no big deal, these students believe, to fall back upon the same utilitarian philosophy in deciding to torture the terrorist.

But a vast body of philosophy does underlie the supposition that "simple arithmetic" is the proper focal point. That philosophy is utilitarianism, the notion of the greatest good for the greatest number. It is true that much of Western social policy today is built upon utilitarian scaffolding. The justification for the principle of redistributing wealth that animates many government programs, from graduated income taxes to historic preservation, is the idea that the number of people who will benefit is greater than the number of people who will be harmed.

But utilitarianism, like the natural rights approach, has its difficulties. Utilitarianism can lead to horrific social policies. A majority may somehow be "happier" if all men are required to wear crew cuts, or if all women are required to wear burkas, or if all "infidels" are put to death. How do we answer that majority?

Moreover, "empirical" though it may be, utilitarianism is not without its own presuppositions. Central among them is precisely the same assumption of the moral bindingness of logic that occurs in the natural rights argument. Why ought we give the greatest good to the greatest number? . . .

So the easy answers to the hypothetical are too easy. Each approach, in the end, opens the door to precisely the evils that it seeks to preclude. Each ultimately is arbitrary in that it relies upon premises that cannot be rationally proven but must, rather, be assumed. Each leaves us looking further.

Some years ago, Justice Hugo Black (1886–1971) reportedly gave an intriguing answer to the ticking time bomb hypothetical. There's a particular reason to be interested in Black. He was one of the leading liberals of the Warren Court. Appointed by President Franklin D. Roosevelt, he had a strong commitment to civil liberties and individual freedom. Black was also the quintessential constitutional "absolutist." He liked "bright line" tests—legal standards that were easy to apply and that admitted of no exceptions. When Black read the words, "Congress shall make no law. . ." in the First Amendment, he read them to mean that Congress shall make no law—not some law, not a few laws, but *no* law.

Black disdained "balancing tests"—standards that permitted judges to weigh competing interests case by case to reach different outcomes in different circumstances. Balancing tests, he believed, gave judges too much discretion, allowing them to substitute their own judgment for that of legislators. The job of judges, Black knew, is to interpret the law, not to make the law. Balancing tests reduce the law to mashed potatoes, to be shaped into anything any judge wants it to be, able to support any conclusion the judge desires. Black was the perfect person to whom the hypothetical could be addressed: How would the ultimate no-nonsense, "no exceptions" jurist who had an abiding respect for the dignity of the individual apply a rule that seemed to cry out for an exception? Should we torture the terrorist?

Black's reported answer was, "Yes—but we could never say that."

It is hard to resist reveling in the pithy wisdom of these words. In one sentence, Black reconciles down-home common sense with a profound recognition of the limits of the law—I should say, with a recognition of the limits of human cognitive and linguistic capacity.

Common sense kept Black, in the end, from being a true absolutist, at least within the realm of morality, if not law. By a true absolutist I mean one who refuses to balance competing values. An absolutist would say that a certain act is always, in every situation, wrong. Killing, lying, stealing, assassination—and, of course, torture—are examples of the kinds of acts some absolutists believe are always wrong, regardless of "exigent" circumstances. In his answer to the ticking time bomb hypothetical, Black reveals that he is willing to balance one value against another, weighing the evil of torture against the preservation of human life. So in a moral sense, the hypothetical seemed to have its intended purpose of "smoking him out," of showing that even the most dedicated constitutional absolutist could, under the right conditions, be forced to jump ship.

But Black does not jump ship in the legal realm. *We could never say that.* He is unwilling to allow the law to reflect his moral judgment. It is one thing to acknowledge the moral propriety of torturing the terrorist, but quite another to conclude that such an admission should be acted upon by a court (or, presumably, by a legislature). Why? We can only speculate, but Black might have responded that courts and legislatures, unlike the police, speak with words, not deeds. Don't spell it out in a rule—don't even try to spell it out—just do it. Because the human mind simply is not capable of finding words precise enough to eliminate all unwanted discretion. Because words are too slippery to be entrusted with the responsibility of staying out when strange new facts shake them around. Because any rule that would let us torture a terrorist, however carefully drafted, would inevitably be embraced by corrupt police officers or soldiers or prison guards somewhere as justification for doing what our society finds repugnant.

This answer, however, has an obvious shortcoming. It seems to assume that no legal norm is established if one simply intends not to establish a norm. Black's answer brings to mind Abraham Lincoln's quip: How many legs does a dog have if you call a tail a leg? Four; calling a tail a leg does not make it a leg. Calling a precedent a non-precedent does not make it so. Action counts. Intent is expressed in deeds as well as words. And deeds that are allowed to stand are likely to be repeated by others. Even if those deeds are not repeated, it is possible that the police officer who did the torturing could later be hauled into court for the act. What then? Turning a blind eye to manifest illegality could taint the entire legal system—though the law may have enough give at the joints to limit torture's corrupting influence. (Those found guilty of torture where mitigating circumstances exist could be given suspended sentences, for example.)

Despite its flaws, "not saying that" is sometimes our best option. The courts have various ways of "not saying that." One is encapsulated in Justice Oliver Wendell Holmes, Jr.'s famous dictum that hard cases make bad law. To avoid bad law, avoid hard cases; avoid resolving a conflict when two fundamental values clash. To resolve such a case is to risk establishing a formal legal precedent that will require a future case to be decided in a bad way. This is why the Supreme Court, when confronted with a hard case, is inclined to underscore that its decision is restricted to the precise facts of the case before it.

The ticking time bomb hypothetical is, to be sure, a hard and essentially implausible case. Yet it can be made even harder. Assume that the person who knows the location of the bomb is not a terrorist—or even a wrongdoer. Assume that he happens to know where the bomb is located but, acting upon some perverse principle, refuses to answer the authorities' questions. Suppose, for example, that the police know that the bomb is hidden in his mother's house, unknown to her, and that they don't know her address. Suppose that he declines to cooperate out of fear that the police will hurt his mother. Is it permissible to torture a wholly innocent bystander to spare the lives of eight million people?

One might say that the person is a wrongdoer for the simple reason that it is wrong not to reveal the whereabouts of the bomb. But I am aware of no crime that would be committed by his remaining silent. He is not legally a wrongdoer. Morally, one might think otherwise. But one could also argue that choosing one's own mother's life over the lives of strangers is no moral wrong.

Remember, this person, unlike the terrorist, has not chosen to act outside the law. He has every reason to believe that he is protected from community-sponsored violence. After all, he did what the community told him to do in the only way it could communicate authoritatively with him—through the law. If we are to permit the law's guardians to engage in an improvised and unauthorized utilitarian calculus that trumps the law here, why not elsewhere? And if "elsewhere" can be decided by the law's guardians to be anyplace the guardians wish, what has become of the law?

Since September 11 we have often heard potential departures from the legal order defended with the argument that the "Constitution is not a suicide pact." No one can quarrel with these words (Justice Arthur Goldberg's words, actually). Survival is the ultimate right, for societies as well as for individuals. But the proposition has come to be relied upon too often, in contexts in which societal survival is not at stake. The statement has come to be shorthand for the idea that whenever the Constitution seems to be at odds with some transient utilitarian calculus, the Constitution must give way.

In its strong form, this argument is not just a case for occasionally violating the Constitution. It is an objection to the very idea of the rule of law. The rule of law substitutes for the series of utilitarian calculations that would otherwise occur in a lawless "state of nature." It says that we agree not to weigh costs against benefits where a specific rule of law applies. We do not permit a bank robber to excuse himself with the defense that the bank charged the community unconscionable interest rates, or a murderer to excuse himself with the defense that the deceased was a congenital bully. No: If the law provides the answer as to how certain wrongs are to be righted, then the law's answer controls. We do not set the law aside because the benefits of doing so seem to outweigh the costs.

I say "seem to outweigh the costs" because our assessment of costs can vary under different conditions. Recall Homer's story of the Sirens, the sea nymphs whose hypnotic singing lured sailors to crash their ships onto the rocks. And recall Odysseus's solution: Knowing that he would surely succumb to the Sirens' song (yet desperately wanting to hear it), he had himself bound to the ship's mast and told his crew to plug their ears. He ordered them to ignore his pleas to be untied, no matter how forceful. Knowing in calmer times, in other words, that he would assess the cost of succumbing to the Sirens differently than he would in a moment of great stress, Odysseus set down a rule that was not to be superseded by a later rule formulated in distress.

Society is like Odysseus. When it formulates constitutional limits, society says to itself: "When confronted with temptation, we may scream to be untied—untied to censor unwanted speech, to ban unwanted religion, to impose cruel and un-usual punishments—but do not untie us! We know the true costs of these actions, and those costs are too great!"

So I am not making a roundabout case for the use of torture as an interrogation tool. To the contrary: The captives in Guantánamo Bay do not pose anywhere near as clear and present a danger as the ticking time bomb terrorist. As far as we know, no single, identifiable prisoner possesses information that could save thou-sands of lives. Torturing prisoners absent such exigent circumstances would repre-sent a momentous and irreversible step backward toward war as it was fought cen-turies ago, war with no rules, war with no safe havens, war with no limits. No civilized nation can embark upon such a course unless it has decided to write off its future.

My case can be summed up in two words: *balance* and *limits*. The ticking time bomb hypothetical is a useful analytic tool not only for thinking about terrorism but for thinking about thinking. It makes us ponder whether any one value, how-ever central to our culture, can ever be given overriding, controlling weight in any and all circumstances. The hypothetical shows how sticking to any absolute, in-flexible principle come hell or high water can ultimately undermine the purposes that principle is intended to vindicate. It reveals the need to balance competing values, to reconcile countervailing ideals, pragmatically, with an eye to real-world consequences, not abstract theory. . . . ■

The International Context

The idea that human beings have rights, and that governments have a responsibility to protect those rights, is a cornerstone of American constitutionalism. With the creation of the United Nations after World War II, human rights began to emerge as a critical con-cern of the international community as well. The member states of the United Nations formalized their commitment to human rights in 1948 with the adoption of the Univer-sal Declaration of Human Rights.

The Universal Declaration, of course, was not self-enforcing. More than half a century after its adoption, the broad proclamations of the Declaration remain closer to the ideal than the reality of world politics. But the rights proclaimed in the American Declaration of Independence and in the United States Constitution were not self-enforcing either; progress even in the United States was slow and uncertain for much of our history. The United States did not abolish slavery until 1865, for example, and did not even begin to recognize the equality of women until the 1960s.

In recent years, advocates of an aggressive human rights policy have been heartened by several key international developments, including the prosecution of war criminals in Bosnia and Rwanda, international efforts to hold the former Chilean dictator Augusto Pinochet accountable for human rights abuses committed by his government, and the establishment (albeit without American support) of the International Criminal Court.

In this selection, the constitutional scholar Louis Henkin discusses the relationship between the Universal Declaration of Human Rights and the United States Constitution.

Questions

1. In what respects does the Universal Declaration draw on the United States Constitution? In what areas does the Universal Declaration go beyond the Constitution to advance rights not specifically protected under American law?
2. Why did the authors of the Universal Declaration stress the need to make "national rights effective under national laws and through national institutions"? What difficulties face the international community in its efforts to protect human rights and punish abuses in countries that violate the principles of the Universal Declaration?

3.3 The Universal Declaration and the U.S. Constitution (1998)

Louis Henkin

The Universal Declaration of Human Rights has been acclaimed as perhaps the most important international document of the twentieth century. It established human rights as the idea of our times. It is commonly recognized as the birth certificate of the International Human Rights Movement, marking and confirming the new international concern with human rights. It is the authoritative definition and catalog of human rights. It has been the basis for the contemporary international law of human rights—the source of two international human rights covenants and other conventions, and of a customary law of human rights. In what is perhaps its most significant contribution, it has inspired and promoted "constitutionalism" and respect for human rights in national societies around the world.

The Universal Declaration did not invent the idea of human rights, nor did it fill that idea with rights of its own creation. The Declaration adopted an idea hundreds of years old and filled it with particular rights derived from principles of "natural rights," from historic assertions of rights by brave persons and bold peoples, and from bills of rights composed in America and France in the eighteenth century. One notable source for the "catalog" of rights in the Universal Declaration was the Constitution of the United States and its 200 years of interpretive jurisprudence.

In turn, during the half century since the Declaration was proclaimed, it has been a rich source for new "rights instruments" and has enriched rights in older

---

Louis Henkin, "The Universal Declaration and the U.S. Constitution," *PS: Political Science and Politics* (September 1998, Vol. XXXI, No. 3), pp. 512–515 (abridged). Reprinted by permission.

polities. Rights in the United States have not been overt, avowed beneficiaries of the Declaration, but they have not escaped its subtler influences.

International Human Rights as National Rights

Since 1948 the world has seen the birth of more than 100 new states with new constitutions, as well as the adoption of new or significantly amended constitutions by older states. Every new constitution, every old constitution that is importantly revised, bears the mark of the Universal Declaration. Almost all constitutions now have a bill of rights reflecting the spirit and influence of the Declaration, some of them also its letter. National courts have resorted to the Declaration in the application and interpretation of constitutional rights. The Universal Declaration, having linked in its first preambular clause "the inherent dignity" and "the equal and inalienable rights of all members of the human family," helped establish "human dignity" as the touchstone of rights for national constitutional cultures.

The significance of the Universal Declaration for national constitutional cultures reflects the essential character of the International Human Rights Movement and of the international law of human rights. Human rights are legitimate, recognized claims by every individual upon his or her *national society*, which that society is duty-bound to recognize and to realize, to respect and to ensure. Generally, a society gives effect to human rights through national institutions and national laws that prohibit, prevent, and deter violation of human rights and provide domestic remedies for violations that have occurred.

Human rights, then, are national rights, rights of the individual in his or her society, enforced and given effect by national laws. Strictly, there are no "international human rights"; strictly, there is no "international law of human rights." The purpose of international concern with human rights is to make national rights effective under national laws and through national institutions. The purpose of international law relating to human rights and of international human rights institutions is to make national human rights law and institutions effective instruments for securing and ensuring human rights. In an ideal world—if national laws and institutions were fully effective—there would be no need for international human rights laws and institutions. In a sense, if international human rights laws and institutions were wholly successful, they would be self-liquidating, they would lose their *raison d'être*.

The national character of human rights is reflected in the Universal Declaration in various ways. Though prepared by an international body under international auspices, the Declaration is "Universal," not "International." (The word "international" appears only in the clause encouraging resort to international measures to secure national observance of human rights.) The Declaration is a "declaration," not a treaty. As conceived, and by its terms, the Declaration does not create international legal obligations: it does not even urge states to assume international obligations. Rather, it calls on states to recognize the rights of their inhabitants under their national laws, and to take measures to realize human rights through national institutions within their own societies.

The Universal Declaration and U.S. Constitutional Jurisprudence

The U.S. Constitution, and the constitutional culture it engendered, were a principal conduit for the idea of rights later espoused by the Universal Declaration, and a principal source of many—not all—of the rights recognized in the Declaration. U.S. constitutional jurisprudence inspired the Universal Declaration in spirit, in principle, and in detail. A half century of coexistence may have played the Declaration back a little into U.S. constitutional jurisprudence.

U.S. Constitutional Sources of the Declaration   Since human rights are rights under national law, since the Universal Declaration aimed to set forth individual rights for national systems, it was to be expected that those who drafted the Declaration drew heavily on constitutional bills of rights, principally the Bill of Rights of the U.S. Constitution, and the Declaration of the Rights of Man and of the Citizen which was the progeny of the French Revolution.

In fact, and understandably, those who drafted the Universal Declaration bettered the eighteenth-century instruction. The French Declaration had only a short constitutional life; France had no significant constitutional jurisprudence between 1793 and 1946, when the French Declaration was revived and incorporated by reference in the first post-War constitution of the Fourth Republic. But the French Declaration had lived on in French hagiography and in the culture of France, and traces of the French Declaration are clearly visible in the Universal Declaration.

The influence of the United States Constitution and its jurisprudence on the Universal Declaration is substantial. By the time the Declaration came to be drafted, the U.S. Constitution had been the heart of an established and acclaimed constitutional polity and constitutional culture for more than a hundred and fifty years; by 1948, the U.S. Constitution had had more than 150 years of interpretation and application. . . .

The Universal Declaration, drafted in 1947–48, drew heavily on the modifications and extensions of rights in the United States effected by 150 years of Supreme Court interpretation. The right to property is protected in the Declaration in broad terms (Article 17). The presumption of innocence, not expressed in the U.S. Constitution, is explicit in the Declaration (Article 11). So are the freedoms of movement and residence within the country, and the right to leave and return to one's country (Article 13).

But the Universal Declaration bettered the Supreme Court's instruction as well. The Declaration recognizes rights beyond those the Supreme Court has found in the U.S. Constitution—a right to freedom from torture, not only a prohibition on the use of evidence obtained by torture (or other coercion); a right to be free from any inhuman or degrading treatment; and not only from cruel and unusual punishment for crime, but from inhuman or degrading treatment for any purpose (Article 5).

The Universal Declaration went far beyond the U.S. Constitution and its judicial interpretations in a major respect. Famously, the Universal Declaration called on states to secure an array of "welfare rights," now known as economic and social rights including rights to social security, work and leisure, a standard of living adequate for health and well-being, and education. Such rights are not guaranteed by the U.S. Constitution (though some are recognized by a few state constitutions), but are, at best, "legislative entitlements," and subject therefore to budgetary constraints, political whim, and the ebb and flow of compassion and "compassion fatigue."

The Declaration and the Constitution: Reciprocal Influence   The Universal Declaration, proclaimed without dissent in 1948, has not been formally revisited. New states that have come into existence since 1948 have had no way of "adhering" to the Declaration, but all of them have accepted it by reference in numerous resolutions, and some states have done so in other international instruments (such as the Helsinki Final Act) and by reference in national constitutional and other legal instruments. The status in international law of the Declaration (and of some of its particular provisions) continues to be debated, but the Declaration maintains important political and cultural influence, both in international life and in particular states and societies. There have been few formal uses of the Declaration in law, however, and little "jurisprudence" of interpretation of the Declaration to which developments in national jurisprudence—e.g., in that of the United States—might contribute.

The influence of the Declaration on U.S. constitutional jurisprudence, in turn, has not been large or prominent. The Declaration has been cited only five times in the pages of *Supreme Court Reports* and in no instance decisively, and not at all in the past 25 years. Lower federal courts also have invoked the Declaration only infrequently, and not with compelling effect.

It should not be surprising that hard evidence of influence by the Declaration on U.S. constitutional jurisprudence is difficult to find and to demonstrate. The United States had an established rights jurisprudence and was well-set in its constitutional ways when the Declaration was promulgated. In view of the important contribution of the U.S. Constitution to the Declaration, similarities and parallels between them are numerous, but it would not be necessary, and would perhaps be "impolitic," for lawyers and judges to cite the Declaration as authority where there is parallel and equal support in the text of the U.S. Constitution or in established constitutional jurisprudence.

Historically and culturally, moreover, the United States has not been avowedly receptive to external influence, and U.S. constitutional jurisprudence in particular has been notoriously resistant to foreign legal authority. Especially since the end of the Cold War, the United States has again been withdrawing into "self-sufficiency," and the Supreme Court and its constitutional jurisprudence have not escaped that trend. In particular, the commitment to economic and social rights in the Declaration, fostered by the memory of FDR's "freedom from want" and the influence of Eleanor Roosevelt, has dissipated.

But, avowedly or not, U.S. constitutional jurisprudence has not remained impervious to the international rights jurisprudence the Declaration represents. Insofar as the Universal Declaration has reflected a universal ideology and a common morality, its influences, if difficult to prove, ought not be doubted.

I offer a few notable examples. The radical development in the United States of the equal protection of the laws, as epitomized by *Brown* v. *Board of Education* (1954), came while the world was making equality in rights, and nondiscrimination, on grounds of race in particular, a principal norm of international human rights law. Similarly, the United States came to universal suffrage in 1962, when the Supreme Court found it to be required, not by some muffled constitutional commitment to democracy and representative government but by a commitment to equality newly applied to an old problem: If one person is entitled to vote, the Court ruled, all are entitled to vote, and to vote equally (*Wesberry* v. *Sims* 1964; *Reynolds* v. *Sims* 1964). Can it be that the Supreme Court came to those radical results without looking about, outside the United States, without regard to the ideology, and the content, of the Universal Declaration?

The Universal Declaration, moreover, is not only for constitutional consumption. It was also designed to inspire national laws and national legal-political cultures. Was President Lyndon Johnson impervious, was he not responding, to what the Universal Declaration represented, as he led the United States towards the Great Society? Influence is a continuing force, and a process. United States constitutional jurisprudence has developed in quantum leaps and by continuous seepage. Whether knowingly or unconsciously, the Declaration, I am satisfied, and what it represents in the international culture of the past half century, has had its influence on the U.S. Constitution and on the laws of the United States.

One might anticipate further changes to which the Declaration will speak. Some elements in U.S. constitutional jurisprudence are long overdue for change. The notion that U.S. immigration, including alien deportation laws, are not subject to constitutional restraint, sprang full blown from the brow of the Supreme Court more than 100 years ago (*The Chinese Exclusion Case* 1889); was questioned, though reaffirmed, by the Court nearly 50 years ago (*Galvan* v. *Press* 1954); and still begs for change today in the spirit of the Universal Declaration which speaks to the right to return to "one's country," and the right "to seek and to enjoy" asylum. That doctrine was not mandated by anything in the Constitution, and can be changed without formal constitutional amendment. And the doughty "due process clause," which came to the rescue to help reconceive the right to privacy (the "new privacy," as in *Roe* v. *Wade*, 1973), is also available for change.

Similarly, the text of the U.S. Constitution prohibits cruel and unusual punishment for crime, but reinterpretation of the due process clause could bring us closer to the Declaration by banning torture and all other inhuman and degrading treatment in any context. The right to life is the primary right proclaimed by the Universal Declaration; it ought to inform our jurisprudence on capital punishment. And what cannot be, or should not be, done by constitutional interpretation, can be done by federal and state legislation, in the spirit of the Declaration.

In particular, the United States can reinforce its commitment to economic and social rights declared in the Universal Declaration. If we cannot bring ourselves to declare them "rights," we can well legislate them as entitlements. Our ideology, our values, were not frozen in 1791 when the Bill of Rights was adopted, or in 1868 when the 14th Amendment was ratified. The equal protection of the laws came to mean much beyond what was thought in 1868. Universal suffrage came only 35 years ago, without constitutional amendment. By legislation, by civil rights and voting rights acts, we have moved towards our aspirations for the Great Society. It is time for the United States to take the Universal Declaration seriously in other respects, in all respects.

The United States does not have to vote for, or "ratify," the Universal Declaration again. But especially when, in the name of "cultural relativism" and state "sovereignty," the Declaration is under attack by some who fear the human rights idea it represents, the United States should, on every occasion and by every means, reaffirm its identification with the Declaration and its ideology, with its content, its universality, its fundamental commitment to human dignity. ■

View from the Inside

The First Amendment's protection of freedom of speech is most severely tested when the speech in question is dangerous, offensive, or hateful. So it was in *R.A.V. v. St. Paul,* a Supreme Court case decided in 1992. Defendent R.A.V. (initials were used because he was a juvenile) was arrested for burning a cross on the front lawn of an African American family in St. Paul, Minnesota. The burning cross—made famous as a symbol of racial hatred by the Ku Klux Klan—is an example of what legal scholars call "hate speech." Such cross burning was specifically banned in St. Paul by city ordinance.

Representing R.A.V. were two public defenders, who immediately recognized that this was no ordinary case of juvenile delinquency. Instead, the two lawyers eventually found themselves at the center of a major Supreme Court case involving the limits of free speech. In the end, the Court sided with R.A.V., holding the St. Paul ordinance unconstitutional under the First Amendment.*

A decade later, R.A.V.'s attorneys discussed with an interviewer what it is like to defend a great principle by defending an unpopular client who admits to committing a hateful act.

Questions

1. How did the lawyers explain their representation of R.A.V. to critics who accused them of promoting hatred? Are their explanations convincing?
2. Do you agree or disagree with the Supreme Court's decision that R.A.V.'s actions were protected under the First Amendment? How might John Stuart Mill (see selection 3.1) have resolved this case?

---

*The Supreme Court's decision can be found at 505 U.S. 377 (1992).

3.4 Speaking Our Minds (2002)

Joseph Russomanno

" **A**m I crazy, or is this unconstitutional?" With those words, attorney Edward J. Cleary embarked on a journey that would take him through a maelstrom of issues, gross misperceptions and misunderstandings by members of the public, and culminating with his eloquent presentation before the U.S. Supreme Court and a unanimous ruling in his favor. Cleary's question about constitutionality, directed to co-counsel Michael F. Cromett, concerned the St. Paul Bias-Motivated Crime Ordinance. That law read:

> Whoever places on public or private property a symbol, object, appellation, characterization or graffiti, including, but not limited to, a burning cross or Nazi swastika, which one knows or has reasonable grounds to know arouses anger, alarm or resentment in others on the basis of race, color, creed, religion or gender commits disorderly conduct and shall be guilty of a misdemeanor.

Cleary's newest client, Robert A. Viktora (R.A.V.), had just been charged with violating that ordinance. On the first day of summer in 1990, R.A.V. was one of several teenagers who burned a crudely made cross on the front lawn of Russell and Laura Jones, an African-American family in St. Paul, Minnesota. Ed Cleary, an attorney on contract with the Ramsey County Public Defender's office, was assigned the case. . . .

In taking a case such as this one, R.A.V.'s attorneys had a myriad of challenges before them, not the least of which was dealing with public perception. Oftentimes, it was misperception. Even other lawyers failed to grasp just what Cleary and Cromett were doing and why. Their attempts to explain that they were *not* defending R.A.V.'s action—but rather that they were challenging the constitutionality of the law being used to prosecute him—frequently went unheard or misunderstood. The misperceptions grew, with Cleary being labeled at various times a racist, a Fascist, and—in spite of the fact that he was not paid for his work in this case—a lawyer who would do anything for money.

ED CLEARY: I knew right away [our defense of R.A.V.] was going to be misunderstood. And I certainly knew right away that it was going to be misunderstood by minority people, particularly nonlawyer minority people. And I was right. And that's why the media became so important, because the way the media covered it was crucial to anyone who bothered to take the time to read the articles. Now early on, of course, the media weren't covering it at all. All that was known was that I had gone in and suggested that a law that said you couldn't burn crosses was wrong somehow—and there-fore the logical corollary to that was that it was okay to do. But it didn't shock me. I was disappointed, but it didn't shock me.

MICHAEL CROMETT: I guess the biggest hurdle was getting people to look be-yond the conduct to the language of the ordinance. That forever—and still is—the legacy of *R.A.V.* When Ed wrote his book and they came up with the title *Beyond the Burning Cross*, it seemed so natural. That's what we were fighting to do the whole time—get people to see beyond the burning cross. That was the biggest hurdle. Everybody could really follow the prosecutor saying the First Amend-ment doesn't allow a person to burn a cross in someone's yard. It was really hard to get people to see that we were coming at the challenge from a different angle, a different plane.

When you say the biggest challenge was to get people to see beyond that, what "people" are you referring to? People in the judicial system, or outside of it?

MICHAEL CROMETT: Both. The most interesting thing—or perhaps for us the most frustrating—was some of our colleagues. And not to me so much, as to Ed. Some of our colleagues were just in-censed about what we were doing, and couldn't imagine why we were spending so much time on the case. It really showed what later became clear—the rift between the civil rights part of the First Amendment and the civil liberties part. We were never asked by any of our colleagues if we believed in murder when we represented people charged with murder, but here they were asking, "Do you believe in cross burning?" Those kinds of comments. A lot of it was pretty emotional and hostile.

ED CLEARY: Locally here, I knew a number of the reporters so I could trust them to—even if they didn't understand it—they wouldn't take an easy shot. They would at least try to out-line the issue involved to the degree they understood it. And I don't mean to say that in a mean or rude way, but a number of local reporters never really did grasp what was going on, I don't think. And as time wore on, and the *New York Times* and the *Washington Post* and papers like that got involved, you could see the difference in reporting, quite honestly. I don't know how many of those reporters had law degrees, but they clearly were able to educate the pub-lic in a way that wasn't happening locally. So that was kind of a relief when we got to that point. These reporters were flying into town and interviewing us. The initial reaction was fear that these reporters would somehow take a shot. Underlying all of that, which I probably really didn't grasp then but I grasp more now, is that because I was on the First Amendment side—that is to say I was a First Amendment champion of sorts—I think that there were a number of reporters who tried to understand it because they were obviously First Amendment people themselves, a lot of them. Even if they didn't necessarily like it, they tried to understand it. And obviously those in the national press were better at it. But there were some ugly episodes and that really didn't get going until right before the argument and after the decision. There was the terrible experience of going on [the CNN program] "Sonya Live." And that has stayed with me through these years. That to me was one more sign how lucky I had been with the media and how fair so many reporters had been with me, and what it was like to fall under the power of the media when you didn't have someone who bothered to read the pre-interview or bothered to study the issues and take cheap shots. I mean, it just kind of grew. The media left a bad taste, but that comes with the territory.

How would you respond to someone who would ask you, "How can it be that protecting hate speech is a good thing?"

ED CLEARY: Boy that kind of gets to the core of it, doesn't it? I guess first and foremost, if somebody asked me that, I'd challenge their belief that we can always tell what hate speech is. So it's first a matter of definition. And if we can ever get to the point of agreeing what hate speech is—one man's hate speech is another man's free speech—but let's just say that we can all agree on a very small core that is very clearly hateful in nature. Then I think it would be a further line-drawing problem of what degree of "disturbing" or "offensive" or any of those—where do we draw that line? And most importantly, who decides? So even in the most blatant examples, by protecting it we've left the door open to very disturbing speech. And I think history has shown that core political speech—just to put it aside for a minute from hateful speech—is often very disturbing and offensive, and some would call hateful. And no one would argue that core political speech isn't protected. So I guess my attitude simply is it's a matter of protecting all speech, and if that makes me a First Amendment absolutist—I mean I'm not a total absolutist in the sense that I agree with some of the lines that the Supreme Court has drawn—but "hateful" is just one of those words that causes a lot of people, including me, a lot of concern as a line-drawing criterion.

MICHAEL CROMETT: The thing that I've always tried to say—and really, it's something that we fell into pretty early on—was the whole idea that you need to protect the Devil's free speech in order to protect your own free speech. One of the things that we put in the brief to the United States Supreme Court was the quote from Robert Bolt's play *A Man for All Seasons* where Sir Thomas More has a discussion with a young lawyer about that principle. And it turned out that Justice Scalia really likes that quote. We didn't have any clue about that at the time we did it. But it seemed to summarize the position so well. If you're going to allow people to regulate speech that you don't agree with, it can't be too long before *your* speech—speech that *you* agree with—will be limited, too. I think it's probably that slippery slope that we're afraid of. Once you decide that, where does it end? It's that kind of idea that seems to make sense to me. It really seems to me that the defining principle that distinguishes the United States from most other countries is that we allow speech we disagree with, with the hope that it's going to be other speech that wins out in the marketplace of ideas. Now it's at this point that it starts to get a little crumbly for me in terms of the First Amendment part. People say, "Well, what values does a burning cross have?" And I'm not sure that a burning cross does [have value]. But it's the idea of racial supremacy or separatism—those kinds of things—that carry that principle forward and, despite what we may think about it, they have some currency.

ED CLEARY: I'd say in the first year, when it was still kind of a local issue, to the degree that it was known, you'd be introduced as, "The lawyer that's involved in that cross burning." And with nothing further, you can imagine how people reacted. They reacted like maybe you were a little crazy, or a little off, or more importantly, hiding a racist or political agenda of some sort. So that just made it very uncomfortable. But I knew that what I believed in politically was in strong contrast to what the person who I was defending did. But quite clearly I understood that it was my job to do so. The contradiction never bothered me probably because I embrace as much as I do the Sixth Amendment right to counsel. With one of my friends, I used to interrupt her and change the conversation to something else just because I didn't want to get into it. You find yourself just not wanting to try to explain to *everybody* what the issue was. Then afterwards, after it hit, I had more credibility in the sense that the U.S. Supreme Court had taken it. For nonlawyers, they were impressed with the hoopla—that is, that somebody in Washington wanted to talk about it. But they still didn't understand and thought that it was a very bad thing to do—that you were making the world safer for racists.

Therefore you were, in a sense, aiding and abetting the racists and Fascists in this country. I remember very distinctly after the Supreme Court agreed to take [the case], I felt a chill like I had read my obituary—being referred to as the cross-burning lawyer, which would not be the nicest epitaph.

Does some of this sentiment exist to this day?

ED CLEARY: I think so. I mean, I don't get crank calls, or anything. [But] I still get sideward glances and apprehensive looks, particularly when I'm dealing—as I must in this position—like when I go talk to the Black Lawyers Association, for instance. Pretty clearly, in the back of their minds—as lawyers, they know what it was I did and why. But as members of a minority race, they're not necessarily trusting of someone who would do that. ■

Chapter 4

Civil Rights

The civil rights movement was one of the central forces in American politics in the second half of the twentieth century. Nearly a hundred years after Lincoln's Emancipation Proclamation freed the slaves, the United States at last began to address the gross disparities between the promise of racial equality and the reality of racial discrimination.

The legal struggle for racial equality began in the 1930s. By the 1940s, the struggle for racial equality moved to the political arena as well. The legal battles continued through the 1940s and led ultimately to the landmark school desegregation case, *Brown* v. *Board of Education,* decided in 1954. *Brown* (along with its companion case, *Bolling* v. *Sharpe*) overturned the Supreme Court's 1896 decision in *Plessy* v. *Ferguson,* which had upheld "separate but equal" facilities as constitutional. (*Plessy* is selection 4.1; *Brown* and *Bolling* are sections 4.2 and 4.3.)

At the same time, the struggle for racial equality moved to the political arena. The adoption of a civil rights plank in the Democratic party's 1948 platform led thirty-five southern delegates to walk out of the convention, and later six thousand southerners met in a separate convention to nominate J. Strom Thurmond of South Carolina on the so-called Dixiecrat ticket. Also in 1948, President Harry Truman ordered the desegregation of the U.S. armed forces.

The political branches did not really move forward on civil rights, however, until the 1960s. In 1963, President John F. Kennedy proposed major civil rights legislation, although Congress did not act. Pressure was building, however; a series of events in 1963, including police violence in Birmingham, Alabama, and a major march on Washington, D.C., greatly raised the visibility of the movement. The following year, after Kennedy's assassination, President Lyndon B. Johnson pushed through the most important civil rights legislation since the 1860s, the Civil Rights Act of 1964. A year later Congress added the Voting Rights Act of 1965, which at last secured for minorities a meaningful right to vote.

Recent years have seen controversy and divisiveness in the civil rights area. One major area of controversy is affirmative action, which involves race-conscious and race-specific remedies to problems of past and present discrimination. Aspects of the affirmative action debate are discussed in selection 4.2, which presents a rare attempt to find a compromise on the issue, and in selection 4.5, which deals with the problem of minority rights in multicultural societies.

The civil rights movement gave rise to a number of similar attempts to secure equality to other victims of legal and societal discrimination. One offshoot was the women's rights movement, which successfully persuaded the Supreme Court to extend the equal protection of the law to women. Although the idea of equality for women has gained

111

widespread acceptance, there are still areas of disagreement. One such controversy, treated in selection 4.6, involved the admission of women to previously all-male public military colleges, such as the Citadel in South Carolina and the Virginia Military Institute (VMI).

Other minority groups continue to struggle for even the basic protections of the law. Gays and lesbians, for example, still face widespread discrimination, and have had difficulty in many cases in advancing and protecting their rights in court. For women, African Americans, and members of other minority groups, the civil rights movement is an ongoing struggle. This chapter approaches this complex and varied subject from a multitude of different perspectives.

Chapter Questions

1. At the heart of any discussion of civil rights is the meaning of equality. What alternative views on equality are illustrated in the readings in this chapter? How has the meaning of equality changed over the past two hundred years?
2. How have legal conceptions of civil rights changed over the past century? Consider *Plessy, Brown,* and the affirmative action controversy.
3. Consider the new questions and problems faced by advocates of civil rights in the 1990s, among them the extension of civil rights to previously unprotected groups, including women, and tensions both inside and outside the civil rights movement. How are these tensions related to the goals and purposes of the original civil rights movement?

 Foundations

Any discussion of civil rights in the modern era must start with *Brown* v. *Board of Education,* the 1954 school desegregation case. The impact of *Brown* on race and politics in the United States has been immense. Although *Brown* itself had little effect on school segregation in the Deep South, it set in motion a process that led to the civil rights movement, the Civil Rights Act of 1964, and a host of federal and state programs designed to eliminate and address the effects of racial discrimination.

Brown reversed *Plessy* v. *Ferguson* (selection 4.1), an 1896 case that upheld the segregation of railroad cars in Louisiana. *Brown* based its rejection of *Plessy* on narrow grounds relating to the dangers of segregation in the educational process. In practice, however, the elimination of segregation in public schools led quickly to judicial determinations that all state-sponsored segregation was unconstitutional.

Chief Justice Earl Warren, who wrote the *Brown* opinion, avoided a direct attack on segregation in general; note specifically how his 1954 argument differs from the 1896 dissent of Justice John Marshall Harlan in *Plessy.* Warren's concern was twofold: he sought to ensure that the Court would speak with one voice, believing that an approach such as Harlan's might alienate one or more members of the Court; and he wanted to avoid giving potential critics of the decision a broad target to aim at. His opinion, though criticized by some as insufficiently high-minded, got the job done.

The decision in *Brown* was accompanied by a parallel decision in *Bolling* v. *Sharpe* (selection 4.3), which dealt with segregation in the District of Columbia. Because the Equal Protection Clause applies to the states and not to the federal government, the Court used the Due Process Clause to strike down segregation in the District.

The first *Brown* decision simply announced that segregated schools were unconstitutional. Implementation of that decision was postponed one year, until 1955, when the Court ordered the federal district courts to implement *Brown* "with all deliberate speed."

Questions

1. Why, in Earl Warren's view, are "separate educational facilities inherently unequal"?
2. Does Justice Harlan's dissent in *Plessy* provide an alternative approach to deciding *Brown?* What are the advantages and disadvantages of this approach?

4.1 *Plessy* v. *Ferguson* (1896)

Justice Henry B. Brown
Justice John Marshall Harlan, dissenting

This case turns upon the constitutionality of an act of the General Assembly of the State of Louisiana, passed in 1890, providing for separate railway carriages for the white and colored races.

• • •

The constitutionality of this act is attacked upon the ground that it conflicts with the Thirteenth Amendment of the Constitution, abolishing slavery, and the Fourteenth Amendment, which prohibits certain restrictive legislation on the part of the States.

1. That it does not conflict with the Thirteenth Amendment, which abolished slavery and involuntary servitude, except as a punishment for crime, is too clear for argument. Slavery implies involuntary servitude—a state of bondage; the ownership of mankind as a chattel, or at least the control of the labor and services of one man for the benefit of another, and the absence of a legal right to the disposal of his own person, property and services. This amendment was said in the *Slaughter-house cases* to have been intended primarily to abolish slavery, as it had been previously known in this country, and that it equally forbade Mexican peonage or the Chinese coolie trade, when they amounted to slavery or involuntary servitude, and that the use of the word "servitude" was intended to prohibit the use of all forms of involuntary slavery, of whatever class or nature. It was

---

163 U.S. 537 (1896).

intimated, however, in that case that this amendment was regarded by the states-men of that day as insufficient to protect the colored race from certain laws which had been enacted in the Southern States, imposing upon the colored race onerous disabilities and burdens, and curtailing their rights in the pursuit of life, liberty and property to such an extent that their freedom was of little value; and that the Fourteenth Amendment was devised to meet this exigency.

So, too, in the *Civil Rights cases* it was said that the act of a mere individual, the owner of an inn, a public conveyance or place of amusement, refusing accommo-dations to colored people, cannot be justly regarded as imposing any badge of slav-ery or servitude upon the applicant, but only as involving an ordinary civil injury, properly cognizable by the laws of the State, and presumably subject to redress by those laws until the contrary appears. "It would be running the slavery argument into the ground," said Mr. Justice Bradley, "to make it apply to every act of dis-crimination which a person may see fit to make as to the guests he will entertain, or as to the people he will take into his coach or cab or car, or admit to his concert or theatre, or deal with in other matters of intercourse or business."

A statute which implies merely a legal distinction between the white and col-ored races—a distinction which is founded in the color of the two races, and which must always exist so long as white men are distinguished from the other race by color—has no tendency to destroy the legal equality of the two races, or reestablish a state of involuntary servitude. Indeed, we do not understand that the Thirteenth Amendment is strenuously relied upon by the plaintiff in error in this connection.

2. By the Fourteenth Amendment, all persons born or naturalized in the United States, and subject to the jurisdiction thereof, are made citizens of the United States and of the State wherein they reside; and the States are forbidden from making or enforcing any law which shall abridge the privileges or immunities of citizens of the United States, or shall deprive any person of life, liberty or prop-erty without due process of law, or deny to any person within their jurisdiction the equal protection of the laws.

The proper construction of this amendment was first called to the attention of this court in the *Slaughter-house cases*, which involved, however, not a question of race, but one of exclusive privileges. The case did not call for any expression of opin-ion as to the exact rights it was intended to secure to the colored race, but it was said generally that its main purpose was to establish the citizenship of the negro; to give definitions of citizenship of the United States and of the States, and to protect from the hostile legislation of the States the privileges and immunities of citizens of the United States, as distinguished from those of citizens of the States.

The object of the amendment was undoubtedly to enforce the absolute equality of the two races before the law but in the nature of things it could not have been intended to abolish distinctions based upon color, or to enforce social, as distin-guished from political equality, or a commingling of the two races upon terms un-satisfactory to either. Laws permitting, and even requiring, their separation in places where they are liable to be brought into contact do not necessarily imply the inferiority of either race to the other, and have been generally, if not univer-sally, recognized as within the competency of the state legislatures in the exercise of their police power. The most common instance of this is connected with the establishment of separate schools for white and colored children, which has been held to be a valid exercise of the legislative power even by courts of States where the political rights of the colored race have been longest and most earnestly enforced.

• • •

So far, then, as a conflict with the Fourteenth Amendment is concerned, the case reduces itself to the question whether the statute of Louisiana is a reasonable regulation, and with respect to this there must necessarily be a large discretion on the part of the legislature. In determining the question of reasonableness it is at liberty to act with reference to the established usages, customs and traditions of the people, and with a view to the promotion of their comfort, and the preservation of the public peace and good order. Gauged by this standard, we cannot say that a law which authorizes or even requires the separation of the two races in public conveyances is unreasonable, or more obnoxious to the Fourteenth Amendment than the acts of Congress requiring separate schools for colored children in the District of Columbia, the constitutionality of which does not seem to have been questioned, or the corresponding acts of state legislatures.

We consider the underlying fallacy of the plaintiff's argument to consist in the assumption that the enforced separation of the two races stamps the colored race with a badge of inferiority. If this be so, it is not by reason of anything found in the act, but solely because the colored race chooses to put the construction upon it. The argument necessarily assumes that if, as has been more than once the case, and is not unlikely to be so again, the colored race should become the dominant power in the state legislature, and should enact a law in precisely similar terms, it would thereby relegate the white race to an inferior position. We imagine that the white race, at least, would not acquiesce in this assumption. The argument also assumes that social prejudices may be overcome by legislation, and that equal rights cannot be secured to the negro except by an enforced commingling of the two races. We cannot accept this proposition. If the two races are to meet upon terms of social equality, it must be the result of natural affinities, a mutual appreciation of each other's merits and a voluntary consent of individuals. As was said by the Court of Appeals of New York in *People v. Gallagher*, "this end can neither be accomplished nor promoted by laws which conflict with the general sentiment of the community upon whom they are designed to operate. When the government, therefore, has secured to each of its citizens equal rights before the law and equal opportunities for improvement and progress, it has accomplished the end for which it was organized and performed all of the functions respecting social advantages with which it is endowed." Legislation is powerless to eradicate racial instincts or to abolish distinctions based upon physical differences, and the attempt to do so can only result in accentuating the difficulties of the present situation. If the civil and political rights of both races be equal one cannot be inferior to the other civilly or politically. If one race be inferior to the other socially, the Constitution of the United States cannot put them upon the same place.

• • •

Mr. Justice Harlan dissenting.

By the Louisiana statute, the validity of which is here involved, all railway companies (other than street railroad companies) carrying passengers in that State are required to have separate but equal accommodations for white and colored persons, "by providing two or more passenger coaches for each passenger train, *or* by dividing the passenger coaches by a *partition* so as to secure separate accommodations." Under this statute, no colored person is permitted to occupy a seat in a coach assigned to white persons; nor any white person, to occupy a seat in a coach assigned to colored persons. The managers of the railroad are not allowed to exercise any discretion in the premises, but are required to assign each passenger to some coach or compartment set apart for the exclusive use of his race. If a passenger insists upon going into a coach or compartment not set apart for persons of his race, he is subject to be fined, or to be imprisoned in the parish jail. Penalties are prescribed for the refusal or neglect of the officers, directors, conductors and employees of railroad companies to comply with the provisions of the act.

• • •

In respect of civil rights, common to all citizens, the Constitution of the United States does not, I think, permit any public authority to know the race of those entitled to be protected in the enjoyment of such rights. Every true man has pride of race, and under appropriate circumstances when the rights of others, his equals before the law, are not to be affected, it is his privilege to express such pride and to take such action based upon it as to him seems proper. But I deny that any legislative body or judicial tribunal may have regard to the race of citizens when the civil rights of those citizens are involved. Indeed, such legislation, as that here in question, is inconsistent not only with that equality of rights which pertains to citizenship, National and State, but with the personal liberty enjoyed by every one within the United States.

• • •

The white race deems itself to be the dominant race in this country. And so it is, in prestige, in achievements, in education, in wealth and power. So, I doubt not, it will continue to be for all time, if it remains true to its great heritage and holds fast in the principles of constitutional liberty. But in view of the Constitution, in the eye of the law, there is in this country no superior, dominant, ruling class of citizens. There is no caste here. Our Constitution is color-blind, and neither knows nor tolerates classes among citizens. In respect of civil rights, all citizens are equal before the law. The humblest is the peer of the most powerful. The law regards man as man, and takes no account of his surroundings or of his color when his civil rights as guaranteed by the supreme law of the land are involved. It is, therefore, to be regretted that this high tribunal, the final expositor of the fundamental law of the land, has reached the conclusion that it is competent for a State to regulate the enjoyment by citizens of their civil rights solely upon the basis of race. ■

4.2 *Brown v. Board of Education* (1954)

Chief Justice Earl Warren

Mr. Chief Justice Warren delivered the opinion of the Court.

These cases come to us from the States of Kansas, South Carolina, Virginia, and Delaware. They are premised on different facts and different local conditions, but a common legal question justifies their consideration together in this consolidated opinion.

In each of the cases, minors of the Negro race, through their legal representatives, seek the aid of the courts in obtaining admission to the public schools of the community on a nonsegregated basis. In each instance, they had been denied admission to schools attended by white children under laws requiring or permitting segregation according to race. This segregation was alleged to deprive the plaintiffs of the equal protection of the laws under the Fourteenth Amendment. In each of the cases other than the Delaware case, a three-judge federal district court denied relief to the plaintiffs on the so-called "separate but equal" doctrine announced by this Court in *Plessy v. Ferguson.* Under that doctrine, equality of treatment is accorded when the races are provided substantially equal facilities, even though these facilities be separate. In the Delaware case, the Supreme Court of Delaware adhered to that doctrine, but ordered that the plaintiffs be admitted to the white schools because of their superiority to the Negro schools.

The plaintiffs contend that segregated public schools are not "equal" and cannot be made "equal," and that hence they are deprived of the equal protection of the laws. Because of the obvious importance of the question presented, the Court took jurisdiction. Argument was heard in the 1952 Term, and reargument was heard this Term on certain questions propounded by the Court.

Reargument was largely devoted to the circumstances surrounding the adoption of the Fourteenth Amendment in 1868. It covered exhaustively consideration of the Amendment in Congress, ratification by the states, then existing practices in racial segregation, and the views of proponents and opponents of the Amendment. This discussion and our own investigation convince us that, although these sources cast some light, it is not enough to resolve the problem with which we are faced. At best, they are inconclusive. The most avid proponents of the post-War Amendments undoubtedly intended them to remove all legal distinctions among "all persons born or naturalized in the United States." Their opponents, just as certainly, were antagonistic to both the letter and the spirit of the Amendments and wished them to have the most limited effect. What others in Congress and the state legislatures had in mind cannot be determined with any degree of certainty.

An additional reason for the inconclusive nature of the Amendment's history, with respect to segregated schools, is the status of public education at that time. In the South, the movement toward free common schools, supported by general

347 U.S. 483 (1954).

taxation, had not yet taken hold. Education of white children was largely in the hands of private groups. Education of Negroes was almost nonexistent, and practically all of the race were illiterate. In fact, any education of Negroes was forbidden by law in some states. Today, in contrast, many Negroes have achieved outstanding success in the arts and sciences as well as in the business and professional world. It is true that public school education at the time of the Amendment had advanced further in the North, but the effect of the Amendment on Northern States was generally ignored in the congressional debates. Even in the North, the conditions of public education did not approximate those existing today. The curriculum was usually rudimentary; ungraded schools were common in rural areas; the school term was but three months a year in many states; and compulsory school attendance was virtually unknown. As a consequence, it is not surprising that there should be so little in the history of the Fourteenth Amendment relating to its intended effect on public education.

In the first cases in this Court construing the Fourteenth Amendment, decided shortly after its adoption, the Court interpreted it as proscribing all state-imposed discriminations against the Negro race. The doctrine of "separate but equal" did not make its appearance in this Court until 1896 in the case of *Plessy* v. *Ferguson*, involving not education but transportation. American courts have since labored with the doctrine for over half a century. In this Court, there have been six cases involving the "separate but equal" doctrine in the field of public education. In *Cumming* v. *County Board of Education* and *Gong Lum* v. *Rice* the validity of the doctrine itself was not challenged. In more recent cases, all on the graduate school level, inequality was found in that specific benefits enjoyed by white students were denied to Negro students of the same educational qualifications. In none of these cases was it necessary to re-examine the doctrine to grant relief to the Negro plaintiff. And in *Sweatt* v. *Painter*, the Court expressly reserved decision on the question whether *Plessy* v. *Ferguson* should be held inapplicable to public education.

In the instant cases, that question is directly presented. Here, unlike *Sweatt* v. *Painter*, there are findings below that the Negro and white schools involved have been equalized, or are being equalized, with respect to buildings, curricula, qualifications and salaries of teachers, and other "tangible" factors. Our decision, therefore, cannot turn on merely a comparison of these tangible factors in the Negro and white schools involved in each of the cases. We must look instead to the effect of segregation itself on public education.

In approaching this problem, we cannot turn the clock back to 1868 when the Amendment was adopted, or even to 1896 when *Plessy* v. *Ferguson* was written. We must consider public education in the light of its full development and its present place in American life throughout the Nation. Only in this way can it be determined if segregation in public schools deprives these plaintiffs of the equal protection of the laws.

Today, education is perhaps the most important function of state and local governments. Compulsory school attendance laws and the great expenditures for education both demonstrate our recognition of the importance of education to our democratic society. It is required in the performance of our most basic public responsibilities, even service in the armed forces. It is the very foundation of good citizenship. Today it is a principal instrument in awakening the child to cultural values, in preparing him for later professional training, and in helping him to adjust normally to his environment. In these days, it is doubtful that any child may reasonably be expected to succeed in life if he is denied the opportunity of an education. Such an opportunity, where the state has undertaken to provide it, is a right which must be made available to all on equal terms.

We come then to the question presented: Does segregation of children in public schools solely on the basis of race, even though the physical facilities and other "tangible" factors may be equal, deprive the children of the minority group of equal educational opportunities? We believe that it does.

In *Sweatt* v. *Painter,* in finding that a segregated law school for Negroes could not provide them equal educational opportunities, this Court relied in large part on "those qualities which are incapable of objective measurement but which make for greatness in a law school." In *McLaurin* v. *Oklahoma State Regents,* the Court, in requiring that a Negro admitted to a white graduate school be treated like all other students, again resorted to intangible considerations: ". . . his ability to study, to engage in discussions and exchange views with other students, and, in general, to learn his profession." Such considerations apply with added force to children in grade and high schools. To separate them from others of similar age and qualifications solely because of their race generates a feeling of inferiority as to their status in the community that may affect their hearts and minds in a way unlikely ever to be undone. The effect of this separation on their educational opportunities was well stated by a finding in the Kansas case by a court which nevertheless felt compelled to rule against the Negro plaintiffs:

> Segregation of white and colored children in public schools has a detrimental effect upon the colored children. The impact is greater when it has the sanction of the law; for the policy of separating the races is usually interpreted as denoting the inferiority of the negro group. A sense of inferiority affects the motivation of a child to learn. Segregation with the sanction of law, therefore, has a tendency to [retard] the educational and mental development of negro children and to deprive them of some of the benefits they would receive in a racial[ly] integrated school system.

Whatever may have been the extent of psychological knowledge at the time of *Plessy* v. *Ferguson,* this finding is amply supported by modern authority.* Any language in *Plessy* v. *Ferguson* contrary to this finding is rejected.

We conclude that in the field of public education the doctrine of "separate but equal" has no place. Separate educational facilities are inherently unequal. Therefore, we hold that the plaintiffs and others similarly situated for whom the actions have been brought are, by reason of the segregation complained of, deprived of

---

*[This footnote, number 11 in the original, has become famous. It is frequently referred to simply as "footnote 11."] K. B. Clark, Effect of Prejudice and Discrimination on Personality Development (Midcentury White House Conference on Children and Youth, 1950); Witmer and Kotinsky, Personality in the Making (1952), c. VI; Deutscher and Chein, The Psychological Effects of Enforced Segregation: A Survey of Social Science Opinion, 26 J. Psychol 259 (1948); Chein, What Are the Psychological Effects of Segregation Under Conditions of Equal Facilities?, 3 Int. J. Opinion and Attitude Res. 229 (1949); Brameld, Educational Costs, in Discrimination and National Welfare (MacIver, ed., 1949), 44–48; Frazier, The Negro in the United States (1949), 674–681. And see generally Myrdal, An American Dilemma (1944).

the equal protection of the laws guaranteed by the Fourteenth Amendment. This disposition makes unnecessary any discussion whether such segregation also violates the Due Process Clause of the Fourteenth Amendment.

Because these are class actions, because of the wide applicability of this decision, and because of the great variety of local conditions, the formulation of decrees in these cases presents problems of considerable complexity. On reargument, the consideration of appropriate relief was necessarily subordinated to the primary question—the constitutionality of segregation in public education. We have now announced that such segregation is a denial of the equal protection of the laws. In order that we may have the full assistance of the parties in formulating decrees, the cases will be restored to the docket, and the parties are requested to present further argument on Questions 4 and 5 previously propounded by the Court for the reargument this Term. The Attorney General of the United States is again invited to participate. The Attorneys General of the states requiring or permitting segregation in public education will also be permitted to appear as *amici curiae* upon request to do so by September 15, 1954, and submission of briefs by October 1, 1954.

It is so ordered. ■

4.3 *Bolling* v. *Sharpe* (1954)

Chief Justice Earl Warren

Mr. Chief Justice Warren delivered the opinion of the Court.

This case challenges the validity of segregation in the public schools of the District of Columbia. The petitioners, minors of the Negro race, allege that such segregation deprives them of due process of law under the Fifth Amendment. They were refused admission to a public school attended by white children solely because of their race. They sought the aid of the District Court for the District of Columbia in obtaining admission. That court dismissed their complaint. The Court granted a writ of certiorari before judgment in the Court of Appeals because of the importance of the constitutional question presented.

We have this day held that the Equal Protection Clause of the Fourteenth Amendment prohibits the states from maintaining racially segregated public schools. The legal problem in the District of Columbia is somewhat different, however. The Fifth Amendment, which is applicable in the District of Columbia, does not contain an equal protection clause as does the Fourteenth Amendment which applies only to the states. But the concepts of equal protection and due process, both stemming from our American ideal of fairness, are not mutually exclusive. The "equal protection of the laws" is a more explicit safeguard of prohibited unfairness than "due process of law," and, therefore, we do not imply that the two are always interchangeable phrases. But, as this Court has recognized, discrimination may be so unjustifiable as to be violative of due process.

347 U.S. 497 (1954).

Classifications based solely upon race must be scrutinized with particular care, since they are contrary to our traditions and hence constitutionally suspect. As long ago as 1896, this Court declared the principle "that the Constitution of the United States, in its present form, forbids, so far as civil and political rights are concerned, discrimination by the General Government, or by the States, against any citizen because of his race." And in *Buchanan* v. *Warley*, the Court held that a statute which limited the right of a property owner to convey his property to a person of another race was, as an unreasonable discrimination, a denial of due process of law.

Although the Court has not assumed to define "liberty" with any great precision, that term is not confined to mere freedom from bodily restraint. Liberty under law extends to the full range of conduct which the individual is free to pursue, and it cannot be restricted except for a proper governmental objective. Segregation in public education is not reasonably related to any proper governmental objective, and thus it imposes on Negro children of the District of Columbia a burden that constitutes an arbitrary deprivation of their liberty in violation of the Due Process Clause.

In view of our decision that the Constitution prohibits the states from maintaining racially segregated public schools, it would be unthinkable that the same Constitution would impose a lesser duty on the Federal Government. We hold that racial segregation in the public schools of the District of Columbia is a denial of the due process of law guaranteed by the Fifth Amendment to the Constitution.

It is so ordered. ■

 # American Politics Today

Few areas of law and social policy have been as controversial in recent years as that of affirmative action. Such programs give preferences to women or members of various minority groups in competition for jobs, education, or other valuable resources. Defenders of affirmative action claim that only such preferences can compensate for past discrimination, ensure diversity in the classroom and the workplace, and ensure a level playing field for current and future generations. Opponents object to affirmative action because it allows or requires individuals to be judged on the basis of characteristics such as race or gender instead of on their merits as individuals.

Neither side, as the political scientist Peter H. Schuck suggests in this selection, has a monopoly on the truth. So rather than choose between them, Schuck suggests a compromise. Under his proposal, the government would not participate in affirmative action programs, but it would allow private corporations or universities to do so. Such an approach would recognize the need for government neutrality while allowing private actors the freedom to act as they see fit.

Question

1. Why, in Schuck's view, should the government be held to a different standard than private actors when it comes to affirmative action? Is his distinction between public and private affirmative action convincing?

4.4 Affirmative Action: Don't Mend or End It—Bend It (2002)

Peter H. Schuck

Affirmative action policy—by which I mean ethnoracial preferences in the allocation of socially valuable resources—is even more divisive and unsettled today than at its inception more than 30 years ago.

Affirmative action's policy context has changed dramatically since 1970. One change is legal. Since the Supreme Court's 1978 Bakke decision, when Justice Lewis Powell's pivotal fifth vote endorsed certain "diversity"-based preferences in higher education, the Court has made it increasingly difficult for affirmative action plans to pass constitutional muster unless they are carefully designed to remedy specific past acts of discrimination. Four other changes [provide evidence of] the triumph of the nondiscrimination principle: blacks' large social gains; evidence on the size, beneficiaries, and consequences of preferences; and new demographic realities—persuade me that affirmative action as we know it should be abandoned even if it is held to be constitutional.

"As we know it" is the essential qualifier in that sentence. I propose neither a wholesale ban on affirmative action ("ending" it) nor tweaks in its administration ("mending" it). Rather, I would make two structural changes to curtail existing preferences while strengthening the remaining ones' claim to justice. First, affirmative action would be banned in the public sector but allowed in the private sector. Second, private-sector institutions that use preferences would be required to disclose how and why they do so. These reforms would allow the use of preferences by private institutions that believe in them enough to disclose and defend them, while doing away with the obfuscation, duplicity, and lack of accountability that too often accompany preferences. Affirmative action could thus be localized and customized to suit the varying requirements of particular contexts and sponsors.

Triumph of the Nondiscrimination Principle

Why is change necessary? To explain, one must at the outset distinguish affirmative action entailing preferences from nondiscrimination, a principle that simply requires one to refrain from treating people differently because of their race, eth-

Peter H. Schuck, "Affirmative Action—Don't Mend or End It—Bend It." This is excerpted and adapted from Peter H. Schuck. *Diversity in America: Keeping Government at a Safe Distance* (Harvard University Press, 2003), Chapter 5. Reprinted by permission of the author.

nicity, or other protected characteristics. Although this distinction can blur at the edges, it is clear and vital both in politics and in principle.

When affirmative action became federal policy in the late 1960s, the nondiscrimination principle, though fragile, was gaining strength. Preferences, by contrast, were flatly rejected by civil rights leaders like Hubert Humphrey, Ted Kennedy, and Martin Luther King, Jr. In the three decades that followed, more and more Americans came to embrace nondiscrimination and to oppose affirmative action, yet as John Skrentny shows in his *Ironies of Affirmative Action*, federal bureaucrats extended affirmative action with little public notice or debate. Today, nondiscrimination, or equal opportunity, is a principle questioned by only a few bigots and extreme libertarians, and civil rights law is far-reaching and remedially robust. In contrast, affirmative action is widely seen as a demand for favoritism or even equal outcomes.

Social Gains by Blacks

Blacks, the intended beneficiaries of affirmative action, are no longer the insular minority they were in the 1960s. Harvard sociologist Orlando Patterson shows their "astonishing" progress on almost every front. "A mere 13% of the population," he notes, "Afro-Americans dominate the nation's popular culture....[A]t least 35 percent of Afro-American adult, male workers are solidly middle class." The income of young, intact black families approaches that of demographically similar whites. On almost every other social index (residential integration is a laggard), the black-white gap is narrowing significantly; indeed, the income gap for young black women has disappeared.

Even these comparisons understate black progress. Much of racism's cruel legacy is permanently impounded in the low education and income levels of older blacks who grew up under Jim Crow; their economic disadvantages pull down the averages, obscuring the gains of their far better-educated children and grandchildren. These gains, moreover, have coincided with the arrival of record numbers of immigrants who are competing with blacks. To ignore this factor, economist Robert Lerner says, is like analyzing inequality trends in Germany since 1990 without noting that it had absorbed an entire impoverished country, East Germany. In addition, comparisons that fail to age-adjust social statistics obscure the fact that blacks, whose average age is much lower than that of whites, are less likely to have reached their peak earning years.

My point, emphatically, is not that blacks have achieved social equality—far from it—but that the situation facing them today is altogether different than it was when affirmative action was adopted. Advocates, of course, say that this progress just proves that affirmative action is effective; hence it should be continued or even increased. But this post hoc ergo propter hoc reasoning is fallacious and ignores the policy's growing incoherence and injustice.

Size, Beneficiaries, and Consequences of Preferences

When we weigh competing claims for scarce resources—jobs, admission to higher education, public and private contracts, broadcast or other spectrum licenses, credit, housing, and the like—how heavy is the thumb that affirmative action places on the scales? This is a crucial question. The larger the preference, the more it conflicts with competing interests and values, especially the ideal of merit—almost regardless of how one defines merit.

The best data concern higher education admissions where (for better or for worse) schools commonly use standardized test scores as a proxy for aptitude, preparation, and achievement. William Bowen and Derek Bok, the former presidents of Princeton and Harvard, published a study in 1999 based largely on the academic records of more than 80,000 students who entered 28 highly selective institutions in three different years. Affirmative action, they claimed, only applies to these institutions, although a more recent study suggests that the practice now extends to some second- and even third-tier schools.

Selective institutions, of course, take other factors into account besides race. Indeed, some whites who are admitted have worse academic credentials than the blacks admitted under preferences. Still, Bowen and Bok find a difference of almost 200 points in the average SAT scores of the black and white applicants, and even this understates the group difference. First, the deficit for black applicants' high school grade point average (GPA), the other main admission criterion, is even larger. Thomas Kane finds that black applicants to selective schools "enjoy an advantage equivalent to an increase of two thirds of a point in [GPA]—on a four-point scale—or [the equivalent of] 400 points on the SAT." Second, although the SAT is often criticized as culturally biased against blacks, SAT (and GPA) scores at every level actually overpredict their college performance. Third, the odds were approximately even that black applicants with scores between 1100 and 1199 would be admitted, whereas the odds for whites did not reach that level until they had scores in the 1450–1499 range. With a score of 1500 or above, more than a third of whites were rejected while every single black gained admission. The University of Michigan, whose affirmative action program is detailed in a pending lawsuit, weighs race even more heavily than the average school in the Bowen and Bok sample. At Michigan, being black, Hispanic, or Native American gives one the equivalent of a full point of GPA; minority status can override any SAT score deficit. And a recent study of 47 public institutions found that the odds of a black student being admitted compared to a white student with the same SAT and GPA were 173 to 1 at Michigan and 177 to 1 at North Carolina State.

These preferences, then, are not merely tie-breakers; they are huge—and they continue at the graduate and professional school levels. It is encouraging that an identical share (56 percent) of black and white graduates of the institutions in the Bowen and Bok sample earned graduate degrees; the share of blacks earning professional or doctoral degrees was actually slightly higher than for whites (40 percent vs. 37 percent). But black students' college grades and postgraduate test scores are so much lower on average that their admission to these programs, disproportionately at top-tier institutions, also depends on affirmative action. In the early 1990s, for example, only a few dozen of the 420 blacks admitted to the 18 most selective law schools would have been admitted absent affirmative action. A high percentage of these schools' black graduates eventually pass the bar examination, but some 22 percent of blacks from these schools who take the exam never pass it (compared with 3 percent of whites), and only 61 percent of blacks pass it the first time compared with 92 percent of whites. Blacks who enter the professions do enjoy solid status, income, civic participation and leadership, and career satisfaction. But this hardly makes the case for affirmative action, for the higher-scoring applicants whom they displaced would presumably have done at least as well.

How much of blacks' impressive gains is due to reduced discrimination resulting from changing white attitudes and civil rights enforcement, as distinct from preferences? How would they have fared had they attended the somewhat less prestigious schools they could have attended without preferences? What would the demographics of higher education be without those preferences? We cannot answer these vital questions conclusively. We know that black gains were substantial even before preferences were adopted, that preference beneficiaries are overwhelmingly from middle- and upper-class families, and that most black leaders in all walks of life did not go to elite universities. We also know that many institutions are so committed to affirmative action that they will find ways to prefer favored groups—minorities, legacies, athletes, and others—no matter what the formal rules say. Although California voters banned affirmative action in state programs, their politicians press the university system to jigger the admission criteria until it finds a formula that can skirt the ban and produce the "correct" number of the favored minorities (excluding Asians, who are thought not to need the help).

New Demographic Realities

The moral case for affirmative action rests on the bitter legacy of black slavery, Jim Crow, and the violent dispossession of Native Americans. Yet the descendants of slaves and Native Americans constitute a shrinking share of affirmative action's beneficiaries. Political logrolling has extended preferential treatment to the largest immigrant group, Hispanics, as well as to blacks from Africa, the Caribbean, and elsewhere, Asians and Pacific Islanders, and in some programs to women, a majority group.

Some affirmative action advocates acknowledge this problem and want to fix it. Orlando Patterson, for example, would exclude "first-generation persons of African ancestry" but not "their children and later generations...in light of the persistence of racist discrimination in America." He would also exclude all Hispanics except for Puerto Ricans and Mexican Americans of second or later generations and would exclude "all Asians except Chinese-Americans descended from pre-1923 immigrants. . . ." With due respect for Patterson's path-breaking work on race, his formula resembles a tax code provision governing depreciation expenses more than a workable formula for promoting social justice.

Centuries of immigration and intermarriage have rendered the conventional racial categories ever more meaningless. The number of Americans who consider themselves multiracial and who wish to be identified as such (if they must be racially identified at all) was 7 million in the 2000 census, including nearly 2 million blacks (5 percent of the black population) and 37 percent of all Native Americans. This is why advocacy groups who are desperate to retain the demographic status quo lobbied furiously to preempt a multiracial category.

In perhaps the most grimly ironic aspect of the new demographic dispensation, the government adopted something like the one-drop rule that helped enslave mulattos and self-identifying whites before Emancipation. Under OMB's [Office of

Management and Budget] rules, any response combining one minority race and the white race must be allocated to the minority race. This, although 25 percent of those in the United States who describe themselves as both black and white consider themselves white, as do almost half of Asian-white people and more than 80 percent of Indian-white people. The lesson is clear: making our social policy pivot on the standard racial categories is both illogical and politically unsustainable.

Alternatives

Even a remote possibility that eliminating affirmative action would resegregate our society deeply distresses almost all Americans. Nothing else can explain the persistence of a policy that, contrary to basic American values, distributes valuable social resources according to skin color and surname. But to say that we must choose between perpetuating affirmative action and eliminating it entirely is false. To be sure, most suggested reforms—using social class or economic disadvantage rather than race, choosing among minimally qualified students by lottery, and making preferences temporary—are impracticable or would make matters worse. Limiting affirmative action to the descendants of slaves and Native Americans would minimize some objections to the policy but, as Patterson's proposal suggests, would be tricky to implement and would still violate the nondiscrimination and merit principles.

Most Americans who favor affirmative action would probably concede that it fails to treat the underlying problem. Black applicants will continue to have worse academic credentials until they can attend better primary and secondary schools and receive the remediation they need. A root cause of their disadvantage is inferior schooling, and affirmative action is simply a poultice. We must often deal with symptoms rather than root causes because we do not know how to eliminate them, or consider it too costly to do so, or cannot muster the necessary political will. If we know which social or educational reforms can substantially improve low-income children's academic performance, then we should by all means adopt them. But this does not mean that we should preserve affirmative action until we can eliminate the root causes of inequality.

I propose instead that we treat governmental, legally mandated preferences differently than private, voluntary ones. While prohibiting the former (except in the narrow remedial context approved by the Supreme Court), I would permit the latter—but only under certain conditions discussed below. A liberal society committed to freedom and private autonomy has good reasons to maintain this difference; racial preferences imposed by law are pernicious in ways that private ones are not. To affirmative action advocates, it is a Catch-22 to bar the benign use of race now after having used it against minorities for centuries. But to most Americans (including many minorities), affirmative action is not benign. It is not [a] Catch-22 to recognize what history teaches—that race is perhaps the worst imaginable category around which to organize political and social relations. The social changes I have described only reinforce this lesson. A public law that affirms our common values should renounce the distributive use of race, not perpetuate it.

There are other differences between public and private affirmative action. A private preference speaks for and binds only those who adopt it and only for as long as they retain it. It does not serve, as public law should, as a social ideal. As I explained in *The Limits of Law: Essays on Democratic Governance* (2000), legal rules tend to be cruder, more simplistic, slower to develop, and less contextualized than voluntary ones, which are tailored to more specific needs and situations. Legal rules reflect interest group politics or the vagaries of judicial decision; voluntary ones reflect the chooser's own assessment of private benefits and costs. Legal rules are more difficult to reform, abandon, or escape. Voluntary ones can assume more diverse forms than mandated ones, a diversity that facilitates social learning and problem solving.

Still, many who believe in nondiscrimination and merit and who conscientiously weigh the competing values still support affirmative action. If a private university chooses to sacrifice some level of academic performance to gain greater racial diversity and whatever educational or other values it thinks diversity will bring, I cannot say—nor should the law say—that its choice is impermissible. Because even private affirmative action violates the nondiscrimination principle, however, I would permit it only on two conditions: transparency and protection of minorities. First, the preference—its criteria, weights, and reasons—must be fully disclosed. If it cannot withstand public criticism, it should be scrapped. The goal is to discipline preferences by forcing institutions to reveal their value choices. This will trigger market, reputational, and other informal mechanisms that make them bear more of the policy's costs rather than just shifting them surreptitiously to nonpreferred applicants, as they do now. Second, private affirmative action must not disadvantage a group to which the Constitution affords heightened protection. A preference favoring whites, for example, would violate this condition.

The Commitment to Legal Equality

For better and for worse, American culture remains highly individualistic in its values and premises, even at some sacrifice (where sacrifice is necessary) to its goal of substantive equality. The illiberal strands in our tangled history that enslaved, excluded, and subordinated individuals as members of racial groups should chasten our efforts to use race as a distributive criterion. Affirmative action in its current form, however well-intended, violates the distinctive, deeply engrained cultural and moral commitments to legal equality, private autonomy, and enhanced opportunity that have served Americans well—even though they have not yet served all of us equally well. ■

 # The International Context

The Western political tradition, writes the political scientist Will Kymlicka, "has been surprisingly silent" on questions involving the rights of ethnic, racial, linguistic, and cultural minorities. Instead, "political theorists have operated with an idealized model" of politics in which "fellow citizens share a common descent, language, and culture." This theoretical gap has serious practical implications—in particular, in his view, Western political systems are ill-equipped to deal with the increasingly important and divisive issues arising from their diversity.

In this selection, Kymlicka provides a theoretical model for recognizing what he calls "group-differentiated rights"—the idea that citizens may be entitled to certain rights because of their membership in a particular group. Although it runs counter to much of our political tradition, the idea of group rights, Kymlicka suggests, is legitimate and ought to be taken seriously.

Questions

1. Why are traditional rights principles insufficient to deal with the problem of minority groups? Why is it necessary to "supplement traditional human rights principles with a theory of minority rights"?
2. What are the implications of Kymlicka's approach for affirmative action? For "English-only" legislation? For minority representation in Congress and in state legislatures?

4.5 Multicultural Citizenship (1995)

Will Kymlicka

1. The Issues

Most countries today are culturally diverse. According to recent estimates, the world's 184 independent states contain over 600 living language groups, and 5,000 ethnic groups. In very few countries can the citizens be said to share the same language, or belong to the same ethnonational group.

This diversity gives rise to a series of important and potentially divisive questions. Minorities and majorities increasingly clash over such issues as language rights, regional autonomy, political representation, education curriculum, land claims, immigration and naturalization policy, even national symbols, such as the choice of national anthem or public holidays. Finding morally defensible and politically viable answers to these issues is the greatest challenge facing democracies today. In Eastern Europe and the Third World, attempts to create liberal democratic institutions are being undermined by violent nationalist conflicts. In the West, volatile disputes over the rights of immigrants, indigenous peoples, and other cultural minorities are throwing into question many of the assumptions which have governed political life for decades. Since the end of the Cold War, ethnocultural conflicts have become the most common source of political violence in the world, and they show no sign of abating.

Will Kymlicka, *Multicultural Citizenship: A Theory of Minority Rights*, pp. 1–6, 26–28, 30–33. Copyright © 1995. Reprinted by permission of Oxford University Press.

. . . There are no simple answers or magic formulas to resolve all these questions. Some conflicts are intractable, even when the disputants are motivated by a sense of fairness and tolerance, which all too often is lacking. Moreover, every dispute has its own unique history and circumstances that need to be taken into account in devising a fair and workable solution. My aim is to step back and present a more general view of the landscape—to identify some key concepts and principles that need to be taken into account, and so clarify the basic building blocks for a liberal approach to minority rights.

The Western political tradition has been surprisingly silent on these issues. Most organized political communities throughout recorded history have been multiethnic, a testament to the ubiquity of both conquest and long-distance trade in human affairs. Yet most Western political theorists have operated with an idealized model of the polis in which fellow citizens share a common descent, language, and culture. Even when the theorists themselves lived in polyglot empires that governed numerous ethnic and linguistic groups, they have often written as if the culturally homogeneous city-states of Ancient Greece provided the essential or standard model of a political community.

To achieve this ideal of a homogeneous polity, governments throughout history have pursued a variety of policies regarding cultural minorities. Some minorities were physically eliminated, either by mass expulsion (what we now call "ethnic cleansing") or by genocide. Other minorities were coercively assimilated, forced to adopt the language, religion, and customs of the majority. In yet other cases, minorities were treated as resident aliens, subjected to physical segregation and economic discrimination, and denied political rights.

Various efforts have been made historically to protect cultural minorities, and to regulate the potential conflicts between majority and minority cultures. Early in this century, bilateral treaties regulated the treatment of fellow nationals in other countries. For example, Germany agreed to accord certain rights and privileges to ethnic Poles residing within its borders, so long as Poland provided reciprocal rights to ethnic Germans in Poland. This treaty system was extended, and given a more multilateral basis, under the League of Nations.

However, these treaties were inadequate. For one thing, a minority was only ensured protection from discrimination and oppression if there was a "kin state" nearby which took an interest in it. Moreover, the treaties were destabilizing, because where such kin states did exist, they often used treaty provisions as grounds for invading or intervening in weaker countries. Thus Nazi Germany justified its invasion of Poland and Czechoslovakia on the grounds that these countries were violating the treaty rights of ethnic Germans on their soil.

After World War II, it was clear that a different approach to minority rights was needed. Many liberals hoped that the new emphasis on "human rights" would resolve minority conflicts. Rather than protecting vulnerable groups directly, through special rights for the members of designated groups, cultural minorities would be protected indirectly, by guaranteeing basic civil and political rights to all individuals regardless of group membership. Basic human rights such as freedom of speech, association, and conscience, while attributed to individuals, are typically exercised in community with others, and so provide protection for group life. Where these individual rights are firmly protected, liberals assumed, no further rights needed to be attributed to the members of specific ethnic or national minorities:

> the general tendency of the postwar movements for the promotion of human rights has been to subsume the problem of national minorities under the broader problem of ensuring basic individual rights to all human beings, without reference to membership in ethnic groups. The leading assumption has been that members of national minorities do not need, are not entitled to, or cannot be granted rights of a special character. The doctrine of human rights has been put forward as a substitute for the concept of minority rights, with the strong implication that minorities whose members enjoy individual equality of treatment cannot legitimately demand facilities for the maintenance of their ethnic particularism.

Guided by this philosophy, the United Nations deleted all references to the rights of ethnic and national minorities in its Universal Declaration of Human Rights.

The shift from group-specific minority rights to universal human rights was embraced by many liberals, partly because it seemed a natural extension of the way religious minorities were protected. In the sixteenth century, European states were being torn apart by conflict between Catholics and Protestants over which religion should rule the land. These conflicts were finally resolved, not by granting special rights to particular religious minorities, but by separating church and state, and entrenching each's individual freedom of religion. Religious minorities are protected indirectly, by guaranteeing individual freedom of worship, so that people can freely associate with other co-religionists, without fear of state discrimination or disapproval.

Many post-war liberals have thought that religious tolerance based on the separation of church and state provides a model for dealing with ethnocultural differences as well. On this view, ethnic identity, like religion, is something which people should be free to express in their private life, but which is not the concern of the state. The state does not oppose the freedom of people to express their particular cultural attachments, but nor does it nurture such expression—rather, to adapt Nathan Glazer's phrase, it responds with "benign neglect." The members of ethnic and national groups are protected against discrimination and prejudice, and they are free to try to maintain whatever part of their ethnic heritage or identity they wish, consistent with the rights of others. But their efforts are purely private, and it is not the place of public agencies to attach legal identities or disabilities to cultural membership or ethnic identity. This separation of state and ethnicity precludes any legal or governmental recognition of ethnic groups, or any use of ethnic criteria in the distribution of rights, resources, and duties.

Many liberals, particularly on the left, have made an exception in the case of affirmative action for disadvantaged racial groups. But in a sense this is the exception that proves the rule. Affirmative action is generally defended as a temporary measure which is needed to move more rapidly towards a "colour-blind" society. It is intended to remedy years of discrimination, and thereby move us closer to the sort of society that would have existed had we observed the separation of state and ethnicity from the beginning. Thus the UN Convention on Racial Discrimination endorses affirmative action programmes only where they have this temporary and remedial character. Far from abandoning the ideal of the separation of state and ethnicity, affirmative action is one method of trying to achieve that ideal.

Some liberals, particularly on the right, think it is counterproductive to pursue a "colour-blind" society through policies that "count by race." Affirmative action, they argue, exacerbates the very problem it was intended to solve, by making people more conscious of group differences, and more resentful of other groups. This dispute amongst liberals over the need for remedial affirmative action programmes is a familiar one in many liberal democracies.

But what most post-war liberals on both the right and left continue to reject is the idea of *permanent* differentiation in the rights or status of the members of certain groups. In particular, they reject the claim that group-specific rights are needed to accommodate enduring cultural differences, rather than remedy historical discrimination. As we will see in subsequent chapters, post-war liberals around the world have repeatedly opposed the idea that specific ethnic or national groups should be given a permanent political identity or constitutional status.

However, it has become increasingly clear that minority rights cannot be subsumed under the category of human rights. Traditional human rights standards are simply unable to resolve some of the most important and controversial questions relating to cultural minorities: which languages should be recognized in the parliaments, bureaucracies, and courts? Should each ethnic or national group have publicly funded education in its mother tongue? Should internal boundaries (legislative districts, provinces, states) be drawn so that cultural minorities form a majority within a local region? Should governmental powers be devolved from the central level to more local or regional levels controlled by particular minorities, particularly on culturally sensitive issues of immigration, communication, and education? Should political offices be distributed in accordance with a principle of national or ethnic proportionality? Should the traditional homelands of indigenous peoples be reserved for their benefit, and so protected from encroachment by settlers and resource developers? What are the responsibilities of minorities to integrate? What degree of cultural integration can be required of immigrants and refugees before they acquire citizenship?

The problem is not that traditional human rights doctrines give us the wrong answer to these questions. It is rather that they often give no answer at all. The right to free speech does not tell us what an appropriate language policy is; the right to vote does not tell us how political boundaries should be drawn, or how powers should be distributed between levels of government; the right to mobility does not tell us what an appropriate immigration and naturalization policy is. These questions have been left to the usual process of majoritarian decision-making within each state. The result, I will argue, has been to render cultural minorities vulnerable to significant injustice at the hands of the majority, and to exacerbate ethnocultural conflict.

To resolve these questions fairly, we need to supplement traditional human rights principles with a theory of minority rights. The necessity for such a theory has become painfully clear in Eastern Europe and the former Soviet Union. Disputes over local autonomy, the drawing of boundaries, language rights, and naturalization policy have engulfed much of the region in violent conflict. There is little hope that stable peace will be restored, or that basic human rights will be respected, until these minority rights issues are resolved.

It is not surprising, therefore, that minority rights have returned to prominence in international relations. For example, the Conference on Security and Co-operation in Europe (CSCE) adopted a declaration on the Rights of National Minorities in 1991, and established a High Commissioner on National Minorities in 1993. The United Nations has been debating both a Declaration on the Rights of Persons Belonging to National or Ethnic, Religious and Linguistic Minorities (1993), and a Draft Universal Declaration on Indigenous Rights (1988). The Council of Europe adopted a declaration on minority language rights in 1992 (the European Charter for Regional or Minority Languages). Other examples could be given.

However, these declarations remain controversial. Some were adopted hastily, to help prevent the escalation of conflict in Eastern Europe. As a result, they are quite vague, and often seem motivated more by the need to appease belligerent minorities than by any clear sense of what justice requires. Both the underlying justification for these rights, and their limits, remain unclear.

I believe it is legitimate, and indeed unavoidable, to supplement traditional human rights with minority rights. A comprehensive theory of justice in a multicultural state will include both universal rights, assigned to individuals regardless of group membership, and certain group-differentiated rights or "special status" for minority cultures.

Recognizing minority rights has obvious dangers. The language of minority rights has been used and abused not only by the Nazis, but also by apologists for racial segregation and apartheid. It has also been used by intolerant and belligerent nationalists and fundamentalists throughout the world to justify the domination of people outside their group, and the suppression of dissenters within the group. A liberal theory of minority rights, therefore, must explain how minority rights coexist with human rights, and how minority rights are limited by principles of individual liberty, democracy, and social justice.

• • •

2. Three Forms of Group-Differentiated Rights

Virtually all liberal democracies are either multinational or polyethnic, or both. The "challenge of multiculturalism" is to accommodate these national and ethnic differences in a stable and morally defensible way. In this section, I will discuss some of the most important ways in which democracies have responded to the demands of national minorities and ethnic groups.

In all liberal democracies, one of the major mechanisms for accommodating cultural differences is the protection of the civil and political rights of individuals. It is impossible to overstate the importance of freedom of association, religion, speech, mobility, and political organization for protecting group difference. These rights enable individuals to form and maintain the various groups and associations which constitute civil society, to adapt these groups to changing circumstances, and to promote their views and interests to the wider population. The protection afforded by these common rights of citizenship is sufficient for many of the legitimate forms of diversity in society.

Various critics of liberalism—including some Marxists, communitarians, and feminists—have argued that the liberal focus on individual rights reflects an atomistic, materialistic, instrumental, or conflictual view of human relationships. I believe that this criticism is profoundly mistaken, and that individual rights can be and typically are used to sustain a wide range of social relationships. Indeed, the most basic liberal right—freedom of conscience—is primarily valuable for the protection it gives to intrinsically social (and non-instrumental) activities.

However, it is increasingly accepted in many countries that some forms of cultural difference can only be accommodated through special legal or constitutional measures, above and beyond the common rights of citizenship. Some forms of group difference can only be accommodated if their members have certain group-specific rights—what Iris Young calls "differentiated citizenship."

For example, a recent government publication in Canada noted that:

> In the Canadian experience, it has not been enough to protect only universal individual rights. Here, the Constitution and ordinary laws also protect other rights accorded to individuals as members of certain communities. This accommodation of both types of rights makes our constitution unique and reflects the Canadian value of equality that accommodates difference. The fact that community rights exist alongside individual rights goes to the very heart of what Canada is all about.

It is quite misleading to say that Canada is unique in combining universal individual rights and group-specific "community rights." Such a combination exists in many other federal systems in Europe, Asia, and Africa. As I noted earlier, even the constitution of the United States, which is often seen as a paradigm of individualism, allows for various group-specific rights, including the special status of American Indians and Puerto Ricans.

It is these special group-specific measures for accommodating national and ethnic differences that I will focus on. There are at least three forms of group-specific rights: (1) self-government rights; (2) polyethnic rights; and (3) special representation rights. I will say a few words about each. . . .

1. Self-government Rights   In most multination states, the component nations are inclined to demand some form of political autonomy or territorial jurisdiction, so as to ensure the full and free development of their cultures and the best interests of their people. At the extreme, nations may wish to secede, if they think their self-determination is impossible within the larger state.

The right of national groups to self-determination is given (limited) recognition in international law. According to the United Nations' Charter, "all peoples have the right to self-determination." However, the UN has not defined "peoples," and it has generally applied the principle of self-determination only to overseas colonies, not internal national minorities, even when the latter were subject to the same sort of colonization and conquest as the former. This limitation on self-determination to overseas colonies (known as the "salt-water thesis") is widely seen as arbitrary, and many national minorities insist that they too are "peoples" or "nations," and, as such, have the right of self-determination. They demand certain powers of self-government which they say were not relinquished by their (often involuntary) incorporation into a larger state.

One mechanism for recognizing claims to self-government is federalism, which divides powers between the central government and regional subunits (provinces/

states/cantons). Where national minorities are regionally concentrated, the boundaries of federal subunits can be drawn so that the national minority forms a majority in one of the subunits. Under these circumstances, federalism can provide extensive self-government for a national minority, guaranteeing its ability to make decisions in certain areas without being outvoted by the larger society.

For example, under the federal division of powers in Canada, the province of Quebec (which is 80 per cent francophone) has extensive jurisdiction over issues that are crucial to the survival of the French culture, including control over education, language, culture, as well as significant input into immigration policy. The other nine provinces also have these powers, but the major impetus behind the existing division of powers, and indeed behind the entire federal system, is the need to accommodate the Québecois. At the time of Confederation, most English Canadian leaders were in favour of a unitary state, like Britain, and agreed to a federal system primarily to accommodate French Canadians. . . .

2. Polyethnic Rights   As I noted earlier, immigrant groups in the last thirty years have successfully challenged the "Anglo-conformity" model which assumed that they should abandon all aspects of their ethnic heritage and assimilate to existing cultural norms and customs. At first, this challenge simply took the form of demanding the right freely to express their particularity without fear of prejudice or discrimination in the mainstream society. It was the demand, as Walzer put it, that "politics be separated from nationality—as it was already separated from religion."

But the demands of ethnic groups have expanded in important directions. It became clear that positive steps were required to root out discrimination and prejudice, particularly against visible minorities. For this reason, anti-racism policies are considered part of the "multiculturalism" policy in Canada and Australia, as are changes to the education curriculum to recognize the history and contribution of minorities. However, these policies are primarily directed at ensuring the effective exercise of the common rights of citizenship, and so do not really qualify as group-differentiated citizenship rights.

Some ethnic groups and religious minorities have also demanded various forms of public funding of their cultural practices. This includes the funding of ethnic associations, magazines, and festivals. Given that most liberal states provide funding to the arts and museums, so as to preserve the richness and diversity of our cultural resources, funding for ethnic studies and ethnic associations can be seen as falling under this heading. Indeed, some people defend this funding simply as a way of ensuring that ethnic groups are not discriminated against in state funding of art and culture. Some people believe that public funding agencies have traditionally been biased in favour of European-derived forms of cultural expression, and programmes targeted at ethnic groups remedy this bias. A related demand . . . is for the provision of immigrant language education in schools.

Perhaps the most controversial demand of ethnic groups is for exemptions from laws and regulations that disadvantage them, given their religious practices. For example, Jews and Muslims in Britain have sought exemption from Sunday closing or animal slaughtering legislation; Sikh men in Canada have sought exemption from motorcycle helmet laws and from the official dress-codes of police forces, so that they can wear their turban; Orthodox Jews in the United States have sought the right to wear the yarmulka during military service; and Muslim girls in France have sought exemption from school dress-codes so that they can wear the *chador*.

These group-specific measures—which I call "polyethnic rights"—are intended to help ethnic groups and religious minorities express their cultural particularity and pride without it hampering their success in the economic and political institutions of the dominant society. Like self-government rights, these polyethnic rights are not seen as temporary, because the cultural differences they protect are not something we seek to eliminate. But, ... unlike self-government rights, polyethnic rights are usually intended to promote integration into the larger society, not self-government.

3. Special Representation Rights   While the traditional concern of national minorities and ethnic groups has been with either self-government or polyethnic rights, there has been increasing interest by these groups, as well as other non-ethnic social groups, in the idea of special representation rights.

Throughout the Western democracies, there is increasing concern that the political process is "unrepresentative," in the sense that it fails to reflect the diversity of the population. Legislatures in most of these countries are dominated by middle-class, able-bodied, white men. A more representative process, it is said, would include members of ethnic and racial minorities, women, the poor, the disabled, etc. The under-representation of historically disadvantaged groups is a general phenomenon. In the United States and Canada, women, racial minorities, and indigenous peoples all have under one-third of the seats they would have based on their demographic weight. People with disabilities and the economically disadvantaged are also significantly underrepresented.

One way to reform the process is to make political parties more inclusive, by reducing the barriers which inhibit women, ethnic minorities, or the poor from becoming party candidates or party leaders; another way is to adopt some form of proportional representation, which has historically been associated with greater inclusiveness of candidates.

However, there is increasing interest in the idea that a certain number of seats in the legislature should be reserved for the members of disadvantaged or marginalized groups. During the debate in Canada over the Charlottetown Accord, for example, a number of recommendations were made for the guaranteed representation of women, ethnic minorities, official language minorities, and Aboriginals.

Group representation rights are often defended as a response to some systemic disadvantage or barrier in the political process which makes it impossible for the group's views and interests to be effectively represented. In so far as these rights are seen as a response to oppression or systemic disadvantage, they are most plausibly seen as a temporary measure on the way to a society where the need for special representation no longer exists—a form of political "affirmative action." Society should seek to remove the oppression and disadvantage, thereby eliminating the need for these rights.

However, the issue of special representation rights for groups is complicated, because special representation is sometimes defended, not on grounds of oppression, but as a corollary of self-government. A minority's right to self-government would be severely weakened if some external body could unilaterally revise or revoke its powers, without consulting the minority or securing its consent. Hence it would seem to be a corollary of self-government that the national minority be guaranteed representation on any body which can interpret or modify its powers of self-government (e.g. the Supreme Court). Since the claims of self-government are seen as inherent and permanent, so too are the guarantees of representation which flow from it (unlike guarantees grounded on oppression).

This is just a brief sketch of three mechanisms used to accommodate cultural differences. . . . Virtually every modern democracy employs one or more of these mechanisms. Obviously, these three kinds of rights can overlap, in the sense that some groups can claim more than one kind of right. For example, indigenous groups may demand both special representation in the central government, in virtue of their disadvantaged position, and various powers of self-government, in virtue of their status as a "people" or "nation." But these rights need not go together. An oppressed group, like the disabled, may seek special representation, but have no basis for claiming either self-government or polyethnic rights. Conversely, an economically successful immigrant group may seek polyethnic rights, but have no basis for claiming either special representation or self-government, etc. ■

View from the Inside

Only in the 1970s did the Supreme Court begin to enforce the rights of women—and men—to be free from sex discrimination. In a series of cases, the Court held that sex discrimination is permissible only if the government can show an "exceedingly persuasive justification" for its actions, and that laws or policies should be based on "reasoned analysis" rather than the "mechanical application of traditional, often inaccurate assumptions about the proper roles of men and women."* Applying this standard in 1982, for example, the Court held that a public university in Mississippi could not exclude men from its nursing program.

The Court's decisions brought into question the constitutionality of excluding women from public military colleges, such as the Citadel in South Carolina and the Virginia Military Institute (VMI). Suits were filed against both universities by otherwise-qualified female applicants who had been rejected for admission solely because of their gender. The universities mounted a spirited defense, but the Supreme Court (in the VMI case) ruled that males-only admissions policies were unconstitutional under the Fourteenth Amendment.

The following selection draws heavily from the testimony of witnesses for VMI during the trial phase of the litigation, which (after the U.S. government joined in) was known as *United States* v. *Virginia.*

Mississippi University for Women v. Hogan, 458 U.S. 718 (1982), at 724, 726.

Question

1. How do the VMI officials justify the exclusion of women from the university? Do their arguments reflect "reasoned analysis" or the "mechanical application of traditional, often inaccurate assumptions about the proper roles of men and women?"

4.6 Women in the Barracks (2002)

Philippa Strum

... There were two teams of attorneys crowding the counsel tables. Judith Keith, Nathaniel Douglas (chief of the Educational Opportunities Section), John Moore (his deputy), and Michael Maurer were there for the Justice Department. VMI and the VMI Foundation were represented by Robert Patterson, Anne Marie Whittemore, William G. Broaddus, and J. William Boland—all from Patterson's firm—and former U.S. attorney general Griffin Bell. ... They rose as Judge [Jackson L.] Kiser stepped to his seat behind the bench, and Douglas remained standing to introduce his colleagues. He then turned the floor over to John Moore, who made the opening statement for the government: "May it please the Court, distinguished counsel, while this is a very important case and in some ways a very emotional case, it is not a complicated case. ... It is not disputed that VMI does not admit women. ... This constitutes sex discrimination."

That was the government's overarching assertion: the case was about gender discrimination. The Justice Department lawyers had decided to emphasize a few crucial arguments: VMI was a state-funded school, its admissions policy was exclusionary, there was no similar program for women available elsewhere in the commonwealth, and there was no persuasive justification for keeping women out. The last point had two prongs: women could meet the challenges at VMI, and there was a demand by women for the VMI experience. When Judith Keith was asked by friends and colleagues why any young woman would want to subject herself to life at VMI as it was described at the trial—or, for that matter, why any young man would choose to do so—her answer was that VMI did not attract the average guy and would not attract the average woman. But if Virginia provided that kind of education for men, it had to make it equally available for women. The legal standard to that effect was clear, she maintained, but more important, it was a simple matter of fundamental fairness. ...

Because the government considered it obvious that the case was a simple one about gender discrimination, its attorneys saw no need for a long opening statement. The differences between its approach and VMI's, in both style and substance, became apparent as soon as Robert Patterson rose to introduce the case for VMI.

> We had a little trouble getting used to this case, Your Honor, because when the representatives from the Civil Rights Division stand up and say the United States against VMI, it just strikes a chord in my soul, because always before it has been VMI *for* the United States. When the chips are down, VMI has never let this country down and they never will. So it troubles me and I wonder what is the motivation, which I think any lawyer would speculate on, as to why the United States Government would pick a little tiny school in a little town, 1300 students, come down with the entire forces of this government arrayed against us.

Having established Virginia as a bewildered but feisty David confronted by the federal government's Goliath, Patterson argued that the dispute was entirely Washington's fault: "It is fairly apparent to me that the Justice Department, especially the Civil Rights Division, still does not understand VMI." As a result, federal bureaucrats were attacking the sovereignty of the state, asserting that "the federal government does things one way, Virginia should be forced to do it that way, too." The government said that it was merely enforcing the law, but that was not true: "The Constitution doesn't require what they ask for here."

As Patterson saw it, something else was at the heart of the case, and the government was avoiding the real question. "The issue before you, Your Honor, is a simple one. It is whether VMI's system of education...is going to be permitted to survive. And in the largest sense, one might say that single sex education in and of itself, certainly for men, and logically also for women, is on trial here today."

That was what the case was about to the VMI team: would the radicals in Washington destroy both VMI and single-sex education throughout the United States in their attempt to deny biological realities and remake the world in an unnatural image? As for the equal protection clause, well, Patterson firmly believed that it meant whatever the Supreme Court decided it meant. And he could not believe that the Court intended it to exclude single-sex colleges. . . .

[As its first witness, the government] called [VMI superintendent] General [John William] Knapp. . . . Knapp was asked to describe the mission of VMI ("To produce educated and honorable men") and to define a citizen-soldier ("It's a person who is educated for the work of civil life but prepared in time of national peril to defend the country"), admitting that nothing in the definition precluded the admission of women. Didn't other state institutions produce honorable citizen-soldiers, Douglas asked? Yes, replied Knapp, but "the method is distinctive."

> Q: Now, has the same system been in place since VMI has started?
> A: The same object has been in place. There have been natural changes.

The word *change* would be a battle front throughout the trial. VMI maintained that it would be destroyed if it was forced to change; the Justice Department sought to show that VMI had embraced and thrived under change. Douglas pushed Knapp:

> Q: What have been the natural changes?
> A: Electricity and plumbing in the barracks.

At this point, Kiser interjected:

> THE COURT: It was tough in the old days, wasn't it?
>
> THE WITNESS: Yes, sir. It's still tough, but those are the kinds of changes I mean and I could go on with the electronic analogy. We even have computers now, but very few telephones.

The questioning continued:

> Q: When you say change, you would have to make the change, is it your judgment that there is no other system that will work, or that you just like the one you have, and therefore, it should not be changed?
>
> A: Well, it's my position that we have a successful one now that we would have to set aside, and I can't really tell you what the new one would look like.
>
> THE COURT: Why would the females, assuming, as we have been so far, that the number of females that might demand education at VMI would be small, why would they have to participate in [the hazing rituals engaged in by male cadets]? Once you say you have two classes, couldn't they function separately?
>
> THE WITNESS: Well, yes, sir, but I think you are building another school for the females that is not VMI.
>
> THE COURT: It would still be the same VMI for the males, wouldn't it?
>
> THE WITNESS: I think it would become a coed educational institution. I don't think you could run a separate one. You might as well set it up in some other town.
>
> THE COURT: Well, if you have a limited number of females and you want to continue your. . . [hazing rituals] basically in the male portion of the barracks, why can't you do it?
>
> THE WITNESS: Well, sir, I think we could go ahead and try to run it, but our system is to have 100 percent residents in the barracks and everybody takes the same thing.
>
> THE COURT: I understand that, but as Mr. Douglas has said, is that just a matter of preference, or is it a matter of necessity?
>
> THE WITNESS: Your Honor, I think for us to keep VMI, it's a necessity. We don't have any other classification of students, they don't live off post, they don't go to VMI without going through [hazing rituals] and establishing their class and having the class system, and the—and we might as well be told to start that, what Mr. Patterson referred to as an all female military academy somewhere nearby but not on post.

The exchange showed as much about Kiser's assumptions as it did about Knapp's: if women were admitted to VMI, it would be a "matter of necessity" either to change the. . . [hazing rituals] or to excuse women from it. Knapp listed other aspects of VMI life that he presumed would have to be altered: the lack of locks on the doors, the all-revealing windows in them, the absence of lights around the post. The details were telling in their suggestion of a safe, self-contained, homogeneous institution and of the all-pervasive and ultimately cohesive atmosphere that VMI was fighting to preserve.

Judith Keith stood to call Colonel Norman M. Bissell as the government's next witness. "Mike" Bissell had graduated from VMI in 1961. After spending twenty-six years in the army and a few in industry, he had become VMI's commandant of cadets in the summer of 1990. . . .

Keith put Bissell through a grueling series of questions about life at VMI.... At each stage in the testimony, she asked whether a determination had been made that women could not successfully complete the activity he described; at each stage, the answer was no. His answers to her questions and to Whittemore's during cross-examination, however, made it clear that he did not consider that to be the issue. They also provided the media with their first clear glimpse of life at VMI and so would be quoted with both bemusement and awe over the next five years. . . .

> A: I like to think VMI literally dissects the young student that comes in there, kind of pulls him apart, and through the stress, everything that goes on in that environment, would teach him to know everything about himself. He truly knows how far he can go with his anger, he knows how much he can take under stress, he knows how much he can take when he is totally tired, he knows just exactly what he can do when he is physically exhausted, he fully understands himself and his limits and capabilities.... I think every VMI man that leaves there knows a great deal about his human capacity to do things under all kinds of duress and stress.
>
> Q: At VMI is mental and physical stress critical to the leadership training?
>
> A: I would agree totally, ma'am. . . . I think our theme is to create a stressful environment and to put as much stress on a cadet as possible to see how he reacts and handles situations under that duress . . . stress is the key fundamental of what we do.
>
> Q: Is it correct, then, that stress is purposely imposed at VMI? In other words, there is stress for the purpose of inducing stress?
>
> A: Yes, ma'am.

Bissell described the rigors of [cadet life] and then went on to the cadets' living quarters. "Basically," he said, "the rooms are very, very spartan"—a word that became synonymous with VMI during the trial—and [cadet life] had "far more dramatic, more pressure, more stress than boot camp or basic camp" in the military. If a rat [cadet] was expelled for having violated the honor code, his disgrace was emphasized by his having to creep out of VMI in the dark hours after midnight when the other cadets were asleep.

Bissell depicted [these rituals] as symbolic of what VMI was trying to accomplish, and his description of himself—a middle-aged colonel—slithering through the muck because he "wanted to see what the rats experienced" conveyed something of the VMI spirit. (He would later say that he was glad he had gone through it once but would not dream of putting himself through the experience again.)

[This], he implicitly suggested, was not the kind of activity he would recommend for mixed groups of men and women.

> A: You are in close contact with each other, you are working with each other, in some cases hanging onto each other, as you are moving up that cliff and moving across. . . . Frequently there is a lot of exposure to bodies where clothes are ripped, as you can well imagine from pulling and tugging, there are a lot of body exposure factors that go on there.

Keith asked about VMI's demanding physical education program, which Bissell said was designed both to get the cadets into "good shape" and "to bond them together."

> Q: To your knowledge, has VMI made any determination that women students could not satisfactorily participate in this military drill or any of these PE exercises?
>
> A: No, I don't feel that VMI or anybody has determined that probably they could or could not do it. I don't think that's the issue at all.... [But] once they penetrated VMI, it would break up that totally knit value system where we are all down to the same common

base, all taking showers together, all working together, all living together, without any difference whatsoever.... It would change it dramatically.

During cross-examination, Bissell elaborated on his fear that [life at VMI] would be changed by women:

> I have visions of standing there and watching a young lady...with five upperclassmen standing around her, and I can see one screaming at the top of his lungs, jump down and give me 20 push ups, another one standing there saying, give me the menu for lunch, the third one standing there saying, let's have the [list of] superintendents since the inception of the institute, a fourth one sending her up... because of a dirty belt buckle and a fifth sending her up for conduct [un]becoming a cadet. I see that young lady is going to have trouble with these people all putting full force on her.

The trouble the "young lady" would have was inherent in her more sensitive nature:

> My experience in the Army has told me that women basically have not the same threshold on emotion as men do. . . . When I was a commander of a group and a battalion once . . . my battalion commanders and I had several sessions over that, how do you handle this, they break down emotionally, only because it's the culture and society.
>
> You don't treat them the same. You back off, you say come back in again when you have your composure, you have yourself back together and we will address your punishment. Inevitably you soften or reconsider the punishment over that period of time. I take that same analogy and I put a young lady. . . with a bunch of upperclassmen all over her, she breaks down crying, not only is it going to be terribly demeaning to her, but I wonder how the 18 to 20 year old upperclassmen are going to handle that.... I could see after that happened two or three times, the upperclassmen would back off, wouldn't even bother her, stop her...she would not be part of the. . . [hazing system], be walking around the barracks and not part of the system.

One of Keith's goals in questioning Bissell was to demonstrate that there were no activities at VMI that could not be done by women, and she thought she had been successful in that. She saw his testimony as a reflection of the kind of gender stereotyping the law forbade, and she believed that the VMI lawyers had reserved their cross-examination and questioned him later in the trial to give both him and themselves time to recoup. Bissell remembered Keith getting angrier and angrier as she repeatedly demanded, "Can't women do that? Can't women do that?" At the end of his testimony, as he recalled it, she was so irate that she crumpled up a piece of paper and threw it to the floor, announcing, "That's all I have" in a tone of disgust. To her, his attempts to depict . . . [the hazing system] as "a real rite of passage" rang hollow. To Patterson, however, Bissell's description of VMI rang entirely true. That was the school as he knew it; that was the egalitarian institution about which he would say, "this is an especially good system for people like me, who come from a modest background."

When Bissell stepped down, Kiser adjourned court for the day. Neither side had made any impact on the other. Bissell had perhaps unwittingly typified VMI's sense of horror at the prospect of female cadets: they would have "penetrated" VMI, the way an enemy penetrates a line of defense. The government maintained that when a public institution was involved, women had a right to be on the inside along with the men. What Kiser thought was as yet unknown. ■

 Chapter 5

Political Culture and Public Opinion

Political culture and public opinion are closely interrelated. Both refer to the beliefs, values, and ideas held by the people of a nation. But there is a key difference: political culture involves beliefs, values, and ideas that are deeply held and widely shared, whereas public opinion focuses on the people's views on a wide range of issues and controversies. Thus public opinion may change from moment to moment, while a nation's political culture may remain remarkably stable over time—even over many generations.

In modern times, public opinion is weighed and measured on an ongoing basis, primarily through the use of public opinion polls. Many such polls are conducted by news organizations; others are carried out by academic researchers, commercial polling firms, and political organizations and campaigns. Polls can be manipulated or mismanaged, of course, but on the whole they provide an accurate snapshot of Americans' views on a variety of subjects.

By contrast, American political culture is notoriously difficult to measure. Pronouncements on the subject are likely to be filled with assumptions and overgeneralizations, and often neglect minority viewpoints and subcultures. Used judiciously, however, political culture is an important concept that can provide keen insights into the nature of American society and politics.

Because we are immersed in our own political culture, Americans may have difficulty even seeing that we have an identifiable and common set of beliefs about government and politics. Perhaps the best way to understand American political culture, therefore, is to see ourselves through the eyes of people from other cultures.

The most noteworthy foreign observer of American politics in our history was Alexis de Tocqueville (selection 5.1). Tocqueville visited the United States in the 1830s and, like many other observers of the American scene, was struck by the American commitment to equality, liberty, participation in politics, and religion. To this day, visitors to the United States often remark on the informal, easy manner in which Americans relate to one another, on our deep-seated religiosity, and—at least until recently—on our passion for politics. We are, in a word, a *democratic* society—not only in politics but also in our attitudes toward public and private life. Our underlying belief in democracy and all it connotes forms an essential part of the American polity.

This chapter examines several different aspects of political culture and public opinion in the United States. In addition to an excerpt from Tocqueville, the chapter presents a report on the "culture war" that seems to divide America (selection 5.2), a discussion of the long-running argument as to whether American political culture is fundamentally different from that of other nations (selection 5.3), and an analysis of the ways in which the Bush administration uses public opinion polling data (selection 5.4). Throughout, the common theme is to explore the underlying beliefs and values upon which the American political system rests.

Chapter Questions

1. What attitudes and assumptions about politics are distinctly "American"—that is, seem to be widely held by most Americans no matter what their background or political affiliation? How do these attitudes and assumptions differ from those of other nations?
2. How have American political culture and Americans' political beliefs changed since Tocqueville visited 170 years ago? Since the 1960s? Since the early 1990s? Are these changes permanent and fundamental, or fleeting and insignificant?

 # Foundations

Alexis de Tocqueville, a French nobleman, traveled to the United States in 1831 to study and report back to the French government on the American prison system. As a result of his nine-month trip, he produced not only a report on the prison system but also *Democracy in America,* which, published in 1835, was immediately hailed as a masterpiece of political and social commentary. It remains one of the most important books ever written about American political life. (Tocqueville, incidentally, was accompanied on his trip by his friend Gustave de Beaumont, who also wrote a book on America. It was a novel about a slave woman in Baltimore, titled *Marie,* or *Slavery in the United States.*)

Although he wrote more than 170 years ago, Tocqueville's keen observations of life in the United States offer insights into American political culture that are still valid. The following excerpt highlights the nature of American democracy and the centrality of equality to Americans' understanding of politics.

Questions

1. To what extent is American politics today still based on the idea of equality? Consider not only questions of legal or political equality but also questions of social equality.
2. What examples from modern life support Tocqueville's views on the nature of American democracy? What examples contradict his analysis?

5.1 Democracy in America (1835)

Alexis de Tocqueville

Social Condition of the Anglo-Americans

A social condition is commonly the result of circumstances, sometimes of laws, oftener still of these two causes united; but wherever it exists, it may justly be considered as the source of almost all the laws, the usages, and the ideas, which regulate the conduct of nations: whatever it does not produce, it modifies.

It is, therefore, necessary, if we would become acquainted with the legislation and the manners of a nation, to begin by the study of its social condition.

The Striking Characteristic of the Social Condition of the Anglo-Americans Is Its Essential Democracy

Many important observations suggest themselves upon the social condition of the Anglo-Americans; but there is one which takes precedence of all the rest. The social condition of the Americans is eminently democratic; this was its character at the foundation of the colonies, and is still more strongly marked at the present day.

[Great] equality existed among the emigrants who settled on the shores of New England. The germ of aristocracy was never planted in that part of the Union. The only influence which obtained there was that of intellect; the people were used to reverence certain names as the emblems of knowledge and virtue. Some of their fellow-citizens acquired a power over the rest which might truly have been called aristocratic, if it had been capable of invariable transmission from father to son.

This was the state of things to the east of the Hudson: to the southwest of that river, and in the direction of the Floridas, the case was different. In most of the states situated to the southwest of the Hudson some great English proprietors had settled, who had imported with them aristocratic principles and the English law of descent. I have explained the reasons why it was impossible ever to establish a powerful aristocracy in America; these reasons existed with less force to the southwest of the Hudson. In the south, one man, aided by slaves, could cultivate a great extent of country: it was therefore common to see rich landed proprietors. But their influence was not altogether aristocratic as that term is understood in Europe, since they possessed no privileges; and the cultivation of their estates being carried on by slaves, they had no tenants depending on them, and consequently no patronage. Still, the great proprietors south of the Hudson constituted a superior class, having ideas and tastes of its own, and forming the center of political action. This kind of aristocracy sympathized with the body of the people, whose passions and interests it easily embraced; but it was too weak and too short-lived to excite either love or hatred for itself. This was the class which headed the insurrection in the south, and furnished the best leaders of the American revolution.

At the period of which we are now speaking, society was shaken to its center: the people, in whose name the struggle had taken place, conceived the desire of exercising the authority which it had acquired; its democratic tendencies were awakened; and having thrown off the yoke of the mother-country, it aspired to independence of every kind. The influence of individuals gradually ceased to be felt, and custom and law united together to produce the same result.

But the law of descent was the last step to equality. I am surprised that ancient and modern jurists have not attributed to this law a greater influence on human affairs. It is true that these laws belong to civil affairs: but they ought nevertheless to be placed at the head of all political institutions; for, while political laws are only the symbol of a nation's condition, they exercise an incredible influence upon its social state. They have, moreover, a sure and uniform manner of operating upon society, affecting, as it were, generations yet unborn.

Through their means man acquires a kind of preternatural power over the future lot of his fellow-creatures. When the legislator has once regulated the law of inheritance, he may rest from his labor. The machine once put in motion will go on for ages, and advance, as if self-guided, toward a given point. When framed in a particular manner, this law unites, draws together, and vests property and power in a few hands: its tendency is clearly aristocratic. On opposite principles its action is still more rapid; it divides, distributes, and disperses both property and power. Alarmed by the rapidity of its progress, those who despair of arresting its motion endeavor to obstruct by difficulties and impediments; they vainly seek to counteract its effect by contrary efforts: but it gradually reduces or destroys every obstacle, until by its incessant activity the bulwarks of the influence of wealth are ground down to the fine and shifting sand which is the basis of democracy. When the law of inheritance permits, still more when it decrees, the equal division of a father's property among all his children, its effects are of two kinds: it is important to distinguish them from each other, although they tend to the same end.

In virtue of the law of partible inheritance, the death of every proprietor brings about a kind of revolution in property: not only do his possessions change hands, but their very nature is altered; since they are parcelled into shares, which become smaller and smaller at each division. This is the direct, and, as it were, the physical effect of the law. It follows, then, that in countries where equality of inheritance is established by law, property, and especially landed property, must have a tendency to perpetual diminution. The effects, however, of such legislation would only be perceptible after a lapse of time, if the law was abandoned to its own working; for supposing a family to consist of two children (and in a country peopled as France is, the average number is not above three), these children, sharing among them the fortune of both parents, would not be poorer than their father or mother.

But the law of equal division exercises its influence not merely upon the property itself, but it affects the minds of the heirs, and brings their passions into play. These indirect consequences tend powerfully to the destruction of large fortunes, and especially of large domains.

Among the nations whose law of descent is founded upon the right of primogeniture, landed estates often pass from generation to generation without undergoing division. The consequence of which is, that family feeling is to a certain degree incorporated with the estate. The family represents the estate, the estate the family; whose name, together with its origin, its glory, its power, and its virtues, is thus perpetuated in an imperishable memorial of the past, and a sure pledge of the future.

When the equal partition of property is established by law, the intimate connection is destroyed between family feeling and the preservation of the paternal estate; the property ceases to represent the family; for, as it must inevitably be divided after one or two generations, it has evidently a constant tendency to diminish, and must in the end be completely dispersed. The sons of the great landed proprietor, if they are few in number, or if fortune befriend them, may indeed entertain the hope of being as wealthy as their father, but not that of possessing the same property as he did; their riches must necessarily be composed of elements different from his.

Now, from the moment when you divest the land-owner of that interest in the preservation of his estate which he derives from association, from tradition, and from family pride, you may be certain that sooner or later he will dispose of it; for there is a strong pecuniary interest in favor of selling, as floating capital produces higher interest than real property, and is more readily available to gratify the passions of the moment.

Great landed estates which have once been divided, never come together again; for the small proprietor draws from his land a better revenue in proportion, than the large owner does from his; and of course he sells it at a higher rate. The calculations of gain, therefore, which decided the rich man to sell his domain, will still more powerfully influence him against buying small estates to unite them into a large one.

What is called family pride is often founded upon an illusion of self-love. A man wishes to perpetuate and immortalize himself, as it were, in his great-grandchildren. Where the *esprit de famille* ceases to act, individual selfishness comes into play. When the idea of family becomes vague, indeterminate, and uncertain, a man thinks of his present convenience; he provides for the establishment of the succeeding generation, and no more.

Either a man gives up the idea of perpetuating his family, or at any rate he seeks to accomplish it by other means than that of a landed estate.

Thus not only does the law of partible inheritance render it difficult for families to preserve their ancestral domains entire, but it deprives them of the inclination to attempt it, and compels them in some measure to cooperate with the law in their own extinction.

The law of equal distribution proceeds by two methods: by acting upon things, it acts upon persons; by influencing persons, it affects things. By these means the law succeeds in striking at the root of landed property, and dispersing rapidly both families and fortunes.

Most certainly it is not for us, Frenchmen of the nineteenth century, who daily behold the political and social changes which the law of partition is bringing to pass, to question its influence. It is perpetually conspicuous in our country, overthrowing the walls of our dwellings and removing the landmarks of our fields. But although it has produced great effects in France, much still remains for it to do. Our recollections, opinions, and habits, present powerful obstacles to its progress.

In the United States it has nearly completed its work of destruction, and there we can best study its results. The English laws concerning the transmission of property were abolished in almost all the states at the time of the revolution. The law of entail was so modified as not to interrupt the free circulation of property. The first having passed away, estates began to be parcelled out; and the change became more and more rapid with the progress of time. At this moment, after a lapse of little more than sixty years, the aspect of society is totally altered; the families of the great landed proprietors are almost all commingled with the general mass. In the state of New York, which formerly contained many of these, there are but two who still keep their heads above the stream; and they must shortly disappear. The sons of these opulent citizens have become merchants, lawyers, or physicians. Most of them have lapsed into obscurity. The last trace of hereditary ranks and distinctions is destroyed—the law of partition has reduced all to one level.

I do not mean that there is any deficiency of wealthy individuals in the United States; I know of no country, indeed, where the love of money has taken stronger hold on the affections of men, and where a profounder contempt is expressed for the theory of the permanent equality of property. But wealth circulates with inconceivable rapidity, and experience shows that it is rare to find two succeeding generations in the full enjoyment of it.

This picture, which may perhaps be thought overcharged, still gives a very imperfect idea of what is taking place in the new states of the west and southwest. At the end of the last century a few bold adventurers began to penetrate into the valleys of the Mississippi, and the mass of the population very soon began to move in that direction: communities unheard of till then were seen to emerge from their wilds: states, whose names were not in existence a few years before, claimed their place in the American Union; and in the western settlements we may behold democracy arrived at its utmost extreme. In these states, founded off hand, and as it were by chance, the inhabitants are but of yesterday. Scarcely known to one another, the nearest neighbors are ignorant of each other's history. In this part of the American continent, therefore, the population has not experienced the influence of great names and great wealth, nor even that of the natural aristocracy of knowledge and virtue. None are there to wield that respectable power which men willingly grant to the remembrance of a life spent in doing good before their eyes. The new states of the west are already inhabited; but society has no existence among them.

It is not only the fortunes of men which are equal in America; even their acquirements partake in some degree of the same uniformity. I do not believe there is a country in the world where, in proportion to the population, there are so few uninstructed, and at the same time so few learned individuals. Primary instruction is within the reach of everybody; superior instruction is scarcely to be obtained by any. This is not surprising; it is in fact the necessary consequence of what we have advanced above. Almost all the Americans are in easy circumstances, and can therefore obtain the first elements of human knowledge.

In America there are comparatively few who are rich enough to live without a profession. Every profession requires an apprenticeship, which limits the time of instruction to the early years of life. At fifteen they enter upon their calling, and thus their education ends at the age when ours begins. Whatever is done afterward, is with a view to some special and lucrative object; a science is taken up as a matter of business, and the only branch of it which is attended to is such as admits of an immediate practical application.

In America most of the rich men were formerly poor: most of those who now enjoy leisure were absorbed in business during their youth; the consequence of which is, that when they might have had a taste for study they had no time for it, and when the time is at their disposal they have no longer the inclination.

There is no class, then, in America in which the taste for intellectual pleasures is transmitted with hereditary fortune and leisure, and by which the labors of the intellect are held in honor. Accordingly there is an equal want of the desire and the power of application to these objects.

A middling standard is fixed in America for human knowledge. All approach as near to it as they can; some as they rise, others as they descend. Of course, an immense multitude of persons are to be found who entertain the same number of ideas on religion, history, science, political economy, legislation, and government. The gifts of intellect proceed directly from God, and man cannot prevent their unequal distribution. But in consequence of the state of things which we have here represented, it happens, that although the capacities of men are widely different, as the Creator has doubtless intended they should be, they are submitted to the same method of treatment.

In America the aristocratic element has always been feeble from its birth; and if at the present day it is not actually destroyed, it is at any rate so completely disabled that we can scarcely assign to it any degree of influence in the course of affairs.

The democratic principle, on the contrary, has gained so much strength by time, by events, and by legislation, as to have become not only predominant but all-powerful. There is no family or corporate authority, and it is rare to find even the influence of individual character enjoy any durability.

America, then, exhibits in her social state a most extraordinary phenomenon. Men are there seen on a greater equality in point of fortune and intellect, or in other words, more equal in their strength, than in any other country of the world, or, in any age of which history has preserved the remembrance.

Political Consequences of the Social Condition of the Anglo-Americans

The political consequences of such a social condition as this are easily deductible.

It is impossible to believe that equality will not everywhere find its way into the political world as it does everywhere else. To conceive of men remaining for ever unequal upon one single point, yet equal on all others, is impossible; they must come in the end to be equal upon all.

Now I know of only two methods of establishing equality in the political world: every citizen must be put in possession of his rights, or rights must be granted to no one. For nations which have arrived at the same stage of social existence as the Anglo-Americans, it is therefore very difficult to discover a medium between the sovereignty of all and the absolute power of one man: and it would be vain to deny that the social condition which I have been describing is equally liable to each of these consequences.

There is, in fact, a manly and lawful passion for equality, which excites men to wish all to be powerful and honored. This passion tends to elevate the humble to the rank of the great; but there exists also in the human heart a depraved taste for equality, which impels the weak to attempt to lower the powerful to their own level, and reduces men to prefer equality in slavery to inequality with freedom. Not that those nations whose social condition is democratic naturally despise liberty; on the contrary, they have an instinctive love of it. But liberty is not the chief and constant object of their desire; equality is their idol: they make rapid and sudden efforts to obtain liberty, and if they miss their aim, resign themselves to their disappointment; but nothing can satisfy them except equality, and rather than lose it they resolve to perish.

On the other hand, in a state where the citizens are nearly on an equality, it becomes difficult for them to preserve their independence against the aggressions of power. No one among them being strong enough to engage singly in the struggle with advantage, nothing but a general combination can protect their liberty: and such a union is not always to be found.

From the same social position, then, nations may derive one or the other of two great political results; these results are extremely different from each other, but they may both proceed from the same cause.

The Anglo-Americans are the first who, having been exposed to this formidable alternative, have been happy enough to escape the dominion of absolute power. They have been allowed by their circumstances, their origin, their intelligence, and especially by their moral feeling, to establish and maintain the sovereignty of the people.

• • •

Political Associations in the United States

In no country in the world has the principle of association been more successfully used, or more unsparingly applied to a multitude of different objects, than in America. Beside the permanent associations which are established by law under the names of townships, cities, and counties, a vast number of others are formed and maintained by the agency of private individuals.

The citizen of the United States is taught from his earliest infancy to rely upon his own exertions, in order to resist the evils and the difficulties of life; he looks upon the social authority with an eye of mistrust and anxiety, and he only claims its assistance when he is quite unable to shift without it. This habit may even be traced in the schools of the rising generation, where the children in their games are wont to submit to rules which they have themselves established, and to punish misdemeanors which they have themselves defined. The same spirit pervades every act of social life. If a stoppage occurs in a thoroughfare, and the circulation of the public is hindered, the neighbors immediately constitute a deliberative body; and this extemporaneous assembly gives rise to an executive power, which remedies the inconvenience, before anybody has thought of recurring to an authority superior to that of the persons immediately concerned. If the public pleasures are concerned, an association is formed to provide for the splendor and the regularity of the entertainment. Societies are formed to resist enemies which are exclusively of a moral nature, and to diminish the vice of intemperance: in the United States associations are established to promote public order, commerce, industry, morality, and religion; for there is no end which the human will, seconded by the collective exertions of individuals, despairs of attaining.

I shall hereafter have occasion to show the effects of association upon the course of society, and I must confine myself for the present to the political world. When once the right of association is recognized, the citizens may employ it in several different ways.

An association consists simply in the public assent which a number of individuals give to certain doctrines; and in the engagement which they contract to promote the spread of those doctrines by their exertions. The right of associating with these views is very analogous to the liberty of unlicensed writing; but societies thus formed possess more authority than the press. When an opinion is represented by a society, it necessarily assumes a more exact and explicit form. It numbers its partisans, and compromises their welfare in its cause; they, on the other hand, become acquainted with each other, and their zeal is increased by their number. An association unites the efforts of minds which have a tendency to diverge, in one single channel, and urges them vigorously toward one single end which it points out.

The second degree in the right of association is the power of meeting. When an association is allowed to establish centers of action at certain important points in the country, its activity is increased, and its influence extended. Men have the opportunity of seeing each other; means of execution are more readily combined; and opinions are maintained with a degree of warmth and energy which written language cannot approach. . . .

Why Democratic Nations Show a More Ardent and Enduring Love of Equality Than of Liberty

The first and most intense passion which is engendered by the equality of conditions is, I need hardly say, the love of that same equality. My readers will therefore not be surprised that I speak of it before all others.

Everybody has remarked, that in our time, and especially in France, this passion for equality is every day gaining ground in the human heart. It has been said a hundred times that our contemporaries are far more ardently and tenaciously attached to equality than to freedom; but, as I do not find that the causes of the fact have been sufficiently analyzed, I shall endeavor to point them out.

It is possible to imagine an extreme point at which freedom and equality would meet and be confounded together. Let us suppose that all the members of the community take a part in the government, and that each one of them has an equal right to take a part in it. As none is different from his fellows, none can exercise a tyrannical power: men will be perfectly free, because they will all be entirely equal; and they will all be perfectly equal, because they will be entirely free. To this ideal state democratic nations tend. Such is the completest form that equality can assume upon earth; but there are a thousand others which, without being equally perfect, are not less cherished by those nations.

The principle of equality may be established in civil society, without prevailing in the political world. Equal rights may exist of indulging in the same pleasures, of entering the same professions, of frequenting the same places—in a word, of living in the same manner and seeking wealth by the same means, although all men do not take an equal share in the government.

A kind of equality may even be established in the political world, though there should be no political freedom there. A man may be the equal of all his country-men save one, who is the master of all without distinction, and who selects equally from among them all the agents of his power.

Several other combinations might be easily imagined, by which very great equality would be united to institutions more or less free, or even to institutions wholly without freedom.

Although men cannot become absolutely equal unless they be entirely free, and consequently equality, pushed to its furthest extent, may be confounded with free-dom, yet there is good reason for distinguishing the one from the other. The taste which men have for liberty, and that which they feel for equality, are, in fact, two different things; and I am not afraid to add, that, among democratic nations, they are two unequal things.

Upon close inspection, it will be seen that there is in every age some peculiar and preponderating fact with which all others are connected; this fact almost al-ways gives birth to some pregnant idea or some ruling passion, which attracts to it-self, and bears away in its course, all the feelings and opinions of the time: it is like a great stream, toward which each of the surrounding rivulets seem to flow.

Freedom has appeared in the world at different times and under various forms; it has not been exclusively bound to any social condition, and it is not confined to democracies. Freedom cannot, therefore, form the distinguishing characteristic of democratic ages. The peculiar and preponderating fact which marks those ages as its own is the equality of conditions; the ruling passion of men in those periods is the love of this equality. Ask not what singular charm the men of democratic ages find in being equal, or what special reasons they may have for clinging so tena-ciously to equality rather than to the other advantages which society holds out to them: equality is the distinguishing characteristic of the age they live in; that, of itself, is enough to explain that they prefer it to all the rest.

But independently of this reason there are several others, which will at all times habitually lead men to prefer equality to freedom.

If a people could ever succeed in destroying, or even in diminishing, the equal-ity which prevails in its own body, this could only be accomplished by long and laborious efforts. Its social condition must be modified, its laws abolished, its opin-ions superseded, its habits changed, its manners corrupted. But political liberty is more easily lost; to neglect to hold it fast, is to allow it to escape.

Men therefore not only cling to equality because it is dear to them; they also adhere to it because they think it will last for ever.

That political freedom may compromise in its excesses the tranquillity, the property, the lives of individuals, is obvious to the narrowest and most unthinking minds. But, on the contrary, none but attentive and clear-sighted men perceive the perils with which equality threatens us, and they commonly avoid pointing them out. They know that the calamities they apprehend are remote, and flatter themselves that they will only fall upon future generations, for which the present generation takes but little thought. The evils which freedom sometimes brings with it are immediate; they are apparent to all, and all are more or less affected by them. The evils which extreme equality may produce are slowly disclosed; they creep gradually into the social frame; they are only seen at intervals, and at the moment at which they become most violent, habit already causes them to be no longer felt.

The advantages which freedom brings are only shown by length of time; and it is always easy to mistake the cause in which they originate. The advantages of equality are instantaneous, and they may constantly be traced from their source.

Political liberty bestows exalted pleasures, from time to time, upon a certain number of citizens. Equality every day confers a number of small enjoyments on every man. The charms of equality are every instant felt, and are within the reach of all: the noblest hearts are not insensible to them, and the most vulgar souls exult in them. The passion which equality engenders must therefore be at once strong and general. Men cannot enjoy political liberty unless it has been purchased by some sacrifices, and they never obtain it without great exertions. But the pleasures of equality are self-proffered: each of the petty incidents of life seems to occasion them, and in order to taste them nothing is required but to live.

Democratic nations are at all times fond of equality, but there are certain epochs at which the passion they entertain for it swells to the height of fury. This occurs at the moment when the old social system, long menaced, completes its own destruction after a last intestine struggle, and when the barriers of rank are at length thrown down. At such times men pounce upon equality as their booty, and they cling to it as to some precious treasure which they fear to lose. The passion for equality penetrates on every side into men's hearts, expands there, and fills them entirely. Tell them not that by this blind surrender of themselves to an exclusive passion, they risk their dearest interests: they are deaf. Show them not freedom escaping from their grasp, while they are looking another way: they are blind—or rather, they can discern but one sole object to be desired in the universe.

What I have said is applicable to all democratic nations: what I am about to say concerns the French alone. Among most modern nations, and especially among all those of the continent of Europe, the taste and the idea of freedom only began to exist and to extend itself at the time when social conditions were tending to equality, and as a consequence of that very equality. Absolute kings were the most efficient levellers of ranks among their subjects. Among these nations equality preceded freedom: equality was therefore a fact of some standing, when freedom was still a novelty: the one had already created customs, opinions, and laws belonging to it, when the other, alone and for the first time, came into actual existence. Thus the latter was still only an affair of opinion and of taste, while the former had already crept into the habits of the people, possessed itself of their manners, and given a particular turn to the smallest actions in their lives. Can it be wondered that the men of our own time prefer the one to the other?

I think that democratic communities have a natural taste for freedom: left to themselves, they will seek it, cherish it, and view any privation of it with regret. But for equality, their passion is ardent, insatiable, incessant, invincible: they call for equality in freedom; if they cannot obtain that, they still call for equality in slavery. They will endure poverty, servitude, barbarism—but they will not endure aristocracy.

This is true at all times, and especially true in our own. All men and all powers seeking to cope with this irresistible passion, will be overthrown and destroyed by it. In our age, freedom cannot be established without it, and despotism itself cannot reign without its support. ■

American Politics Today

Politics in the modern era hardly seems to support the idea that Americans are united in a common political culture. Instead, politics today seems to emphasize a wide range of conflicts over fundamental values. Some Americans have even proclaimed the existence of a "culture war" starkly dividing the nation as never before.

Never was this cultural divide more readily apparent than on election night 2000. As the networks tallied the state-by-state vote for president, they colored in a wall map of the United States—red for Bush, blue for Gore. Most of America—geographically speaking, at least—was covered in a red swath that blanketed the South, the heartland of the Midwest, and the states of the Rocky Mountains. Small dots of blue could be seen mostly in the populous (but physically small) states of the Northeast and along the Atlantic coast, and in a narrow strip alongside the Pacific Ocean.

The journalist David Brooks—a resident of Montgomery County, Maryland, in "Blue America"—set out on a journey to discover "Red America." His report is not always accurate, but it is revealing and provocative. In the end, Brooks decides that Red and Blue America are indeed parts of the same country.

Questions

1. What are the predominant characteristics of Red and Blue America? In what ways are Brooks's descriptions of Red and Blue America accurate? In what ways are they inaccurate?
2. What values do Red and Blue America share? On what values do they disagree?
3. Why do Red and Blue America vote so differently on election night? What was it about George W. Bush that appealed to Red America? What was it about Al Gore that appealed to Blue America?

5.2 One Nation, Slightly Divisible (2001)

David Brooks

• • •

Montgomery County is one of the steaming-hot centers of the great espresso machine that is Blue America. It is just over the border from northwestern Washington, D.C., and it is full of upper-middle-class towns inhabited by lawyers, doctors, stockbrokers, and establishment journalists like me—town like Chevy Chase, Potomac, and Bethesda (where I live). Its central artery is a burgeoning high-tech corridor with a multitude of sparkling new office parks housing technology companies such as United Information Systems and Sybase, and pioneering biotech firms such as Celera Genomics and Human Genome Sciences....

Franklin County is Red America. It's a rural county, about twenty-five miles west of Gettysburg, and it includes the towns of Waynesboro, Chambersburg, and Mercersburg. It was originally settled by the Scotch-Irish, and it has plenty of Brethren and Mennonites along with a fast-growing population of evangelicals. The joke that Pennsylvanians tell about their state is that it has Philadelphia on one end, Pittsburgh on the other, and Alabama in the middle. Franklin County is in the Alabama part. It strikes me as I drive there that even though I am going north across the Mason-Dixon line, I feel as if I were going south. The local culture owes more to Nashville, Houston, and Daytona than to Washington, Philadelphia, or New York....

Some of the biggest differences between Red and Blue America show up on statistical tables. Ethnic diversity is one. In Montgomery County 60 percent of the population is white, 15 percent is black, 12 percent is Hispanic, and 11 percent is Asian. In Franklin County 95 percent of the population is white. White people work the gas-station pumps and the 7-Eleven counters. (This is something one doesn't often see in my part of the country.) Although the nation is growing more diverse, it's doing so only in certain spots. According to an analysis of the 2000 census by Bill Frey, a demographer at the Milken Institute, well over half the counties in America are still at least 85 percent white.

Another big thing is that, according to 1990 census data, in Franklin County only 12 percent of the adults have college degrees and only 69 percent have high school diplomas. In Montgomery County 50 percent of the adults have college degrees and 91 percent have high school diplomas. The education gap extends to the children. At Walt Whitman High School, a public school in Bethesda, the average SAT scores are 601 verbal and 622 math, whereas the national average is 506 verbal and 514 math. In Franklin County, where people are quite proud of their schools, the average SAT scores at, for example, the Waynesboro area high school are 495 verbal and 480 math. More and more kids in Franklin County are

---

From "One Nation, Slightly Divisible," by David Brooks, *Atlantic Monthly* 288 (December 2001): pp. 53–65. Reprinted by permission.

going on to college, but it is hard to believe that their prospects will be as bright as those of the kids in Montgomery County and the rest of upscale Blue America.

Because the information age rewards education with money, it's not surprising that Montgomery County is much richer than Franklin County. According to some estimates, in Montgomery County 51 percent of households have annual incomes above $75,000, and the average household income is $100,365. In Franklin County only 16 percent of households have incomes above $75,000, and the average is $51,872.

A major employer in Montgomery County is the National Institutes of Health, which grows like a scientific boomtown in Bethesda. A major economic engine in Franklin County is the interstate highway Route 81. Trucking companies have gotten sick of fighting the congestion on Route 95, which runs up the Blue corridor along the northeast coast, so they move their stuff along 81, farther inland. Several new distribution centers have been built along 81 in Franklin County, and some of the workers who were laid off when their factories closed, several years ago, are now settling for $8.00 or $9.00 an hour loading boxes.

The two counties vote differently, of course—the differences, on a nationwide scale, were what led to those red-and-blue maps. Like upscale areas everywhere, from Silicon Valley to Chicago's North Shore to suburban Connecticut, Montgomery County supported the Democratic ticket in last year's presidential election, by a margin of 63 percent to 34 percent. Meanwhile, like almost all of rural America, Franklin County went Republican, by 67 percent to 30 percent.

However, other voting patterns sometimes obscure the Red-Blue cultural divide. For example, minority voters all over the country overwhelmingly supported the Democratic ticket last November. But—in many respects, at least—blacks and Hispanics in Red America are more traditionalist than blacks and Hispanics in Blue America, just as their white counterparts are. For example, the Pew Research Center for the People and the Press, in Washington, D.C., recently found that 45 percent of minority members in Red states agree with the statement "AIDS might be God's punishment for immoral sexual behavior," but only 31 percent of minority members in Blue states do. Similarly, 40 percent of minorities in Red states believe that school boards should have the right to fire homosexual teachers, but only 21 percent of minorities in Blue states do.

• • •

"The People Versus the Powerful"

There are a couple of long-standing theories about why America is divided. One of the main ones holds that the division is along class lines, between the haves and the have-nots. This theory is popular chiefly on the left, and can be found in the pages of *The American Prospect* and other liberal magazines; in news reports by liberal journalists such as Donald L. Barlett and James B. Steele, of *Time;* and in books such as *Middle Class Dreams* (1995), by the Clinton and Gore pollster Stanley Greenberg, and *America's Forgotten Majority: Why the White Working Class Still Matters* (2000), by the demographer Ruy Teixeira and the social scientist Joel Rogers.

According to this theory, during most of the twentieth century gaps in income between the rich and the poor in America gradually shrank. Then came the information age. The rich started getting spectacularly richer, the poor started getting poorer, and wages for the middle class stagnated, at best. Over the previous decade, these writers emphasized, remuneration for top-level executives had skyrocketed: now the average CEO made 116 times as much as the average rank-and-file worker. Assembly-line workers found themselves competing for jobs against Third World workers who earned less than a dollar an hour. Those who had once labored at well-paying blue-collar jobs were forced to settle for poorly paying service-economy jobs without benefits. . . .

Driving from Bethesda to Franklin County, one can see that the theory of a divide between the classes has a certain plausibility. In Montgomery County we have Saks Fifth Avenue, Cartier, Anthropologie, Brooks Brothers. In Franklin County they have Dollar General and Value City, along with a plethora of secondhand stores. It's as if Franklin County has only forty-five coffee tables, which are sold again and again.

When the locals are asked about their economy, they tell a story very similar to the one that Greenberg, Teixeira, Rogers, and the rest of the wage-stagnation liberals recount. There used to be plenty of good factory jobs in Franklin County, and people could work at those factories for life. But some of the businesses, including the textile company J. Schoeneman, once Franklin County's largest manufacturer, have closed. Others have moved offshore. The remaining manufacturers, such as Grove Worldwide and JLG Industries, which both make cranes and aerial platforms, have laid off workers. The local Army depot, Letterkenny, has radically shrunk its work force. The new jobs are in distribution centers or nursing homes. People tend to repeat the same phrase: "We've taken some hits."

And yet when they are asked about the broader theory, whether there is class conflict between the educated affluents and the stagnant middles, they stare blankly as if suddenly the interview were being conducted in Aramaic. I kept asking, Do you feel that the highly educated people around, say, New York and Washington are getting all the goodies? Do you think there is resentment toward all the latte sippers who shop at Nieman Marcus? Do you see a gulf between high-income people in the big cities and middle-income people here? I got only polite, fumbling answers as people tried to figure out what the hell I was talking about.

When I rephrased the question in more-general terms, as Do you believe the country is divided between the haves and the have-nots?, everyone responded decisively: yes. But as the conversation continued, it became clear that the people saying yes did not consider themselves to be among the have-nots. Even people with incomes well below the median thought of themselves as haves. . . .

Hanging around Franklin County, one begins to understand some of the reasons that people there don't spend much time worrying about economic class lines. The first and most obvious one is that although the incomes in Franklin County are lower than those in Montgomery County, living expenses are also lower—very much so. Driving from Montgomery County to Franklin County is like driving through an invisible deflation machine. Gas is thirty, forty, or even fifty cents a gallon cheaper in Franklin County. I parked at meters that accepted only pennies and nickels. When I got a parking ticket in Chambersburg, the fine was $3.00. At the department store in Greencastle there were racks and racks of blouses for $9.99. . . .

Another thing I found is that most people don't think sociologically. They don't compare themselves with faraway millionaires who appear on their TV screens. They compare themselves with their neighbors. "One of the challenges we face is that it is hard to get people to look beyond the four-state region," Lynne Woehrle, a sociologist at Wilson College, in Chambersburg, told me, referring to the cultural zone composed of the nearby rural areas in Pennsylvania, West Virginia, Maryland, and Virginia. Many of the people in Franklin County view the lifestyles of the upper class in California or Seattle much the way we in Blue America might view the lifestyle of someone in Eritrea or Mongolia—or, for that matter, Butte, Montana. Such ways of life are distant and basically irrelevant, except as a source of academic interest or titillation. One man in Mercersburg, Pennsylvania, told me about a friend who had recently bought a car. "He paid twenty-five thousand dollars for that car!" he exclaimed, his eyes wide with amazement. "He got it fully loaded." I didn't tell him that in Bethesda almost no one but a college kid pays as little as $25,000 for a car.

Franklin County is a world in which there is little obvious inequality, and the standard of living is reasonably comfortable. Youth-soccer teams are able to raise money for a summer trip to England; the Lowe's hardware superstore carries Laura Ashley carpets; many people have pools, although they are almost always above ground; the planning commission has to cope with an increasing number of cars in the county every year, even though the population is growing only gradually. But the sort of high-end experiences that are everywhere in Montgomery County are entirely missing here. . . .

No wonder people in Franklin County have no class resentment or class consciousness; where they live, they can afford just about anything that is for sale. (In Montgomery County, however—and this is one of the most striking contrasts between the two counties—almost nobody can say that. In Blue America, unless you are very, very rich, there is always, all around you, stuff for sale that you cannot afford.) And if they sought to improve their situation, they would look only to themselves. If a person wants to make more money, the feeling goes, he or she had better work hard and think like an entrepreneur. . . .

Ted Hale, a Presbyterian minister in the western part of the county, spoke of the matter this way: "There's nowhere near as much resentment as you would expect. People have come to understand that they will struggle financially. It's part of their identity. But the economy is not their god. That's the thing some others don't understand. People value a sense of community far more than they do their portfolio." Hale, who worked at a church in East Hampton, New York, before coming to Franklin County, said that he saw a lot more economic resentment in New York.

Hale's observations are supported by nationwide polling data. Pew has conducted a broad survey of the differences between Red and Blue states. The survey found that views on economic issues do not explain the different voting habits in the two regions. There simply isn't much of the sort of economic dissatisfaction that could drive a class-based political movement. Eighty-five percent of Americans with an annual household income between $30,000 and $50,000 are satisfied with their housing. Nearly 70 percent are satisfied with the kind of car they can afford. Roughly two thirds are satisfied with their furniture and their ability to afford a night out. These levels of satisfaction are not very different from those found in upper-middle-class America.

The Pew researchers found this sort of trend in question after question. Part of the draft of their report is titled "Economic Divide Dissolves."

A Lot of Religion but Few Crusaders

This leaves us with the second major hypothesis about the nature of the divide between Red and Blue America, which comes mainly from conservatives: America is divided between two moral systems. Red America is traditional, religious, self-disciplined, and patriotic. Blue America is modern, secular, self-expressive, and discomfited by blatant displays of patriotism. Proponents of this hypothesis in its most radical form contend that America is in the midst of a culture war, with two opposing armies fighting on behalf of their views. The historian Gertrude Himmelfarb offered a more moderate picture in *One Nation, Two Cultures* (1999), in which she argued that although America is not fatally split, it is deeply divided, between a heartland conservative population that adheres to a strict morality and a liberal population that lives by a loose one. The political journalist Michael Barone put it this way in a recent essay in *National Journal:* "The two Americas apparent in the 48 percent to 48 percent 2000 election are two nations of different faiths. One is observant, tradition-minded, moralistic. The other is unobservant, liberation-minded, relativistic."

The values-divide school has a fair bit of statistical evidence on its side. Whereas income is a poor predictor of voting patterns, church attendance—as Barone points out—is a pretty good one. Of those who attend religious services weekly (42 percent of the electorate), 59 percent voted for Bush, 39 percent for Gore. Of those who seldom or never attend religious services (another 42 percent), 56 percent voted for Gore, 39 percent for Bush.

The Pew data reveal significant divides on at least a few values issues. Take, for example, the statement "We will all be called before God on Judgment Day to answer for our sins." In Red states 70 percent of the people believe that statement. In Blue states only 50 percent do.

One can feel the religiosity in Franklin County after a single day's visit. It's on the bumper stickers: WARNING: IN CASE OF RAPTURE THIS VEHICLE WILL BE UNMANNED. REAL TRUCKERS TALK ABOUT JESUS ON CHANNEL 10. It's on the radio. The airwaves are filled not with the usual mixture of hit tunes but with evangelicals preaching the gospel. The book section of Wal-Mart features titles such as *The Beginner's Guide to Fasting, Deepen Your Conversation with God,* and *Are We Living in the End Times?* Some general stores carry the "Heroes of the Faith" series, which consists of small biographies of William Carey, George Müller, and other notable missionaries, ministers, and theologians—notable in Red America, that is, but largely unknown where I live. . . .

Franklin County is probably a bit more wholesome than most suburbs in Blue America. (The notion that deviance and corruption lie underneath the seeming conformism of suburban middle-class life, popular in Hollywood and in creative-writing workshops, is largely nonsense.) But it has most of the problems that af-flict other parts of the country: heroin addiction, teen pregnancy, and so on. No-body I spoke to felt part of a pristine culture that is exempt from the problems of the big cities. There are even enough spectacular crimes in Franklin County to make a devoted *New York Post* reader happy. During one of my visits the front pages of the local papers were ablaze with the tale of a young woman arrested for assault and homicide after shooting her way through a Veterans of the Vietnam War post. It was reported that she had intended to rob the post for money to run away with her lesbian girlfriend.

If the problems are the same as in the rest of America, so are many of the solu-tions. Franklin County residents who find themselves in trouble go to their clergy first, but they are often referred to psychologists and therapists as part of their re-covery process. Prozac is a part of life.

Almost nobody I spoke with understood, let alone embraced, the concept of a culture war. Few could see themselves as fighting such a war, in part because few have any idea where the boundary between the two sides lies. People in Franklin County may have a clear sense of what constitutes good or evil (many people in Blue America have trouble with the very concept of evil), but they will say that good and evil are in all neighborhoods, as they are in all of us. People take the Scriptures seriously but have no interest in imposing them on others. One finds little crusader zeal in Franklin County. For one thing, people in small towns don't want to offend people whom they'll be encountering on the street for the next fifty years. Potentially controversial subjects are often played down. "We would never take a stance on gun control or abortion," Sue Hadden, the editor of the Waynesboro paper, told me. Whenever I asked what the local view of abortion was, I got the same response: "We don't talk about it much," or "We try to avoid that subject." Bill Pukmel, the former Chambersburg newspaper editor, says, "A majority would be opposed to abortion around here, but it wouldn't be a big ma-jority." It would simply be uncivil to thrust such a raw disagreement in people's faces. . . .

Certainly Red and Blue America disagree strongly on some issues, such as ho-mosexuality and abortion. But for the most part the disagreements are not large. For example, the Pew researchers asked Americans to respond to the statement "There are clear guidelines about what's good or evil that apply to everyone re-gardless of their situation." Forty-three percent of people in Blue states and 49 percent of people in Red states agreed. Forty-seven percent of Blue America and 55 percent of Red America agreed with the statement "I have old-fashioned val-ues about family and marriage." Seventy percent of the people in Blue states and 77 percent of the people in Red states agreed that "too many children are being raised in day-care centers these days." These are small gaps. And, the Pew re-searchers found, there is no culture gap at all among suburban voters. In a Red state like Arizona suburban voters' opinions are not much different from those in a Blue state like Connecticut. The starkest differences that exist are between peo-ple in cities and people in rural areas, especially rural areas in the South.

The conservatism I found in Franklin County is not an ideological or a reac-tionary conservatism. It is a temperamental conservatism. People place tremen-dous value on being agreeable, civil, and kind. They are happy to sit quietly with one another. They are hesitant to stir one another's passions. They appreciate what they have. They value continuity and revere the past. They work hard to reinforce community bonds. Their newspapers are filled with items about fundraising drives, car washes, bake sales, penny-collection efforts, and auxiliary thrift shops. Their streets are lined with lodges: VFW, Rotarians, Elks, Moose. Luncheons go on everywhere. Retired federal employees will be holding their weekly luncheon at one restaurant, Harley riders at another. I became fascinated by a group called the Tuscarora Longbeards, a local chapter of something called the National Wild Turkey Federation. The Longbeards go around to schools distributing Wild About Turkey Education boxes, which contain posters, lesson plans, and CD-ROMs on turkey preservation.

These are the sorts of things that really mobilize people in Franklin County. Building community and preserving local ways are far more important to them than any culture war.

The Ego Curtain

The best explanation of the differences between people in Montgomery and Franklin Counties has to do with sensibility, not class or culture. If I had to describe the differences between the two sensibilities in a single phrase, it would be conception of the self. In Red America the self is small. People declare in a million ways, "I am normal. Nobody is better, nobody is worse. I am humble before God." In Blue America the self is more commonly large. People say in a million ways, "I am special. I have carved out my own unique way of life. I am independent. I make up my own mind."

In Red America there is very little one-upmanship. Nobody tries to be avant-garde in choosing a wardrobe. The chocolate-brown suits and baggy denim dresses hanging in local department stores aren't there by accident; people conspicuously want to be seen as not trying to dress to impress.

For a person in Blue America the blandness in Red America can be a little oppressive. But it's hard not to be struck by the enormous social pressure not to put on airs. If a Franklin County resident drove up to church one day in a shiny new Lexus, he would face huge waves of disapproval. If one hired a nanny, people would wonder who died and made her queen.

In Franklin County people don't go looking for obscure beers to demonstrate their connoisseurship. They wear T-shirts and caps with big-brand names on them—Coke, McDonald's, Chevrolet. In Bethesda people prefer cognoscenti brands—the Black Dog restaurant, or the independent bookstore Politics and Prose. In Franklin County it would be an affront to the egalitarian ethos to put a Princeton sticker on the rear window of one's car. In Montgomery County some proud parents can barely see through their back windows for all the Ivy League stickers. People in Franklin County say they felt comfortable voting for Bush, because if he came to town he wouldn't act superior to anybody else; he could settle into a barber's chair and fit right in. They couldn't stand Al Gore, because they thought he'd always be trying to awe everyone with his accomplishments. People in Montgomery County tended to admire Gore's accomplishments. They were leery of Bush, because for most of his life he seemed not to have achieved anything. . . .

A Cafeteria Nation

These differences in sensibility don't in themselves mean that America has become a fundamentally divided nation. As the sociologist Seymour Martin Lipset pointed out in *The First New Nation* (1963), achievement and equality are the two rival themes running throughout American history. Most people, most places, and most epochs have tried to intertwine them in some way.

Moreover, after bouncing between Montgomery and Franklin Counties, I became convinced that a lot of our fear that America is split into rival camps arises from mistaken notions of how society is shaped. Some of us still carry the old Marxist categories in our heads. We think that society is like a layer cake, with the upper class on top. And, like Marx, we tend to assume that wherever there is class division there is conflict. Or else we have a sort of *Crossfire* model in our heads: where would people we meet sit if they were guests on that show?

But traveling back and forth between the two counties was not like crossing from one rival camp to another. It was like crossing a high school cafeteria. Remember high school? There were nerds, jocks, punks, bikers, techies, druggies, God Squadders, drama geeks, poets, and Dungeons & Dragons weirdoes. All these cliques were part of the same school: they had different sensibilities; sometimes they knew very little about the people in the other cliques; but the jocks knew there would always be nerds, and the nerds knew there would always be jocks. That's just the way life is.

And that's the way America is. We are not a divided nation. We are a cafeteria nation. We form cliques (call them communities, or market segments, or whatever), and when they get too big, we form subcliques. Some people even get together in churches that are "nondenominational" or in political groups that are "independent." These are cliques built around the supposed rejection of cliques.

We live our lives by migrating through the many different cliques associated with the activities we enjoy and the goals we have set for ourselves. Our freedom comes in the interstices; we can choose which set of standards to live by, and when.

We should remember that there is generally some distance between cliques—a buffer zone that separates one set of aspirations from another. People who are happy within their cliques feel no great compulsion to go out and reform other cliques. The jocks don't try to change the nerds. David Rawley, the Greencastle minister who felt he was clinging to a rock, has been to New York City only once in his life. "I was happy to get back home," he told me. "It's a planet I'm a little scared of. I have no desire to go back."

What unites the two Americas, then, is our mutual commitment to this way of life—to the idea that a person is not bound by his class, or by the religion of his fathers, but is free to build a plurality of connections for himself. We are participants in the same striving process, the same experimental journey.... ■

The International Context

The idea that American political culture differs fundamentally from the political cultures of Europe and elsewhere in the world has long been central to discussions of American politics. As we have seen, this so-called American exceptionalism thesis was first put forward by Tocqueville (see selection 5.1) in the 1830s. Later, it reemerged as part of the effort to explain why the United States—unlike virtually every other industrialized society—failed to develop a viable socialist or communist movement. In this essay, the political scientist Seymour Martin Lipset examines the history of the American exceptionalism thesis and explains how America's distinctive political culture helps illuminate the peculiar nature of American liberalism and conservatism.

Questions

1. Why, according to advocates of the American exceptionalism thesis, did the United States develop a political culture different and distinct from those of Europe? What role did the American Revolution play in the development of this unique political culture?
2. How do American conceptions of liberalism and conservatism differ from their European counterparts? How does the American exceptionalism thesis help explain these differences?

5.3 American Exceptionalism: A Double-Edged Sword (1996)

Seymour Martin Lipset

Born out of revolution, the United States is a country organized around an ideology which includes a set of dogmas about the nature of a good society. Americanism, as different people have pointed out, is an "ism" or ideology in the same way that communism or fascism or liberalism are isms. As G. K. Chesterton put it: "America is the only nation in the world that is founded on a creed. That creed is set forth with dogmatic and even theological lucidity in the Declaration of Independence. . . ." [The] . . . nation's ideology can be described in five words: liberty, egalitarianism, individualism, populism, and laissez-faire. The revolutionary ideology which became the American Creed is liberalism in its eighteenth- and nineteenth-century meanings, as distinct from conservative

Toryism, statist communitarianism, mercantilism, and *noblesse oblige* dominant in monarchical, state-church-formed cultures.

Other countries' senses of themselves are derived from a common history. Winston Churchill once gave vivid evidence to the difference between a national identity rooted in history and one defined by ideology in objecting to a proposal in 1940 to outlaw the anti-war Communist Party. In a speech in the House of Commons, Churchill said that as far as he knew, the Communist Party was composed of Englishmen and he did not fear an Englishman. In Europe, nationality is related to community, and thus one cannot become un-English or un-Swedish. Being an American, however, is an ideological commitment. It is not a matter of birth. Those who reject American values are un-American.

The American Revolution sharply weakened the *noblesse oblige,* hierarchically rooted, organic community values which had been linked to Tory sentiments, and enormously strengthened the individualistic, egalitarian, and anti-statist ones which had been present in the settler and religious background of the colonies. These values were evident in the twentieth-century fact that, as H. G. Wells pointed out close to ninety years ago, the United States not only has lacked a viable socialist party, but also has never developed a British or European-type Conservative or Tory party. Rather, America has been dominated by pure bourgeois, middle-class individualistic values. As Wells put it: "Essentially America is a middle-class [which has] become a community and so its essential problems are the problems of a modern individualistic society, stark and clear." He enunciated a theory of America as a liberal society, in the classic anti-statist meaning of the term:

> It is not difficult to show for example, that the two great political parties in America represent only one English party, the middle-class Liberal party. . . . There are no Tories . . . and no Labor Party. . . . [T]he new world [was left] to the Whigs and Nonconformists and to those less constructive, less logical, more popular and liberating thinkers who became Radicals in England, and Jeffersonians and then Democrats in America. All Americans are, from the English point of view, Liberals of one sort or another. . . .
>
> The liberalism of the eighteenth century was essentially the rebellion . . . against the monarchical and aristocratic state—against hereditary privilege, against restrictions on bargains. Its spirit was essentially anarchistic—the antithesis of Socialism. It was anti-State.

Comparative Perspectives

In dealing with national characteristics it is important to recognize that comparative evaluations are never absolutes, that they always are made in terms of more or less. The statement that the United States is an egalitarian society obviously does not imply that all Americans are equal in any way that can be defined. This proposition usually means (regardless of which aspect is under consideration—social relations, status, mobility, etc.) that the United States is more egalitarian than Europe.

Comparative judgments affect all generalizations about societies. This is such an obvious, commonsensical truism that it seems almost foolish to enunciate it. I only do so because statements about America or other countries are frequently challenged on the ground that they are not absolutely true. Generalizations may invert when the unit of comparison changes. For example, Canada looks different when compared to the United States than when contrasted with Britain. Figuratively, on a scale of 0 to 100, with the United States close to 0 on a given trait and Britain at 100, Canada would fall around 30. Thus, when Canada is evaluated by reference to the United States, it appears as more elitist, law-abiding, and statist, but when considering the variations between Canada and Britain, Canada looks more anti-statist, violent, and egalitarian.

The notion of "American exceptionalism" became widely applied in the context of efforts to account for the weakness of working-class radicalism in the United States. The major question subsumed in the concept became why the United States is the only industrialized country which does not have a significant socialist movement or Labor party. That riddle has bedeviled socialist theorists since the late nineteenth century. Friedrich Engels tried to answer it in the last decade of his life. The German socialist and sociologist Werner Sombart dealt with it in a major book published in his native language in 1906, *Why Is There No Socialism in the United States?* As we have seen, H. G. Wells, then a Fabian, also addressed the issue that year in *The Future in America*. Both Lenin and Trotsky were deeply concerned because the logic of Marxism, the proposition expressed by Marx in *Das Kapital* that "the more developed country shows the less developed the image of their future," implied to Marxists prior to the Russian Revolution that the United States would be the first socialist country.

Since some object to an attempt to explain a negative, a vacancy, the query may of course be reversed to ask why has America been the most classically liberal polity in the world from its founding to the present? Although the United States remains the wealthiest large industrialized nation, it devotes less of its income to welfare and the state is less involved in the economy than is true for other developed countries. It not only does not have a viable, class-conscious, radical political movement, but its trade unions, which have long been weaker than those of almost all other industrialized countries, have been steadily declining since the mid-1950s. . . .

An emphasis on American uniqueness raises the obvious question of the nature of the differences. There is a large literature dating back to at least the eighteenth century which attempts to specify the special character of the United States politically and socially. One of the most interesting, often overlooked, is Edmund Burke's speech to the House of Commons proposing reconciliation with the colonies, in which he sought to explain to his fellow members what the revolutionary Americans were like. He noted that they were different culturally, that they were not simply transplanted Englishmen. He particularly stressed the unique character of American religion. J. Hector St. John Crèvecoeur, in his book *Letters from an American Farmer*, written in the late eighteenth century, explicitly raised the question, "What is an American?" He emphasized that Americans behaved differently in their social relations, were much more egalitarian than other nationalities, that their "dictionary" was "short in words of dignity, and names of honor," that is, in terms through which the lower strata expressed their subservience to the higher. Tocqueville, who observed egalitarianism in a similar fashion, also stressed individualism, as distinct from the emphasis on "group ties" which marked Europe.

These commentaries have been followed by a myriad—thousands upon thousands—of books and articles by foreign travelers. The overwhelming majority are by educated Europeans. Such writings are fruitful because they are comparative; those who wrote them emphasized cross-national variations in behavior and institutions. Tocqueville's *Democracy*, of course, is the best known. As we have seen, he noted that he never wrote anything about the United States without thinking of France. As he put it, in speaking of his need to contrast the same institutions and behavior in both countries, "without comparisons to make, the mind doesn't know how to proceed." Harriet Martineau, an English contemporary, also wrote a first-rate comparative book on America. Friedrich Engels and Max Weber were among the contributors to the literature. There is a fairly systematic and similar logic in many of these discussions.

Beyond the analysis of variations between the United States and Europe, various other comparisons have been fruitful. In previous writings, I have suggested that one of the best ways to specify and distinguish American traits is by contrast with Canada. There is a considerable comparative North American literature, written almost entirely by Canadians. They have a great advantage over Americans since, while very few of the latter study their northern neighbor, it is impossible to be a literate Canadian without knowing almost as much, if not more, as most Americans about the United States. Almost every Canadian work on a given subject (the city, religion, the family, trade unions, etc.) contains a great deal about the United States. Many Canadians seek to explain their own country by dealing with differences or similarities south of the border. Specifying and analyzing variations among the predominantly English-speaking countries—Australia, Canada, Great Britain, New Zealand, and the United States—is also useful precisely because the differences among them generally are smaller than between each and non-Anglophonic societies. I have tried to analyze these variations in *The First New Nation*. The logic of studying societies which have major aspects in common was also followed by Louis Hartz in treating the overseas settler societies—United States, Canada, Latin America, Australia, and South Africa—as units for comparison. Fruitful comparisons have been made between Latin America and Anglophonic North America, which shed light on each.

Some Latin Americans have argued that there are major common elements in the Americas which show up in comparisons with Europe. Fernando Cardoso, a distinguished sociologist and now president of Brazil, once told me that he and his friends (who were activists in the underground left in the early 1960s) consciously decided not to found a socialist party as the military dictatorship was breaking down. They formed a populist party because, as they read the evidence, class-conscious socialism does not appeal in the Americas. With the exceptions of Chile and Canada (to a limited extent), major New World left parties from Argentina to the United States have been populist. Cardoso suggested that consciousness of social class is less salient throughout most of the Americas than in postfeudal Europe. However, I do not want to take on the issue of how exceptional the Americas are; dealing with the United States is more than enough.

Liberalism, Conservatism, and Americanism

The United States is viewed by many as the great conservative society, but it may also be seen as the most classically liberal polity in the developed world. To understand the exceptional nature of American politics, it is necessary to recognize, with H. G. Wells, that conservatism, as defined outside of the United States, is particularly weak in this country. Conservatism in Europe and Canada, derived from the historic alliance of church and government, is associated with the emergence of the welfare state. The two names most identified with it are Bismarck and Disraeli. Both were leaders of the conservatives (Tories) in their countries. They represented the rural and aristocratic elements, sectors which disdained capitalism, disliked the bourgeoisie, and rejected materialistic values. Their politics reflected the values of *noblesse oblige*, the obligation of the leaders of society and the economy to protect the less fortunate.

The semantic confusion about liberalism in America arises because both early and latter-day Americans never adopted the term to describe the unique American polity. The reason is simple. The American system of government existed long before the word "liberal" emerged in Napoleonic Spain and was subsequently accepted as referring to a particular party in mid-nineteenth-century England, as distinct from the Tory or Conservative Party. What Europeans have called "liberalism," Americans refer to as "conservatism": a deeply anti-statist doctrine emphasizing the virtues of laissez-faire. Ronald Reagan and Milton Friedman, the two current names most frequently linked with this ideology, define conservatism in America. And as Friedrich Hayek, its most important European exponent noted, it includes the rejection of aristocracy, social class hierarchy, and an established state church. As recently as the April and June 1987 issues of the British magazine *Encounter*, two leading trans-Atlantic conservative intellectuals, Max Beloff (Lord Beloff) and Irving Kristol, debated the use of titles. Kristol argued that Britain "is soured by a set of very thin, but tenacious, aristocratic pretensions . . . [which] foreclose opportunities and repress a spirit of equality that has yet to find its full expression. . . ." This situation fuels many of the frustrations that make "British life . . . so cheerful, so abounding in *ressentiment*." Like Tocqueville, he holds up "social equality" as making "other inequalities tolerable in modern democracy." Beloff, a Tory, contended that what threatens conservatism in Britain "is not its remaining links with the aristocratic tradition, but its alleged indifference to some of the abuses of capitalism. It is not the Dukes who lose us votes, but the 'malefactors of great wealth. . . .'" He wondered "why Mr. Kristol believes himself to be a 'conservative,'" since he is "as incapable as most Americans of being a conservative in any profound sense." Lord Beloff concluded that "Conservatism must have a 'Tory' element or it is only the old 'Manchester School,'" i.e., liberal.

Canada's most distinguished conservative intellectual, George Grant, emphasized in his *Lament for a Nation* that "Americans who call themselves 'Conservatives' have the right to that title only in a particular sense. In fact, they are old-fashioned liberals. . . . Their concentration on freedom from governmental interference has more to do with nineteenth century liberalism than with traditional conservatism, which asserts the right of the community to restrain freedom in the name of the common good." Grant bemoaned the fact that American conservatism, with its stress on the virtues of competition and links to business ideology, focuses on the rights of individuals and ignores communal rights and obligations. He noted that there has been no place in the American political philosophy "for the organic conservatism that predates the age of progress. Indeed, the United States is the only society on earth that has no traditions from before the age of progress." The recent efforts, led by Amitai Etzioni, to create a "communitarian" movement are an attempt to transport Toryism to America. British and German Tories have recognized the link and have shown considerable interest in Etzioni's ideas.

Still, it must be recognized that American politics have changed. The 1930s produced a qualitative difference. As Richard Hofstadter wrote, this period brought a "social democratic tinge" to the United States for the first time in its history. The Great Depression produced a strong emphasis on planning, on the welfare state, on the role of the government as a major regulatory actor. An earlier upswing in statist sentiment occurred immediately prior to World War I, as evidenced by the significant support for the largely Republican Progressive movement led by Robert LaFollette and Theodore Roosevelt and the increasing strength (up to a high of 6% of the national vote in 1912) for the Socialist Party. They failed to change the political system. Grant McConnell explains the failure of the Progressive movement as stemming from "the pervasive and latent ambiguity in the movement" about confronting American anti-statist values. "Power as it exists was antagonistic to democracy, but how was it to be curbed without the erection of superior power?"

Prior to the 1930s, the American trade union movement was also in its majority anti-statist. The American Federation of Labor (AFL) was syndicalist, believed in more union, not more state power, and was anti-socialist. Its predominant leader for forty years, Samuel Gompers, once said when asked about his politics, that he guessed he was three quarters of an anarchist. And he was right. Europeans and others who perceived the Gompers-led AFL as a conservative organization because it opposed the socialists were wrong. The AFL was an extremely militant organization, which engaged in violence and had a high strike rate. It was not conservative, but rather a militant anti-statist group. The United States also had a revolutionary trade union movement, the Industrial Workers of the World (IWW). The IWW, like the AFL, was not socialist. It was explicitly anarchist, or rather, anarcho-syndicalist. The revived American radical movement of the 1960s, the so-called New Left, was also not socialist. While not doctrinally anarchist, it was much closer to anarchism and the IWW in its ideology and organizational structure than to the Socialists or Communists.

The New Deal, which owed much to the Progressive movement, was not socialist either. Franklin Roosevelt clearly wanted to maintain a capitalist economy. In running for president in 1932, he criticized Herbert Hoover and the Republicans for deficit financing and expanding the economic role of the government, which they had done in order to deal with the Depression. But his New Deal, also rising out of the need to confront the massive economic downsizing, drastically increased the statist strain in American politics, while furthering public support for trade unions. The new labor movement which arose concomitantly, the Committee for (later Congress of) Industrial Organization (CIO), unlike the American Federation of Labor (AFL), was virtually social democratic in its orientation. In fact, socialists and communists played important roles in the movement. The CIO was much more politically active than the older Federation and helped to press the Democrats to the left. The Depression led to a kind of moderate "Europeanization" of American politics, as well as of its labor organizations. Class factors became more important in differentiating party support. The conservatives, increasingly concentrated among the Republicans, remained anti-statist and laissez-faire, but many of them grew willing to accommodate an activist role for the state.

This pattern, however, gradually inverted after World War II as a result of long-term prosperity. The United States, like other parts of the developed world, experienced what some have called an economic miracle. The period from 1945 to the 1980s was characterized by considerable growth (mainly before the mid-1970s), an absence of major economic downswings, higher rates of social mobility both on a mass level and into the elites, and a tremendous expansion of higher educational systems—from a few million to 11 or 12 million going to colleges and universities—which fostered that mobility. America did particularly well economically, leading Europe and Japan by a considerable margin in terms of new job creation. A consequence of these developments was a refurbishing of the classical liberal ideology, that is, American conservatism. The class tensions produced by the Depression lessened, reflected in the decline of the labor movement and lower correlations between class position and voting choices. And the members of the small (by comparative standards) American labor movement are today significantly less favorable to government action than European unionists. Fewer than half of American union members are in favor of the government providing a decent standard of living for the unemployed, as compared with 69 percent of West German, 72 percent of British, and 73 percent of Italian unionists. Even before Ronald Reagan entered the White House in 1981, the United States had a lower rate of taxation, a less developed welfare state, and many fewer government-owned industries than other industrialized nations. ■

View from the Inside

Public opinion polls are not simply neutral devices used to measure American public opinion. They have become tools of the trade for politicians and presidents, especially in recent years. Pollsters play a key role in helping candidates shape their campaigns and in helping political leaders govern.

The use of pollsters by presidents and other politicians has become the source of some controversy. Critics point out that the overuse of public opinion polls tends to turn leaders into followers and also encourages politicians to tell the public only what it wants to hear—a practice that can lead to erratic public policy, a dangerous short-term point of view, and a loss of critically needed perspective. Paradoxically, critics suggest, politicians who rely too much on public opinion polls may end up losing touch with the people; they would be better off relying instead on their own political instincts and leadership abilities.

The Clinton administration was well known for its almost obsessive use of polling. Bill Clinton's critics accused him of using polls to shape public policy, in effect following the public instead of leading it. Such claims eventually became part of George W. Bush's presidential campaign, and the new Bush administration soon cultivated the image that it governed, as Joshua Green writes in this selection, "based upon principle and not polls and focus groups."

In fact, Green argues, the Bush administration has not abandoned polls and focus groups. Although Bush remains as reliant on pollsters as any modern president, his pollsters have been banished to the back room and kept out of sight, allowing the administration to benefit from the best techniques of market research while maintaining an anti-polling image.

Questions

1. What advantages do polls and focus groups bring to the president? What dangers do they present? In answering, consider especially the experiences of the Clinton and Bush presidencies.
2. Consider the role of the political pollster in American governance in light of the arguments concerning democracy presented by James Madison in *Federalist* No. 10 (selection 1.1). Do public opinion polls increase the possibility that majority factions will exert an overpowering influence at the national level?

5.4 The Other War Room (2002)

Joshua Green

On a Friday afternoon late last year [2001], press secretaries from every recent administration gathered in the War Room of the White House at the invitation of Ari Fleischer, press secretary to President Bush. There was no agenda. It was just one of those unexpectedly nice things that seemed to transpire during the brief period after September 11 when people thought of themselves as Americans first and Democrats and Republicans second. Over a lunch of crab cakes and steak, Republicans such as Fleischer and Marlin Fitzwater traded war stories with Joe Lockhart, Mike McCurry, and assorted other Democrats. Halfway through lunch, President Bush dropped by unexpectedly and launched into an impromptu briefing of his own, ticking off the items on his agenda until he arrived at the question of whether it was preferable to issue vague

Joshua Green, "The Other War Room: President Bush Doesn't Believe in Polling—Just Ask His Pollsters." Washington Monthly 34 (April 2002): pp. 11–16. Reprinted with permission from *The Washington Monthly*. Copyright by Washington Monthly Publishing, LLC, 733 15th St. NW, Suite 520, Washington, D.C. 20005. (202) 393-5155. Web site: www.washingtonmonthly.com

warnings of possible terrorist threats or to stay quietly vigilant so as not to alarm people. At this point, former Clinton press secretary Dee Dee Myers piped up, "What do the poll numbers say?" All eyes turned to Bush. Without missing a beat, the famous Bush smirk crossed the president's face and he replied, "In this White House, Dee Dee, we don't poll on something as important as national security."

This wasn't a stray comment, but a glimpse of a larger strategy that has served Bush extremely well since he first launched his campaign for president—the myth that his administration doesn't use polling. As Bush endlessly insisted on the campaign trail, he governs "based upon principle and not polls and focus groups."

It's not hard to understand the appeal of this tactic. Ever since the Clinton administration's well-noted excesses—calling on pollsters to help determine vacation spots and family pets—polling has become a kind of shorthand for everything people dislike about Washington politics. "Pollsters have developed a reputation as Machiavellian plotters whose job it is to think up ways to exploit the public," says Andrew Kohut, director of the Pew Research Center for the People and the Press. Announcing that one ignores polls, then, is an easy way of conveying an impression of leadership, judgment, and substance. No one has recognized and used this to such calculated effect as Bush. When he announced he would "bring a new tone to Washington," he just as easily could have said he'd banish pollsters from the White House without any loss of effect. One of the most dependable poll results is that people don't like polling.

But in fact, the Bush administration is a frequent consumer of polls, though it takes extraordinary measures to appear that it isn't. This administration, unlike Clinton's, rarely uses poll results to ply reporters or congressional leaders for support. "It's rare to even hear talk of it unless you give a Bush guy a couple of drinks," says one White House reporter. But Republican National Committee filings show that Bush actually uses polls much more than he lets on, in ways both similar and dissimilar to Clinton. Like Clinton, Bush is most inclined to use polls when he's struggling. It's no coincidence that the administration did its heaviest polling last summer [2001], after the poorly received rollout of its energy plan, and amid much talk of the "smallness" of the presidency. A *Washington Monthly* analysis of Republican National Committee disbursement filings revealed that Bush's principal pollsters received $346,000 in direct payments in 2001. Add to that the multiple boutique polling firms the administration regularly employs for specialized and targeted polls and the figure is closer to $1 million. That's about half the amount Clinton spent during his first year; but while Clinton used polling to craft popular policies, Bush uses polling to spin unpopular ones—arguably a much more cynical undertaking.

Bush's principal pollster, Jan van Lohuizen, and his focus-group guru, Fred Steeper, are the best-kept secrets in Washington. Both are respected but low-key, proficient but tight-lipped, and, unlike such larger-than-life Clinton pollsters as Dick Morris and Mark Penn, happy to remain anonymous. They toil in the background, poll-testing the words and phrases the president uses to sell his policies to an often-skeptical public; they're the Bush administration's Cinderella. "In terms of the modern presidency," says Ron Faucheux, editor of *Campaigns & Elections*, "van Lohuizen is the lowest-profile pollster we've ever had." But as Bush shifts his focus back toward a domestic agenda, he'll be relying on his pollsters more than ever.

Bush's Brain

On the last day of February [2002], the Bush administration kicked off its renewed initiative to privatize Social Security in a speech before the National Summit on Retirement Savings in Washington, D.C. Rather than address "Social Security," Bush opted to speak about "retirement security." And during the brief speech he repeated the words "choice" (three times), "compound interest" (four times), "opportunity" (nine times) and "savings" (18 times). These words were not chosen lightly. The repetition was prompted by polls and focus groups. During the campaign, Steeper honed and refined Bush's message on Social Security (with key words such as "choice," "control," and "higher returns"), measuring it against Al Gore's attack through polls and focus groups ("Wall Street roulette," "bankruptcy" and "break the contract"). Steeper discovered that respondents preferred Bush's position by 50 percent to 38 percent, despite the conventional wisdom that tampering with Social Security is political suicide. He learned, as he explained to an academic conference last February, that "there's a great deal of cynicism about the federal government being able to do anything right, which translated to the federal government not having the ability to properly invest people's Social Security dollars." By couching Bush's rhetoric in poll-tested phrases that reinforced this notion, and adding others that stress the benefits of privatization, he was able to capitalize on what most observers had considered to be a significant political disadvantage. (Independent polls generally find that when fully apprised of Bush's plan, including the risks, most voters don't support it.)

This is typical of how the Bush administration uses polls: policies are chosen beforehand, polls used to spin them. Because many of Bush's policies aren't necessarily popular with a majority of voters, Steeper and van Lohuizen's job essentially consists of finding words to sell them to the public. Take, for instance, the Bush energy plan. When administration officials unveiled it last May [2001], they repeatedly described it as "balanced" and "comprehensive," and stressed Bush's "leadership" and use of "modern" methods to prevent environmental damage. As *Time* magazine's Jay Carney and John Dickerson revealed, van Lohuizen had poll-tested pitch phrases for weeks before arriving at these as the most likely to conciliate a skeptical public. (Again, independent polls showed weak voter support for the Bush plan.) And the "education recession" Bush trumpeted throughout the campaign? Another triumph of opinion research. Same with "school choice," [and] the "death tax." . . . Even the much-lauded national service initiative Bush proposed in his State of the Union address was the product of focus grouping. Though publicly Bush prides himself on never looking in the mirror (that's "leadership"), privately, he's not quite so secure. His pollsters have even conducted favorability ratings on Ari Fleischer and [Bush adviser] Karen Hughes.

• • •

Poll Vault

The practice of presidents poll-testing their message dates back to John F. Kennedy, who wished to pursue a civil rights agenda but knew that he would have to articulate it in words that the American public in the 1960s would accept.

Alarm about being known to use polls is just as old. Kennedy was so afraid of being discovered that he kept the polling data locked in a safe in the office of his brother, the attorney general. Lyndon Johnson polled more heavily than Kennedy did and learned, through polling, that allowing Vietnam to become an issue in 1964 could cost him re-election. Richard Nixon brought polling—and paranoia over polling—to a new level, believing that his appeal to voters was his reputation as a skilled policymaker, and that if people discovered the extent to which he was polling, they would view him as "slick" and desert him. So he kept his poll data in a safe in his home. But though presidents considered it shameful, polling became an important tool for governing well. Nixon was smart enough to make good use of his polls, once opting to ban oil drilling off the California coast after polling revealed it to be highly unpopular with voters. Jimmy Carter's pollster, Pat Caddell, was the first rock-star pollster, partying with celebrities and cultivating a high-profile image as the president's Svengali (an image considerably tarnished when Caddell's polling for another client, Coca-Cola, became the rationale for the disastrous "New Coke" campaign in the 1980s).

Ronald Reagan polled obsessively throughout his presidency. His pollster, Richard Wirthlin, went so far as to conduct them "before Reagan was inaugurated, while he was being inaugurated, and the day after he was inaugurated," says an administration veteran. He was the first to use polls to sell a right-wing agenda to the country, but he knew enough to retreat when polls indicated that he couldn't win a fight. (Wirthlin's polls convinced Reagan not to cut Social Security, as he'd planned.) By contrast, his successor, George H. W. Bush, practically eschewed polls altogether. "There was a reaction against using polls because they reacted against everything Reagan," says Ron Hinckley, a Bush pollster. "They wanted to put their own name on everything. But their efforts to not be like Reagan took them into a framework of dealing with things that ultimately proved fatal." Indeed, in his first two years in office, Bush is said to have conducted just two polls. Even at Bush's highest point—after the Gulf War, when his approval rating stood at 88 percent—Hinckley says that his economic numbers were in the 40s. "We were in a hell of a lot of trouble," he says, "and nobody wanted to listen."

Bill Clinton, of course, polled like no other president. In addition to polling more often and in greater detail than his predecessors, he put unprecedented faith in his pollsters, elevating them to the status of senior advisers. His tendency to obsess over polls disconcerted even those closest to him, and his over-reliance on polls led to some devastating errors, such as following a Morris poll showing that voters wouldn't accept a candid acknowledgment of his relationship with Monica Lewinsky. . . .

"The Circle is Tight"

When George W. Bush launched his campaign for president, he did so with two prevailing thoughts in mind: to avoid his father's mistakes and to distinguish himself from Bill Clinton. To satisfy the first, Bush needed a tax cut to rival the one being offered by Steve Forbes, at the time considered Bush's most formidable rival for the GOP nomination. But to satisfy the second, Bush needed to engage in some tricky maneuvering. A van Lohuizen poll conducted in late 1998 showed tax cuts to be "the least popular choice" on his agenda among swing voters. So Bush faced a dilemma: He had to sell Americans a tax cut most didn't want, using a poll-crafted sales pitch he didn't want them to know about. In speeches, Bush started listing the tax cut after more popular items like saving Social Security and education. In March 2001, with support still flagging, he began pitching "tax cuts and debt relief" rather than just tax cuts—his polling showed that the public was much more interested in the latter. After plenty of creative math and more poll-tested phrases, Bush's tax cut finally won passage (a larger one, in fact, than he'd been offering in '98).

In a way, Bush's approach to polling is the opposite of Clinton's. He uses polls but conceals that fact, and, instead of polling to ensure that new policies have broad public support, takes policies favored by his conservative base and polls on how to make them seem palatable to mainstream voters. This pattern extends to the entire administration. Whereas Clinton's polling data were regularly circulated among the staff, Bush limits his to . . . [a] handful of senior advisers. . . . According to White House aides, the subject is rarely broached with the president or at other senior staff meetings. "The circle is tight," Matthew Dowd, Bush's chief of polling, testifies. "Very tight." As with Kennedy and Nixon, the Bush administration keeps its polling data under lock and key. Reagan circulated favorable polling data widely among congressional Republicans in an effort to build support. Clinton did likewise and extended this tactic to the media, using polls as political currency to persuade reporters that he was on the right side of an issue. "You don't see it like you did in the Dick Wirthlin days," says a top Republican congressman. "The White House pollster won't meet with the caucus to go through poll data. It just doesn't happen." Says a White House reporter, "The Clinton folks couldn't wait to call you up and share polling data, and Democratic pollsters who worked for the White House were always calling you to talk about it. But there's a general dictate under Bush that they don't use polls to tell them what to think." This policy extends to the president's pollsters, who are discouraged from identifying themselves as such. The strategy seems to be working. A brief, unscientific survey of White House reporters revealed that most couldn't name van Lohuizen as the Bush's primary pollster (most guessed Dowd, who doesn't actually poll). For his part, van Lohuizen sounded genuinely alarmed when I contacted him.

Crafted Talk

It's no mystery why the Bush administration keeps its polling operation in a secure, undisclosed location. Survey after survey shows that voters don't want a president slavishly following polls—they want "leadership" (another word that crops up in Bush's speeches with suspicious frequency). So it's with undisguised relish that Dowd tells me, "It was true during the campaign, it's true now: We don't poll policy positions. Ever."

But voters don't like a president to ignore their desires either. One of the abiding tensions in any democracy is between the need for leaders to respond to public opinion but also to be willing to act in ways that run counter to it. Good presidents strike the right balance. And polls, rightly used, help them do it. . . .

Presidents, of course, must occasionally break with public opinion. But there's a thin line between being principled and being elitist. For many years, Democrats hurt themselves and the country by presuming they knew better than voters when it came to things like welfare, crime, and tax increases. Clinton used polling to help Democrats break this habit. Bush is more intent on using it to facilitate the GOP's own peculiar political elitism—the conviction that coddling corporations and cutting taxes for the rich will help the count, regardless of the fact that a majority of voters disagree.

Bush's attempt to slip a conservative agenda past a moderate public could come back to hurt him, especially now that his high approval ratings might tempt him to overreach. Recent history shows that poll-tested messages are often easy to parry. During the debate over Clinton's healthcare plan, for instance, Republican opponents launched their own poll-tested counterattack, the famous "Harry and Louise" ads, which were broadcast mainly on airport cable networks such as "CNN Airport" where well-traveled congressmen would be sure to spot them and assume they were ubiquitous. Because lawmakers and voters never fully bought Clinton's policy, it couldn't withstand the carefully tested GOP rebuttal. . . .

A similar fate befell the GOP when it took over Congress in 1995, after campaigning on a list of promises dubbed the "Contract With America." As several pollsters and political scientists have since pointed out, the Contract's policies were heavily geared toward the party's conservative base but didn't register with voters—things like corporate tax cuts and limiting the right to sue. The GOP's strategy was to win over the press and the public with poll-tested "power phrases." Education vouchers, for instance, were promoted as a way of "strengthening rights of parents in their children's education," and Republicans were instructed by RNC chairman Haley Barbour to repeat such phrases "until you vomit." But when it came to proposals such as cutting Medicare, Republicans discovered that their confidence in being able to move public opinion—"preserving" and "protecting" Medicare—was misplaced. Clinton successfully branded them as "extremists," and this proposal, along with many of the Contract's provisions, never made it beyond the House.

Like so many other Republican ideas, Barbour's has been reborn under Bush. "What's happened over time is that there's a lot more polling on spin," says Jacobs. "That's exactly where Bush is right now. He's not polling to find out issues that the public supports so that he can respond to their substantive interests. He's polling on presentation. To those of us who study it, most of his major policy statements come off as completely poll concocted." Should this continue, the administration that condemns polling so righteously may not like what the polls wind up saying. ■

 # Chapter 6

Interest Groups

Interest groups play a vital role in American politics. Along with political parties, they are the most important way that Americans organize to express their views and make their demands on government. Interest groups play key roles in the electoral arena and in government policy making. They are active in all three branches of the federal government and in the states.

Interest groups are by no means free of controversy. Government responsiveness to interest groups, if carried too far, can lead to the triumph of special interests at the expense of the public interest. Group involvement in support of particular candidates can be a legitimate way for citizens to advance their interests, but such activity can all too easily cross the line into influence peddling and vote buying.

Above all, the controversy over interest groups rests on a critical debate in modern political science: whether the clash of group interests, if fought on a level playing field where all groups are represented fairly and equitably, will inevitably or even generally result in the victory of the public interest. Those who believe that the public interest is, in effect, the sum of the private interests advocate a large number of effective interest groups. Those on the other side look for ways to limit the power and influence of interest groups in order to allow the public interest to emerge.

This chapter examines the roles played by interest groups in American politics, with particular attention to the dramatic changes in interest group activity over recent decades. Selection 6.1 presents a classic analysis of interest groups by the political scientist E.E. Schattschneider. Selection 6.2 provides an up-to-date account of the roles played by interest groups, written by the political scientists Allan J. Cigler and Burdett A. Loomis; they argue that interest groups are "always involved," but "rarely central" in American politics. Selection 6.3 examines interest groups in comparative perspective, with a look at lobbying in the European Union. Finally, Selection 6.4 puts the spotlight on how Washington lobbyists advance their client's interests by generating (or at least appearing to generate) popular, grass-roots support.

Taken together, these selections probe critical questions: What role should interest groups play in American politics, and should their role be expanded or diminished in order to serve the public interest?

Chapter Questions

1. Is a system of interest group politics consistent with the idea of democracy? Reread Madison's *Federalist* No. 10 and *Federalist* No. 51 (selections 1.1 and 1.4) as you consider your answer.
2. Why are interest groups important in the American political system? What roles do they play? How have the roles of interest groups changed in the past several decades?

 # Foundations

What exactly is an interest group? What is a public interest group, and what distinguishes it from a special interest group? Before examining interest groups in any detail, we need to have an accurate understanding of the meaning of these terms and the nature of interest group politics.

The following selection presents a classic explanation and description of interest group politics. Central to the political scientist E.E. Schattschneider's understanding of interest groups are their size and their narrow focus. Interest groups, by definition, are small and specialized. As such, they can be distinguished from political parties, which, to be effective, must be both large and broad-based. A political system that encourages the formation of interest groups, and responds to their arguments, demands, and pressures, will of necessity differ from one in which citizens express their views and make their demands felt primarily through political parties.

Since Schattschneider's book was published in 1960, American politics has, if anything, become even more focused around interest groups. The role of parties as effective mechanisms for transmitting the demands of citizens to their elected representatives has correspondingly diminished.

Schattschneider's analysis, though more than a generation old, remains an excellent introduction to the theoretical underpinnings of interest group politics.

Questions

1. What characteristics distinguish a special interest group from a public interest group? Is this distinction meaningful, in Schattschneider's view?
2. What would one expect to be the logical result of a political system in which small interest groups dominate? What are the implications of such a system for the role of political parties? For the structure of government institutions? For the nature of public policy?

6.1 The Scope and Bias of the Pressure System (1961)

E.E. Schattschneider

Pressure groups have played a remarkable role in American politics, but they have played an even more remarkable role in American political theory. Considering the political condition of the country in the first third of the twentieth century, it was probably inevitable that the discussion of special-interest pressure groups should lead to development of "group" theories of politics in which an attempt is made to explain everything in terms of group activity, i.e., an attempt to formulate a universal group theory. Since one of the best ways to test an idea is to ride it into the ground, political theory has unquestionably been improved by the heroic attempt to create a political universe revolving about the group. Now that we have a number of drastic statements of the group theory of politics pushed to a great extreme, we ought to be able to see what the limitations of the idea are. . . .

We might begin to break the problem into its component parts by exploring the distinction between public and private interests. If we can validate this distinction, we shall have established one of the boundaries of the subject.

As a matter of fact, the distinction between *public* and *private* interests is a thoroughly respectable one; it is one of the oldest known to political theory. In the literature of the subject, the public interest refers to general or common interests shared by all or by substantially all members of the community. Presumably no community exists unless there is some kind of community of interests, just as there is no nation without some notion of national interests. If it is really impossible to distinguish between private and public interests, the group theorists have produced a revolution in political thought so great that it is impossible to foresee its consequences. For this reason the distinction ought to be explored with great care.

At a time when nationalism is described as one of the most dynamic forces in the world, it should not be difficult to understand that national interests actually do exist. It is necessary only to consider the proportion of the American budget devoted to national defense to realize that the common interest in national survival is a great one. Measured in dollars this interest is one of the biggest things in the world. Moreover, it is difficult to describe this interest as special. The diet on which the American leviathan feeds is something more than a jungle of disparate special interests. In the literature of democratic theory the body of common agreement found in the community is known as the "consensus," without which it is believed that no democratic system can survive.

The reality of the common interest is suggested by demonstrated capacity of the community to survive. There must be something that holds people together.

In contrast with the common interests are the special interests. The implication of this term is that these are interests shared by only a few people or a fraction of the community; they *exclude* others and may be *adverse* to them. A special interest is exclusive in about the same way as private property is exclusive. In a complex society it is not surprising that there are some interests that are shared by all or substantially all members of the community and some interests that are not shared so widely. The distinction is useful precisely because conflicting claims are made by people about the nature of their interests in controversial matters.

Perfect agreement within the community is not always possible, but an interest may be said to have become public when it is shared so widely as to be substantially universal. Thus, the difference between 99 percent agreement and perfect agreement is not so great that it becomes necessary to argue that all interests are special, that the interests of the 99 percent are as special as the interests of the 1 percent. For example, the law is probably doing an adequate job of defining the public interest in domestic tranquility despite the fact that there is nearly always one dissenter at every hanging. That is, the law defines the public interest in spite of the fact that there may be some outlaws.

Since one function of theory is to explain reality, it is reasonable to add that it is a good deal easier to explain what is going on in politics by making a distinction between public and private interests than it is to attempt to explain *everything* in terms of special interests. The attempt to prove that all interests are special forces us into circumlocutions such as those involved in the argument that people have special interests in the common good. The argument can be made, but it seems a long way around to avoid a useful distinction.

What is to be said about the argument that the distinction between public and special interests is "subjective" and is therefore "unscientific"?

All discussions of interests, special as well as general, refer to the motives, desires, and intentions of people. In this sense the whole discussion of interests is subjective. We have made progress in the study of politics because people have observed some kind of relation between the political behavior of people and certain wholly impersonal data concerning their ownership of property, income, economic status, professions, and the like. All that we know about interests, private as well as public, is based on inferences of this sort. Whether the distinction in any given case is valid depends on the evidence and on the kinds of inferences drawn from the evidence.

The only meaningful way we can speak of the interests of an association like the National Association of Manufacturers is to draw inferences from the fact that the membership is a select group to which only manufacturers may belong and to try to relate that datum to what the association does. The implications, logic, and deductions are persuasive only if they furnish reasonable explanations of the facts. That is all that any theory about interests can do. It has seemed persuasive to students of politics to suppose that manufacturers do not join an association to which only manufacturers may belong merely to promote philanthropic or cultural or religious interests, for example. The basis of selection of the membership creates an inference about the organization's concerns. The conclusions drawn from this datum seem to fit what we know about the policies promoted by the association; i.e., the policies seem to reflect the exclusive interests of manufacturers. The method is not foolproof, but it works better than many other kinds of analysis and is useful precisely because special-interest groups often tend to rationalize their special interests as public interests.

Is it possible to distinguish between the "interests" of the members of the National Association of Manufacturers and the members of the American League to Abolish Capital Punishment? The facts in the two cases are not identical. First, *the members of the A.L.A.C.P. obviously do not expect to be hanged.* The membership of the A.L.A.C.P. is not restricted to persons under indictment for murder or in jeopardy of the extreme penalty. *Anybody* can join A.L.A.C.P. Its members oppose capital punishment, although they are not personally likely to benefit by the policy they advocate. The inference is therefore that the interest of the A.L.A.C.P. is not adverse, exclusive, or special. It is not like the interest of the Petroleum Institute in depletion allowances. . . .

. . . The question here is not whether the distinction can be made but whether or not it is worth making. Organization has been described as "merely a stage or degree of interaction" in the development of a group.

The proposition is a good one, but what conclusions do we draw from it? We do not dispose of the matter by calling the distinction between organized and unorganized groups a "mere" difference of degree because some of the greatest differences in the world are differences of degree. As far as special-interest politics is concerned the implication to be avoided is that a few workmen who habitually stop at a corner saloon for a glass of beer are essentially the same as the United States Army because the difference between them is merely one of degree. At this point we have distinction that makes a difference. The distinction between organized and unorganized groups is worth making because it ought to alert us against an analysis which begins as a general group theory of politics but ends with a defense of pressure politics as inherent, universal, permanent, and inevitable. This kind of confusion comes from the loosening of categories involved in the universalization of group concepts.

Since the beginning of intellectual history, scholars have sought to make progress in their work by distinguishing between things that are unlike and by dividing their subject matter into categories to examine them more intelligently. It is something of a novelty, therefore, when group theorists reverse this process by discussing their subject in terms so universal that they wipe out all categories, because this is the dimension in which it is least possible to understand anything.

If we are able, therefore, to distinguish between public and private interests and between organized and unorganized groups we have marked out the major boundaries of the subject; *we have given the subject shape and scope.* We are now in a position to attempt to define the area we want to explore. Having cut the pie into four pieces, we can now appropriate the piece we want and leave the rest to someone else. For a multitude of reasons *the most likely field of study is that of the organized, special-interest groups.* The advantage of concentrating on organized groups is that they are known, identifiable, and recognizable. The advantage of concentrating on special-interest groups is that they have one important characteristic in common; they are all exclusive. This piece of the pie (the organized special-interest groups) we shall call the *pressure system*. The pressure system has boundaries we can define; we can fix its scope and make an attempt to estimate its bias.

It may be assumed at the outset that all organized special-interest groups have some kind of impact on politics. A sample survey of organizations made by the Trade Associations Division of the United States Department of Commerce in 1942 concluded that "From 70 to 100 percent (of these associations) are planning activities in the field of government relations, trade promotion, trade practices, public relations, annual conventions, cooperation with other organizations, and information services."

The subject of our analysis can be reduced to manageable proportions and brought under control if we restrict ourselves to the groups whose interests in politics are sufficient to have led them to unite in formal organizations having memberships, bylaws, and officers. A further advantage of this kind of definition is, we may assume, that the organized special-interest groups are the most self-conscious, best developed, most intense and active groups. Whatever claims can be made for a group theory of politics ought to be sustained by the evidence concerning these groups, if the claims have any validity at all.

The organized groups listed in the various directories (such as *National Associations of the United States*, published at intervals by the United States Department of Commerce) and specialty yearbooks, registers, etc. and the *Lobby Index*, published by the United States House of Representatives, probably include the bulk of the organizations in the pressure system. All compilations are incomplete, but these are extensive enough to provide us with some basis for estimating the scope of the system.

By the time a group has developed the kind of interest that leads it to organize, it may be assumed that it has also developed some kind of political bias because *organization is itself a mobilization of bias in preparation for action*. Since these groups can be identified and since they have memberships (i.e., they include and exclude people), it is possible to think of the *scope* of the system.

When lists of these organizations are examined, the fact that strikes the student most forcibly is that *the system is very small*. The range of organized, identifiable, known groups is amazingly narrow; there is nothing remotely universal about it. There is a tendency on the part of the publishers of directories of associations to place an undue emphasis on business organizations, an emphasis that is almost inevitable because the business community is by a wide margin the most highly organized segment of society. Publishers doubtless tend also to reflect public demand for information. Nevertheless, the dominance of business groups in the pressure system is so marked that it probably cannot be explained away as an accident of the publishing industry.

The business character of the pressure system is shown by almost every list available. *National Associations of the United States* lists 1,860 business associations out of a total of 4,000 in the volume, though it refers without listing (p. VII) to 16,000 organizations of businessmen. One cannot be certain what the total content of the unknown associational universe may be, but, taken with the evidence found in other compilations, it is obvious that business is remarkably well represented. Some evidence of the over-all scope of the system is to be seen in the estimate that 15,000 national trade associations have a gross membership of about one million business firms. The data are incomplete, but even if we do not have a detailed map this is the shore dimly seen.

Much more directly related to pressure politics is the *Lobby Index, 1946–1949* (an index of organizations and individuals registering or filing quarterly reports under the Federal Lobbying Act), published as a report of the House Select Committee on Lobbying Activities. In this compilation, 825 out of a total of 1,247 entries (exclusive of individuals and Indian tribes) represented business. A selected list of the most important of the groups listed in the *Index* (the groups spending the largest sums of money on lobbying) published in the *Congressional Quarterly Log* shows 149 business organizations in a total of 265 listed.

The business or upper-class bias of the pressure system shows up everywhere. Businessmen are four or five times as likely to write to their congressmen as manual laborers are. College graduates are far more apt to write to their congressmen than people in the lowest educational category are.

The limited scope of the business pressure system is indicated by all available statistics. Among business organizations, the National Association of Manufacturers (with about 20,000 corporate members) and the Chamber of Commerce of the United States (about as large as the N.A.M.) are giants. Usually business associations are much smaller. Of 421 trade associations in the metal-products industry listed in *National Associations of the United States,* 153 have a membership of less than 20. The median membership was somewhere between 24 and 50. Approximately the same scale of memberships is to be found in the lumber, furniture, and paper industries where 37.3 percent of the associations listed had a membership of less than 20 and the median membership was in the 25 to 50 range.

The statistics in these cases are representative of nearly all other classifications of industry.

Data drawn from other sources support this thesis. Broadly, the pressure system has an upper-class bias. There is overwhelming evidence that participation in voluntary organizations is related to upper social and economic status; the rate of participation is much higher in the upper strata than it is elsewhere. The general proposition is well stated by Lazarsfeld:

> People on the lower SES levels are less likely to belong to any organizations than the people on high SES (Social and Economic Status) levels. (On an A and B level, we find 72 percent of these respondents who belong to one or more organizations. The proportion of respondents who are members of formal organizations decreases steadily as SES level descends until, on the D level only 35 percent of the respondents belong to any associations.)

The bias of the system is shown by the fact that *even nonbusiness organizations reflect an upper-class tendency.*

Lazarsfeld's generalization seems to apply equally well to urban and rural populations. The obverse side of the coin is that large areas of the population appear to be wholly outside the system of private organization. A study made by Ira Reid of a Philadelphia area showed that in a sample of 963 persons, 85 percent belonged to no civic or charitable organization and 74 percent belonged to no occupational, business, or professional associations, while another Philadelphia study of 1,154 women showed that 55 percent belonged to no associations of any kind.

A *Fortune* farm poll taken some years ago found that 70.5 percent of farmers belonged to no agricultural organizations. A similar conclusion was reached by two Gallup polls showing that perhaps no more than one third of the farmers of the country belonged to farm organizations, while another *Fortune* poll showed that 86.8 percent of the low-income farmers belonged to no farm organizations. All available data support the generalization that the farmers who do not participate in rural organizations are largely the poorer ones.

A substantial amount of research done by other rural sociologists points to the same conclusion. Mangus and Cottam say, on the basis of a study of 556 heads of Ohio farm families and their wives:

> The present study indicates that comparatively few of those who ranked low on the scale of living took any active part in community organizations as members, attendants, contributors, or leaders. On the other hand, those families that ranked high on the scale of living comprised the vast majority of the highly active participants in formal group activities. . . . Fully two-thirds of those in the lower class as defined in this study were non-participants as compared with only one-tenth of those in the upper class and one-fourth of those in the middle class. . . . When families were classified by the general level-of-living index, 16 times as large a proportion of those in the upper classes as of those in the lower class were active participants. . . .

Along the same line Richardson and Bauder observe, "Socio-economic status was directly related to participation." In still another study it was found that "a highly significant relationship existed between income and formal participation." It was found that persons with more than four years of college education held twenty times as many memberships (per one hundred persons) as did those with less than a fourth-grade education and were forty times as likely to hold office in nonchurch organizations, while persons with an income over $5,000 hold ninety-four times as many offices as persons with incomes less than $250.

D. E. Lindstrom found that 72 percent of farm laborers belonged to no organizations whatever.

There is a great wealth of data supporting the proposition that participation in private associations exhibits a class bias.

The class bias of associational activity gives meaning to the limited scope of the pressure system, because *scope and bias are aspects of the same tendency.* The data raise a serious question about the validity of the proposition that special-interest groups are a universal form of political organization reflecting *all* interests. As a matter of fact, to suppose that everyone participates in pressure-group activity and that all interests get themselves organized in the pressure system is to destroy the meaning of this form of politics. The pressure system makes sense only as the political instrument of a segment of the community. It gets results by being selective and biased; *if everybody got into the act, the unique advantages of this form of organization would be destroyed, for it is possible that if all interests could be mobilized the result would be a stalemate.*

Special-interest organizations are most easily formed when they deal with small numbers of individuals who are acutely aware of their exclusive interests. To describe the conditions of pressure-group organization in this way is, however, to say that it is primarily a business phenomenon. Aside from a few very large organizations (the churches, organized labor, farm organizations, and veterans' organizations) the residue is a small segment of the population. *Pressure politics is essentially the politics of small groups.*

The vice of the groupist theory is that it conceals the most significant aspects of the system. The flaw in the pluralist heaven is that the heavenly chorus sings with a strong upper-class accent. Probably about 90 percent of the people cannot get into the pressure system.

The notion that the pressure system is automatically representative of the whole community is a myth fostered by the universalizing tendency of modern group theories. *Pressure politics is a selective process* ill designed to serve diffuse interests. The system is skewed, loaded, and unbalanced in favor of a fraction of a minority.

On the other hand, pressure tactics are not remarkably successful in mobilizing general interests. When pressure-group organizations attempt to represent the interests of large numbers of people, they are usually able to reach only a small segment of their constituencies. Only a chemical trace of the fifteen million Negroes in the United States belong to the National Association for the Advancement of Colored People. Only one five hundredths of 1 percent of American women belong to the League of Women Voters, only one sixteen hundredths of 1 percent of the consumers belong to the National Consumers' League, and only 6 percent of American automobile drivers belong to the American Automobile Association, while about 15 percent of the veterans belong to the American Legion.

The competing claims of pressure groups and political parties for the loyalty of the American public revolve about the difference between the results likely to be achieved by small-scale and large-scale political organization. Inevitably, the outcome of pressure politics and party politics will be vastly different. ■

 # American Politics Today

Interest groups exert their influence throughout the American system of government. They lobby Congress, the White House, and executive agencies; are active in Washington and in the state capitals; and file lawsuits and briefs in both state and federal courts. All of this activity and influence has led some analysts to conclude that interest groups are at the center of American politics—and that any theory attempting to explain the American political system has to start with a theory of groups and their behavior.

The political scientists Allan J. Cigler and Burdett A. Loomis disagree. They see interest groups as "always involved" in American politics, but "rarely central." With this distinction in mind, they highlight four trends in interest group activity over recent decades. In the end, they conclude that "organized interests have their say on almost all issues, yet they rarely dominate the process" or dictate the outcomes.

Questions

1. What are the four main trends that Cigler and Loomis identify in the activities and influence of organized interest groups in American politics? How have these trends affected the political process? How have they affected public policy outcomes?
2. What strategies do organized interest groups use in their attempts to influence government officials? Why do different groups employ different strategies?
3. What do Cigler and Loomis mean when they conclude that organized interests are "rarely central" to American politics?

6.2 Always Involved, Rarely Central: Organized Interests in American Politics (2002)

Allan J. Cigler and Burdett A. Loomis

Looking at the broad sweep of American politics at the start of the twenty-first century, we are struck by the omnipresence of interest groups. Whatever the issue, organized interests are at the table. In electoral politics groups offer tremendous financial assistance and provide increasing numbers of activists and strategists to do everything from getting out the vote to sponsoring polls. Organized interests mount highly sophisticated public relations campaigns and advertise heavily on behalf of candidates and issues. Interests consistently weigh in on judicial and administrative appointments and represent nearly all sectors of social and economic life, albeit with unequal effectiveness. Although this is especially true at the national level, all states and most large cities have their own corps of groups and lobbyists.

In short, interest groups are ubiquitous. [We have argued] that this ubiquity has led to a state of "hyperpluralism"—or excessive representation—in which groups protect their interests tenaciously and effectively. This makes governmental policymaking highly responsive to individual interests, but much less so to broad societal challenges. Such a conclusion might lead some to believe that organized interests lie at the center of American politics, and that some kind of group-based theory would offer a coherent way to think about our political system. But this isn't the case. Although interest groups are important across the board, no group-based theory can explain the whole of American politics. At the same time, organized interests are influential in the contexts of other political models—whether

---

these emphasize political institutions, policymaking, or mobilization of the electorate.

In general, we see four major trends that complement one another. First, more interests are engaged in more ways to influence policy outcomes. Interests monitor more actions than they used to, and stand ready to swing into action more quickly when a red flag is raised (often by a lobbyist on retainer). Given the high stakes of government decisions, whether by a committee in the House of Representatives or a bureau of the Environmental Protection Agency, the combination of monitoring and action is a worthwhile investment for most interests.

Second, the distinction between "outside" lobbying (public relations and grass-roots contacts) and "inside" lobbying (personal relationships) is blurring. Interest groups must use both to get their ideas across. To be sure, a key provision can still find its way into an omnibus bill without a ripple, but battles over most major issues are fought simultaneously on multiple fronts. . . . At the first sign of trouble in a committee hearing or, more likely, a casual conversation, a lobbyist can instruct influential constituents to call, fax, or email their representative. Jack Bonner and a dozen other constituent-lobbying experts can construct a set of grassroots (or elite "grasstops") entreaties within a few days, if not a few hours. And a media buyer can target any sample of legislators for advertisements that run in their districts, thus showing the legislators that their constituents and key Washington interests are watching their action on an important bill.

Third, the distinction between the politics of elections and the politics of policymaking is blurring. Though always linked in a democracy, these two phenomenons have strengthened their ties recently—in many ways reflecting the "permanent campaign" of presidential election politics that emerged in the 1970s and 1980s. Sidney Blumenthal sees this as combining "image-making with strategic calculation. Under the permanent campaign government is turned into the perpetual campaign." In the 1990s many interests have come to see the combination of electoral and policy politics in much the same light, with the issue advocacy ads of 1996 serving as the initial demonstration of this new era. In addition, many interests are now viewing the "campaign" idea as one that defines their broader lobbying strategies, and the boundaries between electoral campaigns and public relations efforts are diminishing.

Fourth, political parties and organized interests are becoming increasingly integrated. The tremendous growth in soft money donations to parties and candidates makes interest groups more important to the financial viability of both. Although some interests give roughly equal amounts to Republicans and Democrats, most groups contribute heavily to one party or the other. And organized interests are now intruding directly into congressional campaigns, mounting large issue advocacy advertising campaigns as well as independent campaigns in competitive districts and states. . . . In addition, many large membership organizations, from labor unions to the National Rifle Association to the Sierra Club, have financed sweeping get-out-the-vote drives, using both volunteers and paid staff to complement candidates' efforts. This influence is enhanced by highly partisan voting among members of many such groups. In 1998 House Minority Whip Tom DeLay publicly chastised the Electronic Industries Association for hiring former Democratic representative David McCurdy as its president rather than a more acceptable former Republican legislator.

In light of these trends organized interests can best be understood by examining their effect on parties, policymaking, and political institutions, rather than by trying to view the political process through the lens of group politics. . . .

Partisan Parity

Although the results of the 2000 elections—for president, the Senate, and the House of Representatives—produced a snapshot of almost total partisan balance, parity between Republicans and Democrats has been a political fact of life since at least 1994, and probably since the elections of 1980. The key elements of even partisan division include divided government, narrow majorities in both houses of Congress, and a relatively small number of competitive seats in the House, as well as an overall balance in the voting public.*

Parity affects interest group politics in terms of individual groups' strategies and tactics and these groups' significance in the political system. In 1990 Robert Salisbury noted that despite an increase in the number of organized interests, their overall "clout" was diminished. Our take is a little different. Partisan parity may make it difficult for groups, like parties, to push through large policy changes. But parity may also mean that interest group activities will be important both in modestly adjusting policies and in protecting past gains. Moreover, partisan parity may not be a defining condition for all decisions. Some issues, like aid to farmers, have rarely reflected pure partisan divisions; others, like national security, especially in the wake of September 11, strongly encourage bipartisanship. Still, the even divisions between the parties dominate the political landscape of the post-2000 era.

Partisan parity has implications for organized interests. Above all, it means that control of Congress is always within reach of the minority party at the next election, which is never more than two years away. Organized interests know that they can "invest" in a party with the hope that it will become the majority—or retain its control. Congress today has few competitive seats, perhaps twenty in 2000 and probably not more than thirty-five in the postredistricting year of 2002, so the chances for a major shift in policy direction are modest. Still, holding a majority is important for parties and groups, as was illustrated by Sen. James M. Jeffords's, I-Vt., decision to leave the GOP and become an Independent (who caucused with the Democrats). Thus a 50–50 Republican Senate (with Vice President Dick Cheney casting the decisive vote) became a 50–49–1 Democratic Senate.

Although this power shift may have altered policy outcomes only modestly (given the need for sixty votes in the Senate on many issues that attract filibusters), Democratic control enhanced opportunities for unions, environmentalists, and similar groups to affect the policy agenda. In addition, tight margins in both chambers mean that almost all legislators seek substantial funds from interest

---

*Editor's note: "Partisan parity" remains a key feature of American politics even after 2002. Although the Republican party now controls not only the White House but also both houses of Congress, its margins of control are razor-thin. This is particularly true in the Senate, where Republicans do not have enough votes to block a Democratic filibuster.

groups—both through political action committee donations and soft money contributions.

Electoral Strategies and Actions   The electoral role of organized interests has increased in recent decades as candidates and parties demand high-tech information gathering and timely communication with the electorate, activities that cost a lot of money. But interest groups are far more than financial resources during election years. The prevalence of permanent campaign politics, with its continual fund-raising and campaign-style attempts at influence, makes distinguishing lobbying from electoral activity difficult. For example, in competitive legislative races, sorting out the messages of political parties, interest groups, and candidates is next to impossible, especially for would-be voters who evince precious little interest in the campaign to begin with.

One consequence of the permanent campaign is that organizations such as the AFL-CIO, the Christian Coalition, and the National Rifle Association now participate in electoral politics full-time. Such groups have emerged as distinct electoral entities, often operating without formal cooperation or collaboration with parties or candidates. In fact, many groups operate like traditional political parties: they recruit and train candidates to run for public office, serve as advisors in primary and general elections, and communicate with voters on candidates' behalf or against their opponents.

The 1999–2000 election cycle represented a continuation of the upward spiral of interest group involvement in federal elections. Although political action committee spending and soft money contributions by organized interests garnered some attention, the major financial story of the 2000 elections was money raised and spent outside the limits of the Federal Election Campaign Act's (FECA) disclosure and expenditure provisions. Political scientist Anthony Corrado contends that campaign finance in the 2000 elections ("bore a greater resemblance to campaign finance prior to the passage of FECA than to the patterns that were supposed to occur after it." That is, interest groups' activities for or against candidates running for federal office were only modestly constrained by law. Much group activity occurred out of the public eye, with more and more interests learning to influence electoral politics through such devices as issue advocacy advertising.

And more groups than ever were involved early in the election cycle; a number played key roles in the 2000 presidential primaries, especially for the Republican Party. One study found that more than one hundred groups, many of which spent huge sums, were active in issue advocacy efforts leading up to the 2000 mid-March Super Tuesday primaries. Interest groups were limited more by imagination and lack of resources than by federal law.

Though it is hard to say precisely how much money was invested in issue advocacy campaigns during the 2000 election cycle, estimates can be made. New York University's Brennan Center, which tracks interest group radio and television ads in seventy-five of the nation's largest media markets, found that interest groups spent $57 million on issue advocacy ads to influence races in 2000. This was roughly one-tenth of all candidate-centered advertising in these markets, and it was overwhelmingly concentrated in a few competitive races.

The 2000 election also saw an escalation in interest groups' "ground war," where a few groups invested in sharply targeted get-out-the-vote efforts, direct mail, and telephone banks. If such efforts do not explicitly advocate a candidate's election or defeat and are not coordinated with either political party or candidate campaigns, they may remain undisclosed to the public and outside the confines of federal regulations. In 2000, for example, the AFL-CIO used roughly three-quarters of its $46 million in election expenses on get-out-the-vote and direct mail voter education efforts. Organized labor claimed it had registered 2.3 million new union household members, had made 8 million phone calls to union households, and distributed more than 14 million leaflets at union work sites. Union get-out-the-vote efforts on election day were crucial in swing states such as Michigan and Pennsylvania. Republican Governor John Engler, explaining Al Gore's victory in Michigan, pointed to the fact that the United Auto Workers had negotiated a paid holiday in their contract, calling it the "largest soft money contribution in history."

The NAACP, using its National Voter Fund as a vehicle, organized a massive get-out-the-vote campaign in forty targeted congressional districts and several key swing states like Michigan, Ohio, and Pennsylvania, spending some $9 million to boost African-American turnout. The NAACP coordinated with the American Federation of Teachers to reach young voters in Philadelphia, arranging to speak at high school assemblies and compiling lists of students eligible to vote. Magleby and his associates were able to identify 211 interest groups that communicated in some way with the electorate in the seventeen competitive races the authors monitored in 2000—and 159 of these groups used telephone contacts and targeted direct mail extensively. Almost all of this get-out-the-vote activity happened outside the confines of federal election law.*. . .

Lobbying Strategies and Actions   Despite organized interests' huge investments in electoral politics, rarely do elections produce definitive victories for a group. Indeed, having your party of choice control Congress or the presidency (or even both) does not guarantee success, as health care reform advocates discovered in 1993–1994 when President Clinton's health care reform package failed. Organized interests have therefore adopted—even pioneered—many "permanent campaign" techniques to advance their own issues. In the early to mid-1990s dozens of telecommunications firms used survey research, public relations campaigns, advertising, campaign contributions, personal contacts by well-paid Washington lobbyists, extensive grassroots lobbying from local and state executives, and broad coalitions to affect the content of the Telecommunications Reform Act eventually passed in 1996.

By the lobbying did not stop there. The act gave continuing decision making power to the Federal Communications Commission, and so the commission—and then Congress again—became targets for further policy change. *Roll Call*, a newspaper that covers Capitol Hill, has been filled with advertisements for and against

---

*The Bipartisan Campaign Reform Act, signed into law by President Bush in March 2002, aims to ban "soft money" contributions to political parties and to restrict the campaign activities of interest groups. As of this writing, the constitutionality of the act is under review by the federal courts.

modifications in the Telecommunications Reform Act, and local notables have been mobilized and remobilized to loosen restrictions on the ability of the Regional Bell companies to offer long distance phone service.

More generally, organized interests emphasize a campaign style of lobbying dedicated to marshalling information that demonstrates the political power of an idea or proposal. For example, groups have begun to use the Internet for grassroots lobbying by identifying, recruiting, and segmenting large numbers of supporters in a fairly short time. Groups from handicapped citizens to the U.S. Chamber of Commerce can encourage and provide the means for constituents to bombard their legislators with well-conceived, focused emails.

In the politics of problem definition, everyone can participate by calling a press conference, releasing a study, going on a talk show, commissioning a poll, or buying an advertisement. Nor is there any shortage in Washington of well-defined problems and potential solutions, as the capital is awash in arguments and evidence that define problems, set agendas, and suggest remedies. More difficult to understand is how certain definitions come to prevail in a system of political institutions that often, though not always, resist new—or newly packaged—ideas.

As problem definition and agenda status become increasingly important elements of policymaking, organized interests are stepping up their attempts to expand, restrict, or redirect conflict. The public interest and environmental movements of the 1960s often led the way in employing those strategies, leaving business to catch up in the 1970s and 1980s. Jeffrey Berry, a long-time student of public interest groups, has concluded that citizen groups have driven the policy agenda since the 1960s, thus forcing business interests to respond to issues developed by groups such as Common Cause and environmental organizations. We do not fully agree with Berry's assessment, but citizen groups have surely changed the governmental agenda in hundreds of cases.

Following on the heels of these agenda successes has been the institutionalization of interests within government, especially when broad public concerns are at stake. For example, many of the 1995 battles over the Republicans' Contract with America pitted legislators against members of government agencies such as the Environmental Protection Agency. Moreover, many interests have found homes in Congress in caucuses composed of sitting legislators.

And there's the rub. *As more interests seek to define problems and push agenda items, more messages emanate from more sources.* Threatened interests—whether corporate, environmental, or professional—compete with one another to publicize their issues and win converts. Some interests can cut through the cacophony of voices. Those in E.E. Schattschneider's "heavenly chorus" of affluent groups can—at a price—get their message across through public relations campaigns or advertisements. In addition, if such messages are directed toward legislators who have received substantial campaign contributions from the sponsoring interests, the messages typically reach a receptive audience.

The emphasis on problem definition looms large when major public policy issues are on the table amid tremendous uncertainty. Lots of substantive interests are in play, many competing scenarios are put forward, legislative decisions are always contingent, and public policy outcomes are often filled with unanticipated consequences. As loose, ill-defined policy communities replace cozy policymaking triangles of interest groups, congressional committees, and administrative agencies, decision making amid great uncertainty has become the rule, not the exception.

• • •

Always at the Table

Organized groups are integral to American politics, as they have been for a century. . ., and they represent a wide variety of interests in electoral campaigns, agenda setting, decision making, and policy implementation at all levels of government. Whether forging breast cancer victims into a formidable political force. . ., reasserting the power of a traditionally strong group. . ., or embarking on sophisticated media lobbying campaigns. . ., organized interests demonstrate their resilience in a political system that affords multiple points of access and influence.

However important money may be in American politics, useful information is usually worth more. Much of this information is technical, and group representatives provide reams of data and analyses to elected and appointed officials. Increasingly, however, the information comes with explicitly political overtones from constituents activated with breathtaking efficiency and armed with well-tested messages tailored to each legislator. . . . [I]nside lobbying [remains relevant,] but much of this complements constituency-based efforts that employ highly sophisticated campaign techniques.

So, interest group activity is vigorous. But is it effective, too? Success and failure can be difficult to assess; political parties, individual legislators, and the media come into play, as does competition among interests. In the end organized interests have their say on almost all issues, yet they rarely dominate the process. Nor can we explain all outcomes on the basis of their activities. [As many] studies demonstrate, the politics of organized interests is messy, frustrating, and fully integrated into our system of checks and balances. In that sense, there are few permanent victories and even fewer unassailable generalizations. Rather, groups interact with government officials, sometimes influencing outcomes, sometimes not, and sometimes operating at the direction of elected officials rather than the reverse. Things do change, from the increasing use of telephones at the turn of the twentieth century to the growth of the Internet at the advent of the twenty-first. But much remains the same as legislators and lobbyists combine to represent constituents and interests in distinct, but overlapping, ways. ■

 # The International Context

The activities of American interest groups are not limited to the United States. In an increasingly interdependent world, American corporations and other organized interests must also be aware of—and attempt to influence—political decisions in other countries.

The decisions of the European Union (EU), as the journalist Samuel Loewenberg suggests, are often of particularly importance to American interests. In recent years, for example, European policy makers have played key roles in approving or preventing mergers involving American companies, and in imposing regulations that impact American efforts to export products to the European market. American corporations and interest groups have responded by stepping up their efforts to lobby the European Union.

But lobbying in Europe, as Loewenberg points out, can be very different from lobbying in the United States. To succeed, American interest groups have to observe, learn, and adapt their behavior as needed.

Question

1. What are the differences between the lobbying environment in Europe and the lobbying environment in the United States? What factors account for these differences?

6.3 Lobbying, Euro-Style (2001)

Samuel Loewenberg

You've heard plenty about their battles with the Bush Administration over global warming and missile defense, but the issue that really has Europeans in an uproar these days is exploding television sets. At least that's the view being pushed by the global public relations and lobbying firm Burson-Marsteller, which has been waging a campaign on behalf of its clients in the bromine industry against legislation in the European Union that would ban the chemical as a flame retardant in household appliances.

Burson-Marsteller's lobbyists and their clients, which include Great Lakes Chemical Corp. and the Dead Sea Bromine Group, have a big fight on their hands. The regulation is being pushed by the Green Party—a powerful force in Western Europe—and has the support of several countries. Critics of bromine are concerned because the chemical is toxic and they fear it will leach into the environment. After wending its way through the European Union's three governmental bodies, the bill is now going before the EU Parliament for a second time.

During its long campaign, Burson-Marsteller has created the Bromine Science and Environmental Forum, which publishes scientific studies and has an annual conference. It has also established the Alliance for Consumer Fire Safety in Europe, which operates a Web site in English, French, Dutch, and German. The site gives examples of horrific fires from around the Continent, and implies that the combustion of household products causes 4,000 deaths and 80,000 injuries in Europe each year.

"This is an incredibly technical piece of legislation," said Jeremy Galbraith, who heads the Burson-Marsteller lobbying operation in this city [Brussels] that serves as the European Union's capital. After four years of public relations and lobbying, he said, the firm is making "progress" in demonstrating the benefits of bromine to European Union officials.

That the European Union became engulfed in this lobbying battle royal over such a narrow issue might surprise people in the U.S. policy world. If the bromine initiative arose in Washington, it would likely be stuck in the bowels of a regulatory agency and not in Congress. Were it to get to Capitol Hill, industry lobbyists could probably quash the legislation by applying political pressure or by neutralizing it during the appropriations process.

But as American companies are slowly learning, the rules of the influence trade are very different in the European Union from what they are in Washington.

Indeed, for most Washingtonians, the European Union is hard to fathom. When the European Union's actions do attract notice in the United States—such as in the recent scuttling of the merger between General Electric Co. and Honeywell International Inc.—they are usually greeted with shock and indignation and then explained away as being driven by politics, protectionism, and elitism. But in fact, the quashing of the merger by Brussels, and the astonishment it generated on the other side of the Atlantic, shows that U.S. corporations are often behind the curve in figuring out how to play the influence game at the European Union.

Eighty percent of the regulations that affect businesses in Europe originate with the European Union, according to the public affairs firm Hill & Knowlton. Yet it is only in the past few years that U.S. companies peddling their wares in Europe's 340 million-person market have started to realize that they can no more ignore regulators and politicians in Brussels than they can their counterparts in Washington. This summer [2001], for instance, the European Union's reach has ranged far beyond merger approvals to issues such as food safety, securities regulation, and the prohibiting of television advertisements aimed at children. In late August, European Union regulators moved against Microsoft Corp., arguing that the software giant was attempting to monopolize the browser market on the Continent.

And yet this is a world largely without campaign contributions, where the revolving door would be considered crass, and where "astroturf"—the American practice in which industry lobbyists manufacture grassroots support for their clients—is almost nonexistent.

Although the internal dynamics of lobbying differ considerably in Brussels from those in Washington, the overriding principles of access and influence remain constant. Both cities operate in a bubble, little understood or observed by the public, where often-overworked and understaffed politicians and bureaucrats decide on complex policy issues. Thus in both places, lobbyists exercise influence as providers of substantive information and political intelligence.

But as some of the biggest U.S. companies have been slow to learn, simply transporting K Street tactics and personnel to Brussels can be a recipe for failure. As early as March, Euro lobbyists were talking about how General Electric CEO Jack Welch's bluster over the proposed GE-Honeywell merger had poisoned the waters with European officials, repeating mistakes made by executives from Monsanto Co. and Coca-Cola Co. in previous years. Even Jack Valenti, the president of the Motion Picture Association of America, who is regarded as a paragon of K Street smooth, made serious mistakes during his visit to the European Union several years ago when trying to counter French-led attempts to curtail the invasion of American movies. The U.S. film industry, according to a Brussels lobbyist for a multinational entertainment company, is still trying to regain ground lost by Valenti. "Valenti talked about culture as if it was a commodity to be traded," said the lobbyist. "We are still in a post-Jack recovery mode, even years later."

Different Geometry

For lobbyists who touch down in Brussels, navigating the European Union system is in some ways geometrically more complicated than lobbying in the United States. In Washington, although Republicans and Democrats constantly vie for control, the general lines of power are firmly established. Issues and players vary, but one lobby campaign follows much the same format as another. Not so in the still evolving European Union, formed in 1993, where lobbyists face a monumental task in simply trying to figure out where to focus their efforts.

"In Washington lobbying, you get access to people. In Brussels lobbying, you get people who show you the way through the big, untransparent maze," said Maurits Bruggink, the managing director of the Brussels lobbying shop Grayling Political Strategy. K Street's trend of going bipartisan isn't enough here: The 12 lobbyists in Bruggink's office hail from seven different countries and speak nine different languages. Bruggink, who is Dutch, speaks five languages himself. Grayling, which is headquartered in London, has offices in seven countries.

The nature of lobbying on the Continent is different—and so are the fees, which fall on the low end of the K Street scale. Brussels firms report hourly charges of from $100 to $200, and monthly fees ranging from $5,000 to $10,000.

The entity called the European Union is actually made up of a variety of institutions, all vying with each other for power; even defining where power begins and ends is difficult. In cases ranging from human rights to banking, EU officials have issued guidelines that member states interpret and put into law. How they choose to do so can vary widely. In other instances, though, such as the fight over the use of bromine as a flame retardant, the European Union spends many months debating narrow issues that are smaller than anything that would rise to the level of a congressional floor debate.

For lobbyists, there are three vital EU decision-making bodies. The Council of Ministers is composed of leaders from member nations and senior Cabinet officials who propose and approve legislation. The European Commission is the giant multinational bureaucracy that promulgates regulations. And the 625-member European Parliament has taken on an increasingly powerful oversight role, particularly on environmental and consumer affairs issues. Within these institutions are members who hold allegiances to a multitude of political parties, among them Socialists, Greens, Thatcherite Conservatives, and ultra-rightists. EU regulators are technically nonpartisan, but are quite activist by American standards. As many companies have learned, while they may have the support of one EU body, another always seems ready to pop up and make life difficult with inconvenient laws and rules. . . .

The drawn-out and contentious policy-making process in Brussels further complicates influence-peddling. These days, European lobbyists are focusing their efforts on Parliament, which has gained power in the past few years. Elaine Cruikshanks, Hill & Knowlton's European chairman, noted in a recent article that Parliament has become a favorite for lobbyists because it "is open and accessible and has members with relatively few staff to support them," and the members are thus eager for input from helpful lobbyists. To Washington lobbyists, that probably sounds a lot like Capitol Hill.

Many Players

The aspect that is perhaps most underestimated by U.S. companies is the European Union's essential makeup: The union consists of 15 sovereign countries, which, unlike American states, do not share the same underlying ideological and economic interests. American lobbyists often focus on decision makers in Brussels without realizing that it is equally, if not more important, to concentrate first on the capitals of some or all of the 15 member nations—all the countries of Western Europe, except Norway and Switzerland.

"If I want a positive outcome, I have to have the message coming from the member states," said Ivan Hodac, a Czech who runs AOL Time Warner's lobbying operation in Brussels and whose other lobbyists are from Spain, Italy, and Holland.

In Washington, campaign contributions and entrenched party politics enable most issues to be dealt with in a few congressional cycles as companies hire lobbyists who can enlist the help of the party leadership and the relevant committee chairmen, regardless of what state they are from. But for a company in trouble in Europe, it is not simply a matter of hiring the local Haley Barbour, Tommy Boggs, or other star lobbyist to straighten out the mess. Given the European Union's decentralized nature, it is hard to imagine that such a person exists.

The golden rule of Euro lobbying is to get four things right: timing, intelligence, targeting, and sensitivity, said veteran EU lobbyist David Earnshaw, who had been a senior parliamentary aide for a Socialist member and then worked as a lobbyist for pharmaceutical giant SmithKline Beecham.

Connections simply do not mean as much in Brussels, because of the high number of players and because the policy-making process is drawn out and consensus-based. Slipping in a last-minute provision or neutering a bill in appropriations is usually not an option. European lobbyists place much less importance on "getting a meeting" than do their American counterparts. One lobbyist for a U.S. investment bank maintains that the bank has well-connected former high-level officials on retainer in almost every European country. "We can get access to anybody we want to," said the American. But most European lobbyists scoff at such claims, emphasizing that technical knowledge and a good case are more important than political connections.

Lobbying in Brussels is more low-key than in the United States, said Cruikshanks. "It's much more workmanlike, I would say. We are not the stars—the client is." Cruikshanks said that the role of her lobbyists—who, as a group, speak nine of the 11 EU languages—is to act as facilitators.

For Americans, adjusting to this different culture takes time. One lobbyist for a U.S. company that is currently under fire said she uses a European firm because "a lot of times I don't want to show my face. You send people in so as not to leave fingerprints." In Washington, corporations and industries often send out hired guns with political connections to fix problems with the government. But this is not an accepted practice in Brussels, where most European lobbyists say they rarely talk to officials on behalf of their clients. In fact, lobbyists say they often do not even accompany their clients to meetings. A lobbyist for a European liquor trade group expressed horror at the idea of sending an advocate on his industry's behalf.

"When you go and talk to politicians here, they like to see the whites of your eyes," said Ken Baker, who lobbies for Monsanto in Brussels. Baker, a New Zealander, speaks French, Dutch, Italian, and some German, and said he is perceived as a fellow European.

Even that sacred K Street tradition, the revolving door, is a rarity for Euro lobbying shops. Europeans have a professional bureaucracy, and the concept that regulators might cash in by going to work for corporations they once oversaw is a foreign one. Further, old contacts can go stale, as the presidency of the Council of Ministers rotates among countries every six months, and the heads of the Commission's various agencies are reappointed every five years. One head of a lobby shop said she prefers to hire not former legislators but former journalists, because they tend to have a broad range of contacts and know how to write.

Of course, politicians here are no strangers to the back-room deal and the under-the-table envelope. Last year, the Commission was dissolved in a cloud of scandal and then reorganized, while corruption at the highest levels was revealed recently in France and Germany.

The American system involves the widespread passing of money through mostly regulated (and disclosed) campaign contributions. Comparing their work to that of their Washington counterparts, Brussels lobbyists point to the lack of campaign donations as the biggest difference. Corporations can give money to political parties in most European countries, but they are usually limited in their donations to individuals, as much by custom as by law. Another difference is that European politicians do not face the same fundraising pressures as Americans do: David Robert Bowe, a two-term British member of the European Parliament, said that his last campaign cost 30,000 [pounds sterling]—about $43,000.

In England, where the public is quite sensitive to any perceived ties between government and industry, a few intermediaries have popped up to facilitate contact. "There is a lot more suspicion of vested corporate interests influencing the democratic process here," said Phil Royal, a lobbyist with the London firm of Butler Kelly, who directs the Environment Forum, a bipartisan group that brings together companies and politicians. The group holds dinners and lunches so that corporate representatives can chat informally with regulatory officials and members of Parliament.

While the lack of campaign contributions removes a crucial tool from the lobbyist's tool kit, American corporations face an even bigger difficulty: learning to negotiate the European Union and its multilateral policy-making process. Each of the union's 15 member states has substantial power to push through or veto policy initiatives. Brent Staples, who heads the Brussels office of APCO Worldwide, a huge PR and lobbying firm, compares EU lobbying to "three-dimensional chess." And that means that public opinion often plays a greater role here than in the United States, particularly on environmental issues. Burson-Marsteller, for instance, created a unit dedicated to working on environmental issues, the company's only such issue-specific division.

Indeed, American companies often hit a wall when confronted by the fact that many European countries are social democracies built in very different political foundations from those of the United States. Thus, when a company tries to make the case that its position will benefit the general populace, invoking the name of the Chamber of Commerce or the National Association of Manufacturers does not carry the same cachet as it does in Washington. A recent article in *The New York Times* on the Daimler-Chrysler merger pointed out that American executives were shocked that their German counterparts were used to dining in the same company cafeterias as low-level employees. For American lobbyists in Brussels struggling to form a personal connection with European officials, the differing political mores can be confounding.

"There is a whole kind of underlying socialist suspicion" of corporations, said a lobbyist for a U.S. investment bank. "Consumers are treated like children in Europe. It's all part of the tradition of Big Government here."

The American penchant for trying to substitute self-regulation for government oversight has little credibility with officials in Brussels, who tend to take the view that companies will misbehave if left to themselves. But it's not only European regulators who hold this view. Bertel Heerink, government affairs director for the European Chemical Industry Council, said that public demands for corporate responsibility have caused his group to publicly disagree with at least one of its American members, ExxonMobil Corp., which is seeking to eliminate a variety of regulations on chemicals. "Sometimes you come to the limit of where you can stretch" in terms of principle versus public perception, Heerink said. "It's the political reality of today."

Environmentalists Hold Sway

Corporate lobbyists in the European Union also face an obstacle that does not exist in the United States: a powerful environmental and consumer movement that has elected members of governments. The green movement began in Germany, the industrial giant; France fights heated trade wars on behalf of family farmers and fresh pastries; and England, home of Thatcherism and privatization, is also a nation of militant bird-watchers and gardening-club members.

"You have U.S. companies that don't see it in the U.S., and it comes as a terribly rude shock to them in Europe," said Gavin Grant, a managing director at Burson-Marsteller's London office, who formerly worked on cruelty-to-animal issues for an NGO [nongovernmental organization]. "Often, American corporations don't understand the pace at which this stuff moves over here.". . .

[L]obbyists such as [David] Earnshaw, the former aide to a Socialist member of the British Parliament, thinks it will be some time before most American lobbyists and their corporate clients become truly effective in Brussels. Earnshaw, who has worked in the past for corporate clients but who is now the chief lobbyist for the global charity organization Oxfam International, said that the United States is rooted in the ideology of free markets and a hostile view of regulation, both of which come into sharp conflict with fundamental European Union values.

"The American context is so neoliberal that it is very hard for any American, whether they are a consumer organization or a corporation, to understand what drives Europeans," he said. ■

 # View from the Inside

A few decades ago, interest group activity in Washington was dominated by what the journalist Hedrick Smith called "old-breed lobbying"—an insider's game that thrives on the "clubbiness of the old-boy network" and that "turns on the camaraderie of personal friendships" of Washington power-brokers. In recent years, however, "old-breed lobbying" has given way to "new-breed lobbying"—an approach that combines techniques borrowed from mass marketing and public relations, and that takes advantage of new technologies, including the fax machine, e-mail, and the Internet.*

In this selection, the *New York Times* reporter Alison Mitchell examines the new style of lobbying in the nation's capital.

Questions

1. What are the advantages and disadvantages of new-breed as opposed to old-breed lobbying from the interest groups' point of view?
2. Is "new-breed" lobbying an improvement over "old-breed" lobbying from the point of view of American democracy?

6.4 A New Form of Lobbying Puts Public Face on Private Interest (1998)

Alison Mitchell

From the nondescript headquarters of his Houston construction firm, Leo E. Linbeck Jr., a lanky, bow-tied executive with a drawl, is masterminding a crusade to overturn the nation's tax system.

Alison Mitchell, "A New Form of Lobbying Puts Public Face on Private Interest," *The New York Times,* September 30, 1998, pp. A1, A14. Copyright © 1998 by The New York Times Company. Reprinted with permission.

*Hedrick Smith, *The Power Game: How Washington Really Works* (New York: Random House, 1988).

Once, someone like him might have hired some of Washington's "Gucci Gulch" lobbyists to prowl the well-trod marble corridors outside Congress's tax committees. But Mr. Linbeck, with Texas-style audacity, wants to engineer a populist uprising to replace the income tax code with a national sales tax. And so with $15 million from some initial investors and mass fund-raising, he has run a media advertising campaign and employed an army of consultants, pollsters, political strategists, marketers, academics and yes, even a few lobbyists, to energize the citizenry.

"Imagine what it would be like if you were in Congress and you got a thousand phone calls a week and letters and E-mails and faxes," Mr. Linbeck said. "Not people from all over the country, but your constituents, people whose names you recognize, the people who were at the polls with you, who live down the street."

Mr. Linbeck and his fellow investors in Americans for Fair Taxation are unusual in the scale of their ambition. But their methods have become commonplace as lobbying has undergone a revolution over the past decade.

Rarely now does a well-connected Washington lobbyist work alone. Instead, the lobbyist has become just one of many players running national campaigns designed to create a "grass-roots" groundswell in support, or more often in opposition, to legislation before Congress.

In their million-dollar costs and in their reliance on television, polling and grass-roots constituency building, these efforts most resemble Presidential campaigns. And they are now so pervasive and sophisticated that it has become difficult to distinguish between a lobbying effort, an issue advocacy campaign and a citizens movement.

Some of these efforts are genuinely grass-roots movements. But others are deceptions in which a special interest pays to create the appearance of a popular groundswell. The growth of these techniques has spread the wealth of the influence industry beyond the lawyer-lobbyists to a new class of political professionals who often play overlapping roles as advisers to Presidential and Congressional candidates, corporate tacticians and media pundits.

In a world where the distinctions and conflicts between their multiple roles seem to matter less and less and can even be a business advantage, strategists who are ideological enemies in politics put their differences aside to work together on large-scale corporate campaigns.

The trend is the outgrowth of several developments in technology and politics. E-mail, computer databases, talk radio and 24-hour cable television all make it easier to organize and send a political message across the country at warp speed.

At the same time, power in Washington has been dispersed so that new ways are needed to influence more legislators. The media-age politician is far more likely to be moved by polls, television ads and mass constituent contacts than by party discipline, a committee chairman or a Washington wise man. And the Republicans in Congress know that they came to power with the help of several groups with grass-roots memberships: the National Federation of Independent Business, the National Rifle Association, the Christian Coalition.

"There's a couple of evolutions happening simultaneously," said Keith Appell, of Creative Response Concepts, a Republican public relations firm. "There's Republican sensitivity to grass-roots and certain lobbying methods you didn't have before and the explosion of media in the communications age."

Public policy experts debate whether the new methods of lobbying have made it more democratic by taking it out of the back rooms of the Capitol or whether they have simply made it harder for interests without money to compete in the public arena.

"It's part of a trend in Washington where rational debate on issues gets buried in big-budget sound bites," said Edward L. Yingling, the chief lobbyist for the American Bankers Association.

Mr. Linbeck said of his way of moving Congress: "It's not as orderly. It's not as predictable. It's not as controlled as some might want it to be. But I think those are positive attributes."

The convergence of lobbying and politics is evident in how Mr. Linbeck has gone about his crusade. He estimated that the effort would take several years and ultimately cost an extraordinary $90 million, a sum possible only if hundreds of thousands of Americans join his cause. Right now, tax reform is only a glimmer far on the horizon of Congress.

Some of the initial money spent by Mr. Linbeck's group went to hire prominent academics and research organizations to work on the 23 percent national sales tax. But to speed the organizing and make the sales tax proposal as politically appealing as possible, Americans for Fair Taxation also turned to national experts in politics, using Denis Calabrese, a Houston Republican consultant and onetime aide to Representative Dick Armey of Texas, as his chief strategist. With Mr. Calabrese's help, Americans for Fair Taxation has hired an all-star cast from both parties to propel the sales tax. . . .

"Clients and industries have come to appreciate there are no solo pilots in this town," said Jack Quinn, who returned to the law firm of Arnold & Porter after resigning as White House counsel. "Now you send armies, ships, tanks, aircraft, infantry, Democrats and Republicans, grass-roots specialists, people with special relationships."

In many cases, much about these campaigns remains undisclosed, from the cost to the proponents. Many consultants who were willing to explain their techniques would not identify their clients.

In 1995 the new Republican-led Congress approved major changes in how Congress does business. It imposed a ban on gifts and passed tough new disclosure requirements for lobbyists. But the legislation did not include reporting requirements for "grass-roots" lobbying such as telephone and letter-writing campaigns, even if the campaigns were generated by hired lobbyists and organizers. An earlier effort to pass a disclosure law that would have required reporting on such lobbying faltered in the Democratic-led Congress in 1994 when Representative Newt Gingrich, then the House Republican whip, branded the measure an "anti-religious" attempt to chill growing grass-roots conservative movements.

Numerous movements on the political scene have genuine grass-roots memberships, from the Christian Coalition to the Sierra Club. But creating citizens' movements, or the semblance of citizens' movements, on demand has also become big business.

Public relations firms and boutique shops advertise such arcane-sounding specialities as: "development of third-party allies" or "grass-roots recruitment and mobilization" or "grass-tops lobbying." The goal of these campaigns is to persuade ordinary voters to serve as the front-line advocates for the paying clients.

"In terms of the concept, you move beyond candidate advertising and beyond party organizations and form your own free-standing operation around an issue," said Brian A. Lunde, a former executive director of the Democratic National Committee who specializes in this kind of organizing. "The day of the P.A.C. check and the steak dinner and the golf dinner is over."

Practitioners said a grass-roots effort can cost from $40,000 for a small-scale attempt to sway the vote of just one or two crucial members of a subcommittee to many millions of dollars to sway a majority.

Three years ago, *Campaigns & Elections* magazine, a trade journal, conducted a painstaking survey and concluded that "grass-roots lobbying," apart from more traditional lobbying, had become an $800 million industry in 1993 and 1994.

And advertising adds to the cost.

"The inside game of lobbying is in decline," said Mike Murphy, who was a media consultant in 1996 to the Republican Presidential candidates Lamar Alexander and Bob Dole. "The outside game of consumer messaging, of marshaling public opinion, is advancing and increasing, and savvy companies have figured out that the best experts to hire to do this kind of work are political consultants."

The Evolution: Reaching the Masses Is Easier Than Ever

Two decades ago, corporations rarely used any of these techniques. Grass-roots mobilizations were the province of environmentalists, the civil rights movement or opponents of the war in Vietnam. Television advertising on legislation would have been considered an extravagant waste of money.

But in the early 1980's, campaign strategists looking for business during years without major elections and corporations looking for a better way to argue their case found common ground.

Mr. Sewell, who made the transition from Democratic politics, recalled that his first experience with issue campaigning came when the AT&T Corporation, in the wake of divestiture, hired the political public relations firm where he then worked.

"They didn't know what they were asking for," he said. "They thought they needed something like what was in a political campaign. We didn't know quite what to make of it, but we started developing programs whereby we understood that just like a member of Congress has a constituency, a corporation has a constituency. Our job was to go and identify that constituency and mobilize that constituency to advocate a point of view."

Since then such campaigns have become prevalent.

The Internet, E-mail, talk radio and computerized fax machines have made it far easier to organize national constituencies and instruct them on when to deluge Congress with letters and telephone calls.

At the same time, the Congressional gift ban cut down on opportunities for traditional lobbyists to wine and dine lawmakers.

And as party discipline has waned, members of Congress have also proved ever more responsive to television advertising or contacts from home, or the ups and downs of instantly sampled public opinion.

"You have entrepreneurial politicians not disciplined by the party but by their own images," Mr. Murphy said. "The mainspring in this is that public opinion counts."

Or at least the element of public opinion that is marshaled by the paid organizers and image makers. "There may be a lot of people who agree with your position but they will never get involved," Mr. Sewell said. "It's our job to find the people who would agree with the position and get them involved."

Television Advertising: Small Screen Helps Make a Big Statement

Often these days, it is television advertising that frames the terms of discussion for the Congress.

Five years ago, when the Health Insurance Association of America used its $17 million "Harry and Louise" commercials to help defeat President Clinton's plan for universal health insurance, the effort was pioneering.

"It was a big gamble in that nobody had done this kind of thing on that scale before," said Ben Goddard, a partner in the Malibu-based Goddard-Claussen firm that made the commercials.

Now Mr. Goddard's firm has its own Washington office. And media advertising on a legislative issue recently passed another milestone: the estimated $40 million radio and television advertising campaign that the five largest tobacco companies used this spring to defeat anti-tobacco legislation was the most expensive and sustained issue advocacy campaign ever undertaken on legislation, according to the Annenberg Public Policy Center of the University of Pennsylvania.

Such advertising campaigns are usually accompanied by mobilizations designed to make average citizens the advocates for the paying clients. Sometimes the advertisements help lobbyists find those sympathizers by running 800-numbers.

Some of these efforts amount to easily spotted carpet-bombing of Congress with form letters and patch-through telephone calls.

Senator John McCain, the Arizona Republican who sponsored the anti-tobacco bill, was swamped with form letters opposing it sent by members of the National Smokers Alliance, which receives financing from the Philip Morris Companies Inc., the Brown & Williamson Tobacco Corporation and the Lorillard Tobacco Company.

Senator Tom Harkin, Democrat of Iowa, also received letters opposing his position on tobacco, but from one part of his state.

"I couldn't figure out why I would get all these letters from one area," Mr. Harkin said. "It turns out they work for a Kraft food plant owned by R. J. Reynolds. But there was no disclosure of that."

Many of the creators of grass-roots lobbying campaigns for business say that, at their best, the campaigns mobilize real people with a sincere interest in the cause: sometimes company employees, shareholders, retirees, or vendors and sometimes individuals carefully selected through sophisticated demographic research.

Take the campaign waged this year by the nation's credit unions to preserve their expanded memberships in the face of a Supreme Court ruling that Federal regulators had overstepped when they allowed employee groups too small to form their own credit union to join others.

To pass their legislation over the opposition from the banks, the credit unions hired a large Washington cast of lobbyists, strategists and public relations specialists to mount an issue campaign that would take advantage of the fact that credit unions have loyal customers who favor them over banks. One person familiar with the campaign said it cost about $12 million over two years. The strategists deployed every weapon in the lobbying arsenal, from television commercials to talk radio to letter-writing campaigns to 800-numbers in credit unions that customers could use to call Congress. The campaign culminated in a rally of 7,000 supporters on the West Lawn of the Capitol.

Buddy Gill, a former Democratic campaign coordinator who was the credit unions' strategist, said, "Members of Congress had a classic dilemma. They want the support of their local banks and their campaign contributions, but they also want the votes of over 100,000 credit union people."

The credit unions raised money, too. Some credit union members paid $25 to $100 apiece to hold special fund-raisers for certain lawmakers.

The American Bankers Association had its own in-house specialists in "grass-roots" lobbying, but decided that it would not run the same kind of campaign as the credit unions. "We knew from our polling and focus groups and others this was not a battle we would be able to win in terms of grass-roots volume," said Mr. Yingling, the chief lobbyist for the association. "We had to win it in terms of the quality of the debate." But in the last two weeks before the Senate was to vote, the banks did turn to an 800-number to generate thousands of telegrams to Congress.

After this summer's loss, Mr. Yingling said his group was re-examining its budget for future grass-roots efforts. "This is just going to continue to escalate," he said.

What Does It Mean? Private Interests, Not People, Call the Shots

These changes in lobbying are taking place at the same time that party politics is metamorphosing in the television age, with fund-raisers replacing block captains and the public increasingly cut off from either party. And some say these lobbying efforts are the politics of the future. "It's like the election industry back in the 70's," Mr. Lunde said. "This is the same thing. It's the next generation of political campaign in the country."

Practitioners differed over whether the new practices were reinvigorating participation or squelching it.

Mr. Linbeck of Texas said that his sales tax movement gives citizens a chance to dictate an agenda to Congress instead of acting like vassals.

"I think we have a form of contemporary feudalism," he said. "Now how do you reverse that in a relatively benign way? A loud demonstration to the electorate that they do not have to be a supplicant with respect to a very important issue for them. And if they are interested in this and run with it to the extent that the polling, focus groups and test markets suggest they will, it will be a leverage point for creating a different view of government by the average person."

Critics argue that so much money is being poured into these efforts that their true purpose is to drown out competing viewpoints. "The whole effort of these campaigns is to prevent a second opinion from occurring," said David Cohen, a co-director of the Advocacy Institute, which teaches citizens groups how to make their cases.

Senator Carl Levin, a Michigan Democrat who was one of the leaders of the fight for lobbying disclosure, said that the problem with some of the techniques was that they could create a distorted picture when firms are paid to generate a certain number of telephone calls or telegrams.

"Suddenly a member of Congress is getting 50 phone calls on something," Mr. Levin said. "That's a lot of phone calls. What the member doesn't know is that 950 other people were contacted and said, 'No way.'"

The Grass Tops: Advice From Sources Lawmakers Will Heed

Because mass mobilizations have become so prevalent, a number of firms have become experts in a technique known as "grass-tops" lobbying, aimed at mobilizing an elite as opposed to the masses.

The goal is to figure out to whom a member of Congress cannot say no: his chief donor, his campaign manager, a political mentor. The lobbyist then tries to persuade that person to take his client's side. If the method works, the member of Congress may never know that a person contacting him had been revved up by a lobbyist.

To pull off this feat, Washington lobbying and public relations firms keep databases of organizers across the country, most of them with backgrounds in politics. Richard Pinsky, of West Palm Beach, Fla., who managed Mr. Dole's Florida primary campaign in 1996, is one of them.

Last year, with Florida a swing delegation in a House fight over trade, the Dewey Square Group, a public relations firm, relied on Mr. Pinsky to find prominent citizens to lobby certain House members to support giving President Clinton "fast-track" trade negotiating authority.

In one case, Mr. Pinsky said, he asked Bob Martinez, Florida's former Republican governor, who has an international trade practice, to contact Representative Jim Davis, a Democratic freshman. "It wasn't necessarily that a former Republican governor would have influence on a Democratic Congressman," Mr. Pinsky said, "as that the Governor lived in his district."

Mr. Davis, who did come to support the President, said that he had independently sought to talk to the former governor. And he said it did not matter if Mr. Pinsky had also contacted Mr. Martinez because, "I knew he had a business interest in promoting trade. I took it into account."

But he added that if someone without an obvious interest contacted him on an issue because of the involvement of a Washington lobbying firm, he would want to know about the role of the intermediaries. ■

Chapter 7

The Media

A free and unbridled press is one of the safeguards of American liberty. The United States, as Supreme Court Justice William Brennan wrote in 1964, has maintained a "profound national commitment to the principle that debate on public issues should be uninhibited, robust, and wide-open."* The press plays a critical role in promoting democracy by exposing official mismanagement and corruption, providing data on which citizens can make key decisions, and generally providing the people with a window on the activities of their government and the government with feedback on the opinions and viewpoints of the people.

The role of the media in the United States today, however, is not so simple. The media not only report the news; they also decide what is and what is not news. The media not only report on public opinion; they also play a vital role in shaping public opinion. In theory, the media may be free and unencumbered, but journalists live and work in a complex environment: their employers are themselves large corporations, which depend on other larger corporations for necessary advertising revenue; they have their own agendas to pursue, both professionally and, some would say, ideologically; they must both entertain and inform, especially on television; they are easily manipulated and used by government officials and candidates; they must cope with short deadlines and often with limited information; and they must continually try to fight off boredom, bias, and a pack mentality.

All of this is complicated by television, which has become the dominant medium in the United States. More Americans get their news on television than in any other form. Campaigns are waged and the country is governed through media performances, sound bites, and photo opportunities. Understanding television and knowing how to use it can get a candidate elected—and help him or her govern—consider, for example, John F. Kennedy and Ronald Reagan. Failing to project the right media image can ruin both a candidate and a president, as an endless trail of defeated politicians could easily testify.

This chapter examines these themes from four vantage points. Selection 7.1 examines the constitutional commitment to freedom of the press through the prism of *New York Times Co.* v. *United States,* a 1971 Supreme Court decision that refused to allow government censorship of the media, even when national security was arguably at stake. Selections 7.2 and 7.3 investigate the vexing question of media bias. Selection 7.4 looks at a new and unusual player in the worldwide media game—the Arab television network Al Jazeera, which has become a staple feature of post–September 11 terrorism coverage in the United States. Finally, selection 7.5 provides an insight into the uneasy relationship between the White House press corps and the president's press secretary.

New York Times v. Sullivan, 376 U.S. 254 (1964), at 270.

Chapter Questions

1. What roles do the media play in American politics? How do these roles conflict with one another; with the economic, personal, or professional interests of journalists; or with the interests of the corporations for which most journalists work?
2. What influences the media's decisions on what news to report and how to report it? To what extent do the media control the agenda in American politics? To what extent are the media manipulated by politicians and government officials?

 # Foundations

The media's critical role in the American political system is grounded in the First Amendment to the United States Constitution, which protects both freedom of speech and freedom of the press. The American commitment to a free press can be traced back as far as 1735 when the printer John Peter Zenger was acquitted by a New York jury even though he admitted to violating the law by publishing criticisms of the colonial government. It was not until the twentieth century, however, that the Supreme Court translated that commitment into legally enforceable doctrine.

The media are not at liberty to publish or broadcast anything they want, of course. Newspapers can still be sued for libel, which involves the publication of false statements damaging to the reputation of an individual or organization, although the rules laid down by the Supreme Court make it difficult for public officials and public figures to win such suits. The broadcast media are more heavily regulated, with television and radio stations subjected to licensing requirements and to rules prohibiting or limiting certain kinds of speech, including sexually explicit materials. In general, however, the American press remains remarkably free from governmental control or interference.

One of the Supreme Court's landmark decisions on press freedom was the 1971 case *New York Times Co. v. United States*. The case arose when the *Times* began to publish the so-called Pentagon Papers, a series of secret documents concerning the Vietnam War. Citing national security considerations, the Nixon administration immediately went to court, asking a federal judge for an injunction (or order) forcing the newspaper to cease publication of the papers. The judge agreed, at least until the issue could be resolved by the courts. Meanwhile, several other newspapers—including the *Washington Post*—began publishing the papers and joined the lawsuit. Within a matter of weeks, the matter was argued before the Supreme Court, which threw out the lower court order by a vote of six to three, clearing the way for publication.

There was no majority opinion in the case. Instead, eight justices submitted separate opinions. The opinion of Justice Hugo L. Black, which was joined by Justice William O. Douglas, is a passionate and eloquent statement by one of the First Amendment's strongest supporters. Black's opinion underscores the importance of a free press in any democratic society.

Questions

1. What was the purpose of the First Amendment, according to Black? Why is a free press, in his view, essential to the creation and maintenance of a free society?
2. Why does Black reject the Nixon administration's argument that the injunctions in this case were justified by considerations of national security?

7.1 *New York Times Co. v. United States* (1971)

Justice Hugo L. Black

I adhere to the view that the Government's case against the Washington Post should have been dismissed and that the injunction against the New York Times should have been vacated without oral argument when the cases were first presented to this Court. I believe that every moment's continuance of the injunctions against these newspapers amounts to a flagrant, indefensible, and continuing violation of the First Amendment. . . . In my view it is unfortunate that some of my Brethren are apparently willing to hold that the publication of news may sometimes be enjoined. Such a holding would make a shambles of the First Amendment.

Our Government was launched in 1789 with the adoption of the Constitution. The Bill of Rights, including the First Amendment, followed in 1791. Now, for the first time in the 182 years since the founding of the Republic, the federal courts are asked to hold that the First Amendment does not mean what it says, but rather means that the Government can halt the publication of current news of vital importance to the people of this country.

In seeking injunctions against these newspapers and in its presentation to the Court, the Executive Branch seems to have forgotten the essential purpose and history of the First Amendment. When the Constitution was adopted, many people strongly opposed it because the document contained no Bill of Rights to safeguard certain basic freedoms. They especially feared that the new powers granted to a central government might be interpreted to permit the government to curtail freedom of religion, press, assembly, and speech. In response to an overwhelming public clamor, James Madison offered a series of amendments to satisfy citizens that these great liberties would remain safe and beyond the power of government to abridge. Madison proposed what later became the First Amendment in three parts, two of which are set out below, and one of which proclaimed: "The people shall not be deprived or abridged of their right to speak, to write, or to publish their sentiments; and the freedom of the press, as one of the great bulwarks of liberty, shall be inviolable." The amendments were offered to curtail and restrict the general powers granted to the Executive, Legislative, and Judicial Branches two

---

403 U.S. 713 (1971).

years before in the original Constitution. The Bill of Rights changed the original Constitution into a new charter under which no branch of government could abridge the people's freedoms of press, speech, religion, and assembly. . . . Madison and the other Framers of the First Amendment, able men that they were, wrote in language they earnestly believed could never be misunderstood: "Congress shall make no law . . . abridging the freedom . . . of the press. . . ." Both the history and language of the First Amendment support the view that the press must be left free to publish news, whatever the source, without censorship, injunctions, or prior restraints.

In the First Amendment the Founding Fathers gave the free press the protection it must have to fulfill its essential role in our democracy. The press was to serve the governed, not the governors. The Government's power to censor the press was abolished so that the press would remain forever free to censure the Government. The press was protected so that it could bare the secrets of government and inform the people. Only a free and unrestrained press can effectively expose deception in government. And paramount among the responsibilities of a free press is the duty to prevent any part of the government from deceiving the people and sending them off to distant lands to die of foreign fevers and foreign shot and shell. In my view, far from deserving condemnation for their courageous reporting, the New York Times, the Washington Post, and other newspapers should be commended for serving the purpose that the Founding Fathers saw so clearly. In revealing the workings of government that led to the Vietnam war, the newspapers nobly did precisely that which the Founders hoped and trusted they would do.

The Government's case here is based on premises entirely different from those that guided the Framers of the First Amendment. The Solicitor General [on behalf of the U.S. government] has carefully and emphatically stated:

> Now, Mr. Justice [BLACK], your construction of . . . [the First Amendment] is well known, and I certainly respect it. You say that no law means no law, and that should be obvious. I can only say, Mr. Justice, that to me it is equally obvious that "no law" does not mean "no law," and I would seek to persuade the Court that is true. . . . [T]here are other parts of the Constitution that grant powers and responsibilities to the Executive, and . . . the First Amendment was not intended to make it impossible for the Executive to function or to protect the security of the United States.

And the Government argues in its brief that in spite of the First Amendment, "[t]he authority of the Executive Department to protect the nation against publication of information whose disclosure would endanger the national security stems from two interrelated sources: the constitutional power of the President over the conduct of foreign affairs and his authority as Commander-in-Chief."

In other words, we are asked to hold that despite the First Amendment's emphatic command, the Executive Branch, the Congress, and the Judiciary can make laws enjoining publication of current news and abridging freedom of the press in the name of "national security." The Government does not even attempt to rely on any act of Congress. Instead it makes the bold and dangerously far-reaching contention that the courts should take it upon themselves to "make" a law abridging freedom of the press in the name of equity, presidential power and national security, even when the representatives of the people in Congress have adhered to the command of the First Amendment and refused to make such a law. To find that the President has "inherent power" to halt the publication of news by resort to the courts would wipe out the First Amendment and destroy the fundamental liberty and security of the very people the Government hopes to make "secure." No one can read the history of the adoption of the First Amendment without being convinced beyond any doubt that it was injunctions like those sought here that Madison and his collaborators intended to outlaw in this Nation for all time.

The word "security" is a broad, vague generality whose contours should not be invoked to abrogate the fundamental law embodied in the First Amendment. The guarding of military and diplomatic secrets at the expense of informed representative government provides no real security for our Republic. The Framers of the First Amendment, fully aware of both the need to defend a new nation and the abuses of the English and Colonial governments, sought to give this new society strength and security by providing that freedom of speech, press, religion, and assembly should not be abridged. This thought was eloquently expressed in 1937 by Mr. Chief Justice Hughes—great man and great Chief Justice that he was—when the Court held a man could not be punished for attending a meeting run by Communists.

> The greater the importance of safeguarding the community from incitements to the overthrow of our institutions by force and violence, the more imperative is the need to preserve inviolate the constitutional rights of free speech, free press and free assembly in order to maintain the opportunity for free political discussion, to the end that government may be responsive to the will of the people and that changes, if desired, may be obtained by peaceful means. Therein lies the security of the Republic, the very foundation of constitutional government. ■

American Politics Today

Critics on both sides of the American political debate have accused the media of bias. Liberals argue that the media are dominated by large corporations, which are themselves dependent on other corporations for advertising revenue. They also point to the conservatives' dominance of the radio talk show circuit, and in particular the influence of media giant Rush Limbaugh. Conservatives emphasize the liberal orientation of most reporters and editors, and argue that their side rarely gets a fair shake from the major television networks or from newspapers like the *New York Times* or the *Washington Post*.

The debate over media bias has been raging on and off for several decades, but the rhetoric heated up in 2002 with the publication of *Bias*, a self-proclaimed exposé of the media's liberal bias by the former CBS journalist Bernard Goldberg. An excerpt from Goldberg's book is followed by a brief rebuttal to Goldberg by the journalist Jonathan Chait.

Questions

1. On what basis does Bernard Goldberg argue that the media are biased toward the liberal side of the political spectrum? How does Jonathan Chait counter Goldberg's argument?
2. What factors other than alleged bias might influence the behavior of reporters and editors?

7.2 Bias (2002)

Bernard Goldberg

On December 6, 1998, on a *Meet the Press* segment about Bill Clinton and his relationship with the Washington news corps, one of the capital's media stars, the *Washington Post*'s Sally Quinn, felt she needed to state what to her was the obvious.

The Washington press corps, she insisted, was not some "monolith." "We all work for different organizations," she said, "we all think differently."

Not really, Sally.

Two years earlier, in 1996, the Freedom Forum and the Roper Center released the results of a now famous survey of 139 Washington bureau chiefs and congressional correspondents. The results make you wonder what in the world Sally Quinn was talking about.

The Freedom Forum is an independent foundation that examines issues that involve the media. The Roper Center is an opinion research firm, also with a solid reputation. "No way that the data are the fruit of right-wing press bashers," as the journalist Ben Wattenberg put it.

What these two groups found was that Washington journalists are far more liberal and far more Democratic than the typical American voter:

♦ 89 percent of the journalists said they voted for Bill Clinton in 1992, compared with just 43 percent of the nonjournalist voters.
♦ 7 percent of the journalists voted for George Bush; 37 percent of the voters did.
♦ 2 percent of the news people voted for Ross Perot while 19 percent of the electorate did.

Eighty-nine percent voted for Bill Clinton. This is incredible when you think about it. There's hardly a candidate in the entire United States of America who carries his or her district with 89 percent of the vote. This is way beyond mere landslide numbers. The only politicians who get numbers like that are called Fidel Castro or Saddam Hussein. The same journalists that Sally Quinn tells us do not constitute a "monolith" certainly vote like one.

Sally says they "all think differently." About what? Picking the best appetizer at the Ethiopian restaurant in Georgetown?

What party do journalists identify with?

♦ 50 percent said they were Democrats.
♦ *4 percent* said they were Republicans.

When they were asked, "How do you characterize your political orientation?" 61 percent said "liberal" or "moderate to liberal." Only 9 percent said they were "conservative" or "moderate to conservative."

In the world of media elites, Democrats outnumber Republicans by twelve to one and liberals outnumber conservatives by seven to one. Yet Dan Rather believes that "most reporters don't know whether they're Republican or Democrat, and vote every which way." In your dreams, Dan.

After the survey came out, the *Washington Post* media writer, Howard Kurtz, said on *Fox News Sunday*, "Clearly anybody looking at those numbers, if they're even close to accurate, would conclude that there is a diversity problem in the news business, and it's not just the kind of diversity we usually talk about, which is not getting enough minorities in the news business, but political diversity, as well. Anybody who doesn't see that is just in denial."

James Glassman put it this way in the *Washington Post*: "The people who report the stories are liberal Democrats. This is the shameful open secret of American journalism. That the press itself . . . chooses to gloss over it is conclusive evidence of how pernicious the bias is."

Tom Rosenstiel, the director of the Project for Excellence in Journalism, says, "Bias is the elephant in the living room. We're in denial about it and don't want to admit it's there. We think it's less of a problem than the public does, and we just don't want to get into it."

Even *Newsweek*'s Evan Thomas (the one who thought Ronald Reagan had "a kind of intuitive idiot genius") has said, "There is a liberal bias. It's demonstrable. You look at some statistics. About 85 percent of the reporters who cover the White House vote Democratic; they have for a long time. There is a, particularly at the networks, at the lower levels, among the editors and the so-called infrastructure, there is a liberal bias."

Nonsense!

That's the response from Elaine Povich, who wrote the Freedom Forum report. No way, she said, that the survey confirms any liberal bias in the media.

"One of the things about being a professional," she said, "is that you attempt to leave your personal feelings aside as you do your work," she told the *Washington Times*.

"More people who are of a liberal persuasion go into reporting because they believe in the ethics and the ideals," she continued. "A lot of conservatives go into the private sector, go into Wall Street, go into banking. You find people who are idealistic tending toward the reporting end."

"Right," says Ben Wattenberg in his syndicated column. "These ethical, idealistic journalists left their personal feelings aside to this extent: When queried [in the Freedom Foundation/Roper poll in 1996] whether the 1994 Contract with

America was an 'election-year campaign ploy' rather than 'a serious reform proposal,' 59 percent said 'ploy' and only 3 percent said 'serious.'"

It's true that only 139 Washington journalists were polled, but there's no reason to think the results were a fluke. Because this wasn't the first survey that showed how liberal so many journalists are.

A poll back in 1972 showed that of those reporters who voted, 70 percent went for McGovern, the most liberal presidential nominee in recent memory, while 25 percent went for Nixon—the same Richard Nixon who carried every single state in the union except Massachusetts.

In 1985 the *Los Angeles Times* conducted a nationwide survey of about three thousand journalists and the same number of people in the general public to see how each group felt about the major issues of the day:

♦ 23 percent of the public said they were liberal; 55 percent of the journalists described themselves as liberal.
♦ 56 percent of the public favored Ronald Reagan; 30 percent of the journalists favored Reagan.
♦ 49 percent of the public was for a woman's right to have an abortion; 82 percent of the journalists were pro-choice.
♦ 74 percent of the public was for prayer in public schools; 25 percent of the journalists surveyed were for prayer in the public schools.
♦ 56 percent of the nonjournalists were for affirmative action; 81 percent of the journalists were for affirmative action.
♦ 75 percent of the public was for the death penalty in murder cases; 47 percent of the journalists were for the death penalty.
♦ Half the public was for stricter handgun controls; 78 percent of the journalists were for tougher gun controls.

A more recent study, released in March 2000, also came to the conclusion that journalists are different from most of the people they cover. Peter Brown, an editor at the *Orlando Sentinel* in Florida, did a mini-census of 3,400 journalists and found that they are less likely to get married and have children, less likely to do volunteer community service, less likely to own homes, and less likely to go to church than others who live in the communities where they work.

"How many members of the *Los Angeles Times* and the *St. Louis Post-Dispatch*," he asks, "belong to the American Legion or the Kiwanis or go to prayer breakfasts?"

But it's not just that so many journalists are so different from mainstream America. It's that some are downright hostile to what many Americans hold sacred.

On April 14, 1999, I sat in on a *CBS Weekend News* conference call from a speakerphone in the Miami bureau. It's usually a routine call with CBS News producers all over the country taking part, telling the show producers in New York about the stories coming up in their territories that weekend. Roxanne Russell, a longtime producer out of the Washington bureau, was telling about an event that Gary Bauer would be attending. Bauer was the conservative, family-values activist who seven days later would announce his candidacy for the Republican nomination for president.

Bauer was no favorite of the cultural Left, who saw him as an annoying right-wing moralist. Anna Quindlen, the annoying left-wing moralist and columnist who writes for *Newsweek,* once called him "a man best known for trying to build a bridge to the 19th century."

So maybe I shouldn't have been surprised by what I heard next, but I was. Without a trace of timidity, without any apparent concern for potential consequences, Roxanne Russell, sitting at a desk inside the CBS News Washington bureau, nonchalantly referred to this conservative activist as "Gary Bauer, the little nut from the Christian group."

The little nut from the Christian group!

Those were her exact words, uttered at exactly 12:36 P.M. If any of the CBS News producers on the conference call were shocked, not one of them gave a clue. Roxanne Russell had just called Gary Bauer, the head of a major group of American Christians, "the little nut from the Christian group" and merrily went on with the rest of her list of events CBS News in Washington would be covering.

What struck me was not the obvious disrespect for Bauer. Journalists, being as terribly witty and sophisticated as we are, are always putting someone down. Religious people are especially juicy targets. In a lot of newsrooms, they're seen as odd and viewed with suspicion because their lives are shaped by faith and devotion to God and an adherence to rigid principles—opposition to abortion, for one—that seem archaic and closed-minded to a lot of journalists who, survey after survey suggests, are not especially religious themselves.

So it wasn't the hostility to Bauer in and of itself that threw me. It was the lack of concern of any kind in showing that disrespect *so openly.* Producers from CBS News bureaus all over the country were on the phone. And who knows who else was listening, just as I was.

So I wondered: would a network news producer ever make such a disparaging remark, so openly, about the head of a Jewish group? Or a gay group? Or a black group? . . . ■

7.3 Victim Politics (2002)

Jonathan Chait

• • •

W hen [former CBS journalist Bernard] Goldberg goes beyond his first-person observations at CBS, . . . he does little more than recycle long-standing conservative complaints. He notes, for instance, that news accounts describe Republicans as "right-wing" far more than they call Democrats "left-wing." This may sound like a perfectly impartial objection—mustn't there be

Jonathan Chait, "Victim Politics." *The New Republic,* March 18, 2002, pp. 22–25. Reprinted by permission of *The New Republic,* © 2002, The New Republic, LLC.

as many left-wingers in American politics as right-wingers? If you consider Clinton a leftist, as many conservatives do, then the answer is yes. But the center of American politics has moved rightward over the last 25 years. By historical standards—not to mention the standards of other democracies—American liberals today are rather conservative. Clinton was probably further to the right on domestic policy than Richard Nixon, and he was almost certainly further to the right than European conservatives such as Helmut Kohl and Jacques Chirac. So from these broader perspectives, it's entirely natural that reporters would label more contemporary American politicians "right-wing" than "left-wing."

This same rightward drift has made liberalism less fashionable. So, over the last decade, major newspapers have used the pejorative phrase "unreconstructed liberal" more than five times as often as they've used "unreconstructed conservative." Why isn't this disparity evidence of anti-liberal bias? For basically the same reason Goldberg's example isn't. Reporters are more likely to call liberals "unreconstructed" not because they consider liberalism out of date, but because in recent years liberals have indeed felt the need to reconstruct themselves more than conservatives have. . . .

Another bias that Goldberg repeatedly notes stems from the crass imperative for commercial success. Ratings, he writes—again, apparently without recognition that he is undermining his thesis—are "the reason television people do almost everything." But if networks care only about ratings, why do they risk their profits by offending the political views of their audience? Indeed, in a free market, how could an overwhelmingly liberal media even exist? Even though the conservative FOX NEWS network has increased its share in recent years, "liberal" networks like ABC, CBS, CNN, and NBC still control the bulk of the TV news market and "liberal" newspapers the bulk of the newspaper market. If you believe that the media tilt left, then you must either believe that the public has no objection to this slant, or that the news business is unaffected by the forces of supply and demand.

To avoid such sticky questions, most conservatives ignore the political inclinations of both media owners and media consumers, and concentrate instead on the biases of reporters and editors. And here the right has its strongest case. Reporters, as numerous studies have established, overwhelmingly vote for Democrats. The most famous survey, taken after the 1992 elections, found that 89 percent of Washington journalists had voted for Clinton, 7 percent for Bush père, and only 2 percent for Ross Perot (as compared with 43, 37, and 19 percent, respectively, for the voters at large).

But this doesn't prove quite as much as one might suspect. Reporters may hold liberal views, but not on everything. Fairness and Accuracy in Reporting, a left-wing media watchdog, polled Washington journalists and compared the results with those of the public. It found that, while reporters generally hold more liberal views on social issues, they often take more conservative stances on economic questions. The public was far more likely than were media elites to think that Clinton's tax hike for the wealthy didn't go far enough and that the government should guarantee medical care. Reporters were far more inclined to support free trade and cutting entitlement programs.

This should come as no surprise. The views of the Beltway press reflect the ideology of the socioeconomic stratum in which they reside: secular, educated, urban or suburban, liberal on the environment and social issues, moderately conservative on economics. Indeed, the greatest statistical discrepancy in the 1992 voting pattern is not Washington reporters' lack of support for Bush, but their lack of support for Perot—they were one-fifth as likely as the public to cast a ballot for the GOP candidate, but only one-tenth as likely to support the Texas billionaire. Perot, of course, appealed to the disaffected working class, railing against free trade and immigration. Naturally, this brand of populism held little appeal for the media elite. . . .

On the whole, this set of biases disproportionately benefits Democrats and liberals. The media's aversion to the cultural right is more pronounced than its aversion to the economic left, and, since reporters tend to label politicians according to their social views, they're more apt to consider Democrats moderate. This is the kernel of truth underlying Goldberg's hyperbolic screed.

But there are two important caveats. First, the professional constraints and institutional tendencies of political journalism—which value neutrality, tend to follow compelling story lines, and place a premium on maintaining good sources within both parties—often overwhelm reporters' ideological predilections. Second, conservative Republicans who understand these predilections can turn them to their own advantage. The recent revelation that the 2000 Bush presidential campaign kept Ralph Reed off its payroll is instructive: The reason, according to the *Times*, was that associating Bush too publicly with a former director of the Christian Coalition would complicate his efforts to portray himself as a "compassionate conservative." Bush's advisers understood that reporters would gauge his moderation largely by his distance from social conservatives. (They also no doubt understood that retaining Larry Lindsey, a fervent supply-sider, as his main economic adviser would set off no such alarms in the press.)

Bush outlined his plan to handle the press in a 1999 interview with *National Review*. "I do think [the media] are biased against conservative thought," he said in a forum that received little attention outside the right. "And the reason is that they think conservative thinkers are not compassionate people. And that's one of the reasons I've attached a moniker to the philosophy that I espouse, because I want people to hear a different message." As the Bush campaign understood, reporters are predisposed to seeing conservatives as temperamentally mean-spirited—an idiotic notion (think of Ronald Reagan or Jack Kemp), but a deeply rooted one nonetheless. Therefore, they viewed Bush's cheerful demeanor and apparent affinity for the poor as evidence that he was not all that conservative, and this conclusion permeated coverage of the entire campaign. . . .

It is ironic, then, that at this moment in history, a book alleging liberal media bias would top the best-seller list. And more ironic still that Bush would give it his tacit endorsement. Conservatives like Goldberg may believe that he overcame the systematic liberal bias of a hostile media, but Bush, surely, knows better. ∎

The International Context

Before September 11, 2001, few Americans had even heard of Al Jazeera. But the Qatar-based Arab television network soon became a household name. Not only was Al Jazeera the only network with correspondents and cameras on the ground in Afghanistan, it also made headlines as the recipient of a series of videotapes featuring Osama bin Laden and other leaders of the al Qaeda terrorist network. Al Jazeera's video thus became a staple of cable news programming in the United States.

This selection provides a rare glimpse into the world of this unusual, and controversial, television network.

Questions

1. In what ways is Al Jazeera's operation similar to that of American cable television news networks? In what ways is Al Jazeera different?
2. Should American networks run news feeds from Al Jazeera, or should they avoid doing so? Why or why not?

7.4 Inside Al Jazeera (2002)

Rick Zednik

Considering its influence, Al Jazeera's newsroom is puny. When Egyptian President Hosni Mubarak peeked in during a visit to Doha, Qatar, a couple of years ago, he asked, "All this noise comes from this matchbox?" Behind a glass wall at one end is the smallest of Al Jazeera's three broadcast studios, where anchors read five-minute newscasts every hour. On the opposite side of the room an illuminated map of the world, flanked by thirty-two television screens, serves as a backdrop for the newscasts. In between are forty-eight computer terminals.

It feels like an American newsroom at first, until you notice the details. While a few of the monitors are tuned to CNN, BBC, and AP Television News, most are set to stations from across the Arab world: Palestine, Iraq, Egypt, Abu Dhabi, Beirut-based Al Manar, and the Middle East Broadcasting Centre (MBC), soon to move from London to Dubai. Journalists bang away at keyboards with Arabic characters, which they read on their screens from right to left. Many of them wear khakis or Western business suits, but some men dress in traditional white thoubs and several women wear headscarves. Virtually all employees are Arab Muslims, although Al Jazeera's headquarters is a secular place. Employees who choose to pray during work hours do so in a tiny mosque behind the main building.

Rick Zednik, "Inside Al Jazeera," reprinted with permission from *Columbia Journalism Review* 40 (March/April 2002): pp. 44–47. Copyright © 2002 by *Columbia Journalism Review*.

The journalists are a loose, sociable bunch, representing almost all twenty-two members of the Arab League. Moroccan producers, Syrian talk show hosts, Iraqi translators, Algerian fixers, Sudanese librarians, Palestinian secretaries, and Qatari executives all speak together in Arabic.

A few paces away from the newsroom is the corner office of Mohamed Jasem Al Ali, Al Jazeera's managing director. Al Ali strides around his office, his thoub flowing and white kaffiyeh held on his head by black cords, pointing out some of the dozens of plaques, trophies, and framed certificates jamming the sill along two walls. He points to citations from the Netherlands, Germany, Lebanon, Egypt, and Russia, clearly proud of the honors his satellite network has garnered in barely five years.

But he is especially eager to explain the significance of one framed newspaper page: the cover of the *Times* of London from December 18, 1998, on which a color photo taken from a television broadcast fills most of the space above the fold. The photo shows a cruise missile exploding over Baghdad. More significant to Al Ali than the picture itself, however, is the logo in the screen's bottom right corner. There, partially obscured by the logo of CNN, is that of Al Jazeera—then barely two years old—which originally shot the pictures. That design, Arabic letters in the shape of a flame or a teardrop, has become recognized across the Arab world as the symbol of a television network that stirs more emotions than any news medium the region has ever seen.

Wide Open

Al Jazeera, which translates as "the Peninsula," was established by emiri decree in February 1996. Sheikh Hamad bin Khalifa Al Thani, who seized power in 1995 from his father, created Al Jazeera as part of an effort to modernize and democratize Qatar. He allocated $137 million to Al Jazeera with the goal that the station would be self-sustaining within five years of its November 1, 1996, debut.

It has grown rapidly, expanding from its original six hours a day to twelve and then, on January 1, 1999, to twenty-four hours. It employs 500 people, including seventy journalists. Among its twenty-seven bureaus are offices in Washington, New York, London, Paris, Brussels, Moscow, Djakarta, and Islamabad.

Al Jazeera is the only twenty-four-hour Arab news station. In addition to its fast-moving, video-heavy newscasts, it has built an audience through its talk shows, which probe political, social, and religious issues previously untouched by Arab media. Perhaps the most popular program is The Opposite Direction, hosted by Faisal Al Qasim, a British-educated Syrian who has a talent for drawing out guests with opposing views and goading them to mix it up on air. He has pitted an Egyptian supporting normalization of relations with Israel against another Egyptian who quoted anti-Semitic writings. A woman opposed to the abolition of polygamy walked off the set, fed up with her counterpart's insistence that it was an anachronistic practice.

Allowing guests to speak freely was radical enough, but then Al Qasim introduced viewer call-ins. Al Jazeera's microphone was not just open, but wide open. Some of his shows have become such shouting matches that some viewers are convinced Al Qasim filters out the moderate voices in favor of extreme ones.

Another popular program is Islamic Law and Life, in which the host, Yusif Al Qardhawi, a professor of Islam at the University of Qatar, has discussed sensitive topics, such as female circumcision and rules that forbid women to work.

The U.S., meanwhile, was introduced to Al Jazeera in the days following the September terrorist attacks. And some here didn't like what they saw.

The Taliban quickly forced all foreign journalists to leave Kabul, allowing only Al Jazeera, which had a history of covering Afghanistan, to stay. When the U.S. launched strikes on Afghanistan on October 7, the world wanted what only Al Jazeera had: war video, including live footage of bombs falling on Kabul. And soon the network aired something even more jolting. In a tape that Al Jazeera staffers say was probably recorded about two weeks after September 11 and delivered via many Taliban hands to their Kabul bureau once U.S. airstrikes began, Osama bin Laden denounced the U.S.

Suddenly, Al Jazeera was not only delivering the news to its thirty-five million viewers, including 150,000 in the U.S., it was telling the world's top story to billions of people around the planet via international media that had little choice but to use Al Jazeera's pictures. It was not simply covering the war; it became an important player in the global battle for public opinion. Al Jazeera also rebroadcast portions of the ninety-minute interview with bin Laden it had aired in June 1999. In that program, the al Qaeda leader said he had "high regard and respect" for the people who bombed U.S. forces in Saudi Arabia in 1995 and 1996. Americans "violate our land and occupy it and steal the Muslims' possessions," he declared, "and when faced with resistance by Muslims they call it terrorism."

Al Jazeera's programming irked the United States so much that Colin Powell expressed concern about its inflammatory rhetoric to the Qatari emir during their October 3 meeting. Six weeks later, on November 13, a pair of 500-pound U.S. bombs destroyed Al Jazeera's Kabul bureau.

In early December, Al Ali received a letter from Victoria Clarke, assistant secretary of defense, asserting that the U.S. did not know the facility was used by Al Jazeera. "Whether it was targeted or not, I can't answer," Al Ali says, slowly rotating his worry beads. "But I can say for 100 percent that the United States knew about the office. Everyone knew we had an office in Kabul. It was very easy to find." On January 31, the New York–based Committee to Protect Journalists formally asked the Department of Defense for an explanation of the bombing.

"Are We a Mouthpiece?"

The U.S. government has not been the only American voice critical of Al Jazeera. A particularly scathing cover story, by Fouad Ajami, a professor of Middle East Studies at Johns Hopkins, ran in the November 18 *New York Times Magazine*. Ajami's piece was based on his viewing of the station's news and talk programming in October, not long after U.S. air strikes on Afghanistan began. He argued that the station had made bin Laden its "star." "One clip juxtaposes a scowling George Bush with a poised, almost dreamy bin Laden," Ajami writes. "Between them is an image of the World Trade Center engulfed in flame." Ajami asserted that "in its rough outlines, the message of Al Jazeera is similar to that of the Taliban: there is a huge technological imbalance between the antagonists, but the foreign power will nonetheless come to grief," and he accused the station of "mimicking Western norms of journalistic fairness while pandering to pan-Arabic sentiments." He cited an October 30 report by Al Jazeera's main man in Kabul, Tayseer Allouni, about which Ajami wrote:

> As Allouni presented it there appeared to be nobody in Kabul who supported America's campaign to unseat the Taliban. A man in a telephone booth, wearing a traditional white cap, offered a scripted-sounding lament that even Kabul's telephone lines had been destroyed. "We have lost so much," he said, "because of the American bombing." Allouni then closed his survey with gruesome images of wounded Afghans. The camera zoomed in on an old man lying on his back, his beard crusted with blood; this was followed by the image of a heavily bandaged child who looked propped up, as if to face the camera. The parting shot was an awful close-up of a wounded child's face.

The *Washington Post*, two weeks later, ran a thinner but also critical piece. Sharon Waxman quoted Jamal Khashoggi, a prominent Saudi Arabian journalist. "They are being led by the masses, they don't lead the masses," he said of Al Jazeera. "They know the taste of the Arab street, and the Arab street is anti-American. They are just like the *New York Post*. This is not very good."

Al Jazeera's journalists do not seem particularly worried about this or any criticism, but they do say that critics frequently confuse the network with the newsmakers and talk-show guests that appear on it. "Are we a mouthpiece for bin Laden?" says Dana Suyyagh, an Al Jazeera news producer who was educated in Canada. "Maybe, but that would make us Bush's mouthpiece as well. He gets more airtime, actually."

Hafiz al-Mirazi, Al Jazeera's Washington bureau chief, sounds weary when asked about accusations of bias. "The network is much more balanced than it gets credit for," he says. "During this crisis we have been criticized for making Al Jazeera a mouthpiece for the U.S. government. Why? Almost on a daily basis we bring on spokespersons for the administration."

Al Ali points out that Al Jazeera provides Arab news from an Arab perspective, with journalists who hail from Mauritania to Iraq—no single nation dominates—and that it has bureaus in almost all Arab countries, including one in the Palestinian West Bank.

The question of what an Arab perspective means comes to the fore in coverage of the struggle between the Israelis and the Palestinians, Al Jazeera's top story before September 11. No other issue so rouses or unites Arabs. . . .

In four days of viewing Al Jazeera's hourlong news roundup, Al Hasad, or The Harvest, in mid-January, the primacy of the Israeli-Palestinian conflict was clear. It was the lead story almost every night. And in its reporting from the West Bank and Gaza Strip, the show featured only one brief interview with an Israeli spokesman. In reporting on the assassination of a young militant leader in the West Bank by the Israelis that week, there was no effort to provide the context for Israelis. Questions from anchors and reporters, meanwhile, sometimes betrayed clear sympathies. On January 15, Jumana Namour interviewed Mohammed Dahlan, a high-ranking security chief for the Palestinians from the Gaza Strip:

> Q. Before September 11, you were viewed as resistance fighters. After September 11 it is as if the right to resistance was taken away.

A. After September 11, we, who were victims in the eyes of the world, became the terrorist Palestinian Authority.

Still, the station did go twice to Washington to talk to U.S. experts on the Middle East, who offered points of view clearly at odds with the Palestinians. Indeed, as the State Department was pressuring Al Jazeera to limit anti-American content, it was offering the station its own officials for interviews. Colin Powell, Donald Rumsfeld, and Condoleezza Rice all appeared on Al Jazeera, as did Christopher Ross, a former American ambassador to Syria who speaks fluent Arabic. The Americans were not alone. British Prime Minister Tony Blair also made his case for "dismantling the network of international terrorism" directly to Al Jazeera viewers.

"I Want My Al Jazeera"

If American officials were to claim that Al Jazeera is against them, their Middle Eastern counterparts likely would reply, "Join the club." According to Yousef Al Shouly, a Palestinian senior producer for Al Jazeera, Western leaders are now absorbing the lesson that Arab heads of state learned over the past five years: "Use Al Jazeera to spread your views; use Al Jazeera to your own benefit." When there is controversy in a country, he says, his station allows both "the government and the opposition to give their point of view. Al Jazeera gives both sides a chance. Al Jazeera has not changed its policy. Governments have changed their policy" to adapt to the network, he says.

Before Al Jazeera began broadcasting in 1996, Arab leaders were accustomed to state-owned media that did not question the status quo. In the choice between pleasing governments or pleasing viewers, Al Jazeera chose the latter.

There's hardly an Arab government that the station has not offended. Al Jazeera staff say the Qatari foreign ministry has received more than 400 complaints. When the network aired a program probing Algeria's civil war, the government in Algiers cut the signal. Nadia Tabib, an Al Jazeera employee, says Algerians soon flooded phone lines with cries of "I want my Al Jazeera!"

Egypt's state media ran a campaign against Al Jazeera's "yellow programs," denouncing the station's "sinister salad of sex, religion and politics" topped with "sensationalist seasoning." Yasir Arafat was reportedly incensed by Al Jazeera's frequent interviews with the Hamas spiritual leader Sheikh Ahmed Yassin. And the network upset Palestinian authorities with a preview for a March 2001 documentary that explored the role of Palestinian guerillas as players in Lebanon's 1975–1990 civil war. Security personnel entered the Palestine bureau and demanded that images insulting to Arafat be removed. Al Jazeera refused, and continued to air the footage.

Saudi Arabia bars Al Jazeera from its territory, except to cover special events like the annual pilgrimage to Mecca. Jordan temporarily closed Al Jazeera's bureau there after a guest on a debate program criticized the regime in Amman. Tunisia, Morocco, and Libya recalled their ambassadors from Doha in protest of Al Jazeera coverage, reinstating them once their point was made. . . .

One of Al Jazeera's profitable revenue streams lately has been its exclusive videos of Osama bin Laden. Three-minute clips of bin Laden have reportedly fetched the station as much as $250,000 apiece. But bin Laden tapes, it appears, can be a double-edged sword.

On January 31, CNN aired a previously unseen interview with bin Laden. It had been conducted by an Al Jazeera correspondent on October 21, two weeks after the bombs began falling on Afghanistan and some three weeks before the fall of Kabul. Al Jazeera had not aired the interview on the ground that it was not newsworthy. The tape reportedly had been circulating in intelligence circles, and had been quoted, though not identified, by British Prime Minister Tony Blair last November. CNN, which said it obtained the tape from "a nongovernmental source," found the interview newsworthy indeed. In it bin Laden first denies "carrying out" the September 11 attacks, but Al Jazeera's reporter presses him. "If inciting people to do that is terrorism and if killing those who kill our sons is terrorism," bin Laden says, "then let history be witness that we are terrorists." And he adds later, "I say it's permissible in Islamic law and logic."

CNN says its agreement with Al Jazeera gave it a right to broadcast the tape, but a furious Al Ali said the network would sever its partnership with CNN. "Al Jazeera would have expected CNN to . . . respect its special relationship with Al Jazeera by not airing material that al Jazeera itself chose not to broadcast."

Al Ali has declined to discuss the reasons that the network did not run the interview.

Joshua Micah Marshall, a senior correspondent for *The American Prospect*, theorized (without evidence) in *Salon* on February 2 that the network buried the interview because "it was too unfavorable to bin Laden" at a time when the Arab world was not convinced of his guilt.

On the other hand, the interview came not long after Vice President Dick Cheney met with the emir of Qatar to complain about the broadcasts, and at a time of ferocious Western criticism of the network for broadcasting the October 7 bin Laden tapes that had been supplied to it. An anonymous Al Jazeera journalist told Reuters that the bin Laden interview had been ditched for such reasons. "We decided, under the circumstances at that time, that airing the interview would have strengthened the belief that we are a mouthpiece for bin Laden." Which, if true, must have been an awkward decision for a network that prides itself on standing up to everybody. ■

[Editor's note: The controversy surrounding Al Jazeera after September 11 was minor compared to the storm that swirled around the network during the Iraq War of 2003. The network was frequently accused of pro-Iraqi bias, and was especially criticized for showing video footage of American prisoners of war being interrogated by their Iraqi captors.]

View from the Inside

The president's press secretary plays a critical role. On a day-to-day basis, he or she is the president's main link to the White House press corps and, through them, to the American people. The press secretary's main job is to "spin" actual or potential news stories in order to make the president look good.

The press secretary's relationship with the White House press corps is by nature adversarial. The press secretary's constant aim is to tell every story from the president's point of view, minimizing controversy and making the president look good at every turn. The media, by contrast, want a good story—and that means conflict, controversy, or evidence of incompetence or scandal.

Every press secretary handles the media in his or her own way. Mike McCurry, who served as President Bill Clinton's press secretary from 1995 to 1999, was a master of charm, gaining the confidence and even friendship of the White House reporters even as he spun every story in the president's direction. Ari Fleischer, who served as President Bush's spokesman from 2001 to 2003, played the game differently. His approach, as the journalist Howard Kurtz explains in this selection, was to hold his cards very close to his vest, giving the news media as little information as he could get away with. Fleischer's tactics were frustrating to the press, but, in general, they served the president well.

Questions

1. What tactics do members of the media employ to get the information they need and want from Fleischer? Why, according to Kurtz, are they usually unsuccessful?
2. Evaluate Ari Fleischer's performance as press secretary from the standpoint of the president, from the standpoint of the White House press corps, and from the standpoint of a citizen of the United States.

7.5 Keeper of Secrets (2002)

Howard Kurtz

• • •

No one has come to epitomize the administration's buttoned-down, tightly disciplined style more than Lawrence Ari Fleischer. He's smart, knows the game and never forgets whose side he is on. A relative newcomer, he has melded perfectly into Bush World, a place that rarely springs a leak, except for the

Excerpted from Howard Kurtz, "Straight Man: George W. Bush's Message Is That Everything's Under Control in a Tightly Disciplined White House That Knows How to Keep a Secret. Ari Fleischer is the Messenger," *Washington Post Magazine* (May 19, 2002), pp. W14–W20, W25–W29. © 2002, *The Washington Post*. Reprinted with permission.

fully authorized kind. He seems far more concerned with staying in the boss's good graces than in currying favor with reporters.

As President Bush, in an interview for this article, describes his spokesman: "He understands the fine line between the need to know and the need to say."

Bush stresses that Fleischer sits in on his high-level meetings with world leaders, and occasionally listens in on their phone calls. "Ari must know not only what's on my mind, but be in a position to see what I see, hear what I hear . . . Knowledge is important to deal with the press corps . . . The one thing about the press corps is they know a lot of stuff."

The president keeps returning to the theme of loyalty. "The thing I like most about him is he cares about me...I appreciate his sensitivity. If he ever thinks he's done something to hurt the administration or my standing, it bothers him. And I admire that in a man."

[White House aide] Karen Hughes says many of her colleagues prefer "to say as little as possible" to the press, but that Fleischer often prods them for information. "Sometimes people will tell me, 'Ari's kind of nosy,'" she says. "Well, he's supposed to be."

Fleischer, 41, agreed to a series of interviews over the last four months to talk about how the Bush White House deals with the media. It quickly became apparent that Bush World runs on time; his assistant once called to reschedule an appointment for five minutes later. Fleischer brings the same controlled style to his personal life, plotting to keep the name of his girlfriend out of the press until the moment he proposed marriage. "I had to maintain operational secrecy," he explains.

Fleischer's by-the-book approach has exposed him to a certain degree of ridicule. "Doonesbury" has Fleischer earnestly telling reporters: "The president has a core belief that he's entitled to unvarnished opinion from a diverse group of campaign contributors." *New York Times* columnist Maureen Dowd calls him "opaque."

Slate's Michael Kinsley describes him as "a great evasive bore . . . Fleischer speaks a sort of imperial court English, in which any question, no matter how specific, is parried with general assurances that the emperor is keenly aware and deeply concerned and fully resolved and infallibly right and the people are fully supportive and further information should be sought elsewhere."

Fleischer professes to be utterly unaffected by these barbs. He responds with The Smile. It's an ear-to-ear grin that he regularly flashes at briefings, even while discussing matters of war and peace. The Smile says Fleischer is relaxed. The Smile says he has a sense of humor. He smilingly points to the wall of his spacious West Wing office, where he has hung the "Doonesbury" cartoons satirizing him.

Besides, he says, "in this White House, if Michael Kinsley and Maureen Dowd start to praise you, you're probably in big trouble." In Bush World, it's uncool to get too exercised over the liberal media.

"As long as the president's happy and my co-workers are happy, I'm happy," Fleischer says. No mention of the reporters whose care and feeding are part of his job. If they're less than happy, so be it.

● ● ●

From the outset, Fleischer's fierce sense of loyalty left many reporters exasperated. Unlike some spokesmen who deliver the day's spin with a wink and a nod, Fleischer played it agonizingly straight. If you woke him at 3 in the morning, he would be on message. On or off the record, he never hinted at the slightest criticism of his boss. And he wasn't shy about elbowing those who got out of line. When *Houston Chronicle* reporter Bennett Roth asked about underage drinking by the president's daughters, Fleischer called to chastise him and said his question had been "noted in the building."

Sometimes Fleischer was too blunt for his own good. After "Politically Incorrect" host Bill Maher announced that "we have been the cowards" in the war in Afghanistan by firing cruise missiles from 2,000 miles away, Fleischer warned that Americans "need to watch what they say." He didn't quite grasp how chilling that statement sounded from the White House podium.

Each day Fleischer tried to anticipate where a story was headed, pressing his administration colleagues for answers. "My job is to think like a reporter," he says. After the morning gaggle, he often told the president what reporters were asking. And like a good reporter, Fleischer had to make sure the boss had the details right, lest the White House be accused of misleading the press.

When Bush told NBC's Tom Brokaw during a limousine ride that his mother-in-law had lost money on Enron stock, Fleischer took it up with the president. Reporters are going to ask when she bought the stock, how many shares. The president called Jenna Welch. It turned out he was wrong in saying that she had bought the shares the previous summer; it was actually in 1999. They also checked with Welch's accountant, who confirmed the $8,000 loss. Bush later used the anecdote with reporters as a way of identifying with Enron's victims.

Still, the press continued to excavate the links between Enron and Bush World. White House economic adviser Lawrence Lindsey, who had been an Enron consultant, had launched a review of the possible financial impact of the company's bankruptcy. Vice President Cheney had interceded on Enron's behalf with officials in India. Army Secretary Thomas White, a former Enron executive, had had 29 meetings and phone calls with senior officials from his old company. Reporters demanded to know why Fleischer hadn't revealed such details sooner.

Fleischer tried to remain patient at these briefings, often flashing The Smile under tough questioning. "I've been at this too long to get frustrated by it," he says. "I accept that the press controls the questions. I try to defuse the tension by letting reporters vent." He made a point of giving reporters two and three follow-up questions. One colleague called his approach the "rope-a-dope strategy."

But in the White House pressroom on January 16, Fleischer lost his legendary patience. He got into it with Ron Fournier, a dogged Associated Press reporter, who asked whether the White House would release a list of all calls related to Enron.

"See, again, there you go, you're asking me are we doing something that you can't even define," Fleischer said. "You're saying to me, are you engaged in a— hold it, hold it—you're asking me are you engaged in a . . ."

Fournier stood his ground. "You can just give me a 'yes' or 'no' if you can. Is the White House determining whether or not administration officials or White House aides have received any calls from Enron since the summer of 2001?"

"On any topic, on anything?" Fleischer asked.

"That's my question, have they received—"

"On any topic, on anything?"

"Have they received any calls, are you guys determining whether or not White House officials or administration officials have received calls from Enron since the summer of 2001?"

"Again, the standard the White House has put in place is that if you have any suggestion of any wrongdoing, as opposed to such a broad, open-ended question—"

"I'm asking whether or not you guys are determining whether these calls were made," Fournier said.

"'These' calls meaning which calls?"

"I'm asking you whether or not, yes or no—"

"You said, 'these calls.' Describe the calls."

"Yes or no, is the administration determining who in this administration got calls from Enron in the last six or 10 months."

"About any—now it's six or 10 months."

"Since the summer of 2001."

"About any topic or anything? Again, the administration is interested, if anybody has any evidence of wrongdoing—"

"I'm asking yes or no—"

"I think you've heard the answer."

Fournier kept at it. Why wouldn't Fleischer answer yes or no?

"Because it is not being handled in the way that I think you all are looking for it to be handled, because you're trying to make comparisons to previous administrations. That is not the White House approach."

Perhaps, Fleischer thought later, he had mishandled the matter. Although he rarely second-guessed himself, he felt he probably should have acknowledged there was no internal investigation into Enron-related calls. Still, Fleischer had his reasons. He didn't like to play the reporters' game of having to talk about what the White House wasn't doing.

He had come to understand the strange habits of the media beast. He knew that journalists were paid to pursue each lead to the ends of the earth, that they were skeptical because they had been lied to in the past, sometimes in the very same pressroom. But he didn't want to encourage their worst excesses.

Sure, he told Karen Hughes, he was worried about looking like the president's team was hiding something. But if he provided a list of phone calls, the journalists would ask for any notes of the calls. The demands would never end.

The reporters had no evidence of administration wrongdoing, just insinuations and suspicions. It was nothing but a fishing expedition, Fleischer believed. And he was determined not to be the dock off which they fished.

To the White House press corps, Fleischer is part propaganda minister, part babysitter, part punching bag. Its members find him endlessly frustrating, yet grudgingly admire his ability to stymie them.

"This White House maintains pretty tight control over information," says CBS's Bill Plante. "They don't want him out there spilling his guts, and he doesn't. He's very careful to say what they want him to say. But in the heat of any crisis, it drives people nuts."

"Ari's an advocate," says CNN's John King. "It is not Ari's job to say, yes, we've changed our position. We have to connect the dots ourselves."

"I like Ari and respect Ari," says NBC's David Gregory. "But it is virtually impossible to get something out of Ari that he doesn't want to say. Ari's very disciplined . . . Sometimes we walk out of those briefings banging our heads against the wall, and he knows that and doesn't worry about it."

• • •

There are times when Fleischer's role is to bob and weave and duck and dodge, even if he looks faintly ridiculous in the process.

As a House vote on campaign finance reform drew closer, everyone knew that Bush was resisting the measure being pushed by Congressmen Chris Shays and Marty Meehan. He had, after all, campaigned against a ban on unlimited soft money donations while facing John McCain in the 2000 primaries. Everyone also knew that Bush didn't want to publicly oppose campaign reform—not in an Enron-frenzied climate in which the administration was being accused of excessive coziness with big corporations.

Fleischer was convinced that journalists had an inherent conflict of interest in covering campaign finance. If candidates had less money to pay for television ads, the news media's role would be more influential. Most journalists believed—and barely hid their view—that big money had corrupted politics and should be greatly restricted.

He could see it in the language that reporters used. People like McCain and Shays and Meehan were "reformers"; those who challenged the legislation were "opponents of reform." The press would never describe Bush as a reformer, even though he had promised to sign a campaign finance bill.

Day after day, White House reporters pressed Fleischer: Did the president support Shays-Meehan? Would the president veto Shays-Meehan? Each time, Fleischer would deflect the questions. Bush would sign a reform bill, Fleischer kept saying, but he wouldn't lobby lawmakers and wouldn't say what should be in the bill.

On February 12, the *New York Times* reported that this stance was basically a sham. "Advisers" to Bush were saying that "the White House is working through the Republican Party to scuttle campaign finance legislation before the House this week while protecting President Bush from any political fallout."

Once again, the president was angry. "It's not true," he told Fleischer. The press secretary checked with political adviser Karl Rove and other aides to make sure no one on the White House staff was actively working against Shays-Meehan.

Of course, the story was absolutely true in the sense that the Republican National Committee would not have been working to undermine the bill without Bush's acquiescence. But at the briefing that day, Fleischer stuck to the script.

"The president would very much like to see the House of Representatives pass a campaign finance reform measure that improves the current system," he said. "The president does see a number of weaknesses in the current system that he thinks can be improved."

Then why wasn't Bush doing any lobbying?

"Because individual members are entitled to exercise their individual will," Fleischer said.

The next day, though, Fleischer suddenly switched tactics. At the morning gaggle, he amended his usual boilerplate about the president wanting to improve the system by declaring that the Shays-Meehan measure would accomplish that. He did this without consulting anyone, he says, just based on his gut. Fleischer figured the bill would pass and decided it would look phony for Bush to embrace it after the fact.

It was just a rhetorical nuance, but Fleischer's words had impact. Supporters of the bill made hundreds of copies of his remarks. Republican leaders on the Hill, who were twisting arms in an effort to torpedo the bill, were infuriated. Fleischer hated the idea of making trouble for his old pals; he had come from the House Republican ranks, after all. But he was the president's man now, and the president's interests had diverged from those of his party. By essentially endorsing the measure, Fleischer felt, he would be taking the Republican arrows that otherwise would be fired at Bush.

There were more battles to come. Just after 1 P.M., at a policy briefing in the Oval Office, congressional lobbyist Nick Calio told Bush that a late-night provision had been quietly slipped into the bill. It would allow lawmakers to use soft money to pay off debts—a subject of special interest because the Democratic National Committee had $10 million in debts, while the RNC had none.

"You should highlight this," Bush told Fleischer.

An hour later, Fleischer was decrying "a multimillion-dollar soft money loophole," saying that "the president views this as an unfair, unwise and unwarranted change."

Would Bush veto the bill with that provision?

"The president, again, wants to sign something that improves the system," Fleischer said, returning to his previous noncommittal language.

"What's the answer to the question?"

"The president wants to sign something that will improve the system."

Fleischer's pivot toward the Shays-Meehan effort was prominently noted by one newspaper the next morning. "You seem to have found your way into *The Washington Post*," Bush told him with a grin.

On this issue, Fleischer had become a player. Shortly before the House passed Shays-Meehan in the early-morning hours, the lawmakers tossed out the loophole provision that he had assailed. That, he felt, was the power of the podium. . . . ■

Chapter 8

Parties and Elections

Elections are a critical part of any democratic political system. They provide the clearest and most important opportunity for citizens to participate in self-government. They help ensure that the government respects the will of the people, at least in a general way. And by providing a mechanism to demonstrate "the consent of the governed," elections help to make government legitimate.

In the modern world, elections are typically fought not just by candidates but also by political parties. Political parties help organize political life, making it easier for voters to make choices and to effect results, and making it easier for public officials to organize governing majorities. In the United States, parties also form a bridge between the legislative and executive branches by providing natural allies for the president in both Houses of Congress.

Parties and elections, however, raise profound questions about the nature and efficacy of democratic politics. American parties, in particular, have been notoriously weak; members of the same political party may have little in common with one another, and even one-party control of both branches of government is no guarantee of success in policy making. Moreover, American elections are strongly influenced by special interest groups, most importantly through the campaign finance system, and by the media, which influence the process and which, in turn, are easily manipulated by candidates and public officials.

The selections in this chapter explore a variety of themes. Selection 8.1 presents a classic critique of American political parties as weak and ineffectual. Selections 8.2 and 8.3 attempt to make sense of the election of 2002, in which the Republican party regained control of the Senate and extended its margin of control in the House of Representatives. Selection 8.4 examines the American two-party system in comparison with the multiparty systems common elsewhere in the world, and selection 8.5 presents an inside account of election night 2000 from the point of view of CNN analyst Jeff Greenfield.

Chapter Questions

1. The ideal party system, according to the Committee on Political Parties of the American Political Science Association (selection 8.1), would be "accountable to the public," would "respect and express ... differences of opinion," and would be "able to cope with the great problems of modern government." How

well does the modern American party system live up to this standard? Would a multiparty system do a better or a worse job?

2. With recent national elections so closely divided, what strategies might the Democratic party use to regain control of Congress and the White House? How might these strategies be countered by the Republicans?

 # Foundations

More than fifty years ago, a group of political scientists representing the Committee on Political Parties of the American Political Science Association (APSA) issued a report on the weaknesses and inadequacies of the American party system. In its report, the APSA committee argued that the nation's political parties needed to be both "responsible and effective"—in other words, they needed to be "accountable to the public" while "able to cope with the great problems of modern government."

The APSA committee's critique remains valid today. Although the American party system has changed greatly in the past half century, American parties remain relatively weak and, except in rare circumstances, are unable to propose a coherent program to the American people and, if elected, carry that program into law. To make matters worse, the modern American electorate seems to prefer divided government, with one party in control of Congress and the other in control of the White House. Thus even if the two parties were each able to operate responsibly and effectively, they would probably have difficulty doing so together.

Questions

1. What does the committee mean by a "responsible and effective" party system? In what ways are modern American parties more responsible and/or effective than their counterparts in 1950? In what ways are they less responsible and/or effective?

2. Would American government be improved or harmed by the emergence of a party system in line with the APSA recommendations? Why?

8.1 Towards a More Responsible Two Party System (1950)

APSA Committee on Political Parties

Americans are reasonably well agreed about the purposes served by the two major parties as long as the matter is discussed in generalities. When specific questions are raised, however, agreement is much more limited. We cannot assume, therefore, a commonly shared view about the essential characteristics of the party system. But we can and must state our own view.

In brief, our view is this: *The party system that is needed must be democratic, responsible and effective*—a system that is accountable to the public, respects and expresses differences of opinion, and is able to cope with the great problems of modern government. Some of the implications warrant special statement, which is the purpose of this section.

I. A Stronger Two-party System

1. *The Need for an Effective Party System.* In an era beset with problems of unprecedented magnitude at home and abroad, it is dangerous to drift without a party system that helps the nation to set a general course of policy for the government as a whole. In a two-party system, when both parties are weakened or confused by internal divisions or ineffective organization it is the nation that suffers. When the parties are unable to reach and pursue responsible decisions, difficulties accumulate and cynicism about all democratic institutions grows.

An *effective party system requires, first, that the parties are able to bring forth programs to which they commit themselves and, second, that the parties possess sufficient internal cohesion to carry out these programs.* In such a system, the party program becomes the work program of the party, so recognized by the party leaders in and out of the government, by the party body as a whole, and by the public. This condition is unattainable unless party institutions have been created through which agreement can be reached about the general position of the party.

Clearly *such a degree of unity within the parties cannot be brought about without party procedures that give a large body of people an opportunity to share in the development of the party program.* One great function of the party system is to bring about the widest possible consent in relation to defined political goals, which provides the majority party with the essential means of building public support for the policies of the government. Democratic procedures in the internal affairs of the parties are best suited to the development of agreement within each party.

2. *The Need for an Effective Opposition Party.* The argument for a stronger party system cannot be divorced from measures designed to make the parties more fully

"Towards a More Responsible Two-Party System" (Report of the APSA Committee on Political Parties), *American Political Science Review* 44 (1950), pp. 17–24.

accountable to the public. *The fundamental requirement of such accountability is a two-party system in which the opposition party acts as the critic of the party in power, developing, defining and presenting the policy alternatives which are necessary for a true choice in reaching public decisions.*

Beyond that, the case for the American two-party system need not be restated here. The two-party system is so strongly rooted in the political traditions of this country and public preference for it is so well established that consideration of other possibilities seems entirely academic. When we speak of the parties without further qualification, we mean throughout our report the two major parties. The inference is not that we consider third or minor parties undesirable or ineffectual within their limited orbit. Rather, we feel that the minor parties in the longer run have failed to leave a lasting imprint upon both the two-party system and the basic processes of American government.

In spite of the fact that the two-party system is part of the American political tradition, it cannot be said that the role of the opposition party is well understood. This is unfortunate because democratic government is greatly influenced by the character of the opposition party. The measures proposed elsewhere in our report to help the party in power to clarify its policies are equally applicable to the opposition.

The opposition most conducive to responsible government is an organized party opposition, produced by the organic operation of the two-party system. When there are two parties identifiable by the kinds of action they propose, the voters have an actual choice. On the other hand, the sort of opposition presented by a coalition that cuts across party lines, as a regular thing, tends to deprive the public of a meaningful alternative. When such coalitions are formed after the elections are over, the public usually finds it difficult to understand the new situation and to reconcile it with the purpose of the ballot. Moreover, on that basis it is next to impossible to hold either party responsible for its political record. This is a serious source of public discontent.

II. Better Integrated Parties

1. *The Need for a Party System with Greater Resistance to Pressure.* As a consciously defined and consistently followed line of action keeps individuals from losing themselves in irresponsible ventures, so a program-conscious party develops greater resistance against the inroads of pressure groups.

The value of special-interest groups in a diversified society made up of countless groupings and specializations should be obvious. But organized interest groups cannot do the job of the parties. Indeed, it is only when a working formula of the public interest in its *general* character is made manifest by the parties in terms of coherent programs that the claims of interest groups can be adjusted on the basis of political responsibility. Such adjustment, once again, calls for the party's ability to honor its word.

There is little to suggest that the phenomenal growth of interest organizations in recent decades has come to its end. Organization along such lines is a characteristic feature of our civilization. To some extent these interest groups have replaced or absorbed into themselves older local institutions in that they make it possible for the government and substantial segments of the nation to maintain contact with each other. It must be obvious, however, that *the whole development makes necessary a reinforced party system that can cope with the multiplied organized pressures*. The alternative would be a scheme perhaps best described as government by pressure groups intent upon using the parties to deflect political attention from themselves.

By themselves, the interest groups cannot attempt to define public policy democratically. Coherent public policies do not emerge as the mathematical result of the claims of all of the pressure groups. The integration of the interest groups into the political system is a function of the parties. Any tendency in the direction of a strengthened party system encourages the interest groups to align themselves with one or the other of the major parties. Such a tendency is already at work. One of the noteworthy features of contemporary American politics is the fact that not a few interest groups have found it impossible to remain neutral toward both parties. To illustrate, the entry of organized labor upon the political scene has in turn impelled antagonistic special interests to coalesce in closer political alignments.

In one respect the growth of the modern interest groups is exerting a direct effect upon the internal distribution of power within the parties. They counteract and offset local interests; they are a nationalizing influence. Indeed, the proliferation of interest groups has been one of the factors in the rise of national issues because these groups tend to organize and define their objectives on a national scale.

Parties whose political commitments count are of particular significance to interest organizations with large membership such as exist among industrial workers and farmers, but to a lesser extent also among businessmen. Unlike the great majority of pressure groups, these organizations through their membership—and in proportion to their voting strength—are able to play a measurable role in elections. Interest groups of this kind are the equivalent of organizations of voters. For reasons of mutual interest, the relationship between them and the parties tends to become explicit and continuing.

A stronger party system is less likely to give cause for the deterioration and confusion of purposes which sometimes passes for compromise but is really an unjustifiable surrender to narrow interests. *Compromise among interests is compatible with the aims of a free society only when the terms of reference reflect an openly acknowledged concept of the public interest.* There is every reason to insist that the parties be held accountable to the public for the compromises they accept.

2. *The Need for a Party System with Sufficient Party Loyalty.* It is here not suggested, of course, that the parties should disagree about everything. Parties do not, and need not, take a position on all questions that allow for controversy. The proper function of the parties is to develop and define policy alternatives on matters likely to be of interest to the whole country, on issues related to the responsibility of the parties for the conduct of either the government or the opposition.

Needed clarification of party policy in itself *will not cause the parties to differ more fundamentally or more sharply than they have in the past.* The contrary is much more likely to be the case. The clarification of party policy may be expected to produce a more reasonable discussion of public affairs, more closely related to the political performance of the parties in their actions rather than their words. *Nor is it to be assumed that increasing concern with their programs will cause the parties to erect between themselves an ideological wall*. There is no real ideological division in the American electorate, and hence programs of action presented by responsible parties for the voter's support could hardly be expected to reflect or strive toward such division.

It is true at the same time that ultimately any political party must establish some conditions for membership and place some obligations on its representatives in government. Without so defining its identity the party is in danger of ceasing to be a party. To make party policy effective the *parties have the right and the duty to announce the terms to govern participation in the common enterprise*. This basic proposition is rarely denied, nor are precedents lacking. But there are practical difficulties in the way of applying restraints upon those who disregard the stated terms.

It is obvious that an effective party cannot be based merely or primarily on the expulsion of the disloyal. To impose discipline in any voluntary association is possible only as a last resort and only when a wide consensus is present within the association. Discipline and consensus are simply the front and rear sides of the same coin. *The emphasis in all consideration of party discipline must be,* therefore, *on positive measures to create a strong and general agreement on policies*. Thereafter, the problem of discipline is secondary and marginal.

When the membership of the party has become well aware of party policy and stands behind it, assumptions about teamwork within the party are likely to pervade the whole organization. Ultimately it is the electorate itself which will determine how firmly it wants the lines of party allegiance to be drawn. Yet even a small shift of emphasis toward party cohesion is likely to produce changes not only in the structure of the parties but also in the degree to which members identify themselves with their party.

Party unity is always a relative matter. It may be fostered, but the whole weight of tradition in American politics is against very rigid party discipline. As a general rule, the parties have a basis for expecting adherence to the party program when their position is reasonably explicit. Thus it is evident that the disciplinary difficulties of the parties do not result primarily from a reluctance to impose restraints but from the neglect of positive measures to give meaning to party programs.

As for party cohesion in Congress, the parties have done little to build up the kind of unity within the congressional party that is now so widely desired. Traditionally congressional candidates are treated as if they were the orphans of the political system, with no truly adequate party mechanism available for the conduct of their campaigns. Enjoying remarkably little national or local party support, congressional candidates have mostly been left to cope with the political hazards of their occupation on their own account. *A basis for party cohesion in Congress will be established as soon as the parties interest themselves sufficiently in their congressional candidates to set up strong and active campaign organizations in the constituencies*. Discipline is less a matter of what the parties do *to* their congressional candidates than what the parties do *for* them.

III. More Responsible Parties

1. *The Need for Parties Responsible to the Public. Party responsibility means the responsibility of both parties to the general public, as enforced in elections.*

Responsibility of the party in power centers on the conduct of the government, usually in terms of policies. The party in power has a responsibility, broadly defined, for the general management of the government, for its manner of getting results, for the results achieved, for the consequences of inaction as well as action, for the intended and unintended outcome of its conduct of public affairs, for all that it plans to do, for all that it might have foreseen, for the leadership it provides, for the acts of all of its agents, and for what it says as well as for what it does.

Party responsibility includes the responsibility of the opposition party, also broadly defined, for the conduct of its opposition, for the management of public discussion, for the development of alternative policies and programs, for the bipartisan policies which it supports, for its failures and successes in developing the issues of public policy, and for its leadership of public opinion. The opposition is as responsible for its record in Congress as is the party in power. It is important that the opposition party be effective but it is equally important that it be responsible, for an irresponsible opposition is dangerous to the whole political system.

Party responsibility to the public, enforced in elections, implies that there be more than one party, for the public can hold a party responsible only if it has a choice. Again, unless the parties identify themselves with programs, the public is unable to make an intelligent choice between them. The public can understand the general management of the government only in terms of policies. When the parties lack the capacity to define their actions in terms of policies, they turn irresponsible because the electoral choice between the parties becomes devoid of meaning.

As a means of achieving responsibility, the clarification of party policy also tends to keep public debate on a more realistic level, restraining the inclination of party spokesmen to make unsubstantiated statements and charges. When party policy is made clear, the result to be expected is a more reasonable and profitable discussion, tied more closely to the record of party action. When there is no clear basis for rating party performance, when party policies cannot be defined in terms of a concrete program, party debate tears itself loose from the facts. Then wild fictions are used to excite the imagination of the public.

2. The Need for Parties Responsible to Their Members. Party responsibility includes also the responsibility of party leaders to the party membership, as enforced in primaries, caucuses and conventions. To this end the internal processes of the parties must be democratic, the party members must have an opportunity to participate in intraparty business, and the leaders must be accountable to the party. Responsibility demands that the parties concern themselves with the development of good relations between the leaders and the members. Only thus can the parties act as intermediaries between the government and the people. Strengthening the parties involves, therefore, the improvement of the internal democratic processes by which the leaders of the party are kept in contact with the members.

The external and the internal kinds of party responsibility need not conflict. Responsibility of party leaders to party members promotes the clarification of party policy when it means that the leaders find it necessary to explain the policy to the membership. Certainly the lack of unity within the membership cannot be overcome by the fiat of an irresponsible party leadership. A democratic internal procedure can be used not merely to test the strength of the various factions within a party but also to resolve the conflicts. The motives for enlarging the areas of agreement within the parties are persuasive because unity is the condition of success.

Intraparty conflict will be minimized if it is generally recognized that national, state and local party leaders have a common responsibility to the party membership. Intraparty conflict is invited and exaggerated by dogmas that assign to local party leaders an exclusive right to appeal to the party membership in their area.

Occasions may arise in which the parties will find it necessary to apply sanctions against a state or local party organization, especially when that organization is in open rebellion against policies established for the whole party. There are a variety of ways in which recognition may be withdrawn. It is possible to refuse to seat delegates to the National convention; to drop from the National Committee members representing the dissident state organization; to deny legislative committee assignments to members of Congress sponsored by the disloyal organization; and to appeal directly to the party membership in the state or locality, perhaps even promoting a rival organization. The power to take strong measures is there.

It would be unfortunate, however, if the problem of party unity were thought of as primarily a matter of punishment. Nothing prevents the parties from explaining themselves to their own members. The party members have power to insist that local and state party organizations and leaders cooperate with the party as a whole; all the members need is a better opportunity to find out what party politics is about. The need for sanctions is relatively small when state and local organizations are not treated as the restricted preserve of their immediate leaders. National party leaders ought to have access to party members everywhere as a normal and regular procedure because they share with local party leaders responsibility to the same party membership. It would always be proper for the national party leaders to discuss all party matters with the membership of any state or local party organization. Considering their great prestige, wise and able national party leaders will need very little more than this opportunity.

The political developments of our time place a heavy emphasis on national issues as the basis of party programs. As a result, the party membership is coming to look to the national party leaders for a larger role in intraparty affairs. There is some evidence of growing general agreement within the membership of each party, strong enough to form a basis of party unity, provided the parties maintain close contact with their own supporters.

In particular, *national party leaders have a legitimate interest in the nomination of congressional candidates*, though normally they try hard to avoid the appearance of any intervention. Depending on the circumstances, this interest can be expressed quite sufficiently by seeking a chance to discuss the nomination with the party membership in the congressional district. On the other hand, it should not be assumed that state and local party leaders usually have an interest in congressional nominations antagonistic to the interest of the national leaders in maintaining the general party policy. As a matter of fact, congressional nominations are not considered great prizes by the local party organization as generally as one might think. It is neglect of congressional nominations and elections more than any other factor that weakens party unity in Congress. It should be added, however, that what is said here about intraparty relations with respect to congressional nominations applies also to other party nominations. ∎

American Politics Today

The election of 2000 was one of the closest in American history. When all the votes were counted, the Democrat Al Gore had won the popular vote by a margin of just over 500,000 ballots (or one-half of 1 percent of the votes cast). But presidential elections are conducted on a state-by-state basis, and so the election came down to Florida, which was divided so narrowly that it took five weeks—and two Supreme Court decisions—to award the election to the Republican George W. Bush. The congressional elections were nearly as close; the Republicans retained control of the House of Representatives by just nine seats, while the Senate was so closely divided that control shifted from one party to the other on the basis of one Senator's switch from Republican to Independent.

Both parties had high hopes for 2002. The Democrats hoped to win back the House and extend their razor-thin lead in the Senate, while the Republicans aimed to keep the House and win back the Senate. The election was too close to call until election night, but in the end the Republicans prevailed. That left the Democrats—and political analysts—wondering what had happened.

The selections here provide some answers. In the first, James A. Barnes argues that the Republicans prevailed in 2002 because they won the battle for America's suburban vote. In the second, the journalist John B. Judis gives credit for the Republican victory to a popular president fighting a war against terrorism.

Questions

1. On the basis of these two analyses, what might the Democrats have done differently in 2002? What lessons might both Democrats and Republicans learn for 2004 and beyond?
2. Compare and contrast the analyses in these selections with the cultural observations presented by David Brooks in selection 5.2.

8.2 The Crabgrass Wars (2002)

James A. Barnes

Think Ozzie and Harriet. Or, better still, think Ozzy and Sharon Osbourne. That's what the Democratic Party needs to do if it wants to understand why it lost the Senate. Want to put a label on the party's problem? Call it "white, married with children."

James A. Barnes, "The Crabgrass Wars," *National Journal* (November 16, 2002): pp. 3392–3394. Copyright 2002 by National Journal Group, Inc. All rights reserved. Reprinted by permission.

In several key Senate races this year, Republicans swept the suburban counties where the growth in households headed by white, married couples with children is among the fastest in the nation. Generally, Democratic Senate nominees need to win big in metropolitan areas in order to offset poor showings in small towns and rural areas. But this year, GOP success in suburbs with rapidly growing populations of white-married-with-children households enabled Republicans to severely cut into the Democrats' metro-area advantage—and to sometimes even capture the territory outright.

And while population trends do not indicate that the number of white, married couples with children is going to surge across the whole crabgrass frontier, the growth of these households is likely to continue in the Southeast and West—to which congressional districts and Electoral College votes continue to flow—as well as in other regions' expanding "exurbs," where statewide elections are often won or lost.

"Even though this kind of family is not a large demographic nationally, in these [Southern and Western suburbs] it is," notes University of Michigan demographer William H. Frey, who analyzed census data for this article. "They are big pockets of the new Sun Belt, and they will probably increase."

The GOP advantage among white, married suburbanites with children was particularly telling in the Senate races in North Carolina and Texas this year. Those states have some political terrain that should favor Democrats: North Carolina's Research Triangle around Raleigh, Durham, and Chapel Hill, where the dominant employers are high-tech companies, universities, and the state government; and the Austin–San Marcos metropolitan area in Texas, which has similar characteristics.

These booming, post-industrial communities have attracted the kind of voters that New South Democrats have successfully cultivated in the past—transplanted Yankees who tend to have less-conservative views on social issues than their homegrown white neighbors. But quite a few of these northern migrants are also white, married suburbanites with children.

In fact, from 1990 to 2000, the Austin–San Marcos and Raleigh–Durham–Chapel Hill metro areas posted the nation's second- and third-highest growth rates for suburban households of white, married couples with children. And both of these places voted more Republican this year.

The GOP candidates who can attract these suburban swing voters in significant numbers are not their party's culture warriors. In 1998, Democratic trial lawyer John Edwards captured five of the six counties that make up the Raleigh-Durham metro area on his way to defeating GOP Sen. Lauch Faircloth, a cultural conservative. Edwards won 38,000 more votes than Faircloth in the six counties, almost half of the Democrat's statewide margin of victory.

But this year [2002], it was former Red Cross President Elizabeth Dole who was carrying the Republican standard. She successfully campaigned to succeed retiring GOP Sen. Jesse Helms, a die-hard founder of the Religious Right. Although Dole promised to carry on in Helms's tradition and talked of being a born-again Christian, she is still the Duke University sorority sister who graduated from Harvard Law School and went on to become the secretary of two Cabinet departments—

making her a successful career woman who is more inspiring than frightening to many swing voters in the Research Triangle.

With the help of Baby Boomers who still have kids at home, and of Gen X-ers who now have families of their own, Dole eked out a 500-vote victory in the Raleigh-Durham metro area over her Democratic opponent, Erskine B. Bowles, who was chief of staff in the Clinton White House. This was never Helms country. In his successful 1990 bid for a fourth term, Helms lost the Raleigh-Durham metro counties by more than 45,000 votes.

In the six counties of the Charlotte-Gastonia metro area, where the growth of white, married suburbanites with kids ranked in 12th place nationally, Dole romped. She outpolled Bowles, a Charlotte investment banker, in his own backyard by more than 50,000 votes. Four years earlier, Edwards had carried this turf by more than 2,000 votes.

The Texas Senate race was not even close. The Republican nominee, state Attorney General John Cornyn, defeated his Democratic opponent, former Dallas Mayor Ron Kirk, by more than half a million votes, in part because Kirk could not capitalize on Democratic opportunities in the Austin and San Marcos metro area. Although Kirk won Travis County—home of the University of Texas, the state capital, and Dell Computer—by more than 30,000 votes, that edge was almost completely offset by Cornyn's showing in three of the four surrounding counties where white, suburban families are on the rise. Most of the increases in white-married-with-children-households came in Williamson County, where the number of such families has jumped by more than 55 percent in the last decade. Its voters cast nearly two-thirds of their ballots for Cornyn.

Yet in 1990, when Democratic state Treasurer Ann Richards ran successfully for governor, she won all five Austin-area counties, racking up a 73,000-vote margin. In contrast, Kirk beat Cornyn in metropolitan Austin by fewer than 6,000 votes, a lead that was dwarfed by the Republican's strong showing in the suburbs around Dallas, where white-married-with-children families are rapidly growing, and in West and East Texas.

For Democrats, the Republicans' success in winning the votes of white, married suburbanites with children is a serious problem. "If you look at the Democratic-leaning, post-industrial areas and these white, married households with children, if the Republicans are able to swing too many people to their side, that is going to compress the Democrats' margin in the counties that they tend to dominate," said Ruy Teixeira, a senior fellow at the Century Foundation who has studied how demographic and political trends could resurrect the Democratic Party's majority status.

If Democrats can't win big in their traditional territory, they must compete on GOP turf. "It puts Democrats too much on the edge," Teixeira says. "They'd have to pick up more swing [votes] in exurbs and rural areas where the cultural worries are in the other direction"—that Democrats are too liberal.

In Georgia, Democratic Sen. Max Cleland lost his bid for a second term when his Republican challenger, Rep. Saxby Chambliss, was able to ride President Bush's post-9/11 popularity to victory. But Republican strength in the ring of suburban counties around Atlanta, where the white, married households with children are exploding, clearly contributed to Cleland's defeat. Cleland held his own in Atlanta's inner suburban counties. But the 133,000-vote lead he posted there was overtaken by the 171,000-vote margin that Chambliss rolled up in the 12 surrounding counties.

Tom Murphy, the longtime speaker of the Georgia House, also fell victim to the trend. According to Merle Black, a political science professor at Emory University, Murphy lost his re-election bid because part of Paulding County, in the far western suburbs of Atlanta, was added to his territory during redistricting. In Paulding, the number of white, married households with children exploded by 74 percent in the 1990s. "The only thing they may have known about the speaker is that he's a Democrat," Black says. "And that was enough."

Although Republicans lost a Senate seat in Arkansas, that race might have been over before it began, because incumbent Tim Hutchinson was a "family values" politician who had divorced his wife and married a former aide. But the Republicans will have a new opportunity to resume their momentum in the South in the December 7 Senate runoff that pits Louisiana Democratic Sen. Mary L. Landrieu against Republican state Elections Commissioner Suzanne Haik Terrell. When Landrieu won her seat in 1996 by just over 5,000 votes, she had the benefit of facing veteran GOP state legislator Woody Jenkins, who ran as a culture warrior and assailed her for supporting abortion rights and gay rights.

Terrell, who is viewed warily by some conservative activists in the state, is unlikely to attack Landrieu from the far right. While Landrieu must mobilize black voters in New Orleans, one of the keys to the race may be how many Republican votes Terrell can turn out in St. Tammany Parish, north of the city. That parish is one of the few areas in the state showing growth in both the overall population and in the number of white, suburban families. St. Tammany is only about half the size of Jefferson Parish, which includes the traditional GOP suburban stronghold of Metairie, east of New Orleans. But in the 2000 presidential election, Bush's margin over Vice President Gore in St. Tammany was 36,471 votes, compared with 34,592 in Jefferson.

GOP candidates want to emulate their president. "The role model, increasingly, for Southern Republicans is President George W. Bush," says Rice University political scientist Earl Black, who, along with his brother Merle, has written extensively on Dixie's politics. Bush's moderate style "is the inspiration that will become the new way of running as a Republican across the South, but it will not be just limited to the South."

In the border state of Missouri, former GOP Rep. Jim Talent narrowly defeated Democratic Sen. Jean Carnahan. The incumbent dominated Kansas City, St. Louis, and their close-in suburbs, while Talent turned out the GOP rural base. But the Republican landed decisive blows in the fastest-growing counties in the state, which had notable increases in white, married households with children: Christian and Webster counties, which include the Springfield suburbs; Stone County; Taney County, home of the country music magnet of Branson; and St. Charles County, the rapidly growing GOP exurb of St. Louis, where Bush attended a Talent campaign rally the day before the election. Talent's advantage over Carnahan in these five counties was larger than his statewide margin of victory.

After the death of Sen. Paul Wellstone, D-Minn., former Vice President Mondale became the Democrats' replacement candidate. But his state had changed since he was last on the ballot, as his party's 1984 presidential nominee. Back then, Mondale carried Hennepin and Ramsey counties, where Minneapolis and St. Paul are located, by 64,436 votes—more than enough to offset the 15,534-vote advantage that President Reagan posted in the nine suburban counties that ring the Twin Cities.

This year, the Democratic icon racked up a similar lead of just over 60,500 votes in Hennepin and Ramsey against the GOP Senate nominee, former St. Paul Mayor Norm Coleman. And Mondale ran stronger than most Democrats do in the state's rural farm and mining belts.

But the Minneapolis–St. Paul suburbs are one of the few northern metro areas that have seen white, married households with children rise in recent years. Coleman drew 116,000 more votes than Mondale in the nine "collar" counties, and won the election there.

Meanwhile, in Colorado, former Democratic U.S. Attorney Tom Strickland again came up short in his efforts to defeat Republican Wayne Allard, despite cutting into the Republican's 1996 margins in the slow-growing Denver suburbs in Arapahoe and Jefferson counties. Allard countered by boosting his margins in Douglas County, south of Denver, where the number of white, married households with children had exploded by 177 percent, and in El Paso County (Colorado Springs), where these families grew modestly.

The demographic and political challenge that Democrats face in suburban counties where households of white, married couples with children are growing is not likely to diminish any time soon. In the 1970s and 1980s, the growth of these households collapsed as the main cohort of the Baby Boomers flocked to college and then focused on their careers instead of having children. The feminist tide of the times put many women in the workforce rather than on the mommy track, and they delayed having children.

But now, demographer Frey notes, that decline may have bottomed out. "The newer generations have come along, and they are holding their own," Frey says. "We're not going to have a smaller share of Ozzie and Harriets in the future."

Democrats can expect to see the number of white-married-with-children households growing in suburbs that will be key electoral battlegrounds in 2004 and beyond. So the party had better figure out a way to make itself more appealing to them—or resign itself to its minority status. ■

8.3 Why There's Nothing the Democrats Could Have Done (2002)

John B. Judis

Democrats are gradually coalescing around an interpretation of why their party did so poorly [in 2002]. The party, the argument goes, failed to get out its base; and the reason it failed to do so was because it didn't draw a clear enough distinction between its policies and the Republicans'. As former political consultant Paul Begala argued on CNN, "The Democrats didn't fight Bush hard enough on the tax cut, and they didn't campaign on it. They didn't fight him hard enough on the war. That means that base Democrats are very depressed on this Election Day." The party's rank and file, said California Representative Nancy Pelosi, faulted party leadership for its timidity in presenting an alternative to the GOP.

This seems like a plausible explanation for the Democrats' defeats—until you actually look at what happened on the ground. In most of the crucial Senate races that the Democrats lost, the Democratic candidate did proportionately as well as ever among the Democratic base. Turnout did go down from 2000, but it wasn't unusually low compared to the last off-year election in 1998. In Missouri, for instance, losing Democratic Senate candidate Jean Carnahan garnered the same percentage of the vote in St. Louis and Kansas City that her late husband had gotten in 2000 when he defeated incumbent Republican John Ashcroft. What made the difference in her race—and in others around the country—was that the GOP did so much better at turning out voters in Republican-leaning areas and in the mostly white suburbs where Independents and swing voters predominate. The Democrats didn't lose the election in the cities but in the suburbs.

Would the Democrats have done better in the suburbs had they been less timid about defining their differences with the GOP? Probably not. If you look closely at the political context in which these races occurred—in particular, the overwhelming popularity of George W. Bush as a war president and the overriding importance of national security as a campaign issue—it is far from apparent that more strident attacks from the Democrats would have reversed any of the outcomes. Indeed, while such an approach might have improved Democrats' standing among their base, it would likely have eroded their position among swing voters still further.

Take Georgia, where Republican Saxby Chambliss defeated Democratic incumbent Max Cleland. Cleland won Atlanta's highly Democratic Fulton County by 58 percent to 40 percent, while successful Senate candidate Zell Miller won it by a somewhat better 66 percent to 31 percent in 2000 when he ran against Republican Matt Mattingly. But the real turnaround came in white, upscale Cobb County, north of Atlanta. Chambliss defeated Cleland there by 59 percent to 39 percent, whereas Miller had defeated Mattingly by 52 percent to 44 percent. That's a swing of 28 points. Similarly, in white suburban Gwinett County, northeast of Atlanta, Chambliss bested Cleland by a whopping 64 percent to 34 percent; in 2000, by contrast, Miller edged out Mattingly by 50 percent to 46 percent. These suburban counties are where Cleland lost the race. Likewise, in Missouri, Carnahan won her urban base but did significantly worse than her late husband in places like predominately white suburban St. Louis County and Osage County, outside of Jefferson.

Commentators on Tuesday night made much of New Hampshire Democrat Jeanne Shaheen's failure to carry the city of Manchester against Republican John Sununu. But Manchester has long ceased to be a Democratic stronghold. Even as she coasted to reelection in her 2000 governor's race, Shaheen barely defeated far-right Republican Gordon Humphrey in Manchester, 48 percent to 47 percent. Where Shaheen really lost votes to Sununu was in suburban towns, where Sununu did even better than Bush had done in 2000. In that election, Bush carried Merrimack by 50 percent to 45 percent, while Shaheen's gubernatorial challenger, Gordon Humphrey, beat her 48 percent to 47 percent. This week, Sununu carried Merrimack by 55 percent to 43 percent over Shaheen. She, like Carnahan, Cleland, and Mondale, lost the election in the suburbs.

In Minnesota, where Walter Mondale was defeated by Republican Norm Coleman, Mondale—following on the heels of the late Paul Wellstone—got out the Democratic vote. Turnout was up in Minnesota, but Mondale still didn't do as well in key suburban areas as victorious Democratic candidate Mark Dayton had done in 2000 against Republican Rod Grams. Dayton had won Hennepin County, which includes Democratic Minneapolis, but which also includes suburban areas that have swung between Democrats and Republicans, by 53 percent to 37 percent in 2000; yet Mondale only won it by 51 percent to 46 percent this year. And Coleman easily defeated Mondale in rural counties where Dayton had been competitive. Coleman won Cass County in central Minnesota by 54 percent to 40 percent, while Grams had won it by only 47 percent to 46 percent.

What explains the Republicans' success in the suburbs? Primarily, Bush's popularity as the leader of the war against terrorism, which carried over to the Republican Party and to Republican candidates. Prior to September 11, 2001, Bush's job-approval ratings hovered at 51 percent in the Gallup poll, and more people viewed the Republican Party unfavorably than favorably. After September 11, however, Bush's popularity soared and has never fallen back to its pre–September 11 levels. On the eve of this year's election, Gallup found that 63 percent of Americans approved of the president's handling of his job and only 29 percent disapproved, while 53 percent viewed the Republicans favorably and only 35 percent viewed them unfavorably. And, while Bush's popularity has fallen among self-identified Democrats, it remains high among Independents. In a CBS/*New York Times* poll conducted at the end of October, Independents approved of Bush's job as president by 60 percent to 27 percent and of his job on foreign policy by 54 percent to 33 percent; they also viewed Republicans favorably by 54 percent to 35 percent.

Bush's popularity as a war leader translated into voter support for Republican candidates in general. According to the CBS/*New York Times* poll, 31 percent of voters, including 28 percent of Independents and 15 percent of Democrats, thought of their vote for Congress as "a vote for George Bush." Bush crystallized that support during his five-day campaign on behalf of Republican candidates in the key battleground states.

Republican candidates capitalized on their party's reputation among Independents, as well as among their own followers, by painting their Democratic opponents as weak on defense. Republican Senate candidates in Georgia, South Carolina, New Hampshire, South Dakota, Missouri, Colorado, and Texas, to name a few, challenged their Democratic opponents' support for the war against terror. In Georgia, Chambliss attacked Cleland for opposing Bush's version of the homeland security bill and for questioning the need for a national missile defense. Likewise, in New Hampshire, Sununu attacked Shaheen for accepting contributions from the Council for a Livable World—which has been critical of the administration's missile defense plans—and for opposing the administration's homeland security bill.

Democrats hoped that by quickly passing the president's resolution on Iraq they could put national security issues behind them and focus the electorate on Social Security and prescription drugs. Many political analysts, including myself, thought this ploy would work and preserve the Democrats' Senate majority. It didn't. Not only did voters accord more importance to fighting the war against terrorism than to reducing prescription-drug prices, but their view of the war on terrorism—and of Bush's leadership in fighting it—colored their perception of the nation's economic problems. Most Americans did not blame Bush and the Republicans for the economic downturn that began last year. Asked last month by pollsters Fabrizio, McLaughlin and Associates who was "most responsible for the economy," 23 percent of Americans blamed the business cycle, 21 percent the September 11 attacks, 15 percent former President Clinton, and 14 percent Bush. Given the nation's economic doldrums, it is remarkable that the preelection Ipsos-Reid survey found 54 percent of Americans approving of Bush's handling of the economy. Meanwhile, the CBS/*New York Times* survey found that the public, by 41 percent to 37 percent, believed that Republicans were "more likely to make sure the country is prosperous."

Democrats did do well in governors' races, where they took over Republican statehouses in Pennsylvania, Illinois, Wisconsin, Wyoming, Oklahoma, Arizona, Tennessee, and Kansas. But these exceptions prove the rule. Gubernatorial candidates were least likely to be judged on national security issues. In these races, the Democrats' advantage on economic and social issues came to the fore. Bush's popularity as a war president—except, perhaps, in Florida and Texas—was not an important factor. Suburban voters were more likely to care what a Democrat thought about social spending or abortion or gun control. But, in judging House and Senate candidates in the same states, swing voters and Independents paid more attention to national security than to Social Security.

So what if Democrats had followed Begala and Pelosi's advice and come out strong against the tax cut and war with Iraq? It's hard to imagine the outcome would have been any different. If Shaheen had come out against the president's tax cut in taxophobic New Hampshire, she would have likely suffered the same fate as Democratic gubernatorial candidate Mark Fernald, who, because he advocated an income tax, was routed by 21 points. Cleland's campaign would have been a lot more coherent if he had opposed Bush's tax cut, but he would have lost even more votes in Cobb County. And opposition to the war would have doomed Democratic Senate candidates in the South—and probably in South Dakota and Colorado as well. In Minnesota, Mondale did draw the lines very clearly on taxes and the war in his November 4 debate with Coleman—and he subsequently lost the election.

The country might have been better off had Democrats tried to develop a coherent foreign policy and advocated the repeal of Bush's disastrous tax cut. Even as a party, the Democrats might be better off now if they had articulated clearer positions in opposition to the Bush administration. But, if they had, they would have still lost the Senate—possibly by an even larger margin than they did. Although it wasn't apparent until the final days of the election, the Republicans were borne to victory this fall by Bush's energetic response to Osama bin Laden. And there was probably nothing that the Democrats could have done to stop them. ■

The International Context

The two-party system is a characteristic feature of the American polity. Most of the other democracies in the world, by contrast, have *multiparty* systems, in which one or more major parties are joined by several (and in some cases many) smaller ones.

The historical persistence of the American two-party system is due, in part at least, to the rules of the electoral game. Most American elections reward only the candidate with the most votes—other candidates, no matter how many votes they receive, win nothing. Such "single-member plurality" (or SMP) rules apply in both presidential elections and congressional elections. In the 1992 presidential election, for example, H. Ross Perot won 19 percent of the popular vote, but because he did not finish first in any state, he received no electoral votes. Third-party candidates have historically fared poorly in congressional elections as well; at present, there is only one member of Congress who is not a Democrat or Republican.

The SMP system has distinct advantages for a political system. Perhaps most important, single-member plurality rules require candidates to reach out to a large bloc of voters, and encourage compromise and cooperation. But as the political scientist Douglas J. Amy argues in this selection, the SMP system also raises serious concerns. As an alternative, Amy suggests that the United States consider a proportional representation (or PR) system, which is used by most other democracies in the world today. In a PR system, the number of legislative seats won by a particular party would be roughly proportional to the number of votes it receives—whether or not it attains a plurality in any particular district.

Questions

1. What are the disadvantages of the single-member plurality system, according to Amy? How, in his view, would a PR system address the problems with the SMP system?
2. What arguments would you make in opposition to Amy's proposal? What are the advantages of the SMP system as used in the United States? What problems might arise if we adopted a PR system?
3. How would a PR system change the relationships between members of Congress and party leaders? Between the White House and Congress? Between members of Congress and their constituents?

8.4 Breaking the Two-Party Monopoly (1993)

Douglas J. Amy

The Problem of Only Two Parties

For the sake of argument assume that the Democrats and Republicans were to develop into parties offering detailed and distinctly different policy options to the voters. Would this eliminate the problems surrounding our two-party system? The answer is no—because having only two parties from which to choose is itself limiting and problematic. It unreasonably restricts the political options available to the electorate. Many combinations of positions can be taken on the pressing issues of the day, but in our party system they are automatically reduced to two. A simple example illustrates the extent of the problem. Assume that we face only five political issues in an election—say, defense, education, welfare, farm policy, and health policy—and that we can choose to increase or decrease expenditures in each area. Even this simplified situation presents thirty-two combinations of positions that could be offered by parties. In a two-party system, one party might advocate increasing defense spending and cutting the others, and the other party might advocate the opposite. But where does that leave all the voters who desire any of the other combinations? They are left with no choice they can enthusiastically endorse and with the task of deciding which is the lesser of two evils. And that is the basic problem with a two-party system—it simply cannot offer anything approaching a reasonable variety of positions on the issues.

Again, the inherent limitations of choice in our party system become even more obvious when compared with European party systems—systems that offer not only a larger number of parties but also a wider variety of parties with distinct

---

ideologies and policy programs. Voters there have the option of moderate parties in the middle, as well as a socialist party on the far left or a conservative party on the right, or even a Green party that claims to be neither left nor right. In these multiparty systems, voters have a much better chance of finding parties and candidates with policy positions close to their own.

Supporters of the two-party system sometimes suggest that limiting the public to two choices may in fact be an advantage—that reducing our options conveniently minimizes the complexity and difficulty of election choices. The assumption is that any more than two options would strain the intellectual capacity of most voters. But this logic is hardly accepted in other areas of American life. American consumers would be outraged if they were offered only two choices of houses or cars to meet their different needs. As political consumers we should hardly be less infuriated with the same overly restricted electoral choices.

One-Party Systems

Having only two options in the election booth is bad enough, but our choices are often even more restricted than that. In many areas of the country we do not even have a two-party system; we have a one-party system. In cities, counties, and states in which one party has a reliable majority of the voters, that dominant party is usually the only viable option. Indeed, for most of this century, one-party systems have been the rule in most areas of the United States. Until the 1950s the South had a one-party system dominated by the Democrats, while several northern states were often controlled by Republicans. Similar situations remain in many parts of the country today. Recent years have seen some increase in party competition in some states, but one part of the state often is dominated by the Democrats and another by the Republicans.

In this sense, our current party system often closely resembles a corporate oligopoly in which the two dominant companies divide up their territories and agree not to compete with each other in them. Indeed, Mayhew and others present evidence that Republicans and Democrats sometimes collude in exactly this way, with legislators agreeing on gerrymandering schemes that ensure safe districts for the representatives of each party. So it is misleading to call ours a competitive two-party system; often it is more accurately described as a pair of one-party monopolies. The big loser in this situation is the same one that suffers in a one-company territory—the public. Such arrangements severely curtail the choices of American voters and ultimately undermine their power to control the political system. Americans have long been aware of the evils of economic monopolies and oligopolies, but we have been slow to awaken to the dangers of the same arrangements in our party system.

The Electoral Connection

If our two-party system is so frustrating, why does it persist? Why haven't we developed a multiparty system that offers a set of genuine political choices? The first reason is the power of tradition. Most Americans are socialized in our party system and learn to view our political universe in those limited terms. We come to think of having only two parties as natural. The media contribute to this view by giving little coverage to any minor-party candidates who do happen to run, making it more difficult for these challengers to get their messages out and to build larger bases of public support. Equally important, the two parties have also devised numerous election procedures that discourage minor parties. Many states, for example, still require excessively large numbers of voter signatures on petitions before minor parties can even get access to the ballot.

But the electoral rule that is by far the biggest obstacle to the emergence of viable minor parties in the United States is plurality voting. Plurality rules tend to foster two-party systems by systematically discriminating against minor parties and making it extremely difficult for them to achieve any electoral success. In the 1950s the French political scientist Maurice Duverger described the supportive relationship between plurality rules and two-party systems, and it remains one of the most extensively examined propositions in political science. Duverger noted that plurality voting rules tend to work against minor parties in two ways. First is what Duverger called the *mechanical effect* of these rules: The tendency of the plurality system to give the largest party more seats than it deserves and to give smaller parties fewer seats than they deserve. Such underrepresentation is often a problem for the second party, but it can prove disastrous for third or fourth parties.

As a rule, the smaller the party, the larger the proportion of seats out of which it is cheated. For example, in the 1987 British elections for Parliament, the Conservative party won 42.3 percent of the vote and received 57.7 percent of the seats. The second-place Labor party was actually slightly overrepresented as well, winning 30.8 percent of the vote and 35.5 percent of the seats. But the third party, the Alliance of Social Democrats and Liberals, suffered the brunt of the underrepresentation. It received a respectable 22.8 percent of the vote, but was given a minuscule 3.4 percent of the seats in Parliament. Similar fates have befallen third-party efforts in New Zealand's plurality elections. The Social Credit party received 16.1 percent of the vote in 1978, but won only one seat (1.1%) in the ninety-two-seat national parliament. In 1981 its portion of the vote increased to 20.7 percent, but the party only managed to receive two seats (2.2%).

Underrepresentation is typical of the fate of minor parties under plurality rules. And it is quite possible to imagine worse situations, in which minor parties receive a substantial portion of the votes, only to get no seats at all. For example, in 1989 British elections to the European parliament, the British Green party received 15 percent of the vote, but because of plurality election rules received no seats. Similarly, in 1984 the New Zealand party received 12 percent of the vote in that country and no seats. The only way for minor parties to enjoy any kind of consistent electoral success in plurality systems is by being concentrated in local or regional enclaves, where they can sometimes muster a plurality of the votes. This is the case with the small Welsh and Scottish parties in Great Britain; regional popularity allows them to send several members to Parliament. In the United States some third parties have been concentrated in particular states. In the 1930s the Progressive party in Wisconsin was able to elect a governor and many state legislators; during that same period the Farmer-Labor party in Minnesota captured the governorship for three successive terms. Without such regional sanctuaries, however, it is difficult, if not impossible, for minor-party candidates to win office, making it more likely that these parties will be short-lived in single-member plurality systems.

The tendency of the mechanical effect of plurality systems to discourage minor parties is compounded by what Duverger called the *psychological effect* of those rules. Potential supporters will hesitate to vote for a minor-party candidate if they believe that candidate has little chance of winning a plurality or majority of the vote. They fear wasting their votes on a minor-party candidate. It is much more rational for voters to support a candidate who stands a chance of winning—usually one from the two major parties. Thus even though minor parties and their candidates might enjoy some support among the electorate, supporters will often realize that the only realistic choice is to vote for a major-party candidate. This was the case, for instance, for those who supported the Independent John Anderson in the 1980 presidential elections. Opinion polls indicated that up to 24 percent of voters supported Anderson, but only 7 percent cast ballots for him on election day. Similarly a University of Michigan national survey indicated that of those voters who rated Anderson the highest among the three candidates, only 39 percent actually voted for him. In contrast, Ronald Reagan and Jimmy Carter received 95 percent of the votes of people who rated them the highest. Studies done in other countries support the conclusion that voters often will abandon a preferred minor-party candidate to reluctantly cast a vote for a major-party candidate with a better chance of being elected.

Thus plurality rules subject minor parties to a kind of double penalty: They first ensure that these parties will be severely underrepresented in the legislature, which discourages voters from voting for these candidates in the first place. But the plight of minor parties under plurality rules is actually even worse. Minor-party voters also can be contributing to the election of the very candidate they oppose the most. Imagine, for instance, being a voter faced with a choice of a liberal Democrat, a moderate Republican, and a Libertarian. A far-right conservative may be tempted to support the Libertarian candidate, if only as a protest vote, but doing so only takes that vote away from the moderate Republican and thus boosts the chances of the conservative's least preferable candidate, the Democrat. Or take a real example of this dilemma: the 1980 U.S. Senate race in New York. That year three candidates ran—Alphonse D'Amato (Republican party), Elizabeth Holtzman (Democratic party), and Jacob Javits (Liberal party). Eleven percent of the voters opted for Javits, which took votes away from the other liberal candidate, Holtzman. She lost to D'Amato by one percentage point—45 percent to 44 percent—largely because probable supporters defected to Javits. Polls indicated that most of Javits's votes would have gone to Holtzman in a two-way race between she and D'Amato. But in a plurality system those votes for the Liberal party candidate simply ensured that the most conservative candidate won. Thus an additional punishment often is meted out to those who dare vote for minor-party candidates in the United States—the election of the candidate they most detest.

Plurality election rules undermine minor parties primarily by discouraging voters from supporting their candidates. However, scaring voters away can have several secondary effects that further handicap these parties. For example, because minor parties lack a realistic chance of getting candidates elected under current rules, they usually have trouble recruiting experienced and talented politicians. Such politicians are inevitably attracted to the two mainstream parties where the career opportunities are dramatically better. Also minor parties usually have difficulty attracting financial contributors, who are understandably hesitant to invest money in quixotic campaigns. Thus minor parties are caught in a vicious circle: Plurality rules discourage voter support, which makes potential candidates and contributors reluctant to join up, which further erodes the ability of these parties to conduct effective campaigns and to attract voters, and so on. These effects can quickly seal the fate of a minor party.

Clearly, then, our SMP election rules are much of why ours is one of the few countries that continues to lack viable and ongoing minor parties. These parties have not failed to thrive in the United States because Americans are all political centrists who always prefer our two middle-of-the-road parties. The long history of third-party efforts in the United States—including the Populists, Socialists, Progressives, American Independents, and others—clearly indicates that millions of Americans have frequently been interested in a wider range of political options. But plurality election rules usually squelch such options by putting the minor parties at such a disadvantage that most have found it impossible to survive. By discriminating against minor parties, our plurality rules provide artificial and unfair support for the two major parties. They discourage competition and help to maintain a political oligarchy. Instead of creating an open electoral market in which all parties compete freely for the support of voters, plurality rules put minority parties at a huge competitive disadvantage and virtually ensure the continued dominance of the two major parties.

The Predicament for Nonmainstream Groups

The current U.S. election system also severely limits the organizational options of groups outside the political mainstream. Under SMP rules, political groups on the far left or far right inevitably face a difficult dilemma: they can try to work within the major parties (which will generally tend to ignore them) or they can try to start their own party (which will most likely be doomed). Neither option is particularly attractive or effective. For example, consider the position of those who see themselves to the left of the Democratic party: militant labor unionists, left liberals, democratic socialists, radical environmentalists, feminists, civil rights activists, and others. They often face just this sort of difficult, no-win choice. They can try to work within the Democratic party, but this often turns out to be fruitless. The party generally refuses to adopt genuine leftist political positions out of fear that they might alienate the centrist base. It has also been able to take the support of leftist groups for granted, even without giving them any substantial concessions. Leftists' political impotence within the Democratic party often leads these groups to consider splitting off and starting their own party. But leftist groups intensely disagree on and debate such moves. Many leftists, well aware of the electoral obstacles that exist for minor parties, believe that such efforts are a waste of time and money. In addition, such third-party efforts are often criticized as divisive. For example, NOW's [National Organization for Women] efforts to establish a new women's party created friction with some black political activists who feared that the effort would undercut support for Jesse Jackson, who has chosen to work within the Democratic party.

Forces on the far right have faced similar political predicaments. Some try to fashion a niche within the Republican party, with mixed success. Others strike out on their own and create new parties, including the Right-to-Life party and the U.S. Taxpayers party. But with a few exceptions these parties are quixotic efforts that have failed to elect candidates to office. The main point, of course, is that the frustrating political position of these nonmainstream groups is entirely a creation of the peculiar rules of single-member plurality elections. And the only real way to escape this dilemma is to escape the SMP system itself.

The Need for PR and a Multiparty System

Americans have suffered under our two-party system for so long that we tend to view its problems and limitations as unfortunate but inevitable. In reality, of course, many of these problems are inevitable only under single-member plurality voting rules. The adoption of proportional representation in the United States would go a long way toward addressing many of these shortcomings. PR would allow for the development of a multiparty system with a variety of genuine political alternatives. Minor parties would no longer be unfairly penalized, and they would be able to elect representatives in numbers that reflect their political strength in the electorate. In short, PR would be an antitrust law for the party system. It would discourage party monopolies and oligopolies and allow for free competition among parties. It would create a level playing field on which all parties could vie fairly for public support.

A more hospitable political environment for minor parties under PR would probably result in the expansion of the party system in the United States. Voter support for minor parties would increase as voters realize that voting for minor-party candidates no longer means wasting their votes. Talented politicians would be more attracted to these parties. They could run for office on those tickets without fearing that they are throwing their careers away. Donations to these parties would probably increase as the contributors realize that these investments could actually produce some electoral dividends.

It is important to recognize that the adoption of PR in the United States would not *force* us to have a multiparty system; it simply would *allow* such a system to develop, if it reflected the wishes of the American voter. As political scientists often observe, many factors other than electoral systems help determine the number of parties in a political system—such as the number and depth of political cleavages in a society. Thus if American voters choose to support only the two major parties, PR would produce a two-party system, as has happened in Austria. In this sense, PR does not mandate any particular kind of party system; it simply does not inhibit the development of a multiparty system the way plurality rules do. With proportional representation what the public wants in a party system, it gets.

This principle was evident in the experiments with PR in U.S. cities. The effect of PR on party systems varied from city to city, depending on local political conditions and public preferences. In some cities that adopted PR, such as Cincinnati, essentially two parties still contested local elections, though PR produced a much more accurate representation of those parties in the city council. In cities with more heterogeneous political populations, like New York, a vigorous multiparty system emerged. Before the adoption of proportional representation, New York City was dominated by the Democratic machine, which elected virtually the entire city council. The onset of PR broke the political monopoly of the Democrats, and what was a one-party system became a multiparty system. The PR city council in 1947 reflected the wide variety of political persuasions among the New York City electorate and consisted of twelve Democrats, five Republicans, two Liberals, two Communists, and two American Laborites.

If we were to move toward a multiparty system today, what new parties would be likely to develop in the United States? A coalition of leftists might break from the Democratic party—perhaps something like the recently formed 21st Century party or the New party. A far right party—perhaps resembling a Moral Majority party—could split off from the Republican party. On the right, the Libertarian party probably would see some growth in membership as electing its candidates became more realistic. Another possibility is an independent, nonideological centrist party—perhaps along the lines of the group that supported Ross Perot's presidential candidacy in 1992. In areas with concentrations of racial minorities, we could see the emergence of an African-American party or a Latino party. PR could also spur growth in the several Green parties that have already sprouted in the United States. Other parties are possible—the variety limited only by the wishes of American voters.

Is it likely that the two major parties would fracture into smaller parties and disappear entirely? Probably not. One reason for their persistence is the presence and importance of presidential elections in our political system. Unlike parliamentary systems, the chief executive in our presidential system is elected separately by a plurality vote. The winning presidential candidate must garner a majority or substantial plurality of the vote, and this requirement encourages large political parties like the Democrats and Republicans. These broad-based parties are best equipped to muster the wide voter support required. In fact, the presidential election may be much of why two-party dominance has been stronger in the United States than in other plurality countries, like Great Britain and Canada, which have parliamentary systems. In any case, the most likely scenario for the United States would be for the Democratic and Republican parties to remain in some form, with a number of minor parties emerging.

• • •

PR: Giving Voters a Real Choice

Voting is one of our most fundamental acts of political choice. But a crucial difference exists between simply having a choice and having a real or a meaningful choice. For any choice to be real, we must have some control over the options we are given. Otherwise our choice may be only a fraud or an illusion. If we were told that we were free to choose between being hit in the face and kicked in the stomach, we would probably protest that this is hardly freedom and really no choice at all. Many Americans find themselves in just that situation with our two-party system. Plurality rules artificially limit our choices to two similar parties, and for many voters this does not seem like a real choice at all. In contrast, proportional representation elections would ensure that voters have as wide a variety of distinct political choices as they desire. The adoption of PR in the United States would finally allow the American voter—not our plurality election rules—to decide which political parties and political views deserve to be represented in our legislatures. Putting this power of choice back in the hands of the American voters would help make our election system much more fair and democratic. ■

 # View from the Inside

CNN's Jeff Greenfield had a front-row seat for the nail-biting election of 2000. For hour after hour on election night, Greenfield and his colleagues—along with the rest of the country—watched and waited as both the official election returns (reported by the Associated Press) and the exit poll–based predictions of the Voter News Service (VNS) told their topsy-turvy story. But as night turned into morning, the end of the story still could not be predicted. The stalemate would not be broken until five weeks later when the Supreme Court's decision in *Bush* v. *Gore* at last resolved one of the closest and most dramatic presidential elections in American history.

Question

1. What mistakes did CNN and other networks make on election night? What lessons might they draw from the election of 2000 as they prepare for election night 2004?

8.5 Oh, Waiter! One Order of Crow! (2001)

Jeff Greenfield

[It was now past 2 A.M., and] the VNS count in Florida shows Bush leading by twenty-nine thousand votes, with 96 percent of the vote in—but with some of the strongest Gore counties yet to finish. It is a picture custom-made for restraint—especially when compared with the Associated Press numbers that are showing a steady, sharp drop in Bush's lead. Nobody looking at those numbers would have thought of making a call. But nobody is looking at those numbers. Instead, everyone is watching the VNS count—where a few minutes later, Volusia County's votes are tabulated, and Bush's lead suddenly jumps to more than fifty thousand. And *now* the experts, all of them, know that it is starting to look as if Bush has Florida just about wrapped up. With 97 percent of the precincts in, and with about one hundred eighty thousand votes left to be counted, Gore would have to win some 63 percent of the remaining votes—an almost impossible task, according to past voting patterns.

There are only two small problems with the conclusions: First, Bush does *not* have a fifty-thousand-vote lead; second, there are closer to four hundred thousand votes yet to be counted from heavily Democratic areas.

How did that fifty-thousand-vote spread suddenly appear? Thanks to a faulty computer memory card, a single precinct in Volusia County—Precinct 216—has actually *subtracted* sixteen thousand votes from Gore, and at the same time has incorrectly added votes to Bush's total. Further, a reporting error from Brevard County has added another four thousand phantom votes to Bush's total. Without those mistakes, VNS would not have estimated a final Bush plurality of thirty thousand votes statewide. But here again, simple human nature has reared its ugly head. Authorities in Volusia County had strung up yellow crime-scene tape around the election unit offices, in an effort to keep out interlopers. The local stringer for Voter News Service saw the tape, and concluded that the information lid was on. It was late; she was tired; she went home.

The local AP stringer made a different decision. He gained access to headquarters, and quickly learned that the local officials had discovered their error. He flashed the real numbers to AP, which reported the correct numbers at 2:18 A.M. By then, Fox, NBC, CBS, and CNN had all called Florida, and the presidency, for Bush. It was a scenario right out of one of those death-row dramas, where the hot line from the governor's office to the prison rings just as the warden is throwing the switch. Of course, in the movies, the call always comes just in time.

So at 2:18 A.M., while CNN was in a commercial break, Tom Hannon alerted the four of us at the anchor desk: "We are going to call Florida, and the presidency, for Bush." And so, a moment later, Bernard Shaw announced: "George Bush, governor of Texas, will become the forty-third president of the United States."

It would be a fine thing if I could report to you that my colleagues and I feverishly objected, urged that we hold back until we were absolutely sure, or at least cautioned our viewers that this call was an estimate, that it was our best guess about the probable outcome. But it's been a long time since we've talked that way; and besides, our job was now to flesh out the story, to put it in context, to dazzle the viewers with insights about the next president and how he won this incredibly close election.

Caution? That's not the message we're sending out to the viewer. We are airing a splendid graphic, featuring a heroic picture of Bush and the words: "Bush Wins Presidency." This was no time for second-guessing; besides, we were in no position to second-guess anything. Did we have the VNS screens in front of us? Were we looking at the actual tabulated vote, as reported by AP, or the Florida secretary of state's Web site? Of course not. So we press on.

So we speak of Bush, only the second son of a president to win the White House; we speak of how close the Electoral vote is likely to be, how it is not impossible that Gore might actually overtake Bush in the popular vote. I whip out that dramatic contrast of the rivals on their respective fortieth birthdays that I'd prepared all those hours ago: Gore, the United States senator with a credible run for the presidency behind him; Bush, the failed businessman with an uncertain future and a drinking problem, whose first real success came as the owner of a baseball team. From her perch outside the state capitol in Austin, Texas, where she has been standing, barely protected, under an increasingly hard rain, Candy Crowley recalls Governor Bush's warning to his brother Jeb that if Florida goes Democratic, "'that Thanksgiving turkey is going to be pretty cold.' So Thanksgiving dinner, apparently, is safe now for Jeb Bush."

From his perch outside Nashville's War Memorial auditorium, John King has already begun detailing the outlines of the early recriminations:

"Within the Gore campaign, already that he was hurt on the left from Ralph Nader, and on the right, if you will, among conservative Democrats, conservative elderly voters, by Bill Clinton's character problem—others already questioning the Gore campaign strategy. . . . We will hear from the vice president, we're told, in about fifteen minutes."

In the camps of the candidates, there is no reason to doubt the network calls. In the Four Seasons Hotel in Austin, the close friends and relatives of Bush explode out of every room, into the hall, embracing one another. In the Loew's Vanderbilt Plaza Hotel in Nashville, Tennessee, Elaine Kamarck, who has fallen asleep, has somehow awakened at the precise moment CNN calls the race for Bush. A few moments later, her phone rings; one of Gore's close aides, in tears, is telling her that the vice president is calling Bush to concede, that he will soon make his way to the War Memorial, bedecked with huge hanging American flags, to congratulate the new president. It won't be long now.

In fact, at this defining moment in the majestic pageantry that is our national election process, forged in Valley Forge and Yorktown, in the miracle of Philadelphia's Constitution Hall, in these first moments of the Age of Bush the Second, and all that portends for our future, I am held by one single thought: *If Al Gore concedes by 3 A.M., and Bush claims victory by 3:30, and if my car is still waiting for me outside the CNN center, then I can get back to the hotel, pack up everything, get out to the airport, catch the 6:30 A.M. flight to New York, crash for an hour or so, and meet my friends for our traditional Wednesday lunch.*

Call it shallow, if you will, but at that very moment, there were several hundred reporters, producers, camera operators, sound technicians, and political operatives of every stripe thinking roughly the same way. It is an exciting, exhilarating way of life, the business of covering campaigns, but next to a war, there is nothing like it for ripping you away from any semblance of a normal life. Listen in on the cellphone conversations on a press bus, and you will hear countless snatches of family ties frayed by time and distance: *I'm so sorry I missed the play, I'll bet you were great, I'll watch the video as soon as I get home. . . . What's his temperature now? Did you give him the Tylenol? Dr. Kramer's number is right there on the fridge. . . . Really, two merit badges? I'm really proud of . . . what? . . . I'm losing you, I'll call tonight, no, make it first thing in the morning.* And for everyone caught up in the life, Election Day is the finish line, the promise of shared meals, clean laundry, and the chance to exhale. Days later, I remembered a piece of newsreel footage from my childhood: a marathon runner, entering the stadium far, far ahead of his rivals, needing only to circle the track for his victory. But he is exhausted, drained of all but the last ounce of energy. He falls; the crowd rises, cheering him on; he staggers to his feet, his legs wobbly, his body slack; he hobbles a few more steps, and falls again; slowly gets upright, and half walks, half runs some more, weaving back and forth across the track, until, with one final, heroic effort, he falls across the finish line.

It is the wrong finish line.

Shortly before 3 A.M., as we speculate on the makeup of Bush's cabinet, and the potential Democratic candidates for 2004—Gore? Lieberman? Kerry? Kerrey? Gephardt? Daschle? Edwards?—VNS finally gets the correct Volusia County totals into its calculations. Unsurprisingly, Bush's lead suddenly drops by some sixteen thousand votes. At about this time, someone in Warren Mitofsky's operation checks out the AP wire; according to the news service, Bush's margin continues to drop with gravitational force. Tom Hannon remembers hearing a disembodied voice on the open phone link say: "We better check the [Florida secretary of state's] Web site." And somewhere after 3 A.M., a conference call takes place among VNS and all the major subscribing news organizations.

"If you could have eavesdropped on Hell," Tom Hannon says, "that's what it would have sounded like: fear, anguish, everybody desperately trying to find out. People are yelling, 'Can you guys tell us what the hell is going on?' And they couldn't. It was like . . . you know the woodcut? Munch? *The Scream.* That's what it was like."

For those of us on the air, time seemed to be slowing down. John King had reported at 3 A.M. that Gore had called the governor, and was now in his motorcade on the way to acknowledge defeat. Candy Crowley had reported that Bush had told Gore: "We gave them a cliff-hanger." King went on the air before 3:30 A.M. to report that the motorcade had arrived at the auditorium. The national vote totals were now almost exactly even, and it was becoming more and more likely that Gore would become the first man in more than one hundred years to lose the White House while winning the popular vote. And it was then that Judy Woodruff called up the vote totals from the state of Florida, and noted that, with 99 percent of the votes in, Bush was ahead by 11,000 votes out of 5.6 million cast.

"John King," Bernard Shaw said, "you're standing by in Nashville. Any talk there among the Gore people about a possible recount anywhere, especially given what we've talked about, eleven thousand votes?"

"We have to assume no, Bernie," King said. ". . . if the vice president were actively planning to challenge the results, we assume he would say nothing tonight, or at least say that he was not prepared to concede defeat."

A fair assumption—except that at this moment, at least two players in the Gore campaign were desperately trying to keep the vice president from conceding. Bob Butterworth, Florida attorney general, knew that under state law, any margin of less than one-half of 1 percent automatically triggers a recount—and based on the way the votes were coming in, the final margin was likely to be somewhere around one thousand votes out of six million cast—a margin of about two-hundredths of 1 percent of the vote. Michael Whouley, a veteran Boston operative who had organized the turnout effort for Gore, watched the numbers drop and urgently paged officials, until the message worked up the chain of command to William Daley, and then the candidate: *Whatever you do, do not get on the podium and concede.*

Meanwhile, we waited . . . and waited. We picked apart the Gore campaign decisions: Should he have called on Clinton for more help? Did the debates turn it around? And then, about 3:30 A.M., came the first hints that we had another surprise waiting for us. From Nashville, John King reported that "CNN is double-checking the vote count . . . to make sure the vote is accurate . . . We've been trying to reach [Gore's] senior aides to find out the reason for the delay, but we've been unsuccessful in doing so."

A moment later, King was back—reporting that the Bush margin in Florida was now about six hundred votes, that an automatic recount was certain, and that "what the vice president is working on now is exactly what to say." At almost the same moment, Candy Crowley's producer in Austin got a call on his cell phone from Bush's communications director, Karen Hughes. He listened, handed the phone to Crowley, and said, "You'd better listen to this."

I just thought you should know, Hughes said, *that the vice president has just called the governor, and has retracted his concession.*

Say that again, Crowley said. After twelve hours of cold and rain and sleeplessness, she literally did not trust herself to have heard what she had heard.

Hughes said it again. Crowley immediately told Atlanta to put her on the air.

"Judy," Crowley said simply, "something to report to you here on this very unusual night. The vice president has recalled the governor, and has retracted his concession, saying Florida is too close right now."

And Judy said: "Whoaa."

And I thought: *I don't think I'll be catching that 6:30 A.M. flight to New York.*

We didn't leave the air until almost two hours later, after Gore chairman Daley had told the revived crowd in Nashville, "Our campaign continues," and until after Bush chairman Don Evans told the stunned crowd in Austin, "They're still counting. And I'm confident that when it's all said and done, we will prevail." At CNN, we were privileged to air the single most bizarre moment of the night—at 4:30 A.M., actually—when actor-director Rob Reiner, a hard-core Gore backer, joined John King at his perch.

"Why are you here?" King asked. "You have a comfortable life, you could be home watching this on television."

"Well, you know," Reiner said, "I'm quite attracted to you, John, and that's why I'm here . . . we've had two close moments tonight, so anything can happen. Even an important relationship between you and me could happen."

"Hate to disappoint you," King deadpanned, "but I'm going to rule that out."

It was a badly needed moment of levity. What we faced was a lot less humorous: We were now in the middle of the weirdest political story of our lifetimes, when the machinery of our political system was about to be put to a test it had not faced in nearly 125 years. Moreover, we already knew that the media's machinery for reporting this race had been tested and had failed . . . not once, but twice in the same evening. I'd been at this for twenty years. And over those twenty years, I'd felt absolute exhilaration, absolute embarrassment, and absolute exhaustion. I'd just never felt all of it at exactly the same time.

And so, shortly before six o'clock in the morning, thirteen hours after we began, we left the anchor desk. My parting remarks were a product of that exhilaration, embarrassment, and exhaustion.

"Folks," I said, "in the year 2004, please could you make up your minds a little more conclusively, because I think we can't take another election like this one." Had I known we'd still be at it more than a month later, I'm not sure that my words would have been fit for public consumption—even on cable. ■

Chapter 9

The Congress

Over the long term of American history, it is fair to conclude that Congress has lost political power to the executive branch. Since the New Deal, Congress has been forced to delegate more and more power to the federal bureaucracy, which has the expertise and resources to deal with the increasingly complex and diverse roles of the federal government. Since America's rise to power in international affairs after World War II, Congress has also lost power to what some observers have called the "imperial presidency."

Congress nevertheless remains the focal point of the American national government. Its power in domestic affairs remains paramount, and in recent years it has struggled to regain some of its lost power in foreign policy as well. No president can afford to ignore or slight Congress, especially its leadership, and no agency can afford to ignore or slight a congressional committee or subcommittee with jurisdiction over its affairs. Interest groups direct the lion's share of their energies toward Congress, and the media often take their cues from Congress as to what issues are worth considering. The federal courts, whatever else they do, must focus their energies in large part on interpreting congressional statutes. Presidents may propose, as the saying goes, but Congress disposes. Congress retains the power to investigate wrongdoing in the executive branch; has final budgetary and taxing authority; has the power to confirm executive and judicial appointments; and, as Bill Clinton learned, has the power of impeachment as well.

Two themes dominate the diverse readings in this chapter. The first, and oldest, is the ongoing struggle for power between the legislative and executive branches. The separation of powers as conceived in 1787 did not resolve the division of authority between the two branches: the Framers deliberately created a system in which the two "political branches" would continually joust with each other for power (see Chapter 1).

The second is a fundamental question about the nature of representative government in the United States. Although the Framers clearly wanted congressmen to "refine and filter" the public's views (see *Federalist* No. 10, selection 1.1), members of Congress have always considered themselves "local men, locally minded, whose business began and ended with the interests of their constituency."* This tension between the local interest and the national interest, and between the will of their constituents and their own view

---

*Bernard Bailyn, *The Ideological Origins of the American Revolution* (Cambridge: Belknap Press of Harvard University Press, 1967), p. 162.

of the public interest, remains a problem for members of Congress even today. The Federalists' thoughts on these matters are presented in selections 9.1 and 9.2, and the problem of representation as it relates to public perceptions of Congress is explored in selection 9.3.

The final two selections provide two additional perspectives. Selection 9.4 examines the contrasts between the American system of government (based on the separation of powers) and the British, or parliamentary, system; while selection 9.5 presents a profile of Senate majority leader Bill Frist of Tennessee.

Chapter Questions

1. Review the Federalists' conception of the separation of powers (selections 1.2 through 1.4). In what ways does the operation of the modern Congress underscore the Framers' belief that "ambition must be made to counteract ambition"? What evidence is there in the readings in this chapter to suggest that Congress plays an active role in the administrative process and that the president plays an active role in the legislative process? The readings in Chapter 10 (The Presidency) may cast light on these questions as well.
2. What roles do members of Congress play? How do these roles conflict with one another? How do members of Congress seek to balance their own goals, their constituents' interests, and the public or national interest?

Foundations

The Federalists' view of representation was twofold. Representatives were expected not only to represent their constituents' interests but also to "refine and enlarge the public views, by passing them through the medium of a chosen body of citizens, whose wisdom may best discern the true interest of their country and whose patriotism and love of justice will be least likely to sacrifice it to temporary or partial considerations" (*Federalist* No. 10; see selection 1.1). Congress was expected to be a deliberative body that would think about and consider public questions and resolve them in the public interest. Thus, the Framers made the connection between congressmen and their constituents close but not too close: elections were to be held every two years, not every year, despite the popular eighteenth-century slogan that "when annual election ends, tyranny begins." Senators were to be elected every six years, and by the state legislatures, not by the people directly.

The Framers' views on representation and on Congress's role as the primary decision-making body, at least in matters of domestic policy, form the background for this chapter. *Federalist* No. 55, written by James Madison, defends the small size of the original Congress (only sixty-five members) as a way of securing "the benefits of free consultation and discussion." Moreover, the Framers thought, a small House would encourage representatives to think of the national interest instead of the local interest when they voted on public questions. But as *Federalist* No. 57 points out, the Framers believed the members of Congress would still be close to their constituents and would still faithfully represent their interests in the federal capital.

Questions

1. What does Madison mean when he writes, "Had every Athenian citizen been a Socrates, every Athenian assembly would still have been a mob"?
2. How might a member of Congress seek to balance his or her role as the representative of a local district with the sometimes conflicting role of acting in the interest of the entire nation?

9.1 *Federalist* No. 55 (1788)

James Madison

Outline

I. Critics' objections to the relatively small size of the House of Representatives (sixty-five members).
II. Madison's response.
   A. General remarks on the problem of size of legislatures.
   B. Specific remarks on the United States House of Representatives.
      1. Size of House will increase as population increases.
      2. Size of House is not dangerous to the public liberty.

The number of which the House of Representatives is to consist forms another and a very interesting point of view under which this branch of the federal legislature may be contemplated. Scarce any article, indeed, in the whole Constitution seems to be rendered more worthy of attention by the weight of character and the apparent force of argument with which it has been assailed. The charges exhibited against it are, first, that so small a number of representatives will be an unsafe depositary of the public interests; second, that they will not possess a proper knowledge of the local circumstances of their numerous constituents; third, that they will be taken from that class of citizens which will sympathize least with the feelings of the mass of the people and be most likely to aim at a permanent elevation of the few on the depression of the many; fourth, that defective as the number will be in the first instance, it will be more and more disproportionate, by the increase of the people and the obstacles which will prevent a correspondent increase of the representatives.

In general it may be remarked on this subject that no political problem is less susceptible of a precise solution than that which relates to the number most convenient for a representative legislature; nor is there any point on which the policy of the several States is more at variance, whether we compare their legislative assemblies directly with each other, or consider the proportions which they respectively bear to the number of their constituents. Passing over the difference between the smallest and largest States, as Delaware, whose most numerous branch consists of twenty-one representatives, and Massachusetts, where it amounts to between three and four hundred, a very considerable difference is observable among States nearly equal in population. The number of representatives in Pennsylvania is not more than one fifth of that in the State last mentioned. New York, whose population is to that of South Carolina as six to five, has little more than one third of the number of representatives. As great a disparity prevails between the States of Georgia and Delaware or Rhode Island. In Pennsylvania, the representatives do not bear a greater proportion to their constituents than of one for every four or five thousand. In Rhode Island, they bear a proportion of at least one for every thousand. And according to the constitution of Georgia, the proportion may be carried to one to every ten electors; and must unavoidably far exceed the proportion in any of the other states.

Another general remark to be made is that the ratio between the representatives and the people ought not to be the same where the latter are very numerous as where they are very few. Were the representatives in Virginia to be regulated by the standard in Rhode Island, they would, at this time, amount to between four and five hundred; and twenty or thirty years hence, to a thousand. On the other hand, the ratio of Pennsylvania, if applied to the State of Delaware, would reduce the representative assembly of the latter to seven or eight members. Nothing can be more fallacious than to found our political calculations on arithmetical principles. Sixty or seventy men may be more properly trusted with a given degree of power than six or seven. But it does not follow that six or seven hundred would be proportionably a better depositary. And if we carry on the supposition to six or seven thousand, the whole reasoning ought to be reversed. The truth is that in all cases a certain number at least seems to be necessary to secure the benefits of free consultation and discussion, and to guard against too easy a combination for improper purposes; as, on the other hand, the number ought at most to be kept within a certain limit, in order to avoid the confusion and intemperance of a multitude. In all very numerous assemblies, of whatever characters composed, passion never fails to wrest the scepter from reason. Had every Athenian citizen been a Socrates, every Athenian assembly would still have been a mob.

It is necessary also to recollect here the observations which were applied to the case of biennial elections. For the same reason that the limited powers of the Congress, and the control of the State legislatures, justify less frequent election than the public safety might otherwise require, the members of the Congress need be less numerous than if they possessed the whole power of legislation, and were under no other than the ordinary restraints of other legislative bodies.

With these general ideas in our minds, let us weigh the objections which have been stated against the number of members proposed for the House of Representatives. It is said, in the first place, that so small a number cannot be safely trusted with so much power.

The number of which this branch of the legislature is to consist, at the outset of the government, will be sixty-five. Within three years a census is to be taken, when the number may be augmented to one for every thirty thousand inhabitants; and within every successive period of ten years the census is to be renewed, and augmentations may continue to be made under the above limitations. It will not be thought an extravagant conjecture that the first census will, at the rate of one for every thirty thousand, raise the number of representatives to at least one hundred. Estimating the Negroes in the proportion of three fifths, it can scarcely be doubted that the population of the United States will by that time, if it does not already, amount to three millions. At the expiration of twenty-five years, according to the computed rate of increase, the number of representatives will amount to two hundred; and of fifty years, to four hundred. This is a number which, I presume, will put an end to all fears arising from the smallness of the body. I take for granted here what I shall, in answering the fourth objection, hereafter show, that the number of representatives will be augmented from time to time in the manner provided by the Constitution. On a contrary supposition, I should admit the objection to have very great weight indeed.

The true question to be decided, then, is whether the smallness of the number, as a temporary regulation, be dangerous to the public liberty? Whether sixty-five members for a few years, and a hundred or two hundred for a few more, be a safe depositary for a limited and well-guarded power of legislating for the United States? I must own that I could not give a negative answer to this question, without first obliterating every impression which I have received with regard to the present genius of the people of America, the spirit which actuates the State legislatures, and the principles which are incorporated with the political character of every class of citizens. I am unable to conceive that the people of America, in their present temper, or under any circumstances which can speedily happen, will choose, and every second year repeat the choice of, sixty-five or a hundred men who would be disposed to form and pursue a scheme of tyranny or treachery. I am unable to conceive that the State legislatures, which must feel so many motives to watch and which possess so many means of counteracting the federal legislature, would fail either to detect or to defeat a conspiracy of the latter against the liberties of their common constituents. I am equally unable to conceive that there are at this time, or can be in any short time, in the United States, any sixty-five or a hundred men capable of recommending themselves to the choice of the people at large, who would either desire or dare, within the short space of two years, to betray the solemn trust committed to them. What change of circumstances time, and a fuller population of our country may produce requires a prophetic spirit to declare, which makes no part of my pretensions. But judging from the circumstances now before us, and from the probable state of them within a moderate period of time, I must pronounce that the liberties of America cannot be unsafe in the number of hands proposed by the federal Constitution. . . .

As there is a degree of depravity in mankind which requires a certain degree of circumspection and distrust, so there are other qualities in human nature which justify a certain portion of esteem and confidence. Republican government presupposes the existence of these qualities in a higher degree than any other form. Were the pictures which have been drawn by the political jealousy of some among us faithful likenesses of the human character, the inference would be that there is not sufficient virtue among men for self-government; and that nothing less than the chains of despotism can restrain them from destroying and devouring one another. ■

9.2 *Federalist* No. 57 (1788)

James Madison

Outline

I. Madison's responses to the charge that the members of the House of Representatives will not have sympathy with the common people.

  A. Members of the House will be elected by the people.

  B. Every citizen of the appropriate age will be eligible for election to the House.

  C. For several reasons, the representatives will remain loyal to their constituents.

    1. In general, representatives will be men of high character.

    2. They will show gratitude and affection for those who elected them.

    3. They will be attached to representative government out of pride and vanity.

    4. They will be subject to frequent elections.

    5. Their constituents will insist they subject themselves to every law they make.

The *third* charge against the House of Representatives is that it will be taken from that class of citizens which will have least sympathy with the mass of the people, and be most likely to aim at an ambitious sacrifice of the many to the aggrandizement of the few.

Of all the objections which have been framed against the federal Constitution, this is perhaps the most extraordinary. Whilst the objection itself is leveled against a pretended oligarchy, the principle of it strikes at the very root of republican government.

The aim of every political constitution is, or ought to be, first to obtain for rulers men who possess most wisdom to discern, and most virtue to pursue, the common good of the society; and in the next place, to take the most effectual precautions for keeping them virtuous whilst they continue to hold their public trust. The elective mode of obtaining rulers is the characteristic policy of republican government. The means relied on in this form of government for preventing their degeneracy are numerous and various. The most effectual one is such a limitation of the term of appointments as will maintain a proper responsibility to the people.

Let me now ask what circumstance there is in the constitution of the House of Representatives that violates the principles of republican government, or favors the elevation of the few on the ruins of the many? Let me ask whether every circumstance is not, on the contrary, strictly conformable to these principles, and scrupulously impartial to the rights and pretensions of every class and description of citizens?

Who are to be the electors of the federal representatives? Not the rich, more than the poor; not the learned, more than the ignorant; not the haughty heirs of distinguished names, more than the humble sons of obscure and unpropitious fortune. The electors are to be the great body of the people of the United States. They are to be the same who exercise the right in every State of electing the corresponding branch of the legislature of the State.

Who are to be the objects of popular choice? Every citizen whose merit may recommend him to the esteem and confidence of his country. No qualification of wealth, of birth, of religious faith, or of civil profession is permitted to fetter the judgment or disappoint the inclination of the people.

If we consider the situation of the men on whom the free suffrages of their fellow-citizens may confer the representative trust, we shall find it involving every security which can be devised or desired for their fidelity to their constituents.

In the first place, as they will have been distinguished by the preference of their fellow citizens, we are to presume that in general they will be somewhat distinguished also by those qualities which entitle them to it, and which promise a sincere and scrupulous regard to the nature of their engagements.

In the second place, they will enter into the public service under circumstances which cannot fail to produce a temporary affection at least to their constituents. There is in every breast a sensibility to marks of honor, of favor, of esteem, and of confidence, which, apart from all considerations of interests, is some pledge for grateful and benevolent returns. Ingratitude is a common topic of declamation against human nature; and it must be confessed that instances of it are but too frequent and flagrant, both in public and in private life. But the universal and extreme indignation which it inspires is itself a proof of the energy and prevalence of the contrary sentiment.

In the third place, those ties which bind the representative to his constituents are strengthened by motives of a more selfish nature. His pride and vanity attach him to a form of government which favors his pretensions and gives him a share in its honors and distinctions. Whatever hopes or projects might be entertained by a few aspiring characters, it must generally happen that a great proportion of the men deriving their advancement from their influence with the people would have more to hope from a preservation of the favor than from innovations in the government subversive of the authority of the people.

All these securities, however, would be found very insufficient without the restraint of frequent elections. Hence, in the fourth place, the House of Representatives is so constituted as to support in the members an habitual recollection of their dependence on the people. Before the sentiments impressed on their minds by the mode of their elevation can be effaced by the exercise of power, they will be compelled to anticipate the moment when their power is to cease, when their exercise of it is to be reviewed, and when they must descend to the level from which they were raised; there forever to remain unless a faithful discharge of their trust shall have established their title to a renewal of it.

I will add, as a fifth circumstance in the situation of the House of Representatives, restraining them from oppressive measures, that they can make no law which will not have its full operation on themselves and their friends, as well as on the great mass of the society. This has always been deemed one of the strongest bonds by which human policy can connect the rulers and the people together. It creates between them that communion of interests and sympathy of sentiments of which few governments have furnished examples; but without which every government degenerates into tyranny. If it be asked, what is to restrain the House of Representatives from making legal discriminations in favor of themselves and a particular class of society? I answer: the genius of the whole system; the nature of just and constitutional laws; and, above all, the vigilant and manly spirit which actuates the people of America—a spirit which nourishes freedom, and in return is nourished by it.

If this spirit shall ever be so far debased as to tolerate a law not obligatory on the legislature, as well as on the people, the people will be prepared to tolerate anything but liberty.

Such will be the relation between the House of Representatives and their constituents. Duty, gratitude, interest, ambition itself, are the cords by which they will be bound to fidelity and sympathy with the great mass of the people. It is possible that these may all be insufficient to control the caprice and wickedness of men. But are they not all that government will admit, and that human prudence can devise? Are they not the genuine and the characteristic means by which republican government provides for the liberty and happiness of the people? . . . ■

 # American Politics Today

The American people have always had an uneasy relationship with their representatives in Congress. Americans understand the importance of representation—the American Revolution was fought under the banner of "No Taxation Without Representation." Average citizens have always felt at least some affinity with Congress; incumbent reelection rates, for example, are high, suggesting that Americans have no great desire to trade in their own member of Congress for someone new.

Yet Congress itself has never been a very popular institution. Members of Congress have always been depicted in the public press as corrupt, narrow-minded, and self-interested. And Congress as an institution ranks low in terms of public confidence, especially when compared to the Supreme Court and the presidency.

In the following selection, the political scientists John R. Hibbing and James T. Smith attempt to sort out this confusion. They examine why people like Congress more sometimes than other times; why people like other parts of the political system more than Congress; why people like certain parts of Congress more than others; and why some people like Congress more than other people do. The result is a thoughtful explanation of a very complicated problem.

Questions

1. Under what conditions is Congress most popular? Under what conditions is it least popular?
2. How do popular attitudes toward Congress help explain why Congress behaves the way it does? What are the broader implications of the public's attitudes for the American political system of government?

9.3 What the American Public Wants Congress to Be (2001)

John R. Hibbing and James T. Smith

Congress is designed to be a permeable institution. If it is doing its job, public opinion should be able to enter and affect the policy actions taken by Congress. This reflection of public views in congressional policy decisions is called representation, and Congress is specially designed to facilitate it. Large collections of formally equal officials who are subject to frequent elections and incredibly open operating procedures, and who are all directly responsible for acting in the interests of specific groups of constituents, should generate policy representation if any institutional structure can. Indeed, if Congress were not representative why would we have it? A smaller, more hierarchical body is far better at getting things done, but "getting things done" is not the only goal of government. After all, the cry of the revolution was not "no taxation unless it is enacted by an efficient, hierarchical body"; it was "no taxation without representation."

The question of whether or not Congress is successful in fulfilling its constitutional mission to provide policy representation is one that has occupied observers for quite some time. Although liberals tend to think Congress is too conservative and conservatives tend to think it is too liberal, for the most part the people prefer centrist policies and believe Congress provides centrist policies. Certainly, on some issues, such as gun control, campaign finance reform, and limiting legislative terms, policy is severely out of step with majority public sentiment, but issues of constitutionality hamper the ability of Congress to act in all three of these areas; moreover, these policy inconsistencies seem to be more the exception than the rule. In general, Congress addresses the issues the public believes to be important and acts on those issues in the moderate ways the public prefers. . . .

But public opinion can also affect Congress in a manner quite different from influence on specific policy decisions. The public's opinion of Congress itself can serve as an important institutional constraint on it. If the public strongly

---

From "What the American Public Wants Congress to Be," by John R. Hibbing and James T. Smith, in Lawrence C. Dodd and Bruce L. Oppenheimer, *Congress Reconsidered*, 7/e, pp. 45–65. Copyright © 2001 Congressional Quarterly, Inc. Reprinted by permission of the publisher, CQ Press.

disapproves of Congress, sitting members may decide against seeking reelection and prospective candidates may decide against running for a seat in the first place. If members are sensitive to the public's opinion of them and of Congress, they may be reluctant to address new policy initiatives, especially any that are mildly controversial. And solid evidence even suggests that negative views of Congress render people less likely to comply with the laws it passes.

Given these important consequences of public attitudes toward Congress, it is imperative that we understand the factors that lead the public to regard the institution favorably or unfavorably. . . .

Why People Like Congress More Sometimes than Others

Maybe the public simply detests Congress and that is all that needs to be said on the matter. Perhaps it is erroneous to think that Congress under any circumstances could be even remotely popular. As tempting as it may be to jump to this conclusion and as much as popular press coverage encourages such inclinations, the situation is actually much more complex than that. Survey data from across the decades reveal a surprising amount of variation, as is apparent in Figure 1, which presents the percentage of people approving of Congress from 1975 through the third quarter of 1999, according to various Gallup polls.

The last quarter of the twentieth century began with Congress (and the rest of the political system) struggling to pull itself out of a trying period. In fact, although soundings were taken much less frequently prior to 1975, the data that are available demonstrate that the mid-to-late 1960s was a period of relative popularity for Congress and for all of government. But starting about 1968 and continuing into the first half of the 1970s, the public's approval of political institutions and, indeed, societal institutions generally declined precipitously. Thus, the opening data points in the figure, coming on the heels of the Watergate scandal and other societal frustrations, reflect a disillusioned people, and barely one out of four American adults approved of Congress.

After these initial low ratings, the rest of the figure suggests three phases of congressional approval: high, low, and high again. By 1985 Watergate and perhaps the economic difficulties of the late 1970s and early 1980s were distant memories and the Reagan "feel-good" period had arrived. Well over half of the American public approved of the job Congress was doing in the latter 1980s. But by 1992 approval levels had reverted to 1970s levels or worse, with sometimes just one in five adults approving of Congress. Just before the 1994 midterm election, Congress's popularity bottomed out with a whopping 75 percent of the population *disapproving* of the job Congress was doing.

This high level of dissatisfaction with Congress continued well into the mid-1990s even though by then the economy had long been booming. In fact, it was not until very late 1997 that approval levels turned around. By January 1998 more people approved of Congress than disapproved, a situation that had not been seen since the late 1980s. Approval levels then stayed high until impeachment proceedings were commenced in the House against President Bill Clinton. In August 1998 Congress was enjoying 55 percent public approval, but as soon as impeachment of the president became the dominant congressional issue these marks began

Figure 1 ■ Approval of Congress, 1975–1999

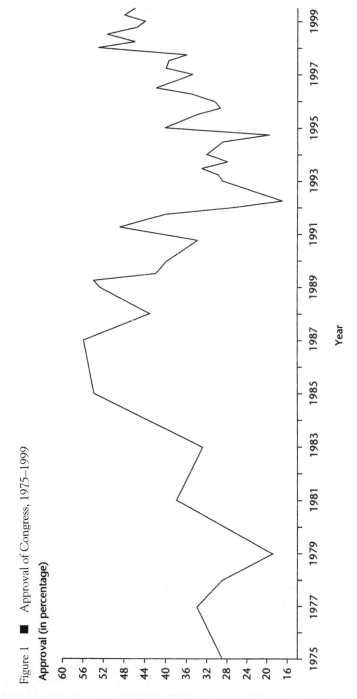

Source: Gallup polls, 1975–1988; *Washington Post*, various issues, 1989–1999. From John R. Hibbing and Elizabeth Theiss-Morse, *Congress as Public Enemy*. Copyright © 1995. Reprinted with the permission of Cambridge University Press.

to drop, although perhaps not as much as might have been expected. By early 1999 approval was down more than 10 points to 44 percent. And then, as the painful national episode faded, approval of Congress improved slightly, to the upper 40s by the end of 1999. The divisive period reduced public approval of Congress but never threatened to return approval to the low levels of the late 1970s or early 1990s.

Taken as a whole, the pattern is not an easy one to explain. Societal conditions seem to affect the public's approval of Congress, but the relationship is not as powerful as is usually anticipated. Economic conditions, for example, are sometimes strong when approval of Congress is weak (the mid-1990s, for example), and vice versa. The authors of the most systematic effort to account for the ups and downs of public approval discovered that economic conditions have far less of an impact on congressional than on presidential approval. A broader analysis of attitudes toward various parts of government, including Congress, notes that "it is by no means clear that economic performance has actually played a decisive role in generating [the] decline in trust." And Katharine Seelye may have put it best: "Most Americans still deeply distrust the federal government despite the end of the cold war, the robust economy and the highest level of satisfaction in their own lives in 30 years."

If societal conditions such as the health of the economy explain only a small portion of changes in the public's attitudes toward Congress (and the entire polity), then what accounts for the rest? One obvious possibility is that people are more influenced by congressional actions than by societal conditions. Rather than holding Congress accountable for society generally, approval of the job Congress is doing may actually depend, sensibly enough, on perceptions of the job Congress is doing. Perhaps not surprisingly, evidence presented in previous research finds support for this possibility, but the particular congressional actions that warm the hearts of most Americans are not the actions that may have been expected. Passage of particular policy proposals traditionally has done little to enhance approval of Congress. In fact, when Congress is engaged in meaningful debate, when it is being newsworthy by passing important legislation and by checking presidential power, people are *least* happy with the institution. One writer correctly observes that "the less people hear from Congress, the higher Congress' ratings soar."

This surprising finding suggests that conflict in the political arena is not something the American public likes to see, largely because the public commonly believes that consensus is wide in the United States and so conflict in the political arena is unnecessary. Many people may prefer divided government but this does not mean they like to see open conflict between Congress and the president and between the parties in Congress. The more that parties and institutions are at odds, the more the people believe the interests of ordinary Americans are being neglected. For most people, the model for how government should work is the balanced budget agreement that dominated the news in the second half of 1997. Here was a case in which the major institutions of government, even though they were controlled by different parties, quietly cooperated in addressing a problem consistently rated as "the most important problem" by the public. People were spared the usual partisan hyperbole and gamesmanship and a reasonable solution was produced (even if the roaring economy made the task of politicians infinitely less difficult). It is probably not a coincidence that approval of Congress went up shortly thereafter, when it became increasingly apparent that the deficit really was trending downward at a brisk rate.

People do not want an activist, contentious, marketplace-of-ideas Congress, and they are unable to fathom why earnest problem-solving cannot be the norm rather than the exception. Citizens are more likely to approve of Congress when it is being still and not rocking the boat. For much of the public, conflict is a sign that elected officials are out of touch with ordinary, centrist Americans and that they are too much "in touch" with nefarious special interests. The leaders of Congress have recognized the public's inclinations and have been known to trim the sails of the legislative agenda when they are concerned about public perceptions of the institution. Thus, Congress may go into "hibernation" when an election is approaching and approval ratings are high.

Why People Like Other Components of the Political System More than Congress

So, public approval of Congress varies and does so in predictable, if in some respect counterintuitive, ways. If conditions (especially economic) are favorable and Congress is not caught in the unforgivable acts of openly debating tough policy issues, serving as a counterweight to presidential initiatives, representing diverse views, and pursuing activist legislative agendas, Congress is likely to be approved of by more than half of the American public. Still, it is unlikely that even under these conditions Congress will be nearly as popular as just about any other feature of government in the United States. Despite ups and downs over time, relative to other institutions and levels of government, Congress is consistently liked the least. . . .

[Consider] a Gallup survey administered in early 1998 to a random national sample of 1,266 adults in the United States. Respondents were asked whether or not they approved of six different aspects of government, including the "overall political system." As may be recalled from Figure 1, this particular (pre-impeachment) time period was one in which Congress was relatively popular, so we see that a respectable 52 percent of the respondents approved of Congress. Compared with other components of the political system, however, approval of Congress fares much worse. Specifically, Congress is the least-liked part of the political system. Even the federal government is more popular (56 percent approval). The overall political system is at 59 percent approval, which is about the same approval level accorded President Clinton at that time (it may be recalled that a few months later, with impeachment proceedings in full swing, his popularity, unlike Congress's, went up several percentage points). Levels of approval for state government are quite a bit higher than for the federal government (69 to 56 percent), and the Supreme Court is easily the most popular political body, with better than three out of four Americans approving of it. . . .

What is it about the Supreme Court that makes it so much more popular than Congress? The answer offered in the previous section—that people are put off by political conflict—fits equally well with the results in this section. Compared with Congress, the Supreme Court has developed an amazing capacity to cloak its conflict. If open warfare occurs among the justices, it is hidden behind curtains and a vow of secrecy; and if conflict occurs between the Court and another political institution, it is not typically the stuff of front-page news stories. Thus, the Supreme Court is popular for all the reasons Congress is not; particularly, its ability to keep the people from seeing what is going on inside. Contrary to common interpretations, political popularity is not enhanced by openness, by democratic accountability, and by representation of diverse popular views. Rather, it is often enhanced by processes that move to some kind of resolution without a lot of fuss and blather, even if some measure of accountability is sacrificed in the process. Congress is relatively unpopular with the public precisely because it is so public.

Why People Like Certain Parts of Congress More than Others

Further information on the reasons people feel as they do about Congress can be obtained by paying careful attention to the aspects of Congress they do and do not like. Congress, of course, is an amazingly multifaceted institution. It is not just organized into many different parts but it is organized along many different lines: parties, committees, caucuses, delegations, leadership structures, staffs, and two separate houses all play important roles in congressional organization, and it is quite likely that, just as the people like some components of the political system more than others, they also like some components of Congress more than others.

Love Our Member but Hate Our Congress?   One of the most off-repeated points about congressional popularity is that people "hate Congress but love their own member of Congress." Survey research consistently provides support for this observation. According to polling conducted by the National Election Studies at the University of Michigan in 1980, 88 percent of the people approved of their own member of the House but only 41 percent approved of Congress itself. By 1998 this gap had diminished a little but was still quite large, with 82 percent approving of their own member and 51 percent approving of Congress. People clearly distinguish between their own member and a generic "Congress."

This conclusion may be only part of the story, however. When people are asked to evaluate "Congress," what comes to their mind? Most of them probably envision a tumultuous collection of 535 members, and they often do not approve of this facet of Congress. But when the public actually thinks of Congress less as a collection of inevitably flawed human beings and more as an important institutional component of the nation's governance, reactions are likely to change noticeably. This speculation is supported by the results obtained from a 1992 survey and that are presented in Figure 2.

In the battery of questions used to compile this figure, respondents were asked whether or not they approved of four different congressional referents. The first was "all members of Congress." The second was "the leaders of Congress." The third was "their own member of Congress." And the fourth was "Congress as an institution of government, no matter who is in office." The different reactions evoked by these various referents are noteworthy. Dissatisfaction is certainly generated by mention of "all members" and of "congressional leaders." Only one in four

Figure 2 ■ Evaluations of Congressional Referents, 1992

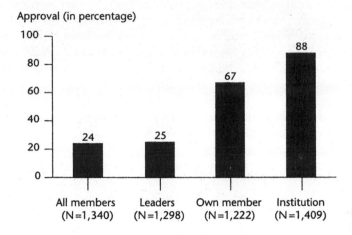

Approval (in percentage)

Source: **Perceptions of Congress Survey, 1992, conducted by the
Bureau of Sociological Research at the University of Nebraska; see
John R. Hibbing and Elizabeth Theiss-Morse,** *Congress as Public
Enemy* **(New York: Cambridge University Press, 1995).**

Americans approved of these groups at the time the survey was taken. Approval
levels of the respondent's "own member" were, as previous research has consistently demonstrated, much higher, with two of three responding favorably. But
people were even more approving of Congress "as an institution," with a remarkable 88 percent approving. Although it is not tremendously surprising that people
would respond positively to a question that weeds human foibles out of the mix, it
is still worth noting that people do not really disapprove of Congress; rather, they
disapprove of the membership of Congress, their own member excepted of course.

• • •

Why Do Some People Like Congress More than Others

It is easy to lose sight of the fact that many people do approve of Congress—over
50 percent, in fact, in the last years of the 1990s. Just as Congress is more popular
at some times than at others, so too is Congress looked upon more favorably by
some people than by others. Identification of the kinds of individuals most likely
to either approve or disapprove of Congress should allow us to say more about why
Congress generates the kind of public reaction that it does. . . .

For example, there has been much talk lately about "angry, white males." Is it
the case, then, that males and whites are less approving of Congress? . . . [T]here is
little difference between males and females and between whites and nonwhites in
attitudes toward Congress. The anticipated patterns are in evidence, but barely.
Males are a little less approving of Congress than females and whites are a little

less approving than nonwhites . . . , but [the] differences . . . are quite modest. The findings for most of the other demographic variables are similar. More education, perhaps surprisingly, does not bring much improvement in attitudes toward Congress. The pattern across income levels is not consistent. The youngest age bracket (eighteen to twenty-five) is the most approving of Congress, but after that there is no apparent pattern. And those who scored well on a four-question political knowledge test were not any more approving of Congress than their less-informed compatriots.

Once we move to the area of simple political attitudes and identifications, relationships are only marginally more visible. With regard to party identification, even though Republicans controlled both houses of Congress at the time the survey was administered (1998), respondents identifying with the Democratic Party were more approving (but only slightly) than Republicans. . . . The only real difference is produced by "independents." They are more negative toward Congress than either Democrats or Republicans . . . and, in fact, are the most negative of virtually any group. With regard to political ideology, the pattern is the opposite of the one that might have been expected on the basis of party identification. Whereas partisan independents are the least supportive of Congress, ideological moderates are the most supportive . . . , and whereas Democrats are the most supportive of Congress, ideological liberals are the least. . . . Conservatives, like their closest partisan equivalent, Republicans, are in the middle. . . . Independents may dislike Congress, but this should not be taken to mean that moderates do.

But the more important point is that the differences across all these standard demographic groups are surprisingly modest. If one attempts to describe the type of individual who is most likely to disapprove of Congress, it is clear that basing a description on people's age, gender, skin color, income, education, political knowledge, and even party identification and ideology will not be particularly helpful. To the extent that there are predictable patterns in who likes and dislikes Congress, we must look beyond demographics toward more specific political attitudes and preferences.

One reasonable expectation is that those who are satisfied with the policies government produces, other things being equal, will be more likely to approve of one of the most important shapers of those policies, the United States Congress. The specific survey item we employ asked if respondents strongly agreed, agreed, disagreed, or strongly disagreed with the statement that they were "generally satisfied with the public policies the government has produced lately." But one of the themes that has surfaced throughout this [article] is that people's attitudes toward Congress are influenced by more than just the policies produced; they also seem to be influenced by people's attitudes toward certain processes of making policy. . . .

What may be more surprising for some readers (but perfectly consistent with our expectations) is that even when controlling for the influence of policy satisfaction, people's attitudes toward the desirability of debate and the need for compromise are important predictors of attitudes toward Congress. . . . Although a favorable attitude toward Congress may lead people to like recent policies, it is less likely to lead them to have positive attitudes toward compromise and debate. But these attitudes toward compromise and debate certainly are related to approval of

Congress. The more that people believe "the country would be helped if elected officials would stop talking" the less likely they are to approve of Congress. And the more that people believe "compromise is unnecessary because of Americans' level of agreement with each other" the less likely they are to approve of Congress. These two relationships are strong and statistically significant.

This means that if more people realized the extent of policy disagreement in American society and the resultant need to discuss our differences and to reach a mutual accord by being willing to compromise with those holding divergent views, Congress would then be a more popular institution. But when people view all debate as bickering and see compromise as selling out, they naturally are less likely to approve of an institution that spends much of its time bickering and selling out. Even if people were given the exact policies they want, . . . some of them would still be unhappy with Congress, assuming Congress continued to rely, as any representative institution in a divided society must, on open presentation of diverse opinions, discussion of those opinions, and brokered solutions.

Summary

When is Congress unpopular? Not surprisingly, when negative economic and other societal conditions exist, but also when Congress is particularly active and newsworthy in proposing and debating important legislative matters and balancing presidential power. Why is Congress less popular than other parts of government? Because more than those other parts, Congress is charged with giving voice to tremendously varied interests from across the country and then, in full public view, coming to a single policy decision in the face of that diversity. Which parts of Congress are particularly unpopular? Any part that can be seen as serving an interest narrower than the entire country whether that interest belongs to a political party intent on winning an election, a special interest intent on securing a benefit for that particular group, or members of Congress (other than one's own member) intent on getting reelected so they can continue to lead the high life at the expense of hard-working American taxpayers. What kind of person is most likely to disapprove of Congress? Not surprisingly, someone who dislikes recent policy actions, but also someone who dislikes debate and who believes there is little need for politicians to compromise.

Taken together, these findings make it difficult to deny that the processes by which decisions are made matter. People are not consumed solely by the desire to obtain a certain policy outcome. Indeed, on an amazing number of issues, most people have weak or, more likely, nonexistent policy preferences. But even when people do not have a pre-existing preference on a policy issue, government action can still affect attitudes. In fact, it is precisely when people see governing officials spending copious amounts of time arguing about what the people regard to be trifling issues that they become most disgusted with government. Moreover, whether or not people have a pre-existing stake in a particular policy outcome, they have a standing preference that all policies result from a process designed to benefit the general welfare of all Americans rather than the specific welfare of fractious, overly influential, individual interests. The public unquestionably errs by assuming there is a reasonably consensual general will in as heterogeneous a country as the United States, but the fact remains that congressional popularity is damaged when the institution is perceived to act on the basis of narrow, selfish interests. And because virtually every congressional action is perceived by the people in precisely these terms, the most popular Congress is usually the most inert Congress. ■

The International Context

In sharp contrast to the United States, most modern democracies operate under *parliamentary* systems of government. In a parliamentary system, the legislative and executive branches are fused, not separated, and the leader of the legislative branch (usually known as the prime minister) also functions as chief executive. Moreover, in such systems the two branches are typically controlled by a single political party, or coalition of parties, and party leaders can expect, and enforce, loyalty from their troops.

The American system of government, of course, is different in all respects. Congress and the White House are independent by constitutional design and, in modern times, are often controlled by different political parties. Congressional leaders, though stronger than they were twenty-five years ago, still cannot compel or count on the unswerving loyalty of their rank-and-file members.

Throughout American history, many political leaders and political scientists have argued that the American system is inferior to the parliamentary system and that the United States should move, more or less radically, in the parliamentary direction. In particular, these would-be reformers argue, a parliamentary system allows the government to act more efficiently and facilitates majority rule. In this essay, the political scientist Leon D. Epstein explains the differences between the two systems of government and analyzes the validity of the reformist arguments. In the end, he suggests, the American system is deeply grounded in American political culture and is thus highly resistant to change.

Questions

1. What are the key differences between the American system of government and most parliamentary systems? What are the advantages and disadvantages of each system?
2. What aspects of American political culture reinforce Americans' commitment to the current system and create resistance to proposals that would make the American system more like most parliamentary systems?

9.4 Changing Perceptions of the British System (1994)

Leon D. Epstein

Since the development of their academic discipline over a century ago, American political scientists have treated British parliamentary democracy as a benchmark in evaluating the American system. For almost half of that century, it is distressing for me to realize, I have tried to contribute to that comparative enterprise. Now I hope only to refurbish previously stated views by taking into account recent political experience and selected scholarly interpretations of that experience. My perspective combines respect for the British political system with a disbelief in the suitability of its parliamentary institutions for the United States. As a corollary, I treat the separation of executive and legislative powers as workable, if not ideal. It is so central in the American system that its drastic transformation, as distinct from marginal changes in its practice, is inconceivable in circumstances short of a catastrophic breakdown of the system itself. These views are hardly unusual. They are at odds only with a scholarly minority that has long advocated American adaptations of British parliamentary government.

Although I should like to think that my views are the product of research and scholarly contemplation, they surely owe something to the place and time of my political education. Wisconsin, where I lived and studied even before World War II, was not an Anglophile stronghold, and I encountered none of the admirers of the British system who reputedly populated academic institutions elsewhere. More importantly, my earliest and presumably formative political engagement was in the 1930s, when the American system appeared successfully responsive to New Deal policies. Later, I learned to appreciate British democracy first by observing it during World War II and then by academically pursuing the subject. But even as I sought to become a British politics specialist, I retained research and teaching interests in American politics. No doubt, the Americanist mark will be recognizable in this article's first two sections on the nature and recent operation of the British political system, and especially plain in the third and concluding section on proposed solutions to American institutional problems.

The Nature of the Model

"British parliamentary democracy" and "British political system" are terms that distinguish a particular version of fused executive and legislative authority from the several other versions of parliamentary government in the universe of democratic nations. "Westminster model" is similarly useful. To be sure, the model resembles

Leon D. Epstein, "Changing Perceptions of the British System." Reprinted with permission from *Political Science Quarterly* 109 (Special Issue, 1994), pp. 483–497.

other versions of parliamentary government in that any fusion of executive and legislative authority stands in broad contrast to the American separation of powers. But fusion alone is not what principally inspires admiration among American political scientists. It is Britain's strong and stable government by the leadership of a single cohesive party holding a majority of seats in a virtually omnipotent parliamentary body. Peace-time deviations from this pattern have been brief and exceptional in Britain, while the pattern itself has been uncharacteristic of most other European parliamentary democracies. I refer not to checks in some of those nations through effective second chambers and judicial review; the importance of their absence in Britain will be noted later. Here, I am thinking of the typical continental multipartism that makes coalition governments normal practice. Such governments often endure from one election to the next, as do the German but not the Italian. Nevertheless, they usually lack the prized virtue of the British model: one party's full responsibility for governmental policy. Responsibility, in this sense, is what first prompted American admiration of British parliamentary government. The admiration has been sustained, indeed strengthened, as party majorities in the House of Commons became more durable than in Walter Bagehot's day, now ordinarily ensuring a government's tenure between general elections and thus making a government more directly responsible to the electorate.

Britain's majority-party government is as readily associated with single-member, simple-plurality (first-past-the-post) elections as continental European multiparty parliaments are with proportional representation. Neither kind of election, to be sure, guarantees the results with which it is associated; but no one doubts that Britain's first-past-the-post arrangement has returned a majority parliamentary party much more often than would the well known alternative arrangements. Only in one of the fourteen general elections between 1945 and 1992 did it fail to do so. Yet, in none of those fourteen elections did the majority party poll even half of the total national vote for its parliamentary candidates, and in several elections its share was either a little below or a little above two-fifths. Accordingly, first-past-the-post election, or something like it, looks like an essential element of British majority-party government. Perhaps for some Americans observing the British system, first-past-the-post election commands little attention, because unlike many other British institutional practices, it is also an American method. Despite interesting variations, American partisan legislative elections are most often decided by simple pluralities in single-member districts. On this score, transplanting the Westminster model to the United States requires no change. The situation is very different for other significant institutional practices associated with that model.

Start with the organizational roles of political parties. British parliamentary party cohesion is undoubtedly salient for Americans frustrated by notoriously less unified congressional parties. The cohesion is not absolutely uniform; occasionally, dissidents do vote against their party positions, and more exceptionally, revolts are substantial enough to force the leadership of a governing majority party to retreat from a policy position either before or after a parliamentary defeat. After a single such defeat, a government does not really have to resign as long as its majority support is renewed in a specifically labeled vote of confidence as well as in subsequent policy votes. The renewal of support occurs because parliamentary cohesion remains the norm, for the majority party and also for its principal opposition, even though rebellions are more frequent and more serious in certain periods than in others. In this respect, British party behavior so nearly resembles that in other parliamentary regimes that one looks to governmental structure to explain the contrast to American practice. Although members of the U.S. Congress most often find it useful to vote with their parties, their incentives to do so regularly or almost uniformly are modest relative to those of parliamentary members whose support is necessary for their party leaders to retain executive offices and for members themselves to avoid the risk of an untimely election campaign.

The structure of parliamentary government in Britain and elsewhere is associated not only with party cohesion in legislative matters but also with a greater party electoral role than American parties possess. British MPs, much more clearly than members of the U.S. Congress, are elected as supporters of their leaders. They are expected to be loyal partisans both by ordinary voters and, more critically, by the organized party members who choose the candidates to bear major-party labels in general elections. Candidate selection in Britain, however, is not highly centralized as it is in many continental European parties. Each British constituency party customarily selects its parliamentary candidate, subject only to national party rules, assistance, and occasional influence; but the procedure is as likely as a more centralized arrangement to produce reliable partisan candidates. Selection is the business of engaged activists in an organized dues-paying branch of the national party, and such activists tend to prefer a candidate who shares their strongly partisan commitment. The process, therefore, is radically different from the American direct primary in which a large portion of the electorate, with only tenuous party identification, bestows the party label.

Britain's more devotedly partisan selectors expect their candidate, if successfully elected with their considerable help, to support their cause and their national leader. The expectation is so customarily fulfilled that constituency parties seldom need to take measures against their sitting MPs. They may even tolerate occasional dissidents, especially those who are most remote from the opposition party and unthreatening to their own party's hold on office. Nevertheless, constituency parties have the power to deny reselection, and Labour in the 1980s made it easier to exercise that power. Conservative MPs also know that deselection is an ultimate sanction of their local party organization. It need not be much used in order for an MP to bear it in mind.

The greater role of the British party than of the American involves a kind of organization absent in the United States. A regularized dues-paying membership, though suffering currently diminished numbers, gives a degree of democratic legitimacy to candidate selection that we seldom attribute to America's more loosely bounded party organizations, for whose nominations we substitute direct primaries. Moreover, British parties are national as the American are not. Members, through constituency units, belong to a national party and not to any equivalent of American state parties.

In addition to the kind of parties I have described, other institutional elements distinguish British parliamentary government from the American system in ways that are also fundamental in understanding the assumed advantages of strong and responsible government. Power is truly centralized in the party commanding the House of Commons as well as the cabinet, because that fusion of legislative and executive branches is subject to virtually none of the effective checks of a kind that exist in many parliamentary regimes, as well as in the United States. With a unitary rather than a federal system and without a codified higher law constitution, a Commons majority produces legislation that is not subject to invalidation by judicial review in anything like the manner practiced by U.S. courts and in several other democratic nations. Insofar as individual rights are nonetheless protected, it is not by a judiciary's treatment of parliamentary enactments as violations of a Bill of Rights.

Nor is a second legislative chamber able to do more than delay for a limited time the will of a determined government backed by a majority in the Commons. The same can be said for the capacity of the opposition within the Commons to check that majority. This is not to say that opposition criticism in the Commons, or even in the House of Lords, is always of no effect. It has been known to cause a government to become less determined, especially in response to pressures in its own party ranks, and thus to compromise or abandon what turn out to be unpopular policies. But checks of this kind, real enough politically, are not formal institutional veto points.

All of this is familiar, I realize, but worth mentioning in order to emphasize that the British system is notably farther removed from the American than are other parliamentary systems—for example, the German and even the Canadian and Australian whose adaptations of the Westminster model add institutional checks absent in Britain itself. America's traditional cultural attachments to Britain must explain why its democratic system, so drastically different from that of the United States, serves as a model for American academic reformers.

• • •

A Model for the United States?

In speaking of Americans who look with favor on British parliamentary government, as Britons do not with respect to the American separation of executive and legislative powers, I have in mind only limited numbers, mainly in the academic community. We have every reason to assume that an overwhelming majority of Americans in and out of active politics prefer the system to which they are accustomed. That system prevails in each of the fifty states as in the national government, and it has so prevailed since the early days of the Republic when states began separately to elect governors and legislatures if they had not done so previously. No new state has fused executive and legislative authorities in the parliamentary pattern. Such fusion, though possibly subject to challenge in Congress when a state sought admission, would almost surely meet the vague standard of "a Republican Form of Government" guaranteed to each state by Section 4 of Article IV of the U.S. Constitution. The absence of even a single state's experiment with parliamentary government is strong evidence of American dedication to the separation of legislative and executive powers. For a political scientist, it is nonetheless regrettable that no state has tried parliamentary government and thus served as an experimental laboratory as have states in other respects. I know of no advocates of that experimentation. Nor is it discussed as a foreseeable result of an otherwise unfortunate Canadian break-up that would lead one or more provinces to become American states while persisting in their fusion of executive and legislative powers.

• • •

Interest . . . is persistently greater in the kind of reform that tries to achieve British-style party government without changing the Constitution. The principal suggestion is to strengthen American political parties mainly by efforts within parties themselves but also with the help of legislation newly favorable to party organizations. Under the rubric of responsible-party government, the advocacy has a hundred-year history and many distinguished academic supporters. Its most famous statement was published in 1950 as a report from a committee of the American Political Science Association.* Then, or on other occasions, proponents of responsible party government wanted to strengthen each of the two potential majority parties by promoting active programmatic memberships, midterm national conventions, closer links between presidential and congressional candidates, cohesive congressional caucuses reflecting national party policies, organizational membership influence in (if not control of) nominations, closed instead of open primaries if there are to be any primaries at all, freedom from burdensome state regulations, public funding of party campaigns, and higher legal limits on private funding of party campaign activities. Fulfilling the entire wish list might come close to establishing indirectly, almost by stealth, the equivalent of British parliamentary party government. So much seems as unrealistic as the straightforward constitutional changes. Both encounter the American political culture's resistance to majoritarian democracy of the British kind. ■

 # View from the Inside

When Senate Republicans elected Bill Frist of Tennessee to be their majority leader in December 2002, they ended an extraordinary episode in American political history. Two weeks earlier, their would-be majority leader, Senator Trent Lott of Mississippi, had embarrassed himself and his party by suggesting that the nation would have been better off if Strom Thurmond, then a segregationist, had been elected president in 1948. The resulting outcry, and a series of bungled attempts to limit the damage, sealed Lott's fate.

Frist, as the journalist Jonathan Cohn writes in this selection, was an unusual choice for majority leader. To understand Frist, Cohn suggests, one must begin with his profession: he is the first practicing physician to be elected to the Senate in nearly a century. Frist's medical background affects his style, his politics, and his approach to public policy.

---

*See selection 8.1.

Questions

1. Why was Frist attractive to Senate Republicans as they sought to recover from the Lott debacle? What qualities and qualifications did he have for the job?
2. How does Frist's background as a physician help explain his political success? His relationship with his peers? His approach to public policy questions?

9.5 Dr. Feelgood (2003)

Jonathan Cohn

Right after New Year's Day, just over a week after his colleagues elected him Senate majority leader, Bill Frist again popped up in the news, not for any political deed but for trying to save the lives of those injured in a gruesome Florida car crash. It sounded too good to be true—except to anyone who knows Frist here in Nashville. The thing that first strikes you when you start talking to friends and former colleagues of the surgeon-turned-senator is that everyone has a different story about his penchant for small acts of kindness. Janie Webb, a social worker at the Vanderbilt Transplant Center that Frist established, remembers the time Frist found out one of his patients didn't have money to cover her electric bill. He promptly paid the bill himself. Tom Nesbitt, a local physician who has known Frist since they started first grade together, recalls the senator making weekly phone calls about a mutual friend's son, stricken with cancer, for months—and then flying down for the funeral smack in the middle of a busy congressional session. Mark Tipps, who was Frist's chief of staff before returning to Nashville to practice law, still marvels at the way Frist declined to attend a 1996 campaign rally with presidential nominee Bob Dole and half of Tennessee's congressional delegation. Frist had promised to accompany his son to the Cub Scouts' Pinewood Derby races that night and wouldn't break his word. "It was at a time when a lot of Republicans were talking about family values," Tipps notes, "and he was actually doing it."

These stories may not have circulated beyond Nashville, but the image they suggest is already taking hold across the United States. Everybody now knows that Frist is a man of good deeds, from his medical crusades in sub-Saharan Africa to his on-the-spot treatment of shooting victims on Capitol Hill in 1998. More fundamentally, everybody now knows that Frist is a doctor—a profession people associate with compassion and intelligence. "[I]t is a particular stroke of genius that Bill Frist has been named Senate majority leader in a time when our political trust is once again on shaky ground," novelist Ann Patchett wrote recently in *The New York Times Magazine*. "I think a healthy dose of doctoring may be what our government needs." Or, as Maureen Dowd memorably put it, Frist is "Dr. Perfect."

Excerpted from Jonathan Cohn, "Dr. Feelgood," *The New Republic* (January 27, 2003): pp. 16–21. Reprinted by permission of *The New Republic*, © 2003, The New Republic, LLC.

And that's exactly what the White House wants him to be. A major reason Bush touted Frist as the successor to Trent Lott was that Frist seemed to be Lott's opposite—thoughtful where Lott was hardheaded, caring where Lott was indifferent, and smart where Lott was just plain dumb. Just as important, Republicans realize that Frist lends them cover on what may be their most salient political vulnerability: health care. Even today, with Republicans having narrowed the public opinion gap on many traditionally Democratic issues, voters trust Democrats more than Republicans on health care by overwhelming margins—53 percent to 33 percent, according to a December ABC News/*Washington Post* poll. "He's very articulate on issues where the Republican Party has been weak, like health care," Long Island Representative Peter King recently told *Newsday*. "We're on the defensive on patients' bill of rights and prescription drugs [for seniors], and Frist is probably the most knowledgeable about these issues as anyone in Washington today."

But, while Frist may understand medicine, that doesn't mean he's the best person to craft health policy. Ironically, his experience as a transplant surgeon—an experience markedly different than, say, a pediatrician's—has reinforced policy notions that could make our health care system, already cruelly insensitive to the uninsured and the underinsured, even harsher. Moreover, he seems to have inherited from his family, which founded one of the nation's largest for-profit health care companies, a tendency to see the market as the solution to most problems, even as the ways the market distorts health care—everything from drug companies pushing unnecessary medications to insurance companies neglecting beneficiaries—are growing ever more evident. So, while Frist's record as a physician certainly suggests he's an uncommonly decent fellow, it also suggests that he's exactly the wrong man to address the nation's health care woes.

● ● ●

...Frist...invokes his medical background at every turn. "Until today, I've always regarded my most profound professional responsibility in my professional life the blessing I had to hold in my hands the human heart, recognizing all its glory and all its potential, and then technically seating it into the chest of a dying woman to give her life and a future she would not otherwise have," Frist said upon being elected majority leader last month. "A few moments ago, my colleagues gave me a responsibility equal to that—some would even say a heavier one." While this cant gets tiresome, Frist's medical background does help explain his interest in such issues as technology and global AIDS funding. It also helps explain one of Frist's boldest political acts, his position on the nomination of Henry Foster as surgeon general in 1995. Although conservatives were attacking Foster for, among other things, his support of abortion rights, Frist knew Foster through the Frist family's long involvement with Nashville's Meharry Medical College, the nation's oldest private African American medical school. Frist voted for Foster, and although Republicans ultimately defeated the nomination anyway, Foster remains a Frist booster to this day: "This man has demonstrated his ability to be courageous and vote his conscience."

Another episode on which Frist's medical expertise came to bear was the controversy over stem-cell research two summers ago. In what had become a familiar ritual to his staff, Frist buried himself in original research, convened briefings by advocates from both sides, then produced a list of ten principles for governing stem-cell research. Under his proposal, scientists would be permitted to use embryos to generate stem cells just so long as they were going to be discarded anyway, as often happens with in vitro fertilization. But there was to be no creation of embryos specifically for stem-cell creation—i.e., no cloning of embryos specifically for harvesting stem cells—and the government would eventually limit the number of stem-cell lines. This position was to the right of the scientific community, which wanted no such restrictions, but to the left of hard-core conservatives, for whom any embryonic stem-cell research was immoral.

Such heresies explain why some conservatives eye him suspiciously. Just before Frist became majority leader, conservative activist Paul Weyrich, president of the Free Congress Foundation, told reporters that "Senator Bill Frist is not somebody conservatives would be comfortable with given his disposition. He's a moderate Republican at heart, who's not really pro-life." After Frist's opening address on December 23, a speech that talked about reducing racial disparities in medicine and getting health care to the uninsured, conservative columnist Robert Novak discerned an ideological heretic of a different sort: "On Dec. 23, Frist did not mention taxes. Instead, he delivered a pronouncement on health care that, with hardly any editing, could have been echoed by Senate Democratic Leader Thomas Daschle." But, as anxious Democrats have pointed out frequently during the last few weeks, Frist has voted with Trent Lott 90 percent of the time over the last eight years, making him one of the Senate's most conservative members. On nearly every important vote during his tenure, Frist has voted with the Republican leadership: for banning partial-birth abortion, against raising the minimum wage, for convicting Bill Clinton on impeachment charges, against the McCain-Feingold campaign finance reforms, and for the Bush tax cut. Notably, Frist's conservative record holds even on his signature issue, health care. In 1996, Frist voted to strip the Domenici-Wellstone mental health parity bill of a core provision, one prohibiting insurance companies from imposing stricter limitations on coverage for psychiatric illness. That same year, Frist voted against a Democratic initiative that would have restored $18 billion in Medicaid cuts.

So how does a man with no history of conspicuously partisan behavior before 1994 end up with such a conspicuously partisan voting record in the years since? One answer is that Frist is determined to win, and, as he did in his 1994 campaign, he's willing to act like a conservative firebrand if that's what it takes. Consider abortion and stem cells. Frist today calls himself "pro-life," and, indeed, the National Right to Life Committee gives him a perfect voting record on their issues. But, of the eight former medical colleagues I interviewed, not one believes that Frist's voting record is indicative of his true thinking. "I saw his comments on television just before Christmas, but I want to see what he really does," says Gus Vlahakes, who trained with Frist at MGH and remains a friend today. "If I had to take a guess, I'd say he's starting from a more moderate viewpoint than his recent comments would suggest."

Frist's floor statement during the stem-cell debate tends to support this interpretation. "Upon fertilization," Frist explained, "there is a continuum from a sperm and an egg, to a blastocyst, to a fetus, to a child, to an adolescent, to an adult. That continuum is indeed life. . . . I wish to make it clear to my colleagues that from my perspective I do value life and give moral significance to the embryo and to the blastocyst and to that full continuum." Parse those sentences carefully: Frist conspicuously refers to "life" rather than "human life." And his use of the word "continuum" suggests that, while Frist may assign "moral significance" to an embryo, it's not necessarily the same significance he applies to a well-developed fetus or a newborn out of the womb. That position would put Frist at odds with the position of anti-abortion activists; indeed, the idea that the moral value of an embryo changes as pregnancy proceeds happens to be the precise logic of *Roe* v. *Wade*, the 1973 Supreme Court decision legalizing abortion.

But if Frist's positions on superheated social issues seem to reflect mostly political posturing, his record on bread-and-butter issues—taxes, welfare, and, most significantly, health care—seems generally consistent with what we know about his character. In a letter to his family written in 1997 and later published as part of a memorial to him, the 87-year-old Thomas Frist Sr. said, "I am a conservative. I believe the free-enterprise system can do a better job at most things than the government can. People should learn to be self-reliant; when they are self-reliant, they will have self-respect." And, while people might assume that Bill Frist's experience as a healer would blunt this perspective, it may have actually enhanced it.

Medicine has an established sociology to it. On one end of the spectrum you have the specialists: orthopedists, ophthalmologists, cardiothoracic surgeons. On the other end, you have the primary care doctors: pediatricians, family practitioners, and some internists. Not only do surgeons make a lot more money than primary care doctors, fostering different worldviews on issues like taxes and government re-imbursement levels; they also practice medicine in strikingly different ways. Surgical specialists, as the term suggests, develop deep but narrow expertise on one part of the body or even one particular procedure that a patient may need just once in a lifetime. Primary care physicians, by contrast, must consider patients as large, interrelated systems whose health they must maintain over the course of years. "The medical profession is not a monolithic community," says Howard Markel, a professor of pediatrics and the history of medicine at the University of Michigan. "Just look at the way different physicians deal with obesity. Getting somebody to go on a diet, not to eat McDonald's so much, to exercise, that's very hard to do and very frustrating, but it's important, and that's how a family doctor would approach the problem. Now what's the surgical solution? Stick a tube in somebody's gut, and suck out the fat."

What's more, surgeons worry a great deal about anything that might stunt technological innovation, a problem they see as related to government regulation and cost controls. Primary care physicians, on the other hand, spend a lot of time watching how outside factors—environment, poverty, lack of insurance—affect their patients' well-being, and they frequently see government as a means for correcting these problems. As Markel explains, "A lot of medicine has become much more organ-based, much more procedure-based, so the cardiologist thinks just about the heart, the surgeon who does gall bladders thinks just about that operation, and so on. The pediatricians, the internists, they tend to look at the body as a whole, thinking not just about the problems within but some of the problems without as well."

These distinctions translate into politics. Surgeons have historically been the most conservative doctors, with organizations like the American Academy of Ophthalmology among the most hostile to Medicare and government regulation. The American Academy of Pediatrics, by contrast, has long been among the nation's most persistent advocates of national health insurance. Today, seven physicians hold positions in Congress. Of the five Republicans, four are surgeons. Of the Democrats, one is a family practitioner while the other is a psychiatrist. (Psychiatrists, whose long-term relationships with patients resemble primary care doctors' more than surgeons', are also pretty liberal as a group.) There's also one physician, former Vermont Governor Howard Dean, who's running for president. He's a former family practitioner, so, naturally, he's a Democrat.

These are stereotypes, to be sure, and Frist doesn't fit them precisely. Everything we know about Frist's medical practice suggests that he was an unusually warm surgeon, and transplant surgery, by its nature, requires more post-operative contact with patients than many other specialties. But transplant surgery also fosters an unusually strong ethos of rugged individualism. With transplants, success often rests ultimately on the patient's willingness and determination to go through rehabilitation and adopt a healthier lifestyle. And transplant surgeons must constantly make decisions about which patients deserve to go on transplant lists and which ones don't. Like his father, a self-made man who disdained handouts and preached the up-by-your-bootstraps ethic, Frist became comfortable with the idea of making sharp judgments about people—something more in tune with Republican values than Democratic ones. A passage in [Frist's memoir] *Transplant* recalls this advice from Frist's father: "Now we have the know-how to save some of them. Some of them—not all of them. Well, I raised you to make that decision. I raised you, and this society trained you specifically for that purpose, and you spent years learning how to make it."

• • •

None of this is to say Frist's perspective on health care is entirely without merit. In keeping with his free-market orientation, he thinks the basic underlying problem with our nation's health care problems—everything from Medicare spending to the uninsured to managed care abuses—is a lack of sufficient economic incentives for patients. The current insurance system insulates people from the cost of their medical care, he says, so they seek more and more of it with little concern for how much it costs. That's why Frist favors his particular health care solutions, each of which would require people to consider the trade-offs between quality and access on the one hand and cost on the other. Under his vision for Medicare, for example, people who wanted lavish coverage—free choice of doctor, unfettered access to experimental treatment, total prescription-drug coverage—could opt to have it, but only if they were willing to pay higher premiums and co-payments. Those willing to live with less could go a cheaper route, presumably a traditional Health Maintenance Organization (HMO). Medical Savings Accounts would accomplish the same goal, by letting people decide whether they wanted to spend their tax-sheltered money on medicine or save it for other uses later on.

As insights into the problems with medical economics, Frist's ideas are sound. But they are also incomplete and ultimately lead to counterproductive policies. Transferring some responsibility for making health care spending decisions onto patients makes sense if it's done in a measured way—say, by modestly increasing premiums or co-payments for each person. But the schemes Frist favors would go much further in that direction, creating financial incentives against seeking expensive care so dramatic that they would disrupt the entire health insurance market. The more costly health care becomes on an individual basis, the more healthy people—who can afford to go without expensive care—will opt for the skimpiest plans. That will leave the truly ill, whose health situations force them to opt for more complete coverage, alone in their plans, driving their costs up. For example, one respected analysis of Medical Savings Accounts, published in 1996 by the Urban Institute, estimated that if large numbers of healthier people opt for medical savings accounts, insurance premiums for everybody else could increase by 60 percent—likely more than many could afford, thereby swelling the ranks of the uninsured even more.

On a more basic level, the fact that Frist has practiced medicine at the very top of his field seems to have insulated him from the experiences of people who suffer most under the current health care regime: the uninsured. Frist apparently saw some charity cases at Vanderbilt, but, as he notes in his memoir, the university had special funding to help pay for many of them. Late in the book, he notes that the high numbers of uninsured in the United States is a growing crisis, but then he insists, as he continues to today, that it's going to be up to private insurance to solve the problem. A physician who had actually spent extensive time working closely with the uninsured—say, in a public clinic, where their financial hardship would be in plain view—would understand instinctively what academics are now showing: that a market approach to the uninsured inevitably leaves out those who need insurance most. "Tax credits for non-group health insurance would not make a major dent in the number of the uninsured," says Jonathan Gruber, a Massachusetts Institute of Technology economist who has done influential research on the subject. "The credits are simply too small relative to the high and variable cost of non-group insurance to make a difference for most low-income uninsured families. Moreover, the small number of uninsured who do take up the credits will be the most young and healthy uninsured who can find affordable policies."

Finally, Frist's views on Medicare also reflect a perspective wildly out of sync with what most people actually on Medicare seem to believe. Frist, a regular critic of the Medicare bureaucracy, frequently speaks of the need to "modernize" the program—as if its antiquity were a source of massive dissatisfaction. That may reflect how most surgeons feel, since they don't like Medicare's paperwork, but it couldn't be further from the sentiments of Medicare recipients. Although they desperately want a drug benefit, seniors want it as part of Medicare as it exists now. And who can blame them? In contrast to private managed care plans, which limit patient choice about doctors and treatment, Medicare allows beneficiaries to see almost anybody. A study in *Health Affairs* released this October compared satisfaction rates between Medicare beneficiaries with people on private insurance. The Medicare beneficiaries were overwhelmingly happier with their insurance, even without the prescription-drug coverage.

Of course, many people assume that Frist will never get to remake Medicare anyway, that the program's popularity will preclude sweeping changes. Many of the same people assume that, however extraordinary Frist's talents, he is bound to fail as Senate majority leader. He's too green, too wonky, too *nice*. But . . . , Frist knows how to play hardball. He got away with it, in part, because voters in 1994 couldn't bring themselves to see a physician—particularly such a compassionate and dedicated one—as the calculating and ambitious politician he had become. Who's to say he can't do it again? ∎

Chapter 10

The Presidency

At first glance, the American presidency is the most powerful office in the world. To the president's vast formal powers are added extraordinary informal powers: to lead Congress, to cope with emergency situations, to take charge of world affairs. The president's constitutional authority, broad and expansive, is supplemented by huge delegations of power from Congress and by the power that comes from the prestige of the office itself.

Yet for all his powers, the president is boxed in by limitations of every kind. He must share his constitutional authority with Congress, with which he must continually negotiate and bargain, and with the federal courts, which he can influence only uncertainly and, usually, only in the long run. His own cabinet officials often have their own political bases and their own agendas, and even his personal staff may become ambitious and unreliable. He must spend much of his first term preparing for reelection, and all of his second term, if he has one, with the knowledge that the Constitution forbids him from running again.

Both the extent and limits of presidential power were amply displayed in the aftermath of the terrorist attacks of September 11, 2001. In the hours and days after the event, as David Frum describes in selection 10.6, millions in America and around the world turned to George W. Bush for leadership and reassurance. Acting on his own authority and providing decisive leadership to Congress, Bush waged war in Afghanistan, rounded up thousands of terrorist suspects, and conducted clandestine operations against terrorist operations across the globe. He set forth a bold agenda in both foreign and domestic policy, and watched as his public approval rating soared toward 90 percent.

But as the months passed, the limits of Bush's power began to show. After declaring his intention to depose Iraq's Saddam Hussein, Bush found it necessary to negotiate with the United Nations Security Council for authorization; eventually he yielded to the demands of our European allies for additional weapons inspections prior to the use of military force. At home, Bush faced a faltering economy, a hostile and still powerful Democratic minority in Congress, and a nation divided on matters of both domestic and foreign policy.

The readings in this chapter share a common theme: they present the paradox of a president whose immense resources are not always sufficient to perform the tasks expected of him by the American people and the world. Selections 10.1 and 10.2, which are drawn from the *Federalist Papers,* provide the classic justification for a strong and unitary presidency. Selection 10.3, by the political scientist Richard Neustadt, argues that the informal powers of the presidency are as important to consider as are his formal powers. Selection 10.4, by the political scientist Fred I. Greenstein, examines the presidency of

George W. Bush both before and after September 11; did the tragic events of that day, Greenstein asks, fundamentally change Bush as a leader? Selection 10.5 looks at presidential power from a comparative perspective, while selection 10.6 presents an inside account of life inside the White House on the day of the terrorist attacks on America.

Chapter Questions

1. What are the sources of the president's formal authority? His informal authority?
2. Consider Richard Neustadt's argument (in selection 10.3) that a president's real power comes from his ability to bargain and persuade effectively. What examples of bargaining and persuading can be found in this chapter? Consider the president's foreign affairs power, his dealings with Congress, and his relationship with his own staff, for starters.
3. The presidency, some suggest, is an eighteenth-century office forced to function in a twentieth-first-century world. How has the presidency adjusted to the extraordinary political, social, and technological changes of the past two hundred years? Has this adaptation been successful?

 # Foundations

The Framers of the Constitution recognized the importance of a unitary executive. Legislative bodies could deliberate and plan policy in the long run, perhaps, but only a unitary executive could act with the speed, decisiveness, and, when appropriate, secretiveness necessary for effective leadership. These qualities were especially important, the Framers believed, in matters of foreign and military policy.

Americans are so used to a strong presidency that it is easy to forget how much opposition there was in the beginning to such an office. The opponents of the Constitution feared that the presidency would quickly be transformed into an oppressive monarchy (the Articles of Confederation, remember, had no federal executive). They feared the Constitution's broad grants of legislative power to the president (especially the veto power and the power to make treaties), the commander-in-chief clause, and the president's power to appoint the federal judiciary.

Alexander Hamilton's strong defense of presidential power in the *Federalist* No. 70 is a clear indication that the Framers favored both efficiency and liberty and indeed believed that one was impossible without the other. It follows *Federalist* No. 68, in which Hamilton defends the mode of appointment of the president; he suggests that the indirect scheme the Framers designed would ensure to a "moral certainty that the office of President will seldom fall to the lot of any man who is not in an eminent degree endowed with the requisite qualifications."

Yet the Antifederalists' fears were not wholly unfounded. Maintaining the balance between a presidency strong enough to do what is required yet constrained enough to be controlled by the people remains a difficult, and daunting, task. The president's only hope of governing under such circumstances, as the political scientist Richard Neustadt suggests, is to rely not only on his formal powers, but also on his informal powers—especially his power to bargain with and persuade his friends, his opponents, and the American people.

Questions

1. Why is a unitary executive necessary, according to Hamilton? What characteristics does a single individual possess that a body of individuals—Congress, for example—lacks?
2. Have Hamilton's arguments become stronger or weaker over the past two hundred years? Has the modern presidency borne out his views or those of his opponents?
3. What advantages does a president have in the bargaining process, according to Richard Neustadt? Does he have any significant advantages or disadvantages in dealing with Congress? With the bureaucracy? With the American people?

10.1 *Federalist* No. 68 (1788)

Alexander Hamilton

Outline

I. Explanation of the means chosen for the appointment of the president of the United States.

   A. The mode of appointment selected—involving the creation of the Electoral College—

      1. Involves the people at large.

      2. Leaves the ultimate choice to those most capable of judging wisely between candidates.

      3. Avoids "tumult and disorder."

      4. Guards against corruption.

      5. Maintains the independence of the chief executive.

   B. Process results in a "moral certainty" that those selected will be qualified.

The mode of appointment of the Chief Magistrate of the United States is almost the only part of the system, of any consequence, which has escaped without severe censure or which has received the slightest mark of approbation from its opponents. The most plausible of these, who has appeared in print, has even deigned to admit that the election of the President is pretty well guarded. [Hamilton refers to the *Letters of a Federal Farmer*, written by an Antifederalist critic of the Constitution.] I venture somewhat further, and hesitate not to affirm that if the manner of it be not perfect, it is at least excellent. It unites in an eminent degree all the advantages the union of which was to be desired.

It was desirable that the sense of the people should operate in the choice of the person to whom so important a trust was to be confided. This end will be answered by committing the right of making it, not to any pre-established body, but to men chosen by the people for the special purpose, and at the particular conjuncture.

It was equally desirable that the immediate election should be made by men most capable of analyzing the qualities adapted to the station and acting under circumstances favorable to deliberation, and to a judicious combination of all the reasons and inducements which were proper to govern their choice. A small number of persons, selected by their fellow-citizens from the general mass, will be most likely to possess the information and discernment requisite to so complicated an investigation.

It was also peculiarly desirable to afford as little opportunity as possible to tumult and disorder. This evil was not least to be dreaded in the election of a magistrate who was to have so important an agency in the administration of the government as the President of the United States. But the precautions which have been so happily concerted in the system under consideration promise an effectual security against this mischief. The choice of *several* to form an intermediate body of electors will be much less apt to convulse the community with any extraordinary or violent movements than the choice of *one* who was himself to be the final object of the public wishes. And as the electors, chosen in each State, are to assemble and vote in the State in which they are chosen, this detached and divided situation will expose them much less to heats and ferments, which might be communicated from them to the people, than if they were all to be convened at one time, in one place.

Nothing was more to be desired than that every practicable obstacle should be opposed to cabal, intrigue, and corruption. These most deadly adversaries of republican government might naturally have been expected to make their approaches from more than one quarter, but chiefly from the desire in foreign powers to gain an improper ascendant in our councils. How could they better gratify this than by raising a creature of their own to the chief magistracy of the Union? But the convention have guarded against all danger of this sort with the most provident and judicious attention. They have not made the appointment of the President to depend on any preexisting bodies of men who might be tampered with beforehand to prostitute their votes; but they have referred it in the first instance to an immediate act of the people of America, to be exerted in the choice of persons for the temporary and sole purpose of making the appointment. And they have excluded from eligibility to this trust all those who from situation might be suspected of too great devotion to the President in office. No senator, representative, or other person holding a place of trust or profit under the United States can be of the number of the electors. Thus without corrupting the body of the people, the immediate agents in the election will at least enter upon the task free from any sinister bias. Their transient existence and their detached situation, already taken notice of, afford a satisfactory prospect of their continuing so, to the conclusion of it. The business of corruption, when it is to embrace so considerable a number of men, requires time as well as means. Nor would it be found easy suddenly to embark them, dispersed as they would be over thirteen States, in any combinations founded upon motives which, though they could not properly be denominated corrupt, might yet be of a nature to mislead them from their duty.

Another and less important desideratum was that the executive should be independent for his continuance in office on all but the people themselves. He might otherwise be tempted to sacrifice his duty to his complaisance for those whose favor was necessary to the duration of his official consequence. This advantage will also be secured, by making his re-election to depend on a special body of representatives, deputed by the society for the single purpose of making the important choice.

All these advantages will be happily combined in the plan devised by the convention; which is, that the people of each State shall choose a number of persons as electors, equal to the number of senators and representatives of such State in the national government who shall assemble within the State, and vote for some fit person as President. Their votes, thus given, are to be transmitted to the seat of the national government, and the person who may happen to have a majority of the whole number of votes will be the President. But as a majority of the votes might not always happen to center on one man, and as it might be unsafe to permit less than a majority to be conclusive it is provided that, in such a contingency, the House of Representatives shall elect out of the candidates who shall have the five highest number of votes the man who in their opinion may be best qualified for the office.

This process of election affords a moral certainty that the office of President will seldom fall to the lot of any man who is not in an eminent degree endowed with the requisite qualifications. Talents for low intrigue, and the little arts of popularity, may alone suffice to elevate a man to the first honors in a single State; but it will require other talents, and a different kind of merit, to establish him in the esteem and confidence of the whole Union, or of so considerable a portion of it as would be necessary to make him a successful candidate for the distinguished office of President of the United States. It will not be too strong to say that there will be a constant probability of seeing the station filled by characters pre-eminent for ability and virtue. And this will be thought no inconsiderable recommendation of the Constitution by those who are able to estimate the share which the executive in every government must necessarily have in its good or ill administration. Though we cannot acquiesce in the political heresy of the poet who says:

> For forms of government let fools contest—
> That which is best administered is best,—

yet we may safely pronounce that the true test of a good government is its aptitude and tendency to produce a good administration. . . . ■

10.2 *Federalist* No. 70 (1788)

Alexander Hamilton

Outline

I. The importance and components of strength and energy in the executive branch.

    A. A strong and energetic executive branch requires unity, duration in office, adequate resources, and sufficient powers.

II. Defense of a unitary (one-person) executive rather than a council.

    A. Importance of limiting dissension and disagreement with the executive branch.

    B. Importance of being able to fix responsibility within the executive branch.

There is an idea, which is not without its advocates, that a vigorous executive is inconsistent with the genius of republican government. The enlightened well-wishers to this species of government must at least hope that the supposition is destitute of foundation; since they can never admit its truth, without at the same time admitting the condemnation of their own principles. Energy in the executive is a leading character in the definition of good government. It is essential to the protection of the community against foreign attacks; it is not less essential to the steady administration of the laws; to the protection of property against those irregular and high-handed combinations which sometimes interrupt the ordinary course of justice; to the security of liberty against the enterprises and assaults of ambition, of faction, and of anarchy. Every man the least conversant in Roman history knows how often that republic was obliged to take refuge in the absolute power of a single man, under the formidable title of dictator, as well against the intrigues of ambitious individuals who aspired to the tyranny, and the seditions of whole classes of the community whose conduct threatened the existence of all government, as against the invasions of external enemies who menaced the conquest and destruction of Rome.

There can be no need, however, to multiply arguments or examples on this head. A feeble executive implies a feeble execution of the government. A feeble execution is but another phrase for a bad execution; and a government ill executed, whatever it may be in theory, must be, in practice, a bad government.

Taking it for granted, therefore, that all men of sense will agree in the necessity of an energetic executive, it will only remain to inquire, what are the ingredients which constitute this energy? How far can they be combined with those other ingredients which constitute safety in the republican sense? And how far does this combination characterize the plan which has been reported by the convention?

The ingredients which constitute energy in the executive are unity; duration; an adequate provision for its support; and competent powers.

The ingredients which constitute safety in the republican sense are a due dependence on the people and a due responsibility.

Those politicians and statesmen who have been the most celebrated for the soundness of their principles and for the justness of their views have declared in favor of a single executive and a numerous legislature. They have, with great propriety, considered energy as the most necessary qualification of the former, and have regarded this as most applicable to power in a single hand; while they have, with equal propriety, considered the latter as best adapted to deliberation and wisdom, and best calculated to conciliate the confidence of the people and to secure their privileges and interests.

That unity is conducive to energy will not be disputed. Decision, activity, secrecy, and dispatch will generally characterize the proceedings of one man in a much more eminent degree than the proceedings of any greater number; and in proportion as the number is increased, these qualities will be diminished.

• • •

Whenever two or more persons are engaged in any common enterprise or pursuit, there is always danger of difference of opinion. If it be a public trust or office in which they are clothed with equal dignity and authority, there is peculiar danger of personal emulation and even animosity. From either, and especially from all these causes, the most bitter dissensions are apt to spring. Whenever these happen, they lessen the respectability, weaken the authority, and distract the plans and operations of those whom they divide. If they should unfortunately assail the supreme executive magistracy of a country, consisting of a plurality of persons, they might impede or frustrate the most important measures of the government in the most critical emergencies of the state. And what is still worse, they might split the community into the most violent and irreconcilable factions, adhering differently to the different individuals who composed the magistracy.

Men often oppose a thing merely because they have had no agency in planning it, or because it may have been planned by those whom they dislike. But if they have been consulted, and have happened to disapprove, opposition then becomes, in their estimation, an indispensable duty of self-love. They seem to think themselves bound in honor, and by all the motives of personal infallibility, to defeat the success of what has been resolved upon contrary to their sentiments. Men of upright, benevolent tempers have too many opportunities of remarking, with horror, to what desperate lengths this disposition is sometimes carried, and how often the great interests of society are sacrificed to the vanity, to the conceit, and to the obstinacy of individuals, who have credit enough to make their passions and their caprices interesting to mankind. Perhaps the question now before the public may, in its consequences, afford melancholy proofs of the effects of this despicable frailty, or rather detestable vice, in the human character.

Upon the principles of a free government, inconveniences from the source just mentioned must necessarily be submitted to in the formation of the legislature; but it is unnecessary, and therefore unwise, to introduce them into the constitution of the executive. It is here too that they may be most pernicious. In the legislature, promptitude of decision is oftener an evil than a benefit. The differences of opinion, and the jarring of parties in that department of the government, though they may sometimes obstruct salutary plans, yet often promote deliberation and circumspection, and serve to check excesses in the majority. When a resolution too is once taken, the opposition must be at an end. That resolution is a law, and resistance to it punishable. But no favorable circumstances palliate or atone for the disadvantages of dissension in the executive department. Here they are pure and unmixed. There is no point at which they cease to operate. They serve to embarrass and weaken the execution of the plan or measure to which they relate, from the first step to the final conclusion of it. They constantly counteract those qualities in the executive which are the most necessary ingredients in its composition—vigor and expedition, and this without any counterbalancing good. In the conduct of war, in which the energy of the executive is the bulwark of the national security, everything would be to be apprehended from its plurality. . . .

But one of the weightiest objections to a plurality in the executive, and which lies as much against the last as the first plan is that it tends to conceal faults and destroy responsibility. Responsibility is of two kinds—to censure and to punishment. The first is the more important of the two, especially in an elective office. Men in public trust will much oftener act in such a manner as to render them unworthy of being any longer trusted, than in such a manner as to make them obnoxious to legal punishment. But the multiplication of the executive adds to the difficulty of detection in either case. It often becomes impossible, amidst mutual accusations, to determine on whom the blame or the punishment of a pernicious measure, or series of pernicious measures, ought really to fall. It is shifted from one to another with so much dexterity, and under such plausible appearances, that the public opinion is left in suspense about the real author. The circumstances which may have led to any national miscarriage or misfortune are sometimes so complicated that where there are a number of actors who may have had different degrees and kinds of agency, though we may clearly see upon the whole that there has been mismanagement, yet it may be impracticable to pronounce to whose account the evil which may have been incurred is truly chargeable. . . . ■

10.3 Presidential Power (1960)

Richard E. Neustadt

The separateness of institutions and the sharing of authority prescribe the terms on which a President persuades. When one man shares authority with another, but does not gain or lose his job upon the other's whim, his willingness to act upon the urging of the other turns on whether he conceives the action right for him. The essence of a President's persuasive task is to convince such men that what the White House wants of them is what they ought to do for their sake and on their authority.

Persuasive power, thus defined, amounts to more than charm or reasoned argument. These have their uses for a President, but these are not the whole of his resources. For the men he would induce to do what he wants done on their own responsibility will need or fear some acts by him on his responsibility. If they share his authority, he has some share in theirs. Presidential "powers" may be inconclusive when a President commands, but always remain relevant as he persuades. The status and authority inherent in his office reinforce his logic and his charm.

Status adds something to persuasiveness; authority adds still more. When Truman urged wage changes on his Secretary of Commerce while the latter was administering the steel mills, he and Secretary Sawyer were not just two men reasoning with one another. Had they been so, Sawyer probably would never have agreed to act. Truman's status gave him special claims to Sawyer's loyalty, or at least attention. In Walter Bagehot's charming phrase "no man can *argue* on his knees." Although there is no kneeling in this country, few men—and exceedingly few Cabinet officers—are immune to the impulse to say "yes" to the President of the United States. It grows harder to say "no" when they are seated in his oval office at the White House, or in his study on the second floor, where almost tangibly he partakes of the aura of his physical surroundings. In Sawyer's case, moreover, the President possessed formal authority to intervene in many matters of concern to the Secretary of Commerce. These matters ranged from jurisdictional disputes among the defense agencies to legislation pending before Congress and, ultimately, to the tenure of the Secretary, himself. There is nothing in the record to suggest that Truman voiced specific threats when they negotiated over wage increases. But given his *formal* powers and their relevance to Sawyer's other interests, it is safe to assume that Truman's very advocacy of wage action conveyed an implicit threat.

A President's authority and status give him great advantages in dealing with the men he would persuade. Each "power" is a vantage point for him in the degree that other men have use for his authority. From the veto to appointments, from publicity to budgeting, and so down a long list, the White House now controls the most encompassing array of vantage points in the American political system. With hardly an exception, the men who share in governing this country are aware that at some time, in some degree, the doing of *their* jobs, the furthering of *their* ambitions, may depend upon the President of the United States. Their need for presidential action, or their fear of it, is bound to be recurrent if not actually continuous. Their need or fear is his advantage.

A President's advantages are greater than mere listing of his "powers" might suggest. The men with whom he deals must deal with him until the last day of his term. Because they have continuing relationships with him, his future, while it lasts, supports his present influence. Even though there is no need or fear of him today, what he could do tomorrow may supply today's advantage. Continuing relationships may convert any "power," any aspect of his status, into vantage points in almost any case. When he induces other men to do what he wants done, a President can trade on their dependence now *and* later.

The President's advantages are checked by the advantages of others. Continuing relationships will pull in both directions. These are relationships of mutual dependence. A President depends upon the men he would persuade; he has to reckon with his need or fear of them. They too will possess status, or authority, or both, else they would be of little use to him. Their vantage points confront his own; their power tempers his.

Persuasion is a two-way street. Sawyer, it will be recalled, did not respond at once to Truman's plan for wage increases at the steel mills. On the contrary, the Secretary hesitated and delayed and only acquiesced when he was satisfied that publicly he would not bear the onus of decision. Sawyer had some points of vantage all his own from which to resist presidential pressure. If he had to reckon with coercive implications in the President's "situations of strength," so had Truman to be mindful of the implications underlying Sawyer's place as a department head, as steel administrator, and as a Cabinet spokesman for business. Loyalty is reciprocal. Having taken on a dirty job in the steel crisis, Sawyer had strong claims to loyal support. Besides, he had authority to do some things that the White House could ill afford. Emulating Wilson, he might have resigned in a huff (the removal power also works two ways). Or emulating Ellis Arnall, he might have declined to sign necessary orders. Or, he might have let it be known publicly that he deplored what he was told to do and protested its doing. By following any of these courses Sawyer almost surely would have strengthened the position of management, weakened the position of the White House, and embittered the union. But the whole purpose of a wage increase was to enhance White House persuasiveness in urging settlement upon union and companies alike. Although Sawyer's status and authority did not give him the power to prevent an increase outright, they gave him capability to undermine its purpose. If his authority over wage rates had been vested by a statute, not by revocable presidential order, his power of prevention might have been complete. So Harold Ickes demonstrated in the famous case of helium sales to Germany before the Second World War.

The power to persuade is the power to bargain. Status and authority yield bargaining advantages. But in a government of "separated institutions sharing powers," they yield them to all sides. With the array of vantage points at his disposal, a President may be far more persuasive than his logic or his charm could make him. But outcomes are not guaranteed by his advantages. ∎

American Politics Today

Few presidencies have been transformed as quickly—and so seemingly completely—as was George W. Bush's on September 11, 2001. On September 10, the Bush administration was largely focused on domestic affairs—a sluggish economy, a raging debate over stem cell research, and plans for education reform. The terrorist attacks changed Bush's focus from domestic to foreign affairs, and from peace to war.

The events of 9/11, as the political scientist Fred I. Greenstein suggests in this selection, not only transformed the Bush presidency—they also transformed Bush himself.

Questions

1. Which of George W. Bush's traits or characteristics most prepared him for the actions he would have to take in the aftermath of 9/11? Which traits or characteristics did he have to overcome?
2. Could Bush's response to 9/11 have been predicted on the basis of what we knew before Bush was elected president?

10.4 The Changing Leadership of George W. Bush (2002)

Fred I. Greenstein

The American presidency is said to be an office in which some incumbents grow and others swell. If ever a president has fallen in the first of these categories, it is George W. Bush. Before the suicide bombings of September 11, 2001, even a number of Bush's strong supporters were not persuaded that he was fully up to his responsibilities. Since then, even many of his critics grant that he has become strikingly more presidential. A Gallup poll completed a day before the bombing of the World Trade Towers and the Pentagon found that only 51 percent of the public expressed approval of his presidential performance. Three days after the attacks, Gallup fielded the first of an extended run of polls in which Bush registered approval levels in excess of 85 percent.

Bush has not only played well with the public. It is widely viewed in the political community that there has been an impressive increase in his political competence, a perception that extends beyond the United States. Five weeks after the terror attacks, a front-page column in the influential *Frankfurter Allgemeine* likened George W. Bush to Harry S Truman. Noting that the unassuming Truman had risen to the challenge of the cold war presidency, the writer declared that Bush had grown "before our eyes," becoming "more profound and more sure-footed."

In what follows, I present my own comparison of the pre- and post-9/11 political leadership style of George W. Bush, bringing up to date an assessment of Bush's strengths and weaknesses that I completed in the spring of 2001. . . . My remarks fall under . . . six headings . . . [that] identify presidential leadership qualities: emotional intelligence, cognitive style, political skill, policy vision, organizational capacity, and effectiveness as a public communicator.

• • •

Excerpted from Fred I. Greenstein, "The Changing Leadership of George W. Bush: A Pre- and Post-9/11 Comparison," *Presidential Studies Quarterly* 32: pp. 387–396, June 2002. Copyright © 2002 by Sage Publications, Inc. Reprinted by permission of Sage Publications, Inc.

Emotional Intelligence

It is not necessary that a chief executive be a paragon of mental health, but the nation may be at risk if he (and someday she) lacks the ability to control his emotions and turn them to productive use. This ability, which has come to be referred to as "emotional intelligence," is—or should be—a threshold requirement for the custodian of the most potentially lethal military arsenal in human experience.

By the standard of emotional intelligence, George W. Bush would have been a poor presidential prospect in his years of excessive drinking and drift. It would not be surprising if someone with such life experiences proved to be an emotional tinder box, but Bush's business and political careers have been largely free of emotional excesses. He bore up well in the seemingly endless presidential campaign that brought him to the White House, rebounding after his defeat in New Hampshire, and he weathered the lengthy post–Election Day stalemate with seeming equanimity. Bush did face a minor national security crisis in April 2001, when an American surveillance plane was forced down on China's Hainan Island and China interned its crew. After a blustery initial statement, he was cool, measured, and patient. Still, it was by no means evident before September 11 how he might respond to a national security crisis of major proportions.

Bush's performance since September 11, 2001, is reassuring from the standpoint of his emotional intelligence. In the chaotic first day of the episode, he came across to some observers as being less than fully confident. But from then on, he radiated a sense of self-assurance and calm determination. It is instructive to contrast Bush's actions with those of Richard Nixon in the 1970 events that led to the killing of four student protestors at Kent State University. In April of that year, Nixon concluded that it was necessary for the United States to attack a concentration of communist troops that were using Cambodia as a sanctuary. Ignoring advice to inform the public of the action as a routine Pentagon statement, Nixon chose to announce it in a confrontational address and went on to refer to student protestors as "bums." By the end of the week, the nation's campuses were wracked with antiwar protests, Washington was under siege by demonstrators, and the moribund peace movement had been reinvigorated.

Cognitive Style

Late-night television comedians notwithstanding, George W. Bush has ample native intelligence. However, he has not been marked by intellectual curiosity or drawn to the play of ideas. Moreover, he is the nation's first MBA chief executive, and he lets it be known that he favors a corporate model of political leadership in which he avoids immersing himself in detail and relies on subordinates to structure his options. As governor of Texas, Bush was sweeping in his acts of delegation. A study of his Texas schedule found, for example, that when he was delivering a lengthy report on a tragedy in which a number of Texas A&M students were killed in a faultily constructed bonfire, he read neither it nor its executive summary, leaving it to his aides to highlight a few paragraphs of the report's conclusions. Even in the sensitive realm of capital punishment, Bush relied heavily on the recommendations of his aides, reducing the time he spent on reviews of death sentences from thirty to fifteen minutes in the course of his governorship.

When Bush went on to Washington, it remained to be seen whether he could remain as remote from specifics as he had in Austin. There were a number of instances during the pre-9/11 period of his presidency when it seemed evident that he needed to dig deeper into policy content than had been his wont. A notable example was his response on April 26 to an interviewer's question about whether it is American policy to defend the island republic of Taiwan against an invasion from mainland China. Bush remarked that the United States would do "whatever it takes" to help Taiwan, but it quickly became evident that he had not meant to signal a departure from the longtime policy of maintaining ambiguity about how the United States would respond to such a contingency.

Bush has exhibited a far firmer grasp of policy specifics after than before September 11. Particularly striking was his masterful review of his administration's policies at his first full-scale East Room press conference, a month to the day following the acts of terror. The impression that he is now delving more deeply into the problems of the day has been strongly confirmed by the legwork on Capitol Hill of Steven Thomma, the Washington correspondent of the Knight Ridder newspaper chain, who quotes a number of members of Congress who found Bush to be disengaged before September 11 and now find him to be thoughtful and focused. As one of them put it, "He's as smart as he wants to be."

Political Skill

The congenitally gregarious George W. Bush resembles his fellow Texan Lyndon Johnson in his aptitude for personal politics and his readiness to seek support on both sides of the aisle. In his December 2000 speech to the Texas legislature immediately following Al Gore's concession, Bush stressed that he intended to apply the bipartisan methods he had used in Texas in the nation's capital. He had chosen to deliver the speech in the chamber of the Texas House of Representatives, he explained, "because it has been home to bipartisan cooperation," adding that "the spirit of cooperation we have seen in this hall is what is needed in Washington, D.C."

In the first several weeks after his inauguration, Bush spent so much time courting Democrats that the press characterized his efforts as a "charm offensive." But he went on to focus almost exclusively on mobilizing his party's narrow congressional majority to advance one of the issues on which he had campaigned—his proposal for a $1.6 billion tax cut. He did so until it became clear that he would have to compromise, at which point he settled for a smaller reduction and declared victory. By the time the political community had engaged in the ritual of assessing the first hundred days of the Bush presidency, the prevailing view was that he is an exceptionally able politician. Still, it was too early to tell what his skill and that of his highly experienced associates would enable him to accomplish given the close balance of forces in the policy-making community. It also remained to be seen whether his gestures toward the Democrats were just that or whether he would be capable of engaging in genuine bipartisan policy making.

In the aftermath of September 11, Bush employed the same face-to-face political skills that marked the earlier months of his presidency, reinforcing his bonds with members of the policy-making community, including key Democrats. Two examples of the latter are noteworthy: on September 20, on the way out of the House chamber following his much-praised address to a joint session of Congress, Bush strode up to Senate Majority Leader Tom Daschle and embraced him. On November 20, Bush presided over the naming of the Justice Department building for Robert Kennedy, doing so in the presence of some fifty members of the Kennedy family. The success of yearlong negotiations that led to passage in December 2000 of a much-modified version of Bush's education bill made it clear that he in fact was willing and able to bring about bipartisan policy outcomes. As Senator Kennedy, who had been one of the bill's negotiators, put it, "President Bush was there every step of the way."

Policy Vision

In contrast to Bill Clinton, who was fascinated with the intricacies of public policy, George W. Bush evinces little interest in policies in and of themselves. When Bush's fellow participants in his father's 1988 election campaign socialized with him, they found that he liked to talk about baseball, not issues. Yet unlike his father, Bush does have the "vision thing," adopting policy positions to preempt his opponents as well as because of their appeal to him. Having seen his father fail to amass a record on which to win reelection, Bush's practice is to campaign and govern on the basis of a clear-cut set of goals. He did this in Texas, and he has done it in his presidency, but he also has been unsentimental about jettisoning portions of his programs if it becomes evident that they are not attainable.

Bush continued to show a clear sense of direction in the aftermath of September 11, but his primary focus shifted to combating terror. He was explicit, but not unrealistic, in stating his administration's war aims, both abroad and on the home front. Meanwhile, he put much of what remained unenacted in his domestic program on hold with one important exception—the aforementioned education bill, a landmark measure that increases school spending by many billions of dollars and targets the expenditures to poorly performing schools and their students.

Organizational Capacity

It speaks well for Bush's organizational capacity that he surrounded himself with a cadre of able loyalists who served him in Texas for the better part of a decade and followed him to Washington. Further evidence of his aptitude for team leadership is to be found in the personnel choices he made during and after the presidential campaign. He has staffed his White House and cabinet with an impressive array of seasoned public servants. Especially notable were his selection of the strategically gifted Washington insider Dick Cheney as his running mate and his appointment of Secretary of State Colin Powell, Secretary of Defense Donald Rumsfeld, and National Security Adviser Condoleezza Rice, who constitute one of the most experienced national security teams in the history of the presidency.

Bush's choice of his national security team has been more than vindicated by the rapid overthrow of the Taliban regime in Afghanistan. That team of what once had been deprecated as "retreads" is impressive in that it reflects a healthy diversity of viewpoints but has not evinced the scarcely concealed bureaucratic conflict that afflicted many earlier national security teams. It is too early to tell how Bush's domestic team will shake down. Its most controversial member by far is Attorney General John Ashcroft, whom Bush may be employing as a lightning rod, much as President Eisenhower left it to Secretary of State John Foster Dulles and Chief of Staff Sherman Adams to promulgate policies that clashed with his own image as an ecumenical head of state.

Effectiveness As a Public Communicator

In a manner that is reminiscent of the early Harry S Truman, George W. Bush began his presidency with an unassertive, less-than-fluent approach to public communication. He did not address the public as often as many of his predecessors had, and his public presentations were awkward and unpolished. He also met with the press infrequently and took a minimalist approach to his responsibilities as the nation's symbolic leader. Thus, he did not seize upon an outbreak of racial disturbances in Cincinnati, Ohio, to address the nation, and he failed to take part in the welcome for the air force personnel who had been interned on Hainan Island. The result, as columnist David Broder commented, was that Bush's political persona lacked "clear definition."

Since September 11, George W. Bush has made himself a public presence. Public communication is the realm in which he has been most dramatically transformed. Bush's brief address to the nation on the evening of September 11 was strong in content but brief and flat in delivery. In the days and weeks that followed, he became strikingly more articulate and assertive. During the three days following the suicide bombings, he made strong presentations at the sites of the World Trade Center and Pentagon disaster and delivered a moving set of remarks at the memorial service for the tragedy's victims in the National Cathedral. He went on in later weeks to give forceful addresses to a joint session of Congress and the United Nations General Assembly and to field the questions of journalists in rich detail at his October 11 press conference. He has even begun to preside over Bill Clinton–style town halls.

Coda

As these remarks were written, the unexpectedly eventful Bush presidency was less than a year old. There remained the lesson of the first President Bush, who in the immediate aftermath of the Gulf War achieved the highest public approval rating in the history of the Gallup poll, a record the younger Bush has now exceeded. A year after the Gulf War, the focus of public attention shifted from military victory to economic malaise and George H.W. Bush was defeated for reelection. How will the second Bush presidency fare? We can only watch and wait. ∎

The International Context

Every political system in the world has some form of executive leadership, explains the political scientist Richard Rose. The American system, which features an independent executive branch, is atypical; the top executive in most modern democracies is the prime minister, who also serves as the head of the legislative branch. Some nations—such as France—have both a president and a prime minister.

In this selection, Rose examines the political systems of the United States, Great Britain, and France in an effort to understand whether these differences in the structure of government make a real difference in the way power is exercised in practice.

Questions

1. What are the main characteristics of a presidential system? Of a prime-ministerial system? Of a hybrid system, such as that of France? What are the implications of these different characteristics for the nature of executive power?
2. How might Richard Neustadt's argument about presidential power (see selection 10.3) be modified if he were writing about executive leadership in Great Britain or France?
3. Do the British and French systems provide lessons for how the American system might be improved?

10.5 Presidents and Prime Ministers (1988)

Richard Rose

The need to give direction to government is universal and persisting. Every country, from Egypt of the pharoahs to contemporary democracies, must maintain political institutions that enable a small group of politicians to make authoritative decisions that are binding on the whole of society. Within every system, one office is of first importance, whether it is called president, prime minister, führer, or dux.

There are diverse ways of organizing the direction of government, not only between democracies and authoritarian regimes, but also among democracies. Switzerland stands at one extreme, with collective direction provided by a federal council whose president rotates from year to year. At the other extreme are countries that claim to centralize authority, under a British-style parliamentary system or in an American or French presidential system, in which one person is directly elected to the supreme office of state.

To what extent are the differences in the formal attributes of office a reflection of substantive differences in how authority is exercised? To what extent do the imperatives of office—the need for electoral support, dependence upon civil servants for advice, and vulnerability to events—impose common responses in practice? Comparing the different methods of giving direction to government in the United States (presidential), Great Britain (prime ministerial and Cabinet), and France (presidential and prime ministerial) can help us understand whether other countries do it—that is, choose a national leader—in a way that is better.

To make comparisons requires concepts that can identify the common elements in different offices. Three concepts organize the comparisons I make: the career that leads to the top; the institutions and powers of government; and the scope for variation within a country, whether arising from events or personalities.

Career Leading to the Top

By definition, a president or prime minister is unrepresentative by being the occupant of a unique office. The diversity of outlooks and skills that can be attributed to white, university-educated males is inadequate to predict how people with the same social characteristics—a Carter or an Eisenhower; a Wilson or a Heath—will perform in office. Nor is it helpful to consider the recruitment of national leaders deductively, as a management consultant or personnel officer would, first identifying the skills required for the job and then evaluating candidates on the basis of a priori requirements. National leaders are not recruited by examination; they are self-selected, individuals whose driving ambitions, personal attributes, and, not least, good fortune, combine to win the highest public office.

To understand what leaders can do in office we need to compare the skills acquired in getting to the top with the skills required once there. The tasks that a president or prime minister must undertake are few but central: sustaining popular support through responsiveness to the electorate, and being effective in government. Success in office encourages electoral popularity, and electoral popularity is an asset in wielding influence within government.

The previous careers of presidents and prime ministers are significant, insofar as experience affects what they do in office—and what they do well. A politician who had spent many years concentrating upon campaigning to win popularity may continue to cultivate popularity in office. By contrast, a politician experienced in dealing with the problems of government from within may be better at dealing effectively with international and domestic problems.

Two relevant criteria for comparing the careers of national leaders are: previous experience of government, and previous experience of party and mass electoral politics. American presidents are outstanding in their experience of campaigning for mass support, whereas French presidents are outstanding for their prior knowledge of government from the inside. British prime ministers usually combine experience in both fields.

Thirteen of the fourteen Americans who . . . [were] nominated for president of the United States by the Democratic or Republican parties . . . [between 1945 and

1984] had prior experience in running for major office, whether at the congressional, gubernatorial or presidential level. Campaigning for office makes a politician conscious of his or her need for popular approval. It also cultivates skill in dealing with the mass media. No American will be elected president who has not learned how to campaign across the continent, effectively and incessantly. Since selection as a presidential candidate is dependent upon winning primaries, a president must run twice: first to win the party nomination and then to win the White House. The effort required is shown by the fact that in 1985, three years before the presidential election, one Republican hopeful campaigned in twenty-four states, and a Democratic hopeful in thirty. Immediately after the 1986 congressional elections ended, the media started featuring stories about the 1988 campaign.

Campaigning is different from governing. Forcing ambitious politicians to concentrate upon crossing and recrossing America reduces the time available for learning about problems in Washington and the rest of the world. The typical postwar president has had no experience working within the executive branch. The way in which the federal government deals with foreign policy, or with problems of the economy is known, if at all, from the vantage point of a spectator. A president is likely to have had relatively brief experience in Congress. As John F. Kennedy's career illustrates, Congress is not treated as a means of preparing to govern; it is a launching pad for a presidential campaign. The last three presidential elections have been won by individuals who could boast of having no experience in Washington. Jimmy Carter and Ronald Reagan were state governors, experienced at a job that gives no experience in foreign affairs or economic management.

A president who is experienced in campaigning can be expected to continue cultivating the media and seeking a high standing in the opinion polls. Ronald Reagan illustrates this approach. A president may even use campaigning as a substitute for coming to grips with government. Jimmy Carter abandoned Washington for the campaign trail when confronted with mid-term difficulties in 1978. But public relations expertise is only half the job; looking presidential is not the same as acting like a president.

A British prime minister, by contrast, enters office after decades in the House of Commons and years as a Cabinet minister. The average postwar prime minister had spent thirty-two years in Parliament before entering 10 Downing Street. Of that period, thirteen years had been spent as a Cabinet minister. Moreover, the prime minister has normally held the important policy posts of foreign secretary, chancellor of the exchequer or both. The average prime minister has spent eight years in ministerial office, learning to handle foreign and/or economic problems. By contrast with the United States, no prime minister has had postwar experience in state or local government, and by contrast with France, none has been a civil servant since World War II.

The campaign experience of a British prime minister is very much affected by the centrality that politicians give Parliament. A politician seeks to make a mark in debate there. Even in an era of mass media, the elitist doctrine holds that success in the House of Commons produces positive evaluation by journalists and invitations to appear on television, where a politician can establish an image with the national electorate. Whereas an American presidential hopeful has a bottom-up strategy, concentrating upon winning votes in early primaries in Iowa and New Hampshire as a means of securing media attention, a British politician has a top-down approach, starting to campaign in Parliament.

Party is the surrogate for public opinion among British politicians, and with good reason. Success in the Commons is evaluated by a politician's party colleagues. Election to the party leadership is also determined by party colleagues. To become prime minister a politician does not need to win an election; he or she only needs to be elected party leader when the party has a parliamentary majority. Jim Callaghan and Sir Alec Douglas-Home each entered Downing Street this way and lost office in the first general election fought as prime minister.

The lesser importance of the mass electorate to British party leaders is illustrated by the fact that the average popularity rating of a prime minister is usually less than that of an American president. The monthly Gallup poll rating often shows the prime minister approved by less than half the electorate and trailing behind one or more leaders of the opposition.

In the Fifth French Republic, presidents and prime ministers have differed from American presidents, being very experienced in government, and relatively inexperienced in campaigning with the mass electorate. Only one president, François Mitterrand, has followed the British practice of making a political career based on Parliament. Since he was on the opposition side for the first two decades of the Fifth Republic, his experience of the problems of office was like that of a British opposition member of Parliament, and different from that of a minister. Giscard d'Estaing began as a high-flying civil servant and Charles de Gaulle, like Dwight Eisenhower, was schooled in bureaucratic infighting as a career soldier.

When nine different French prime ministers are examined, the significance of a civil service background becomes clear. Every prime minister except for Pierre Mauroy has been a civil servant first. It has been exceptional for a French prime minister to spend decades in Parliament before attaining that office. An Englishman would be surprised that a Raymond Barre or a Couve de Murville had not sat there before becoming prime minister. An American would be even more surprised by the experience that French leaders have had in the ministries as high civil servants, and particularly in dealing with foreign and economic affairs.

The traditional style of French campaigning is plebiscitary. One feature of this is that campaigning need not be incessant. Louis Napoleon is said to have compared elections with baptism; something it is necessary to do—but to do only once. The seven-year fixed term of the French president, about double the statutory life of many national leaders, is in the tradition of infrequent consultation with the electorate.

The French tradition of leadership is also ambivalent; a plebiscite is, after all, a mass mobilization. The weakness of parties, most notably on the Right, which has provided three of the four presidents of the Fifth Republic, encourages a personalistic style of campaigning. The use of the two-ballot method for the popular election of a president further encourages candidates to compete against each other as individuals, just as candidates for the presidential nomination compete against fellow-partisans in a primary. The persistence of divisions between Left and Right ensures any candidate successful in entering the second ballot a substantial bloc of votes, with or without a party endorsement.

On the two central criteria of political leadership, the relationship with the mass electorate, and knowledge of government, there are cross-national contrasts in the typical career. A British or French leader is likely to know far more about government than an American president, but an American politician is likely to be far more experienced in campaigning to win popular approval and elections.

Less for the President to Govern

Journalistic and historical accounts of government often focus on the person and office of the national leader. The American president is deemed to be very powerful because of the immense military force that he can command by comparison to a national leader in Great Britain or France. The power to drop a hydrogen bomb is frequently cited as a measure of the awesome power of an American president; but it is misleading, for no president has ever dropped a hydrogen bomb, and no president has used atomic weapons in more than forty years. Therefore, we must ask: What does an American president (and his European counterparts) do when not dropping a hydrogen bomb?

In an era of big government, a national leader is more a chief than an executive, for no individual can superintend, let alone carry out, the manifold tasks of government. A national leader does not need to make major choices about what government ought to do; he inherits a set of institutions that are committed—by law, by organization, by the professionalism of public employees, and by the expectations of voters—to appropriate a large amount of the country's resources in order to produce the program outputs of big government.

Whereas political leadership is readily personalized, government is intrinsically impersonal. It consists of collective actions by organizations that operate according to impersonal laws. Even when providing benefits to individuals, such as education, health care, or pensions, the scale of a ministry or a large regional or local government is such as to make the institution appear impersonal.

Contemporary Western political systems are first of all governed by the rule of law rather than personal will. When government did few things and actions could be derived from prerogative powers, such as a declaration of war, there was more scope for the initiative of leaders. Today, the characteristic activities of government, accounting for most public expenditure and personnel, are statutory entitlements to benefits of the welfare state. They cannot be overturned by wish or will. . . . Instead of the leader dominating government, government determines much that is done in the leader's name.

In a very real sense, the so-called power of a national leader depends upon actions that his government takes, whether or not this is desired by the leader. Instead of comparing the constitutional powers of leaders, we should compare the resources that are mobilized by the government for which a national leader is nominally responsible. The conventional measure of the size of government is public expenditure as a proportion of the gross national product. By this criterion, French or British government is more powerful than American government. Organization for Economic Cooperation and Development (OECD) statistics show that in 1984 French public expenditure accounted for 49 percent of the national product, British for 45 percent, and American for 37 percent. When attention is directed at central government, as distinct from all levels of government, the contrast is further emphasized. British and French central government collect almost two-fifths of the national product in tax revenue, whereas the American federal government collects only one-fifth.

When a national leader leads, others are meant to follow. The legitimacy of authority means that public employees should do what elected officials direct. In an era of big government, there are far more public employees at hand than in an era when the glory of the state was symbolized by a small number of people clustering around a royal court. Statistics of public employment again show British and French government as much more powerful than American government. Public employment in France accounts for 33 percent of all persons who work, more than Britain, with 31 percent. In the United States, public employment is much less, 18 percent.

The capacity of a national leader to direct public employees is much affected by whether or not such officials are actually employed by central government. France is most centralized, having three times as many public employees working in ministries as in regional or local government. If public enterprises are also reckoned as part of central government, France is even more centralized. In the United States and Great Britain, by contrast, the actual delivery of public services such as education and health is usually shipped out to lower tiers of a federal government, or to a complex of local and functional authorities. Delivering the everyday service of government is deemed beneath the dignity of national leaders in Great Britain. In the United States, central government is deemed too remote to be trusted with such programs as education or police powers.

When size of government is the measure, an American president appears weaker than a French or British leader. By international standards, the United States has a not so big government, for its claim on the national product and the national labor force is below the OECD average. Ronald Reagan is an extreme example of a president who is "antigovernment," but he is not the only example. In the past two decades, the United States has not lagged behind Europe in developing and expanding welfare state institutions that make government big. It has chosen to follow a different route, diverging from the European model of a mixed economy welfare state. Today, the president has very few large-scale program responsibilities, albeit they remain significant: defense and diplomacy, social security, and funding the federal deficit.

By contrast, even an "antigovernment" prime minister such as Margaret Thatcher . . . [found] herself presiding over a government that . . . [claimed] more than two-fifths of the national product in public expenditure. Ministers must answer, collectively and individually in the House of Commons, for all that is done under the authority of an Act of Parliament. In France, the division between president and prime minister makes it easier for the president of the republic to avoid direct entanglement in low status issues of service delivery, but the centralization of government accessarily involves the prime minister and his colleagues.

When attention is turned to the politics of government as distinct from public policies, all leaders have one thing in common, they are engaged in political management, balancing the interplay of forces within government, major economic interests, and public opinion generally. It is no derogation of a national leader's position to say that it has an important symbolic dimension, imposing a unifying and persuasive theme upon what government does. The theme may be relatively clear-cut, as in much of Margaret Thatcher's rhetoric. Or it may be vague and symbolic, as in much of the rhetoric of Charles de Gaulle. The comparative success of Ronald Reagan, an expert in manipulating vague symbols, as against Jimmy Carter, whose technocratic biases were far stronger than his presentational skills, is a reminder of the importance of a national political leader being able to communicate successfully to the nation.

In the United States and France, the president is both head of government and head of state. The latter role makes him president of all the people, just as the former role limits his representative character to governing in the name of a majority (but normally, less than 60 percent) of the voters. A British prime minister does not have the symbolic obligation to represent the country as a whole: the queen does that.

The institutions of government affect how political management is undertaken. The separate election of the president and the legislature in the United States and France create a situation of nominal independence, and bargaining from separate electoral bases. By contrast, the British prime minister is chosen by virtue of being leader of the largest party in the House of Commons. Management of Parliament is thus made much easier by the fact that the British prime minister can normally be assured of a majority of votes there.

An American president has a far more difficult task in managing government than do British and French counterparts. Congress really does determine whether bills become laws, by contrast to the executive domination of law and decree-making in Europe. Congressional powers of appropriation provide a basis for a roving scrutiny of what the executive branch does. There is hardly any bureau that is free from congressional scrutiny, and in many congressional influence may be as strong as presidential influence. By contrast, a French president has significant decree powers and most of the budget can be promulgated. A British prime minister can also invoke the Official Secrets Act and the doctrine of collective responsibility to insulate the effective (that is, the executive) side of government from the representative (that is, Parliament).

Party politics and electoral outcomes, which cannot be prescribed in a democratic constitution, affect the extent to which political management must be invested in persuasion. If management is defined as making an organization serve one's purpose, then Harry Truman gave the classic definition of management as persuasion: "I sit here all day trying to persuade people to do the things they ought to have sense enough to do without my persuading them. That's all the powers of the President amount to." Because both Democratic and Republican parties are loose coalitions, any president will have to invest much effort in persuading fellow partisans, rather than whipping them into line. Given different electoral bases, congressmen may vote their district, rather than their party label. When president and Congress are of opposite parties, then strong party ties weaken the president.

In Great Britain, party competition and election outcomes are expected to produce an absolute majority in the House of Commons for a single party. Given that the prime minister, as party leader, stands and falls with members of Parliament in votes in Parliament and at a general election, a high degree of party discipline is attainable. Given that the Conservative and Labor parties are themselves coalitions of differing factions and tendencies, party management is no easy task. But it is far easier than interparty management, a necessary condition of coalition government, including Continental European governments.

The Fifth Republic demonstrates that important constitutional features are contingent upon election outcomes. Inherent in the constitution of the Fifth Republic is a certain ambiguity about the relationship between president and prime minister. Each president has desired to make his office preeminent. The first three presidents had no difficulty in doing that, for they could rely upon the support of a majority of members of the National Assembly. Cooperation could not be coerced, but it could be relied upon to keep the prime minister subordinate. . . .

Whether the criterion is government's size or the authority of the national leader vis-à-vis other politicians, the conclusion is the same: the political leaders of Great Britain and France can exercise more power than the president of the United States. The American presidency is a relatively weak office. America's population, economy, and military are not good measures of the power of the White House. Imagine what one would say if American institutions were transplanted, more or less wholesale, to some small European democracy. We would not think that such a country had a strong leader.

While differing notably in the separate election of a French president as against a parliamentary election of a British prime minister, both offices centralize authority within a state that is itself a major institution of society.

As long as a French president has a majority in the National Assembly, then this office can have most influence within government, for ministers are unambiguously subordinate to the president. The linkage of a British prime minister's position with a parliamentary majority means that as long as a single party has a majority, a British politician is protected against the risks of cohabitation à la française or à la americaine.

Variation Within Nations

An office sets parameters within which politicians can act, but the more or less formal stipulation of the rules and resources of an office cannot determine exactly what is done. Within these limits, the individual performance of a president or prime minister can be important. Events too are significant; everyday crises tend to frustrate any attempt to plan ahead, and major crises—a war or domestic disaster—can shift the parameters, reducing a politician's scope for action (for example, Watergate) or expanding it (for example, the mass mobilization that Churchill could lead after Dunkirk).

In the abstract language of social science, we can say that the actions of a national leader reflect the interaction of the powers of office, of events, and of personality. But in concrete situations, there is always an inclination to emphasize one or another of these terms. For purposes of exposition, I treat the significance of events and personality separately: each is but one variable in a multivariate outcome.

Social scientists and constitutional lawyers are inherently generalizers, whereas critical events are unique. For example, a study of the British prime ministership that ignored what could be done in wartime would omit an example of powers temporarily stretched to new limits. Similarly, a study of Winston Churchill's capacities must recognize that his personality prevented him from achieving the nation's highest office—until the debacle of 1940 thrust office upon him.

In the postwar era, the American presidency has been especially prone to shock events. Unpredictable and nonrecurring events of importance include the outbreak of the Korean War in 1950, the assassination of President Kennedy in 1963, American involvement in the Vietnam War in the late 1960s, and the Watergate scandal, which led to President Nixon's resignation in 1974. . . .

The creation of the Fifth French Republic followed after events in Vietnam and in Algeria that undermined the authority and legitimacy of the government of the Fourth Republic. The events of May 1968 had a far greater impact in Paris than in any other European country. Whereas in 1958 events helped to create a republic with a president given substantial powers, in 1968 events were intended to reduce the authority of the state.

Great Britain has had relatively uneventful postwar government. Many causes of momentary excitement, such as the 1963 Profumo scandal that embarrassed Harold Macmillan, were trivial. The 1956 Suez war, which forced the resignation of Anthony Eden, did not lead to subsequent changes in the practice of the prime ministership, even though it was arguably a gross abuse of power vis-à-vis Cabinet colleagues and Parliament. The 1982 Falklands war called forth a mood of self-congratulation rather than a cry for institutional reform. The electoral boost it gave the prime minister was significant, but not eventful for the office. . . .

While personal factors are often extraneous to government, each individual incumbent has some scope for choice. Within a set of constraints imposed by office and events, a politician can choose what kind of a leader he or she would like to be. Such choices have political consequences. "Do what you can" is a prudential rule that is often overlooked in discussing what a president or prime minister does. The winnowing process by which one individual reaches the highest political office not only allows for variety, but sometimes invites it, for a challenger for office may win votes by being different from an incumbent.

A president has a multiplicity of roles and a multiplicity of obligations. Many—as commander in chief of the armed forces, delivering a State of the Union message to Congress, and presenting a budget—are requirements of the office; but the capacity to do well in particular roles varies with the individual. For example, Lyndon Johnson was a superb manager of congressional relations, but had little or no feel for foreign affairs. By contrast, John F. Kennedy was interested in foreign affairs and defense and initially had little interest in domestic problems. Ronald Reagan . . . [was] good at talking to people, whereas Jimmy Carter and Richard Nixon preferred to deal with problems on paper. Dwight D. Eisenhower brought to the office a national reputation as a hero that he protected by making unclear public statements. By contrast, Gerald Ford's public relations skills, while acceptable in a congressman, were inadequate to the demands of the contemporary presidency.

In Great Britain, Margaret Thatcher . . . [was] atypical in her desire to govern, as well as preside over government. She . . . [applied] her energy and intelligence to problems of government—and to telling her colleagues what to do about them. The fact that she [wanted] . . . to be *the* decision-maker for British government [excited] . . . resentment among civil servants and Cabinet colleagues. This [was] . . . not only a reaction to her forceful personality, but also an expression of surprise: other prime ministers did not want to be the chief decision-maker in government. In the case of an aging Winston Churchill from 1951–55, this could be explained on grounds of ill health. In the case of Anthony Eden, it could be explained by an ignorance of domestic politics.

The interesting prime ministers are those who chose not to be interventionists across a range of government activities. Both Harold Macmillan and Clement Attlee brought to Downing Street great experience of British government. But Attlee was ready to be simply a chairman of a Cabinet in which other ministers were capable and decisive. Macmillan chose to intervene very selectively on issues that he thought important and to leave others to get on with most matters. . . .

In France, the role of a president varies with personality. De Gaulle approached the presidency with a distinctive concept of the state as well as of politics. By contrast, Mitterand [drew] . . . upon his experience of many decades of being a parliamentarian and a republican. Pompidou was distinctive in playing two roles, first prime minister under de Gaulle, and subsequently president.

Differences between French prime ministers may in part reflect contrasting relationships with a president. As a member of a party different from the president, Chirac . . . [had] partisan and personal incentives to be more assertive than does a prime minister of the same party. Premiers who enter office via the Assembly or local politics, like Chaban-Delmas and Mauroy, are likely to have different priorities than a premier who was first a technocrat, such as Raymond Barre.

Fluctuations in Leaders

The fluctuating effect upon leaders of multiple influences is shown by the monthly ratings of the popularity of presidents and prime ministers. If formal powers of office were all, then the popularity rating of each incumbent should be much the same. This is not the case. If the personal characteristics of a politician were all-important, then differences would occur between leaders, but each leader would receive a consistent rating during his or her term of office. In fact, the popularity of a national leader tends to go up and down during a term of office. Since personality is held constant, these fluctuations cannot be explained as a function of personal qualities. Since there is no consistent decline in popularity, the movement cannot be explained as a consequence of impossible expectations causing the public to turn against whoever initially wins its votes.

The most reasonable explanation of these fluctuations in popularity is that they are caused by events. They may be shock events, such as the threat of military action, or scandal in the leader's office. Alternatively, changes may reflect the accumulation of seemingly small events, most notably those that are reflected in the state of the economy, such as growth, unemployment, and inflation rates. A politician may not be responsible for such trends, but he or she expects to lose popularity when things appear to be going badly and to regain popularity when things are going well.

Through the decades, cyclical fluctuations can reflect an underlying long-term secular trend. In Europe a major secular trend is the declining national importance of international affairs. In the United States events in Iran or Central America remain of as much (or more) significance than events within the United States. In a multipolar world a president is involved in and more vulnerable to events in many places. By contrast, leaders of France and Great Britain have an influence limited to a continental scale, in a world in which international relations has become intercontinental. This shift is not necessarily a loss for heads of government in the European Community. In a world summit meeting, only one nation, the United States, has been first. Japan may seek to exercise political influence matching its growing economic power. The smaller scale of the European Community nations with narrower economic interests creates conditions for frequent contact and useful meetings in the European arena which may bring them marginal advantages in world summit meetings too.

If the power of a national leader is measured, as Robert A. Dahl suggests in *Who Governs?*, by the capacity that such an individual has to influence events in the desired direction, then all national leaders are subject to seeing their power eroded as each nation becomes more dependent upon the joint product of the open international economy. This is as true of debtor nations such as the United States has become, as of nations with a positive trade balance. It is true of economies with a record of persisting growth, such as Germany, and of slow growth economies such as Great Britain.

A powerful national leader is very desirable only if one believes that the *Führerprinzip* is the most important principle in politics. The constitutions and politics of Western industrial nations reject this assumption. Each political system is full of constraints upon arbitrary rule, and sometimes of checks and balances that are obstacles to prompt, clear-cut decisions.

The balance between effective leadership and responsiveness varies among the United States, Great Britain, and France. A portion of that variation is organic, being prescribed in a national constitution. This is most evident in a comparison of the United States and Great Britain, but constitutions are variables, as the history of postwar France demonstrates. Many of the most important determinants of what a national leader does are a reflection of changing political circumstances, of trends, and shock events, and of the aspirations and shortcomings of the individual in office. ■

View from the Inside

At the White House—as at millions of other workplaces—September 11, 2001, started out as just another workday. But the routine was soon shattered by news of the worst terrorist attacks in American history. In this memoir, White House speechwriter David Frum recalls the events of that long and painful day.

Question

1. Were critics justified in suggesting that Bush could have handled the events of 9/11 more effectively? What might he have done differently?

10.6 September 11, 2001 (2003)

David Frum

Inside the White House, the events of September 11 began just the way they did for everyone else: on television. But for those of us who worked there, the events did not remain on the screen for very long.

I arrived at work late that morning. Washington's highway traffic, never good, was especially horrible that day, and I had to inch my way to the office from my children's school, too irritated even to listen to the radio. I did not pull into the little strip of parking spaces in front of the old Executive Office Building until a few minutes after nine.

My cell phone rang as I reached my desk. It was my wife's gentle voice that first introduced me to the hard facts of our new life: Two hijacked planes had crashed into the World Trade Center. The twin towers were burning. Thousands of people were in danger. The United States had been attacked.

Hours after the bombing of Pearl Harbor, Eleanor Roosevelt declared on the radio that "the moment we all dreaded had arrived." September 11 was a moment that had been dreaded by almost nobody except for a few terrorism experts. A quiet August was slipping unnoticeably into a golden September. Americans felt safe and remote from the troubles of the rest of the globe. The president's long vacation from Washington had ended; the country's long vacation from history had promised to go on and on.

Now history had exploded on us like a bomb, killing God knows how many thousands of people. I rushed to my desk and turned on my television. And there it was: the worst crime ever recorded on videotape.

I suddenly recollected that I was supposed to cross the Potomac River at noon to have lunch with a friend over at the Pentagon. I telephoned his office to cancel: Nobody, I thought unprophetically, would be leaving his or her desk today. My friend's assistant picked up the phone. I began to say that something terrible in New York had happened, we would all be needed at our posts . . . but she cut me off. "They're evacuating this building," she said grimly. "I cannot talk. We must leave."

I turned the television's sound back on. They were reporting that a third plane had struck the Pentagon—a truck bombing was reported at the State Department—fires had been set on the National Mall. My wife called again, her voice

---

taut and strained. "The White House will be next! You have to get out of there—don't wait, please hurry!"

I felt a surge of . . . what? Battle fever? Mulishness? I only remember how hot my ears felt. "No!" I said fiercely. "*No!* I am not leaving!" I clicked off the phone, ready to . . . well, I don't know what I was ready to do—whatever it is that speechwriters do in times of war. Type, I suppose—but type with renewed patriotism and zeal. And at precisely that blood-boiling moment, a Secret Service agent was pounding on my door, shouting, "Everybody must evacuate this building now—this is an order—everybody must evacuate now!" A face popped through the doorway. "*You!* Out—now! *Now!*"

My heroic moment had lasted less than two minutes. I stepped out into the corridor. The tiled hallways of the Executive Office Building are wide enough and high enough for a chariot race. No matter how many people they hold, they always look and sound half-empty . . . but not that day. Little streams of clicking feet merged into rivers of footsteps, and then into a torrent. "Don't run!" the guards shouted, and the torrent slowed. We poured through the tall, carved oak doors of the building onto the avenue between the Executive Office Building and the West Wing of the White House and were reinforced by another rivulet of secretaries and staffers.

The guards suddenly changed their minds. "*Run!*" they now shouted. "Ladies—if you can't run in heels, kick off your shoes."

The northwest gate to the White House was thrown open, and out we all raced. More guards waited for us on Lafayette Square. "Keep going!" The offices in the town houses along the west side of the square emptied themselves into the crowd. "Don't stop!"

We ran past the statues of Count Rochambeau, the hero of Yorktown, and General Steuben, who drilled Washington's army. We ran alongside Andrew Jackson astride his horse, Sam Patch. We ran under the windows of the house of Commodore Stephen Decatur ("Our country! . . . may she always be in the right—but our country, right or wrong!"). We finally halted on the south side of H Street. "Take your badges off!" shouted another guard, and we pulled over our heads the blue or orange plastic cards that might mark us for a sniper. And there we stood: banished from our offices, stripped of our identifiers, helpless and baffled.

During the fighting in Afghanistan, it became popular for White House staffers to wear red, white, and blue plastic cards around their necks with the motto "These colors don't run." But that day they did run, and I ran with them, and I will never fully extract the sting of that memory.

The crowd of staffers milled aimlessly about the streets. Senior directors of the National Security Council, presidential assistants, and officers in uniform stood on the sidewalks, punching again and again at the dial pads of their cell phones, unable to get a signal, unable to keep a signal if they did get it, uncertain of where to go or what to do. The White House's emergency plans dated back to the cold war and were intended to protect the president, the vice president, and a handful of top aides against a nuclear attack. The rest of the staff, it was quietly assumed, would have been vaporized into radioactive dust.

But here we all were, alive but shaken, knowing less about what was going on in the world than a CNN viewer in Tasmania. I spotted John McConnell, the vice president's speechwriter. "We're just a couple of blocks from the American Enterprise Institute," I proposed. "They'll have land lines and television sets. And maybe we'll be able to think of something useful to do." We struck off across Farragut Square—and arrived to the news that the south tower of the World Trade Center had collapsed, killing unknown thousands of people inside.

Chris DeMuth, AEI's president, greeted McConnell and me like sailors hauled in from the water. He offered us offices and telephones, Internet connections and e-mail—"Whatever you need," he said urgently.

McConnell and I had been trying for an hour to reach Michael Gerson by pager, by phone, by e-mail. We would have sent pigeons if we had had them. We finally found him at his home in Alexandria. He had been late to work that morning, too—and had been stuck in a traffic jam underneath the flight path of American Airlines Flight 77 when it crashed into the Pentagon.

Gerson told us that DaimlerChrysler had volunteered its Washington office as an improvised headquarters for the White House staff. We should walk over and get to work at once on a statement the president could issue on his return to Washington. It would be impossible for Gerson to enter the city. He would work from home.

A statement for the president. But what would it say? What *could* it say?

McConnell and I set off again. It was drawing close to noon. A security perimeter was being drawn around the center of Washington, D.C. To reach the DaimlerChrysler building we had to cross a police line, guarded by uniformed Secret Service agents who scrutinized our passes with unusual minuteness.

I had assumed that the federal government had designated these offices in advance for emergency use. In fact, the only reason we were here was that somebody on the White House staff was married to somebody in DaimlerChrysler's management, who offered up the premises in a spontaneous gesture. It was about 11:45. I was pointed to an office and told it was mine for the day. Its regular tenant gave me his long-distance dialing codes, showed me how to work his e-mail, packed his briefcase, and shook my hand on his way through the door.

There's an old political—okay, Republican—joke about the biggest lie in the world being "I'm from the government, and I'm here to help you." The joke didn't seem very funny on September 11. We were from the government, and as far as the people at DaimlerChrysler were concerned, we *were* here to help them—by helping their president defend their country. And they in turn wanted to help us.

Somehow they had contrived to set out trays of sandwiches, bowls of salad, cookies, cake, coffee, and soft drinks before they left. Anxious, weary, and parched, the ravenous White House staffers wolfed down the food and then settled at DaimlerChrysler's computers and telephones.

The White House was now distributed in three principal places, with stragglers spread throughout the capital. The mid-level staff was here at 1401 H Street. The vice president and his chief of staff, Lewis Libby; National Security Adviser Condoleezza Rice; Deputy Chief of Staff Josh Bolten—they were all beneath the White House in a hardened bunker. And the president, Chief of Staff Andy Card, and the top political and communications aides were flying westward on Air Force One.

The president had been reading to the second-grade class at the Emma E. Booker Elementary School in Sarasota, Florida, when Card whispered into his ear the confirmation that the plane crashes in New York City were terrorist attacks. He finished reading and then approached the microphones. Reprising a line of his father's from ten years before, he declared that terrorism against the United States "would not stand."

It is hard to govern during an age of instantaneous broadcast. There were no microphones to preserve every quaver in Abraham Lincoln's voice after the firing on Fort Sumter; we cannot study Franklin Delano Roosevelt's face for traces of uncertainty in the seconds after Pearl Harbor. There would be much criticism of Bush's seeming disorientation and unease in the early hours after the attack. Well, who that day *wasn't* disoriented and uneasy? Yet we do live in an age of instantaneous media and have no choice but to play by its rules—and those rules would treat Bush harshly from his first remarks that morning until he returned to Washington that night.

The president ordered Air Force One to fly back to Washington as swiftly as possible. But as the president's plane approached the capital, the Secret Service received intelligence suggesting that the plane was a terrorist target, too. It would take many days for that intelligence to be proved false. So the big jet was rerouted to Barksdale Air Force Base in Louisiana. The president disembarked there to address a shocked and terrified nation at 12:40 eastern time: "The resolve of our great nation is being tested," he said. "But make no mistake: We will show the world that we will pass this test. God bless."

The words were correct and reassuring. The images were not. Air force bases do not come equipped with television studios, so the president was obliged to record his message in a bare room over a herky-jerky digital connection. He looked and sounded like the hunted, not the hunter. Even such a good friend of the administration as the editorial page of *The Wall Street Journal* cuttingly commented that Bush's flight from air force base to air force base before finally returning to the capital showed that he "could not be frightened away for long, if at all."

With Air Force One apparently a target, and the White House shuttered and largely useless, Bush proceeded to Strategic Command at Offutt Air Force Base in Nebraska. From Offutt the president can command the defense of the nation's airspace, if need be, and teleconference with his National Security Council.

As Bush flew westward, taking phone calls, gathering information, and deciding upon his and the nation's course, his writers were pacing and talking and drafting and redrafting a formal message that the president could deliver to the nation from the Oval Office that evening.

By now, Matthew Scully had made his way to the DaimlerChrysler building, and he, McConnell, and I gathered around a computer screen, with Gerson on the other end of a phone line. When we finished, we fired the text to Gerson's home; he edited it some more and then forwarded it to Hughes.

Our work was interrupted by a terrible bulletin. McConnell had said to me on our walk through the empty city: "There are going to be thousands and thousands of funerals in this country over the next week. Everybody is going to know someone among the dead." Now it was our turn. My wife telephoned into our office. She could barely speak. She had learned that Barbara Olson, wife of Solicitor General Theodore Olson, had been one of the passengers aboard the flight that crashed into the Pentagon. In the confusion and terror of the hijacking, Barbara Olson had somehow found the cool and courage to call her husband on her cell phone. Her call gave the government early notice of the seizure of a third plane. Her last words expressed her infinite faith in Ted: "The pilot is here with me. Tell him what to do."

I keep a transliteration of the Kaddish, the Jewish prayer for the dead, on my PalmPilot. I stepped out of our little office, retreated to the photocopy room, closed the door, and looked around for something with which to cover my head. I could find nothing, so I pulled my arms out of my jacket, pulled it up and over my head like a shawl, recited the ancient words, and mourned my brave and beautiful friend.

The sun was setting. Information circulated that the president would be returning to Washington at about eight o'clock and that the White House would be reopened to staff. McConnell, Scully, and I decided to return to the office in case we were needed for something. We cleared our desks and gathered up our notes and copies of our e-mails for the presidential record keepers. I left a short note of thanks for the man whose desk I had occupied all day, but I have a bad feeling that the record keepers scooped it up, too. We stepped out of the office, into the elevator, and out of the building—into a world transformed.

Washington was empty and silent, save for the screams of sirens far off in the distance and the periodic roar of F-16s overhead. Entire city blocks were cordoned off by yellow police tape. Uniformed guards checked our passes every fifty feet. Black-clad paramilitary agents clutching murderous automatic weapons surveyed us skeptically. Otherwise, there were no people to be seen. A sad and lonely stillness had settled upon the central precinct of American power.

We were all weary from the emotions that had surged through us that day: fear and rage and grief. But we were not depleted. The fear and the rage receded, the grief had to be postponed. What was left was a budding tenderness toward every symbol of this wounded country. The lights that illuminated the monuments of the capital had been defiantly switched on. The evening air was sweet and soft. And we looked with new and more loving eyes at the familiar streets. There! There was the Treasury Department—where they would mobilize the limitless resources of the nation for war. There! There was the East Wing, the office of the First Lady, who had visited Congress that morning—and who could have easily numbered among the dead had the fourth hijacked jet struck the Capitol. And there! There! There was the flag over the White House. Tomorrow it would be lowered to half-staff. Today it flew high, brilliantly lit, in defiance of all terror—still gallantly streaming, just as it had for an imprisoned poet on the deck of an enemy warship two centuries ago.

The day's violence seemed to be over for the moment. The night was quiet. But tomorrow? What would happen tomorrow? And the next day?

McConnell, Scully, and I drew near the black iron fence around the White House. We showed our passes once more, and a guard radioed our names to some authority inside. A long wait—and then one by one we were permitted to step through the gate.

Even on the dullest day, stepping from the outside to the inside of the White House gate feels like crossing into a forbidden city. But never before had the line of separation felt so thick and high. The silent, patrolled city beyond the lush lawn and the still-thick greenery of the trees, beyond the sensors, the fence, and the gates, fell away behind us into remoteness and invisibility as we trudged along West Executive Avenue to the entrance to the West Wing. We stepped under the white canopy that extends from the side doorway to the avenue—and into a building that was humming back to life after the longest session of inactivity perhaps in its existence.

We entered the small basement suite of offices that Gerson and his assistant shared with another senior staffer and his assistant. We turned on the television, sat on a couch, and watched the president walk briskly across the South Lawn to the Oval Office. There was an hour to wait before he would speak to the country.

The screens began to flash images of the White House as the networks readied themselves for the president's message. My mind traveled backward through all the images of this president those same networks had shown the American people since he had emerged on the national scene two years before. Had they seen a man in whom they could place their trust? It was nine o'clock. We were about to learn. ∎

 # Chapter 11

The Bureaucracy

Bureaucracy is a pervasive and inescapable fact of modern existence. Every large organization in society—not just the government—is managed by a bureaucratic system: tasks are divided among particular experts, and decisions are made and administered according to general rules and regulations. No one who has attended a university, worked for a large corporation, served in the military, or dealt with the government is unfamiliar with the nature of bureaucracies.

Bureaucracies, as the sociologist Max Weber observed, are a necessary feature of modern life. When social organizations are small—as in a small business or a small academic department—decisions can be made and programs carried out by a few individuals using informal procedures and with a minimum of red tape and paperwork. As these organizations grow, it becomes increasingly necessary to delegate authority, develop methods of tracking and assessment, and create general rules instead of deciding matters on a case-by-case basis. Suddenly a bureaucracy has arisen.

In the political realm, bureaucracies serve another purpose. Beginning with the Pendleton Act of 1883, civil service reformers sought to insulate routine governmental decisions from the vagaries of partisan politics—to ensure, in other words, that decisions were made on the basis of merit instead of on the basis of party affiliation. The Pendleton Act greatly reduced the number of presidential appointments in such departments as the Customs Service and the Post Office, putting in place an early version of the merit system. As the federal government's responsibilities grew, the need to keep politics out of such functions as tax collection, administration of social security and welfare, and similar programs became even greater.

The bureaucratization of government therefore serves important purposes: increasing efficiency, promoting fairness, ensuring accountability. Yet at the same time, it creates problems of its own. Bureaucracies have a tendency to grow, to become rigid, to become answerable only to themselves, and to create barriers between citizens and the government. These bureaucratic "pathologies" are well known; they are the subject of frequent editorials and commentaries. Politicians can always count on stories about bureaucratic inefficiency and callousness to strike a chord with the voting public.

The selections in this chapter cover the bureaucracy from several different viewpoints. In selection 11.1, the sociologist Max Weber provides the classic description of the bureaucratic form of governmental power; in selection 11.2, the political scientist James Q. Wilson updates Weber, examining what government agencies do and why they do it.

Selection 11.3 looks at bureaucracies in comparative perspective, while selection 11.4 examines the bureaucracy in action, with a dramatic account of the cooperative effort to track down two snipers suspects in Washington, D.C.

As you read these selections, keep in mind that the alternative to bureaucratic government in the modern world is not some sort of utopian system in which all decisions are fair, all programs efficient, all children above average. Limiting the power of bureaucracies means increasing the power of other institutions: Congress, the presidency, private businesses, or the courts. Reducing the power of the bureaucracy may also create a government that is less fair or less accountable.

Also keep in mind that bureaucrats—like baseball umpires—are most noticeable when they make mistakes. Americans tend to take for granted the extraordinary number of government programs that work well: the letters delivered correctly and on time, the meat inspected properly, the airplanes that land safely. Criticism and evaluation of the bureaucracy must be kept in a reasonable perspective.

Chapter Questions

1. What role does the bureaucracy play in any large social system? What functions does the bureaucracy perform? What are its most significant characteristics?
2. What is the relationship between the bureaucracy and the other political institutions in the United States? What are the alternatives to bureaucratic power? What are the advantages and disadvantages of these other forms of power?

 # Foundations

Any discussion about bureaucracy—in the United States or anywhere else—must begin with Max Weber, who is best known for his work laying the intellectual foundation for the study of modern sociology. Weber wrote extensively on modern social and political organization; his works include the unfinished *Wirtschaft und Gesellschaft* [Economy and Society] (1922) and the influential *The Protestant Ethic and the Spirit of Capitalism* (1904–1905).

Weber was born in Thuringia, in what is now eastern Germany, in 1864; he died in 1920. Although his observations on bureaucracy draw on historical and contemporary European examples, they were heavily informed by his experiences in the United States. While traveling in the New World, Weber was struck by the role of bureaucracy in a democratic society. The problem, as he saw it, was that a modern democracy required bureaucratic structures of all kinds in the administration of government and even in the conduct of professional party politics. Handing over the reins to a class of unelected "experts," however, threatened to undermine the very basis of democracy itself. In particular, Weber stressed two problems: the unaccountability of unelected civil servants and the bureaucratic tendency toward inflexibility in the application of rules.

In this brief selection, Weber describes the essential nature of bureaucracy.

Questions

1. What are the characteristics of the bureaucratic form of governmental power? What are bureaucracy's strong points? Weak points?
2. Why are rules so important in a bureaucracy? What are the advantages and disadvantages of making decisions on the basis of general rules, rather than on a case-by-case basis?

11.1 Bureaucracy (1922)

Max Weber

I: Characteristics of Bureaucracy

Modern officialdom functions in the following specific manner:

I. There is the principle of fixed and official jurisdictional areas, which are generally ordered by rules, that is, by laws or administrative regulations.

1. The regular activities required for the purposes of the bureaucratically governed structure are distributed in a fixed way as official duties.

2. The authority to give the commands required for the discharge of these duties is distributed in a stable way and is strictly delimited by rules concerning the coercive means, physical, sacerdotal, or otherwise, which may be placed at the disposal of officials.

3. Methodical provision is made for the regular and continuous fulfillment of these duties and for the execution of the corresponding rights; only persons who have the generally regulated qualifications to serve are employed.

In public and lawful government these three elements constitute "bureaucratic authority." In private economic domination, they constitute bureaucratic "management." Bureaucracy, thus understood, is fully developed in political and ecclesiastical communities only in the modern state, and, in the private economy, only in the most advanced institutions of capitalism. Permanent and public office authority, with fixed jurisdiction, is not the historical rule but rather the exception. This is so even in large political structures such as those of the ancient Orient, the Germanic and Mongolian empires of conquest, or of many feudal structures of state. In all these cases, the ruler executes the most important measures through personal trustees, table-companions, or court-servants. Their commissions and authority are not precisely delimited and are temporarily called into being for each case.

II. The principles of office hierarchy and of levels of graded authority mean a firmly ordered system of super- and subordination in which there is a supervision of the lower offices by the higher ones. Such a system offers the governed the possibility of appealing the decision of a lower office to its higher authority, in a definitely regulated manner. With the full development of the bureaucratic type, the office hierarchy is monocratically organized. The principle of hierarchical office authority is found in all bureaucratic structures: in state and ecclesiastical structures as well as in large party organizations and private enterprises. It does not matter for the character of bureaucracy whether its authority is called "private" or "public."

When the principle of jurisdictional "competency" is fully carried through, hierarchical subordination—at least in public office—does not mean that the "higher" authority is simply authorized to take over the business of the "lower." Indeed, the opposite is the rule. Once established and having fulfilled its task, an office tends to continue in existence and be held by another incumbent.

III. The management of the modern office is based upon written documents ("the files"), which are preserved in their original or draught form. There is, therefore, a staff of subaltern officials and scribes of all sorts. The body of officials actively engaged in a "public" office, along with the respective apparatus of material implements and the files, make up a "bureau." In private enterprise, "the bureau" is often called "the office."

In principle, the modern organization of the civil service separates the bureau from the private domicile of the official, and, in general, bureaucracy segregates official activity as something distinct from the sphere of private life. Public monies and equipment are divorced from the private property of the official. This condition is everywhere the product of a long development. Nowadays, it is found in public as well as in private enterprises; in the latter, the principle extends even to the leading entrepreneur. In principle, the executive office is separated from the household, business from private correspondence, and business assets from private fortunes. The more consistently the modern type of business management has been carried through the more are these separations the case. The beginnings of this process are to be found as early as the Middle Ages.

It is the peculiarity of the modern entrepreneur that he conducts himself as the "first official" of his enterprise, in the very same way in which the ruler of a specifically modern bureaucratic state spoke of himself as "the first servant" of the state. The idea that the bureau activities of the state are intrinsically different in character from the management of private economic offices is a continental European notion and, by way of contrast, is totally foreign to the American way.

IV. Office management, at least all specialized office management—and such management is distinctly modern—usually presupposes thorough and expert training. This increasingly holds for the modern executive and employee of private enterprises, in the same manner as it holds for the state official.

V. When the office is fully developed, official activity demands the full working capacity of the official, irrespective of the fact that his obligatory time in the bureau may be firmly delimited. In the normal case, this is only the product of a long development, in the public as well as in the private office. Formerly, in all cases, the normal state of affairs was reversed: official business was discharged as a secondary activity.

VI. The management of the office follows general rules, which are more or less stable, more or less exhaustive, and which can be learned. Knowledge of these rules represents a special technical learning which the officials possess. It involves jurisprudence, or administrative or business management.

The reduction of modern office management to rules is deeply embedded in its very nature. The theory of modern public administration, for instance, assumes that the authority to order certain matters by decree—which has been legally granted to public authorities—does not entitle the bureau to regulate the matter by commands given for each case, but only to regulate the matter abstractly. This stands in extreme contrast to the regulation of all relationships through individual privileges and bestowals of favor, which is absolutely dominant in patrimonialism, at least in so far as such relationships are not fixed by sacred tradition. . . .

Technical Advantages of Bureaucratic Organization

The decisive reason for the advance of bureaucratic organization has always been its purely technical superiority over any other form of organization. The fully developed bureaucratic mechanism compares with other organizations exactly as does the machine with the nonmechanical modes of production.

Precision, speed, unambiguity, knowledge of the files, continuity, discretion, unity, strict subordination, reduction of friction and of material and personal costs—these are raised to the optimum point in the strictly bureaucratic administration, and especially in its monocratic form. As compared with all collegiate, honorific, and avocational forms of administration, trained bureaucracy is superior on all these points. And as far as complicated tasks are concerned, paid bureaucratic work is not only more precise but, in the last analysis, it is often cheaper than even formally unremunerated honorific service.

Honorific arrangements make administrative work an avocation and, for this reason alone, honorific service normally functions more slowly; being less bound to schemata and being more formless. Hence it is less precise and less unified than bureaucratic work because it is less dependent upon superiors and because the establishment and exploitation of the apparatus of subordinate officials and filing services are almost unavoidably less economical. Honorific service is less continuous than bureaucratic and frequently quite expensive. This is especially the case if one thinks not only of the money costs to the public treasury—costs which bureaucratic administration, in comparison with administration by notables, usually substantially increases—but also of the frequent economic losses of the governed caused by delays and lack of precision. The possibility of administration by notables normally and permanently exists only where official management can be satisfactorily discharged as an avocation. With the qualitative increase of tasks the administration has to face, administration by notables reaches its limits—today, even in England. Work organized by collegiate bodies causes friction and delay and requires compromises between colliding interests and views. The administration, therefore, runs less precisely and is more independent of superiors; hence, it is less unified and slower. All advances of the Prussian administrative organization have been and will in the future be advances of the bureaucratic, and especially of the monocratic, principle.

Today, it is primarily the capitalist market economy which demands that the official business of the administration be discharged precisely, unambiguously, continuously, and with as much speed as possible. Normally, the very large, modern capitalist enterprises are themselves unequalled models of strict bureaucratic organization. Business management throughout rests on increasing precision, steadiness, and, above all, the speed of operations. This, in turn, is determined by the peculiar nature of the modern means of communication, including, among other things, the news service of the press. The extraordinary increase in the speed by which public announcements, as well as economic and political facts, are transmitted exerts a steady and sharp pressure in the direction of speeding up the tempo of administrative reaction towards various situations. The optimum of such reaction time is normally attained only by a strictly bureaucratic organization.

Bureaucratization offers above all the optimum possibility for carrying through the principle of specializing administrative functions according to purely objective considerations. Individual performances are allocated to functionaries who have specialized training and who by constant practice learn more and more. The "objective" discharge of business primarily means a discharge of business according to *calculable rules* and "without regard for persons."

"Without regard for persons" is also the watchword of the "market" and, in general, of all pursuits of naked economic interests. A consistent execution of bureaucratic domination means the leveling of status "honor." Hence, if the principle of the free-market is not at the same time restricted, it means the universal domination of the "class situation." That this consequence of bureaucratic domination has not set in everywhere, parallel to the extent of bureaucratization, is due to the differences among possible principles by which polities may meet their demands.

The second element mentioned, "calculable rules," also is of paramount importance for modern bureaucracy. The peculiarity of modern culture, and specifically of its technical and economic basis, demands this very "calculability" of results. . . . [The] specific nature [of bureaucracy], which is welcomed by capitalism, develops the more perfectly the more the bureaucracy is "dehumanized," the more completely it succeeds in eliminating from official business love, hatred, and all purely personal, irrational, and emotional elements which escape calculation. This is the specific nature of bureaucracy and it is appraised as its special virtue.

The more complicated and specialized modern culture becomes, the more its external supporting apparatus demands the personally detached and strictly "objective" *expert*, in lieu of the master of older social structures, who was moved by personal sympathy and favor, by grace and gratitude. Bureaucracy offers the attitudes demanded by the external apparatus of modern culture in the most favorable combination. As a rule, only bureaucracy has established the foundation for the administration of a rational law conceptually systematized on the basis of such enactments as the latter Roman imperial period first created with a high degree of technical perfection. During the Middle Ages, this law was received along with the bureaucratization of legal administration, that is to say, with the displacement of the old trial procedure which was bound to tradition or to irrational presuppositions, by the rationally trained and specialized expert. ■

American Politics Today

Critics of the American bureaucracy frequently attack the public sector as wasteful, inefficient, and unaccountable to the public. Such criticisms, however, are frequently nothing more than cheap shots, for they ignore the very great differences between the public and private sectors. A fair appraisal of the public bureaucracy must begin with a clear view of what we expect from the public sector and of the constraints under which it must operate.

The government, as James Q. Wilson points out in the following selection, does indeed compare badly to the private sector when viewed in terms of economic efficiency. The problem, he suggests, is that government is constrained in ways that the private sector is not. And those constraints, he concludes, come from the people themselves. It is the people—expressing themselves individually, by way of interest groups, or through the legislature—who impose the constraints under which the bureaucracy must operate.

Central to Wilson's argument is his attempt to broaden the concept of efficiency to include more than economic efficiency. If we measure governmental action by the simple standard of economic efficiency—that is, the cost per unit output—government compares badly to the private sector. Once we recognize that a true measure of bureaucratic efficiency must take into account *"all* of the valued outputs"—including honesty, accountability, and responsiveness to particular constituents—the equation becomes more complicated, and perhaps more favorable to the government.

Wilson's argument is no whitewash for the government bureaucracy. Even if we allow for all of this, as he points out, government agencies may still be inefficient. Recognizing the multifaceted and complex constraints on government officials will, in any event, provide a reasonable and realistic way to evaluate the bureaucracy.

Questions

1. Wilson suggests that government officials operate under very different constraints from their counterparts in the private sector. What are these differences, and what is their effect? Put another way, why does Wilson assert that "the government can't say 'yes' "?
2. What values other than economic efficiency do we demand of government? Why is the avoidance of arbitrariness so important?

11.2 Bureaucracy: What Government Agencies Do and Why They Do It (1989)

James Q. Wilson

On the morning of May 22, 1986, Donald Trump, the New York real estate developer, called one of his executives, Anthony Gliedman, into his office. They discussed the inability of the City of New York, despite six years of effort and the expenditure of nearly $13 million, to rebuild the ice-skating rink in Central Park. On May 28 Trump offered to take over the rink reconstruction, promising to do the job in less than six months. A week later Mayor Edward Koch accepted the offer and shortly thereafter the city appropriated $3 million on the understanding that Trump would have to pay for any cost overruns out of his own pocket. On October 28, the renovation was complete, over a month ahead of schedule and about $750,000 under budget. Two weeks later, skaters were using it.

For many readers it is obvious that private enterprise is more efficient than are public bureaucracies, and so they would file this story away as simply another illustration of what everyone already knows. But for other readers it is not so obvious what this story means; to them, business is greedy and unless watched like a hawk will fob off shoddy or overpriced goods on the American public, as when it sells the government $435 hammers and $3,000 coffeepots. Trump may have done a good job in this instance, but perhaps there is something about skating rinks or New York City government that gave him a comparative advantage; in any event, no larger lessons should be drawn from it.

Some lessons can be drawn, however, if one looks closely at the incentives and constraints facing Trump and the Department of Parks and Recreation. It becomes apparent that there is not one "bureaucracy problem" but several, and the solution to each in some degree is incompatible with the solution to every other. First there is the problem of accountability—getting agencies to serve agreed-upon goals. Second there is the problem of equity—treating all citizens fairly, which usually means treating them alike on the basis of clear rules known in advance. Third there is the problem of responsiveness—reacting reasonably to the special needs and circumstances of particular people. Fourth there is the problem of efficiency—obtaining the greatest output for a given level of resources. Finally there is the problem of fiscal integrity—assuring that public funds are spent prudently for public purposes. Donald Trump and Mayor Koch were situated differently with respect to most of these matters.

Accountability   The Mayor wanted the old skating rink refurbished, but he also wanted to minimize the cost of the fuel needed to operate the rink (the first effort to rebuild it occurred right after the Arab oil embargo and the attendant increase in energy prices). Trying to achieve both goals led city hall to select a new refrigeration system that as it turned out would not work properly. Trump came on the scene when only one goal dominated: get the rink rebuilt. He felt free to select the most reliable refrigeration system without worrying too much about energy costs.

Equity   The Parks and Recreation Department was required by law to give every contractor an equal chance to do the job. This meant it had to put every part of the job out to bid and to accept the lowest without much regard to the reputation or prior performance of the lowest bidder. Moreover, state law forbade city agencies from hiring a general contractor and letting him select the subcontractors; in fact, the law forbade the city from even discussing the project in advance with a general contractor who might later bid on it—that would have been collusion. Trump, by contrast, was free to locate the rink builder with the best reputation and give him the job.

Fiscal Integrity   To reduce the chance of corruption or sweetheart deals the law required Parks and Recreation to furnish complete, detailed plans to every contractor bidding on the job; any changes after that would require renegotiating the contract. No such law constrained Trump; he was free to give incomplete plans to his chosen contractor, hold him accountable for building a satisfactory rink, but allow him to work out the details as he went along.

Efficiency   When the Parks and Recreation spent over six years and $13 million and still could not reopen the rink, there was public criticism but no city official lost money. When Trump accepted a contract to do it, any cost overruns or delays would have come out of his pocket and any savings could have gone into his pocket (in this case, Trump agreed not to take a profit on the job).

Gliedman summarized the differences neatly: "The problem with government is that government can't say, 'yes' . . . there is nobody in government that can do that. There are fifteen or twenty people who have to agree. Government has to be slower. It has to safeguard the process."

Inefficiency

The government can't say "yes." In other words, the government is constrained. Where do the constraints come from? From us.

Herbert Kaufman has explained red tape as being of our own making: "Every restraint and requirement originates in somebody's demand for it." Applied to the Central Park skating rink Kaufman's insight reminds us that civil-service reformers demanded that no city official benefit personally from building a project; that contractors demanded that all be given an equal chance to bid on every job; and that fiscal watchdogs demanded that all contract specifications be as detailed as possible. For each demand a procedure was established; viewed from the outside, those procedures are called red tape. To enforce each procedure a manager was appointed; those managers are called bureaucrats. No organized group demanded that all skating rinks be rebuilt as quickly as possible, no procedure existed to enforce that demand, and no manager was appointed to enforce it. The political process can more easily enforce compliance with constraints than the attainment of goals.

When we denounce bureaucracy for being inefficient we are saying something that is half true. Efficiency is a ratio of valued resources used to valued outputs produced. The smaller that ratio the more efficient the production. If the valued output is a rebuilt skating rink, then whatever process uses the fewest dollars or the least time to produce a satisfactory rink is the most efficient process. By this test Trump was more efficient than the Parks and Recreation Department.

But that is too narrow a view of the matter. The economic definition of efficiency (efficiency in the small, so to speak) assumes that there is only one valued output, the new rink. But government has many valued outputs, including a reputation for integrity, the confidence of the people, and the support of important interest groups. When we complain about skating rinks not being built on time we speak as if all we cared about were skating rinks. But when we complain that contracts were awarded without competitive bidding or in a way that allowed bureaucrats to line their pockets we acknowledge that we care about many things besides skating rinks; we care about the contextual goals—the constraints—that we want government to observe. A government that is slow to build rinks but is honest and accountable in its actions and properly responsive to worthy constituencies may be a very efficient government, *if* we measure efficiency in the large by taking into account *all* of the valued outputs.

Calling a government agency efficient when it is slow, cumbersome, and costly may seem perverse. But that is only because we lack any objective way for deciding how much money or time should be devoted to maintaining honest behavior, producing a fair allocation of benefits, and generating popular support as well as to achieving the main goal of the project. If we could measure these things, and if we agreed as to their value, then we would be in a position to judge the true efficiency of a government agency and decide when it is taking too much time or spending too much money achieving all that we expect of it. But we cannot measure these things nor do we agree about their relative importance, and so government always will appear to be inefficient compared to organizations that have fewer goals.

Put simply, the only way to decide whether an agency is truly inefficient is to decide which of the constraints affecting its action ought to be ignored or discounted. In fact that is what most debates about agency behavior are all about. In fighting crime are the police handcuffed? In educating children are teachers tied down by rules? In launching a space shuttle are we too concerned with safety? In building a dam do we worry excessively about endangered species? In running the Postal Service is it important to have many post offices close to where people live? In the case of the skating rink, was the requirement of competitive bidding for each contract on the basis of detailed specifications a reasonable one? Probably not. But if it were abandoned, the gain (the swifter completion of the rink) would have to be balanced against the costs (complaints from contractors who might lose business and the chance of collusion and corruption in some future projects).

Even allowing for all of these constraints, government agencies may still be inefficient. Indeed, given the fact that bureaucrats cannot (for the most part) benefit monetarily from their agencies' achievements, it would be surprising if they were not inefficient. Efficiency, in the large or the small, doesn't pay.

But some critics of government believe that inefficiency is obvious and vast. Many people remember the 1984 claim of the Grace Commission (officially, the President's Private Sector Survey on Cost Control) that it had identified over $400 billion in savings that could be made if only the federal government were managed properly. Though the commission did not say so, many people inferred that careless bureaucrats were wasting that amount of money. But hardly anybody remembers the study issued jointly by the General Accounting Office and the Congressional Budget Office in February 1984, one month after the Grace Commission report. The GAO and CBO reviewed those Grace recommendations that accounted for about 90 percent of the projected savings, and after eliminating double-counting and recommendations for which no savings could be estimated, and other problems, concluded that the true savings would be less than one-third the claimed amount.

Of course, $100 billion is still a lot of money. But wait. It turns out that about 60 percent of this would require not management improvements but policy changes: for example, taxing welfare benefits, ending certain direct loan programs, adopting new rules to restrict Medicare benefits, restricting eligibility for retirement among federal civilian workers and military personnel, and selling the power produced by government-owned hydroelectric plants at the full market price.

That still leaves roughly $40 billion in management savings. But most of this would require either a new congressional policy (for example, hiring more Internal Revenue Service agents to collect delinquent taxes), some unspecified increase in "worker productivity," or buying more services from private suppliers. Setting aside the desirable goal of increasing productivity (for which no procedures were identified), it turns out that almost all of the projected savings would require Congress to alter the goals and constraints of public agencies. If there is a lot of waste (and it is not clear why the failure to tax welfare benefits or to hire more IRS agents should be called waste), it is congressionally directed waste.

Military procurement, of course, is the biggest source of stories about waste, fraud, and mismanagement. There cannot be a reader of this book who has not heard about the navy paying $435 for a hammer or the air force paying $3,000 for a coffeepot, and nobody, I suspect, believes Defense Department estimates of the cost of a new airplane or missile. If ever one needed evidence that bureaucracy is inefficient, the Pentagon supplies it.

Well, yes. But what kind of inefficiency? And why does it occur? To answer these questions one must approach the problem just as we approached the problem of fixing up a skating rink in New York City: We want to understand why the bureaucrats, all of whom are rational and most of whom want to go [sic] a good job, behave as they do.

To begin, let us forget about $435 hammers. They never existed. A member of Congress who did not understand (or did not want to understand) government accounting rules created a public stir. The $3,000 coffeepot existed, but it is not clear that it was overpriced. But that does not mean there are no problems; in fact, the real problems are far more costly and intractable than inflated price tags on hammers and coffeemakers. They include sticking too long with new weapons of dubious value, taking forever to acquire even good weapons, and not inducing contractors to increase their efficiency. What follows is not a complete explanation of military procurement problems; it is only an analysis of the contribution bureaucratic systems make to those problems.

When the military buys a new weapons system—a bomber, submarine, or tank—it sets in motion a procurement bureaucracy comprised of two key actors, the military program manager and the civilian contract officer, who must cope with the contractor, the Pentagon hierarchy, and Congress. To understand how they behave we must understand how their tasks get defined, what incentives they have, and what constraints they face.

Tasks   The person nominally in charge of buying a major new weapon is the program manager, typically an army or air force colonel or a navy captain. Officially, his job is to design and oversee the acquisition strategy by establishing specifications and schedules and identifying problems and tradeoffs. Unofficially, his task is somewhat different. For one thing he does not have the authority to make many important decisions; those are referred upward to his military superiors, to Defense Department civilians, and to Congress. For another, the program he oversees must constantly be sold and resold to the people who control the resources (mostly, the key congressional committees). And finally, he is surrounded by inspectors and auditors looking for any evidence of waste, fraud, or abuse and by the advocates of all manner of special interests (contractors' representatives, proponents of small and minority business utilization, and so on). As the Packard Commission observed, the program manager, "far from being the manager of the program . . . is merely one of the participants who can influence it."

Under these circumstances the actual task of the program manager tends to be defined as selling the program and staying out of trouble. Harvard Business School professor J. Ronald Fox, who has devoted much of his life to studying and participating in weapons procurement, found that a program manager must spend 30 to 50 percent of his time defending his program inside DOD and to Congress. It is entirely rational for him to do this, for a study by the General Accounting Office showed that weapons programs with effective advocates survived (including some that should have been terminated) and systems without such advocates were more likely to be ended (even some that should have been completed). Just as with the New York City skating rink, in the Pentagon there is no one who can say "yes" and make it stick. The only way to keep winning the support of the countless people who must say "yes" over and over again is to forge ahead at full speed, spending money at a rate high enough to prevent it from being taken away. . . .

Incentives   In theory, military program managers are supposed to win promotions if they have done a good job supervising weapons procurement. In fact, promotions to the rank of general or admiral usually have been made on the basis of their reputation as combat officers and experience as military leaders. According to Fox, being a program manager is often not a useful ticket to get punched if you want to rise to the highest ranks. In 1985, for example, 94 percent of the lieutenant colonels who had commanded a battalion were promoted by the army to the rank of colonel; the promotion rate for lieutenant colonels without that experience was only half as great. The armed services now claim that they do promote procurement officers at a reasonable rate, but Fox, as well as many officers, remain skeptical. The perceived message is clear: Traditional military specialties are a surer route to the top than experience as a program manager. . . .

Civilian contract officers do have a distinct career path, but as yet not one that produces in them much sense of professional pride or organizational mission. Of the more than twenty thousand civilian contract administrators less than half have a college degree and the great majority are in the lower civil-service grades (GS-5 to GS-12). Even the most senior contract officers rarely earn (in 1988) more than $50,000 a year, less than half or even one-third of what their industry counterparts earn. Moreover, all are aware that they work in offices where the top posts usually are held by military officers; in civil-service jargon, the "head room" available for promotions is quite limited. . . .

The best evidence of the weakness of civilian incentives is the high turnover rate. Fox quotes a former commander of the military acquisition program as saying that "good people are leaving in droves" because "there is much less psychic income today" that would make up for the relatively low monetary income. The Packard Commission surveyed civilian procurement personnel and found that over half would leave their jobs if offered comparable jobs elsewhere in the federal government or in private industry.

In short, the incentives facing procurement officials do not reward people for maximizing efficiency. Military officers are rewarded for keeping programs alive and are encouraged to move on to other assignments; civilian personnel have weak inducements to apply a complex array of inconsistent constraints to contract administration.

Constraints   These constraints are not designed to produce efficiency but to reduce costs, avoid waste, fraud, and abuse, achieve a variety of social goals, and maintain the productive capacity of key contractors.

Reducing costs is not the same thing as increasing efficiency. If too little money is spent, the rate of production may be inefficient and the managerial flexibility necessary to cope with unforeseen circumstances may be absent. Congress typically appropriates money one year at a time. If Congress wishes to cut its spending or if DOD is ordered to slash its budget requests, the easiest thing to do is to reduce the number of aircraft, ships, or missiles being purchased in a given year without reducing the total amount purchased. This stretch-out has the effect of increasing the cost of each individual weapon as manufacturers forgo the economies that come from large-scale production. As Fox observes (but as many critics fail to understand), the typical weapons program in any given year is not overfunded, it is *under*funded. Recognizing that, the Packard Commission called for adopting a two-year budget cycle.

Reducing costs and eliminating fraud are not the same as increasing efficiency. There no doubt are excessive costs and there may be fraud in military procurement, but eliminating them makes procurement more efficient only if the costs of eliminating the waste and fraud exceed the savings thereby realized. To my knowledge no one has systematically compared the cost of all the inspectors, rules, and auditors with the savings they have achieved to see if all the checking and reviewing is worth it. Some anecdotal evidence suggests that the checking does not always pay for itself. In one case the army was required to spend $5,400 to obtain fully competitive bids for spare parts that cost $11,000. In exchange for the $5,400 and the 160 days it took to get the bids, the army saved $100. In short, there is an optimal level of "waste" in any organization, public or private: It is that level below which further savings are worth less than the cost of producing them.

The weapons procurement system must serve a number of "social" goals mandated by Congress. It must support small business, provide opportunities for minority-owned businesses, buy American-made products whenever possible, rehabilitate prisoners, provide employment for the handicapped, protect the environment, and maintain "prevailing" wage rates. One could lower the cost of procurement by eliminating some or all of the social goals the process is obliged to honor; that would produce increases in efficiency, narrowly defined. But what interest group is ready to sacrifice its most cherished goal in the name of efficiency? And if none will volunteer, how does one create a congressional majority to compel the sacrifice?

Weapons procurement also is designed to maintain the productive capacity of the major weapons builders. There is no true market in the manufacture of missiles, military aircraft, and naval vessels because typically there is only one buyer (the government) and no alternative uses for the production lines established to supply this buyer. Northrop, Lockheed, Grumman, McDonnell Douglas, the Bath Iron Works, Martin Marietta—these firms and others like them would not exist, or would exist in very different form, if they did not have a continuous flow of military contracts. As a result, each new weapons system becomes a do-or-die proposition for the executives of these firms. Even if the Pentagon cared nothing about their economic well-being it would have to care about the productive capacity that they represent, for if it were ever lost or much diminished the armed services would have nowhere else to turn when the need arose for a new airplane or ship. And if by chance the Pentagon did not care, Congress would; no member believes he or she was elected to preside over the demise of a major employer.

This constraint produces what some scholars have called the "follow-on imperative": the need to give a new contract to each major supplier as work on an old contract winds down. If one understands this it is not necessary to imagine some sinister "military-industrial complex" conspiring to keep new weapons flowing. The armed services want them because they believe, rightly, that their task is to defend the nation against real though hard to define threats; the contractors want them because they believe, rightly, that the nation cannot afford to dismantle its productive capacity; Congress wants them because its members believe, rightly, that they are elected to maintain the prosperity of their states and districts.

When these beliefs encounter the reality of limited resources and the need to make budget choices, almost everyone has an incentive to overstate the benefits and understate the costs of a new weapons system. To do otherwise—to give a cautious estimate of what the weapon will achieve and a candid view of what it will cost—is to invite rejection. And none of the key actors in the process believe they can afford rejection.

The Bottom Line   The incentives and constraints that confront the military procurement bureaucracy push its members to overstate benefits, understate costs, make frequent and detailed changes in specifications, and enforce a bewildering array of rules designed to minimize criticism and stay out of trouble. There are hardly any incentives pushing officials to leave details to manufacturers or delegate authority to strong program managers whose career prospects will depend on their ability to produce good weapons at a reasonable cost.

In view of all this, what is surprising is that the system works as well as it does. In fact, it works better than most people suppose. The Rand Corporation has been studying military procurement for over thirty years. A summary of its findings suggests some encouraging news, most of it ignored amidst the headlines about hammers and coffeepots. There has been steady improvement in the performance of the system. Between the early 1960s and the mid-1980s, cost overruns, schedule slippages, and performance shortfalls have all decreased. Cost overruns of military programs on the average are now no greater than they are for the civil programs of the government such as highway and water projects and public buildings. Moreover, there is evidence that for all its faults the American system seems to work as well or better than that in many European nations.

Improvements can be made but they do not require bright new ideas, more regulations, or the reshuffling of boxes on the organizational chart. The necessary ideas exist in abundance, the top-down reorganizations have been tried without much effect, and the system is drowning in regulations. What is needed are changes in the incentives facing the key members. ■

 # The International Context

Although the American civil service shares many attributes in common with all other bureaucracies, there are nonetheless certain unique features of public administration in the United States. Those differences include matters of structure and function and extend to the way the bureaucracy is viewed by political scientists. Like the bureaucracy it studies, the field of American public administration itself is unique.

The following brief statement of the differences between American and European public administration highlights both the governmental and academic sides of the question. Some of these differences relate to the American constitutional structure; others stem from historical differences between the United States and Europe; still others are a result of differences in political culture.

Questions

1. Of the nine items discussed in this selection, which seem most fundamental? Which seem least consequential?
2. How do the differences noted by the authors of this selection relate to differences in political culture between the United States and other countries (see selection 5.3 as you consider your answer).

11.3 The Distinctive Nature of American Public Administration (1983)

Gerald E. Caiden, Richard A. Lovard, Thomas J. Pavlak, Lynn F. Sipe, and Molly M. Wong

The scope of American public administration is distinct in at least . . . [nine] ways. First, in contrast to the European tradition, it excludes public law. Public administration is not seen as the exercise of public law. Law is seen as part of the judiciary and the judicial system, and under the American doctrine of the separation of powers it is identified with the judicial branch of government, not the executive branch. Until recently, whenever the two overlapped, public administration gave way to the superior claims of the legal profession. Now, with public and administrative law becoming increasingly important to the practice of government, public administration is reaching out into judicial dimensions which the legal profession has been reluctant to explore. Nonetheless, public administration falls far short of the strong legal inclusion found in other countries where public law and public administration are indistinguishable.

Second, in contrast to the British tradition, it has excluded, until relatively recently, considerations of the ends of government and the uses of public office. Public administration has not been seen as the exercise of power. Public power has been seen as part of the study of political science and in the dichotomy that was propounded by Wilson and Goodnow the study of politics and uses made of public office were separated from the study of administration. Whenever the two overlapped, public administration yielded in this case to political science. With the acceptance of the administrative state and the emergence of Big Government, the processes of government can no longer be separated from the purposes to which they are put. Public administration has come now to include the objectives as well as the practices of public management. It has also been reaching out into policy and public interest dimensions which political scientists have been reluctant to explore. Nonetheless, there is still much diffidence, if not downright reluctance, to go beyond the dimensions of the management of public organizations. American public administration falls far short of the strong political inclusion found in other countries where public affairs have never distinguished between policy and administration and where the ends of government have never been separated from the means. Only recently in American public administration has it been realized that the two are (and probably always have been) fused and only recently have strong ideological differences emerged over the role of the administrative state in modern society.

Gerald E. Caiden, Richard A. Lovard, Thomas J. Pavlak, Lynn F. Sipe, and Molly M. Wong, *American Public Administration: A Bibliographical Guide to the Literature* (New York: Garland Publishing, Inc., 1983), pp. 4–8. Used with permission of the publisher.

Third, the generalist approach to the administration of public affairs has not been embraced in the United States to the extent that it has been elsewhere. The generalist tradition of the British administrative culture and the stress placed on intellectuality among European bureaucratic elites have provided an inclusive administrative profession to which other public management specialists have been subordinate. In contrast, the early emergence of strong professions in this country before the acceptance of a managerial profession (let alone the notion of a superior administrative cadre in the public bureaucracy) has fragmented the public sector into many rival concerns, few of which have accepted the superior imposition of a generalist administrative elite. Consequently, American public administration has been more of a residual than an inclusive entity. The armed forces and the management of defense have always been excluded, so too have the police and the management of justice, fire fighters, social workers, and teachers as well as members of the traditional professions (law, medicine, religion, higher education) employed in the public sector. These independent professions have jealously guarded their territory against intrusions from a generalist profession of public administrator. Since they were on the scene first, public administration has been reluctant to confront them and has tried to devise an amicable modus vivendi for peaceful coexistence. From a strictly logical point of view, the historical and political boundaries drawn between them make little sense. Compared with other countries, American public administration is less inclusory of public sector activities.

Fourth, the business community has been powerful in the United States and its influence over the public sector has probably been stronger than elsewhere. Many activities directly provided by the public bureaucracy in other countries are provided in the United States by the private sector or the significant third sector betwixt business and government, either directly or under contract with public authorities. Although part of the administrative state, they are not considered part of public administration; that is, scholars and practitioners have been reluctant to include them in their domains. On the one hand, this voluntary abstention has left significant gaps in the study of public administration which are now being filled hesitantly and inadequately. On the other hand, the blurred boundaries among the public, private, and third sectors have also opened up opportunities for the study of their interface which have been seized possibly to a greater extent than elsewhere. The same is probably true of intergovernmental administrative arrangements because of the blurred boundaries and jurisdictions among federal, state, regional, local, and community agencies in the United States.

Public administration in this country, fifth, is pragmatic, not ideological. The major concern has been to discover what works best in the public interest, construed in purely American terms in the light of prevailing conditions; rationalizations, justifications, and theoretical underpinnings have come afterwards. Yet this practical emphasis in American public administration should not be allowed to obscure its strong political roots in liberal democracy and the dominance of political principles over administrative practice and convenience. Democratic liberal values are paramount in American public management theory and practice. They are the lifeblood of the public bureaucracy. They are the unwritten premise on which the administrative state is expected to conduct itself. Since this is so well understood, American public administration has not felt the need to articulate its norms as much as other countries where the conduct of the state is subject to strong ideological differences and continuous political bargaining and shifting compromises.

Sixth, there really is no American public administration. It is a theoretical construct. Like Weber's ideal bureaucracy, it exists nowhere. It is a hybrid of common ideas and practices which have been abstracted from what exists. It is not a complete picture of reality, nor is it a photograph of specific circumstances. The United States is too diverse. Administrative arrangements and practices differ from one place to another, sometimes quite remarkably. In dealing with public administration as it really is, one experiences continual culture shock because experience contrasts so much with expectation. There are no common frames of reference; every office seems to be a law to itself, choosing within limits those practices which best suit itself. It is this variety that confuses and forces a level of abstraction that nowhere conforms exactly with reality. As a result, much in the study of public management is what should be rather than what is, and most is analytical not descriptive.

Next, [or seventh,] because of constant change in public administration, history has little contemporary meaning. Historical analysis has little relevance to the present. In any case, administrators are so caught up with the present that they have little time for the past and little interest in having the past reconstructed for them. In brief, there is relatively little administrative history and, as the expense of holding archives for purely historical interest is rarely justifiable, the possibility of reconstructing the past diminishes with every passing year. The task is so daunting that there are few volunteers and precious little market. As a result, there is little historical continuity and many things are continually being rediscovered because often the left hand does not know what the right is doing (or has done). Anyway, Americans are not too proud of their administrative past nor of uncovering administrative skeletons that should remain buried. What is done is done. Only the present counts and making the future better counts even more. Public administration in this country looks forward not back.

Eighth, few figures dominate public administration in the United States. Other countries can point to their administrative heroes, those few individuals who dominated the public bureaucracy in their day or revamped it in their own image which lasted for an appreciable period after them. Not so here. Americans do not indulge in much historical veneration, least of all public administrators. One of the few exceptions is Robert Moses who dominated New York government for decades, but his legacy has almost vanished and his reputation has not lasted. The same applies for the scholastic domain where no figure has emerged comparable in status to a Max Weber or a Maynard Keynes. Leonard White exercised some authority for a period as did Dwight Waldo, but the only Nobel Prize recipient has been Herbert Simon, much of whose pathfinding work was done in public administration, but since the 1950's he has not been associated with the field. If there have been no giants, there have been many persons of commendable stature who between them have made the development of the field a cooperative venture.

Ninth, the absence of an intellectual colossus, lateness in arriving on the American scene, and the tendency to fragmentation, have all caused public administration to fight for its place in the sun. It is frequently overshadowed by such more powerful disciplines as law, political science, and business administration which primarily serve other constituencies. These rivals claim that public administration does not exist or that if it does, it is a minor part of something else (usually themselves), that to be anything more than a minor or subdiscipline, it will have to demonstrate more than it has a proper intellectual or theoretical base, a clear and unquestionable core, well-defined boundaries, and a logically consistent whole. In brief, it should have a distinct and commonly accepted paradigm in order to be accepted as a fully fledged member of the academic community. Outside the United States, public administration does not suffer such intellectual indignity nor react with such an intellectual inferiority complex. In this nation, public administration is continually forced to reaffirm itself, to justify its existence and to protect itself from takeover bids. It is continually searching for its soul, for its *raison d'être*, for its paradigm, for its identity. Periodically, it goes through its "identity crisis" and rediscovers itself. Nowhere else does public administration go through such soul-searching or experience such self-doubts. ■

View from the Inside

Rarely have officials from so many jurisdictions worked together on a common problem as in October 2002 when a pair of snipers terrorized the Washington, D.C., metropolitan area, shooting thirteen people and killing eleven over a period of more than two weeks. Among those hunting the suspects were police officers from two states and the District of Columbia and agents of the Federal Bureau of Investigation (FBI). Logistical help was provided by the armed forces. Key pieces of the puzzle were provided by law enforcement officials in Washington State and Alabama. In the end, critical information and support were provided by members of the general public and the media.

Looking back, one can see missed opportunities, errors in judgment, and failures in communication. Each day's delay meant more shootings, and more victims. But the story is not without heroes—men and women who worked day after day to solve a nearly impossible puzzle. The struggle to find and arrest the sniper suspects—told here by *Newsweek* reporter Evan Thomas—presents a realistic portrait of government in action.

Questions

1. What techniques did government officials use to maximize communication and coordination between the various government agencies involved in the hunt for the sniper suspects? How might these techniques have been improved?
2. The author of this selection points out that law enforcement officials missed several key chances to stop the killers. What led to these missed chances? How might they have been avoided?

11.4   Descent into Evil (2002)

Evan Thomas

• • •

The call came in to Chief [Charles A.] Moose's office at the Montgomery County [Maryland] Police Department on Friday, Oct. 18, two weeks and 11 victims into the sniper nightmare. A public-information officer answered. According to a law-enforcement source, the angry caller said something like, "Do you know who you're dealing with? Don't mess with me." The caller told the Montgomery police to check out a murder-robbery at a liquor store "in Montgomery." Law-enforcement sources offer conflicting accounts about whether the caller specifically said, "Montgomery, Alabama," or just "Montgomery." In retrospect, it is clear that the snipers were showing off. They were pointing police to the shooting of two women at a state liquor store in Montgomery, Ala., on Sept. 21. Ambushed, one woman was shot in the back, the other in the back of the neck. (One died.) The shooter, police now believe, was John Muhammad. The link to the Montgomery, Ala., shooting would prove to be crucial. At the time, however, the hint from the angry caller did not really capture the attention of the sniper task force. The public-information officer who took the call didn't realize he was talking to the sniper. A second call from the same man an hour later was abruptly cut off; apparently, the caller had run out of change at a pay phone.

The investigators were inundated. After a shooting, calls were coming in at the rate of 1,000 an hour. The task-force leaders and their troops—several thousand men and women, some drafted from other government agencies to man the phones 24 hours a day—were exhausted and staggering under the weight of hopes raised and dashed. Top officials muttered about the irresponsibility of the press. They were angry that reporters had let slip that the Pentagon had provided spy planes to track the snipers. "It's a chess move we would rather have made in the dark," one police official said. In the large, cluttered office space in Rockville, Md., that served as a bullpen for all the different investigative agencies, bleary-eyed investigators tracked down tips, mostly nutty or useless, but some that seemed promising and led nowhere.

There was, for instance, the Dentist. He had been fingered by a caller to the tip line, who phoned police to say that he knew of an odd and angry dentist who loved guns. The dentist's home was in what police called "the red zone," the area in Montgomery County where the profilers thought the sniper probably lived. The first time police visited the dentist's house, they heard the double click of a shotgun being cocked. The next day a victim was gunned down in Fredericksburg, Va., 45 minutes away from the dentist's office. Federal agents returned and found the dentist—with a high-powered rifle, capable of shooting .223 ammunition, in his trunk. Peering through the dentist's office window, they observed a map of the region, with the locations of all the sniper attacks marked with colored pins. The cops got a warrant to seize the gun—but the ballistics didn't match the sniper's bullets. The dentist's alibi was "rock solid," said a frustrated gumshoe.

Then there was the Good Ole Boy. He was another gun-crazed white man with suspicious habits. The police put him under surveillance. One night in the middle of the siege, he was observed shooting pool and drinking beer with his buddies until 2 A.M. "Not serial-killer behavior," the cops concluded.

That week, while detectives futilely chased white vans and trucks by the thousand, the sniper had seemed to go quiet. Then on Saturday night, Oct. 19, he struck again, shooting a traveler as he left the Ponderosa Steak House in Ashland, Va. Alerted by an anonymous call (now believed to be Muhammad), the police found a three-page letter. It was sealed in a sandwich bag, tacked to a tree behind the restaurant. "For you, Mr. Police," it read. "Call me God." The words matched those written on a tarot card discovered by investigators after the Oct. 7 shooting of the schoolboy. The letter continued, "We have tried to contact you to start a negotiation" and listed a half-dozen attempts to call police or FBI tip lines that were rebuffed as "a hoax or joke." If the authorities wanted to stop the killings, the letter warned, they would place $10 million in the account of a Visa bank card. The letter provided a PIN and an account number for a card that turned out to be stolen. Police were told to stand ready to take a call at a pay phone near the Ponderosa at 6 A.M. that Sunday. The sniper gave the cops until 9 A.M. Monday to deposit the money. The letter writers warned of more "body bags," and added, "P.S., your children are not safe anywhere at any time."

On the sniper's list of foiled attempts to contact the authorities, one in particular stood out. It said, simply, "Priest at Ashland." (Investigators theorize that the shooter called a priest not for forgiveness but to find a go-between.) Around noontime, after Sunday mass, the FBI visited St. Ann's Catholic Church in Ashland. The pastor, Msgr. William Sullivan, told the investigators that he had indeed received a call from a man who reportedly introduced himself, "I am God." According to the priest, the caller complained that the woman at the Home Depot (FBI cyber analyst Linda Franklin, 47, slain on Oct. 14) would not have died if police had not ignored his calls. It took two visits from the FBI to surface the key detail. The caller had instructed the priest to write down a message for police to "look into Montgomery, Alabama." The caller wanted the police to know about the slaying at the liquor store. The call was garbled; the priest had thought he was talking to a crank. But this time round, the reference to Montgomery seized the attention of investigators. "That call did it," said one top law-enforcement official. After two and a half weeks of flailing and false leads, the trail was about to grow warm.

At about 9 that Sunday, Montgomery, Ala., Police Chief John Wilson was just settling down for an evening of football on TV. He had watched the Atlanta Falcons game with a friend and polished off a steak dinner and a glass of wine. The call came from his chief of detectives, Maj. Pat Downing. "You're not going to believe this," said Downing. A detective from the sniper task force in Montgomery County, Md., had called. He told his Alabama counterpart that the sniper task force had received a phone call from a man who claimed to be the sniper. Faced with skepticism, the angry caller had reportedly said, "I know something about a murder-robbery at an ABC liquor store in Montgomery, Alabama, near Ann Street."

Wilson and Downing were surprised. They knew all about the Sept. 21 slaying. A Montgomery cop had chased the killer on foot for a quarter of a mile before he got away (a blue car had pulled out and suddenly cut off the policeman). The case was languishing, unsolved. Could the missing Alabama killer turn out to be the Washington sniper? "It sounded so farfetched and too good to be true," says Wilson. Nonetheless, the Montgomery police turned over a stack of evidence from the shooting to the local FBI office. On Monday afternoon, a Montgomery-based FBI agent, Margaret Faulkner, flew to Washington with the package.

The most important piece in the pile, it turned out, was the fingerprints pulled off a copy of a gun magazine, an ArmaLite catalog, apparently dropped near the scene of the liquor-store killing. No match had been found in state records. But the fingerprints had never been entered into the federal database (Alabama does not belong to the service that provides it). On Monday night, task-force investigators searched for a match—and found one. The fingerprints belonged to one Lee Malvo, a juvenile who was facing illegal immigration charges in the small town of Bellingham, Wash. He had been reported to the INS [Immigration and Naturalization Service] after police were called in to deal with a dispute involving the boy's mother and another man. That man's name, it appeared, was John Muhammad. Investigators finally had a name; in fact, two names.

The task force was finally beginning to get somewhere. But there was no eureka moment, say investigators. News of the fingerprint match was not widely shared, and many investigators learned of the breakthrough only from water-cooler gossip. Communication between locals and Feds and rival agencies like the ATF [Bureau of Alcohol, Tobacco, and Firearms] and FBI was erratic. If anything, the gumshoes seemed to be stumbling in the dark. The missed phone calls from the sniper (which the press had found out about) were an embarrassment, however understandable under the stressed circumstances. Because they wanted to be meticulous about handling and preserving evidence, ever so carefully fingerprinting and tagging the plastic sandwich bag tacked to the tree and its contents, investigators had not read the sniper's letter until Sunday morning—after the 6 A.M. time set in the letter for the phone call from the sniper. That is why Chief Moose abruptly went before the cameras on Sunday night to deliver a cryptic message: "To the person who left us a message at the Ponderosa last night, you gave us a telephone number. We do want to talk to you. Call us at the number you provided."

On Monday morning, the shooter called police again. But when the cops traced the call to a phone booth in Richmond, Va., they caught the wrong men: two illegal immigrants who just happened to be in the wrong place at the wrong time. One was driving a white van. A beleaguered Chief Moose was forced to deliver more mysterious messages: "We are going to respond to a message that we have received. We will respond later. We are preparing that response at this time," the chief announced. Later that afternoon, he begged the callers to try again. "The audio was unclear," he said, "and we want to get it right."

The snipers delivered their response at 5:57 the next morning, Tuesday, Oct. 22. A Montgomery County bus driver was fatally shot as he stood in the vehicle's lit, open doorway, taking a break before beginning his morning run. In the woods, investigators found another letter—again insisting that money be deposited in the bank-card account and threatening the lives of children. (Once again, the investigators read the letter too late to take a scheduled phone call from the snipers.) The snipers demanded that the authorities respond not just with money but also by repeating what appeared to be a cheeky taunt: "We have caught the sniper like a duck in a noose." The duck reference is from a folk tale in which a boastful rabbit tries to catch a duck in a noose—only to have the duck fly away, dragging the rabbit, then dropping him inside a tree stump, where the rabbit is trapped.

To the average TV viewer, the investigators were beginning to look like cornered rabbits. But behind the scenes, the FBI thought they might have found a clever ruse to catch the killers. The Feds deposited $100,000 in the bank-card account, *Newsweek* has learned. The card had been stolen from a woman in Arizona, so the bureau had to go to the bank and ask it to reopen the account and increase the daily withdrawal limit to $1,000. As it turned out, the trap was not sprung because the pair never got the chance to use the card. By Wednesday, the noose was beginning to tighten around the duck's neck in a chokehold that would permit no escape.

In Washington state, the Feds were learning some very interesting information about 17-year-old John Lee Malvo and his older friend John Muhammad, 41. The two, who lived together for a time at a homeless shelter, seemed to have a curious bond. Muhammad referred to Malvo as his "stepson," but he was not. At one point, the gumshoes learned, the duo had stayed in Tacoma with Robert Edward Holmes, an old Army buddy of Muhammad's. Holmes told investigators that Muhammad had appeared in the spring of 2002 toting an AR-15, a semiautomatic assault rifle that shoots a .223 round. The gun had a telescopic sight, and Muhammad concealed it in an aluminum case. "Can you imagine the damage you could do if you could shoot with a silencer?" Muhammad had exclaimed, according to Holmes. Neighbors had heard shooting with a high-powered rifle in the backyard. On Wednesday morning, federal investigators began combing the yard with a metal detector, looking for shell casings.

Back at task-force headquarters, the sniper investigation was turning up a lead that was at once embarrassing and promising. The Feds ran a check on Muhammad's license and found, to their astonishment, that he had been discovered by Baltimore police asleep in his car on the night of Oct. 8, about a half-hour's drive from the scene of the shooting the day before at Tasker Middle School in Bowie, Md. The Baltimore cops had run a check on the car—a blue 1990 Chevy Caprice—and found nothing amiss. Muhammad had been allowed to go about his business.

Moving quickly now, police traced the registration on the car to Camden, N.J. It turned out that Muhammad had bought the battered clunker with roughly 150,000 miles on it for $250 from the Sure Shot Auto Shop in Camden. (The car's last use: as an undercover vehicle by the cops.) Last week federal agents arrested Nathaniel Osbourne, 26, in Flint, Mich. Osbourne was listed as co-owner of the car with Muhammad. Held as a material witness, he is not a suspect in the shootings, but an FBI spokesman said, "We believe he has valuable information about the sniper case."

Remarkably, law-enforcement sources tell *Newsweek,* some investigators continued to cling to the belief that the sniper or snipers were driving a white van or truck. Like the talking heads on TV, they had convinced themselves that the snipers must be white men driving a white truck. They had trouble accepting that they should have been looking for two black men driving a blue car. They were fixated on cars fleeing the scene. It does not seem to have really occurred to them that the shooters would hang around—as they almost surely did. As it turned out, a witness had reported seeing a Caprice driving slowly with its lights off near the scene of the Oct. 3 shooting in northeast D.C. But in the dark, the witness remembered the car's color as burgundy, not blue, and the lead was lost in the chatter over white vehicles. A witness outside the Fredericksburg, Va., Michaels craft store, scene of a shooting on Oct. 4, reported a "dark-colored vehicle with New Jersey tags" leaving the scene. A woman calling the tip line on Oct. 7 said she had spotted a black man crouching beneath the dashboard in a dark Chevy Caprice. The woman was struck by the intensity of the man's stare. The agent on the tip line brushed her off. "We're looking for a white truck," she said.

Finally, by Wednesday night, Muhammad and Malvo were at the "top of the list" of suspects, Montgomery County Executive Douglas Duncan told *Newsweek.* "Wednesday, it kept going back and forth," he said. Doubts remained. The investigators had been burned by false leads before. "I expected calls on at least three other days telling me 'We got him'—and they turned out not to be the ones," said Duncan. There was still the question of how to run down the suspects. SWAT [special weapons and tactics] and . . . [hostage rescue] teams were looking through cheap hotels. D.C. cops were patrolling with the Caprice's New Jersey license-plate number written on Post-It notes stuck on their dashboards. The investigators hotly debated whether to release the suspects' photographs. Some feared that would only tip them off and make them flee. Or worse, provoke them to strike again. Others feared the suspects would be found first by vigilantes. "The concern was that, God forbid, it's not the people [the real snipers] and someone takes matters into their own hands," said Duncan.

The debate raged until almost midnight, when Moose finally emerged to tell reporters that police were on the lookout for Muhammad and Malvo. The investigators did not release the description of the blue 1990 Chevy Caprice or its New Jersey license-plate number, NDA21Z. But reporters with police scanners had already heard the identifying information being relayed to patrol officers in their cruisers.

It was that fortuitous leak that led to the snipers' arrest. At a rest stop off I-70, near the Pennsylvania border, a truck driver, Ronald Lantz, was listening to his favorite program, "Truckin' Bozo Radio Show," out of WLW-AM in Cincinnati, when he heard the host broadcast a description of the blue Caprice. Lantz looked out his window, and there it was. He immediately called 911. It was 12:54 A.M. At just about the same time, the rest-stop custodian, Larry Blank, was hunkered down in a white van with another man who had spotted the blue Caprice. They, too, dialed 911. After the first police arrived, Lantz and another trucker blocked the rest-stop exits until the SWAT teams came storming in, some two hours later.

Top officials on the sniper task force could hardly believe that the ordeal was over. When he awoke Thursday morning, the first question that popped into

County Executive [Douglas] Duncan's head was: "Has anyone gotten shot?" By evening, the state and local law-enforcement chiefs and top federal officials jammed into Chief Moose's office. No one wanted to declare victory until the ATF had made a match between the gun found in the car—a Bushmaster XM-15—and the bullet fragments extracted from 11 of the sniper's victims. They waited and waited, until ATF Special Agent Joe Riehl finally walked into Moose's office at about 8 P.M. and shut the door. Outside, lower-level investigators listened anxiously for some sign. There was silence. Then, at last, the sound of clapping. Moose emerged, looking stern as usual. Duncan teased him, "Can you smile now?" The chief looked up and a huge grin spread across his face.

The suspects were whisked away to an "undisclosed location" and placed in separate interrogation rooms. When prosecutors stepped out for a moment and left Malvo alone, he tried to escape. He somehow broke the table leg to which he had been handcuffed and started climbing up through the ceiling tiles. Pulled back down, he soiled himself, and had to be given a new prisoner's jumpsuit.

The spirit of good cheer on the sniper task force lasted less than a day. By Friday, state and federal prosecutors were bitterly vying for the chance to prosecute Muhammad and Malvo. A meeting between the various agencies and jurisdictions broke down in acrimony. When FBI agents were called on their cell phones and ordered to take the suspects from the interrogation room, task-force cops and prosecutors exploded in anger. Malvo had sat in stony silence, but Muhammad was beginning to answer a few questions. Hoping that he would warm up and begin to spill, agents and officials crowded around closed-circuit monitors to watch the questioning. The Feds insisted that the suspects had to be taken before a federal magistrate and formally charged with a federal crime—or risk having the case thrown out for an illegal arrest. But local officials blamed Thomas Dibiagio, the U.S. Attorney in Baltimore, for hogging the limelight and ruining any chance of getting the suspects to talk before they were silenced by defense lawyers. "We may never know why they [Muhammad and Malvo] did what they did because of what Dibiagio did," said an angry local official. Montgomery County State's Attorney Douglas Gansler went ahead and charged the two men with six counts of murder in Maryland. Virginia officials also say they are eager to try the men for murder, and the authorities in Montgomery, Ala., also filed homicide charges. It is unclear how the legal wrangling will sort itself out. If the Feds charge Muhammad with extortion that results in murder (the demand for $10 million, or else), he could get the death penalty. He could also be executed under state law if the Maryland governor, as expected, goes along. Minors generally escape capital punishment, though not in Virginia, and under some circumstance Malvo could be "certified" as an adult.

The trials are sure to be media circuses. The cable-TV experts will come back out to psychoanalyze the defendants, to make some sense out of what they did in the month of October 2002. The prosecutors will try to make Muhammad coldly sane. "He may be talking nonsense, but that doesn't mean he's delusional," says one prosecutor involved in the investigation. Psychiatrist Dorothy Otnow Lewis, a professor at New York University School of Medicine and one of the few talking heads to get it right during the long sniper siege, cautions against expecting clear-cut or rational answers. "You have to suspend logic," she says, when asked questions like why a Muslim killer would turn to a Roman Catholic priest. "We don't know what his underlying fantasy was."

We do know what his overlying reality may have been. It stretched far beyond the corpses and crime scenes and well beyond the Beltway. With one rifle, an old car and a teenage disciple, authorities believe, he brought terror to the nation's capital. For almost three weeks, he kept schoolchildren in a state of "lockdown," a term normally associated with prisons. He forced high-school homecoming games to be played on undisclosed secure military bases. He made children run when they got off the school bus—not to the playground, but for cover. He caused thousands of sad conversations between parents and their children, who were painfully learning to adapt to an age in which everyone, old and young, feels less safe than before. ■

 Chapter 12

The Judiciary

Some forty years ago, the constitutional scholar Robert G. McCloskey surveyed the history of the Supreme Court of the United States and concluded, "Surely the record teaches that no useful purpose is served when the judges seek the hottest political cauldrons of the moment and dive into the middle of them." Instead, "The Court's greatest successes have been achieved when it has operated near the margins of rather than in the center of political controversy, when it has nudged and gently tugged the nation, instead of trying to rule it."* Writing after the Court's 1954 school desegregation decision but before the controversies over reapportionment of state legislatures, abortion, busing, and school prayer, McCloskey feared for the Court's future if it did not learn the lessons of its past.

The Court, of course, did not follow McCloskey's advice. Over the past four decades, the Supreme Court has become an increasingly important force in American politics and the subject of intense, and at times bitter, political controversy. In the 1960s and 1970s, the Court's most controversial decisions involved questions of civil rights and civil liberties. Although such cases remain prominent on the Court's agenda, in recent years the justices have also turned their attention to other controversial issues, including those arising from the separation of powers, federalism, and economic rights. In 2000, the Court even injected itself into the contentious arena of electoral politics, making a ruling in *Bush* v. *Gore* (see selection 12.5) that, in effect, decided who would be the next president of the United States.

All of this judicial activity has created a highly charged political debate over the proper role of the courts in American society. Presidents Ronald Reagan and George H.W. Bush endeavored to reshape the Court along more conservative lines; several of their nominees provoked considerable controversy, and the nomination of Judge Robert Bork was defeated by the Senate. When their turns came, first Bill Clinton and then George W. Bush tried to push the Court in one direction or the other. Each new nomination, and each controversial Court decision, sets off a new round of debate.

This chapter surveys the many aspects of the judiciary's role in American politics and society. Selections 12.1 and 12.2 present two classic arguments on behalf of judicial review—the first by Alexander Hamilton, the second by Chief Justice John Marshall. Selection 12.3, by the *New York Times* reporter Linda Greenhouse, examines how well the

*Robert McCloskey, *The American Supreme Court* (Chicago: University of Chicago Press, 1960), p. 229.

current Supreme Court discharges its responsibilities to the legal community and to the American people. Selection 12.4 compares judicial activism in the United States and Canada, while selection 12.5 presents an unusual behind-the-scenes view of the Supreme Court's internal negotiations over *Bush* v. *Gore.*

Chapter Questions

1. What are the advantages and disadvantages of leaving political decisions to the courts instead of to the political branches of the federal government or to the states? What qualities do the courts have that make such activism attractive? Unattractive, or even dangerous?

2. What is the relationship between the federal judiciary and the other branches of the federal government? In what ways do the three branches of government work together to make policy? In what ways is the relationship competitive or adversarial?

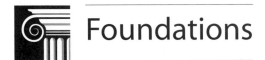 Foundations

The Supreme Court's power to review acts of Congress and decide whether they are un-constitutional is perhaps the most extraordinary power possessed by any court in the world; the decision of five of nine justices can nullify the expressed will of the people's representatives in Congress. Moreover, the Court can strike down laws passed by state or local officials based on a conflict with federal law. Although Supreme Court decisions striking down major acts of Congress have been relatively infrequent, the Court has acted often to nullify unconstitutional measures passed by the states.

Despite the enormity of the Court's power of judicial review, as it is known, this power was not explicitly granted to the Court by the Constitution. The lack of specific language in the Constitution on this point—probably because the delegates could not agree as to whether the state or the federal courts should have the last word—made it necessary for the Supreme Court to claim and defend its power of judicial review later. The justices who were most influential in this struggle were Chief Justice John Marshall and his ally, Justice Joseph Story.

The following two selections trace the highlights of this struggle. The first is Alexander Hamilton's classic defense of judicial review in the *Federalist Papers* No. 78. The second is Marshall's 1803 decision in *Marbury* v. *Madison,* in which the Supreme Court first claimed the power of judicial review.

Questions

1. Hamilton begins his argument with a defense of the Constitution's provision for life appointment of justices of the Supreme Court. How does this argument relate to his and John Marshall's defense of judicial review?

2. Considering the other readings in this chapter, how reasonable is Hamilton's observation that the courts possess "neither FORCE nor WILL, but merely judgment"?

3. Consider the validity of this statement by Justice Oliver Wendell Holmes: "I do not think the United States would come to an end if we lost our power to declare an Act of Congress void. I do think the Union would be imperiled if we could not make that declaration as to the laws of the several States."*

12.1 *Federalist* No. 78 (1788)

Alexander Hamilton

Outline

I. Mode of appointment of federal judges.

II. Necessity of lifetime appointments for federal judges.

 A. The judiciary is the least dangerous and the weakest branch; life tenure is essential to preserving its independence from the other branches.

 B. Life tenure is particularly important in a system with a limited Constitution, which cannot be preserved in practice except if judges have the authority to strike down laws that are inconsistent with the Constitution (a power known as judicial review).

 1. Defense of judicial review.

 i. Congress merely acts as the agent of the people; the Constitution sets out the terms of agency and must take precedence over acts of Congress.

 ii. The Constitution is a fundamental law; it belongs to the judges to give it meaning and to enforce it in preference to any legislative act.

 iii. The Courts cannot substitute their own judgment for that of the legislature; they must exercise judgment, not will.

 iv. Judges must be independent (and thus hold life tenure) in order to play this role without legislative interference.

 2. An independent judiciary also protects against legislative acts which do not violate the Constitution but do interfere with private rights.

 3. There are a few individuals in society who combine the necessary skill and integrity to be federal judges; life tenure may be necessary to encourage such people to leave the private practice of law for the federal bench.

*Oliver Wendell Holmes, "Law and the Court," address delivered February 15, 1913, in *Collected Legal Papers* (New York: Peter Smith, 1952), pp. 295–296.

Wwe proceed now to an examination of the judiciary department of the proposed government.

In unfolding the defects of the existing Confederation, the utility and necessity of a federal judicature have been clearly pointed out. It is the less necessary to recapitulate the considerations there urged, as the propriety of the institution in the abstract is not disputed; the only questions which have been raised being relative to the manner of constituting it, and to its extent. To these points, therefore, our observations shall be confined.

The manner of constituting it seems to embrace these several objects: 1st. The mode of appointing the judges. 2d. The tenure by which they are to hold their places. . . .

First. As to the mode of appointing the judges; this is the same with that of appointing the officers of the Union in general. . . .

Second. As to the tenure by which the judges are to hold their places; this chiefly concerns their duration in office; the provisions for their support; the precautions for their responsibility.

According to the plan of the convention, all judges who may be appointed by the United States are to hold their offices DURING GOOD BEHAVIOR; which is conformable to the most approved of the State constitutions and among the rest, to that of this State. Its propriety having been drawn into question by the adversaries of that plan, is no light symptom of the rage for objection, which disorders their imaginations and judgments. The standard of good behavior for the continuance in office of the judicial magistracy, is certainly one of the most valuable of the modern improvements in the practice of government. In a monarchy it is an excellent barrier to the despotism of the prince; in a republic it is a no less excellent barrier to the encroachments and oppressions of the representative body. And it is the best expedient which can be devised in any government, to secure a steady, upright, and impartial administration of the laws.

Whoever attentively considers the different departments of power must perceive, that, in a government in which they are separated from each other, the judiciary, from the nature of its functions, will always be the least dangerous to the political rights of the Constitution; because it will be least in a capacity to annoy or injure them. The Executive not only dispenses the honors, but holds the sword of the community. The legislature not only commands the purse, but prescribes the rules by which the duties and rights of every citizen are to be regulated. The judiciary, on the contrary, has no influence over either the sword or the purse; no direction either of the strength or of the wealth of the society; and can take no active resolution whatever. It may truly be said to have neither FORCE nor WILL, but merely judgment; and must ultimately depend upon the aid of the executive arm even for the efficacy of its judgments.

This simple view of the matter suggests several important consequences. It proves incontestably, that the judiciary is beyond comparison the weakest of the three departments of power; that it can never attack with success either of the other two; and that all possible care is requisite to enable it to defend itself against their attacks. It equally proves, that though individual oppression may now and then proceed from the courts of justice, the general liberty of the people can never be endangered from that quarter; I mean so long as the judiciary remains truly distinct from both the legislature and the Executive. For I agree, that "there is no liberty, if the power of judging be not separated from the legislative and executive powers." And it proves, in the last place, that as liberty can have nothing to fear from the judiciary alone, but would have every thing to fear from its union with either of the other departments; that as all the effects of such a union must ensue from a dependence of the former on the latter, notwithstanding a nominal and apparent separation; that as, from the natural feebleness of the judiciary, it is in continual jeopardy of being overpowered, awed, or influenced by its coordinate branches; and that as nothing can contribute so much to its firmness and independence as permanency in office, this quality may therefore be justly regarded as an indispensable ingredient in its constitution, and, in a great measure, as the citadel of the public justice and the public security.

The complete independence of the courts of justice is peculiarly essential in a limited Constitution. By a limited Constitution, I understand one which contains certain specified exceptions to the legislative authority; such, for instance, as that it shall pass no bills of attainder, no *ex-post-facto* laws, and the like. Limitations of this kind can be preserved in practice no other way than through the medium of courts of justice, whose duty it must be to declare all acts contrary to the manifest tenor of the Constitution void. Without this, all the reservations of particular rights or privileges would amount to nothing.

Some perplexity respecting the rights of the courts to pronounce legislative acts void, because contrary to the Constitution, has arisen from an imagination that the doctrine would imply a superiority of the judiciary to the legislative power. It is urged that the authority which can declare the acts of another void, must necessarily be superior to the one whose acts may be declared void. As this doctrine is of great importance in all the American constitutions, a brief discussion of the ground on which it rests cannot be unacceptable.

There is no position which depends on clearer principles, than that every act of a delegated authority, contrary to the tenor of the commission under which it is exercised, is void. No legislative act, therefore, contrary to the Constitution, can be valid. To deny this, would be to affirm, that the deputy is greater than his principal; that the servant is above his master; that the representatives of the people are superior to the people themselves; that men acting by virtue of powers, may do not only what their powers do not authorize, but what they forbid.

If it be said that the legislative body are themselves the constitutional judges of their own powers, and that the construction they put upon them is conclusive upon the other departments, it may be answered, that this cannot be the natural presumption, where it is not to be collected from any particular provisions in the Constitution. It is not otherwise to be supposed, that the Constitution could intend to enable the representatives of the people to substitute their WILL to that of their constituents. It is far more rational to suppose, that the courts were designed to be an intermediate body between the people and the legislature, in order, among other things, to keep the latter within the limits assigned to their authority. The interpretation of the laws is the proper and peculiar province of the courts. A constitution is, in fact, and must be regarded by the judges, as a fundamental law. It therefore belongs to them to ascertain its meaning, as well as the meaning of any particular act proceeding from the legislative body. If there should happen to be an irreconcilable variance between the two, that which has the superior obligation and validity ought, of course, to be preferred; or, in other words, the Constitution ought to be preferred to the statute, the intention of the people to the intention of their agents.

Nor does this conclusion by any means suppose a superiority of the judicial to the legislative power. It only supposes that the power of the people is superior to both; and that where the will of the legislature, declared in its statutes, stands in opposition to that of the people, declared in the Constitution, the judges ought to be governed by the latter rather than the former. They ought to regulate their decisions by the fundamental laws, rather than by those which are not fundamental.

This exercise of judicial discretion, in determining between two contradictory laws, is exemplified in a familiar instance. It not uncommonly happens, that there are two statutes existing at one time, clashing in whole or in part with each other, and neither of them containing any repealing clause or expression. In such a case, it is the province of the courts to liquidate and fix their meaning and operation. So far as they can, by any fair construction, be reconciled to each other, reason and law conspire to dictate that this should be done; where this is impracticable, it becomes a matter of necessity to give effect to one, in exclusion of the other. The rule which has obtained in the courts for determining their relative validity is, that the last in order of time shall be preferred to the first. But this is a mere rule of construction, not derived from any positive law, but from the nature and reason of the thing. It is a rule not enjoined upon the courts by legislative provision, but adopted by themselves, as consonant to truth and propriety, for the direction of their conduct as interpreters of the law. They thought it reasonable, that between the interfering acts of an EQUAL authority, that which was the last indication of its will should have the preference.

But in regard to the interfering acts of a superior and subordinate authority, of an original and derivative power, the nature and reason of the thing indicate the converse of that rule as proper to be followed. They teach us that the prior act of a superior ought to be preferred to the subsequent act of an inferior and subordinate authority; and that accordingly, whenever a particular statute contravenes the Constitution, it will be the duty of the judicial tribunals to adhere to the latter and disregard the former.

It can be of no weight to say that the courts, on the pretense of a repugnancy, may substitute their own pleasure to the constitutional intentions of the legislature. This might as well happen in the case of two contradictory statutes; or it might as well happen in every adjudication upon any single statute. The courts must declare the sense of the law; and if they should be disposed to exercise WILL instead of JUDGMENT, the consequence would equally be the substitution of their pleasure to that of the legislative body. The observation, if it prove any thing, would prove that there ought to be no judges distinct from that body.

If, then, the courts of justice are to be considered as the bulwarks of a limited Constitution against legislative encroachments, this consideration will afford a strong argument for the permanent tenure of judicial offices, since nothing will contribute so much as this to that independent spirit in the judges which must be essential to the faithful performance of so arduous a duty.

This independence of the judges is equally requisite to guard the Constitution and the rights of individuals from the effects of those ill humors, which the arts of designing men, or the influence of particular conjunctures, sometimes disseminate among the people themselves, and which, though they speedily give place to better information, and more deliberate reflection, have a tendency, in the meantime, to occasion dangerous innovations in the government, and serious oppressions of the minor party in the community. Though I trust the friends of the proposed Constitution will never concur with its enemies, in questioning that fundamental principle of republican government, which admits the right of the people to alter or abolish the established Constitution, whenever they find it inconsistent with their happiness, yet it is not to be inferred from this principle, that the representatives of the people, whenever a momentary inclination happens to lay hold of a majority of their constituents, incompatible with the provisions in the existing Constitution, would, on that account, be justifiable in a violation of those provisions; or that the courts would be under a greater obligation to connive at infractions in this shape, than when they had proceeded wholly from the cabals of the representative body. Until the people have, by some solemn and authoritative act, annulled or changed the established form, it is binding upon themselves collectively, as well as individually; and no presumption, or even knowledge, of their sentiments, can warrant their representatives in a departure from it, prior to such an act. But it is easy to see, that it would require an uncommon portion of fortitude in the judges to do their duty as faithful guardians of the Constitution, where legislative invasions of it had been instigated by the major voice of the community.

But it is not with a view to infractions of the Constitution only, that the independence of the judges may be an essential safeguard against the effects of occasional ill humors in the society. These sometimes extend no farther than to the injury of the private rights of particular classes of citizens, by unjust and partial laws. Here also the firmness of the judicial magistracy is of vast importance in mitigating the severity and confining the operation of such laws. It not only serves to moderate the immediate mischiefs of those which may have been passed, but it operates as a check upon the legislative body in passing them; who, perceiving that obstacles to the success of iniquitous intention are to be expected from the scruples of the courts, are in a manner compelled, by the very motives of the injustice they meditate, to qualify their attempts. This is a circumstance calculated to have more influence upon the character of our governments, than but few may be aware of. The benefits of the integrity and moderation of the judiciary have already been felt in more States than one; and though they may have displeased those whose sinister expectations they may have disappointed, they must have commanded the esteem and applause of all the virtuous and disinterested. Considerate men, of every description, ought to prize whatever will tend to beget or fortify that temper in the courts: as no man can be sure that he may not be to-morrow the victim of a spirit of injustice, by which he may be a gainer to-day. And every man must now feel, that the inevitable tendency of such a spirit is to sap the foundations of public and private confidence, and to introduce in its stead universal distrust and distress.

That inflexible and uniform adherence to the rights of the Constitution, and of individuals, which we perceive to be indispensable in the courts of justice, can certainly not be expected from judges who hold their offices by a temporary commission. Periodical appointments, however regulated, or by whomsoever made, would, in some way or other, be fatal to their necessary independence. If the power of making them was committed either to the Executive or legislature, there would be danger of an improper complaisance to the branch which possessed it; if to both, there would be an unwillingness to hazard the displeasure of either; if to the people, or the persons chosen by them for the special purpose, there would be too great a disposition to consult popularity, to justify a reliance that nothing would be consulted but the Constitution and the laws.

There is yet a further and a weightier reason for the permanency of the judicial offices, which is deducible from the nature of the qualifications they require. It has been frequently remarked, with great propriety, that a voluminous code of laws is one of the inconveniences necessarily connected with the advantages of a free government. To avoid an arbitrary discretion in the courts, it is indispensable that they should be bound down by strict rules and precedents, which serve to define and point out their duty in every particular case that comes before them; and it will readily be conceived from the variety of controversies which grow out of the folly and wickedness of mankind, that the records of those precedents must unavoidably swell to a very considerable bulk, and must demand long and laborious study to acquire a competent knowledge of them. Hence it is, that there can be but few men in the society who will have sufficient skill in the laws to qualify them for the stations of judges. And making the proper deductions for the ordinary depravity of human nature, the number must be still smaller of those who unite the requisite integrity with the requisite knowledge. These considerations apprise us, that the government can have no great option between fit character; and that a temporary duration in office, which would naturally discourage such characters from quitting a lucrative line of practice to accept a seat on the bench, would have a tendency to throw the administration of justice into hands less able, and less well qualified, to conduct it with utility and dignity. In the present circumstances of this country, and in those in which it is likely to be for a long time to come, the disadvantages on this score would be greater than they may at first sight appear; but it must be confessed, that they are far inferior to those which present themselves under the other aspects of the subject.

Upon the whole, there can be no room to doubt that the convention acted wisely in copying from the models of those constitutions which have established GOOD BEHAVIOR as the tenure of their judicial offices, in point of duration; and that so far from being blamable on this account, their plan would have been inexcusably defective, if it had wanted this important feature of good government. The experience of Great Britain affords an illustrious comment on the excellence of the institution. ■

12.2 *Marbury* v. *Madison* (1803)

Chief Justice John Marshall

[In 1801, at the very end of his presidential term, John Adams made a number of last-minute judicial appointments, hoping to install members of his own Federalist party in key positions before the Republican president, Thomas Jefferson, took over. One of these appointments was given to William Marbury, who was appointed to be a justice of the peace of the District of Columbia. In the confusion of the last few days of Adams's term, however, Marbury's commission was never delivered to him. When President Jefferson came into the White House, he held up Marbury's commission. Marbury sued in the Supreme Court, asking the Court to order the new secretary of state, James Madison, to deliver the commission to him.

The legal and political aspects of the case are extremely complex. Chief Justice Marshall, a staunch Federalist, did not want to condone Jefferson's actions, but he also did not want to risk ordering the administration to deliver the commission; he would be a laughing stock if Jefferson and Madison simply ignored him. He solved this dilemma by writing a strong opinion condemning Jefferson's acts as illegal but refusing to issue a compliance order. To do so, Marshall concluded, would be unconstitutional.

In one stroke, Marshall embarrassed Jefferson, protected his own position, and claimed for the first time the power to review acts of Congress as unconstitutional. The part of the argument making the last point follows.]

• • •

The question, whether an act, repugnant to the constitution, can become the law of the land, is a question deeply interesting to the United States; but, happily, not of an intricacy proportioned to its interest. It seems only necessary to recognize certain principles, supposed to have been long and well established, to decide it.

That the people have an original right to establish, for their future government, such principles as, in their opinion, shall most conduce to their own happiness, is the basis on which the whole American fabric has been erected. The exercise of this original right is a very great exertion; nor can it, nor ought it, to be frequently repeated. The principles, therefore, so established, are deemed fundamental. And as the authority from which they proceed, is supreme, and can seldom act, they are designed to be permanent.

This original and supreme will organizes the government, and assigns, to different departments, their respective powers. It may either stop here; or establish certain limits not to be transcended by those departments.

The government of the United States is of the latter description. The powers of the legislature are defined, and limited; and that those limits may not be mistaken, or forgotten, the constitution is written. To what purpose are powers limited, and to what purpose is that limitation committed to writing, if these limits may, at any time, be passed by those intended to be restrained? The distinction,

5 U.S. (1 Cranch) 137 (1803).

between a government with limited and unlimited powers, is abolished, if those limits do not confine the persons on whom they are imposed, and if acts prohibited and acts allowed, are of equal obligation. It is a proposition too plain to be contested, that the constitution controls any legislative act repugnant to it; or, that the legislature may alter the constitution by an ordinary act.

Between these alternatives there is no middle ground. The constitution is either a superior, paramount law, unchangeable by ordinary means, or it is on a level with ordinary legislative acts, and, like other acts, is alterable when the legislature shall please to alter it.

If the former part of the alternative be true, then a legislative act contrary to the constitution is not law: if the latter part be true, then written constitutions are absurd attempts, on the part of the people, to limit a power, in its own nature illimitable.

Certainly all those who have framed written constitutions contemplate them as forming the fundamental and paramount law of the nation, and consequently the theory of every such government must be, that an act of the legislature, repugnant to the constitution, is void.

This theory is essentially attached to a written constitution, and is, consequently to be considered, by this court, as one of the fundamental principles of our society. It is not therefore to be lost sight of in the future consideration of this subject.

If an act of the legislature, repugnant to the constitution, is void, does it, notwithstanding its invalidity, bind the courts, and oblige them to give it effect? Or, in other words, though it be not law, does it constitute a rule as operative as if it was a law? This would be to overthrow in fact what was established in theory; and would seem, at first view, an absurdity too gross to be insisted on. It shall, however, receive a more attentive consideration.

It is emphatically the province and duty of the judicial department to say what the law is. Those who apply the rule to particular cases, must of necessity expound and interpret that rule. If two laws conflict with each other, the courts must decide on the operation of each.

So if a law be in opposition to the constitution; if both the law and the constitution apply to a particular case, so that the court must either decide that case conformably to the law, disregarding the constitution; or conformably to the constitution, disregarding the law; the court must determine which of these conflicting rules governs the case. This is of the very essence of judicial duty.

If, then, the courts are to regard the constitution; and the constitution is superior to any ordinary act of the legislature; the constitution, and not such ordinary act, must govern the case to which they both apply.

Those then who controvert the principle that the constitution is to be considered, in court, as a paramount law, are reduced to the necessity of maintaining that courts must close their eyes on the constitution, and see only the law.

This doctrine would subvert the very foundation of all written constitutions. It would declare that an act which, according to the principles and theory of our government, is entirely void; is yet, in practice, completely obligatory. It would declare, that if the legislature shall do what is expressly forbidden, such act, notwithstanding the express prohibition, is in reality effectual. It would be giving to the legislature a practical and real omnipotence, with the same breath which professes to restrict their powers within narrow limits. It is prescribing limits, and declaring that those limits may be passed at pleasure.

That it thus reduces to nothing what we have deemed the greatest improvement on political institutions—a written constitution—would of itself be sufficient, in America, where written constitutions have been viewed with so much reverence, for rejecting the construction. But the peculiar expressions of the constitution of the United States furnish additional arguments in favour of its rejection.

The judicial power of the United States is extended to all cases arising under the constitution.

Could it be the intention of those who gave this power, to say that, in using it, the constitution should not be looked into? That a case arising under the constitution should be decided without examining the instrument under which it arises?

This is too extravagant to be maintained.

In some cases, then, the constitution must be looked into by the judges. And if they can open it at all, what part of it are they forbidden to read, or to obey?

There are many other parts of the constitution which serve to illustrate this subject. It is declared that "no tax or duty shall be laid on articles exported from any state." Suppose a duty on the export of cotton, of tobacco, or of flour; and a suit instituted to recover it. Ought judgment to be rendered in such a case? ought the judges to close their eyes on the constitution, and only see the law?

The constitution declares that "no bill of attainder or *ex post facto* law shall be passed."

If, however, such a bill should be passed and a person should be prosecuted under it; must the court condemn to death those victims whom the constitution endeavors to preserve?

"No person," says the constitution, "shall be convicted of treason unless on the testimony of two witnesses to the same overt act, or on confession in open court."

Here the language of the constitution is addressed especially to the courts. It prescribes, directly for them, a rule of evidence not to be departed from. If the legislature should change that rule, and declare one witness, or a confession out of court, sufficient for conviction, must the constitutional principle yield to the legislative act?

From these, and many other selections which might be made, it is apparent, that the framers of the constitution contemplated that instrument, as a rule for the government of *courts*, as well as of the legislature.

Why otherwise does it direct the judges to take an oath to support it? This oath certainly applies, in an especial manner, to their conduct in their official character. How immoral to impose it on them, if they were to be used as the instruments, and the knowing instruments, for violating what they swear to support!

The oath of office, too, imposed by the legislature, is completely demonstrative of the legislative opinion on this subject. It is in these words: "I do solemnly swear that I will administer justice without respect to persons, and do equal right to the poor and to the rich; and that I will faithfully and impartially discharge all the duties incumbent on me as according to the best of my abilities and understanding, agreeably to *the constitution*, and laws of the United States."

Why does a judge swear to discharge his duties agreeably to the constitution of the United States, if that constitution forms no rule for his government? If it is closed upon him, and cannot be inspected by him?

If such be the real state of things, this is worse than solemn mockery. To prescribe, or to take this oath, becomes equally a crime.

It is also not entirely unworthy of observation that in declaring what shall be the *supreme* law of the land, the *constitution* itself is first mentioned; and not the laws of the United States generally, but those only which shall be made in *pursuance* of the constitution, have that rank.

Thus, the particular phraseology of the constitution of the United States confirms and strengthens the principle, supposed to be essential to all written constitutions, that a law repugnant to the constitution is void; and that *courts*, as well as other departments, are bound by that instrument. . . . ■

 # American Politics Today

Linda Greenhouse—who for many years has covered the United States Supreme Court for the *New York Times*—has a unique vantage point from which to view the Court. She sees the Court not only as a legal analyst, but also as a journalist and as a representative of the public. In this selection, Greenhouse focuses not on specific doctrines or cases, but on the Court's overall roles and responsibilities. Her goal is to set out a series of "performance standards" by which the American people can judge the Court's performance.

Questions

1. How does the Court's role as a political institution change its responsibilities to the general public? In what ways do Greenhouse's "performance standards" reflect the political role of the Court?
2. What are the implications of Greenhouse's arguments for the selection of judges to serve on the United States Supreme Court? Based on Greenhouse's analysis, what qualities or qualifications might a president look for in appointing new justices?

12.3 Beyond *Bush* v. *Gore* (2002)

Linda Greenhouse

• • •

There is a Rehnquist Court revolution in progress, and it is definitely not an equal protection revolution. Nor is it a states' rights revolution, as I had often thought and written in the six years since the Court in *United States* v. *Lopez* struck down an exercise of Congress' commerce power for the first time in sixty years. Rather, it is a separation of powers revolution that has to do with the primacy of the judicial branch and of the Court itself. . . .

Where do we go from here? That depends on many variables, including the timing of any retirements and the politics of filling the vacancies. That is beyond our collective power to predict. One thing of which I am certain is that we need to maintain an active and informed civic dialogue about the Court. Everyone has done their screaming and venting or possibly, cheering, about *Bush* v. *Gore,* but there are seventy-five other cases for decision this Term, many of them quite important, and it is important that they receive full attention.

I thought I might spend a few minutes putting the election case aside, if that is possible. I obviously cannot analyze the entire docket. What might be more helpful is for me to offer a generic road map, a template for observing the Court and assessing its work regardless of the particular doctrinal area involved and one's view of the merits of a particular decision. I think, that as citizens, we are entitled to hold the Court to a set of performance standards, and I will sketch these out briefly and offer some examples from the past few Terms of what I am talking about.

At the most basic level, the Court owes the public an obligation to speak clearly. Obviously, there will be specialized language in any legal opinion, but an educated person ought to be able to pick up a Supreme Court opinion, make sense of the reasoning, find a clear bottom line, and count the vote, without making a two-color chart. . . .

As consumers of the Court's work, it seems to me we have a right to expect opinions that we can understand, at least structurally. After all, the power of judicial review is an extraordinary power—one of America's major gifts to democracy and political theory. That great power gives the Court what Professor Burke Marshall of Yale Law School has called the "preeminent duty of principled explanation of what is actually going on in constitutional decision-making," or what Professor Joseph Goldstein described as "the Supreme Court's obligation to maintain the Constitution as something we the people can understand."

That raises another question: Who is the Court's audience, after all? Yes, it is, in Professor Goldstein's words, "we the people," but I think that is a bit romantic and not too realistic. Judges of other courts in the federal and state systems are an

"Thinking About the Supreme Court After *Bush* v. *Gore*," by Linda Greenhouse, *Indiana Law Review*. 35 Ind. L. Rev. 435, 2002. Reprinted by permission.

important audience, of course, and I know, from my conversations with judges over the years, that they are as frustrated as anyone else when the Supreme Court fails to attain a basic level of coherence.

However, I want to focus on the wider audience for the Court's work. The public learns about Supreme Court opinions only derivatively, through the media, or as mediated by politicians or leaders of other sectors of society. How many people believe that the Court's school prayer decisions of the 1960s expelled God from the classroom, because that is what sloppy journalism and political demagoguery told them the Court did? Does the distinction matter? It absolutely does.

In evaluating whether the Court is doing a good job of communicating, we must look at how the Court communicates to the specialized audience that in turn is going to carry the message to the wider audience of people who will never in their entire lives hold a Supreme Court opinion in their hands.

The Court's relationship with the press is problematic at best. The Court is not so much hostile to the press as it is, often, oblivious to what the press needs in order to do an adequate job of describing the Court's work. I do not mean this comment as special pleading. To the extent the Court is oblivious to the needs of the press, it is oblivious to its need to communicate to the public.

I do not mean background briefings on the real meaning of opinions; I'm a realist. I understand the culture of an institution that has not changed much since the late Justice William Brennan spoke to a group of law students in 1959:

A great Chief Justice of my home State [Arthur Vanderbilt of New Jersey] was asked by a reporter to tell him what was meant by a passage in an opinion which had excited much lay comment. Replied the Chief Justice, "Sir, we write opinions, we don't explain them." This wasn't arrogance—it was his picturesque, if blunt, way of reminding the reporter that the reasons behind the social policy fostering an independent judiciary also require that the opinions by which judges support decisions must stand on their own merits without embellishment or comment from the judges who write or join them.

Now I do not mean sitting at the Justices' elbows or interviewing them behind the scenes on the deeper meanings of their opinions. Rather, I would have a more modest wish list. The spacing of opinions, for example, sounds almost foolishly trivial as an issue. However, considering the number of finite commodities involved in digesting and reporting news about the Supreme Court (or about anything else for that matter), a finite amount of time to make the evening news or next day's newspaper, the finite amount of broadcast time or space in the paper, the finite number of human beings to handle the material, timing emerges as an important issue.

The Court always finishes its Term with a bang, with most of the major decisions coming in the last few weeks of June. That is only human. Like any other institution, the Justices save the hardest work for the end. In the Term that ended last June [2001], for example, the Court on its final day issued 391 pages of opinions deciding four major cases: the Boy Scouts' right to exclude gay members, the Nebraska partial birth abortion case, a case on the permissible limits of federal aid to parochial schools, and a First Amendment case on restrictions on demonstrations outside abortion clinics. Earlier in the same week, the Court issued its decisions reaffirming *Miranda* v. *Arizona*, striking down California's blanket primary system, and issuing highly significant new rules requiring jury participation in criminal sentencing. Now, this was nothing compared to the last day of the 1987 Term when the Court handed down an entire volume of *U.S. Reports*.

Ideally, newspapers and television networks would expand to fit the news from the Court, and people would be able to cover it all. I have written three, and on rare occasions, four Court stories in a day—not particularly well, by the third or fourth story, but if I can write them, my newspaper will probably print them. However, most of the media do not have my employer's priorities, and when opinions come in a huge rush like this, the triage is brutal.

I once mentioned this problem to Chief Justice [William] Rehnquist, who listened sympathetically and then said, quite cordially, "Well, just because we put them out on one day doesn't mean you have to write them all on one day—save some for the next day." At that point, I lost all hope that we could ever have a meeting of the minds on the subject of the desirability of the Court—in its own interest and in the public interest—to accommodate the needs of the press.

Let us move on: assuming some minimal level of coherence and some minimal accommodation to the realities of press coverage—I would like to focus on candor. Is the Court being honest with its audience? Is the Court dealing squarely with precedent, or is it playing games with precedent? These are not just questions of style. They go to the reliable and orderly development of the law.

There are numerous recent examples of the Court not dealing squarely with precedent . . . [An example is] *Romer* v. *Evans*, the decision that struck down, on equal protection grounds, Colorado's constitutional amendment that barred any public entity in the state from adopting gay rights legislation. Justice [Anthony] Kennedy's majority opinion did not even cite *Bowers* v. *Hardwick*, the Court's 1986 decision holding that homosexual relations between consenting adults are not protected by the constitutional right to privacy. There were no doubt strong strategic reasons for Justice Kennedy to avoid any mention to *Bowers*, which is still on the books. He was not on the Court when it decided *Bowers*, but Justice Sandra Day O'Connor was a member of the *Bowers* majority, and avoiding mention of *Bowers* may have freed her to join the *Romer* majority without the explicit need to reconcile the two votes. Nonetheless, and despite the considerable merit of the *Romer* opinion, this was scarcely the most intellectually honest way of dealing with the state of the law. In fact, if a purpose of a Supreme Court decision is to guide the lower courts in the consistent development of the law, the success of the *Romer* decision is quite problematic. . . .

A subset of the candor issue is the question of consistency. Two recent decisions provided a striking example of the absence of consistency—might I suggest, of the result-orientation—in the Court's treatment of what it likes to call "bright line rules."

Both decisions were in criminal cases, both were Fourth Amendment cases, and both had to do with the encounter between police officers and people in cars. The first was *Ohio* v. *Robinette*. The Ohio Supreme Court had ruled that once a police officer makes an otherwise valid traffic stop, that officer may not, in the absence of any suspicion of further, hidden wrongdoing, begin interrogating the driver about whether he has drugs or other contraband in the car unless the officer first advises the driver that he does not have to answer these questions and is legally free to go. Only that explicit advice can make a subsequent search, even one the driver has agreed to, truly consensual.

Not surprisingly, the Court, in *Robinette* overturned this decision, by an 8–1 vote, in an opinion by Chief Justice Rehnquist. The Chief Justice said, in a rather weary tone, that the Court had said over and over again that the test under the Fourth Amendment was "reasonableness" and that the Ohio court had gone astray in trying to construct a bright line rule. "[W]e have consistently eschewed bright line rules," he said, "instead emphasizing the fact-specific nature of the reasonableness inquiry."

Then came *Maryland* v. *Wilson*, another state appeal from a ruling by a state court. In this case, the Maryland Court of Special Appeals ruled that a police officer may not, as a matter of course and in the absence of any suspicion, order a passenger out of a car that was stopped because the driver was speeding or for some other routine reason. The Maryland court refused to extend to passengers the rule of *Pennsylvania* v. *Mimms*, a 1977 Supreme Court case holding that the police, for their own safety, may routinely order the driver out of the car during a routine traffic stop.

Not surprisingly, the Supreme Court overturned this decision as well, in another opinion by Chief Justice Rehnquist. The Court said the Maryland court was wrong in not adopting a bright line rule. "While there is not the same basis for ordering the passengers out of the car as there is for ordering the driver out, the additional intrusion on the passenger is minimal," the Chief Justice said. "We therefore hold that an officer making a traffic stop may order passengers to get out of the car pending completion of the stop." Well, so much for case by case assessment of Fourth Amendment reasonableness. . . .

Let me turn now to a different subject, the question of the Court's voice, or specifically, the voice of dissent. We certainly have to expect differences of opinion on the Court, especially on questions that divide the society of which, after all, the Court is only a mirror. But I think we can also expect these differences to be expressed without personal invective. In his dissenting opinion in *Romer*, Justice [Antonin] Scalia's invocation of a "Kulturkampf," his excoriation of "the elite class from which the Members of this institution are selected," did not leave readers with confidence that the constitutionality of Colorado's Amendment 2 was being debated on the basis of legal principles rather than emotional invective.

Before we leave the question of the Court's voice, I want to touch on an elusive subject that for lack of a better word we might call institutional compassion. I do not mean compassion in the touchy-feely sense. Rather, what I want to convey is my sense that good judging requires some institutional ability to look at the world, or at the complaint, or at the appeal, from a point of view other than what might come naturally to the judge. I am not advocating knocking down precedents that stand inconveniently in the way of a sympathetic outcome. Nonetheless, I was rather amused recently by a pair of criminal cases, decided within a week of one another, that seemed to call for some comment along this line.

In one case, *Minnesota* v. *Carter*, the question was whether the police violated the Fourth Amendment rights of the occupants of a ground floor apartment whom a police officer observed, while standing on the grass and looking through the crooked and not quite closed venetian blinds, engaged in the task of preparing cocaine for distribution. In upholding the criminal convictions, Chief Justice Rehnquist's majority opinion did not reach the underlying issue of the validity of the search, but rather held that the defendants did not even have standing to challenge the search because they were not the owners or renters of the apartment, but were just passing through, as temporary guests engaging in a business transaction.

The next week, in *Knowles* v. *Iowa*, the Court decided a criminal case with a different outcome and quite a different flavor. The question was whether a simple speeding ticket could justify a police officer in conducting a search of the entire car. In this case the Court quickly and unanimously, in another opinion by Chief Justice Rehnquist, said no, overturning a conviction for the marijuana the police had found in the speeding motorist's car. There was no justification for the further search, the Chief Justice said.

I do not want to be unfair, but looking at these two cases, it was hard to escape the sense that the Justices may have identified a bit more with someone stopped for speeding—as several of them have been—than with temporary denizens of a ground floor apartment in a housing project. The Justices were downright solicitous of the interests of the driver and quite dismissive of the privacy interests of the apartment's occupants, even though both had drug offenses in common. Is it possible the Justices could see themselves standing in the shoes of the one and not the other?

Let me move from voice to, what for lack of a better word, I will call reach. What should be the Court's stance toward its work? How directly should the Court confront the myth of judicial infallibility—what Professor Paul Gewirtz calls "the ideology of perfectionism"? And should we give the Court points or demerits for admitting that some cases and some questions are just too hard for the Court to speak definitively about? After all, it was Justice Robert Jackson who said, in his great opinion in the flag salute case, "we act in these matters not by authority of our competence but by force of our commissions." We need a Supreme Court that at the end of the day is going to tell us what the law is.

But there is a new academic interest in what Professor Cass Sunstein of the University of Chicago calls "decisional minimalism" or "the constructive uses of silence." Minimalism is to be favored, according to this school of thought, when the Court is dealing with issues that are in flux, and on which democratic debate has not yet run its course. Professor Sunstein has high praise for the *Romer* opinion, which he calls "puzzling and opaque" and unsatisfying from a theoretical point of view, but from a broader institutional and political point of view, "a masterful stroke—an extraordinary and salutary moment in American law" precisely because it said no more than it had to say to decide the case at hand while not foreclosing further development.

By the same token, Justice [Stephen] Breyer's unusual opinion in the Denver cable indecency case . . . has won wide praise from academics although not, I hasten to add, from either practicing lawyers or lower court judges, who have criticized the opinion for not giving adequate guidance on cable television's place in the First Amendment pantheon. Perhaps this disparity between academia and practitioners just goes to show how out of touch the law professors are, but I will use it to make a different point—it illustrates the different premises that go into evaluating the Court's work.

What Justice Breyer basically said in *Denver* was that the technology was moving so fast that the Court should not lock itself into a hard and fast set of First Amendment rules for evaluating indecency on cable television or more generally, for how traditional First Amendment doctrine applies to nontraditional media. Specifically, Justice Breyer said, "aware as we are of the changes taking place in the law, the technology, and the industrial structure related to telecommunications, . . . we believe it unwise and unnecessary definitively to pick one analogy or one specific set of words now."

Indeterminacy of this sort can undoubtedly sometimes be the better part of wisdom. Just as clearly, it has its dangers in the hands of a Court that does not quite know how to get where it wants to go. The Court's recent decisions involving affirmative action and, particularly, race-based redistricting, strike me as examples of inconclusiveness being more troublesome than helpful. Justice O'Connor's 1993 opinion in *Shaw* v. *Reno,* which launched the Court on its ongoing examination of majority-black congressional districts, was extremely unsettling to the law and was highly charged rhetorically, using words such as "bizarre" and "apartheid." But it never really explained whether the Equal Protection problem with these districts was their shape, the race consciousness with which they were created, or some inchoate and unpredictable combination of the two. Proof of how much difficulty the Court created for itself is that it had to review the constitutionality of the twelfth congressional district of North Carolina four times in seven years, because the rules were so unclear that the case kept coming back. . . .

On the other hand, I think the Court deserves substantial credit for the clarity with which it addressed the question of free speech on the Internet when it finally did reach that issue a couple of years ago, in a case that is not necessarily the Court's last word on the subject but was a very important first word. In striking down the Communications Decency Act, in its essentially unanimous opinion in *Reno* v. *American Civil Liberties Union,* the Court announced with great clarity that First Amendment principles apply fully to speech on the Internet and that the government can regulate speech in that forum only with the most compelling of justifications. Not only the result of that case, but the Court's clarity of expression, will have a major impact on the further development of this new medium.

The Court also deserves credit for setting out clear rules for both employers and employees on the question of sexual harassment in the workplace, and I give Justice Scalia credit for the clarity of his opinion for a unanimous Court recently, upholding the authority of the Environmental Protection Agency to issue regulations under the Clean Air Act and re-burying the non-delegation doctrine that the D.C. Circuit had so provocatively revived two years before.

As I said earlier, my goal was to offer a kind of road map out of the election case that might help guide you in thinking about the Court in the months and years ahead. Much as we need and deserve a competent, candid, and comprehensive Supreme Court, the Court needs an attentive, informed citizenry to monitor, critique, and build upon its efforts. ■

The International Context

Compared with judicial institutions in other countries, the United States Supreme Court plays a major role in making public policy. While some view the Court's policy-making activities as necessary and justifiable, others charge the Court with "judicial activism," arguing that the justices should focus on interpreting and applying the law, leaving policy making to Congress, the White House, and the states.

Whatever the merits of this debate, few doubt that the American Supreme Court plays an important role in resolving questions that, in other nations, are left to the legislative and executive branches. In this selection, the political scientist Mark C. Miller uses a comparison between the United States and Canada to examine why an activist judiciary developed in one country but not the other.

Questions

1. What is judicial activism? Why do some suggest that judicial activism is defensible and appropriate while others argue that judicial activism undermines the principles of federalism and the separation of powers?
2. What, according to Miller, accounts for the presence of a more activist judiciary in the United States than in Canada?

12.4 Judicial Activism in Canada and the United States (1998)

Mark C. Miller

The legal systems of Canada and the United States share many common characteristics. Both have their roots in British Common Law. Legal training is similar, and both countries draw their judges primarily from the practicing bar. But despite their similarities, Canadian and U.S. judges have approached their policy-making roles quite differently.

Why? Perhaps the traditional lack of judicial activism in Canada may in part be due to the less political judicial selection system used in that country when compared to the highly public and contested judicial selection processes used for the more activist U.S. courts.

While scholars use the terms judicial activism and judicial restraint often, these concepts can be difficult to define and remain controversial. In general, judicial activism means that the courts are willing to make public policy when the other

Mark C. Miller, "Judicial Activism in Canada and the United States," *Judicature* 81 (May–June 1998), pp. 262–265. Reprinted by permission of the American Judicature Society.

institutions of government either cannot or will not. In *The Global Expansion of Judicial Power* (1995), Neal Tate and Torbjorn Vallinder define judicial activism as "The transfer of decision-making rights from the legislature, the cabinet, or the civil service to the courts." Judicial activism in the United States also means interpreting the U.S. Constitution with a modern eye and adapting the interpretation of the document for contemporary society.

Judicial restraint usually means that the courts defer to the decisions of other political institutions, and in the United States it also means that the federal Constitution is interpreted as intended by the framers. Some opponents of judicial activism use the pejorative "judicial legislating" or similar terms to refer to the policy-making activities of judges.

Activism in Canada

Canadian courts have a long tradition of attempting to separate law and politics, and therefore they also have a long tradition of attempting to avoid judicial activism. As Carl Baar stated in *Judicial Activism in Comparative Perspective* (1991), "The judiciary played an important but largely invisible role in the Canadian political system for over a century." And as Peter Russell notes in his 1987 book *The Judiciary in Canada: The Third Branch of Government*, "Canadians are not conditioned to think of courts as part of the political system. . . . The role of the judiciary is perceived as being essentially technical and non-political; it is there to apply the laws made by the political branches of government."

The passage of the Canadian Charter of Rights and Freedoms in 1982 changed the perception and the role of the courts as policy makers. The charter gave the Canadian courts much greater powers of judicial review. Because it included difficult concepts and provisions, the Canadian courts were almost forced to interpret the new constitutional rights contained within it in order to clarify issues of human rights in a complex modern society. After the passage of the charter, the courts in Canada and especially the supreme court became quite activist for a period. But after 1986 it backed away from activist charter decisions. Even though the Canadian Supreme Court has now taken on a policy-making role as it interprets the charter, it nonetheless remains less activist than many courts in the United States.

Judicial activism today still remains foreign to most Canadian judges. In a 1990 study involving interviews with many judges in Alberta and Ontario, Peter McCormick and Ian Greene found little support among Canadian judges for an activist role. As these scholars explain, "Although the interviews clearly suggest that many judges see some law-making as a legitimate component of their duties, this by no means implies that they see this as an activist role for the judiciary in promoting the causes of social reform or political challenge. In fact, quite the reverse is true." For example, of the 51 Alberta judges interviewed, only 11 described their role orientation as activist. In a study published in 1997, Greene, Baar, and McCormick were able to interview 89 court of appeal and supreme court judges in Canada— only two reported seeing their judicial role as primarily "law-makers."

Most of the judges interviewed in connection with this article were certainly uncomfortable with the judicial activist role because they clearly felt that judges should not be policy makers unless absolutely necessary. In fact, most were quite critical of other activist judges in the country. In the Canadian tradition, most of the interviewees articulated a strong belief that political questions should remain separate from legal questions. They also stressed the need for the courts to remain independent from politics. Judges in Canada have generally avoided the public debate on judicial activism that has often occurred in the United States. Thus, even after the enactment of the charter, Canadian judges seem hesitant to take on a judicial activist role.

While judicial activism is a relatively new phenomenon in Canada, most social scientists argue that the U.S. courts have long practiced it. And in recent decades many U.S. courts have become even more activist. According to Larry Baum (*American Courts: Process and Policy*, 1998) from 1960 to 1996 the U.S. Supreme Court struck down 63 federal statutes and 549 state and local ones. These figures are nearly half of the total number of times that the U.S. Supreme Court has struck down legislation throughout its history. Of course, in the United States the lower federal courts and the state courts can also be quite activist.

Court Structure

Although both Canada and the United States have adopted federal systems, the two have structured their courts quite differently. The United States has two distinct and separate parallel court systems—state and federal—sharing the same geographical space. The U.S. Supreme Court's precedents are binding on all courts in both systems, although that court will only hear cases with a significant federal question. Thus the structure of the U.S. court systems is quite complex.

In contrast, the Canadian court system follows a much more unified and singular structure. Minor cases are heard by the provincial trial courts in each province. More serious civil cases begin in superior trial courts located in each province, and each province also has a court of appeal. All judges at the superior court level and above are appointed by the federal government. Since 1949, when appeals to the Judicial Committee of the Privy Council in Britain were finally abolished, the supreme court has served at the apex of this unified pyramid structure.

This rather simple court structure gives the Canadian Supreme Court more ability than the U.S. Supreme Court to increase federal power over the provinces. In interviews, many of the provincial court of appeal judges commented about the power of the Canadian Supreme Court to centralize law in that country. These judges were often concerned that a potentially activist supreme court would increase the power of the federal government over the provinces and the courts located in the provinces. This concern was especially strong in Quebec province, where there is a growing mistrust of federally appointed judges. The court of appeals judges in Quebec feel caught in a difficult position because they serve in Quebec but were appointed by the federal government.

Selection

Judges in the United States are selected using a wide variety of formal selection systems, although it is worth highlighting the fact that each selection system retains a highly political component. U.S. federal judges are appointed for life terms by the president and confirmed by the Senate in a highly political confirmation process. State judges are generally elected in some manner, including retention elections in merit selection states or partisan elections in other states for relatively short terms of office. Thus, in the United States, politics plays a role in the selection of both state and federal judges.

In Canada, all judges at the superior trial court level and above are appointed by the prime minister or the federal minister of justice. The lowest level provincial trial judges are appointed by the provincial cabinets on recommendation of the provincial attorneys general. There is no legislative confirmation process for any of these judges. By tradition, almost all judges in Canada are appointed from the ranks of practicing lawyers or legal academics.

Peter Russell and Jacob Ziegel argue in an influential 1991 *University of Toronto Law Journal* article that, in Canada, "Partisan connections should be irrelevant in identifying the most talented candidates for judicial office." In a study of judicial appointments in Canada, they found that only about half of the federal appointees had any real ties to the prime minister's party, and some of these seemed quite weak. Although these scholars complained about the "patronage" nature of some of the Canadian judicial appointments, in the United States most federal judicial appointees have close ties to the appointing party.

The Canadian judges interviewed for this article prided themselves on not being chosen for their politics. Several went out of their way to note that they were appointed to the superior trial courts by one party and then elevated to the provincial court of appeal by another. They repeatedly stressed how important judicial independence is in the relatively nonpolitical Canadian court system. When asked to state the main differences between judges in the United States and judges in Canada, almost all the Canadian judges interviewed stated that the biggest difference was the political nature of judicial selection and judicial decision making in the United States.

Federalism

Although both Canada and the United States have federal systems of government, the two have chosen very different ways to implement the concept of federalism. At first glance, the division of power between the levels of government seems less vague in Canada than in the United States. The documents that constitute the Canadian constitution, especially the British North America Act of 1867 (after 1982 renamed the Constitution Act of 1867), are much more specific than the U.S. Constitution about which powers are under the jurisdiction of the provinces and which are reserved for the national government. But this clarity may be deceiving. Both societies continue to struggle with the concept of federalism in practice.

Historically, both in the United States and in Canada, the courts have been very active in determining questions of federalism. In the United States, questions of federal constitutional law have occupied the U.S. Supreme Court for almost all of American history. Until very recently, the U.S. courts have generally favored federal power over the states. In the summer of 1997, however, the Supreme Court curtailed the power of the U.S. Congress by declaring that the federal government had no right to require local police officials to perform federally required background checks before an individual could purchase a handgun. It is too early to tell if *Printz* v. *U.S.* signals a severe shift in the balance of power between the federal government and the states, although it does clearly indicate that the U.S. Supreme Court will not allow federal power to increase without any limits.

Canada also has a long history of debate over federalism, and the uncertainty continues today. As Wayne Thompson notes in *Canada 1996*, "The forces of decentralization and centralization are always at work in Canada." In fact, disagreement over questions of federalism have prevented Canada from becoming a truly sovereign people. As Christopher Manfredi has noted in *Judicial Power and the Charter: Canada and the Paradox of Liberal Constitutionalism* (1993), "The complex realities of the division of powers inevitably meant that the judiciary would be forced to become the 'umpire' of federalism." Because questions of federalism have remained so unsettled in Canada, these issues have often become judicial questions.

For example, in February 1998, at the request of the federal government, the Canadian Supreme Court heard oral arguments on the crucial question of what procedures must be followed if a province attempts to leave the federation. The three specific questions before the court were: (1) Does the Canadian Constitution allow Quebec to secede unilaterally? (2) Does international law give Quebec the right to secede? (3) If there is a conflict between these two sources of law, which one would take precedence?

Since it became the final court of appeal in Canada in 1949, the Canadian Supreme Court has been widely perceived as a centralist force in Canadian politics. With the passage of the Constitution Act of 1982, which included the enactment of the Canadian Charter of Rights and Freedoms, the Canadian Supreme Court was faced with a clear mandate to determine the future of constitutional law and federalism. The charter went into effect despite the objections of Quebec, when the supreme court ruled that provincial consent to the new Constitution Act of 1982 did not require unanimous approval among the provinces. Thus the passage of the charter has increased the power of the courts in Canadian society.

But the effects on Canadian federalism of the charter's passage should not be overemphasized. As Peter Russell has concluded, "Thus far, the Supreme Court's application of the charter has not had the predicted centralizing effects on the Canadian federation. There has been very little of the most obvious form of centralization—that is, the Supreme Court's imposition of *national* standards on provincial legislatures. . . . [In fact], some of the Supreme Court's Charter decisions have actually had a decentralizing effect on policy-making" [emphasis in original]. Although given the opportunity to be activist on questions of federalism, the Canadian courts have generally attempted to avoid the activist role on these issues. In part because Canadian courts have not taken an activist approach, questions regarding federalism in Canada have generally been settled through means other than by judicial decision making.

The Activism-Selection Link

Although there may be some convergence occurring, clearly the courts in Canada are less activist than most courts in the United States. U.S. courts also employ the most politically based judicial selection systems on the globe. Are there links between the judicial selection system and the level of judicial activism in that sys-tem? Could it be that the higher the number of political actors involved in the informal judicial selection process, the more likely that judges in that system will be willing to adopt an activist role?

Most of the empirical scholarly work concerning judicial selection processes has focused solely on differences among the formal systems used to select U.S. state and federal judges. But Charles Sheldon and Nicholas Lovrich have argued that scholars should look beyond differences among formal selection systems to exam-ine important differences in the informal procedures and norms used to select judges. In their model, informal judicial selection systems can be compared using the number of participants involved in the initiation, screening, and affirmation stages of the recruitment process. Thus a highly articulated system would have many actors involved in these three stages of judicial recruitment, while a low ar-ticulation system would have very few actors involved. Using this model of the informal procedures used for judicial selection, one can begin to draw the links between judicial selection and the level of judicial activism in any legal system.

Among the industrialized democracies of the world, probably England, France, and Japan have the least activist judges. Using Sheldon and Lovrich's terms, these countries also have some of the lowest judicial selection articulation levels. Thus there appears to be a clear link between the articulation level of the selection sys-tem and the level of judicial activism in that system.

The U.S. and Canadian judicial systems also illustrate this point. The Cana-dian court system certainly maintains a very low articulation level because so few actors are involved at any of the judicial recruitment stages. Although the provinces (especially Quebec) would like more say in who is selected as a judge to serve in their province, to date the debate has not revolved around specific judi-cial appointments. Thus, Canada remains a low articulation system for judicial se-lection, and its judges practice relatively little judicial activism.

On the other hand, the U.S. generally has a very high articulation system for judicial recruitment because so many political actors (including bar associations, interest groups, political parties, elected politicians, voters, the media, and others) take an interest in who is selected at every level of the judicial recruitment stages. And, of course, the United States has a high level of judicial activism. The link between the number of actors involved in the judicial selection system and the level of judicial activism seems clear.

Although it is more difficult to prove empirically, one could also argue that within the United States relatively different articulation levels among the states' informal judicial selection processes could produce differences in the levels of ju-dicial activism among U.S. state judges. For example, Massachusetts has one of the lowest articulation judicial selection processes in the country, and it has a very low level of judicial activism among judges on its highest state court. On the other hand, Ohio has a very highly articulated judicial selection system, and it has a very activist state supreme court. This pattern appears to hold for various other U.S. state court systems as well.

Clearly, judicial activism is more common and more accepted among American judges. Although the level of judicial activism may be increasing in Canada,

Canadian judges still seem uncomfortable with the concept of judicial policy making. Perhaps one reason for this difference is the possible links between judicial activism and the number of political actors involved in the judicial selection system. When comparing court systems in industrialized democracies, the Canadian and U.S. examples seem to point to such a link. ■

View from the Inside

The inner workings of the Supreme Court of the United States have always been shrouded in secrecy. The justices deliberate and vote in private—not even a secretary or law clerk is present at the judicial conference—and the long process of writing and negotiating the justices' written opinions takes place entirely outside the public view. Leaks of information from inside the Court are exceedingly rare; news reporters, who are briefed routinely on what goes on inside the other branches of government, can do little more than guess at what is happening in the marble temple of justice.

In this selection, David A. Kaplan provides a rare glimpse inside the United States Supreme Court at one of the critical moments in its history—during its deliberations in *Bush* v. *Gore*, which overturned a Florida Supreme Court decision and banned a recount of the presidential vote in that state. The result of *Bush* v. *Gore* was nothing less than to decide the outcome of the 2000 presidential election.

Questions

1. Does knowledge of the inner workings of the Supreme Court during its consideration of *Bush* v. *Gore* make that decision seem more or less legitimate? Why?
2. Compare the Court's behavior in *Bush* v. *Gore* with the "performance standards" laid out by Linda Greenhouse in selection 12.3. Did the Court live up to what Greenhouse regards as its responsibilities to the American body politic?

12.5 The "Accidental President" (2001)

David A. Kaplan

• • •

[*Bush* v. *Gore*] pitted the Court's five conservatives against its four liberals, producing vitriolic opinions not seen in a generation, in a case many thought the Court should not have taken in the first place because state elections weren't federal judicial matters. Yet within weeks of *Bush* v. *Gore*, many of the justices gave speeches trying to defuse the controversy. All was well at the High Court, they said; everybody had moved on. Given the public record, that seemed plausible. And because the Court's "conference"—where the Supremes, without clerks or anyone else, debate cases and render their votes—is ultra-secret, it's hard to pierce the judicial veil.

But behind the scenes, in remarkable post-decision moments previously unreported, the justices were stewing. In particular, the dissenters—Justices Stephen Breyer, Ruth Bader Ginsburg, David Souter and John Paul Stevens—couldn't believe what their conservative brethren had wrought. How could the conservative Court majority decide to step into a presidential election, all the more so using the doctrinal excuse of "equal protection"? Equal protection? That's the constitutional rationale the liberals had used for a generation to expand rights, and the conservatives despised it. But now the conservatives were embracing the doctrine, claiming that different recount standards in Florida counties amounted to unequal protection? The whole thing smelled bad.

When the justices' counterparts on the Russian Constitutional Court came to town for a private gathering, the American justices let slip the recriminations. Those scenes shed light on what transpired inside the High Court as the justices determined who'd be the next president—and on the raw emotional fallout from the fateful decision.

Given the hard feelings, the amazing aspect of *Bush* v. *Gore* is that it just might've gone the other way. Justice Anthony Kennedy—the key swing vote, the man the Court's law clerks once dubbed "Flipper" for his equivocations—had wavered, enough that Souter thought until the very end that he'd get him. If Kennedy could be flipped, the 5-to-4 ruling for Bush would become a 5-to-4 win for Gore. They'd find an equal-protection violation, send the case back to the Florida justices to fix standards and administer the best recount they could under the circumstances and before December 18, and then leave it to the political branches—the Florida Legislature and, if need be, the U.S. Congress—to settle for good. (The political composition of Congress and the Legislature suggests Bush probably would've won in the end anyway.) But the High Court's decision short-circuited the process. The vote was close. But we never knew—until now—just how close.

A month after the decision, Souter met at the Court with a group of prep-school students from Choate. Souter was put on the Court in 1990 by Bush's father, advertised as a "home run" for such constitutional crusades as overturning *Roe* v. *Wade*. Instead, Souter turned out to be a non-doctrinaire New Englander who typically sided with the liberal justices. It didn't make him a liberal—this was a passionately modest man in matters of law as well as life—as much as it reflected how far the rest of the court had yawed starboard. Souter told the Choate students how frustrated he was that he couldn't broker a deal to bring in one more justice—Kennedy being the obvious candidate. Souter explained that he had put together a coalition back in 1992, in *Planned Parenthood* v. *Casey*, the landmark abortion case in which the Court declined by a 5-to-4 vote to toss out *Roe*; Souter, along with Kennedy and Justice Sandra Day O'Connor, took the unusual gesture of writing a joint opinion for the majority in that case.

If he'd had "one more day—one more day," Souter now told the Choate students, he believed he would have prevailed. Chief Justice William Rehnquist, along with Justices Antonin Scalia and Clarence Thomas, had long ago become part of the Dark Side. O'Connor appeared beyond compromise. But Kennedy seemed within reach. *Just give me 24 more hours on the clock,* Souter thought. While a political resolution to the election—in the Florida Legislature or in the Congress—might not be quick and might be a brawl, Souter argued that the nation would still accept it. "It should be a political branch that issues political decisions," he said to the students. Kennedy, though, wouldn't flip. He thought the trauma of more recounts, more fighting—more politics—was too much for the country to endure. (Souter and Kennedy, as well as the other justices, declined to be interviewed on the record.)

Mild-mannered by nature, Kennedy had a grandiose view of his role. In a memorable profile of the justice in *California Lawyer* magazine back in 1992, Kennedy had agreed to let the writer into chambers just before going into the courtroom to announce a major ruling. "Sometimes you don't know if you're Caesar about to cross the Rubicon or Captain Queeg cutting your own towline," Kennedy ruminated to his listener. Then the justice self-consciously asked for solitude. "I need to brood," Kennedy said. "I generally brood, as all of us do on the bench, just before we go on." The difference was that most of them didn't do it on cue.

The margin of victory for George W. Bush wasn't 154, 165, 193 or 204 votes (depending on which numbers you believe from the abbreviated recounts). Nor is the operative margin Florida Secretary of State Katherine Harris's initial number of 930. The sands of history will show Bush won by a single vote, cast in a 5-to-4 ruling of the U.S. Supreme Court. The vote was Tony Kennedy's. One justice had picked the president.

In a Virginia hotel, near the makeshift Bush transition office, Karl Rove—the campaign's political guru—was watching MSNBC when the Court ruling was announced. He called Bush in Texas; the governor was watching CNN, which took longer to decipher the opinions. "This is good news," Rove told Bush. "This is great news."

"No, no, this is bad news," Bush replied. Rove was the first person Bush talked to as the verdict came in—Bush had no sense initially he'd just been declared the winner by the stroke of the Court's pen. It was very confusing. "Where are you now?" he asked Rove.

"In the McLean Hilton—standing in my pajamas."

"Well, I'm in my pajamas, too," said the new president-elect.

Rove laughed at the vision of them both, at this historic moment, in their PJs. Soon enough, Bush talked to his field general, Jim Baker, who talked to Ted Olson and the other lawyers on the team. Within half an hour, Bush was convinced Gore had finally run out of tricks.

A month later, the animosities within the Court finally spilled over at a gathering inside the marble temple. It was a meeting known only to the participants, as well as a few translators and guests. Yet, in illuminating how *Bush* v. *Gore* came to be, it was the seminal event. It happened in January as Inauguration Day approached—after the 37 days of Florida, but while emotions were still raging. It was the time when the justices let their guards down, without knowing they were providing an X-ray into their hearts.

The Americans were playing host to special visitors from Russia. Their guests were six judges, all part of that country's decade-long experiment with freedom after Communism. It was the fifth gathering between the judges and their counterparts at the Supreme Court—an attempt by the most powerful tribunal in the world to impart some of its wisdom to a nascent system trying to figure out how constitutional law really worked in a democracy. It was by no means obvious. To outsiders, the idea that unelected judges who served for life could ultimately dictate the actions of the other two branches of American government, both popularly elected, was nothing short of unbelievable.

These were always collegial meetings inside the Supreme Court. This time— over the course of two days, January 9 and 10—seven American justices participated, everyone but Souter and Thomas. The justices from the Constitutional Court of the Russian Federation—Yuri Rudkin, Nikolai Seleznev, Oleg Tyunov, and Gennady Zhilin—were joined by judges from the Constitutional Court of the Republic of Dagestan and the Constitutional Supervision Committee of the Republic of Northern Ossetia–Alania. They all met in the Court's private ceremonial conference rooms: for an informal reception, the blue-motif West Conference Room; for hours of discussions about law and American heritage, the rose-motif East Conference Room, with a portrait of the legendary 19th-century chief justice John Marshall above the fireplace.

But this year, the discussions weren't about general topics such as due process or free expression or separation of powers. Some of the Russians wanted to know how *Bush* v. *Gore* had come to pass—how it was that somebody other than the electorate decided who ran the government. That was the kind of thing that gave Communism a bad name. "In our country," a Russian justice said, bemused, "we wouldn't let judges pick the president." The justice added that he knew that, in various nations, judges were in the pocket of executive officials—he just didn't know that was so in the United States. It was a supremely ironic moment.

Bush v. *Gore* was the elephant in the room—the ruling was on the minds of the Russians, but would it be rude to raise it? Once one of them did, it elicited an extraordinary exchange, played out spontaneously and viscerally among the American justices, according to people in the room. It could have been a partial replay of the Court conference itself in *Bush* v. *Gore*.

Justices don't discuss their decisions with others. That's because their views are supposed to be within the four corners of their written opinions. A good legal opinion isn't supposed to need further explanation. Memorialized in the law books, a Court opinion spoke for itself to future generations. But *Bush* v. *Gore* was so lean in its analysis, so unconvincing in its reasoning, that it led all manner of observers to wonder just where the Court had been coming from. Maybe that's why some of the justices so readily engaged their guests.

Stephen Breyer, one of the dissenters and a Clinton appointee, was angry and launched into an attack on the decision, right in front of his colleagues. It was "the most outrageous, indefensible thing" the Court had ever done, he told the visiting justices. "We all agree to disagree, but this is different." Breyer was defiant, brimming with confidence he'd been right in his dissent. "However awkward or difficult" it might've been for Congress to resolve the presidency, Breyer had written, "Congress, being a political body, expresses the people's will far more accurately than does an unelected Court. And the people's will is what elections are about." To have judges do it instead—as the country learned in the Hayes-Tilden presidential stalemate of 1876—not only failed to legitimize the outcome, but stained the judiciary. That was "a self-inflicted wound" harming "not just the Court, but the nation."

In contrast to Breyer, Ginsburg—Clinton's other appointee—was more baffled than annoyed, attempting to rationalize the legitimacy of the ruling that so ripped away her confidence in the neutrality of the Court. "Are we so highly political, after all?" she said. "We've surely done other things, too, that were activist, but here we're applying the Equal Protection Clause in a way that would de-legitimize virtually every election in American history."

"I'm so tired," offered Justice John Paul Stevens. "I am just so exhausted." His weariness may have reflected the fact that he was the oldest member of the Court at 80—or that he'd been fighting these battles from the left for 24 years, and the number he won was decreasing.

O'Connor talked pedantically about the Electoral College, which, of course, had nothing to do with the Russians' curiosity. Rehnquist and Scalia—the intellectual firebrands on the Court's right flank—said almost nothing, leaving it up to a floundering Kennedy to try to explain a 5-to-4 ruling in which he was the decisive vote, the justice who gave the presidency to Bush. The virtual silence of Rehnquist and Scalia led some in the room to wonder if the two justices were basically admitting their ruling was intellectually insupportable, all the more in a setting where there might be give-and-take. Maybe they didn't think this was the right forum or audience in which to engage a debate. In any event, Kennedy was left holding the bag.

"Sometimes you have to be responsible and step up to the plate," Kennedy told the Russians. "You have to take responsibility." He prized order and stability. Chaos was the enemy. This was vintage Kennedy, who loved to thump his chest about the burden of it all. For example, back in the controversial 1989 decision that flag-burning was protected by the First Amendment, Kennedy joined the 5-to-4 majority, but dramatized his discomfort. "This case, like others before us from time to time, exacts its personal toll," he wrote. "The hard fact is that sometimes we must make decisions we do not like."

Everything Kennedy did or thought seemed to him to carry great weight. It had to—he was a justice of the Supreme Court. It was as if Kennedy kept telling himself, and us, that—but for him and his role—the Republic might topple. In *Bush* v. *Gore*, that meant entering the breach to save the Union from an electoral muddle that could go on and on. The equal-protection stuff? That was the best he could come up with on short notice. It was apparently no big deal that there was another branch of the government right across the street—democratically elected, politically accountable, and specifically established by the Constitution, as well as by federal statute, to finally determine a disputed presidential election. "Congress" wasn't even mentioned in the opinions by the Court's conservatives. Congress was the appropriate, co-equal branch not because it was wisest, but because it was legitimate.

What was Kennedy's explanation for becoming the deus ex machina? It was Bush and Gore who should be blamed for bringing their problems to the Court. "When contending parties invoke the process of the courts," he wrote, "it becomes our unsought responsibility to resolve the federal and constitutional issues the judicial system has been forced to confront." But that was theatrical nonsense. The justices refused to hear 99 percent of the appeals they were asked to take. Since 1925, their discretion was unbridled—they could decline to take a case because it failed to raise significant issues, because the questions involved were purely state affairs, because they'd decided a similar appeal in recent years, or for no reason at all. Accepting jurisdiction in the presidential election of 2000 showed not respect for the rule of law, but the hubris of kings. Any imminent constitutional "crisis" was only in the imaginations of the justices.

Nobody "forced" Kennedy or four of his brethren to hear *Bush* v. *Gore*. In the very first instance, they had to choose who chose—whether the Court or Congress was the proper branch to settle the presidential dispute. The justices chose themselves. ■

Chapter 13

Public Policy

The purpose and function of government is to make policy—that is, to create and implement the rules and programs under which society is to be governed. In a sense, all of the previous chapters have been examining the policy-making process: the institutions that interact to create policy and the constitutional foundation on which they operate, the relationship of policy making to public opinion and the electoral process, and the role of nongovernmental actors—like the media and interest groups—in policy development. In this chapter, we turn to examining the total picture.

Political scientists typically divide policy into two broad categories—domestic policy and foreign policy. Domestic policy involves a broad range of issues, including health care, education, the economy, and criminal justice. Foreign policy includes not only diplomacy but also military affairs.

Domestic policy making in the United States underwent several transformations in the twentieth century. The New Deal greatly expanded the federal government's role in economic regulation and social policy making. In the 1960s, Lyndon Johnson's Great Society widened the scope of federal welfare programs, a trend continued under President Richard Nixon. In the 1980s, the election of Ronald Reagan initiated a period of struggle for control over the scope and direction of federal social policy. That struggle has grown even more intense in recent years.

At bottom, the debate over social policy in the United States is marked by a contest between those who believe that the national government should take the lead in solving society's social problems and those who believe that state and local governments and the private sector should carry the load. As for foreign policy, Americans tend to agree on the broad goals the United States should pursue, but frequently disagree on how best to pursue those goals in a complex and often hostile world.

The selections in this chapter cover a wide range of issues related to public policy. Selection 13.1 introduces the concept of public policy, and draws distinctions between different types of policies, and among the different stages of policy making. Selection 13.2 examines the continuing controversy over Social Security reform, while selection 13.3 probes the advantages and disadvantages of American unilateralism in foreign policy. Finally, selection 13.4 provides an inside look at how government officials can succeed in influencing the making of public policy.

Chapter Questions

1. How have the larger trends and currents in American politics over the past thirty years affected domestic policy? Consider in particular the increasingly bitter conflict between liberal and conservative ideologies.
2. How has American foreign policy changed since the terrorist attacks of September 11, 2001? In addition to fighting terrorism, what other goals should the United States pursue in foreign policy, and how should it pursue them?

 # Foundations

Government policy is made by all three branches and is heavily influenced and constrained by public opinion and by the electoral process. The Framers designed a system that prevents any one branch from making policy on its own, and to a great extent the system in fact works just that way. Policy making, in general, involves cooperation, negotiation, and, at times, conflict among many different players. Nor is that process completed once a policy is enacted into law. The law must be implemented by the executive branch, under congressional and judicial supervision. When necessary, the program must be modified to fit new or unexpected circumstances. Each year the program must be funded through the congressional budget process, and periodically, it must be reauthorized by Congress as well.

Political scientists have categorized public policy making along several dimensions; for example, one can look at the various stages of the process, at the different types of policy, or at the different political actors involved. The following selection, by two political scientists, examines public policy making from a variety of perspectives.

Questions

1. What are the major stages of public policy making? Which institutions are most effective at each stage? Why?
2. Define these terms: *distributive policies*, *regulatory policies*, and *redistributive policies*. What are the defining characteristics of each?

13.1 Domestic Policy Making (1994)

Roger H. Davidson and Walter J. Oleszek

Definitions of Policy

Because policies ultimately are what government is about, it is not surprising that definitions of policy and policy making are diverse and influenced by the beholder's eye. David Easton's celebrated definition of public policy as society's "authoritative allocations" of values or resources is one approach to the question. To put it another way, policies can be regarded as reflecting "who gets what, when, and how" in a society. A more serviceable definition of policy is offered by Randall Ripley and Grace Franklin: policy is what the government says and does about perceived problems. . . .

Stages of Policy Making

Whatever the time frame, policy making normally has four distinct stages: setting the agenda, formulating policy, adopting policy, and implementing policy.

Setting the Agenda   At the initial stage, public problems are spotted and moved onto the national agenda, which can be defined as "the list of subjects to which government officials and those around them are paying serious attention." In a large, pluralistic country like the United States, the national agenda at any given moment is extensive and vigorously debated.

How do problems get placed on the agenda? Some are heralded by a crisis or some other prominent event—the hijacking of a plane by terrorists, the demise of savings and loan associations, or a campaign-funding scandal. Others are occasioned by the gradual accumulation of knowledge—for example, increasing awareness of an environmental hazard like acid rain or ozone depletion. Still other agenda items represent the accumulation of past problems that no longer can be avoided or ignored. Finally, agendas may be set in motion by political processes—election results, turnover in Congress, or shifts in public opinion. The 1994 election results are an example of how the GOP's control of the 104th Congress and its Contract with America drove the national agenda.

Agenda items are pushed by *policy entrepreneurs*, people willing to invest time and energy to promote a particular issue. Numerous Washington "think tanks" and interest groups, especially at the beginning of a new president's term, issue reports that seek to influence the economic, social, or foreign policy agenda of the nation. Usually, however, elected officials and their staffs or appointees are more likely to shape agendas than are career bureaucrats or nongovernmental actors. Notable policy entrepreneurs on Capitol Hill are congressional leaders who push their party's policy initiatives. Speaker Newt Gingrich with his advocacy of a min-

Roger H. Davidson and Walter J. Oleszek, *Congress and Its Members*, 6th Edition (Washington DC: CQ Press, 1998), pp. 349–356. Reprinted by permission of Congressional Quarterly.

imalist role for the central government (the "Republican revolution") is a good example.

Lawmakers frequently are policy entrepreneurs because they are expected to voice the concerns of constituents and organized groups and to seek legislative solutions. Politicians generally gravitate toward issues that are visible, salient, and solvable. Tough, arcane, or conflictual problems may be shunned because they offer few payoffs and little hope of success.

Sometimes only a crisis—such as the oil price increases in the 1970s—can force lawmakers to address difficult questions. Yet, despite enactment of legislation designed to ameliorate future energy problems, Americans today are as dependent on imported oil as they were two decades ago. Forecasters predict another energy crisis unless steps are taken to develop alternative fuels, change habits of consumption, and reduce the spiraling demand for oil, especially from the volatile Middle East. This kind of "creeping crisis" is often difficult for members of Congress to grapple with, in part because of the "two Congresses" dilemma. As conscientious lawmakers, members might want to forge long-term solutions. But as representatives of their constituents, they are deterred from acting when most citizens see no problems with the immediate situation.

Formulating Policy   In the second stage of policy making, items on the political agenda are discussed and potential solutions are explored. Members of Congress and their staffs play crucial roles by conducting hearings and writing committee reports. They are aided by policy experts in executive agencies, interest groups, and the private sector.

Another term for this stage is *policy incubation*, which entails "keeping a proposal alive while it picks up support, or waits for a better climate, or while a consensus begins to form that the problem to which it is addressed exists." Sometimes this process takes only a few months; more often it requires years. During Dwight D. Eisenhower's administration, for example, congressional Democrats explored and refined policy options that, while not immediately accepted, were ripe for adoption by the time their party's nominee, John F. Kennedy, was elected president in 1960.

The incubation process not only brings policies to maturity but also refines solutions to the problems. The process may break down if workable solutions are not available. The seeming intractability of many modern issues complicates problem solving. Thomas S. Foley, D-Wash. (Speaker, 1989–1995), held that issues had become far more perplexing since he came to Congress in 1965. At that time "the civil rights issue facing the legislators was whether the right to vote should be federally guaranteed for blacks and Hispanics. Now members are called on to deal with more ambiguous policies like affirmative action and racial quotas."

Solutions to problems normally involve "some fairly simple routines emphasizing the tried and true (or at least not discredited)." A repertoire of proposals exists—for example, blue-ribbon commissions, trust funds, or pilot projects—that can be applied to a variety of unsolved problems. Problem solvers also must guard against recommending solutions that will be viewed as worse than the problem.

Adopting Policy   Laws are ideas whose time has come. The right time for a policy is what scholar John Kingdon calls the *policy window:* the opportunity presented by circumstances and attitudes to enact a policy into law. Policy entre-preneurs must seize the opportunity before the policy window closes and the idea's time has passed.

Once policies are ripe for adoption, they must gain popular acceptance. This is the function of *legitimation*, the process through which policies come to be viewed by the public as right or proper. Inasmuch as citizens are expected to comply with laws or regulations—pay taxes, observe rules, or make sacrifices of one sort or an-other—the policies themselves must appear to have been properly considered and enacted. A nation whose policies lack legitimacy is in deep trouble.

Symbolic acts, such as members voting on the House or Senate floor or the president signing a bill, signal to everyone that policies have been duly adopted according to traditional forms. Hearings and debates, moreover, serve not only to fine-tune policies but also to cultivate support from affected interests. Responding to critics of Congress's slowness in adopting energy legislation, Sen. Ted Stevens, R-Alaska, asked these questions:

> Would you want an energy bill to flow through the Senate and not have anyone consider the impacts on housing or on the automotive industry or on the energy industries that provide our light and power? Should we ignore the problems of the miner or the producer or the distributor? Our legislative process must reflect all of the problems if the public is to have confidence in the government.

Legitimating, in other words, often demands a measured pace and attention to procedural details. (Another strategy is to move quickly—before opposition forces can mobilize—to enact bold changes and then work to gain the public's accep-tance of them.)

Implementing Policy   In the final stage, policies shaped by the legislature and the highest executive levels are put into effect, usually by a federal agency. Poli-cies are not self-executing: they must be promulgated and enforced. A law or ex-ecutive order rarely spells out exactly how a particular policy will be implemented. Congress and the president usually delegate most decisions about implementation to the responsible agencies under broad but stated guidelines. Implementation de-termines the ultimate effect of policies. Officials of the executive branch can thwart a policy by foot dragging or sheer inefficiency. By the same token, overzeal-ous administrators can push a policy far beyond its creators' intent.

Congress therefore must exercise its oversight role. It may require executive agencies to report or consult with congressional committees or to follow certain formal procedures. Members of Congress get feedback on the operation of federal programs through a variety of channels: media coverage, interest group protests, and even constituent casework. With such information Congress can and often does pass judgment by adjusting funding, introducing amendments, or recasting the basic legislation governing a particular policy.

Types of Domestic Policies

One way to understand public policies is to analyze the nature of the policies themselves. Scholars have classified policies in many different ways. The typology we shall use identifies three types of domestic policies: distributive, regulatory, and redistributive.

Distributive Policies   Distributive policies or programs are government actions that convey tangible benefits to private individuals, groups, or firms. Invariably, they involve subsidies to favored individuals or groups. The benefits are often called "pork" (special-interest spending for projects in members' states or districts), although that appellation is sometimes difficult to define. After all, "one person's pork is another person's steak." The projects come in several different varieties:

> Dams, roads and bridges, known as "green pork," are old hat. These days, there is also "academic pork" in the form of research grants to colleges, "defense pork" in the form of geographically specific military expenditures and lately "high-tech pork," for example the intense fight to authorize research into super computers and high-definition television (HDTV).

The presence of distributive politics—which makes many interests better off and few, if any, visibly worse off—is natural in Congress, which as a nonhierarchical institution must build coalitions in order to function. A textbook example was the $1-billion-plus National Parks and Recreation Act of 1978. Dubbed the "Park Barrel" bill, it created so many parks, historical sites, seashores, wilderness areas, wild and scenic rivers, and national trails that it sailed through the Interior (now Resources) Committee and passed the House by a 341-61 vote. "Notice how quiet we are. We all got something in there," said one House member, after the Rules Committee cleared the bill in five minutes flat. Another member quipped, "If it had a blade of grass and a squirrel, it got in the bill." Distributive politics of this kind throws into sharp relief the "two Congresses" notion: national policy as a mosaic of local interests.

The politics of distribution works best when tax revenues are expanding, fueled by high productivity and economic growth—characteristics of the U.S. economy from the end of World War II through the mid-1970s. When productivity declines or tax cutting squeezes revenues, it becomes difficult to add new benefits or expand old ones. Such was the plight of lawmakers in the 1980s and 1990s. Yet distributive impulses remained strong, adding pressure to wring distributive elements out of tight budgets. Even in the tight-fisted 104th Congress, lawmakers in both parties ensured that money would be spent for particular purposes in their districts or states. As one account noted:

> With Republicans cutting non-military spending but protecting the defense budget from reductions, the huge $243 billion Pentagon spending bill this year has taken the place of pork-barrel public works measures of old. Instead of seeking bridges and roads, members of Congress in both parties have been clamoring for defense contracts to protect home-state jobs and businesses.

House GOP freshman John Ensign of Nevada highlighted both the "two Congresses" and the prevailing legislative sentiments toward distributive policy making when he said, "I hate the idea of pork, but if there's a pot of money, I want to make sure that Nevada gets its fair share."

Regulatory Policies   Regulatory policies are designed to protect the public against harm or abuse that might result from unbridled private activity. For example, the Food and Drug Administration (FDA) monitors standards for foodstuffs and tests drugs for purity, safety, and effectiveness, and the Federal Trade Commission (FTC) guards against illegal business practices, such as deceptive advertising.

Federal regulation against certain abuses dates from the late nineteenth century, when the Interstate Commerce Act and the Sherman Antitrust Act were enacted to protect against transport and monopoly abuses. As the twentieth century dawned, scandalous practices in slaughterhouses and food processing plants, colorfully described by reform-minded muckraking reporters, led to meatpacking, food, and drug regulations. The stock market collapse in 1929 and the Great Depression paved the way for the New Deal legislation that would regulate the banking and securities industries and labor-management relations. Consumer rights and environmental protection came of age in the 1960s and 1970s. Dramatic attacks on unsafe automobiles by Ralph Nader and others led to new laws mandating tougher safety standards. Concern about smog produced by auto exhausts led to the Clean Air Act of 1970. And concern about airline delays, congestion, and safety prompted Congress to consider new regulatory controls for the nation's air traffic system. . . .

Redistributive Policies   Redistribution, which visibly shifts resources from one group to another, is the most difficult of all political feats. Because it is controversial, redistributive policy engages a broad spectrum of political actors—not only in the House and Senate chambers but also in the executive branch and among interest groups and the public at large. Redistributive issues tend to be ideological: they often separate liberals and conservatives because they upset relationships between social and economic classes. Theodore R. Marmor described the thirty-year fight over medical care for the aged as "cast in terms of class conflict":

> The leading adversaries . . . brought into the opposing camps a large number of groups whose interests were not directly affected by the Medicare outcome. . . . [I]deological charges and countercharges dominated public discussion, and each side seemed to regard compromise as unacceptable.

Most of the divisive socioeconomic issues of the past generation—civil rights, affirmative action, school busing, aid to education, homelessness, abortion, tax reform—were redistributive problems. Fiscal policy making has taken on a redistributive character as federal expenditures outpace revenues, and lawmakers are forced to find ways to close the gap. Cutting federal benefits and opening up new revenue sources both involve redistribution because they turn "haves" into "have nots." That is why politicians today find budget and revenue issues so burdensome. "I wasn't here in the glory days, when a guy with a bright idea of a scholarship program or whatever could get a few hundred million dollars to pursue it," lamented Rep. Richard J. Durbin, D-Ill. "Now you've got to take from one to give to the other."

Federal budgeting is marked not only by extreme conflict but also by techniques to disguise the redistributions or make them more palatable. Omnibus budget packages permit legislators to approve cuts *en bloc* rather than one by one, and across-the-board formulas (like "freezes") give the appearance of spreading the misery equally to affected groups. In all such vehicles, distributive elements are added to placate the more vocal opponents of change. Such is the unhappy lot of politicians consigned to lawmaking in a redistributive mode. ■

 # American Politics Today

Few public policy issues are as important to Americans of every generation as social security. This combination retirement and insurance system has served Americans since 1935. It is largely responsible for the tremendous reduction in poverty among America's elderly population.

Many Americans have lost faith in the social security system, however. By the government's own admission, the system must be reformed if it is to remain solvent after the "baby boom" generation retires. Some argue that the government should allow workers to manage their own social security accounts, investing their money as they see fit. Others maintain that only modest changes are needed to keep the system intact.

In this essay, the author Dean Baker analyzes and debunks nine "misconceptions" about social security that, in his view, have clouded the national debate on this vital issue.

Questions

1. Why do many Americans believe that the social security program will face a crisis in this century? How does Baker respond to these arguments?
2. What goals was social security designed to achieve? Evaluate the various reform proposals discussed by Baker in terms of these diverse goals.

13.2 Nine Misconceptions About Social Security (1998)

Dean Baker

1. *The Social Security Trust Fund Is an Accounting Fiction.*

The Social Security tax has been raising more money than is needed to pay for current benefits, in order to build up a surplus to help finance the retirement of the Baby Boom generation. All of this surplus is lent to the U.S. Treasury when

Dean Baker, "Nine Misconceptions About Social Security," *The Atlantic Monthly* (July 1998), pp. 34–39. Reprinted by permission of the author, a senior research fellow at the Preamble Center in Washington, D.C. and the Century Foundation in New York City.

the Social Security Trust Fund buys bonds from it. The money is then used to finance the federal deficit, just like any other money the government borrows. The bonds held by the fund pay the same interest as bonds held by the public. These bonds are every bit as real (or as much of a fiction) as the bonds held by banks, corporations, and individuals. Throughout U.S. history the federal government has always paid its debts. As a result, government bonds enjoy the highest credit ratings and are considered one of the safest assets in the world. Thus the fund has very real and secure assets.

It is true that the interest the government pays on these bonds is a drain on the Treasury, as will be the money paid by the government when the fund ultimately cashes in its bonds. But this drain has nothing to do with Social Security. If the Social Security Trust Fund were not currently building up a surplus, and lending the money to the government, the government would still be running a deficit of approximately $60 billion in its non–Social Security operations. It would then have to borrow this money from individuals like H. Ross Perot and Peter G. Peterson and to pay out more interest each year to the people it borrowed from. Therefore, the government's debt to the fund is simply a debt it would have incurred in any event. The government's other spending and tax policies, not Social Security, will be the cause if there is any problem in the future in paying off the bonds held by the fund.

The government bonds held by the Social Security Trust Fund will always be a comparatively small portion of the government's debt, and therefore a relatively minor burden. They will hit a peak of about 14.4 percent of gross domestic product in 2015, whereas the debt now held by individuals and corporations is about 47 percent of GDP. Therefore, at its peak the burden of interest payments to the fund will be less than a third as large as the interest burden the government now bears.

2. The Government Uses Overly Optimistic Numbers to Convince People That Social Security Will Be There for Them. The Situation is Much Worse Than the Government Admits.

Actually, Social Security projections are based on extremely pessimistic economic assumptions: that growth will average just 1.8 percent over the next twenty years, a lower rate than in any comparable period in U.S. history; that growth will slow even further in later years, until the rate is less than half the 2.6 percent of the past twenty years; that there will be no increase in immigration even when the economy experiences a labor shortage because of the retirement of the Baby Boom generation; and that this labor shortage will not lead to a rapid growth in wages. Both possibilities excluded in these projections—increased immigration and rapid wage growth—would increase the fund's revenues. These projections are genuinely a worst-case scenario.

3. The Demographics of the Baby Boom Will Place an Unbearable Burden on the Social Security System.

Those who want to overhaul Social Security make their case with the following numbers: in 1960 there were more than five workers for each beneficiary; today there are 3.3 workers; by 2030 there will be only two workers for each beneficiary. At present the fund is running an annual surplus of more than $80 billion, approximately 20 percent as much as its current expenditures. This surplus will generate interest revenue to help support the system as the ratio of workers to beneficiaries continues to fall in the next century. Also, the fact that workers are becoming more productive year by year means that it will take fewer workers to support each retiree. The United States had 10.5 farm workers for every hundred people in 1929; it has fewer than 1.1 farm workers for every hundred people today. Yet the population is well fed, and we even export food. Rising farm productivity made this possible. Similarly, increases in worker productivity (which have been and should be reflected in higher incomes), however small compared with those of the past, will allow each retiree to be supported by an ever smaller number of workers.

In fact the demographics of the Baby Boom have very little to do with the long-range problems of Social Security. The main reason the fund will run into deficits in future years is that people are living longer. If people continue to retire at the same age but live longer, then a larger percentage of their lives will be spent in re-tirement. If people want to spend a larger portion of their lives in retirement, ei-ther they will have to accept lower incomes (reduced benefits) in their retirement years relative to those of their working years, or they will have to increase the por-tion of their incomes (higher taxes) that they put aside during their working years for retirement.

This is the main long-range problem facing Social Security. Current projections show that the annual deficit will be 5.71 percent of taxable payroll in 2070, long after the Baby Boom will have passed into history. But the annual deficit is ex-pected to be only 4.44 percent of taxable payroll in 2035, when the worst crunch from retired Baby Boomers will be felt.

Examining just the change in the ratio of beneficiaries to workers overstates the burden that workers will face in the future. To assess the burden accurately it is necessary to examine the total number of dependents—beneficiaries and chil-dren—each worker will have to support. It is projected that this ratio will rise from 0.708 per worker at present to 0.795 in 2035. But even this number is well below the ratio of 0.946 that prevailed in 1965. And the fund's trustees project a lower birth rate, meaning that the increased costs of providing for a larger retired population will be largely offset by the reduction of expenses associated with car-ing for children.

4. Future Generations Will Experience Declining Living Standards Be-cause of the Government Debt and the Burden Created by Social Security.

Projections indicate that workers' real wages will increase by approximately one percent a year. If Social Security benefits are left unchanged, in order to meet the fund's obligations it will be necessary to raise the Social Security tax by 0.1 percent a year (0.05 percent on the employer and 0.05 percent on the employee) for thirty-six years, beginning in 2010. This will be a total tax increase of 3.6 percent, approx-imately the same as the increase in Social Security taxes from 1977 to 1990.

Even with this schedule of tax increases, real wages after Social Security taxes are deducted will continue to rise. By 2046, when the tax increases are fully phased in, the average wage after Social Security taxes will be more than 45 percent higher than at present. As noted earlier, this is based on pessimistic projections about wage growth.

5. By 2030 Federal Spending on Entitlement Programs for the Elderly Will Consume All the Revenue Collected by the Government.

By far the greatest part of the projected increases in federal spending on entitlement programs for the elderly is attributable to a projected explosion in national health-care costs, both public and private. According to projections from the Health Care Financing Administration, average health-care spending for a family of four in 2030 will be more than 80 percent of the median family's before-tax income. If such an explosion in health-care costs actually occurred, the economy would be destroyed even if we eliminated entitlement programs altogether. If health-care costs in the public and private sectors are brought under control, the problems posed by demographic trends will be quite manageable.

It is very deceptive to combine other spending categories with health care; projected health-care costs by themselves will consume most of the budget. For example, projected federal spending on education, highways, and health care combined should be more than 80 percent of federal revenues in 2030; defense spending plus projected health-care spending should come close to 70 percent of federal revenues.

6. If Social Security Were Privatized, It Would Lead to a Higher National Saving Rate and More Growth.

By itself, privatizing Social Security would not create a penny of additional savings. All the privatization plans call for the government to continue to pay Social Security benefits to current recipients and those about to retire; therefore spending would be exactly the same after privatization as it was before privatization. Yet the government would no longer be collecting Social Security taxes. Each dollar an individual put into a private retirement account rather than paying it to the government in Social Security taxes would still be a dollar the government must borrow. Individuals would be saving more, but the government would have reduced its saving (increased its borrowing) by exactly the same amount. Most of the privatization schemes being put forward call for additional taxes and additional borrowing to finance a transition while benefits were being paid out under the old system. Any additions to national savings attributable to these plans would stem entirely from the tax increase. This tax increase would have the identical effect on national savings if it were not linked to privatizing Social Security. In other words, raising taxes is one way to increase national savings, and if we are willing to raise taxes, we need not privatize Social Security.

The fact that individuals might put their savings in the stock market or in other private assets, whereas the Social Security Trust Fund buys government bonds, doesn't affect the level of saving at all. If it did, the government could increase the level of saving in the economy by borrowing money and then investing it in the stock market, or by borrowing money and giving it to individuals with the requirement that they invest it in the stock market. If either step could increase the level of saving in the economy, the government should take it independent of any changes in the Social Security system.

In fact, all else being equal, if individuals invested the money they would otherwise pay out in Social Security taxes, less saving would result, because a large portion of this money would be siphoned off by the financial industry. Currently stock brokers, insurance companies, and other financial institutions charge their customers an average of more than one percent a year on the value of the money they hold. Thus if $1,000 is invested through a brokerage firm for forty years, the investor will have been charged in excess of $400 in fees on the original investment, plus an additional one percent a year on all gains. These fees are a big cost from the standpoint of the individual investor, and a complete waste from the standpoint of the economy as a whole. Meanwhile, the operating expenses of the Social Security system are less than $8.00 for every $1,000 paid out to beneficiaries.

It is easy to see why costs in the private financial sector are so much higher. The private sector pays hundreds of thousands of insurance agents and brokers to solicit business. It also incurs enormous costs in television, radio, newspaper, and magazine advertising. In addition, many executives and brokers in the financial industry receive huge salaries. Million-dollar salaries are not uncommon, and some executives earn salaries in the tens of millions. Privatization would add these expenses, which are currently absent from the Social Security system.

7. If People Invest Their Money Themselves, They Will Get a Higher Return Than If They Leave It with the Government.

This may be true for some people, but it cannot be true on average, for much the same reasons as noted above. Some people may end up big winners by picking the right stocks, but if the national saving rate has not increased, the economy will not have increased its growth rate, and the economic pie will be no larger in the future with privatization than it would have been without it. Thus high returns for some must come at the expense of others. In fact, since the cost of operating a retirement system is so much greater through the financial markets than through the Social Security system, the average person will actually be worse off.

Some advocates of government-mandated saving plans argue that individual investors can get real returns of seven percent on money invested in the stock market (the historical rate of return), and that this would ensure a comfortable retirement for everyone. Certainly people have gotten far better returns in the market in the past few years, but if Social Security projections are accurate, such rates of return cannot be sustained. Profits can rise only as fast as the economy grows (unless wages fall as a share of national income, which no one is projecting). If stock prices maintain a fixed relationship to profits, then stock prices will grow at the same rate as the economy. The total return will therefore approximate the ratio of dividends to the stock price (currently about three percent) plus the rate of economic growth (two percent over the next ten years, but projected to fall to 1.2

percent in the middle of the next century). This means that the returns people can expect from investing in the stock market will be five percent in the near future and 4.2 percent later in the next century. For stock prices to rise enough to maintain a real return of seven percent, price-to-earnings ratios would have to exceed 400:1 by 2070.

8. The Consumer Price Index Overstates the True Rate of Increase in the Cost of Living. Social Security Recipients Are Therefore Getting a Huge Bonanza Each Year, Because Their Checks Are Adjusted in Accordance with the CPI.

There is considerable dispute about the accuracy of the CPI. The Boskin Commission, which was appointed by the Senate Finance Committee to examine the CPI, stated in its final report, in 1996, that overall the CPI had been overstating the cost of living by 1.3 percentage points a year. However, the Bureau of Labor Statistics found that the CPI understated the cost of living when compared with an index that measured the cost of living for the elderly. This is because the elderly spend an unusually large share of their income on health care and housing, which have risen relatively rapidly in price. Questions remain about the accuracy of the CPI, and they cannot be resolved without further research.

However, one point is clear. If the CPI has been overstating inflation, then future generations will be much better off than we imagined. If inflation has been overstated, then real wage growth must have been *understated*, since real wage growth is actual wage growth minus the rate of inflation. If we accept the Boskin Commission's midrange estimate of CPI overstatement, average real wages in 2030 will be more than $54,000 (measured in today's dollars). If the commission's high-end estimate is right, average wages will be nearly $65,000. By 2050 average wages will be at least $82,000 and possibly as much as $108,000.

Another implication of a CPI that overstates inflation is that people were much poorer in the recent past than is generally recognized. This conclusion is inescapable: if the rate of inflation is lower than indicated by the CPI, then real wages and living standards have been rising faster than is indicated by calculations that use the CPI. If wages and living standards have been rising faster than we thought, then past levels must have been lower. Projecting backward, the Boskin Commission's estimate of the overstatement of the CPI gives a range for the median family income in 1960 of $15,000 to $18,000 (in today's dollars)—or 95 to 110 percent of income at the current poverty level.

If the Boskin Commission's evaluation of the CPI is accepted, any assessment of generational equity looks very bad from the standpoint of the elderly: they lived most of their lives in or near poverty. And the future looks extremely bright for the young. Average annual wages in 1960, when today's seventy-three-year-olds were thirty-five, was between $10,006 and $11,902 in today's dollars. Average annual wages in 2030, when today's newborns are thirty-two, will be between $54,000 and $65,000 in today's dollars. Such numbers make it hard to justify cutting Social Security for the elderly in order to enrich future generations, on the grounds of generational equity.

9. Social Security Gives Tens of Billions of Dollars Each Year to Senior Citizens Who Don't Need It. This Money Could Be Better Used to Support Poor Children.

Most of the elderly are not very well off. Their median household income is only about $18,000. However, even if they were better off, it would be hard to justify taking away their Social Security on either moral or economic grounds.

Social Security is a social-insurance program, not a welfare program. People pay into it during their working lives. They have a right to expect something in return, just as they expect interest payments when they buy a government bond. Social Security is already progressive: the rate of return on tax payments is much lower for the wealthy than for the poor. This progressivity is enhanced by the fact that Social Security income is taxable for middle- and high-income retirees but not for low-income retirees. If benefits for higher-income retirees were cut back further, those people would be receiving virtually no return for the taxes they paid in. This would be certain to undermine support for the program.

From an economic standpoint, means testing or any other way of denying benefits to the wealthy would be foolish, because it would give people a great incentive to hide income and thereby pass the means test. There are many ways this could be done. Parents could pass most of their assets on to their children and then continue to collect full benefits. People could move their money into assets that don't yield an annual income, such as land or some kinds of stock. Most of the income of retirees is from accumulated assets, which makes it much easier to hide than wage income. Means testing would in effect place a very high marginal tax rate on senior citizens, giving them a strong incentive to find ways to evade taxes. It may be desirable to get more revenue from the wealthy, but means testing for Social Security makes about as much sense as means testing for interest on government bonds. ∎

The International Context

The 2003 Iraq War brought to the foreground a critical question for those who make American foreign policy: when should the United States act alone (or with selected allies), and when should it act in cooperation with the broader international community? At first, President George W. Bush sought a broad coalition for the Iraq war, operating under the auspices of the United Nations; when that effort failed, Bush led a "coalition of the willing" instead.

A foreign policy based on actions in concert with the broader international community is known as *multilateralism*. Its opposite—acting alone or with just a handful of allies—is known as *unilateralism*. In this selection, written before the Iraq war, the journalist Michael Hirsh examines the advantages and disadvantages of these two approaches. In practice, he concludes, "it is never easy to find the right mix of unilateralism and multilateralism."

Question

1. What are the advantages and disadvantages of the multilateral and unilateral approaches to foreign policy? Does the experience of the Iraq War and its aftermath provide evidence in support of one approach or the other?

13.3 America and the World (2002)

Michael Hirsh

• • •

The day after September 11, General Richard Myers was asked at a congressional hearing why the mightiest military in history had failed to protect the heart of American power from a band of men brandishing box cutters. In those early, shell-shocked hours, before the spin set in, the incoming chairman of the Joint Chiefs of Staff had no ready reply but the unvarnished truth: "We're pretty good if the threat is coming from the outside," Myers said. "We're not so good if it's coming in from the inside."

A year later, Americans still seem stunned by how hard it is to tell which threats are coming from the outside and which are on the inside. Whereas other nations, such as the United Kingdom, have long accommodated themselves to domestic surveillance because of the infiltration of terrorists, the United States is just getting started on this road. This confusion is at the heart of the divisions in the American intelligence community, long neglected but now critical to the war on terror. The old clash of interests between the CIA and the FBI had been getting ever more aggravated in the post–Cold War period. The CIA began moving into the FBI's traditional bailiwick as crime grew more transnational, involving drugs and the proliferation of weapons of mass destruction (WMD). In more recent years, the FBI began elbowing into the CIA's territory, "running" agents overseas in response to the Khobar Towers and the U.S.S. Cole bombings. But these mutual efforts barely improved communications, and the two agencies seemed to feel little urgency about doing so—until September 11.

Even now, the idea that borders do not mean much anymore is not an easy one for Americans to stomach. Clinton, the "globalization" president, was constantly harping on this theme, but it never really resonated. One of the nation's founding myths, after all, is that of exceptionalism: America is a place apart, protected by its oceans. Such hopes as George Washington's farewell plea for insularity in 1796 or Thomas Jefferson's warning against entangling alliances sprang from the fact that Americans had a national life of their own, gloriously isolated from Europe and Asia, lording over the western hemisphere.

By the late nineteenth century, without even trying, the United States was already the largest economy in the world. These victories imbued its exceptionalism

---

Excerpted from Michael Hirsh, "Bush and the World," *Foreign Affairs* 81 (Sept.–Oct. 2002), pp. 18–43. Reprinted by permission of *Foreign Affairs*. Copyright 2002 by the Council on Foreign Relations, Inc.

and its spawn, isolationism and unilaterialism, with physical, palpable reality. The founding myth had come true. America's success in building a continental empire only fed into the certainty that it could act with total freedom of action. Its pride in its values and ideals made Americans certain that they were always right.

By the twentieth century, the United States was getting pulled into the great wars, starting the now-familiar pattern of intense involvement followed by withdrawal. During the Cold War, withdrawal was not possible as global entanglement with the Soviets followed the war on fascism. But if the vast oceans no longer protected the United States from nuclear attack once the era of nuclear brinksmanship began, Americans still thought of the threat as "out there," coming from the sky and across the sea from an alien, less perfect world. And when that conflict ended, it should have been no surprise to anyone that George W. Bush, his conservative impulses unchecked by the need for Cold War–style engagement, sought to shrink America's presence abroad to a more manageable size and to give voice once again to America's irrepressible exceptionalism.

A number of European commentators have consoled themselves with the idea that at least America is not isolationist any longer. That is true. But unilaterialism and isolationism are ideological twins. They both spring from the same exceptionalist impulse, a deep well of American mistrust about the rest of the world, especially Europe. This is still American scripture, cited by fundamentalists such as Pat Buchanan and John Bolton, a conservative "Americanist" who argues that international treaties are not legally valid. (In fox-guarding-the-henhouse fashion, Bolton became Bush's undersecretary of state for arms control policy and promptly dismantled or obstructed nearly every multilateral treaty in sight.) Unilateralism is more politically acceptable today, but like isolationism, it does not accept the encumbrances of the international system.

What many Americans, including the Bush hard-liners, must grasp is this: during America's periods of intense (if reluctant) engagement overseas, the world that they had wanted to keep at ocean's length became largely their world. For a century now, Americans have built a global order bit by bit, era by era, all the while listing homeward, like a guest at a party who is yearning for an excuse to leave politely. What many Americans have not understood at a gut level is that it is their party. Every major international institution—the UN, the World Bank, the International Monetary fund (IMF), NATO, the General Agreement on Tariffs and Trade—was made in America. And taken together, all this institution building has amounted to a workable international system, one in which democracy and free markets seem to be an ever-rising tide.

Is there any better way, for example, of coopting the putative next superpower, China, into the international system than to mold its behavior through the WTO [World Trade Organization] and the UN Security Council? Neoconservatives would call this approach "appeasement"; they want to "solve" the problem of China with regime change. But they offer no practical program: Washington is certainly not going to invade and occupy a nuclear-armed nation of 1.3 billion people. And while we await the advent of democracy there, the international system offers Beijing a real alternative to the old geopolitical power struggle, both by holding out the possibility of achieving national prosperity within such a system and by giving the Chinese a face-saving way to say they have no other choice but to bow to the American hegemony. The same policy of institutional envelopment goes for Russia.

Americans must now embrace what might seem a contradiction in terms: a more inclusive exceptionalism, which recognizes that what separates the United States from the world is no longer nearly as significant as what binds it to the world. Especially in today's world, where both opportunities and threats have become globalized, the task of securing freedom means securing the international system. The United States faces a tradeoff of time-honored American ideals: to preserve the most central of its founding principles, freedom, it must give up one of it founding myths, that of a people apart. America is now, ineluctably, part of a global community of its own making.

Accepting the International Community

For the Bush administration, it is a sharp irony that America's main ally in the war on terror has turned out to be the global community, and that they now need this despised liberal entity to flesh out the Bush doctrine. As it took power, the new administration insisted it would, as Bush adviser and now National Security Adviser Condoleezza Rice wrote in 2000, "proceed from the firm ground of the national interest and not from the interest of an illusory international community." Conservatives wanted to roll back what they saw as the rabid globalism of the Clinton years; they deplored how this globalized society sought to influence the issues that they wanted to reserve for U.S. sovereignty—from land mines to international war crimes tribunals to taxes.

In truth, by the time they took office, these so-called sovereigntists were already putting their fingers in a very leaky dike. Globalization and the world of complex interdependence had rendered many of their arguments moot. U.S. businesses had set up transnational production networks that left them vulnerable both to the desires of overseas governments and to the whims of transnational actors such as nongovernmental organizations (ngos). The latter, empowered by the global information revolution, have found it easier and easier to pursue their interests divorced from national bases; as Clinton State Department official Strobe Talbott has observed, al Qaeda may be the ultimate ngo. The U.S. economy, meanwhile, had become addicted to the Wall Street–centered international financial system. America had become a net user of other nations' capital, enabling Americans to habitually buy more goods from abroad than they sell to others. This trend became critical to the health of the U.S. economy throughout the 1990s, a decade in which U.S. savings dropped to nearly nothing.

By Bush's inaugural, American dependence on the international system had gone beyond savings and investment, jobs and markets. It was also about maintaining America's military superiority—the very source of its unilateralist pride. As the campaign in Afghanistan showed, much of the best U.S. defense technology is produced by high-tech commercial companies, which supply a lot of the technology that goes into robotic drones, airborne cameras, satellites, handheld global-positioning-system equipment, and systems-integration and telecommunications equipment.

Little of this equipment is produced now by a military-industrial complex sequestered in the United States, as it was during the Cold War. Nor will it be produced that way in the future, despite Bush's huge increase in defense spending. The Internet may have begun, famously, as a top-secret Defense Department project, but those days are long gone. Today Silicon Valley is so far ahead in R&D and product generation that it is simply too expensive and inefficient for the Pentagon to order up its own computer and telecommunications equipment from scratch. And here is the crucial point: these high-tech companies depend on the international marketplace to survive. Indeed, the "dual-use" technologies they produce represent the lion's share of what America's economy has to sell in the global marketplace these days. Supercomputers, for example, are necessary for twenty-first-century warfare—determining everything from warhead design to weather patterns in the event of an air strike—and every U.S. supercomputer company now gets at least half of its revenues from overseas sales. America's defense edge, in other words, depends on the stability and openness of the international economy in a way it never has before.

It is easy for conservatives, of course, to acknowledge the importance of the international economy. The "international community" is another thing. This is still such a nebulous idea that it has always been easy to dismiss as a Wilsonian myth. Yet the international economy no longer exists in a vacuum; there is a growing nexus of markets, governments, and peoples that share common interests and values, and that nexus in turn deepens the international economy. There are old working institutions, such as the Security Council, that sometimes give voice to these interests and values, and new institutions such as the WTO that adjudicate disputes when that nexus breaks down.

Proof that the international community exists—or at least that something other than anarchy prevails—is all around us. It can be found in the lack of serious attempts by other major powers to balance or build alliances against the United States, as realists have predicted. It can be found in the fact that none of the major powers—the EU [European Union], Japan, Russia, even China—is engaged in a major military buildup to challenge the lone superpower decades hence. Despite the war on terror and all the disputes it has provoked between Americans and Europeans, the forces of order are clearly much more powerful than the forces of chaos in the world today. In the last decade, financial markets have collapsed several times, and the global economy has held (so far). Antiglobalization protests raged, and the open-market system has remained intact (for the most part). Terror struck down the World Trade Center towers, and the clash of civilizations has not ensued (yet). If there is a coming anarchy, as some realists warn, then the burden of proof still lies with them, because there is hardly a glimmer of it on the horizon. The structure of the post–Cold War world has stayed together through its many stresses and strains, not least because there is no viable alternative.

Even so, scholars such as Joseph Stiglitz and Kevin Phillips increasingly warn that the engine of the international community, the global economy, is choking on its inequalities and cannot sustain itself without some assiduous repair work. All the more reason why Bush must do far more to make the rich-poor divide part of his global vision; the United States still ranks near last among major powers in foreign aid as a percentage of GDP [Gross Domestic Product].

But nothing demonstrates more than the war on terror the need for Americans to make the conceptual leap into accepting that they are part of an international community. To fight what have become disaffiliated cells, at least since the al Qaeda leadership was partially destroyed in Afghanistan, the United States desperately needs information on terror groups from Berlin to Kuala Lumpur. This approach cries out for a much more conciliatory attitude by the Bush administration, but again it was slow in coming. Washington was even reluctant to share intelligence with key allies such as France and Germany. Not surprisingly, cooperation in shutting down terror cells and rolling up their financial support networks has flagged.

The arcane but critical issue of WMD proliferation is another reason why Americans must work harder to flesh out a fuller international community. As the decades pass, it will only grow easier for terrorist groups to obtain such weapons. The likely main threat to Americans will not be ballistic missiles launched from a rogue state that knows it will face massive retaliation; it will be a WMD loaded into a boat or truck by a small number of hate-filled people who lack a "return address" and are undaunted by the threat of retaliation. Missile defense will not work in those cases, and a beefed-up homeland defense will improve only marginally America's ability to stop them before they are used.

Preemptive action can certainly help, but if overused it could establish a dangerous new precedent for international behavior. So it is clearly in the U.S. national interest to control or cut down the number of such weapons proliferating around the world. That means reducing—or at least holding in place—the number of states that produce them, and curbing the rest. As the Bush administration took office, it had access to a whole slew of useful if flawed tools for helping to accomplish this task, all of them globalist regimes launched by the United States, all of them regimes that would tend to lock in U.S. military superiority. Among these tools are the Comprehensive Test Ban Treaty, the Biological Weapons Convention, and the Chemical Weapons Convention. And yet the Bush administration, pursuing its old agenda against sovereignty-crimping treaties much as it continued to resist the nation building that would give terrorists fewer hiding places, abjured most of these tools rather than trying to fix them.

● ● ●

The Temptations of Unilateralism

Some Europeans have all but given up on Bush—the "Toxic Texan," as he was called by one continental editorialist—and are merely waiting until they can get back to a Clinton-like administration, which is now remembered as happily multilateralist. They have faulty memories. True, the Clintonites may have done a better job of papering over transatlantic differences and sounding multilateralist. Clinton fudged U.S. opposition to the ICC [International Criminal Court] and the Biological Weapons Convention, and he deferred far more to European sensitivities over the ABM [Anti-Ballistic Missile] Treaty. But when the going got tough . . . the Clintonites could act just as unilaterally as the current Bush team.

Today's unilateralism, in other words, has less to do with the peculiarities of Bush's "cowboy" mindset or even exceptionalism than with the sheer inequality in hard power between the United States and the rest of the world—especially

Europe, which is where most of the complaints come from. America behaves unilaterally because it can, and it is always at moments of national crisis when this
impulse is strongest. This fact of life is not going away anytime soon. The Europeans are learning during the war on terror what the Japanese learned in the Persian Gulf War: vast economic power gives you leverage mainly in economics, unless the will exists to turn it into something more. Europe can be a big dog at
WTO talks and on issues such as antitrust, harrying giant U.S. multinationals
such as GE and Microsoft. But as Japan found out upon Saddam Hussein's invasion of Kuwait in 1990, global security is another matter. Tokyo proved during the
Gulf War that it was not ready, it turned out, to be the new Rome of the "Pacific
Century." And in this now-critical realm of hard power, Europe has, like Japan,
been shown to be a "pygmy," to quote the rueful words used by NATO Secretary-
General George Robertson.

Few Europeans have appreciated the extent to which, when the Cold War
ended, their relevance to Washington ended too. The institutions of the transatlantic community were built on the idea of great-power cooperation, a "concert of
power," in Wilson's phrase, with America the superpower as first among equals.
Never mind that the disparity of power between the United States and Europe
was just as great at the end of World War II. The limitations of technology and
the delicate balancing act of Cold War deterrence, of forward-based missiles and
troops directed against the Soviet bloc, required real cooperation.

After the Cold War, George H. W. Bush and Clinton made a good show of pre-
tending nothing had changed. But in fact everything had. In a broad strategic sense
there was no concert anymore; there was only a one-man band. NATO, even as it
expands as a political organization, is less relevant than ever to America's strategic
considerations. NATO is still useful—as it proved in the latter stages of the Afghan
campaign—but as an outpost of American power, rather than a partner to it.

Well before September 11, the contours of this new world system began to
take shape. But neither the Americans nor the Europeans fully acknowledged
that their roles were being newly defined, and that was one reason for all the ill
feeling as the war on terror commenced. Whether the world likes it or not,
American power is now the linchpin of stability in every region, from Europe to
Asia to the Persian Gulf to Latin America. It oversees the global system from
unassailable heights, from space and from the seas. Since September 11, this is
becoming true in long-neglected Central and South Asia as well. And if Bush
has his way, this rise to hegemony will continue. As he said in his West Point
speech, "America has, and intends to keep, military strengths beyond
challenge."

If America now faces the problem of how to behave on the world stage with too
much power, Europe must confront the fact that its rhetoric too often outstrips its
lack of power. If Europe is increasingly speaking with one voice on world crises
such as the Middle East, this voice remains unbacked by a unified power structure.
As German Foreign Minister Joschka Fischer told me last May, "We are 200 years
behind you. In an institutional way we have just now reached the level of the Federalist Papers." And European governments are still spending only tiny amounts
on the much-touted European rapid-reaction force, which underneath the po-
litesse of Foggy Bottom most of Washington mocks.

So both sides, in truth, must make some adjustments. U.S. allies must accept that some U.S. unilateralism is inevitable, even desirable. This mainly involves accepting the reality of America's supreme might—and, truthfully, appreciating how historically lucky they are to be protected by such a relatively benign power. It means understanding, for example, why the United States, as the global stabilizer most often called on for robust intervention, should get special consideration from the ICC. The standing division of labor should be acknowledged and expanded: the Europeans must chip in with peacekeeping just as the oil-guzzling Japanese, during the Gulf War, paid for much of that effort. With the nuclear shadow mostly lifted, many Europeans can no longer stomach the idea of being led by those simplistic, moralistic Americans. But if they want to be "postmodern" states that no longer wage war, they will have to pay the piper: Washington must take the lead in setting the agenda, even if it should not entirely dictate it.

Yet the adjustment Americans must make is just as great. It is precisely because American power is so dominant that Americans must bend over backward to play down, rather than harp on, the disparities. This is not just a matter of being nice, or doing "coalitions for coalitions' sake," as some internal critics of Powell's lonely multilateralist efforts contend.

If the Europeans no longer play a big part in America's military planning, they remain an essential ally in the strategy of institutional envelopment, coopting the Chinas and the Russias into the international system. And if the Bush team wants to see a global division of labor that works, it cannot expect the Europeans and others to blindly sign on to peacekeeping and nation building without being genuinely consulted on overall strategy beforehand. It would be much easier to win converts on Iraq, for example, if the Europeans were being asked to help develop a long-term strategy for turning that nation, post-Saddam, into a stable, Western ally. For these reasons, the administration cannot simply swat aside institutional constraints it does not like. In the case of the ICC, for example, it would have been far more effective for the administration to argue as a signatory for safeguards for U.S. troops—even to hamstring the court, if necessary, from the inside—than to simply reject it as an outsider.

One problem with proposing a new Wilsonianism is that because America is so dominant, any attempt to trumpet universal values from Washington is likely to be resented more than it was in the past. Presidents such as Wilson or Reagan were able to bring the world along with them because the world was far more afraid of the alternative. But now there is no alternative: there is only the big, bad superpower. The saving grace is that America no longer needs to work as hard to build a world anew: that structure now exists. Washington simply has to back it up.

Bush himself said it best during his campaign in 2000: "Our nation stands alone right now in the world in terms of power. And that's why we've got to be humble and yet project strength in a way that promotes freedom. . . . If we are an arrogant nation, they'll view us that way, but if we're a humble nation, they'll respect us." The mystery is why the Bush administration now thinks it must carry a big stick and speak loudly at the same time—why it feels it must declare its values "nonnegotiable." That only turns one into the schoolyard bully. And bullies always have their comeuppance.

A New Consensus

There is a middle choice between the squishy globalism that the Bush sovereign-tists despise and the take-it-or-leave-it unilateralism they offer up as an alterna-tive. A new international consensus, built on a common vision of the interna-tional system, is possible. In today's world, American military and economic dominance is a decisive factor and must be maintained—as the right believes—but mainly to be the shadow enforcer of the international system Americans have done so much to create in the last century, in which the left places much of its trust. It is this international system and its economic and political norms that again must do the groundwork of keeping order and peace: deepening the ties that bind nations together; coopting failed states such as Afghanistan, potential rogues, and "strategic competitors"; and isolating, if not destroying, terrorists. As Henry Kissinger wrote, "the dominant trend in American foreign-policy thinking must be to transform power into consensus so that the international order is based on agreement rather than reluctant acquiescence." Or, as Senator Chuck Hagel, a Republican increasingly critical of the administration, recently summed it up, "We need friends."

In terms of practical policy, it is never easy to find the right mix of unilateralism and multilateralism to make this work. Washington must strike the proper bal-ance, warning the world that it will permit no other power to challenge America without being overbearing about it, and reassuring the world of America's essen-tial benignness without encouraging the idea that it has gone "soft" or will with-draw. Achieving this will be a task of long-term, assiduous diplomacy requiring "the virtuosity of a Bismarck to pull it off," in the words of Washington analyst Andrew Krepinevich.

It will also require some political sacrifice. The peculiarity of American foreign policy is that it must be sold to the American people. And unilateralism is so much easier to sell and conceptually so much cleaner than multilaterialism. The benefits are immediate: a strong image for the president, higher poll ratings, and in Bush's case, preserving a conservative base. But the costs are long-term and dif-fuse: the threat of WMD slipping through, the distant notion that Europe or China may start to oppose U.S. hegemony decades hence, the degree-by-degree warming of the globe. As for multilateralism, on the other hand, its benefits are long-term and diffuse for the same reasons and its costs immediate: an image of compromise and weakness, which is something no American president likes, espe-cially when fighting a war.

But American presidents, Bush included, must bite the bullet (or the ballot) and accept this consummate responsibility, even if it costs them some votes. That blithe Cold War description, "leader of the free world," must be restored and broadened. If America wants to maintain its primacy, direct, if not constitutional, responsibility for the entire global system must be written into the job description of every American president. In practical terms, Bush must talk forthrightly about the international system that benefits all; he must systematically support its insti-tutions even if he does not always agree with them; and he must dwell somewhat less on what is purely good for "America.". . . ■

View from the Inside

Kenneth Ashworth—currently a public administration professor but once a bureaucrat himself—draws on his experiences in the public sector to dispense wisdom in a series of letters from "Uncle Ken" to his niece Kim, who is interested in a career in public service. In this selection, Uncle Ken dispenses some practical advice on how government officials can succeed in influencing public policy.

Question

1. Ashworth suggests that Kim "will by now be hearing a lot about theories and models as to how decisions and public policies are made." Consider the theories presented in selection 13.1. What types of policy will government officials most likely be able to influence? At what stage in the policy-making process?

13.4 Taking the Initiative, or Risk Taking Inside Government (2001)

Kenneth Ashworth

Dear Kim

You will by now be hearing a lot about theories and models as to how decisions and public policies are made. And you will probably have run across some criticism of these conceptual frameworks, such as that they ignore the role played by opportunity and chance events in how things get done in government. Politicians are forever being criticized for being opportunists. I want to see if I can't defend to you opportunism as an effective approach to promoting government programs and policies.

In the first place, why would we believe that a person who feels strongly about a cause or goal should not eagerly take advantage of circumstances that can advance that cause or goal? Since a primary requirement for moving governments to address public issues is the political will to act and since a responsibility of public executives is to infuse that political will into policymakers, anything that can solidify or influence political will is too good to be ignored or discarded.

In the 1950s it was suddenly discovered that the popular use in Europe of thalidomide to ease sleeping problems of pregnant women was the cause of severe birth defects. With that the mounting criticisms of the Federal Drug Administration (FDA) as being too slow in approving new drugs immediately stopped. Those defending and wishing to reinforce the agency's rigorous review procedures for new drugs seized on the circumstances to strengthen the FDA's legal and regulatory position.

Since opportunities and chance events can have such an impact on policy development, government officials endeavor to find ways to shape and influence events to their advantage, that is, to create "opportunities." Odd as it may seem for a public administrator not to run from criticism, one way to create opportunities is to build opposition to an existing condition. For example, if you are convinced that a change in policy needs to be made, one sure way to get shot down quickly is to propose the change because you personally can look ahead and foresee its need. You can help kill such a good policy change by saying it is your personal sense that it is a good idea. This is particularly true when there is no visible or audible objection to the present situation or existing policy.

Politicians and many policymakers do follow the old adage, "If it ain't broke, don't fix it." And if you alone say something is broke, you are likely to be ignored. It is far better for you to propose a modification to a policy in response to vigorous criticism of the status quo. In other words, it sometimes helps to have countervailing opposition to how you and your agency are doing things at the moment. This may mean that you need to stimulate an opposition group, or even to create one, to attack you for doing nothing about their concerns. This criticism then allows you to modify your rules or to propose to your policymaking body a compromise position that moves away from the old policy. You aren't out on a limb by yourself. Rather you are trying to find a reasonable new policy to accommodate those people who are complaining.

When there was reluctance and hesitancy by the state government to move quickly enough in responding to minority underrepresentation in higher education, I appointed an advisory committee and arranged for the minority co-chairs (Hispanic and African American) to address our board on the committee's findings. They used this meeting as a public forum to present facts and projections that would have drawn yawns or tut-tuts if presented by our own staff. The emotional quality of the reports, presented by minorities, was essential to give the issue personal and human interest for press coverage and visibility. Much of the criticism was directed at our agency and some of it at me personally. This created a situation that demanded a reaction by us and by the legislature. In their zeal, the critics—those I had appointed as co-chairs—moved on in their enthusiasm to visit legislators and other state leaders as well. And in doing so, they were presenting data my own staff had put together. In the meantime we and our board were busy setting new directions and goals in anticipation of coming pressures from the legislature and the governor's office. Even if I were represented as unresponsive and dilatory in not taking action before the report, it was a small price to pay for the progress we were able to make afterward.

When the Federal Fifth Circuit Court ruled in 1996 that Texas could no longer take race into consideration in admissions and financial aid decisions, I appointed a committee of fifteen sociologists, consisting of a majority of minority members. Their task was to study the feasibility of identifying markers and social characteristics that we might use as a surrogate for race. When they reported their findings to our board, the committee told us that they had found that using combinations of all other sociological categories, but not race, would still result in a fifty percent reduction in minority admissions in coming years. But these negative findings were not useless. They were picked up by the legislature in drafting bills to ease the impact of the court ruling. The findings had a particular impact on the conservative legislators, who did not want minority enrollments to decline sharply because they recognized that Texas will soon become "majority minorities." They might object to favoritism of any kind based on race or ethnicity, but as a result of our study they suddenly became very interested in finding other approaches the schools and the legislature could still use to recruit and retain minority students.

I have always thought that Alice Roosevelt Longworth, Theodore Roosevelt's daughter, was talking about this approach to policymaking when she was in her nineties. A reporter asked her if she had developed a philosophy of life from her experience. She replied, "I have. Empty what's full, fill what's empty, and scratch where it itches." I think she believed in this definition of the primary responsibility of the public servant: "Comfort the afflicted and afflict the comfortable." I'll bet she would have been among the first to agree that from time to time you have to introduce a few gnats and fleas to start some itching.

Once when I was addressing an annual meeting of the Mexican American Legal Defense and Education Fund (MALDEF), I was commending them for how effectively we had been working together despite our apparent differences in public. We were getting results even if we were a long way from conspiring. They had been impatiently pushing the state to move off the dime to increase Hispanic enrollments in higher education, and our agency had been progressively making things somewhat better by responding to their pushing. As a metaphor in my talk I used Mark Twain's comment that every dog should have a few fleas; it keeps him from forgetting he's a dog. Several of them apologized later after some of their colleagues had left the meeting to report that the commissioner was now calling Mexican Americans fleas.

This reminds me of a blooper during a campaign for governor. The campaign staff of one candidate tried out the new capacity of computers to use first names in the salutation of letters to voters to personalize the governor's campaign messages. For example, you would have received a "Dear Kim" letter from this candidate whom you did not know at all. A friend from the Mexican American Legal Defense and Education Fund sent me a copy of a note he had written to a colleague with the African American Students Association at a nearby university. My MALDEF friend wrote, "I am enclosing a campaign letter I just received beginning, 'Dear Mexican.' It is with fear and trepidation that I wait to learn how yours was addressed."

The opportunities that come your way may be in small things, not big nation-shaking policies. In 1965, I was working with the U.S. Office of Education (before it became a department), running a grant program of several hundred million dollars for constructing college classrooms and laboratories. At the end of the fiscal year in June we had about $5 million left over that we could not commit because some states had not fully used up their allotted shares. I was in my office over lunch trying to figure out how to allocate these remaining funds among the states. My division director, Jay du Von, came in and said President [Lyndon] Johnson had just talked with the secretary of Health, Education and Welfare and the secretary had, in turn, called him to say the president wanted all federal agencies to do everything they could to help Topeka, Kansas, and Washburn University. Just the night before the city had been hit by a devastating tornado and the university had been largely destroyed. Jay said to let him know right away if I had any ideas on how we might help.

When he left I turned back to the problem on my desk, how to deal with the $5 million figuratively lying there awaiting my decision. I saw an opportunity and I quickly dashed off a briefing memo which made these points:

We have $5 million for construction grants left for the year.

Our rules say to divide it among states with remaining demand.

All states have received funds under the program.

Congress likes the program so much they have *doubled* our appropriation for next year.

With everybody counting on more money next year and Washburn U so badly hurt, I doubt any state or university president would want to appear a "dog in the manger" and complain if President Johnson were to announce that he has given the $5 million to Washburn University.

No bureaucratic delays here. As I recall, the White House announced the commitment of the funds within the hour. Our offer was the first to reach the president's desk since his directive to the federal agencies and departments. And when my direct boss returned from lunch and found out what we had done, he was livid at our having violated written rules and regulations in such a cavalier manner.

Lessons: (a) Learn to quickly write short and convincing briefing memos, and (b) when the big boss is in the stew with you, you'll probably survive being unorthodox. Incidentally, I will make a note to tell you in a later letter a few things about writing briefing memos.

The greatest fun in being a government executive is the ability from time to time to create a new program. One day I had to go to Corpus Christi to give a commencement talk and as I read over my speech before leaving my office I was not particularly pleased with it. So I grabbed a handful of my business cards. That night, after congratulating the graduates, I said, "But I'm talking to the wrong group here. You are sitting there in your caps and gowns all prepared for success. I want to address the younger people here tonight. To be successful you will need a network of influential people so in a few years you can also be sitting down there in your own caps and gowns. I want to be part of your network to help you get ahead. After the ceremony is over if you young people will come up here on the stage I will give you my business card. I want you to take it home and stick it on your mirror where you'll see it every day to remind you of our deal we are going to make tonight. Our deal is this: You graduate from high school and I will guarantee that you will get the financial aid you need to go to college."

Of course I ran out of cards, but I wrote names and addresses on the back of my speech and the next week we sent those students cards and letters as well. This was no big commitment on my part because the state already guaranteed student financial aid to needy high school graduates. Students and parents just don't always know this. Our agency turned what I did that evening into a statewide program. Today we still send a newsletter to the eighth grade students across the state as we try to reach the most economically deprived young people. We have received hundreds of letters over the years from students I have promised to help, calling on me to meet my end of our bargain since they have met theirs by graduating from high school. One letter I remember particularly. A thirteen-year-old girl wrote saying, "I have lost the card you gave me. Does that mean I can't go to college?"

The point here is that entrepreneurship is not limited to the business sector. You need to learn to be a risk taker in government too. You must learn to recognize opportunities when they come your way and be prepared to grab them. Often those opportunities are ephemeral and will disappear quickly. "Wild Bill" Donovan, chief spy and director of the OSS [Office of Strategic Services] in World War II, frequently used to say, "The perfect is the enemy of the good." A perfect or better decision or plan of action late by a day or even an hour may prove worthless. A timely but merely good decision or plan of action may serve to seize an opportunity that will otherwise be lost. Of course you must learn to expect the Monday morning quarterbacks who will later criticize you for not having used a more perfect approach to the circumstances you faced at the moment. . . .

I have been telling you about opportunity and the role it plays in government decisions and policies. But there is a corollary and that is patience. When I first took on higher level positions I constantly worried about how to be ready for every problem that I saw coming at me or likely to come. I spent enormous amounts of energy and time trying to develop responses and to be ready for those eventualities. Then in time several things became clear to me. I have gained confidence that I can handle the problems when they actually arrive. Second, I have found that some of the problems never came to full bloom and I was wasting my time planning ahead too far. Third, that the problems, when they do come into full bloom, are so different from what I had imagined and spent time preparing for that an entirely different response is often required. And last, I have found I can be more effective in trying to influence the circumstances and conditions related to the developing problems rather than focusing on the imagined problems to come. I have learned I can sometimes shape the development of the problem more to my liking. I look constantly for opportunities to change the way problems come to me. I have discovered this is a better and more effective use of my time and energy than worrying about detailed solutions and responses for possible use in the future.

Another point about patience. There was a time when I became convinced that I could not survive in my job because the governor wanted me out. The governor had just appointed one-third of my eighteen-member board every two years, and the new governor had just appointed six who seemed committed to questioning my every move and recommendation and to make my job as agency executive miserable. I reasoned that with his next set of six appointees he'd have the two-thirds necessary to have me removed. I considered, metaphorically speaking, turning off my engine when I saw a flat, green pasture ahead and gliding down to an easy landing, that is, taking a job in one of our universities, from whence I had come to this job. But the more I thought about it the more I came to the realization that I had come into the public service to have at least one really good fight someday, and this might be it. I decided, to continue the metaphor, I'd rather be shot down in flames. So I was unremitting in my staff recommendation to the board and refused to quit. Then two years later, when the next six appointees arrived, I found that I had underestimated the educability of the governor's first six appointees. I still had twelve solid supporters on the board, who immediately set out to educate the new, entering freshman class of board members that the governor might be wrong about their executive.

I have had the impression that every new governor wanted me fired. It is not so much that the governors have disliked me—and several of them truly have—but because I have worked for the previous governor and because they would prefer to have their own person in the commissioner's position. There is clearly a good argument to be made for the cabinet form of government, wherein every new governor should be able to appoint his or her own people to all top state agency positions. How else can the new governor carry out policies and be responsive to the voters who elected him or her to do certain things and change government in accordance with the platform if he or she cannot put his or her own appointees into the key jobs?

On the other hand, I can argue, with a strong personal interest, that the higher education commissioner's job should not be politicized and that it should remain nonpartisan. Under a cabinet form of government, the commissioner and other offices filled by a governor become lame duck positions when the governor is in his last term. Moreover, there would be a great loss of continuity and expertise with frequent turnovers in the office. This argument can be made for other specialized fields in government as well, such as health, the public schools, and the state police. The structure wherein governors appoint boards which, in turn, hire and fire commissioners and agency heads seems to me to provide sufficient accountability to the governor and the voters, even if there is a time delay during which the governor is not able to force immediate turnover in all agency executives. In any event, you can see why I like this system better than the cabinet form of state government. This is the principal reason I have survived in my job for over twenty years.

One lesson I learned is to have patience and to keep on working and playing the game. I gained an appreciation for the Arab story about the camel driver caught in the sheik's harem. When he returned to the prison yard from his scheduled execution, everyone was amazed and asked how he had managed to survive. He explained that he had convinced the sheik that he would teach his horse to fly. They all exclaimed this was impossible, why bother to try? To which he replied, "Perhaps. But while I am teaching the horse to fly many things might happen. The sheik might die. The horse might die. I might die. And, who knows, I may teach that horse to fly." Keep your options open. Keep playing the game.

You asked in your last letter for me to write to you about leadership. I have been, haven't you noticed? Everybody wants the formula or the secrets or they want the books and instructional tapes that reveal the formulas and secrets. In any event, I will think on it after I've written you on several other topics I've jotted down—if there's anything special left over to say on the topic.

Your transgressive kinsman,

Uncle Ken ∎